Catholic

Daily & Sunday Mass Missal

Liturgy of the word 2021 (year B)

Sisters of the Holy Rosary I N C

JANUARY 1ST, 2021

The Octave Day of Christmas

Solemnity of the Blessed Virgin Mary, the Mother of God

1st Reading NM 6:22-27

The LORD said to Moses: "Speak to Aaron and his sons and tell them: This is how you shall bless the Israelites. Say to them: The LORD bless you and keep you! The LORD let his face shine upon you, and be gracious to you! The LORD look upon you kindly and give you peace! So shall they invoke my name upon the Israelites, and I will bless them.

Responsorial Psalm PS 67:2-3, 5, 6, 8.

R. (2a) May God bless us in his mercy.

May God have pity on us and bless us; may he let his face shine upon us. So may your way be known upon earth; among all nations, your salvation.

R. May God bless us in his mercy.

May the nations be glad and exult because you rule the peoples in equity; the nations on the earth you guide.

R. May God bless us in his mercy.

May the peoples praise you, O God; may all the peoples praise you! May God bless us, and may all the ends of the earth fear him!

R. May God bless us in his mercy.

2nd Reading GAL 4:4-7

Brothers and sisters: When the fullness of time had come, God sent his Son, born of a woman, born under the law, to ransom those under the law, so that we might receive adoption as sons. As proof that you are sons, God sent the Spirit of his Son into our hearts, crying out, "Abba, Father!" So you are no longer a slave but a son, and if a son then also an heir, through God.

Alleluia HEB 1:1-2

R. Alleluia, alleluia.

In the past God spoke to our ancestors through the prophets; in these last days, he has spoken to us through the Son.

R. Alleluia, alleluia.

Gospel LK 2:16-21
The shepherds went in haste to Bethlehem and found Mary and Joseph, and the infant lying in the manger. When they saw this, they made known the message that had been told them about this child. All who heard it were amazed by what had been told them by the shepherds. And Mary kept all these things, reflecting on them in her heart. Then the shepherds returned, glorifying and praising God for all they had heard and seen, just as it had been told to them. When eight days were completed for his circumcision, he was named Jesus, the name given him by the angel before he was conceived in the womb.

JANUARY 2ND, 2021
Memorial of Saints Basil the Great and Gregory Nazianzen, Bishops and Doctors of the Church

1st Reading 1 JN 2:22-28
Beloved: Who is the liar? Whoever denies that Jesus is the Christ. Whoever denies the Father and the Son, this is the antichrist. Anyone who denies the Son does not have the Father, but whoever confesses the Son has the Father as well. Let what you heard from the beginning remain in you. If what you heard from the beginning remains in you, then you will remain in the Son and in the Father. And this is the promise that he made us: eternal life. I write you these things about those who would deceive you. As for you, the anointing that you received from him remains in you, so that you do not need anyone to teach you. But his anointing teaches you about everything and is true and not false; just as it taught you, remain in him. And now, children, remain in him, so that when he appears, we may have confidence and not be put to shame by him at his coming.

Responsorial Psalm PS 98:1, 2-3AB, 3CD-4
R. (3cd) All the ends of the earth have seen the saving power of God.

Sing to the LORD a new song, for he has done wondrous deeds; His right hand has won victory for him, his holy arm.

R. All the ends of the earth have seen the saving power of God.

The LORD has made his salvation known: in the sight of the nations, he has revealed his justice. He has remembered his kindness and his faithfulness toward the house of Israel.

R. All the ends of the earth have seen the saving power of God.

All the ends of the earth have seen the salvation by our God. Sing joyfully to the LORD, all you land; break into song; sing praise.

R. All the ends of the earth have seen the saving power of God.

Alleluia HEB 1:1-2

R. Alleluia, alleluia.

In times, past, God spoke to our ancestors through the prophets: in these last days, he has spoken to us through his Son.

R. Alleluia, alleluia.

Gospel JN 1:19-28

This is the testimony of John. When the Jews from Jerusalem sent priests and Levites to him to ask him, "Who are you?" He admitted and did not deny it, but admitted, "I am not the Christ." So they asked him, "What are you then? Are you Elijah?" And he said, "I am not." "Are you the Prophet?" He answered, "No." So they said to him, "Who are you, so we can give an answer to those who sent us? What do you have to say for yourself?" He said: "I am the voice of one crying out in the desert, 'Make straight the way of the Lord,' as Isaiah the prophet said." Some Pharisees were also sent. They asked him, "Why then do you baptize if you are not the Christ or Elijah or the Prophet?" John answered them, "I baptize with water; but there is one among you whom you do not recognize, the one who is coming after me, whose sandal strap I am not worthy to untie." This happened in Bethany across the Jordan, where John was baptizing

JANUARY 3RD, 2021
The Epiphany of the Lord

1st Reading Is 60:1-6

Rise up in splendor, Jerusalem! Your light has come, the glory of the Lord shines upon you. See, darkness covers the earth, and thick clouds cover the peoples; but upon you the LORD shines, and over you appears his glory.

Nations shall walk by your light, and kings by your shining radiance. Raise your eyes and look about; they all gather and come to you: your sons come from afar, and your daughters in the arms of their nurses.

Then you shall be radiant at what you see, your heart shall throb and overflow, for the riches of the sea shall be emptied out before you, the wealth of nations shall be brought to you.

Caravans of camels shall fill you, dromedaries from Midian and Ephah; all from Sheba shall come bearing gold and frankincense, and proclaiming the praises of the LORD.

Responsorial Ps 72:1-2, 7-8, 10-11, 12-13

R. (cf. 11) Lord, every nation on earth will adore you.

O God, with your judgment endow the king, and with your justice, the king's son;

He shall govern your people with justice and your afflicted ones with judgment.

R. Lord, every nation on earth will adore you. Justice shall flower in his days, and profound peace, till the moon be no more.

May he rule from sea to sea, and from the River to the ends of the earth.

R. Lord, every nation on earth will adore you.

The kings of Tarshish and the Isles shall offer gifts; the kings of Arabia and Seba shall bring tribute.

All kings shall pay him homage, all nations shall serve him.

R. Lord, every nation on earth will adore you.

For he shall rescue the poor when he cries out, and the afflicted when he has no one to help him.

He shall have pity for the lowly and the poor; the lives of the poor he shall save.

R. Lord, every nation on earth will adore you.

2nd Reading EPH 3:2-3A, 5-6

Brothers and sisters: You have heard of the stewardship of God's grace that was given to me for your benefit, namely, that the mystery was made known to me by revelation. It was not made known to people in other generations as it has now been revealed to his holy apostles and prophets by the Spirit: that the Gentiles are coheirs, members of the same body, and copartners in the promise in Jesus through the gospel.

Alleluia MT 2:2

R. Alleluia, alleluia.

We saw his star at its rising and have come to do him homage.

R. Alleluia, alleluia.

Gospel MT 2:1-12

When Jesus was born in Bethlehem of Judea, in the days of King Herod, behold, magi from the east arrived in Jerusalem, saying, "Where is the newborn king of the Jews? We saw his star at its rising and have come to do him homage." When King Herod heard this, he was greatly troubled, and all Jerusalem with him. Assembling all the chief priests and the scribes of the people, He inquired of them where the Christ was to be born. They said to him, "In Bethlehem of Judea, for thus it has been written through the prophet: And you, Bethlehem, land of Judah, are by no means least among the rulers of Judah; since from you shall come a ruler, who is to shepherd my people Israel." Then Herod called the magi secretly and ascertained from them the time of the star's appearance. He sent them to Bethlehem and said, Go and search diligently for the child. When you have found him, bring me word, that I too may go and do him homage." After their audience with the king they set out. And behold, the star that they had seen at its rising preceded them, until it came and stopped over the place where the child was. They were overjoyed at seeing the star, and on entering the house they saw the child with Mary his mother. They prostrated themselves and did him homage. Then they opened their treasures and offered him gifts of gold, frankincense, and myrrh. And having been warned in a dream not to return to Herod, they departed for their country by another way

JANUARY 4TH, 2021

Memorial of Saint Elizabeth Ann Seton, Religious

1st Reading 1 Jn 3:22–4:6

Beloved:

We receive from him whatever we ask, because we keep his commandments and do what pleases him.

And his commandment is this: we should believe in the name of his Son, Jesus Christ, and love one another just as he commanded us.

Those who keep his commandments remain in him, and he in them, and the way we know that he remains in us is from the Spirit whom he gave us.

Beloved, do not trust every spirit but test the spirits to see whether they belong to God, because many false prophets have gone out into the world.

This is how you can know the Spirit of God: every spirit that acknowledges Jesus Christ come in the flesh belongs to God, and every spirit that does not acknowledge Jesus does not belong to God.

This is the spirit of the antichrist who, as you heard, is to come, but in fact is already in the world.

You belong to God, children, and you have conquered them, for the one who is in you is greater than the one who is in the world.

They belong to the world; accordingly, their teaching belongs to the world, and the world listens to them.

We belong to God, and anyone who knows God listens to us, while anyone who does not belong to God refuses to hear us.

This is how we know the spirit of truth and the spirit of deceit.

Responsorial Psalm PS 2:7bc-8, 10-12a

R. (8ab) I will give you all the nations for an inheritance.

The LORD said to me, "You are my Son; this day I have begotten you.

Ask of me and I will give you the nations for an inheritance and the ends of the earth for your possession."

R. I will give you all the nations for an inheritance.

And now, O kings, give heed; take warning, you rulers of the earth.

Serve the LORD with fear, and rejoice before him; with trembling rejoice.

R. I will give you all the nations for an inheritance.

Alleluia: Mt 4:23

R. Alleluia, alleluia.

Jesus proclaimed the Gospel of the Kingdom and cured every disease among the people.

R. Alleluia, alleluia.

Gospel: Mt 4:12-17, 23-25
When Jesus heard that John had been arrested, he withdrew to Galilee.

He left Nazareth and went to live in Capernaum by the sea, in the region of Zebulun and Naphtali, that what had been said through Isaiah the prophet might be fulfilled:

Land of Zebulun and land of Naphtali, the way to the sea, beyond the Jordan,

Galilee of the Gentiles, the people who sit in darkness have seen a great light, on those dwelling in a land overshadowed by death light has arisen.

From that time on, Jesus began to preach and say,

"Repent, for the Kingdom of heaven is at hand."

He went around all of Galilee, teaching in their synagogues, proclaiming the Gospel of the Kingdom, and curing every disease and illness among the people.

His fame spread to all of Syria, and they brought to him all who were sick with various diseases and racked with pain, those who were possessed, lunatics, and paralytics, and he cured them.

And great crowds from Galilee, the Decapolis, Jerusalem, and Judea, and from beyond the Jordan followed him.

JANUARY 5TH, 2021
Memorial of Saint John Neumann, Bishop

Beloved, let us love one another, because love is of God; everyone who loves is begotten by God and knows God.

Whoever is without love does not know God, for God is love.

In this way the love of God was revealed to us:

God sent his only-begotten Son into the world so that we might have life through him.

In this is love: not that we have loved God, but that he loved us and sent his Son as expiation for our sins.

R. (see 11) Lord, every nation on earth will adore you.

O God, with your judgment endow the king, and with your justice, the king's son;

He shall govern your people with justice and your afflicted ones with judgment.

R. Lord, every nation on earth will adore you.

The mountains shall yield peace for the people, and the hills justice.

He shall defend the afflicted among the people, save the children of the poor.

R. Lord, every nation on earth will adore you.

Justice shall flower in his days, and profound peace, till the moon be no more.

May he rule from sea to sea, and from the River to the ends of the earth.

R. Lord, every nation on earth will adore you.

Alleluia: Lk 4:18

R. Alleluia, alleluia.

The Lord has sent me to bring glad tidings to the poor and to proclaim liberty to captives.

R. Alleluia, alleluia.

Gospel Mk 6:34-44

When Jesus saw the vast crowd, his heart was moved with pity for them, for they were like sheep without a shepherd; and he began to teach them many things.

By now it was already late and his disciples approached him and said,

"This is a deserted place and it is already very late.

Dismiss them so that they can go to the surrounding farms and villages and buy themselves something to eat."

He said to them in reply, "Give them some food yourselves."

But they said to him, "Are we to buy two hundred days' wages worth of food and give it to them to eat?"

He asked them, "How many loaves do you have? Go and see."

And when they had found out they said, "Five loaves and two fish."

So he gave orders to have them sit down in groups on the green grass. The people took their places in rows by hundreds and by fifties.

Then, taking the five loaves and the two fish and looking up to heaven, he said the blessing, broke the loaves, and gave them to his disciples to set before the people; he also divided the two fish among them all.

They all ate and were satisfied.

And they picked up twelve wicker baskets full of fragments and what was left of the fish. Those who ate of the loaves were five thousand men.

JANUARY 6TH, 2021
Wednesday after Epiphany

1st Reading 1 Jn 4:11-18

Beloved, if God so loved us, we also must love one another. No one has ever seen God. Yet, if we love one another, God remains in us, and his love is brought to perfection in us. This is how we know that we remain in him and he in us, that he has given us of his Spirit. Moreover, we have seen and testify that the Father sent his Son as savior of the world. Whoever acknowledges that Jesus is the Son of God, God remains in him and he in God. We have come to know and to believe in the love God has for us. God is love, and whoever remains in love remains in God and God in him. In this is love brought to perfection among us, that we have confidence on the day of judgment because as he is, so are we in this world. There is no fear in love, but perfect love drives out fear because fear has to do with punishment, and so one who fears is not yet perfect in love.

Responsorial Psalm PS 72:1-2, 10, 12-13

R. (see 11) Lord, every nation on earth will adore you.

O God, with your judgment endow the king, and with your justice, the king's son; He shall govern your people with justice and your afflicted ones with judgment.

R. Lord, every nation on earth will adore you.

The kings of Tarshish and the Isles shall offer gifts; kings of Arabia and Seba shall bring tribute.

R. Lord, every nation on earth will adore you.

For he shall rescue the poor when he cries out, and the afflicted when he has no one to help him He shall have pity for the lowly and the poor; the lives of the poor he shall save.

R. Lord, every nation on earth will adore you.

Alleluia 1 TM 3:16

R. Alleluia, alleluia.

Glory to you, O Christ, proclaimed to the Gentiles. Glory to you, O Christ, believed in throughout the world.

R. Alleluia, alleluia.

10

Gospel MK 6:45-52

After the five thousand had eaten and were satisfied, Jesus made his disciples get into the boat and precede him to the other side toward Bethsaida, while he dismissed the crowd. And when he had taken leave of them, he went off to the mountain to pray. When it was evening, the boat was far out on the sea and he was alone on shore. Then he saw that they were tossed about while rowing, for the wind was against them. About the fourth watch of the night, he came toward them walking on the sea. He meant to pass by them. But when they saw him walking on the sea, they thought it was a ghost and cried out. They had all seen him and were terrified. at once he spoke with them, "Take courage, it is I, do not be afraid!" He got into the boat with them and the wind died down. They were completely astounded. They had not understood the incident of the loaves. On the contrary, their hearts were hardened.

JANUARY 7TH, 2021
Thursday after Epiphany

1st Reading 1 JN 4:19–5:4

Beloved, we love God because he first loved us. If anyone says, "I love God," but hates his brother, he is a liar; for whoever does not love a brother whom he has seen cannot love God whom he has not seen. This is the commandment we have from him: Whoever loves God must also love his brother. Everyone who believes that Jesus is the Christ is begotten by God, and everyone who loves the Father loves also the one begotten by him. In this way we know that we love the children of God when we love God and obey his commandments. For the love of God is this, that we keep his commandments. And his commandments are not burdensome, for whoever is begotten by God conquers the world. And the victory that conquers the world is our faith.

Responsorial Psalm   PS 72:1-2, 14 AND 15BC, 17

R. (see 11) Lord, every nation on earth will adore you.

O God, with your judgment endows the king, and with your justice, the king's son; He shall govern your people with justice and your afflicted ones with judgment.

R. Lord, every nation on earth will adore you.

From fraud and violence he shall redeem them, and precious shall their blood be in his sight. May they be prayed for continually; day by day shall they bless him.

R. Lord, every nation on earth will adore you.

May his name be blessed forever; as long as the sun his name shall remain. In him shall all the tribes of the earth be blessed; all the nations shall proclaim his happiness.

R. Lord, every nation on earth will adore you.

Alleluia LK 4:18

R. Alleluia, alleluia.

The Lord has sent me to bring glad tidings to the poor and to proclaim liberty to captives.

R. Alleluia, alleluia.

Gospel LK 4:14-22

Jesus returned to Galilee in the power of the Spirit, and news of him spread throughout the whole region. He taught in their synagogues and was praised by all. He came to Nazareth, where he had grown up, and went according to his custom into the synagogue on the Sabbath day. He stood up to read and was handed a scroll of the prophet Isaiah. He unrolled the scroll and found the passage where it was written: The Spirit of the Lord is upon me, because he has anointed me to bring glad tidings to the poor. He has sent me to proclaim liberty to captives and recovery of sight to the blind, to let the oppressed go free ,and to proclaim a year acceptable to the Lord. Rolling up the scroll, he handed it back to the attendant and sat down, and the eyes of all in the synagogue looked intently at him. He said to them, "Today this Scripture passage is fulfilled in your hearing." And all spoke highly of him and were amazed at the gracious words that came from his mouth.

JANUARY 8TH, 2021
Friday after Epiphany

1st Reading 1 JN 5:5-13

Beloved: Who indeed is the victor over the world but the one who believes that Jesus is the Son of God? This is the one who came through water and

Blood, Jesus Christ, not by water alone, but by water and Blood. The Spirit is the one who testifies, and the Spirit is truth. So there are three who testify, the Spirit, the water, and the Blood, and the three are of one accord. If we accept human testimony, the testimony of God is surely greater. Now the testimony of God is this that he has testified on behalf of his Son.

Whoever believes in the Son of God has this testimony within himself. Whoever does not believe God has made him a liar by not believing the testimony God has given about his Son. And this is the testimony: God gave us eternal life, and this life is in his Son. Whoever possesses the Son has life; whoever does not possess the Son of God does not have life. I write these things to you so that you may know that you have eternal life, you who believe in the name of the Son of God.

Responsorial Psalm   PS 147:12-13, 14-15, 19-20
R. (12a) Praise the Lord, Jerusalem.

or:

R. Alleluia.

Glorify the LORD, O Jerusalem;

Praise your God, O Zion. For he has strengthened the bars of your gates; he has blessed your children within you.

R. Praise the Lord, Jerusalem.

or:

R. Alleluia.

He has granted peace in your borders; with the best of wheat he fills you. He sends forth his command to the earth; swiftly runs his word!

R. Praise the Lord, Jerusalem.

or:

R. Alleluia.

He has proclaimed his word to Jacob, his statutes and his ordinances to Israel. He has not done thus for any other nation; his ordinances he has not made known to them. Alleluia.

13

R. Praise the Lord, Jerusalem.

or:

R. Alleluia.

Alleluia MT 4:23

R. Alleluia, alleluia.

Jesus proclaimed the Gospel of the Kingdom and cured every disease among the people.

R. Alleluia, alleluia.

Gospel   LK 5:12-16

It happened that there was a man full of leprosy in one of the towns where Jesus was; and when he saw Jesus, he fell prostrate, pleaded with him, and said, "Lord, if you wish, you can make me clean." Jesus stretched out his hand, touched him, and said, "I do will it. Be made clean." And the leprosy left him immediately. Then he ordered him not to tell anyone, but "Go, show yourself to the priest and offer for your cleansing what Moses prescribed; that will be proof for them." The report about him spread all the more, and great crowds assembled to listen to him and to be cured of their ailments, but he would withdraw to deserted places to pray.

JANUARY 9TH, 2021
Saturday after Epiphany

1st Reading 1 JN 5:14-21

Beloved: We have this confidence in him that if we ask anything according to his will, he hears us. And if we know that he hears us in regard to whatever we ask, we know that what we have asked him for is ours. If anyone sees his brother sinning, if the sin is not deadly, he should pray to God and he will give him life. This is only for those whose sin is not deadly. There is such a thing as deadly sin, about which I do not say that you should pray. All wrongdoing is sin, but there is sin that is not deadly. We know that anyone begotten by God does not sin; but the one begotten by God he protects, and the Evil One cannot touch him. We know that we belong to God, and the whole world is under the power of the Evil One. We also know that the Son of God has come and has given us discernment to know the one who is true.

And we are in the one who is true, in his Son Jesus Christ. He is the true God and eternal life. Children, be on your guard against idols.

Responsorial Psalm PS 149:1-2, 3-4, 5-6A AND 9B
R. The Lord takes delight in his people.

or:

R. Alleluia.

Sing to the LORD a new song of praise in the assembly of the faithful. Let Israel be glad in their maker, let the children of Zion rejoice in their king.

R. The Lord takes delight in his people.

or:

R. Alleluia.

Let them praise his name in the festive dance, let them sing praise to him with timbrel and harp. For the LORD loves his people and he adorns the lowly with victory.

R... The Lord takes delight in his people.

or:

R. Alleluia.

Let the faithful exult in glory; let them sing for joy upon their couches; Let the high praises of God be in their throats. This is the glory of all his faithful. Alleluia.

R... The Lord takes delight in his people.

or:

R. Alleluia.

Alleluia MT 4:16

R. Alleluia, alleluia.

The people who sit in darkness have seen a great light, on those dwelling in a land overshadowed by death light has arisen.

R. Alleluia, alleluia.

Gospel JN 3:22-30

Jesus and his disciples went into the region of Judea, where he spent some time with them baptizing. John was also baptizing in Aenon near Salim, because there was an abundance of water there, and people came to be baptized, for John had not yet been imprisoned. Now a dispute arose between the disciples of John and a Jew about ceremonial washings. So, they came to John and said to him, "Rabbi, the one who was with you across the Jordan, to whom you testified, here he is baptizing and everyone is coming to him. "John answered and said, "No one can receive anything except what has been given from heaven. You yourselves can testify that I said that I am not the Christ, but that I was sent before him.

The one who has the bride is the bridegroom; the best man, who stands and listens for him, rejoices greatly at the bridegroom's voice. So this joy of mine has been made complete. He must increase; I must decrease."

JANUARY 10TH, 2021
The Baptism of the Lord

1st Reading   IS 42:1-4, 6-7

Thus says the LORD: Here is my servant whom I uphold, my chosen one with whom I am pleased, upon whom I have put my spirit; he shall bring forth justice to the nations, not crying out, not shouting, not making his voice heard in the street. a bruised reed he shall not break, and a smoldering wick he shall not quench, until he establishes justice on the earth; the coastlands will wait for his teaching. I, the LORD, have called you for the victory of justice, I have grasped you by the hand; I formed you, and set you as a covenant of the people, a light for the nations, to open the eyes of the blind, to bring out prisoners from confinement, and from the dungeon, those who live in darkness.

Or   Is 55:1-11

Thus, says the LORD: All you who are thirsty come to the water!

You who have no money, come, receive grain and eat; come, without paying and without cost, drink wine and milk!

Why spend your money for what is not bread, your wages for what fails to satisfy? Heed me, and you shall eat well, you shall delight in rich fare. Come to me heedfully; listen, that you may have life.

I will renew with you the everlasting covenant, the benefits assured to David. As I made him a witness to the peoples, a leader and commander of nations, so shall you summon a nation you knew not, and nations that knew you not shall run to you, because of the LORD, your God, the Holy One of Israel, who has glorified you.

Seek the LORD while he may be found, call him while he is near.

Let the scoundrel forsake his way, and the wicked man his thoughts; let him turn to the LORD for mercy; to our God, who is generous in forgiving.

For my thoughts are not your thoughts, nor are your ways my ways, says the LORD. As high as the heavens are above the earth so high are my ways above your ways and my thoughts above your thoughts.

For just as from the heavens the rain and snow come down and do not return there till, they have watered the earth, making it fertile and fruitful, giving seed to the one who sows and bread to the one who eats, so shall my word be that goes forth from my mouth; my word shall not return to me void, but shall do my will, achieving the end for which I sent it.

Responsorial Psalm   PS 29:1-2, 3-4, 3, 9-10.
R. (11b) The Lord will bless his people with peace.

Give to the LORD, you sons of God, give to the LORD glory and praise, give to the LORD the glory due his name; adore the LORD in holy attire.

R... The Lord will bless his people with peace.

The voice of the LORD is over the waters, the LORD, over vast waters. The voice of the LORD is mighty; the voice of the LORD is majestic.

R... The Lord will bless his people with peace.

The God of glory thunders, and in his temple, all say, "Glory!"

The LORD is enthroned above the flood; the LORD is enthroned as king forever.

R... The Lord will bless his people with peace.

Or   Is 12:2-3, 4bcd, 5-6
R (3) You will draw water joyfully from the springs of salvation.

God indeed is my savior; I am confident and unafraid.

My strength and my courage is the LORD, and he has been my savior. With joy you will draw water at the fountain of salvation.

R. You will draw water joyfully from the springs of salvation.

Give thanks to the LORD, acclaim his name; among the nations make known his deeds, proclaim how exalted is his name.

R. You will draw water joyfully from the springs of salvation.

Sing praise to the LORD for his glorious achievement; let this be known throughout all the earth.

Shout with exultation, O city of Zion, for great in your midst is the Holy One of Israel!

R. You will draw water joyfully from the springs of salvation.

2nd Reading ACTS 10:34-38

Peter proceeded to speak to those gathered in the house of Cornelius, saying: "In truth, I see that God shows no partiality. Rather, in every nation whoever fears him and acts uprightly is acceptable to him. You know the word that he sent to the Israelites as he proclaimed peace through Jesus Christ, who is Lord of all, what has happened all over Judea, beginning in Galilee after the baptism that John preached, how God anointed Jesus of Nazareth with the Holy Spirit and power. He went about doing good and healing all those oppressed by the devil, for God was with him."

Or 1 Jn 5:1-9

Beloved:

Everyone who believes that Jesus is the Christ is begotten by God, and everyone who loves the Father loves also the one begotten by him.

In this way we know that we love the children of God when we love God and obey his commandments.

For the love of God is this, that we keep his commandments. And his commandments are not burdensome, for whoever is begotten by God conquers the world. And the victory that conquers the world is our faith.

Who indeed is the victor over the world but the one who believes that Jesus is the Son of God?

This is the one who came through water and blood, Jesus Christ, not by water alone, but by water and blood. The Spirit is the one who testifies, and the Spirit is truth.

So there are three that testify, the Spirit, the water, and the blood, and the three are of one accord.

If we accept human testimony, the testimony of God is surely greater. Now the testimony of God is this, that he has testified on behalf of his Son

Alleluia Cf. Jn 1:29

R. Alleluia, alleluia.

John saw Jesus approaching him, and said:

Behold the Lamb of God who takes away the sin of the world.

R. Alleluia, alleluia.

Gospel Mk 1:7-11
This is what John the Baptist proclaimed:

"One mightier than I is coming after me.

I am not worthy to stoop and loosen the thongs of his sandals. I have baptized you with water; he will baptize you with the Holy Spirit."

It happened in those days that Jesus came from Nazareth of Galilee and was baptized in the Jordan by John.

On coming up out of the water he saw the heavens being torn open and the Spirit, like a dove, descending upon him.

And a voice came from the heavens, "You are my beloved Son; with you I am well pleased.

JANUARY 11TH, 2021

Monday of the First Week in Ordinary Time

1st Reading HEB 1:1-6

Brothers and sisters: In times past, God spoke in partial and various ways to our ancestors through the prophets; in these last days, he spoke to us through the Son, whom he made heir of all things and through whom he created the universe, who is the refulgence of his glory, the very imprint of his being, and who sustains all things by his mighty word. When he had accomplished purification from sins, he took his seat at the right hand of the Majesty on high, as far superior to the angels as the name he has inherited is more excellent than theirs.

For to which of the angels did God ever say: You are my Son; this day I have begotten you? Or again: I will be a father to him, and he shall be a Son to me? And again, when he leads the first born into the world, he says: Let all the angels of God worship him

Responsorial Psalm PS 97:1 AND 2B, 6 AND 7C, 9

R. (see 7c) Let all his angels worship him.

The LORD is king; let the earth rejoice; let the many isles be glad. Justice and judgment are the foundation of his throne.

R. Let all his angels worship him.

The heavens proclaim his justice, and all peoples see his glory. Let all his angels worship him.

R. Let all his angels worship him.

Because you, O LORD, are the Most High over all the earth, exalted far above all gods.

R. Let all his angels worship him.

Alleluia MK 1:15

R. Alleluia, alleluia.

The Kingdom of God is at hand; repent and believe in the Gospel.

R. Alleluia, alleluia.

After John had been arrested, Jesus came to Galilee proclaiming the Gospel of God: "This is the time of fulfillment. The Kingdom of God is at hand. Repent, and believe in the Gospel." As he passed by the Sea of Galilee, he saw Simon and his brother Andrew casting their nets into the sea; they were fishermen. Jesus said to them, "Come after me, and I will make you fishers of men. "Then they left their nets and followed him. He walked along a little farther and saw James, the son of Zebedee, and his brother John. They too were in a boat mending their nets. Then he called them. So they left their father Zebedee in the boat along with the hired men and followed him.

JANUARY 12TH, 2021

Tuesday of the First Week in Ordinary Time

1st Reading HEB 2:5-12

It was not to angels that God subjected the world to come, of which we are speaking. Instead, someone has testified somewhere: What is man that you are mindful of him, or the son of man that you care for him? You made him for a little while lower than the angels; you crowned him with glory and honor, subjecting all things under his feet. In "subjecting" all things to him, he left nothing not "subject to him. "Yet at present we do not see "all things subject to him," but we do see Jesus "crowned with glory and honor" because he suffered death, he who "for a little while" was made "lower than the angels," that by the grace of God he might taste death for everyone. For it was fitting that he, for whom and through whom all things exist, in bringing many children to glory, should make the leader to their salvation perfect through suffering. He who consecrates and those who are being consecrated all have one origin. Therefore, he is not ashamed to call them "brothers" saying: I will proclaim your name to my brethren, in the midst of the assembly I will praise you.

Responsorial Psalm   PS 8:2AB AND 5, 6-7, 8-9

R. You have given your Son rule over the works of your hands.

O LORD, our Lord, how glorious is your name over all the earth! What is man that you should be mindful of him, or the son of man that you should care for him?

R. You have given your Son rule over the works of your hands.

You have made him little less than the angels, and crowned him with glory and honor. You have given him rule over the works of your hands, putting all things under his feet.

R. You have given your Son rule over the works of your hands.

All sheep and oxen, yes, and the beasts of the field, The birds of the air, the fishes of the sea, and whatever swims the paths of the seas.

R. You have given your Son rule over the works of your hands.

Alleluias   SEE 1 THES 2:13

R. Alleluia, alleluia.

Receive the word of God, not as the word of men, but as it truly is, the word of God.

R. Alleluia, alleluia.

Gospel MK 1:21-28
Jesus came to Capernaum with his followers, and on the Sabbath he entered the synagogue and taught. The people were astonished at his teaching, for he taught them as one having authority and not as the scribes. In their synagogue was a man with an unclean spirit; he cried out, "What have you to do with us, Jesus of Nazareth? Have you come to destroy us? I know who you are—the Holy One of God!" Jesus rebuked him and said, "Quiet! Come out of him. The unclean spirit convulsed him and with a loud cry came out of him. All were amazed and asked one another, "What is this? A new teaching with authority. He commands even the unclean spirits and they obey him." His fame spread everywhere throughout the whole region of Galilee.

JANUARY 13TH, 2021
Wednesday of the First Week in Ordinary Time

1st Reading   HEB 2:14-18
Since the children share in blood and Flesh, Jesus likewise shared in them, that through death he might destroy the one who has the power of death, that is, the Devil, and free those who through fear of death had been subject to slavery all their life. Surely he did not help angels but rather the descendants of Abraham; therefore, he had to become like his brothers and

sisters in every way, that he might be a merciful and faithful high priest before God to expiate the sins of the people. Because he himself was tested through what he suffered, he is able to help those who are being tested.

Responsorial Psalm PS 105:1-2, 3-4, 6-7, 8-9
R. (8a) The Lord remembers his covenant forever.

or:

R. Alleluia.

Give thanks to the LORD, invoke his name; make known among the nations his deeds. Sing to him, sing his praise, proclaim all his wondrous deeds.

R... The Lord remembers his covenant forever.

or:

R. Alleluia.

Glory in his holy name; rejoice, O hearts that seek the LORD! Look to the LORD in his strength; seek to serve him constantly.

R... The Lord remembers his covenant for ever.

or:

R. Alleluia.

You descendants of Abraham, his servants, sons of Jacob, his chosen ones! He, the LORD, is our God; throughout the earth his judgments prevail.

R. The Lord remembers his covenant for ever.

or:

R. Alleluia.

He remembers forever his covenant which he made binding for a thousand generations. Which he entered into with Abraham and by his oath to Isaac.

R. The Lord remembers his covenant for ever.

or:

R. Alleluia.

Alleluia JN 10:27

R. Alleluia, alleluia.

My sheep hear my voice, says the Lord. I know them, and they follow me.

R. Alleluia, alleluia.

Gospel MK 1:29-39

On leaving the synagogue Jesus entered the house of Simon and Andrew with James and John. Simon's mother-in-law lay sick with a fever. They immediately told him about her. He approached, grasped her hand, and helped her up. Then the fever left her and she waited on them. When it was evening, after sunset, they brought to him all who were ill or possessed by demons. The whole town was gathered at the door. He cured many who were sick with various diseases, and he drove out many demons, not permitting them to speak because they knew him. Rising very early before dawn, he left and went off to a deserted place, where he prayed. Simon and those who were with him pursued him and on finding him said, "Everyone is looking for you." He told them, "Let us go on to the nearby villages that I may preach there also. For this purpose have I come." So he went into their synagogues, preaching and driving out demons throughout the whole of Galilee.

JANUARY 14TH, 2021
Memorial of Saint Anthony, Abbot

1st Reading HEB 3:7-14

The Holy Spirit says: Oh, that today you would hear his voice, "Harden not your hearts as at the rebellion in the day of testing in the desert, where your ancestors tested and tried me and saw my works for forty years. Because of this I was provoked with that generation and I said, 'They have always been of erring heart, and they do not know my ways.' As I swore in my wrath, 'They shall not enter into my rest.'" Take care, brothers and sisters, that none of you may have an evil and unfaithful heart, so as to forsake the living God. Encourage yourselves daily while it is still "today," so that none of you may grow hardened by the deceit of sin. We have become partners of Christ if only we hold the beginning of the reality firm until the end.

R. If today you hear his voice, harden not your hearts.

Come, let us bow down in worship; let us kneel before the LORD who made us. For he is our God, and we are the people he shepherds, the flock he guides.

R. If today you hear his voice, harden not your hearts.

Oh, that today you would hear his voice: "Harden not your hearts as at Meribah, as in the day of Massah in the desert, Where your fathers tempted me; they tested me though they had seen my works."

R. If today you hear his voice, harden not your hearts.

Forty years I was wearied of that generation; I said: "This people's heart goes astray; they do not know my ways." Therefore I swore in my anger: "They shall never enter my rest."

R. If today you hear his voice, harden not your hearts.

Alleluia MT 4:23

R. Alleluia, alleluia.

Jesus preached the Gospel of the Kingdom and cured every disease among the people.

R. Alleluia, alleluia.

Gospel MK 1:40-45

A leper came to him and kneeling down begged him and said, "If you wish, you can make me clean." Moved with pity, he stretched out his hand, touched the leper, and said to him, "I do will it. Be made clean." The leprosy left him immediately, and he was made clean. Then, warning him sternly, he dismissed him at once. Then he said to him, "See that you tell no one anything, but go, show yourself to the priest and offer for your cleansing what Moses prescribed; that will be proof for them." The man went away and began to publicize the whole matter. He spread the report abroad so that it was impossible for Jesus to enter a town openly. He remained outside in deserted places, and people kept coming to him from everywhere.

1st Reading HEB 4:1-5, 11

Let us be on our guard while the promise of entering into his rest remains, that none of you seem to have failed. For in fact we have received the Good News just as our ancestors did. But the word that they heard did not profit them, for they were not united in faith with those who listened. For we who believed enter into that rest, just as he has said: As I swore in my wrath, "They shall not enter into my rest," and yet his works were accomplished at the foundation of the world. For he has spoken somewhere about the seventh day in this manner, And God rested on the seventh day from all his works; and again, in the previously mentioned place. They shall not enter into my rest. Therefore, let us strive to enter into that rest, so that no one may fall after the same example of disobedience.

Responsorial Psalm   PS 78:3 AND 4BC, 6C-7, 8
R (see 7b) Do not forget the works of the Lord!

What we have heard and know, and what our fathers have declared to us, we will declare to the generation to come.

The glorious deeds of the LORD and his strength.

R. Do not forget the works of the Lord!

That they too may rise and declare to their sons that they should put their hope in God, And not forget the deeds of God but keep his commands.

R. Do not forget the works of the Lord!

And not be like their fathers, a generation wayward and rebellious, A generation that kept not its heart steadfast nor its spirit faithful toward God.

R. Do not forget the works of the Lord!

Alleluia LK 7:16

R. Alleluia, alleluia.

A great prophet has arisen in our midst and God has visited his people.

R. Alleluia, alleluia.

Gospel   MK 2:1-12

When Jesus returned to Capernaum after some days, it became known that he was at home. Many gathered together so that there was no longer room for them, not even around the door, and he preached the word to them. They came bringing to him a paralytic carried by four men. Unable to get near Jesus because of the crowd, they opened up the roof above him. After they had broken through, they let down the mat on which the paralytic was lying. When Jesus saw their faith, he said to him, "Child, your sins are forgiven." Now some of the scribes were sitting there asking themselves, "Why does this man speak that way? He is blaspheming. Who but God alone can forgive sins?" Jesus immediately knew in his mind what they were thinking to themselves, so he said, "Why are you thinking such things in your hearts? Which is easier, to say to the paralytic, 'Your sins are forgiven,' or to say, 'Rise, pick up your mat and walk'? But that you may know that the Son of Man has authority to forgive sins on earth" –he said to the paralytic, "I say to you, rise, pick up your mat, and go home." He rose, picked up his mat at once, and went away in the sight of everyone. They were all astounded and glorified God, saying, "We have never seen anything like this."

JANUARY 16TH, 2021
Saturday of the First Week in Ordinary Time

1st Reading HEB 4:12-16

The word of God is living and effective, sharper than any two-edged sword, penetrating even between soul and spirit, joints and marrow, and able to discern reflections and thoughts of the heart. No creature is concealed from him, but everything is naked and exposed to the eyes of him to whom we must render an account. Since we have a great high priest who has passed through the heavens, Jesus, the Son of God, let us hold fast to our confession. For we do not have a high priest who is unable to sympathize with our weaknesses, but one who has similarly been tested in every way, yet without sin. So let us confidently approach the throne of grace to receive mercy and to find grace for timely help.

Responsorial Psalm PS 19:8, 9, 10, 15
R. Your words, Lord, are Spirit and life.

The law of the LORD is perfect, refreshing the soul. The decree of the LORD is trustworthy, giving wisdom to the simple.

R. Your words, Lord, are Spirit and life.

The precepts of the LORD are right, rejoicing the heart; The command of the LORD is clear, enlightening the eye.

R. Your words, Lord, are Spirit and life.

The fear of the LORD is pure, enduring forever; The ordinances of the LORD are true, all of them just.

R. Your words, Lord, are Spirit and life.

Let the words of my mouth and the thought of my heart find favor before you, O LORD, my rock and my redeemer.

R. Your words, Lord, are Spirit and life.

Alleluia LK 4:18

R. Alleluia, alleluia.

The Lord sent me to bring glad tidings to the poor and to proclaim liberty to captives.

R. Alleluia, alleluia.

Gospel MK 2:13-17

Jesus went out along the sea. All the crowd came to him and he taught them. As he passed by, he saw Levi, son of Alphaeus, sitting at the customs post. Jesus said to him, "Follow me." And he got up and followed Jesus. While he was at table in his house, many tax collectors and sinners sat with Jesus and his disciples; for there were many who followed him. Some scribes who were Pharisees saw that Jesus was eating with sinners and tax collectors and said to his disciples, "Why does he eat with tax collectors and sinners?" Jesus heard this and said to them, "Those who are well do not need a physician, but the sick do. I did not come to call the righteous but sinners."

JANUARY 17TH, 2021
Second Sunday in Ordinary Time

1st Reading   1 Sm 3:3b-10, 19

Samuel was sleeping in the temple of the LORD where the ark of God was.

The LORD called to Samuel, who answered, "Here I am." Samuel ran to Eli and said, "Here I am. You called me." "I did not call you," Eli said. "Go back to sleep." So he went back to sleep.

Again the LORD called Samuel, who rose and went to Eli. "Here I am," he said. "You called me."

But Eli answered, "I did not call you, my son. Go back to sleep."

At that time Samuel was not familiar with the LORD, because the LORD had not revealed anything to him as yet.

The LORD called Samuel again, for the third time. Getting up and going to Eli, he said, "Here I am. You called me." Then Eli understood that the LORD was calling the youth. So he said to Samuel, "Go to sleep, and if you are called, reply,

Speak, LORD, for your servant is listening." When Samuel went to sleep in his place, the LORD came and revealed his presence, calling out as before, "Samuel, Samuel!" Samuel answered, "Speak, for your servant is listening."

Samuel grew up, and the LORD was with him, not permitting any word of his to be without effect.

Responsorial Psalm   Ps 40:2, 4, 7-8, 8-9, 10
R. (8a and 9a) Here am I, Lord; I come to do your will.

I have waited, waited for the LORD, and he stooped toward me and heard my cry.

And he put a new song into my mouth, a hymn to our God.

R. Here am I, Lord; I come to do your will.

Sacrifice or offering you wished not, but ears open to obedience you gave me.

Holocausts or sin-offerings you sought not; then said I, "Behold I come."

R. Here I am, Lord; I come to do your will.

"In the written scroll it is prescribed for me, to do your will, O my God, is my delight, and your law is within my heart!"

R. Here am I, Lord; I come to do your will.

I announced your justice in the vast assembly; I did not restrain my lips, as you, O LORD, know.

R. Here am I, Lord; I come to do your will.

2nd Reading   1 Cor 6:13c-15a, 17-20
Brothers and sisters:

The body is not for immorality, but for the Lord, and the Lord is for the body;

God raised the Lord and will also raise us by his power.

Do you not know that your bodies are members of Christ?

But whoever is joined to the Lord becomes one Spirit with him.

Avoid immorality. Every other sin a person commits is outside the body, but the immoral person sins against his own body.

Do you not know that your body is a temple of the Holy Spirit within you, whom you have from God, and that you are not your own? For you have been purchased at a price.

Therefore glorify God in your body.

Alleluia   Jn 1:41, 17b

R. Alleluia, alleluia.

We have found the Messiah:Jesus Christ, who brings us truth and grace..

R. Alleluia, alleluia.

Gospel   Jn 1:35-42
John was standing with two of his disciples, and as he watched Jesus walk by, he said,

"Behold, the Lamb of God."

The two disciples heard what he said and followed Jesus. Jesus turned and saw them following him and said to them,

"What are you looking for?" They said to him, "Rabbi" — which translated means Teacher —, "where are you staying?"

He said to them, "Come, and you will see." So they went and saw where Jesus was staying, and they stayed with him that day.

It was about four in the afternoon. Andrew, the brother of Simon Peter, was one of the two who heard John and followed Jesus.

He first found his own brother Simon and told him,

"We have found the Messiah" — which is translated Christ —.

Then he brought him to Jesus. Jesus looked at him and said,

"You are Simon the son of John; you will be called Cephas" — which is translated Peter.

JANUARY 18TH, 2021
Monday of the Second Week in Ordinary Time

1st Reading HEB 5:1-10
Brothers and sisters: Every high priest is taken from among men and made their representative before God, to offer gifts and sacrifices for sins. He is able to deal patiently with the ignorant and erring, for he himself is beset by weakness and so, for this reason, must make sin offerings for himself as well as for the people. No one takes this honor upon himself but only when called by God, just as Aaron was. In the same way, it was not Christ who glorified himself in becoming high priest, but rather the one who said to him: You are my Son: this day I have begotten you; just as he says in another place, You are a priest forever according to the order of Melchizedek. In the days when he was in the Flesh, he offered prayers and supplications with loud cries and tears to the one who was able to save him from death, and he was heard because of his reverence. Son though he was, he learned obedience from what he suffered; and when he was made perfect, he became the source of eternal salvation for all who obey him.

Responsorial Psalm PS 110:1, 2, 3, 4
R. You are a priest for ever, in the line of Melchizedek.

The LORD said to my Lord: "Sit at my right hand till I make your enemies your footstool."

R. You are a priest for ever, in the line of Melchizedek.

The scepter of your power the LORD will stretch forth from Zion: "Rule in the midst of your enemies."

R. You are a priest for ever, in the line of Melchizedek.

"Yours is princely power in the day of your birth, in holy splendor; before the daystar, like the dew, I have begotten you."

R. You are a priest for ever, in the line of Melchizedek.

The LORD has sworn, and he will not repent:

"You are a priest forever, according to the order of Melchizedek."

R. You are a priest for ever, in the line of Melchizedek.

Alleluia   HEB 4:12

R. Alleluia, alleluia.

The word of God is living and effective, able to discern reflections and thoughts of the heart.

R. Alleluia, alleluia.

Gospel   MK 2:18-22

The disciples of John and of the Pharisees were accustomed to fast. People came to Jesus and objected, "Why do the disciples of John and the disciples of the Pharisees fast, but your disciples do not fast?" Jesus answered them, "Can the wedding guests fast while the bridegroom is with them? As long as they have the bridegroom with them they cannot fast. But the days will come when the bridegroom is taken away from them, and then they will fast on that day. No one sews a piece of unshrunken cloth on an old cloak. If he does, its fullness pulls away, the new from the old, and the tear gets worse. Likewise, no one pours new wine into old wineskins. Otherwise, the wine will burst the skins, and both the wine and the skins are ruined. Rather, new wine is poured into fresh wineskins."

JANUARY 19TH, 2021

Tuesday of the Second Week in Ordinary Time

Brothers and sisters: God is not unjust so as to overlook your work and the love you have demonstrated for his name by having served and continuing to serve the holy ones. We earnestly desire each of you to demonstrate the same eagerness for the fulfillment of hope until the end, so that you may not become sluggish, but imitators of those who, through faith and patience, are inheriting the promises. When God made the promise to Abraham, since he had no one greater by whom to swear, he swore by himself, and said, I will indeed bless you and multiply you. And so, after patient waiting, Abraham obtained the promise. Now, men swear by someone greater than themselves; for them an oath serves as a guarantee and puts an end to all argument. So when God wanted to give the heirs of his promise an even clearer demonstration of the immutability of his purpose, he intervened with an oath, so that by two immutable things, in which it was impossible for God to lie, we who have taken refuge might be strongly encouraged to hold fast to the hope that lies before us. This we have as an anchor of the soul, sure and firm, which reaches into the interior behind the veil, where Jesus has entered on our behalf as forerunner, becoming high priest forever according to the order of Melchizedek.

Responsorial Psalm   PS 111:1-2, 4-5, 9 AND 10C

R... The Lord will remember his covenant forever.

or:

R. Alleluia.

I will give thanks to the LORD with all my heart in the company and assembly of the just. Great are the works of the LORD, exquisite in all their delights.

R. The Lord will remember his covenant for ever.

or:

R. Alleluia.

He has won renown for his wondrous deeds; gracious and merciful is the LORD. He has given food to those who fear him; he will forever be mindful of his covenant.

R. The Lord will remember his covenant for ever.

or:

R. Alleluia.

He has sent deliverance to his people; he has ratified his covenant forever; holy and awesome is his name. His praise endures forever.

R... The Lord will remember his covenant for ever.

or:

R. Alleluia.

Alleluia   EPH 1:17-18

R. Alleluia, alleluia.

May the Father of our Lord Jesus Christ enlighten the eyes of our hearts, that we may know what is the hope that belongs to our call.

R. Alleluia, alleluia.

Gospel MK 2:23-28

As Jesus was passing through a field of grain on the Sabbath, his disciples began to make a path while picking the heads of grain. At this the Pharisees said to him, "Look, why are they doing what is unlawful on the Sabbath?" He said to them, "Have you never read what David did when he was in need and he and his companions were hungry? How he went into the house of God when Abiathar was high priest and ate the bread of offering that only the priests could lawfully eat, and shared it with his companions?" Then he said to them, "The Sabbath was made for man, not man for the Sabbath. That is why the Son of Man is lord even of the Sabbath."

JANUARY 20TH, 2021

Wednesday of the Second Week in Ordinary Time

1st Reading HEB 7:1-3, 15-17

Melchizedek, king of Salem and priest of God Most High, met Abraham as he returned from his defeat of the kings and blessed him. And Abraham apportioned to him a tenth of everything. His name first means righteous king, and he was also "king of Salem," that is, king of peace. Without father, mother, or ancestry, without beginning of days or end of life, thus made to resemble the Son of God, he remains a priest forever. It is even more obvious if another priest is raised up after the likeness of Melchizedek, who has become so, not by a law expressed in a commandment concerning physical descent but by the power of a life that cannot be destroyed. For it is testified: You are a priest forever according to the order of Melchizedek.

Responsorial Psalm   PS 110:1, 2, 3, 4

R. (4b) you are a priest for ever, in the line of Melchizedek.

The LORD said to my Lord: "Sit at my right hand till I make your enemies your footstool."

R. You are a priest for ever, in the line of Melchizedek.

The scepter of your power the LORD will stretch forth from Zion: "Rule in the midst of your enemies."

R. You are a priest for ever, in the line of Melchizedek.

"Yours is princely power in the day of your birth, in holy splendor; before the daystar, like the dew, I have begotten you."

R. You are a priest for ever, in the line of Melchizedek.

The LORD has sworn, and he will not repent: "You are a priest forever, according to the order of Melchizedek."

R. You are a priest for ever, in the line of Melchizedek.

Alleluia MT 4:23

R. Alleluia, alleluia.

Jesus preached the Gospel of the Kingdom and cured every disease among the people.

R. Alleluia, alleluia.

Gospel MK 3:1-6

Jesus entered the synagogue. There was a man there who had a withered hand. They watched Jesus closely to see if he would cure him on the Sabbath so that they might accuse him. He said to the man with the withered hand, "Come up here before us." Then he said to the Pharisees, "Is it lawful to do good on the Sabbath rather than to do evil, to save life rather than to destroy it?" But they remained silent. Looking around at them with anger and grieved at their hardness of heart, Jesus said to the man, "Stretch out your hand." He stretched it out and his hand was restored. The Pharisees went out and immediately took counsel with the Herodians against him to put him to death.

JANUARY 21ST, 2021
Memorial of Saint Agnes, Virgin and Martyr

1st Reading   HEB 7:25—8:6
Jesus is always able to save those who approach God through him, since he lives forever to make intercession for them. It was fitting that we should have such a high priest: holy, innocent, undefiled, separated from sinners, higher than the heavens. He has no need, as did the high priests, to offer sacrifice day after day, first for his own sins and then for those of the people; he did that once for all when he offered himself. For the law appoints men subject to weakness to be high priests, but the word of the oath, which was taken after the law, appoints a son, who has been made perfect forever. The main point of what has been said is this: we have such a high priest, who has taken his seat at the right hand of the throne of the Majesty in heaven, a minister of the sanctuary and of the true tabernacle that the Lord, not man, set up. Now every high priest is appointed to offer gifts and sacrifices; thus the necessity for this one also to have something to offer. If then he were on earth, he would not be a priest, since there are those who offer gifts according to the law. They worship in a copy and shadow of the heavenly sanctuary, as Moses was warned when he was about to erect the tabernacle. For God says, "See that you make everything according to the pattern shown you on the mountain." Now he has obtained so much more excellent a ministry as he is mediator of a better covenant, enacted on better promises.

Responsorial Psalm   PS 40:7-8A, 8B-9, 10, 17
R. Here am I, Lord; I come to do your will.

Sacrifice or oblation you wished not, but ears open to obedience you gave me. Burnt offerings or sin-offerings you sought not; then said I, "Behold I come."

R. Here am I, Lord; I come to do your will.

"In the written scroll it is prescribed for me, To do your will, O my God, is my delight, and your law is within my heart!"

R. Here am I, Lord; I come to do your will.

I announced your justice in the vast assembly; I did not restrain my lips, as you, O LORD, know.

R. Here am I, Lord; I come to do your will.

May all who seek you exult and be glad in you, And may those who love your salvation say ever, "The LORD be glorified."

R. Here am I, Lord; I come to do your will.

Alleluia 2 TM 1:10

R. Alleluia, alleluia.

Our Savior Jesus Christ has destroyed death and brought life to light through the Gospel.

R. Alleluia, alleluia.

Gospel MK 3:7-12

Jesus withdrew toward the sea with his disciples. A large number of people followed from Galilee and from Judea. Hearing what he was doing, a large number of people came to him also from Jerusalem, from Idumea, from beyond the Jordan, and from the neighborhood of Tyre and Sidon. He told his disciples to have a boat ready for him because of the crowd, so that they would not crush him. He had cured many and, as a result, those who had diseases were pressing upon him to touch him. And whenever unclean spirits saw him they would fall down before him and shout, "You are the Son of God." He warned them sternly not to make him known.

JANUARY 22ND, 2021
Day of Prayer for the Legal Protection of Unborn Children

1st Reading Heb 8:6-13
Brothers and sisters:

Now our high priest has obtained so much more excellent a ministry as he is mediator of a better covenant, enacted on better promises.

For if that first covenant had been faultless, no place would have been sought for a second one.

But he finds fault with them and says: Behold, the days are coming, says the Lord, when I will conclude a new covenant with the house of

Israel and the house of Judah. It will not be like the covenant I made with their fathers the day I took them by the hand to lead them forth from the land of Egypt; for they did not stand by my covenant and I ignored them, says the Lord.

But this is the covenant I will establish with the house of Israel after those days, says the Lord:

I will put my laws in their minds and I will write them upon their hearts.

I will be their God, and they shall be my people.

And they shall not teach, each one his fellow citizen and kin, saying,

"Know the Lord," for all shall know me, from least to greatest.

For I will forgive their evildoing and remember their sins no more.

When he speaks of a "new" covenant, he declares the first one obsolete.

And what has become obsolete and has grown old is close to disappearing.

Responsorial Psalm   85:8 and 10, 11-12, 13-14
R. (11a) Kindness and truth shall meet.

Show us, O LORD, your mercy, and grant us your salvation.

Near indeed is his salvation to those who fear him, glory dwelling in our land.

R. Kindness and truth shall meet.

Kindness and truth shall meet; justice and peace shall kiss.

Truth shall spring out of the earth, and justice shall look down from heaven.

R. Kindness and truth shall meet.

The LORD himself will give his benefits; our land shall yield its increase.

Justice shall walk before him, and salvation, along the way of his steps.

R. Kindness and truth shall meet.

Alleluia

R. Alleluia, alleluia.

God was reconciling the world to himself in Christ, and entrusting to us the message of reconciliation.

R. Alleluia, alleluia.

Gospel   Mk 3:13-19
Jesus went up the mountain and summoned those whom he wanted and they came to him.

He appointed Twelve, whom he also named Apostles, that they might be with him and he might send them forth to preach and to have authority to drive out demons:

He appointed the Twelve: Simon, whom he named Peter;

James, son of Zebedee, and John the brother of James, whom he named Boanerges, that is, sons of thunder;

Andrew, Philip, Bartholomew,Matthew, Thomas, James the son of Alphaeus;

Thaddeus, Simon the Cananean, and Judas Iscariot who betrayed him.

JANUARY 23RD, 2021
Saturday of the Second Week in Ordinary Time

1st Reading   Heb 9:2-3, 11-14
A tabernacle was constructed, the outer one, in which were the lampstand, the table, and the bread of offering; this is called the Holy Place.

Behind the second veil was the tabernacle called the Holy of Holies.

But when Christ came as high priest of the good things that have come to be, passing through the greater and more perfect tabernacle not made by hands, that is, not belonging to this creation, he entered once for all into the sanctuary, not with the blood of goats and calves but with his own Blood, thus obtaining eternal redemption.

For if the blood of goats and bulls and the sprinkling of a heifer's ashes can sanctify those who are defiled so that their flesh is cleansed, how much more will the Blood of Christ, who through the eternal spirit offered himself unblemished to God, cleanse our consciences from dead works to worship the living God.

Responsorial Psalm PS 47:2-3, 6-7, 8-9
R. (6) God mounts his throne to shouts of joy: a blare of trumpets for the Lord.

All you peoples, clap your hands, shout to God with cries of gladness,

For the LORD, the Most High, the awesome, is the great king over all the earth.

R. God mounts his throne to shouts of joy: a blare of trumpets for the Lord.

God mounts his throne amid shouts of joy; the LORD, amid trumpet blasts.

Sing praise to God, sing praise; sing praise to our king, sing praise.

R. God mounts his throne to shouts of joy: a blare of trumpets for the Lord.

For king of all the earth is God: sing hymns of praise.

God reigns over the nations, God sits upon his holy throne.

R. God mounts his throne to shouts of joy: a blare of trumpets for the Lord.

Alleluia: See Acts 16:14b

R. Alleluia, alleluia.

Open our hearts, O Lord, to listen to the words of your Son.

R. Alleluia, alleluia.

Gospel MK 3:20-21
Jesus came with his disciples into the house. Again the crowd gathered, making it impossible for them even to eat. When his relatives heard of this they set out to seize him, for they said, "He is out of his mind."

JANUARY 24TH, 2021
Third Sunday in Ordinary Time

1st Reading   Jon 3:1-5, 10
The word of the LORD came to Jonah, saying:

"Set out for the great city of Nineveh, and announce to it the message that I will tell you."

So Jonah made ready and went to Nineveh, according to the LORD'S bidding. Now Nineveh was an enormously large city; it took three days to go through it.

Jonah began his journey through the city, and had gone but a single day's walk announcing,

"Forty days more and Nineveh shall be destroyed, "when the people of Nineveh believed God; they proclaimed a fast and all of them, great and small, put on sackcloth.

When God saw by their actions how they turned from their evil way, he repented of the evil that he had threatened to do to them; he did not carry it out.

Responsorial Psalm: Ps 25:4-5, 6-7, 8-9
R. (4a) Teach me your ways, O Lord.

Your ways, O LORD, make known to me; teach me your paths,

Guide me in your truth and teach me, for you are God my savior.

R. Teach me your ways, O Lord.

Remember that your compassion, O LORD, and your love are from of old.

In your kindness remember me, because of your goodness, O LORD.

R. Teach me your ways, O Lord.

Good and upright is the LORD; thus he shows sinners the way.

He guides the humble to justice, and teaches the humble his way.

R. Teach me your ways, O Lord.

2nd Reading 1 Cor 7:29-31

I tell you, brothers and sisters, the time is running out.

From now on, let those having wives act as not having them, those weeping as not weeping, those rejoicing as not rejoicing, those buying as not owning, those using the world as not using it fully.

For the world in its present form is passing away.

Alleluia Mk 1:15

R. Alleluia, alleluia.

The kingdom of God is at hand. Repent and believe in the Gospel..

R. Alleluia, alleluia.

Gospel Mk 1:14-20

After John had been arrested,

Jesus came to Galilee proclaiming the gospel of God: "This is the time of fulfillment. The kingdom of God is at hand. Repent, and believe in the gospel." As he passed by the Sea of Galilee, he saw Simon and his brother Andrew casting their nets into the sea; they were fishermen.

Jesus said to them, "Come after me, and I will make you fishers of men."

Then they abandoned their nets and followed him. He walked along a little farther and saw James, the son of Zebedee, and his brother John. They too were in a boat mending their nets. Then he called them. So they left their father Zebedee in the boat along with the hired men and followed him.

JANUARY 25TH, 2021

Feast of the Conversion of Saint Paul, Apostle

1st Reading   Acts 22:3-16

Paul addressed the people in these words:

"I am a Jew, born in Tarsus in Cilicia, but brought up in this city.

At the feet of Gamaliel I was educated strictly in our ancestral law and was zealous for God, just as all of you are today. I persecuted this Way to death, binding both men and women and delivering them to prison.

Even the high priest and the whole council of elders can testify on my behalf. For from them I even received letters to the brothers and set out for Damascus to bring back to Jerusalem in chains for punishment those there as well.

"On that journey as I drew near to Damascus, about noon a great light from the sky suddenly shone around me. I fell to the ground and heard a voice saying to me, 'Saul, Saul, why are you persecuting me?'

I replied, 'Who are you, sir?'

And he said to me, 'I am Jesus the Nazorean whom you are persecuting.'

My companions saw the light but did not hear the voice of the one who spoke to me. I asked, 'What shall I do, sir?'

The Lord answered me, 'Get up and go into Damascus, and there you will be told about everything appointed for you to do.'

Since I could see nothing because of the brightness of that light, I was led by hand by my companions and entered Damascus.

"A certain Ananias, a devout observer of the law, and highly spoken of by all the Jews who lived there, came to me and stood there and said, 'Saul, my brother, regain your sight.' And at that very moment I regained my sight and saw him.

Then he said, 'The God of our ancestors designated you to know his will, to see the Righteous One, and to hear the sound of his voice; for you will be his witness before all to what you have seen and heard.

Now, why delay? Get up and have yourself baptized and your sins washed away, calling upon his name.'

OR:

Acts 9:1-22

Saul, still breathing murderous threats against the disciples of the Lord, went to the high priest and asked him for letters to the synagogues in Damascus, that, if he should find any men or women who belonged to the Way, he might bring them back to Jerusalem in chains. On his journey, as he was nearing Damascus, a light from the sky suddenly flashed around him. He fell to the ground and heard a voice saying to him,

"Saul, Saul, why are you persecuting me?"

He said, "Who are you, sir?" The reply came, "I am Jesus, whom you are persecuting. Now get up and go into the city and you will be told what you must do."

The men who were traveling with him stood speechless, for they heard the voice but could see no one. Saul got up from the ground, but when he opened his eyes he could see nothing; so they led him by the hand and brought him to Damascus.

For three days he was unable to see, and he neither ate nor drank.

There was a disciple in Damascus named Ananias, and the Lord said to him in a vision, Ananias."

He answered, "Here I am, Lord."

The Lord said to him, "Get up and go to the street called Straight and ask at the house of Judas for a man from Tarsus named Saul.

He is there praying, and in a vision he has seen a man named Ananias come in and lay his hands on him, that he may regain his sight."

But Ananias replied, "Lord, I have heard from many sources about this man, what evil things he has done to your holy ones in Jerusalem.

And here he has authority from the chief priests to imprison all who call upon your name." But the Lord said to him,

"Go, for this man is a chosen instrument of mine to carry my name before Gentiles, kings, and children of Israel, and I will show him what he will have to suffer for my name." So Ananias went and entered the house; laying his hands on him, he said,

"Saul, my brother, the Lord has sent me,

Jesus who appeared to you on the way by which you came, that you may regain your sight and be filled with the Holy Spirit."

Immediately things like scales fell from his eyes and he regained his sight. He got up and was baptized, and when he had eaten, he recovered his strength.

He stayed some days with the disciples in Damascus, and he began at once to proclaim Jesus in the synagogues, that he is the Son of God.

All who heard him were astounded and said, "Is not this the man who in Jerusalem ravaged those who call upon this name, and came here expressly to take them back in chains to the chief priests?"

But Saul grew all the stronger and confounded the Jews who lived in Damascus, proving that this is the Christ.

Responsorial Psalm   PS 117:1bc, 2

R.   (Mark 16:15) Go out to all the world, and tell the Good News.

or:

R.   Alleluia, alleluia.

Praise the LORD, all you nations; glorify him, all you peoples!

R.   Go out to all the world, and tell the Good News.

or:

R.   Alleluia, alleluia.

For steadfast is his kindness toward us, and the fidelity of the Lord endures forever.

R.   Go out to all the world, and tell the Good News.

or:

R.   Alleluia, alleluia.

Alleluia: See Jn 15:16

R. Alleluia, alleluia.

I chose you from the world, to go and bear fruit that will last, says the Lord.

R. Alleluia, alleluia.

Jesus appeared to the Eleven and said to them:

"Go into the whole world and proclaim the Gospel to every creature.

Whoever believes and is baptized will be saved; whoever does not believe will be condemned.

These signs will accompany those who believe: in my name they will drive out demons, they will speak new languages.

They will pick up serpents with their hands, and if they drink any deadly thing, it will not harm them.

They will lay hands on the sick, and they will recover."

JANUARY 26TH, 2021

Memorial of Saints Timothy and Titus, bishops

1st Reading 2 Tm 1:1-8

Paul, an Apostle of Christ Jesus by the will of God for the promise of life in Christ Jesus, to Timothy, my dear child: grace, mercy, and peace from God the Father and Christ Jesus our Lord.

I am grateful to God, whom I worship with a clear conscience as my ancestors did, as I remember you constantly in my prayers, night and day.

I yearn to see you again, recalling your tears, so that I may be filled with joy, as I recall your sincere faith that first lived in your grandmother Lois and in your mother Eunice and that I am confident lives also in you.

For this reason, I remind you to stir into flame the gift of God that you have through the imposition of my hands.

For God did not give us a spirit of cowardice but rather of power and love and self-control.

So do not be ashamed of your testimony to our Lord, nor of me, a prisoner for his sake; but bear your share of hardship for the Gospel with the strength that comes from God.

OR:

Ti 1:1-5

Paul, a slave of God and Apostle of Jesus Christ for the sake of the faith of God's chosen ones and the recognition of religious truth, in the hope of eternal life that God, who does not lie, promised before time began, who indeed at the proper time revealed his word in the proclamation with which I was entrusted by the command of God our savior, to Titus, my true child in our common faith: grace and peace from God the Father and Christ Jesus our savior.

For this reason I left you in Crete so that you might set right what remains to be done and appoint presbyters in every town, as I directed you.

Responsorial Psalm   PS 96:1-2a, 2b-3, 7-8a, 10
R.   (3) Proclaim God's marvelous deeds to all the nations.

Sing to the LORD a new song; sing to the LORD, all you lands.

Sing to the LORD; bless his name.

R.   Proclaim God's marvelous deeds to all the nations.

Announce his salvation, day after day.

Tell his glory among the nations, among all peoples, his wondrous deeds.

R. Proclaim God's marvelous deeds to all the nations.

Give to the LORD, you families of nations, give to the LORD glory and praise; give to the LORD the glory due his name!

R. Proclaim God's marvelous deeds to all the nations.

Say among the nations: The LORD is king.

He has made the world firm, not to be moved; he governs the peoples with equity.

R. Proclaim God's marvelous deeds to all the nations.

Alleluia   MT 11:25

R. Alleluia, alleluia.

Blessed are you, Father, Lord of heaven and earth; you have revealed to little ones the mysteries of the Kingdom.

R. Alleluia, alleluia.

Gospel   MK 3:31-35

The mother of Jesus and his brothers arrived at the house. Standing outside, they sent word to Jesus and called him. A crowd seated around him told him, "Your mother and your brothers and your sisters are outside asking for you." But he said to them in reply, "Who are my mother and my brothers?" And looking around at those seated in the circle he said, "Here are my mother and my brothers. For whoever does the will of God is my brother and sister and mother."

JANUARY 27TH 2021
Wednesday of the Third Week in Ordinary Time

1st Reading HEB 10:11-18

Every priest stands daily at his ministry, offering frequently those same sacrifices that can never take away sins. But this one offered one sacrifice for sins, and took his seat forever at the right hand of God; now he waits until his enemies are made his footstool. For by one offering he has made perfect forever those who are being consecrated. The Holy Spirit also testifies to us, for after saying: This is the covenant I will establish with them after those days, says the Lord: "I will put my laws in their hearts, and I will write them upon their minds,"he also says: Their sins and their evildoing I will remember no more. Where there is forgiveness of these, there is no longer offering for sin.

Responsorial Psalm   PS 110:1, 2, 3, 4

R. You are a priest forever, in the line of Melchizedek.

The LORD said to my Lord: "Sit at my right hand till I make your enemies your footstool."

R. You are a priest for ever, in the line of Melchizedek.

The scepter of your power the LORD will stretch forth from Zion: "Rule in the midst of your enemies."

R. You are a priest for ever, in the line of Melchizedek.

"Yours is princely power in the day of your birth, in holy splendor; before the daystar, like the dew, I have begotten you."

R. You are a priest for ever, in the line of Melchizedek.

The LORD has sworn, and he will not repent: "You are a priest forever, according to the order of Melchizedek."

R. You are a priest for ever, in the line of Melchizedek.

Alleluia

R. Alleluia, alleluia.

The seed is the word of God, Christ is the sower; all who come to him will live for ever.

R. Alleluia, alleluia.

Gospel MK 4:1-20

On another occasion, Jesus began to teach by the sea. A very large crowd gathered around him so that he got into a boat on the sea and sat down.

And the whole crowd was beside the sea on land. And he taught them at length in parables, and in the course of his instruction he said to them, "Hear this! A sower went out to sow .And as he sowed, some seed fell on the path, and the birds came and ate it up. Other seed fell on rocky ground where it had little soil. It sprang up at once because the soil was not deep. And when the sun rose, it was scorched and it withered for lack of roots. Some seed fell among thorns, and the thorns grew up and choked it and it produced no grain. And some seed fell on rich soil and produced fruit. It came up and grew and yielded thirty, sixty, and a hundredfold." He added, "Whoever has ears to hear ought to hear." And when he was alone, those present along with the Twelve questioned him about the parables. He answered them, "The mystery of the Kingdom of God has been granted to you. But to those outside everything comes in parables, so that they may look and see but not perceive, and hear and listen but not understand, in order that they may not be converted and be forgiven." Jesus said to them, "Do you not understand this parable? Then how will you understand any of the parables? The sower sows the word. These are the ones on the path where the word is sown. As soon as they hear, Satan comes at once and takes away the word sown in them. And these are the ones sown on rocky ground who, when they hear the word, receive it at once with joy. But they have no roots; they last only for a time. Then when tribulation or persecution comes because of the word, they quickly fall away. Those sown among thorns are another sort. They are the people who hear the word, but worldly anxiety, the lure of riches, and the craving for other things intrude and choke the word, and it bears no fruit. But those sown on rich soil are the ones who hear the word and accept it and bear fruit thirty and sixty and a hundredfold."

JANUARY 28TH, 2021
Memorial of Saint Thomas Aquinas, Priest and Doctor of the Church

1st Reading HEB 10:19-25
Brothers and sisters: Since through the Blood of Jesus we have confidence of entrance into the sanctuary by the new and living way he opened for us through the veil, that is, his flesh, and since we have "a great priest over the house of God," let us approach with a sincere heart and in absolute trust, with our hearts sprinkled clean from an evil conscience and our bodies washed in pure water. Let us hold unwaveringly to our confession that gives us hope, for he who made the promise is trustworthy. We must consider how to rouse one another to love and good works. We should not stay away from our assembly, as is the custom of some, but encourage one another, and this all the more as you see the day drawing near.

Responsorial Psalm   PS 24:1-2, 3-4AB, 5-6
R. Lord, this is the people that longs to see your face.

The LORD's are the earth and its fullness; the world and those who dwell in it. For he founded it upon the seas and established it upon the rivers.

R. Lord, this is the people that longs to see your face.

Who can ascend the mountain of the LORD? or who may stand in his holy place? He whose hands are sinless, whose heart is clean, who desires not what is vain.

R. Lord, this is the people that longs to see your face.

He shall receive a blessing from the LORD, a reward from God his savior. Such is the race that seeks for him, that seeks the face of the God of Jacob.

R. Lord, this is the people that longs to see your face.

Alleluia   PS 119:105

R. Alleluia, alleluia.

A lamp to my feet is your word, a light to my path.

R. Alleluia, alleluia.

Gospel   MK 4:21-25
Jesus said to his disciples,"Is a lamp brought in to be placed under a bushel basket or under a bed, and not to be placed on a lampstand? For there is nothing hidden except to be made visible; nothing is secret except to come to light. Anyone who has ears to hear ought to hear." He also told them, "Take care what you hear. The measure with which you measure will be measured out to you, and still more will be given to you. To the one who has, more will be given; from the one who has not, even what he has will be taken away."

JANUARY 29TH, 2021
Friday of the Third Week in Ordinary Time

1st Reading HEB 10:32-39
Remember the days past when, after you had been enlightened, you endured a great contest of suffering. At times you were publicly exposed to abuse and affliction; at other times you associated yourselves with those so treated. You even joined in the sufferings of those in prison and joyfully accepted the confiscation of your property, knowing that you had a better and lasting possession. Therefore, do not throw away your confidence; it will have great recompense. You need endurance to do the will of God and receive what he has promised. For, after just a brief moment, he who is to come shall come; he shall not delay. But my just one shall live by faith, and if he draws back I take no pleasure in him. We are not among those who draw back and perish, but among those who have faith and will possess life.

Responsorial Psalm PS 37:3-4, 5-6, 23-24, 39-40
R. The salvation of the just comes from the Lord.

Trust in the LORD and do good, that you may dwell in the land and be fed in security. Take delight in the LORD, and he will grant you your heart's requests.

R. The salvation of the just comes from the Lord.

Commit to the LORD your way; trust in him, and he will act.

He will make justice dawn for you like the light; bright as the noonday shall be your vindication.

R. The salvation of the just comes from the Lord.

By the LORD are the steps of a man made firm, and he approves his way. Though he fall, he does not lie prostrate, for the hand of the LORD sustains him.

R. The salvation of the just comes from the Lord.

The salvation of the just is from the LORD; he is their refuge in time of distress. And the LORD helps them and delivers them; he delivers them from the wicked and saves them, because they take refuge in him.

R. The salvation of the just comes from the Lord.

Alleluia   MT 11:25

R. Alleluia, alleluia.

Blessed are you, Father, Lord of heaven and earth; you have revealed to little ones the mysteries of the Kingdom.

R. Alleluia, alleluia.

Gospel   MK 4:26-34

Jesus said to the crowds: "This is how it is with the Kingdom of God; it is as if a man were to scatter seed on the land and would sleep and rise night and day and the seed would sprout and grow, he knows not how. Of its own accord the land yields fruit, first the blade, then the ear, then the full grain in the ear. And when the grain is ripe, he wields the sickle at once, for the harvest has come. "He said,"To what shall we compare the Kingdom of God, or what parable can we use for it? It is like a mustard seed that, when it is sown in the ground, is the smallest of all the seeds on the earth. But once it is sown, it springs up and becomes the largest of plants and puts forth large branches, so that the birds of the sky can dwell in its shade." With many such parables he spoke the word to them as they were able to understand it. Without parables he did not speak to them, but to his own disciples he explained everything in private.

JANUARY 30TH, 2021
Saturday of the Third Week in Ordinary Time

1st Reading Heb 11:1-2, 8-19
Brothers and sisters:

Faith is the realization of what is hoped for and evidence of things not seen.

Because of it the ancients were well attested.

By faith Abraham obeyed when he was called to go out to a place that he was to receive as an inheritance; he went out, not knowing where he was to go.

By faith he sojourned in the promised land as in a foreign country, dwelling in tents with Isaac and Jacob, heirs of the same promise; for he was looking forward to the city with foundations, whose architect and maker is God.

By faith he received power to generate, even though he was past the normal age and Sarah herself was sterile for he thought that the one who had made the promise was trustworthy.

So it was that there came forth from one man, himself as good as dead, descendants as numerous as the stars in the sky and as countless as the sands on the seashore.

All these died in faith.

They did not receive what had been promised but saw it and greeted it from afar and acknowledged themselves to be strangers and aliens on earth, for those who speak thus show that they are seeking a homeland.

If they had been thinking of the land from which they had come, they would have had opportunity to return.

But now they desire a better homeland, a heavenly one.

Therefore, God is not ashamed to be called their God, for he has prepared a city for them.

By faith Abraham, when put to the test, offered up Isaac, and he who had received the promises was ready to offer his only son, of whom it was said,

Through Isaac descendants shall bear your name. He reasoned that God was able to raise even from the dead, and he received Isaac back as a symbol.

Responsorial Psalm   Luke 1:69-70, 71-72, 73-75
R. (see 68) Blessed be the Lord the God of Israel; he has come to his people.

He has raised up for us a mighty savior, born of the house of his servant David.

R. Blessed be the Lord the God of Israel; he has come to his people.

Through his holy prophets he promised of old. that he would save us from our sins from the hands of all who hate us.

He promised to show mercy to our fathers and to remember his holy covenant.

R. Blessed be the Lord the God of Israel; he has come to his people.

This was the oath he swore to our father Abraham: to set us free from the bonds of our enemies, free to worship him without fear, holy and righteous in his sight all the days of our life.

R. Blessed be the Lord the God of Israel; he has come to his people.

Alleluia: Jn 3:16

R. Alleluia, alleluia.

God so loved the world that he gave his only-begotten Son, so that everyone who believes in him might have eternal life.

R. Alleluia, alleluia.

Gospel   Mk 4:35-41
On that day, as evening drew on, Jesus said to his disciples: "Let us cross to the other side."

Leaving the crowd, they took Jesus with them in the boat just as he was. And other boats were with him.

A violent squall came up and waves were breaking over the boat, so that it was already filling up. Jesus was in the stern, asleep on a cushion. They woke him and said to him,

"Teacher, do you not care that we are perishing?" He woke up, rebuked the wind, and said to the sea, "Quiet! Be still!"

The wind ceased and there was great calm. Then he asked them, "Why are you terrified? Do you not yet have faith?"

They were filled with great awe and said to one another, "Who then is this whom even wind and sea obey?"

JANUARY 31ST, 2021
Fourth Sunday in Ordinary Time

1st Reading Dt 18:15-20
Moses spoke to all the people, saying:

"A prophet like me will the LORD, your God, raise up for you from among your own kin; to him you shall listen.

This is exactly what you requested of the LORD, your God, at Horeb on the day of the assembly, when you said,

'Let us not again hear the voice of the LORD, our God, nor see this great fire any more, lest we die.' And the LORD said to me, 'This was well said.

I will raise up for them a prophet like you from among their kin, and will put my words into his mouth; he shall tell them all that I command him.

Whoever will not listen to my words which he speaks in my name, I myself will make him answer for it.

But if a prophet presumes to speak in my name an oracle that I have not commanded him to speak, or speaks in the name of other gods, he shall die.'"

Responsorial Psalm PS 95:1-2, 6-7, 7-9
R. (8) If today you hear his voice, harden not your hearts.

Come, let us sing joyfully to the LORD; let us acclaim the rock of our salvation.

Let us come into his presence with thanksgiving; let us joyfully sing psalms to him.

R. If today you hear his voice, harden not your hearts.

Come, let us bow down in worship; let us kneel before the LORD who made us.

For he is our God, and we are the people he shepherds, the flock he guides.

R. If today you hear his voice, harden not your hearts.

Oh, that today you would hear his voice: "Harden not your hearts as at Meribah, as in the day of Massah in the desert,

Where your fathers tempted me; they tested me though they had seen my works."

R. If today you hear his voice, harden not your hearts.

Second Reading 1 Cor 7:32-35
Brothers and sisters:

I should like you to be free of anxieties.

An unmarried man is anxious about the things of the Lord, how he may please the Lord.

But a married man is anxious about the things of the world, how he may please his wife, and he is divided.

An unmarried woman or a virgin is anxious about the things of the Lord, so that she may be holy in both body and spirit.

A married woman, on the other hand, is anxious about the things of the world, how she may please her husband.

I am telling you this for your own benefit, not to impose a restraint upon you, but for the sake of propriety and adherence to the Lord without distraction.

Alleluia: Mt 4:16

R. Alleluia, alleluia.

The people who sit in darkness have seen a great light; on those dwelling in a land overshadowed by death, light has arisen.

R. Alleluia, alleluia.

Then they came to Capernaum, and on the sabbath Jesus entered the synagogue and taught.

The people were astonished at his teaching, for he taught them as one having authority and not as the scribes.

In their synagogue was a man with an unclean spirit; he cried out, "What have you to do with us, Jesus of Nazareth?

Have you come to destroy us? I know who you are—the Holy One of God!"

Jesus rebuked him and said, "Quiet! Come out of him!"

The unclean spirit convulsed him and with a loud cry came out of him. All were amazed and asked one another,

"What is this? A new teaching with authority.

He commands even the unclean spirits and they obey him."

His fame spread everywhere throughout the whole region of Galilee.

FEBRUARY 1st, 2021
Monday of the Fourth Week in Ordinary Time

1st Reading HEB 11:32-40
Brothers and sisters: What more shall I say? I have not time to tell of Gideon, Barak, Samson, Jephthah, of David and Samuel and the prophets, who by faith conquered kingdoms, did what was righteous, obtained the promises; they closed the mouths of lions, put out raging fires, escaped the devouring sword; out of weakness they were made powerful, became strong in battle, and turned back foreign invaders. Women received back their dead through resurrection. Some were tortured and would not accept deliverance, in order to obtain a better resurrection. Others endured mockery, scourging, even chains and imprisonment. They were stoned, sawed in two, put to death at sword's point; they went about in skins of sheep or goats, needy, afflicted, and tormented. The world was not worthy of them. They wandered about in deserts and on mountains, in caves and in crevices in the earth. Yet all these, though approved because of their faith, did not receive what had been promised. God had foreseen something better for us, so that without us they should not be made perfect.

R. (25) Let your hearts take comfort, all who hope in the Lord.

How great is the goodness, O LORD, which you have in store for those who
fear you, And which, toward those who take refuge in you, you show in the
sight of the children of men.

R. Let your hearts take comfort, all who hope in the Lord.

You hide them in the shelter of your presence from the plotting's of men;
You screen them within your abode from the strife of tongues.

R. Let your hearts take comfort, all who hope in the Lord.

Blessed be the LORD whose wondrous mercy he has shown me in a
fortified city.

R. Let your hearts take comfort, all who hope in the Lord.

Once I said in my anguish, "I am cut off from your sight";

Yet you heard the sound of my pleading when I cried out to you.

R. Let your hearts take comfort, all who hope in the Lord.

Love the LORD, all you his faithful ones! The LORD keeps those who are
constant, but more than requites those who act proudly.

R. Let your hearts take comfort, all who hope in the Lord.

Alleluia LK 7:16

R. Alleluia, alleluia.

A great prophet has arisen in our midst and God has visited his people.

R. Alleluia, alleluia.

Gospel MK 5:1-20
Jesus and his disciples came to the other side of the sea, to the territory of
the Gerasenes. When he got out of the boat, at once a man from the tombs
who had an unclean spirit met him. The man had been dwelling among the
tombs, and no one could restrain him any longer, even with a chain. In fact,
he had frequently been bound with shackles and chains, but the chains had

been pulled apart by him and the shackles smashed, and no one was strong enough to subdue him. Night and day among the tombs and on the hillsides he was always crying out and bruising himself with stones. Catching sight of Jesus from a distance, he ran up and prostrated himself before him, crying out in a loud voice, "What have you to do with me, Jesus, Son of the Most High God? I adjure you by God, do not torment me!" (He had been saying to him, "Unclean spirit, come out of the man!") He asked him, "What is your name?" He replied, "Legion is my name. There are many of us." And he pleaded earnestly with him not to drive them away from that territory.

Now a large herd of swine was feeding there on the hillside. And they pleaded with him, "Send us into the swine. Let us enter them." And he let them, and the unclean spirits came out and entered the swine. The herd of about two thousand rushed down a steep bank into the sea, where they were drowned. The swineherds ran away and reported the incident in the town and throughout the countryside. And people came out to see what had happened. As they approached Jesus, they caught sight of the man who had been possessed by Legion, sitting there clothed and in his right mind. And they were seized with fear. Those who witnessed the incident explained to them what had happened to the possessed man and to the swine. Then they began to beg him to leave their district. As he was getting into the boat, the man who had been possessed pleaded to remain with him. But Jesus would not permit him but told him instead, "Go home to your family and announce to them all that the Lord in his pity has done for you." Then the man went off and began to proclaim in the Decapolis what Jesus had done for him; and all were amazed.

FEBRUARY 2ND, 2021
Feast of the Presentation of the Lord

1st Reading Mal 3:1-4
Thus says the Lord God:

Lo, I am sending my messenger to prepare the way before me;

And suddenly there will come to the temple the LORD whom you seek,

And the messenger of the covenant whom you desire. Yes, he is coming, says the LORD of hosts.

But who will endure the day of his coming? And who can stand when he appears? For he is like the refiner's fire, or like the fuller's lye.

He will sit refining and purifying silver, and he will purify the sons of Levi, Refining them like gold or like silver that they may offer due sacrifice to the LORD.

Then the sacrifice of Judah and Jerusalem will please the LORD, as in the days of old, as in years gone by.

Responsorial Psalm PS 24:7, 8, 9, 10
R. (8) Who is this king of glory? It is the Lord!

Lift up, O gates, your lintels;   reach up, you ancient portals, that the king of glory may come in!

R. Who is this king of glory? It is the Lord!

Who is this king of glory?   The LORD, strong and mighty,   the LORD, mighty in battle.

R. Who is this king of glory? It is the Lord!

Lift up, O gates, your lintels;   reach up, you ancient portals,   that the king of glory may come in!

R. Who is this king of glory? It is the Lord!

Who is this king of glory?   The LORD of hosts; he is the king of glory.

R. Who is this king of glory? It is the Lord!.

2nd Reading Heb 2:14-18
Since the children share in blood and flesh,

Jesus likewise shared in them, that through death he might destroy the one who has the power of death, that is, the Devil, and free those who through fear of death had been subject to slavery all their life. Surely he did not help angels but rather the descendants of Abraham; therefore, he had to become like his brothers and sisters in every way, that he might be a merciful and faithful high priest before God to expiate the sins of the people.

Because he himself was tested through what he suffered, he is able to help those who are being tested.

Lk 2:32

R. Alleluia, alleluia.

A light of revelation to the Gentiles, and glory for your people Israel.

R. Alleluia, alleluia.

Gospel Lk 2:22-40 or 2:22-32

When the days were completed for their purification according to the Law of Moses,

Mary and Joseph took Jesus up to Jerusalem to present him to the Lord, just as it is written in the law of the Lord,

Every male that opens the womb shall be consecrated to the Lord, and to offer the sacrifice of a pair of turtledoves or two young pigeons, in accordance with the dictate in the law of the Lord.

Now there was a man in Jerusalem whose name was Simeon.

This man was righteous and devout, awaiting the consolation of Israel, and the Holy Spirit was upon him.

It had been revealed to him by the Holy Spirit that he should not see death before he had seen the Christ of the Lord.

He came in the Spirit into the temple; and when the parents brought in the child Jesus to perform the custom of the law in regard to him, he took him into his arms and blessed God, saying:

"Now, Master, you may let your servant go in peace, according to your word, for my eyes have seen your salvation, which you prepared in the sight of all the peoples: a light for revelation to the Gentiles, and glory for your people Israel."

The child's father and mother were amazed at what was said about him; and Simeon blessed them and said to Mary his mother,

"Behold, this child is destined for the fall and rise of many in Israel, and to be a sign that will be contradicted -and you yourself a sword will pierce-so that the thoughts of many hearts may be revealed."

There was also a prophetess, Anna, the daughter of Phanuel, of the tribe of Asher. She was advanced in years, having lived seven years with her husband after her marriage, and then as a widow until she was eighty-four.

She never left the temple, but worshiped night and day with fasting and prayer. And coming forward at that very time, she gave thanks to God and spoke about the child to all who were awaiting the redemption of Jerusalem.

When they had fulfilled all the prescriptions of the law of the Lord, they returned to Galilee, to their own town of Nazareth.

The child grew and became strong, filled with wisdom; and the favor of God was upon him.

OR:

When the days were completed for their purification according to the Law of Moses, Mary and Joseph took Jesus up to Jerusalem to present him to the Lord just as it is written in the law of the Lord,

Every male that opens the womb shall be consecrated to the Lord, and to offer the sacrifice of a pair of turtledoves or two young pigeons, in accordance with the dictate in the law of the Lord.

Now there was a man in Jerusalem whose name was Simeon.

This man was righteous and devout, awaiting the consolation of Israel, and the Holy Spirit was upon him.

It had been revealed to him by the Holy Spirit that he should not see death before he had seen the Christ of the Lord.

He came in the Spirit into the temple; and when the parents brought in the child Jesus to perform the custom of the law in regard to him, he took him into his arms and blessed God, saying:

"Now, Master, you may let your servant go in peace, according to your word, for my eyes have seen your salvation, which you prepared in the sight of all the peoples: a light for revelation to the Gentiles, and glory for your people Israel."

FEBRUARY 3RD, 2021
Wednesday of the Fourth Week in Ordinary Time

1st Reading Heb 12:4-7, 11-15

Brothers and sisters: In your struggle against sin you have not yet resisted to the point of shedding blood. You have also forgotten the exhortation addressed to you as children: My son, do not disdain the discipline of the Lord or lose heart when reproved by him; for whom the Lord loves, he disciplines; he scourges every son he acknowledges. Endure your trials as "discipline"; God treats you as his sons. For what A son" is there whom his father does not discipline? At the time, all discipline seems a cause not for joy but for pain, yet later it brings the peaceful fruit of righteousness to those who are trained by it. So strengthen your drooping hands and your weak knees. Make straight paths for your feet, that what is lame may not be dislocated but healed. Strive for peace with everyone, and for that holiness without which no one will see the Lord. See to it that no one be deprived of the grace of God, that no bitter root spring up and cause trouble, through which many may become defiled.

Responsorial Psalm PS 103:1-2, 13-14, 17-18A

R. (see 17) The Lord's kindness is everlasting to those who fear him.

Bless the LORD, O my soul; and all my being, bless his holy name. Bless the LORD, O my soul, and forget not all his benefits.

R. The Lord's kindness is everlasting to those who fear him.

As a father has compassion on his children, so the LORD has compassion on those who fear him, For he knows how we are formed; he remembers that we are dust.

R.. The Lord's kindness is everlasting to those who fear him.

But the kindness of the LORD is from eternity to eternity toward those who fear him. And his justice toward children's children among those who keep his covenant.

R... The Lord's kindness is everlasting to those who fear him.

Alleluia JN 10:27

R. Alleluia, alleluia.

My sheep hear my voice, says the Lord; I know them, and they follow me.

R. Alleluia, alleluia.

Gospel MK 6:1-6

Jesus departed from there and came to his native place, accompanied by his disciples. When the Sabbath came he began to teach in the synagogue, and many who heard him were astonished. They said, "Where did this man get all this? What kind of wisdom has been given him? What mighty deeds are wrought by his hands! Is he not the carpenter, the son of Mary, and the brother of James and Joseph and Judas and Simon? And are not his sisters here with us?" And they took offense at him. Jesus said to them, "A prophet is not without honor except in his native place and among his own kin and in his own house." So he was not able to perform any mighty deed there, apart from curing a few sick people by laying his hands on them. He was amazed at their lack of faith.

FEBRUARY 4TH, 2021
Thursday of the Fourth Week in Ordinary Time

1st Reading HEB 12:18-19, 21-24

Brothers and sisters: You have not approached that which could be touched and a blazing fire and gloomy darkness and storm and a trumpet blast and a voice speaking words such that those who heard begged that no message be further addressed to them. Indeed, so fearful was the spectacle that Moses said, "I am terrified and trembling. No, you have approached Mount Zion and the city of the living God, the heavenly Jerusalem, and countless angels in festal gathering, and the assembly of the firstborn enrolled in heaven, and God the judge of all, and the spirits of the just made perfect, and Jesus, the mediator of a new covenant, and the sprinkled Blood that speaks more eloquently than that of Abel.

Responsorial Psalm   PS 48:2-3AB, 3CD-4, 9, 10-11
R. (see 10) O God, we ponder your mercy within your temple.

Great is the LORD and wholly to be praised in the city of our God. His holy mountain, fairest of heights, is the joy of all the earth.

R. O God, we ponder your mercy within your temple.

Mount Zion, "the recesses of the North," the city of the great King. God is with her castles; renowned is he as a stronghold.

R. O God, we ponder your mercy within your temple.

As we had heard, so have we seen in the city of the LORD of hosts, In the city of our God; God makes it firm forever.

R. O God, we ponder your mercy within your temple.

O God, we ponder your mercy within your temple. As your name, O God, so also your praise reaches to the ends of the earth. Of justice your right hand is full.

R. O God, we ponder your mercy within your temple.

Alleluia MK 1:15

R. Alleluia, alleluia.

The Kingdom of God is at hand; repent and believe in the Gospel.

R. Alleluia, alleluia.

Gospel MK 6:7-13

Jesus summoned the Twelve and began to send them out two by two and gave them authority over unclean spirits. He instructed them to take nothing for the journey but a walking stick –no food, no sack, no money in their belts. They were, however, to wear sandals but not a second tunic. He said to them, "Wherever you enter a house, stay there until you leave from there. Whatever place does not welcome you or listen to you, leave there and shake the dust off your feet in testimony against them." So they went off and preached repentance.

The Twelve drove out many demons, and they anointed with oil many who were sick and cured them.

FEBRUARY 5TH, 2021
Memorial of Saint Agatha, virgin and martyr

1st Reading HEB13:1-8

Let brotherly love continue. Do not neglect hospitality, for through it some have unknowingly entertained angels. Be mindful of prisoners as if sharing their imprisonment, and of the ill-treated as of yourselves, for you also are in the body. Let marriage be honored among all and the marriage bed be kept undefiled, for God will judge the immoral and adulterers. Let your life be free from love of money but be content with what you have, for he has said, I will never forsake you or abandon you. Thus we may say with confidence: The Lord is my helper, and I will not be afraid. What can anyone do to me? Remember your leaders who spoke the word of God to you. Consider the outcome of their way of life and imitate their faith. Jesus Christ is the same yesterday, today, and forever.

Responsorial Psalm PS 27:1, 3, 5, 8B-9ABC

R. (1a) The Lord is my light and my salvation

The LORD is my light and my salvation; whom should I fear? The LORD is my life's refuge; of whom should I be afraid?

R… The Lord is my light and my salvation.

Though an army encamp against me, my heart will not fear; Though war be waged upon me, even then will I trust.

R. The Lord is my light and my salvation.

For he will hide me in his abode in the day of trouble; He will conceal me in the shelter of his tent, he will set me high upon a rock.

R... The Lord is my light and my salvation.

Your presence, O LORD, I seek. Hide not your face from me; do not in anger repel your servant. You are my helper: cast me not off.

R.. The Lord is my light and my salvation.

Alleluia LK 8:15

R. Alleluia, alleluia.

Blessed are they who have kept the word with a generous heart, and yield a harvest through perseverance.

R. Alleluia, alleluia.

Gospel   MK 6:14-29
King Herod heard about Jesus, for his fame had become widespread, and
people were saying, "John the Baptist has been raised from the dead. That is
why mighty powers are at work in him." Others were saying, "He is Elijah";
still others, "He is a prophet like any of the prophets." But when Herod
learned of it, he said, "It is John whom I beheaded. He has been raised up."
Herod was the one who had John arrested and bound in prison on account
of Herodias, the wife of his brother Philip, whom he had married. John had
said to Herod, "It is not lawful for you to have your brother's wife."
Herodias harbored a grudge against him and wanted to kill him but was
unable to do so. Herod feared John, knowing him to be a righteous and holy
man, and kept him in custody. When he heard him speak he was very much
perplexed, yet he liked to listen to him. Herodias had an opportunity one day
when Herod, on his birthday, gave a banquet for his courtiers, his military
officers, and the leading men of Galilee. His own daughter came in and
performed a dance that delighted Herod and his guests. The king said to the
girl, "Ask of me whatever you wish and I will grant it to you." He even
swore many things to her, "I will grant you whatever you ask of me, even to
half of my kingdom."

She went out and said to her mother, "What shall I ask for?" Her mother
replied, "The head of John the Baptist." The girl hurried back to the king's
presence and made her request, "I want you to give me at once on a platter
the head of John the Baptist." The king was deeply distressed, but because of
his oaths and the guests he did not wish to break his word to her. So he
promptly dispatched an executioner with orders to bring back his head. He
went off and beheaded him in the prison. He brought in the head on a
platter and gave it to the girl. The girl in turn gave it to her mother. When his
disciples heard about it, they came and took his body and laid it in a tomb.

FEBRUARY 6TH, 2021
Memorial of Saint Paul Miki and Companions, Martyrs

1st Reading HEB 13:15-17, 20-21
Brothers and sisters: Through Jesus, let us continually offer God a sacrifice
of praise, that is, the fruit of lips that confess his name. Do not neglect to do
good and to share what you have; God is pleased by sacrifices of that kind.
Obey your leaders and defer to them, for they keep watch over you and will

have to give an account, that they may fulfill their task with joy and not with sorrow, for that would be of no advantage to you. May the God of peace, who brought up from the dead the great shepherd of the sheep by the Blood of the eternal covenant, furnish you with all that is good, that you may do his will. May he carry out in you what is pleasing to him through Jesus Christ, to whom be glory forever and ever. Amen.

Responsorial Psalm PS 23:1-3A, 3B-4, 5, 6
R. (1) The Lord is my shepherd; there is nothing I shall want.

The LORD is my shepherd; I shall not want. In verdant pastures he gives me repose. Beside restful waters he leads me; he refreshes my soul.

R. The Lord is my shepherd; there is nothing I shall want.

He guides me in right paths for his name's sake. Even though I walk in the dark valley I fear no evil; for you are at my side. With your rod and your staff that give me courage.

R.. The Lord is my shepherd; there is nothing I shall want.

You spread the table before me in the sight of my foes; You anoint my head with oil; my cup overflows.

R.. The Lord is my shepherd; there is nothing I shall want.

Only goodness and kindness follow me all the days of my life; And I shall dwell in the house of the LORD for years to come.

R.. The Lord is my shepherd; there is nothing I shall want.

Alleluia JN 10:27

R. Alleluia, alleluia.

My sheep hear my voice, says the Lord; I know them, and they follow me.

R. Alleluia, alleluia.

Gospel   MK 6:30-34
The Apostles gathered together with Jesus and reported all they had done and taught. He said to them, "Come away by yourselves to a deserted place and rest a while." People were coming and going in great numbers, and they had no opportunity even to eat. So they went off in the boat by themselves

to a deserted place. People saw them leaving and many came to know about it. They hastened there on foot from all the towns and arrived at the place before them. When Jesus disembarked and saw the vast crowd, his heart was moved with pity for them, for they were like sheep without a shepherd; and he began to teach them many things.

FEBRUARY 7TH, 2021
Fifth Sunday in Ordinary Time

1st Reading Jb 7:1-4, 6-7

Job spoke, saying: Is not man's life on earth drudgery? Are not his days those of hirelings?

He is a slave who longs for the shade, a hireling who waits for his wages. So I have been assigned months of misery, and troubled nights have been allotted to me.

If in bed I say, "When shall I arise?" then the night drags on; I am filled with restlessness until the dawn. My days are swifter than a weaver's shuttle; they come to an end without hope.

Remember that my life is like the wind; I shall not see happiness again.

Responsorial Psalm Ps 147:1-2, 3-4, 5-6

R. (cf. 3a) Praise the Lord, who heals the brokenhearted.

or:

R. Alleluia.

Praise the LORD, for he is good; sing praise to our God, for he is gracious; it is fitting to praise him. The LORD rebuilds Jerusalem; the dispersed of Israel he gathers.

R. Praise the Lord, who heals the brokenhearted.

or:

R. Alleluia.

He heals the brokenhearted and binds up their wounds.

He tells the number of the stars; he calls each by name.

R. Praise the Lord, who heals the brokenhearted.

or:

R. Alleluia.

Great is our Lord and mighty in power; to his wisdom there is no limit. The LORD sustains the lowly; the wicked he casts to the ground.

R. Praise the Lord, who heals the brokenhearted.

or:

R. Alleluia.

2nd Reading   1 Cor 9:16-19, 22-23
Brothers and sisters:

If I preach the gospel, this is no reason for me to boast, for an obligation has been imposed on me and woe to me if I do not preach it! If I do so willingly, I have recompense, but if unwillingly, and then I have been entrusted with a stewardship.

What then is my recompense? That, when I preach,

I offer the gospel free of charge so as not to make full use of my right in the gospel.

Although I am free in regard to all, I have made myself a slave to all so as to win over as many as possible.

To the weak I became weak, to win over the weak. I have become all things to all, to save at least some. All this I do for the sake of the gospel, so that I too may have a share in it.

Alleluia   Mt 8:17

R. Alleluia, alleluia.

Christ took away our infirmities and bore our diseases

R. Alleluia, alleluia.

On leaving the synagogue Jesus entered the house of Simon and Andrew with James and John. Simon's mother-in-law lay sick with a fever. They immediately told him about her. He approached, grasped her hand, and helped her up.

Then the fever left her and she waited on them.

When it was evening, after sunset, they brought to him all who were ill or possessed by demons. The whole town was gathered at the door. He cured many who were sick with various diseases, and he drove out many demons, not permitting them to speak because they knew him. Rising very early before dawn, he left and went off to a deserted place, where he prayed.

Simon and those who were with him pursued him and on finding him said, "Everyone is looking for you."

He told them, "Let us go on to the nearby villages that I may preach there also. For this purpose have I come." So he went into their synagogues, preaching and driving out demons throughout the whole of Galilee.

FEBRUARY 8TH, 2021
Monday of the Fifth Week in Ordinary Time

1st Reading GN1:1-19
In the beginning, when God created the heavens and the earth, the earth was a formless wasteland, and darkness covered the abyss, while a mighty wind swept over the waters. Then God said, "Let there be light," and there was light. God saw how good the light was. God then separated the light from the darkness. God called the light "day," and the darkness he called "night." Thus evening came, and morning followed–the first day. Then God said, "Let there be a dome in the middle of the waters, to separate one body of water from the other." And so it happened: God made the dome, and it separated the water above the dome from the water below it. God called the dome "the sky." Evening came, and morning followed–the second day. Then God said, "Let the water under the sky be gathered into a single basin, so that the dry land may appear." And so it happened: the water under the sky was gathered into its basin, and the dry land appeared. God called the dry land "the earth," and the basin of the water he called "the sea." God saw how good it was. Then God said, "Let the earth bring forth vegetation: every kind of plant that bears seed and every kind of fruit tree on earth that bears fruit

71

with its seed in it." And so it happened: the earth brought forth every kind of plant that bears seed and every kind of fruit tree on earth that bears fruit with its seed in it. God saw how good it was. Evening came, and morning followed—the third day.

Then God said: "Let there be lights in the dome of the sky, to separate day from night. Let them mark the fixed times, the days and the years, and serve as luminaries in the dome of the sky, to shed light upon the earth. "And so it happened: God made the two great lights, the greater one to govern the day, and the lesser one to govern the night; and he made the stars. God set them in the dome of the sky, to shed light upon the earth, to govern the day and the night, and to separate the light from the darkness. God saw how good it was. Evening came, and morning followed—the fourth day.

Responsorial Psalm   PS 104:1-2A, 5-6, 10 AND 12, 24 AND 35C
R. (31b) May the Lord be glad in his works.

Bless the LORD, O my soul! O LORD, my God, you are great indeed! You are clothed with majesty and glory, robed in light as with a cloak.

R. May the Lord be glad in his works.

You fixed the earth upon its foundation, not to be moved forever; With the ocean, as with a garment, you covered it; above the mountains the waters stood.

R. May the Lord be glad in his works.

You send forth springs into the watercourses that wind among the mountains. Beside them the birds of heaven dwell; from among the branches they send forth their song.

R. May the Lord be glad in his works.

How manifold are your works, O LORD. ! In wisdom you have wrought them all— the earth is full of your creatures;

Bless the LORD, O my soul! Alleluia.

R. May the Lord be glad in his works.

Alleluia MT 4:23

R. Alleluia, alleluia.

Jesus preached the Gospel of the Kingdom and cured every disease among the people.

R. Alleluia, alleluia.

Gospel   MK 6:53-56
After making the crossing to the other side of the sea, Jesus and his disciples came to land at Gennesaret and tied up there. As they were leaving the boat, people immediately recognized him. They scurried about the surrounding country and began to bring in the sick on mats to wherever they heard he was. Whatever villages or towns or countryside he entered, they laid the sick in the marketplaces and begged him that they might touch only the tassel on his cloak; and as many as touched it were healed.

FEBRUARY 9TH, 2021
Tuesday of the Fifth Week in Ordinary Time

1st Reading GN 1:20—2:4A
God said, "Let the water teem with an abundance of living creatures, and on the earth let birds fly beneath the dome of the sky. "and so it happened: God created the great sea monsters and all kinds of swimming creatures with which the water teems, and all kinds of winged birds. God saw how good it was, and God blessed them, saying, "Be fertile, multiply, and fill the water of the seas; and let the birds multiply on the earth." Evening came, and morning followed–the fifth day.

Then God said, "Let the earth bring forth all kinds of living creatures: cattle, creeping things, and wild animals of all kinds." and so it happened: God made all kinds of wild animals, all kinds of cattle, and all kinds of creeping things of the earth. God saw how good it was. Then God said: "Let us make man in our image, after our likeness. Let them have dominion over the fish of the sea, the birds of the air, and the cattle, and over all the wild animals and all the creatures that crawl on the ground." God created man in his image; in the divine image he created him; male and female he created them. God blessed them, saying: "Be fertile and multiply; fill the earth and subdue it. Have dominion over the fish of the sea, the birds of the air, and all the living things that move on the earth." God also said: "See, I give you every seed-bearing plant all over the earth and every tree that has seed-bearing fruit on it to be your food; and to all the animals of the land, all the birds of the air, and all the living creatures that crawl on the ground, I give all the green plants for food." And so it happened. God looked at everything he had made, and he found it very good. Evening came, and morning followed—the sixth day. Thus the heavens and the earth and all their array were completed. Since on the seventh day God was finished with the work he had been doing, he rested on the seventh day from all the work he had undertaken. So God blessed the seventh day and made it holy, because on it he rested from all the work he had done in creation. Such is the story of the heavens and the earth at their creation.

Responsorial Psalm   PS 8:4-5, 6-7, 8-9
R. (2ab) O Lord, our God, how wonderful your name in all the earth!

When I behold your heavens, the work of your fingers, the moon and the stars which you set in place— What is man that you should be mindful of him, or the son of man that you should care for him?

R. O Lord, our God, how wonderful your name in all the earth!

You have made him little less than the angels, and crowned him with glory and honor. You have given him rule over the works of your hands, putting all things under his feet.

R. O Lord, our God, how wonderful your name in all the earth!

All sheep and oxen, yes, and the beasts of the field,

The birds of the air, the fishes of the sea, and whatever swims the paths of the seas.

R. O Lord, our God, how wonderful your name in all the earth!

Alleluia   PS 119:36, 29B

R. Alleluia, alleluia.

Incline my heart, O God, to your decrees; And favor me with your law.

R. Alleluia, alleluia.

Gospel MK 7:1-13
When the Pharisees with some scribes who had come from Jerusalem gathered around Jesus, they observed that some of his disciples ate their

meals with unclean, that is, unwashed, hands. (For the Pharisees and, in fact, all Jews, do not eat without carefully washing their hands, keeping the tradition of the elders. And on coming from the marketplace they do not eat without purifying themselves. And there are many other things that they have traditionally observed, the purification of cups and jugs and kettles and beds.) So the Pharisees and scribes questioned him, "Why do your disciples not follow the tradition of the elders but instead eat a meal with unclean hands?" He responded, "Well did Isaiah prophesy about you hypocrites, as it is written: This people honors me with their lips, but their hearts are far from me; in vain do they worship me, teaching as doctrines human precepts. You disregard God's commandment but cling to human tradition." He went on to say, "How well you have set aside the commandment of God in order to uphold your tradition! For Moses said, Honor your father and your mother, and whoever curses father or mother shall die. Yet you say, 'If someone says to father or mother, "Any support you might have had from me is qorban"' (meaning, dedicated to God), you allow him to do nothing more for his father or mother. You nullify the word of God in favor of your tradition that you have handed on. And you do many such things."

FEBRUARY 10TH, 2021
Memorial of Saint Scholastica, virgin

1st Reading GN 2:4B-9, 15-17
At the time when the LORD God made the earth and the heavens while as yet there was no field shrub on earth and no grass of the field had sprouted, for the LORD God had sent no rain upon the earth and there was no man to till the soil, but a stream was welling up out of the earth and was watering all the surface of the ground the LORD God formed man out of the clay of the ground and blew into his nostrils the breath of life, and so man became a living being.

Then the LORD God planted a garden in Eden, in the east, and he placed there the man whom he had formed. Out of the ground the LORD God made various trees grow that were delightful to look at and good for food, with the tree of life in the middle of the garden and the tree of the knowledge of good and evil. The LORD God then took the man and settled him in the garden of Eden, to cultivate and care for it. The LORD God gave man this order: "You are free to eat from any of the trees of the garden except the tree of knowledge of good and evil. From that tree you shall not eat; the moment you eat from it you are surely doomed to die."

R. (1a) O bless the Lord, my soul!

Bless the LORD, O my soul! O LORD, my God, you are great indeed! You are clothed with majesty and glory, robed in light as with a cloak.

R. O bless the Lord, my soul!

All creatures look to you to give them food in due time. When you give it to them, they gather it; when you open your hand, they are filled with good things.

R. O bless the Lord, my soul!

If you take away their breath, they perish and return to their dust.

When you send forth your spirit, they are created, and you renew the face of the earth.

R. O bless the Lord, my soul!

Alleluia JN 17:17B, 17A

R. Alleluia, alleluia.

Your word, O Lord, is truth: consecrate us in the truth.

R. Alleluia, alleluia.

Gospel MK 7:14-23

Jesus summoned the crowd again and said to them, "Hear me, all of you, and understand. Nothing that enters one from outside can defile that person; but the things that come out from within are what defile." When he got home away from the crowd his disciples questioned him about the parable. He said to them, "Are even you likewise without understanding? Do you not realize that everything that goes into a person from outside cannot defile, since it enters not the heart but the stomach and passes out into the latrine?" (Thus he declared all foods clean.) "But what comes out of the man, that is what defiles him. From within the man, from his heart, come evil thoughts, unchastity, theft, murder, adultery, greed, malice, deceit, licentiousness, envy, blasphemy, arrogance, folly. All these evils come from within and they defile."

FEBRUARY 11TH, 2021

Thursday of the Fifth Week in Ordinary Time

1st Reading GN 2:18-25

The LORD God said: "It is not good for the man to be alone. I will make a suitable partner for him." So the LORD God formed out of the ground various wild animals and various birds of the air, and he brought them to the man to see what he would call them; whatever the man called each of them would be its name. The man gave names to all the cattle, all the birds of the air, and all the wild animals; but none proved to be the suitable partner for the man. So the LORD God cast a deep sleep on the man, and while he was asleep, he took out one of his ribs and closed up its place with flesh. The LORD God then built up into a woman the rib that he had taken from the man. When he brought her to the man, the man said: "This one, at last, is bone of my bones and flesh of my flesh; this one shall be called 'woman,' for out of 'her man' this one has been taken."

That is why a man leaves his father and mother and clings to his wife, and the two of them become one flesh. The man and his wife were both naked, yet they felt no shame.

Responsorial Psalm PS 128:1-2, 3, 4-5

R. (see 1a) Blessed are those who fear the Lord.

Blessed are you who fear the LORD, who walk in his ways! For you shall eat the fruit of your handiwork; blessed shall you be, and favored.

R. Blessed are those who fear the Lord.

Your wife shall be like a fruitful vine in the recesses of your home; Your children like olive plants around your table.

R. Blessed are those who fear the Lord.

Behold, thus is the man blessed who fears the LORD. The LORD bless you from Zion: may you see the prosperity of Jerusalem all the days of your life.

R. Blessed are those who fear the Lord.

Alleluia JAS 1:21BC

R. Alleluia, alleluia.

Humbly welcome the word that has been planted in you and is able to save your souls.

R. Alleluia, alleluia.

Gospel MK 7:24-30
Jesus went to the district of Tyre. He entered a house and wanted no one to know about it, but he could not escape notice. Soon a woman whose daughter had an unclean spirit heard about him. She came and fell at his feet. The woman was a Greek, a Syrophoenician by birth, and she begged him to drive the demon out of her daughter. He said to her, "Let the children be fed first. For it is not right to take the food of the children and throw it to the dogs." She replied and said to him, "Lord, even the dogs under the table eat the children's scraps." Then he said to her, "For saying this, you may go. The demon has gone out of your daughter." When the woman went home, she found the child lying in bed and the demon gone.

FEBRUARY 12TH, 2021
Friday of the Fifth Week in Ordinary Time

1st Reading GN 3:1-8
Now the serpent was the most cunning of all the animals that the LORD God had made. The serpent asked the woman, "Did God really tell you not to eat from any of the trees in the garden?" The woman answered the serpent: "We may eat of the fruit of the trees in the garden; it is only about the fruit of the tree in the middle of the garden that God said, 'You shall not eat it or even touch it, lest you die.'" But the serpent said to the woman: "You certainly will not die! No, God knows well that the moment you eat of it your eyes will be opened and you will be like gods who know what is good and what is evil." The woman saw that the tree was good for food, pleasing to the eyes, and desirable for gaining wisdom. So she took some of its fruit and ate it; and she also gave some to her husband, who was with her, and he ate it.

Then the eyes of both of them were opened, and they realized that they were naked; so they sewed fig leaves together and made loincloths for themselves. When they heard the sound of the LORD God moving about in the garden at the breezy time of the day, the man and his wife hid themselves from the LORD God among the trees of the garden.

R. (1a) Blessed are those whose sins are forgiven.

Blessed is he whose fault is taken away, whose sin is covered. Blessed the man to whom the LORD imputes not guilt, in whose spirit there is no guile.

R. Blessed are those whose sins are forgiven.

Then I acknowledged my sin to you, my guilt I covered not. I said, "I confess my faults to the LORD," and you took away the guilt of my sin.

R. Blessed are those whose sins are forgiven.

For this shall every faithful man pray to you in time of stress. Though deep waters overflow, they shall not reach him.

R. Blessed are those whose sins are forgiven.

You are my shelter; from distress you will preserve me; with glad cries of freedom you will ring me round.

R. Blessed are those whose sins are forgiven.

Alleluia ACTS 16:14B

R. Alleluia, alleluia.

Open our hearts, O Lord, to listen to the words of your Son.

R. Alleluia, alleluia.

Gospel MK 7:31-37

Jesus left the district of Tyre and went by way of Sidon to the Sea of Galilee, into the district of the Decapolis. And people brought to him a deaf man who had a speech impediment and begged him to lay his hand on him. He took him off by himself away from the crowd. He put his finger into the man's ears and, spitting, touched his tongue; then he looked up to heaven and groaned, and said to him, "Ephphatha!" (that is, "Be opened!") And immediately the man's ears were opened, his speech impediment was removed, and he spoke plainly. He ordered them not to tell anyone. But the more he ordered them not to, the more they proclaimed it. They were exceedingly astonished and they said, "He has done all things well. He makes the deaf hear and the mute speak."

FEBRUARY 13TH, 2021
Saturday of the Fifth Week in Ordinary Time

1st Reading GN 3:9-24

The LORD God called to Adam and asked him, "Where are you?" He answered, "I heard you in the garden; but I was afraid, because I was naked, so I hid myself. Then he asked, "Who told you that you were naked? You have eaten, then, from the tree of which I had forbidden you to eat!" The man replied, "The woman whom you put here with me. she gave me fruit from the tree, and so I ate it." The LORD God then asked the woman, "Why did you do such a thing?" The woman answered, "The serpent tricked me into it, so I ate it." Then the LORD God said to the serpent: "Because you have done this, you shall be banned from all the animals and from all the wild creatures; On your belly shall you crawl, and dirt shall you eat all the days of your life. I will put enmity between you and the woman, and between your offspring and hers; He will strike at your head, while you strike at his heel." To the woman he said: "I will intensify the pangs of your childbearing; in pain shall you bring forth children. Yet your urge shall be for your husband, and he shall be your master." To the man he said: "Because you listened to your wife and ate from the tree of which I had forbidden you to eat, "Cursed be the ground because of you! In toil shall you eat its yield all the days of your life. Thorns and thistles shall it bring forth to you, as you eat of the plants of the field.

By the sweat of your face shall you get bread to eat, Until you return to the ground, from which you were taken; For you are dirt, and to dirt you shall return." The man called his wife Eve, because she became the mother of all the living. For the man and his wife the LORD God made leather garments, with which he clothed them. Then the LORD God said: "See! The man has become like one of us, knowing what is good and what is evil! Therefore, he must not be allowed to put out his hand to take fruit from the tree of life also, and thus eat of it and live forever." The LORD God therefore banished him from the garden of Eden, to till the ground from which he had been taken. When he expelled the man, he settled him east of the garden of Eden; and he stationed the cherubim and the fiery revolving sword, to guard the way to the tree of life.

Responsorial Psalm PS 90:2, 3-4ABC, 5-6, 12-13

R... (1). In every age, O Lord, you have been our refuge.

Before the mountains were begotten and the earth and the world were brought forth, from everlasting to everlasting you are God.

R. In every age, O Lord, you have been our refuge.

You turn man back to dust, saying, "Return, O children of men." For a thousand years in your sight are as yesterday, now that it is past, or as a watch of the night.

R. In every age, O Lord, you have been our refuge.

You make an end of them in their sleep; the next morning they are like the changing grass, Which at dawn springs up anew, but by evening wilts and fades.

R. In every age, O Lord, you have been our refuge.

Teach us to number our days aright, that we may gain wisdom of heart. Return, O LORD! How long? Have pity on your servants!

R. In every age, O Lord, you have been our refuge.

Alleluia MT 4:4B

R. Alleluia, alleluia.

One does not live on bread alone, but on every word that comes forth from the mouth of God.

R. Alleluia, alleluia.

Gospel MK 8:1-10

In those days when there again was a great crowd without anything to eat, Jesus summoned the disciples and said, "My heart is moved with pity for the crowd, because they have been with me now for three days and have nothing to eat. If I send them away hungry to their homes, they will collapse on the way, and some of them have come a great distance." His disciples answered him, "Where can anyone get enough bread to satisfy them here in this deserted place?" Still he asked them, "How many loaves do you have?" They replied, "Seven." He ordered the crowd to sit down on the ground. Then, taking the seven loaves he gave thanks, broke them, and gave them to his disciples to distribute, and they distributed them to the crowd. They also had a few fish. He said the blessing over them and ordered them distributed also.

They ate and were satisfied. They picked up the fragments left over—seven baskets. There were about four thousand people. He dismissed the crowd and got into the boat with his disciples and came to the region of Dalmanutha.

FEBRUARY 14TH, 2021
Sixth Sunday in Ordinary Time

1st Reading Lv 13:1-2, 44-46
The Lord said to Moses and Aaron,

"If someone has on his skin a scab or pustule or blotch which appears to be the sore of leprosy, he shall be brought to Aaron, the priest, or to one of the priests among his descendants.

If the man is leprous and unclean, the priest shall declare him unclean by reason of the sore on his head.

"The one who bears the sore of leprosy shall keep his garments rent and his head bare, and shall muffle his beard; he shall cry out, 'Unclean, unclean!'

As long as the sore is on him he shall declare himself unclean,since he is in fact unclean. He shall dwell apart, making his abode outside the camp."

Responsorial Psalm Ps 32:1-2, 5, 11
R. (7) I turn to you, Lord, in time of trouble, and you fill me with the joy of salvation.

Blessed is he whose fault is taken away,   whose sin is covered.

Blessed the man to whom the LORD imputes not guilt,   in whose spirit there is no guile.

R. I turn to you, Lord, in time of trouble, and you fill me with the joy of salvation.

Then I acknowledged my sin to you,   my guilt I covered not.

I said, "I confess my faults to the LORD,"   and you took away the guilt of my sin.

R. I turn to you, Lord, in time of trouble, and you fill me with the joy of salvation.

Be glad in the LORD and rejoice, you just;   exult, all you upright of heart.

R. I turn to you, Lord, in time of trouble, and you fill me with the joy of salvation.

2nd Reading 1 Cor 10:31—11:1
Brothers and sisters,

Whether you eat or drink, or whatever you do, do everything for the glory of God. Avoid giving offense, whether to the Jews or Greeks or the church of God, just as I try to please everyone in every way, not seeking my own benefit but that of the many, that they may be saved.

Be imitators of me, as I am of Christ.

Alleluia   Lk 7:16

R. Alleluia, alleluia.

A great prophet has arisen in our midst, God has visited his people.

R. Alleluia, alleluia.

Gospel   Mk 1:40-45
A leper came to Jesus and kneeling down begged him and said,

"If you wish, you can make me clean." Moved with pity, he stretched out his hand, touched him, and said to him,

"I do will it. Be made clean." The leprosy left him immediately, and he was made clean.

Then, warning the him sternly, he dismissed him at once.

He said to him, "See that you tell no one anything, but go, show yourself to the priest and offer for your cleansing what Moses prescribed; that will be proof for them."

The man went away and began to publicize the whole matter.

He spread the report abroad so that it was impossible for Jesus to enter a town openly. He remained outside in deserted places, and people kept coming to him from everywhere.

FEBRUARY 15TH, 2021
Monday of the Sixth Week in Ordinary Time

1st Reading GN 4:1-15, 25

The man had relations with his wife Eve, and she conceived and bore Cain, saying, "I have produced a man with the help of the LORD." Next she bore his brother Abel. Abel became a keeper of flocks, and Cain a tiller of the soil. In the course of time Cain brought an offering to the LORD from the fruit of the soil, while Abel, for his part, brought one of the best firstlings of his flock. The LORD looked with favor on Abel and his offering, but on Cain and his offering he did not. Cain greatly resented this and was crestfallen. So the LORD said to Cain: "Why are you so resentful and crestfallen. If you do well, you can hold up your head; but if not, sin is a demon lurking at the door: his urge is toward you, yet you can be his master." Cain said to his brother Abel, "Let us go out in the field." When they were in the field, Cain attacked his brother Abel and killed him. Then the LORD asked Cain, "Where is your brother Abel?" He answered, "I do not know. Am I my brother's keeper?" The LORD then said: "What have you done! Listen: your brother's blood cries out to me from the soil! Therefore you shall be banned from the soil that opened its mouth to receive your brother's blood from your hand. If you till the soil, it shall no longer give you its produce. You shall become a restless wanderer on the earth."

Cain said to the LORD: "My punishment is too great to bear. Since you have now banished me from the soil, and I must avoid your presence and become a restless wanderer on the earth, anyone may kill me at sight." "Not so!" the LORD said to him. "If anyone kills Cain, Cain shall be avenged sevenfold." So the LORD put a mark on Cain, lest anyone should kill him at sight. Adam again had relations with his wife, and she gave birth to a son whom she called Seth. "God has granted me more offspring in place of Abel," she said, "because Cain slew him."

Responsorial Psalm PS 50:1 AND 8, 16BC-17, 20-21

R. (14a) Offer to God a sacrifice of praise.

God the LORD has spoken and summoned the earth, from the rising of the sun to its setting. "Not for your sacrifices do I rebuke you, for your burnt offerings are before me always."

R. Offer to God a sacrifice of praise.

"Why do you recite my statutes, and profess my covenant with your mouth. Though you hate discipline and cast my words behind you?"

R. Offer to God a sacrifice of praise.

"You sit speaking against your brother; against your mother's son you spread rumors. When you do these things, shall I be deaf to it? Or do you think that I am like yourself? I will correct you by drawing them up before your eyes."

R. Offer to God a sacrifice of praise.

Alleluia JN 14:6

R. Alleluia, alleluia.

I am the way and the truth and the life, says the Lord; no one comes to the Father except through me.

R. Alleluia, alleluia.

Gospel MK 8:11-13
The Pharisees came forward and began to argue with Jesus, seeking from him a sign from heaven to test him. He sighed from the depth of his spirit and said, "Why does this generation seek a sign? Amen, I say to you, no sign will be given to this generation." Then he left them, got into the boat again, and went off to the other shore.

FEBRUARY 16TH, 2021
Tuesday of the Sixth Week in Ordinary Time

1st Reading GN 6:5-8; 7:1-5, 10
When the LORD saw how great was man's wickedness on earth, and how no desire that his heart conceived was ever anything but evil, he regretted that he had made man on the earth, and his heart was grieved.

So the LORD said: "I will wipe out from the earth the men whom I have created, and not only the men, but also the beasts and the creeping things and the birds of the air, for I am sorry that I made them." But Noah found favor with the LORD. Then the LORD said to Noah: "Go into the ark, you and all your household, for you alone in this age have I found to be truly just. Of every clean animal, take with you seven pairs, a male and its mate; and of the unclean animals, one pair, a male and its mate; likewise, of every clean bird of the air, seven pairs, a male and a female, and of all the unclean birds, one pair, a male and a female. Thus you will keep their issue alive over all the earth. Seven days from now I will bring rain down on the earth for forty days and forty nights, and so I will wipe out from the surface of the earth every moving creature that I have made." Noah did just as the LORD had commanded him. As soon as the seven days were over, the waters of the flood came upon the earth.

Responsorial Psalm   PS 29:1A AND 2, 3AC-4, 3B AND 9C-10
R. (11b) The Lord will bless his people with peace.

Give to the LORD, you sons of God, give to the LORD glory and praise,
Give to the LORD the glory due his name; adore the LORD in holy attire.

R... The Lord will bless his people with peace.

 The voice of the LORD is over the waters, the LORD, over vast waters.
The voice of the LORD is mighty; the voice of the LORD is majestic.

R... The Lord will bless his people with peace.

The God of glory thunders, and in his temple all say, "Glory!" The LORD is enthroned above the flood; the LORD is enthroned as king forever.

R... The Lord will bless his people with peace.

Alleluia JN 14:23

R. Alleluia, alleluia.

Whoever loves me will keep my word, says the Lord; and my Father will love him and we will come to him.

R. Alleluia, alleluia.

The disciples had forgotten to bring bread, and they had only one loaf with them in the boat. Jesus enjoined them, "Watch out, guard against the leaven of the Pharisees and the leaven of Herod." They concluded among themselves that it was because they had no bread. When he became aware of this he said to them, "Why do you conclude that it is because you have no bread? Do you not yet understand or comprehend? Are your hearts hardened? Do you have eyes and not see, ears and not hear? And do you not remember, when I broke the five loaves for the five thousand, how many wicker baskets full of fragments you picked up?" They answered him, "Twelve." "When I broke the seven loaves for the four thousand, how many full baskets of fragments did you pick up?" They answered him, "Seven." He said to them, "Do you still not understand?"

FEBRUARY 17TH, 2021
Ash Wednesday

1st Reading Jl 2:12-18

Even now, says the LORD, return to me with your whole heart, with fasting, and weeping, and mourning; Rend your hearts, not your garments, and return to the LORD, your God.

For gracious and merciful is he, slow to anger, rich in kindness, and relenting in punishment.

Perhaps he will again relent and leave behind him a blessing, Offerings and libations for the LORD, your God.

Blow the trumpet in Zion! Proclaim a fast, call an assembly; Gather the people, notify the congregation; assemble the elders, gather the children and the infants at the breast; Let the bridegroom quit his room and the bride her chamber.

Between the porch and the altar let the priests, the ministers of the LORD, weep, And say, "Spare, O LORD, your people, and make not your heritage a reproach, with the nations ruling over them!

Why should they say among the peoples, 'Where is their God?'"

Then the LORD was stirred to concern for his land and took pity on his people.

Responsorial Psalm PS 51:3-4, 5-6ab, 12-13, 14 and 17

R.. (see 3a) Be merciful, O Lord, for we have sinned.

Have mercy on me, O God, in your goodness, in the greatness of your compassion wipe out my offense.

Thoroughly wash me from my guilt and of my sin cleanse me.

R. Be merciful, O Lord, for we have sinned.

For I acknowledge my offense, and my sin is before me always:

"Against you only have I sinned, and done what is evil in your sight."

R. Be merciful, O Lord, for we have sinned.

A clean heart create for me, O God, and a steadfast spirit renew within me.

Cast me not out from your presence, and your Holy Spirit take not from me.

R. Be merciful, O Lord, for we have sinned.

Give me back the joy of your salvation and a willing spirit sustain in me.

O Lord, open my lips, and my mouth shall proclaim your praise.

R. Be merciful, O Lord, for we have sinned.

2nd Reading 2 Cor 5:20—6:2

Brothers and sisters:

We are ambassadors for Christ, as if God were appealing through us. We implore you on behalf of Christ, be reconciled to God.

For our sake he made him to be sin who did not know sin, so that we might become the righteousness of God in him.

Working together, then, we appeal to you not to receive the grace of God in vain. For he says:

In an acceptable time I heard you, and on the day of salvation I helped you.

Behold, now is a very acceptable time; behold, now is the day of salvation.

Gospel Acclamation

If today you hear his voice, harden not your hearts

Gospel Mt 6:1-6, 16-18
Jesus said to his disciples:

"Take care not to perform righteous deeds in order that people may see them; otherwise, you will have no recompense from your heavenly Father.

When you give alms, do not blow a trumpet before you, as the hypocrites do in the synagogues and in the streets to win the praise of others.

Amen, I say to you, they have received their reward. But when you give alms, do not let your left hand know what your right is doing, so that your almsgiving may be secret.

And your Father who sees in secret will repay you.

"When you pray, do not be like the hypocrites, who love to stand and pray in the synagogues and on street corners so that others may see them.

Amen, I say to you, they have received their reward. But when you pray, go to your inner room, close the door, and pray to your Father in secret. And your Father who sees in secret will repay you.

"When you fast, do not look gloomy like the hypocrites. They neglect their appearance, so that they may appear to others to be fasting.

Amen, I say to you, they have received their reward. But when you fast, anoint your head and wash your face, so that you may not appear to be fasting, except to your Father who is hidden.

And your Father who sees what is hidden will repay you."

FEBRUARY 18TH, 2021
Thursday after Ash Wednesday

1st Reading Dt 30:15-20
Moses said to the people:

"Today I have set before you life and prosperity, death and doom.

If you obey the commandments of the LORD, your God, which I enjoin on you today, loving him, and walking in his ways, and keeping his commandments, statutes and decrees, you will live and grow numerous, and the LORD, your God, will bless you in the land you are entering to occupy.

If, however, you turn away your hearts and will not listen, but are led astray and adore and serve other gods,

I tell you now that you will certainly perish; you will not have a long life on the land that you are crossing the Jordan to enter and occupy.

I call heaven and earth today to witness against you: I have set before you life and death, the blessing and the curse.

Choose life, then, that you and your descendants may live, by loving the LORD, your God, heeding his voice, and holding fast to him.

For that will mean life for you, a long life for you to live on the land that the LORD swore he would give to your fathers Abraham, Isaac and Jacob."

Responsorial Psalm PS 1:1-2, 3, 4 and 6
R.(40:5a) Blessed are they who hope in the Lord.

Blessed the man who follows not the counsel of the wicked Nor walks in the way of sinners, nor sits in the company of the insolent, But delights in the law of the LORD and meditates on his law day and night.

R. Blessed are they who hope in the Lord.

He is like a tree planted near running water, That yields its fruit in due season, and whose leaves never fade. Whatever he does, prospers.

R. Blessed are they who hope in the Lord.

Not so the wicked, not so; they are like chaff which the wind drives away. For the LORD watches over the way of the just, but the way of the wicked vanishes.

R. Blessed are they who hope in the Lord.

Alleluia Mt 4:17

Gospel Acclamation

Repent, says the Lord; the Kingdom of heaven is at hand.

Jesus said to his disciples:

"The Son of Man must suffer greatly and be rejected by the elders, the chief priests, and the scribes, and be killed and on the third day be raised."

Then he said to all, "If anyone wishes to come after me, he must deny himself and take up his cross daily and follow me.

For whoever wishes to save his life will lose it, but whoever loses his life for my sake will save it.

What profit is there for one to gain the whole world yet lose or forfeit himself?"

FEBRUARY 19TH, 2021
Friday after Ash Wednesday

1st Reading Is 58:1-9a
Thus says the Lord GOD:

Cry out full-throated and unsparingly, lift up your voice like a trumpet blast;

Tell my people their wickedness, and the house of Jacob their sins. They seek me day after day, and desire to know my ways,

Like a nation that has done what is just and not abandoned the law of their God; They ask me to declare what is due them, pleased to gain access to God.

"Why do we fast, and you do not see it? Afflict ourselves, and you take no note of it?"

Lo, on your fast day you carry out your own pursuits, and drive all your laborers.

Yes, your fast ends in quarreling and fighting, striking with wicked claw. Would that today you might fast so as to make your voice heard on high! Is this the manner of fasting I wish, of keeping a day of penance?

That a man bows his head like a reed and lie in sackcloth and ashes?

Do you call this a fast, a day acceptable to the LORD?

This, rather, is the fasting that I wish: releasing those bound unjustly, untying the thongs of the yoke; Setting free the oppressed, breaking every yoke; Sharing your bread with the hungry, sheltering the oppressed and the homeless;

Clothing the naked when you see them, and not turning your back on your own. Then your light shall break forth like the dawn, and your wound shall quickly be healed;

Your vindication shall go before you, and the glory of the LORD shall be your rear guard. Then you shall call, and the LORD will answer, you shall cry for help, and he will say: Here I am

Responsorial Psalm PS 51:3-4, 5-6ab, 18-19
R.. (19b) A heart contrite and humbled, O God, you will not spurn.

Have mercy on me, O God, in your goodness; in the greatness of your compassion wipe out my offense. Thoroughly wash me from my guilt and of my sin cleanse me.

R. A heart contrite and humbled, O God, you will not spurn.

For I acknowledge my offense, and my sin is before me always: "Against you only have I sinned, and done what is evil in your sight."

R. A heart contrite and humbled, O God, you will not spurn.

For you are not pleased with sacrifices; should I offer a burnt offering, you would not accept it. My sacrifice, O God, is a contrite spirit; a heart contrite and humbled, O God, you will not spurn.

R. A heart contrite and humbled, O God, you will not spurn.

Gospel Acclamation Am 5:14

Seek good and not evil so that you may live, and the Lord will be with you.

Gospel Mt 9:14-15
The disciples of John approached Jesus and said,

"Why do we and the Pharisees fast much, but your disciples do not fast?"

Jesus answered them, "Can the wedding guests mourn as long as the bridegroom is with them? The days will come when the bridegroom is taken away from them, and then they will fast."

FEBRUARY 20TH, 2021
Saturday after Ash Wednesday

1st Reading Is 58:9b-14
Thus says the LORD:

If you remove from your midst oppression, false accusation and malicious speech;

If you bestow your bread on the hungry and satisfy the afflicted;

Then light shall rise for you in the darkness, and the gloom shall become for you like midday;

Then the LORD will guide you always and give you plenty even on the parched land.

He will renew your strength, and you shall be like a watered garden, like a spring whose water never fails.

The ancient ruins shall be rebuilt for your sake, and the foundations from ages past you shall raise up;

"Repairer of the breach," they shall call you, "Restorer of ruined homesteads."

If you hold back your foot on the sabbath from following your own pursuits on my holy day;

If you call the sabbath a delight, and the LORD's holy day honorable;

If you honor it by not following your ways seeking your own interests, or speaking with malice

Then you shall delight in the LORD and I will make you ride on the heights of the earth;

I will nourish you with the heritage of Jacob, your father, for the mouth of the LORD has spoken.

R. (11ab) Teach me your way, O Lord, that I may walk in your truth.

Incline your ear, O LORD; answer me, for I am afflicted and poor.

Keep my life, for I am devoted to you; save your servant who trusts in you.
You are my God.

R. Teach me your way, O Lord, that I may walk in your truth.

Have mercy on me, O Lord, for to you I call all the day.

Gladden the soul of your servant, for to you, O Lord, I lift up my soul.

R. Teach me your way, O Lord, that I may walk in your truth.

For you, O Lord, are good and forgiving, abounding in kindness to all who
call upon you.

Hearken, O LORD, to my prayer and attend to the sound of my pleading.

R. Teach me your way, O Lord, that I may walk in your truth.

Gospel Acclamation Ez 33:11

I take no pleasure in the death of the wicked man, says the Lord, but rather
in his conversion, that he may live.

Gospel Lk 5:27-32

Jesus saw a tax collector named Levi sitting at the customs post.

He said to him, "Follow me." And leaving everything behind, he got up and
followed him. Then Levi gave a great banquet for him in his house, and a
large crowd of tax collectors and others were at table with them.

The Pharisees and their scribes complained to his disciples, saying, "Why do
you eat and drink with tax collectors and sinners?" Jesus said to them in
reply,

"Those who are healthy do not need a physician, but the sick do. I have not
come to call the righteous to repentance but sinners."

FEBRUARY 21ST, 2021

First Sunday of Lent

1st Reading Gn 9:8-15

God said to Noah and to his sons with him: "See, I am now establishing my covenant with you and your descendants after you and with every living creature that was with you: all the birds, and the various tame and wild animals that were with you and came out of the ark.

I will establish my covenant with you, that never again shall all bodily creatures be destroyed by the waters of a flood; there shall not be another flood to devastate the earth."

God added:" This is the sign that I am giving for all ages to come, of the covenant between me and you and every living creature with you:

I set my bow in the clouds to serve as a sign of the covenant between me and the earth. When I bring clouds over the earth, and the bow appears in the clouds,

I will recall the covenant I have made between me and you and all living beings, so that the waters shall never again become a flood to destroy all mortal beings."

Responsorial Psalm Ps 25:4-5, 6-7, 8-9

R (cf. 10) Your ways, O Lord, are love and truth to those who keep your covenant.

Your ways, O LORD, make known to me; teach me your paths,

Guide me in your truth and teach me, for you are God my savior.

R. Your ways, O Lord, are love and truth to those who keep your covenant.

Remember that your compassion, O LORD, and your love are from of old.

In your kindness remember me, because of your goodness, O LORD.

R. Your ways, O Lord, are love and truth to those who keep your covenant.

Good and upright is the LORD, thus he shows sinners the way.

He guides the humble to justice, and he teaches the humble his way.

R. Your ways, O Lord, are love and truth to those who keep your covenant.

2nd Reading 1 Pt 3:18-22
Beloved:

Christ suffered for sins once, the righteous for the sake of the unrighteous, that he might lead you to God.

Put to death in the flesh, he was brought to life in the Spirit.

In it he also went to preach to the spirits in prison, who had once been disobedient while God patiently waited in the days of Noah during the building of the ark, in which a few persons, eight in all, were saved through water.

This prefigured baptism, which saves you now. It is not a removal of dirt from the body but an appeal to God for a clear conscience, through the resurrection of Jesus Christ, who has gone into heaven and is at the right hand of God, with angels, authorities, and powers subject to him..

Gospel Acclamation Mt 4:4b

One does not live on bread alone, but on every word that comes forth from the mouth of God.

Gospel LK 6:27-38

The Spirit drove Jesus out into the desert, and he remained in the desert for forty days, tempted by Satan.

He was among wild beasts, and the angels ministered to him.

After John had been arrested, Jesus came to Galilee proclaiming the gospel of God:

"This is the time of fulfillment. The kingdom of God is at hand. Repent, and believe in the gospel."

FEBRUARY 22TH, 2021
Feast of the Chair of Saint Peter, Apostle

1st Reading 1 Pt 5:1-4
Beloved:

I exhort the presbyters among you, as a fellow presbyter and witness to the sufferings of Christ and one who has a share in the glory to be revealed.

Tend the flock of God in your midst, overseeing not by constraint but willingly, as God would have it, not for shameful profit but eagerly.

Do not lord it over those assigned to you, but be examples to the flock. And when the chief Shepherd is revealed, you will receive the unfading crown of glory.

Responsorial Psalm PS 23:1-3a, 4, 5, 6
R... (1) The Lord is my shepherd; there is nothing I shall want.

The Lord is my shepherd; I shall not want. In verdant pastures he gives me repose;

Beside restful waters he leads me; he refreshes my soul.

R. The Lord is my shepherd; there is nothing I shall want.

Even though I walk in the dark valley I fear no evil; for you are at my side

With your rod and your staff that give me courage.

R. The Lord is my shepherd; there is nothing I shall want.

You spread the table before me in the sight of my foes;

You anoint my head with oil; my cup overflows.

R. The Lord is my shepherd; there is nothing I shall want.

Only goodness and kindness follow me all the days of my life;

And I shall dwell in the house of the Lord for years to come.

R. The Lord is my shepherd; there is nothing I shall want.

Gospel Acclamation Mt 16:18

You are Peter, and upon this rock I will build my Church; the gates of the netherworld shall not prevail against it.

Gospel Mt 16:13-19
When Jesus went into the region of Caesarea Philippi he asked his disciples,

"Who do people say that the Son of Man is?" They replied, "Some say John the Baptist, others Elijah, still others Jeremiah or one of the prophets."

He said to them, "But who do you say that I am?" Simon Peter said in reply, "You are the Christ, the Son of the living God."

Jesus said to him in reply, "Blessed are you, Simon son of Jonah.

For flesh and blood has not revealed this to you, but my heavenly Father. And so I say to you, you are Peter, and upon this rock I will build my Church, and the gates of the netherworld shall not prevail against it.

I will give you the keys to the Kingdom of heaven. Whatever you bind on earth shall be bound in heaven; and whatever you loose on earth shall be loosed in heaven."

FEBRUARY 23RD, 2021
Optional Memorial of Saint Polycarp, bishop and martyr

1st Reading Is 55:10-11
Thus says the LORD:

Just as from the heavens the rain and snow come down

And do not return there till they have watered the earth, making it fertile and fruitful,

Giving seed to the one who sows and bread to the one who eats,

So shall my word be that goes forth from my mouth;

It shall not return to me void, but shall do my will, achieving the end for which I sent it.

Responsorial Psalm   PS 34:4-5, 6-7, 16-17, 18-19
R.(18b) From all their distress God rescues the just.

Glorify the LORD with me, let us together extol his name.

I sought the LORD, and he answered me and delivered me from all my fears.

R. From all their distress God rescues the just.

Look to him that you may be radiant with joy, and your faces may not blush with shame.

When the poor one called out, the LORD heard, and from all his distress he saved him.

R. From all their distress God rescues the just.

The LORD has eyes for the just, and ears for their cry.

The LORD confronts the evildoers, to destroy remembrance of them from the earth.

R. From all their distress God rescues the just.

When the just cry out, the LORD hears them, and from all their distress he rescues them.

The LORD is close to the brokenhearted; and those who are crushed in spirit he saves.

R. From all their distress God rescues the just.

Gospel Acclamation Mt 4:4b

One does not live on bread alone, but on every word that comes forth from the mouth of God

Gospel   Mt 6:7-15
Jesus said to his disciples:

"In praying, do not babble like the pagans, who think that they will be heard because of their many words.

Do not be like them. Your Father knows what you need before you ask him.

"This is how you are to pray: Our Father who art in heaven, hallowed be thy name, thy Kingdom come, thy will be done, on earth as it is in heaven. Give us this day our daily bread; and forgive us our trespasses, as we forgive those who trespass against us; and lead us not into temptation, but deliver us from evil.

"If you forgive men their transgressions, your heavenly Father will forgive you.

But if you do not forgive men, neither will your Father forgive your transgressions."

FEBRUARY 24TH, 2021
Wednesday of the First Week of Lent

1st Reading Jon 3:1-10

The word of the LORD came to Jonah a second time:

"Set out for the great city of Nineveh, and announce to it the message that I will tell you." So Jonah made ready and went to Nineveh, according to the LORD's bidding.

Now Nineveh was an enormously large city; it took three days to go through it. Jonah began his journey through the city, and had gone but a single day's walk announcing,

"Forty days more and Nineveh shall be destroyed," when the people of Nineveh believed God; they proclaimed a fast and all of them, great and small, put on sackcloth.

When the news reached the king of Nineveh, he rose from his throne, laid aside his robe, covered himself with sackcloth, and sat in the ashes.

Then he had this proclaimed throughout Nineveh, by decree of the king and his nobles:

"Neither man nor beast, neither cattle nor sheep, shall taste anything; they shall not eat, nor shall they drink water.

Man and beast shall be covered with sackcloth and call loudly to God; every man shall turn from his evil way and from the violence he has in hand. Who knows, God may relent and forgive, and withhold his blazing wrath, so that we shall not perish."

When God saw by their actions how they turned from their evil way, he repented of the evil that he had threatened to do to them; he did not carry it out.

Responsorial Psalm PS 51:3-4, 12-13, 18-19
R (19b) A heart contrite and humbled, O God, you will not spurn.

100

Have mercy on me, O God, in your goodness; in the greatness of your compassion wipe out my offense.

Thoroughly wash me from my guilt and of my sin cleanse me.

R.A heart contrite and humbled, O God, you will not spurn.

A clean heart create for me, O God, and a steadfast spirit renew within me. Cast me not out from your presence, and your Holy Spirit take not from me.

R.A heart contrite and humbled, O God, you will not spurn.

For you are not pleased with sacrifices; should I offer a burnt offering, you would not accept it.

My sacrifice, O God, is a contrite spirit; a heart contrite and humbled, O God, you will not spurn.

R. A heart contrite and humbled, O God, you will not spurn.

Gospel Acclamation Jl 2:12-13

Even now, says the LORD, return to me with your whole heart for I am gracious and merciful.

Gospel   Lk 11:29-32
While still more people gathered in the crowd, Jesus said to them,

"This generation is an evil generation; it seeks a sign, but no sign will be given it, except the sign of Jonah.

Just as Jonah became a sign to the Ninevites, so will the Son of Man be to this generation.

At the judgment the queen of the south will rise with the men of this generation and she will condemn them, because she came from the ends of the earth to hear the wisdom of Solomon, and there is something greater than Solomon here.

At the judgment the men of Nineveh will arise with this generation and condemn it, because at the preaching of Jonah they repented, and there is something greater than Jonah here."

1st Reading Est C:12, 14-16, 23-25

Queen Esther, seized with mortal anguish, had recourse to the LORD.

She lay prostrate upon the ground, together with her handmaids, from morning until evening, and said:

"God of Abraham, God of Isaac, and God of Jacob, blessed are you. Help me, who am alone and have no help but you, for I am taking my life in my hand.

As a child I used to hear from the books of my forefathers that you, O LORD, always free those who are pleasing to you. Now help me, who am alone and have no one but you,

O LORD, my God. "And now, come to help me, an orphan.

Put in my mouth persuasive words in the presence of the lion and turn his heart to hatred for our enemy, so that he and those who are in league with him may perish.

Save us from the hand of our enemies; turn our mourning into gladness and our sorrows into wholeness."

Responsorial Psalm   PS 138:1-2ab, 2cdc-3, 7c-8

R. (3a) Lord, on the day I called for help, you answered me.

I will give thanks to you, O LORD, with all my heart, for you have heard the words of my mouth; in the presence of the angels I will sing your praise;

I will worship at your holy temple and give thanks to your name.

R. Lord, on the day I called for help, you answered me.

Because of your kindness and your truth; for you have made great above all things your name and your promise.

When I called, you answered me; you built up strength within me.

R. Lord, on the day I called for help, you answered me.

Your right hand saves me.

The LORD will complete what he has done for me; your kindness, O LORD, endures forever; forsake not the work of your hands.

R. Lord, on the day I called for help, you answered me.

Gospel Acclamation Ps 51:12a, 14a

A clean heart creates for me, O God; give me back the joy of your salvation.

Gospel Mt 7:7-12

Jesus said to his disciples: "Anyone who gives you a cup of water to Jesus said to his disciples:

"Ask and it will be given to you; seek and you will find; knock and the door will be opened to you.

For everyone who asks, receives; and the one who seeks, finds; and to the one who knocks, the door will be opened.

Which one of you would hand his son a stone when he asked for a loaf of bread or a snake when he asked for a fish?

If you then, who are wicked, know how to give good gifts to your children, how much more will your heavenly Father give good things to those who ask him.

"Do to others whatever you would have them do to you.

This is the law and the prophets."

FEBRUARY 26TH, 2021
Friday of the First Week of Lent

1st Reading Ez 18:21-28
Thus says the Lord GOD:

If the wicked man turns away from all the sins he committed, if he keeps all my statutes and does what is right and just, he shall surely live, he shall not die.

None of the crimes he committed shall be remembered against him; he shall live because of the virtue he has practiced.

Do I indeed derive any pleasure from the death of the wicked? says the Lord GOD.

Do I not rather rejoice when he turns from his evil way that he may live?

And if the virtuous man turns from the path of virtue to do evil, the same kind of abominable things that the wicked man does can he do this and still live?

None of his virtuous deeds shall be remembered because he has broken faith and committed sin; because of this, he shall die.

You say, "The LORD's way is not fair!"

Hear now, house of Israel: Is it my way that is unfair, or rather, are not your ways unfair?

When someone virtuous turns away from virtue to commit iniquity, and dies, it is because of the iniquity he committed that he must die.

But if the wicked, turning from the wickedness he has committed, does what is right and just, he shall preserve his life; since he has turned away from all the sins that he committed, he shall surely live, he shall not die.

Responsorial Psalm PS 130:1-2, 3-4, 5-7a, 7bc-8
R. (35a) Guide me, Lord, in the way of your commands.

Blessed are you, O LORD; teach me your statutes.

R. Guide me, Lord, in the way of your commands.

In your statutes I will delight; I will not forget your words.

R. Guide me, Lord, in the way of your commands.

Open my eyes, that I may consider the wonders of your law.

R. Guide me, Lord, in the way of your commands.

Make me understand the way of your precepts, and I will meditate on your wondrous deeds.

R. (3) If you, O Lord, mark iniquities, who can stand?

Out of the depths I cry to you, O LORD; LORD, hear my voice!

Let your ears be attentive to my voice in supplication.

R. If you, O Lord, mark iniquities, who can stand?

If you, O LORD, mark iniquities, LORD, who can stand?

But with you is forgiveness, that you may be revered.

R. If you, O Lord, mark iniquities, who can stand?

I trust in the LORD; my soul trusts in his word.

My soul waits for the LORD more than sentinels wait for the dawn. Let Israel wait for the LORD.

R. If you, O Lord, mark iniquities, who can stand?

For with the LORD is kindness and with him is plenteous redemption;

And he will redeem Israel from all their iniquities.

R. If you, O Lord, mark iniquities, who can stand?

Gospel Acclamation Ez 18:31

Cast away from you all the crimes you have committed, says the LORD, and make for yourselves a new heart and a new spirit.

Gospel Mt 5:20-26
Jesus said to his disciples:

"I tell you, unless your righteousness surpasses that of the scribes and Pharisees, you will not enter into the Kingdom of heaven.

"You have heard that it was said to your ancestors, You shall not kill; and whoever kills will be liable to judgment.

But I say to you, whoever is angry with his brother will be liable to judgment, and whoever says to his brother, Raqa, will be answerable to the Sanhedrin, and whoever says, 'You fool,' will be liable to fiery Gehenna.

Therefore, if you bring your gift to the altar, and there recall that your brother has anything against you, leave your gift there at the altar, go first and be reconciled with your brother, and then come and offer your gift. Settle with your opponent quickly while on the way to court.

Otherwise your opponent will hand you over to the judge, and the judge will hand you over to the guard, and you will be thrown into prison.

Amen, I say to you, you will not be released until you have paid the last penny."

FEBRUARY 27TH, 2021
Saturday of the First Week of Lent

1st Reading Dt 26:16-19
Moses spoke to the people, saying:

"This day the LORD, your God, commands you to observe these statutes and decrees. Be careful, then, to observe them with all your heart and with all your soul.

Today you are making this agreement with the LORD: he is to be your God and you are to walk in his ways and observe his statutes, commandments and decrees, and to hearken to his voice.

And today the LORD is making this agreement with you: you are to be a people peculiarly his own, as he promised you; and provided you keep all his commandments, he will then raise you high in praise and renown and glory above all other nations he has made, and you will be a people sacred to the LORD, your God, as he promised."

Responsorial Psalm PS 119:1-2, 4-5, 7-8
R. (1b) Blessed are they who follow the law of the Lord!

Blessed are they whose way is blameless, who walk in the law of the LORD.

Blessed are they who observe his decrees, who seek him with all their heart.

R. Blessed are they who follow the law of the Lord!

You have commanded that your precepts be diligently kept.

Oh, that I might be firm in the ways of keeping your statutes!

R. Blessed are they who follow the law of the Lord!

I will give you thanks with an upright heart, when I have learned your just ordinances.

I will keep your statutes; do not utterly forsake me.

R. Blessed are they who follow the law of the Lord!

Gospel Acclamation 2 Cor 6:2b

Behold, now is a very acceptable time; behold, now is the day of salvation.

Gospel Mt 5:43-48
Jesus said to his disciples:

"You have heard that it was said, You shall love your neighbor and hate your enemy.

But I say to you, love your enemies, and pray for those who persecute you, that you may be children of your heavenly Father, for he makes his sun rise on the bad and the good, and causes rain to fall on the just and the unjust.

For if you love those who love you, what recompense will you have?

Do not the tax collectors do the same?

And if you greet your brothers and sisters only, what is unusual about that? Do not the pagans do the same? So be perfect, just as your heavenly Father is perfect.".

FEBRUARY 28TH, 2021
Second Sunday of Lent

1st Reading   Gn 22:1-2, 9a, 10-13, 15-18
God put Abraham to the test. He called to him, "Abraham!"

"Here I am!" he replied. Then God said: "Take your son Isaac, your only one, whom you love, and go to the land of Moriah.

There you shall offer him up as a holocaust on a height that I will point out to you."

When they came to the place of which God had told him, Abraham built an altar there and arranged the wood on it.

Then he reached out and took the knife to slaughter his son. But the LORD's messenger called to him from heaven, "Abraham, Abraham!"

"Here I am!" he answered. "Do not lay your hand on the boy," said the messenger. "Do not do the least thing to him.

I know now how devoted you are to God, since you did not withhold from me your own beloved son."

As Abraham looked about, he spied a ram caught by its horns in the thicket.

So he went and took the ram and offered it up as a holocaust in place of his son. Again the LORD's messenger called to Abraham from heaven and said: "I swear by myself, declares the LORD, that because you acted as you did in not withholding from me your beloved son,

I will bless you abundantly and make your descendants as countless as the stars of the sky and the sands of the seashore; your descendants shall take possession of the gates of their enemies, and in your descendants all the nations of the earth shall find blessing—all this because you obeyed my command."

Responsorial Psalm   116:10, 15, 16-17, 18-19
R. (116:9) I will walk before the Lord, in the land of the living.

I believed, even when I said,"I am greatly afflicted."

Precious in the eyes of the LORD is the death of his faithful ones.

R. I will walk before the Lord, in the land of the living.

O LORD, I am your servant; I am your servant, the son of your handmaid; you have loosed my bonds.

To you will I offer sacrifice of thanksgiving, and I will call upon the name of the LORD.

R. I will walk before the Lord, in the land of the living.

My vows to the LORD I will pay in the presence of all his people,

In the courts of the house of the LORD, in your midst, O Jerusalem.

R. I will walk before the Lord, in the land of the living.

2nd Reading Rom 8:31b-34
Brothers and sisters:

If God is for us, who can be against us?

He who did not spare his own Son but handed him over for us all, how will he not also give us everything else along with him?

Who will bring a charge against God's chosen ones?

It is God who acquits us, who will condemn?

Christ Jesus it is who died—or, rather, was raised— who also is at the right hand of God, who indeed intercedes for us.

Gospel Acclamation Mt 17:5

From the shining cloud the Father's voice is heard: This is my beloved Son, listen to him.

Gospel Mk 9:2-10
Jesus took Peter, James, and John and led them up a high mountain apart by themselves.

And he was transfigured before them, and his clothes became dazzling white, such as no fuller on earth could bleach them.

Then Elijah appeared to them along with Moses, and they were conversing with Jesus.

Then Peter said to Jesus in reply, "Rabbi, it is good that we are here! Let us make three tents: one for you, one for Moses, and one for Elijah."

He hardly knew what to say, they were so terrified. Then a cloud came, casting a shadow over them; from the cloud came a voice,

"This is my beloved Son. Listen to him. "Suddenly, looking around, they no longer saw anyone but Jesus alone with them.

As they were coming down from the mountain, he charged them not to relate what they had seen to anyone, except when the Son of Man had risen from the dead.

So they kept the matter to themselves, questioning what rising from the dead meant.

MARCH 1ST, 2021
Monday of the Second Week in Lent

1st Reading Dn 9:4b-10
"Lord, great and awesome God, you who keep your merciful covenant toward those who love you and observe your commandments!

We have sinned, been wicked and done evil; we have rebelled and departed from your commandments and your laws.

We have not obeyed your servants the prophets, who spoke in your name to our kings, our princes, our fathers, and all the people of the land.

Justice, O Lord, is on your side; we are shamefaced even to this day: we, the men of Judah, the residents of Jerusalem, and all Israel, near and far, in all the countries to which you have scattered them because of their treachery toward you.

O LORD, we are shamefaced, like our kings, our princes, and our fathers, for having sinned against you.

But yours, O Lord, our God, are compassion and forgiveness!

Yet we rebelled against you and paid no heed to your command, O LORD, our God, to live by the law you gave us through your servants the prophets."

Responsorial Psalm PS 79:8, 9, 11 and 13
R. (see 103:10a) Lord, do not deal with us according to our sins.

Remember not against us the iniquities of the past; may your compassion quickly come to us, for we are brought very low.

R. Lord, do not deal with us according to our sins.

Help us, O God our savior, because of the glory of your name;

Deliver us and pardon our sins for your name's sake.

R. Lord, do not deal with us according to our sins.

Let the prisoners' sighing come before you; with your great power free those doomed to death.

Then we, your people and the sheep of your pasture, will give thanks to you forever; through all generations we will declare your praise.

R. Lord, do not deal with us according to our sins.

Gospel Acclamation See Jn 6:63c, 68c

Your words, Lord, are Spirit and life; you have the words of everlasting life.

Gospel Lk 6:36-38
Jesus said to his disciples:

"Be merciful, just as your Father is merciful.

"Stop judging and you will not be judged. Stop condemning and you will not be condemned. Forgive and you will be forgiven.

Give and gifts will be given to you; a good measure, packed together, shaken down, and overflowing, will be poured into your lap.

For the measure with which you measure will in return be measured out to you."

MARCH 2TH, 2021
Tuesday of the Second Week of Lent

1st Reading Is 1:10, 16-20
Hear the word of the LORD, princes of Sodom!

Listen to the instruction of our God, people of Gomorrah!

Wash yourselves clean!

Put away your misdeeds from before my eyes; cease doing evil; learn to do good. Make justice your aim: redress the wronged, hear the orphan's plea, defend the widow.

Come now, let us set things right, says the LORD: Though your sins be like scarlet, they may become white as snow;

Though they be crimson red, they may become white as wool.

If you are willing, and obey, you shall eat the good things of the land; But if you refuse and resist, the sword shall consume you: for the mouth of the LORD has spoken!

Responsorial Psalm 50:8-9, 16bc-17, 21 and 23
R. (23b).To the upright I will show the saving power of God."

Gather my faithful ones before me, those who have made a covenant with me by sacrifice." And the heavens proclaim his justice; for God himself is the judge.

R. To the upright I will show the saving power of God.

"Hear, my people, and I will speak; Israel, I will testify against you; God, your God, am I. Not for your sacrifices do I rebuke you, for your burnt offerings are before me always."

R. To the upright I will show the saving power of God.

"Offer to God praise as your sacrifice and fulfill your vows to the Most High. He that offers praise as a sacrifice glorifies me; and to him that goes the right way I will show the salvation of God."

R. To the upright I will show the saving power of God.

Gospel Acclamation Ez 18:31

Cast away from you all the crimes you have committed, says the LORD, and make for yourselves a new heart and a new spirit.

Gospel MK Mt 23:1-12
Jesus spoke to the crowds and to his disciples, saying,

"The scribes and the Pharisees have taken their seat on the chair of Moses.

Therefore, do and observe all things whatsoever they tell you, but do not follow their example. For they preach but they do not practice.

They tie up heavy burdens hard to carry and lay them on people's shoulders, but they will not lift a finger to move them.

All their works are performed to be seen. They widen their phylacteries and lengthen their tassels.

They love places of honor at banquets, seats of honor in synagogues, greetings in marketplaces, and the salutation 'Rabbi.'

As for you, do not be called 'Rabbi.' You have but one teacher, and you are all brothers. Call no one on earth your father; you have but one Father in heaven.

Do not be called 'Master'; you have but one master, the Christ.

The greatest among you must be your servant. Whoever exalts himself will be humbled; but whoever humbles himself will be exalted."

MARCH 3RD, 2021
Wednesday of the Second Week of Lent

1st Reading JER 18:18-20
The people of Judah and the citizens of Jerusalem said, "Come, let us contrive a plot against Jeremiah. It will not mean the loss of instruction from the priests, nor of counsel from the wise, nor of messages from the prophets. And so, let us destroy him by his own tongue; let us carefully note his every word." Heed me, O LORD, and listen to what my adversaries say. Must good be repaid with evil that they should dig a pit to take my life? Remember that I stood before you to speak in their behalf, to turn away your wrath from them

Responsorial Psalm   PS 31:5-6, 14, 15-16
R. (17b) Save me, O Lord, in your kindness.

You will free me from the snare they set for me, for you are my refuge. Into your hands I commend my spirit; you will redeem me, O LORD, O faithful God.

R. Save me, O Lord, in your kindness.

I hear the whispers of the crowd, that frighten me from every side, as they consult together against me, plotting to take my life.

R. Save me, O Lord, in your kindness.

But my trust is in you, O LORD; I say, "You are my God." In your hands is my destiny; rescue me from the clutches of my enemies and my persecutors.

R. Save me, O Lord, in your kindness.

Gospel Acclamation: JN 8:12

I am the light of the world, says the Lord; whoever follows me will have the light of life.

Gospel MT 20:17-28

As Jesus was going up to Jerusalem, he took the Twelve disciples aside by themselves, and said to them on the way, "Behold, we are going up to Jerusalem, and the Son of Man will be handed over to the chief priests and the scribes, and they will condemn him to death, and hand him over to the Gentiles to be mocked and scourged and crucified, and he will be raised on the third day."

Then the mother of the sons of Zebedee approached Jesus with her sons and did him homage, wishing to ask him for something. He said to her, "What do you wish?" She answered him, "Command that these two sons of mine sit, one at your right and the other at your left, in your kingdom." Jesus said in reply, "You do not know what you are asking. Can you drink the chalice that I am going to drink?" They said to him, "We can." He replied, "My chalice you will indeed drink, but to sit at my right and at my left, this is not mine to give but is for those for whom it has been prepared by my Father."

When the ten heard this, they became indignant at the two brothers. But Jesus summoned them and said, "You know that the rulers of the Gentiles lord it over them, and the great ones make their authority over them felt. But it shall not be so among you. Rather, whoever wishes to be great among you shall be your servant; whoever wishes to be first among you shall be your slave. Just so, the Son of Man did not come to be served but to serve and to give his life as a ransom for many."

MARCH 4TH, 2021
Thursday of the Second Week of Lent

1st Reading JER 17:5-10

Thus says the LORD: Cursed is the man who trusts in human beings, who seeks his strength in flesh, whose heart turns away from the LORD. He is like a barren bush in the desert that enjoys no change of season, But stands in a lava waste, a salt and empty earth.

Blessed is the man who trusts in the LORD, whose hope is the LORD. He is like a tree planted beside the waters that stretches out its roots to the stream: It fears not the heat when it comes, its leaves stay green; In the year of drought it shows no distress, but still bears fruit. More tortuous than all else is the human heart, beyond remedy; who can understand it? I, the LORD, alone probe the mind and test the heart, To reward everyone according to his ways, according to the merit of his deeds.

Responsorial Psalm PS 1:1-2, 3, 4 AND 6
R. (40:5a) Blessed are they who hope in the Lord.

Blessed the man who follows not the counsel of the wicked Nor walks in the way of sinners, nor sits in the company of the insolent, But delights in the law of the LORD and meditates on his law day and night.

R. Blessed are they who hope in the Lord.

He is like a tree planted near running water, That yields its fruit in due season, and whose leaves never fade. Whatever he does, prospers.

R. Blessed are they who hope in the Lord.

Not so, the wicked, not so; they are like chaff which the wind drives away. For the LORD watches over the way of the just, but the way of the wicked vanishes.

R. Blessed are they who hope in the Lord.

Gospel Acclamation: LK 8:15

Blessed are they who have kept the word with a generous heart and yield a harvest through perseverance.

Gospel   LK 16:19-31
Jesus said to the Pharisees: "There was a rich man who dressed in purple garments and fine linen and dined sumptuously each day. And lying at his door was a poor man named Lazarus, covered with sores, who would gladly have eaten his fill of the scraps that fell from the rich man's table. Dogs even used to come and lick his sores. When the poor man died, he was carried away by angels to the bosom of Abraham.

The rich man also died and was buried, and from the netherworld, where he was in torment, he raised his eyes and saw Abraham far off and Lazarus at his side. And he cried out, 'Father Abraham, have pity on me. Send Lazarus to dip the tip of his finger in water and cool my tongue, for I am suffering torment in these flames.'

Abraham replied, 'My child, remember that you received what was good during your lifetime while Lazarus likewise received what was bad; but now he is comforted here, whereas you are tormented. Moreover, between us and you a great chasm is established to prevent anyone from crossing who might wish to go from our side to yours or from your side to ours.'

He said, 'Then I beg you, father, send him to my father's house, for I have five brothers, so that he may warn them, lest they too come to this place of torment.' But Abraham replied, 'They have Moses and the prophets. Let them listen to them.' He said, 'Oh no, father Abraham, but if someone from the dead goes to them, they will repent.' Then Abraham said, 'If they will not listen to Moses and the prophets, neither will they be persuaded if someone should rise from the dead.'

MARCH 5TH, 2021
Friday of the Second Week of Lent

1st Reading GN 37:3-4, 12-13A, 17B-28A
Israel loved Joseph best of all his sons, for he was the child of his old age; and he had made him a long tunic. When his brothers saw that their father loved him best of all his sons, they hated him so much that they would not even greet him.

One day, when his brothers had gone to pasture their father's flocks at Shechem, Israel said to Joseph, "Your brothers, you know, are tending our flocks at Shechem. Get ready; I will send you to them." So Joseph went after his brothers and caught up with them in Dothan. They noticed him from a distance, and before he came up to them, they plotted to kill him. They said to one another: "Here comes that master dreamer! Come on, let us kill him and throw him into one of the cisterns here; we could say that a wild beast devoured him. We shall then see what comes of his dreams."

When Reuben heard this, he tried to save him from their hands, saying, "We must not take his life. Instead of shedding blood," he continued, "just throw him into that cistern there in the desert; but do not kill him outright." His

116

purpose was to rescue him from their hands and return him to his father. So when Joseph came up to them, they stripped him of the long tunic he had on; then they took him and threw him into the cistern, which was empty and dry.

They then sat down to their meal. Looking up, they saw a caravan of Ishmaelites coming from Gilead, their camels laden with gum, balm and resin to be taken down to Egypt. Judah said to his brothers: "What is to be gained by killing our brother and concealing his blood? Rather, let us sell him to these Ishmaelites, instead of doing away with him ourselves. After all, he is our brother, our own flesh." His brothers agreed. They sold Joseph to the Ishmaelites for twenty pieces of silver.

Responsorial Psalm   PS 105:16-17, 18-19, 20-21
R. (5a) Remember the marvels the Lord has done.

When the LORD called down a famine on the land and ruined the crop that sustained them, He sent a man before them, Joseph, sold as a slave.

R. Remember the marvels the Lord has done.

They had weighed him down with fetters, and he was bound with chains, Till his prediction came to pass and the word of the LORD proved him true.

R. Remember the marvels the Lord has done.

The king sent and released him, the ruler of the peoples set him free. He made him lord of his house and ruler of all his possessions.

R. Remember the marvels the Lord has done.

Gospel Acclamation: JN 3:16

God so loved the world that he gave his only-begotten Son; so that everyone who believes in him might have eternal life.

Gospel   MT 21:33-43, 45-46
Jesus said to the chief priests and the elders of the people: "Hear another parable. There was a landowner who planted a vineyard, put a hedge around it, dug a wine press in it, and built a tower. Then he leased it to tenants and went on a journey.

When vintage time drew near, he sent his servants to the tenants to obtain his produce. But the tenants seized the servants and one they beat, another they killed, and a third they stoned.

Again he sent other servants, more numerous than the first ones, but they treated them in the same way. Finally, he sent his son to them, thinking, 'They will respect my son.' But when the tenants saw the son, they said to one another,

'This is the heir. Come, let us kill him and acquire his inheritance.' They seized him, threw him out of the vineyard, and killed him. What will the owner of the vineyard do to those tenants when he comes?" They answered him,

He will put those wretched men to a wretched death and lease his vineyard to other tenants who will give him the produce at the proper times." Jesus said to them, have you never read in the Scriptures: The stone that the builders rejected has become the cornerstone; by the Lord has this been done, and it is wonderful in our eyes? Therefore, I say to you, the Kingdom of God will be taken away from you and given to a people that will produce its fruit." When the chief priests and the Pharisees heard his parables, they knew that he was speaking about them.

And although they were attempting to arrest him, they feared the crowds, for they regarded him as a prophet

MARCH 6 TH, 2021
Saturday of the Second Week of Lent

1st Reading MI 7:14-15, 18-20
Shepherd your people with your staff, the flock of your inheritance, that dwells apart in a woodland, in the midst of Carmel. Let them feed in Bashan and Gilead, as in the days of old; As in the days when you came from the land of Egypt, show us wonderful signs. Who is there like you, the God who removes guilt and pardons sin for the remnant of his inheritance; Who does not persist in anger forever, but delights rather in clemency, And will again have compassion on us, treading underfoot our guilt? You will cast into the depths of the sea all our sins; You will show faithfulness to Jacob, and grace to Abraham as you have sworn to our fathers from days of old.

R. (8a) The Lord is kind and merciful.

Bless the LORD, O my soul; and all my being, bless his holy name. Bless the LORD, O my soul, and forget not all his benefits.

R.. The Lord is kind and merciful.

He pardons all your iniquities, he heals all your ills. He redeems your life from destruction, he crowns you with kindness and compassion.

R.. The Lord is kind and merciful.

He will not always chide, nor does he keep his wrath forever. Not according to our sins does he deal with us, nor does he requite us according to our crimes.

R.. The Lord is kind and merciful.

For as the heavens are high above the earth, so surpassing is his kindness toward those who fear him. As far as the east is from the west, so far has he put our transgressions from us.

R.. The Lord is kind and merciful.

Gospel Acclamation: LK 15:18

I will get up and go to my father and shall say to him, Father, I have sinned against heaven and against you.

Gospel LK 15:1-3, 11-32

Tax collectors and sinners were all drawing near to listen to Jesus, but the Pharisees and scribes began to complain, saying, "This man welcomes sinners and eats with them." So to them Jesus addressed this parable. "A man had two sons, and the younger son said to his father, 'Father, give me the share of your estate that should come to me.' So the father divided the property between them.

After a few days, the younger son collected all his belongings and set off to a distant country where he squandered his inheritance on a life of dissipation.

When he had freely spent everything, a severe famine struck that country, and he found himself in dire need. So he hired himself out to one of the local

119

citizens who sent him to his farm to tend the swine. And he longed to eat his fill of the pods on which the swine fed, but nobody gave him any. Coming to his senses he thought, 'How many of my father's hired workers have more than enough food to eat, but here am I, dying from hunger. I shall get up and go to my father and I shall say to him, "Father, I have sinned against heaven and against you. I no longer deserve to be called your son; treat me as you would treat one of your hired workers."' So he got up and went back to his father. While he was still a long way off, his father caught sight of him, and was filled with compassion. He ran to his son, embraced him and kissed him.

His son said to him, 'Father, I have sinned against heaven and against you; I no longer deserve to be called your son. 'But his father ordered his servants, 'Quickly, bring the finest robe and put it on him; put a ring on his finger and sandals on his feet. Take the fattened calf and slaughter it. Then let us celebrate with a feast, because this son of mine was dead, and has come to life again; he was lost, and has been found.' Then the celebration began.

Now the older son had been out in the field and, on his way back, as he neared the house, he heard the sound of music and dancing. He called one of the servants and asked what this might mean. The servant said to him, 'Your brother has returned and your father has slaughtered the fattened calf because he has him back safe and sound.' He became angry, and when he refused to enter the house, his father came out and pleaded with him. He said to his father in reply, 'Look, all these years I served you and not once did I disobey your orders; yet you never gave me even a young goat to feast on with my friends But when your son returns who swallowed up your property with prostitutes, for him you slaughter the fattened calf.' He said to him, 'My son, you are here with me always; everything I have is yours. But now we must celebrate and rejoice, because your brother was dead and has come to life again; he was lost and has been found.'"

MARCH 7TH, 2021

Third Sunday of Lent – Year A Readings

1st Reading   EX 17:3-7

In those days, in their thirst for water, the people grumbled against Moses, saying, "Why did you ever make us leave Egypt? Was it just to have us die here of thirst with our children and our livestock?" So Moses cried out to the LORD, "What shall I do with this people? a little more and they will stone me!"

The LORD answered Moses, "Go over there in front of the people, along with some of the elders of Israel, holding in your hand, as you go, the staff with which you struck the river. I will be standing there in front of you on the rock in Horeb. Strike the rock, and the water will flow from it for the people to drink." This Moses did, in the presence of the elders of Israel. The place was called Massah and Meribah, because the Israelites quarreled there and tested the LORD, saying, "Is the LORD in our midst or not?"

Responsorial Psalm   PS 95:1-2, 6-7, 8-9.
R. (8) If today you hear his voice, harden not your hearts.

Come, let us sing joyfully to the LORD; let us acclaim the Rock of our salvation. Let us come into his presence with thanksgiving; let us joyfully sing psalms to him.

R. If today you hear his voice, harden not your hearts.

Come, let us bow down in worship; let us kneel before the LORD who made us. For he is our God, and we are the people he shepherds, the flock he guides.

R. If today you hear his voice, harden not your hearts.

Oh, that today you would hear his voice: "Harden not your hearts as at Meribah, as in the day of Massah in the desert, Where your fathers tempted me; they tested me though they had seen my works."

R. If today you hear his voice, harden not your hearts.

2nd Reading   ROM 5:1-2, 5-8
Brothers and sisters: Since we have been justified by faith, we have peace with God through our Lord Jesus Christ, through whom we have gained access by faith to this grace in which we stand, and we boast in hope of the glory of God.

And hope does not disappoint, because the love of God has been poured out into our hearts through the Holy Spirit who has been given to us. For Christ, while we were still helpless, died at the appointed time for the ungodly. Indeed, only with difficulty does one die for a just person, though perhaps for a good person one might even find courage to die. But God proves his love for us in that while we were still sinners Christ died for us.

Gospel Acclamation: JN 4:42, 15

Lord, you are truly the Savior of the world; give me living water, that I may never thirst again.

Gospel JN 4:5-42
Jesus came to a town of Samaria called Sychar, near the plot of land that Jacob had given to his son Joseph. Jacob's well was there. Jesus, tired from his journey, sat down there at the well. It was about noon. A woman of Samaria came to draw water. Jesus said to her, "Give me a drink." His disciples had gone into the town to buy food. The Samaritan woman said to him, "How can you, a Jew, ask me, a Samaritan woman, for a drink?" —For Jews use nothing in common with Samaritans.— Jesus answered and said to her, "If you knew the gift of God and who is saying to you, 'Give me a drink, ' you would have asked him and he would have given you living water."

The woman said to him, "Sir, you do not even have a bucket and the cistern deep; where then can you get this living water? Are you greater than our father Jacob, who gave us this cistern and drank from it himself with his children and his flocks?" Jesus answered and said to her, "Everyone who drinks this water will be thirsty again; but whoever drinks the water I shall give will never thirst; the water I shall give will become in him a spring of water welling up to eternal life."The woman said to him, "Sir, give me this water, so that I may not be thirsty or have to keep coming here to draw water." Jesus said to her, "Go call your husband and come back.

"The woman answered and said to him, "I do not have a husband. "Jesus answered her, "You are right in saying, 'I do not have a husband.' For you have had five husbands, and the one you have now is not your husband. What you have said is true. "The woman said to him, "Sir, I can see that you are a prophet. Our ancestors worshiped on this mountain; but you people say that the place to worship is in Jerusalem."

Jesus said to her, "Believe me, woman, the hour is coming when you will worship the Father neither on this mountain nor in Jerusalem. You people worship what you do not understand; we worship what we understand, because salvation is from the Jews. But the hour is coming, and is now here, when true worshipers will worship the Father in Spirit and truth; and indeed the Father seeks such people to worship him. God is Spirit, and those who worship him must worship in Spirit and truth."

The woman said to him, "I know that the Messiah is coming, the one called the Christ; when he comes, he will tell us everything. "Jesus said to her, "I am he, the one speaking with you." At that moment his disciples returned, and were amazed that he was talking with a woman, but still no one said, "What are you looking for?" or "Why are you talking with her?" The woman left her water jar and went into the town and said to the people, "Come see a man who told me everything I have done.

Could he possibly be the Christ?" They went out of the town and came to him. Meanwhile, the disciples urged him, "Rabbi, eat." But he said to them, "I have food to eat of which you do not know." So the disciples said to one another, "Could someone have brought him something to eat?" Jesus said to them, "My food is to do the will of the one who sent me and to finish his work.

Do you not say, 'In four months the harvest will be here'? I tell you, look up and see the fields ripe for the harvest. The reaper is already receiving payment and gathering crops for eternal life, so that the sower and reaper can rejoice together. For here the saying is verified that 'One sows and another reaps.' I sent you to reap what you have not worked for; others have done the work, and you are sharing the fruits of their work."

Many of the Samaritans of that town began to believe in him because of the word of the woman who testified, "He told me everything I have done." When the Samaritans came to him, they invited him to stay with them; and he stayed there two days. Many more began to believe in him because of his word, and they said to the woman, "We no longer believe because of your word; for we have heard for ourselves, and we know that this is truly the savior of the world."

Or   JN 4:5-15, 19B-26, 39A, 40-42

Jesus came to a town of Samaria called Sychar, near the plot of land that Jacob had given to his son Joseph. Jacob's well was there. Jesus, tired from his journey, sat down there at the well. It was about noon.

A woman of Samaria came to draw water. Jesus said to her, "Give me a drink." His disciples had gone into the town to buy food. The Samaritan woman said to him, "How can you, a Jew, ask me, a Samaritan woman, for a drink?" —For Jews use nothing in common with Samaritans.— Jesus answered and said to her,

"If you knew the gift of God and who is saying to you, 'Give me a drink,' you would have asked him and he would have given you living water." The woman said to him, "Sir, you do not even have a bucket and the cistern is

123

deep; where then can you get this living water? Are you greater than our father Jacob, who gave us this cistern and drank from it himself with his children and his flocks?" Jesus answered and said to her, "Everyone who drinks this water will be thirsty again; but whoever drinks the water I shall give will never thirst; the water I shall give will become in him a spring of water welling up to eternal life."

The woman said to him, "Sir, give me this water, so that I may not be thirsty or have to keep coming here to draw water." I can see that you are a prophet. Our ancestors worshiped on this mountain; but you people say that the place to worship is in Jerusalem." Jesus said to her, "Believe me, woman, the hour is coming when you will worship the Father neither on this mountain nor in Jerusalem. You people worship what you do not understand; we worship what we understand, because salvation is from the Jews. But the hour is coming, and is now here, when true worshipers will worship the Father in Spirit and truth; and indeed the Father seeks such people to worship him. God is Spirit, and those who worship him must worship in Spirit and truth."

The woman said to him, "I know that the Messiah is coming, the one called the Christ; when he comes, he will tell us everything." Jesus said to her, "I am he, the one who is speaking with you."

Many of the Samaritans of that town began to believe in him. When the Samaritans came to him, they invited him to stay with them; and he stayed there two days. Many more began to believe in him because of his word, and they said to the woman, "We no longer believe because of your word; for we have heard for ourselves, and we know that this is truly the savior of the world.

MARCH 8TH, 2021
Monday of the Third Week of Lent

1st 2 Kgs 5:1-15ab
Naaman, the army commander of the king of Aram, was highly esteemed and respected by his master, for through him the LORD had brought victory to Aram.

But valiant as he was, the man was a leper. Now the Arameans had captured in a raid on the land of Israel a little girl, who became the servant of Naaman's wife.

"If only my master would present himself to the prophet in Samaria," she said to her mistress, "he would cure him of his leprosy." Naaman went and told his lord just what the slave girl from the land of Israel had said.

"Go," said the king of Aram. "I will send along a letter to the king of Israel." So Naaman set out, taking along ten silver talents, six thousand gold pieces, and ten festal garments.

To the king of Israel he brought the letter, which read:" With this letter I am sending my servant Naaman to you, that you may cure him of his leprosy."

When he read the letter, the king of Israel tore his garments and exclaimed: "Am I a god with power over life and death, that this man should send someone to me to be cured of leprosy? Take note! You can see he is only looking for a quarrel with me!"

When Elisha, the man of God, heard that the king of Israel had torn his garments, he sent word to the king:

"Why have you torn your garments? Let him come to me and find out that there is a prophet in Israel."

Naaman came with his horses and chariots and stopped at the door of Elisha's house. The prophet sent him the message: "Go and wash seven times in the Jordan, and your flesh will heal, and you will be clean."

But Naaman went away angry, saying, "I thought that he would surely come out and stand there to invoke the LORD his God, and would move his hand over the spot, and thus cure the leprosy.

Are not the rivers of Damascus, the Abana and the Pharpar, better than all the waters of Israel? Could I not wash in them and be cleansed?"

With this, he turned about in anger and left.

But his servants came up and reasoned with him. "My father," they said,

"if the prophet had told you to do something extraordinary, would you not have done it? All the more now, since he said to you, 'Wash and be clean,' should you do as he said." So Naaman went down and plunged into the Jordan seven times at the word of the man of God.

His flesh became again like the flesh of a little child, and he was clean.

He returned with his whole retinue to the man of God. On his arrival he stood before him and said, "Now I know that there is no God in all the earth, except in Israel."

Responsorial Psalm   PS 42:2, 3; 43:3, 4
R. (see 42:3) Athirst is my soul for the living God.

When shall I go and behold the face of God? As the hind longs for the running waters, so my soul longs for you, O God.

R. Athirst is my soul for the living God.

When shall I go and behold the face of God? Athirst is my soul for God, the living God. When shall I go and behold the face of God?

R. Athirst is my soul for the living God.

When shall I go and behold the face of God? Send forth your light and your fidelity; they shall lead me on

And bring me to your holy mountain, to your dwelling-place.

R. Athirst is my soul for the living God.

When shall I go and behold the face of God?

Then will I go in to the altar of God, the God of my gladness and joy; Then will I give you thanks upon the harp, O God, my God!

R. Athirst is my soul for the living God.

When shall I go and behold the face of God?

Gospel Acclamation: See Ps 130:5, 7

I hope in the LORD, I trust in his word; with him there is kindness and plenteous redemption.

Gospel   Lk 4:24-30
Jesus said to the people in the synagogue at Nazareth:

"Amen, I say to you, no prophet is accepted in his own native place.

Indeed, I tell you, there were many widows in Israel in the days of Elijah when the sky was closed for three and a half years and a severe famine spread over the entire land.

It was to none of these that Elijah was sent, but only to a widow in Zarephath in the land of Sidon.

Again, there were many lepers in Israel during the time of Elisha the prophet; yet not one of them was cleansed, but only Naaman the Syrian."

When the people in the synagogue heard this, they were all filled with fury. They rose up, drove him out of the town, and led him to the brow of the hill on which their town had been built, to hurl him down headlong.

But he passed through the midst of them and went away.

MARCH 9TH, 2021
Tuesday of the Third Week of Lent

1st Reading   DN 3:25, 34-43

Azariah stood up in the fire and prayed aloud: "For your name's sake, O Lord, do not deliver us up forever, or make void your covenant. Do not take away your mercy from us, for the sake of Abraham, your beloved, Isaac your servant, and Israel your holy one, To whom you promised to multiply their offspring like the stars of heaven, or the sand on the shore of the sea. For we are reduced, O Lord, beyond any other nation, brought low everywhere in the world this day because of our sins.

We have in our day no prince, prophet, or leader, no burnt offering, sacrifice, oblation, or incense, no place to offer first fruits, to find favor with you. But with contrite heart and humble spirit let us be received; As though it were burnt offerings of rams and bullocks, or thousands of fat lambs, So let our sacrifice be in your presence today as we follow you unreservedly; for those who trust in you cannot be put to shame. And now we follow you with our whole heart, we fear you and we pray to you. Do not let us be put to shame, but deal with us in your kindness and great mercy. Deliver us by your wonders, and bring glory to your name, O Lord."

Responsorial Psalm   PS 25:4-5AB, 6 AND 7BC, 8-9

R. (6a) Remember your mercies, O Lord.

Your ways, O LORD, make known to me; teach me your paths, Guide me in your truth and teach me, for you are God my savior.

R. Remember your mercies, O Lord.

Remember that your compassion, O LORD, and your kindness are from of old. In your kindness remember me, because of your goodness, O LORD.

R. Remember your mercies, O Lord.

Good and upright is the LORD; thus he shows sinners the way. He guides the humble to justice, he teaches the humble his way.

R. Remember your mercies, O Lord.

Acclamation: JL 2:12-13

Even now, says the LORD, return to me with your whole heart; for I am gracious and merciful.

Gospel   MT 18:21-35

Peter approached Jesus and asked him, "Lord, if my brother sins against me, how often must I forgive him? As many as seven times?" Jesus answered, "I say to you, not seven times but seventy-seven times. That is why the Kingdom of heaven may be likened to a king who decided to settle accounts with his servants.

When he began the accounting, a debtor was brought before him who owed him a huge amount. Since he had no way of paying it back, his master ordered him to be sold, along with his wife, his children, and all his property, in payment of the debt. At that, the servant fell down, did him homage, and said,

'Be patient with me, and I will pay you back in full.' Moved with compassion the master of that servant let him go and forgave him the loan. When that servant had left, he found one of his fellow servants who owed him a much smaller amount. He seized him and started to choke him, demanding, 'Pay back what you owe.' Falling to his knees, his fellow servant begged him,

'Be patient with me, and I will pay you back.' But he refused. Instead, he had him put in prison until he paid back the debt. Now when his fellow servants saw what had happened, they were deeply disturbed, and went to their master and reported the whole affair.

His master summoned him and said to him, 'You wicked servant! I forgave you your entire debt because you begged me to. Should you not have had pity on your fellow servant, as I had pity on you?' Then in anger his master handed him over to the torturers until he should pay back the whole debt. So will my heavenly Father do to you, unless each of you forgives your brother from your heart."

MARCH 10TH, 2021
Wednesday of the Third Week of Lent

1st Reading DT 4:1, 5-9
Moses spoke to the people and said: "Now, Israel, hear the statutes and decrees which I am teaching you to observe, that you may live, and may enter in and take possession of the land which the LORD, the God of your fathers, is giving you.

Therefore, I teach you the statutes and decrees as the LORD, my God, has commanded me, that you may observe them in the land you are entering to occupy. Observe them carefully, for thus will you give evidence of your wisdom and intelligence to the nations, who will hear of all these statutes and say, 'This great nation is truly a wise and intelligent people.' For what great nation is there that has gods so close to it as the LORD, our God, is to us whenever we call upon him? Or what great nation has statutes and decrees that are as just as this whole law which I am setting before you today?

"However, take care and be earnestly on your guard not to forget the things which your own eyes have seen, nor let them slip from your memory as long as you live, but teach them to your children and to your children's children."

Responsorial Psalm PS 147:12-13, 15-16, 19-20
R. (12a) Praise the Lord, Jerusalem.

Glorify the LORD, O Jerusalem; praise your God, O Zion. For he has strengthened the bars of your gates; he has blessed your children within you.

R. Praise the Lord, Jerusalem.

He sends forth his command to the earth; swiftly runs his word! He spreads snow like wool; frost he strews like ashes.

R. Praise the Lord, Jerusalem.

He has proclaimed his word to Jacob, his statutes and his ordinances to Israel. He has not done thus for any other nation; his ordinances he has not made known to them.

R. Praise the Lord, Jerusalem.

Gospel Acclamation: JN 6:63C, 68C

Your words, Lord, are Spirit and life; you have the words of everlasting life.

Gospel   MT 5:17-19

Jesus said to his disciples: "Do not think that I have come to abolish the law or the prophets. I have come not to abolish but to fulfill. Amen, I say to you, until heaven and earth pass away, not the smallest letter or the smallest part of a letter will pass from the law, until all things have taken place. Therefore, whoever breaks one of the least of these commandments and teaches others to do so will be called least in the Kingdom of heaven. But whoever obeys and teaches these commandments will be called greatest in the Kingdom of heaven."

MARCH 11 TH, 2021
Thursday of the Third Week of Lent

1st Reading   JER 7:23-28

Thus says the LORD: This is what I commanded my people: Listen to my voice; then I will be your God and you shall be my people. Walk in all the ways that I command you, so that you may prosper. But they obeyed not, nor did they pay heed.

They walked in the hardness of their evil hearts and turned their backs, not their faces, to me. From the day that your fathers left the land of Egypt even to this day, I have sent you untiringly all my servants the prophets. Yet they have not obeyed me nor paid heed; they have stiffened their necks and done worse than their fathers. When you speak all these words to them, they will not listen to you either; when you call to them, they will not answer you. Say to them: This is the nation that does not listen to the voice of the LORD, its God, or take correction. Faithfulness has disappeared; the word itself is banished from their speech.

Responsorial Psalm PS 95:1-2, 6-7, 8-9

R. (8) If today you hear his voice, harden not your hearts.

Come, let us sing joyfully to the LORD; let us acclaim the Rock of our salvation. Let us come into his presence with thanksgiving; let us joyfully sing psalms to him.

R. If today you hear his voice, harden not your hearts.

Come, let us bow down in worship; let us kneel before the LORD who made us. For he is our God, and we are the people he shepherds, the flock he guides.

R. If today you hear his voice, harden not your hearts.

Oh, that today you would hear his voice: "Harden not your hearts as at Meribah, as in the day of Massah in the desert, Where your fathers tempted me; they tested me though they had seen my works."

R. If today you hear his voice, harden not your hearts.

Acclamation: JL 2:12-13

Even now, says the LORD, return to me with your whole heart, for I am gracious and merciful.

Gospel   LK 11:14-23

Jesus was driving out a demon that was mute, and when the demon had gone out, the mute man spoke and the crowds were amazed. Some of them said, "By the power of Beelzebul, the prince of demons, he drives out demons." Others, to test him, asked him for a sign from heaven. But he knew their thoughts and said to them, "Every kingdom divided against itself will be laid waste and house will fall against house. And if Satan is divided against himself, how will his kingdom stand? For you say that it is by Beelzebul that I drive out demons. If I, then, drive out demons by Beelzebul, by whom do your own people drive them out?

Therefore they will be your judges. But if it is by the finger of God that I drive out demons, then the Kingdom of God has come upon you. When a strong man fully armed guards his palace, his possessions are safe. But when one stronger than he attacks and overcomes him, he takes away the armor on which he relied and distributes the spoils. Whoever is not with me is against me, and whoever does not gather with me scatters."

MARCH 12TH, 2021
Friday of the Third Week of Lent

1st Reading HOS 14:2-10

Thus says the LORD: Return, O Israel, to the LORD, your God; you have collapsed through your guilt. Take with you words, and return to the LORD; Say to him, "Forgive all iniquity, and receive what is good, that we may render as offerings the bullocks from our stalls. Assyria will not save us, nor shall we have horses to mount; We shall say no more, 'Our god,' to the work of our hands; for in you the orphan finds compassion."

I will heal their defection, says the LORD, I will love them freely; for my wrath is turned away from them. I will be like the dew for Israel: he shall blossom like the lily; He shall strike root like the Lebanon cedar, and put forth his shoots. His splendor shall be like the olive tree and his fragrance like the Lebanon cedar. Again they shall dwell in his shade and raise grain; They shall blossom like the vine, and his fame shall be like the wine of Lebanon.

Ephraim! What more has he to do with idols? I have humbled him, but I will prosper him. "I am like a verdant cypress tree"– Because of me you bear fruit! Let him who is wise understand these things; let him who is prudent know them. Straight are the paths of the LORD, in them the just walk, but sinners stumble in them.

Responsorial Psalm PS 81:6C-8A, 8BC-9, 10-11AB, 14 AND 17

R. (see 11 and 9a) I am the Lord your God: hear my voice.

An unfamiliar speech I hear: "I relieved his shoulder of the burden; his hands were freed from the basket. In distress you called, and I rescued you."

R. I am the Lord your God: hear my voice.

"Unseen, I answered you in thunder; I tested you at the waters of Meribah. Hear, my people, and I will admonish you; O Israel, will you not hear me?"

R. I am the Lord your God: hear my voice.

"There shall be no strange god among you nor shall you worship any alien god. I, the LORD, am your God who led you forth from the land of Egypt."

R. I am the Lord your God: hear my voice.

"If only my people would hear me, and Israel walk in my ways, I would feed them with the best of wheat, and with honey from the rock I would fill them."

R. I am the Lord your God: hear my voice.

Gospel Acclamation: MT 4:17

Repent, says the Lord; the Kingdom of heaven is at hand.

Gospel   MK 12:28-34

One of the scribes came to Jesus and asked him, "Which is the first of all the commandments?" Jesus replied, "The first is this: Hear, O Israel! The Lord our God is Lord alone! You shall love the Lord your God with all your heart, with all your soul, with all your mind, and with all your strength. The second is this: You shall love your neighbor as yourself. There is no other commandment greater than these." The scribe said to him, "Well said, teacher.

You are right in saying, He is One and there is no other than he. And to love him with all your heart, with all your understanding, with all your strength, and to love your neighbor as yourself is worth more than all burnt offerings and sacrifices." And when Jesus saw that he answered with understanding, he said to him, "You are not far from the Kingdom of God." And no one dared to ask him any more questions.

MARCH 13TH, 2021
Saturday of the Third Week of Lent

1st Reading HOS 6:1-6

"Come, let us return to the LORD, it is he who has rent, but he will heal us; he has struck us, but he will bind our wounds. He will revive us after two days; on the third day he will raise us up, to live in his presence. Let us know, let us strive to know the LORD; as certain as the dawn is his coming, and his judgment shines forth like the light of day! He will come to us like the rain, like spring rain that waters the earth."

What can I do with you, Ephraim? What can I do with you, Judah? Your piety is like a morning cloud, like the dew that early passes away. For this reason I smote them through the prophets, I slew them by the words of my mouth; For it is love that I desire, not sacrifice, and knowledge of God rather than burnt offerings.

Responsorial Psalm PS 51:3-4, 18-19, 20-21AB
R. (see Hosea 6:6) It is mercy I desire, and not sacrifice.

Have mercy on me, O God, in your goodness; in the greatness of your compassion wipe out my offense. Thoroughly wash me from my guilt and of my sin cleanse me.

R. It is mercy I desire, and not sacrifice.

For you are not pleased with sacrifices; should I offer a burnt offering, you would not accept it. My sacrifice, O God, is a contrite spirit; a heart contrite and humbled, O God, you will not spurn.

R. It is mercy I desire, and not sacrifice.

Be bountiful, O LORD, to Zion in your kindness by rebuilding the walls of Jerusalem; Then shall you be pleased with due sacrifices, burnt offerings and holocausts.

R. It is mercy I desire, and not sacrifice.

Gospel Acclamation: PS 95:8

If today you hear his voice, harden not your hearts.

Gospel   LK 18:9-14
Jesus addressed this parable to those who were convinced of their own righteousness and despised everyone else. "Two people went up to the temple area to pray; one was a Pharisee and the other was a tax collector. The Pharisee took up his position and spoke this prayer to himself, 'O God, I thank you that I am not like the rest of humanity — greedy, dishonest, adulterous — or even like this tax collector. I fast twice a week, and I pay tithes on my whole income.' But the tax collector stood off at a distance and would not even raise his eyes to heaven but beat his breast and prayed, 'O God, be merciful to me a sinner.' I tell you, the latter went home justified, not the former; for everyone who exalts himself will be humbled, and the one who humbles himself will be exalted."

MARCH 14TH, 2021

Fourth Sunday of Lent – Year A Readings

1st Reading 1 SM 16:1B, 6-7, 10-13A

The LORD said to Samuel: "Fill your horn with oil, and be on your way. I am sending you to Jesse of Bethlehem, for I have chosen my king from among his sons." As Jesse and his sons came to the sacrifice, Samuel looked at Eliab and thought, "Surely the LORD's anointed is here before him." But the LORD said to Samuel:

"Do not judge from his appearance or from his lofty stature, because I have rejected him. Not as man sees does God see, because man sees the appearance but the LORD looks into the heart." In the same way Jesse presented seven sons before Samuel, but Samuel said to Jesse, "The LORD has not chosen any one of these. "Then Samuel asked Jesse, "Are these all the sons you have?"

Jesse replied, "There is still the youngest, who is tending the sheep." Samuel said to Jesse, "Send for him; we will not begin the sacrificial banquet until he arrives here." Jesse sent and had the young man brought to them. He was ruddy, a youth handsome to behold and making a splendid appearance.

The LORD said, "There—anoint him, for this is the one!" Then Samuel, with the horn of oil in hand, anointed David in the presence of his brothers; and from that day on, the spirit of the LORD rushed upon David.

Responsorial Psalm PS 23: 1-3A, 3B-4, 5, 6.
R. (1) The Lord is my shepherd; there is nothing I shall want.

The LORD is my shepherd; I shall not want. In verdant pastures he gives me repose; beside restful waters he leads me; he refreshes my soul.

R... The Lord is my shepherd; there is nothing I shall want.

He guides me in right paths for his name's sake. Even though I walk in the dark valley I fear no evil; for you are at my side With your rod and your staff that give me courage.

R... The Lord is my shepherd; there is nothing I shall want.

You spread the table before me in the sight of my foes; you anoint my head with oil; my cup overflows.

R... The Lord is my shepherd; there is nothing I shall want.

Only goodness and kindness follow me all the days of my life; and I shall dwell in the house of the LORD for years to come.

R... The Lord is my shepherd; there is nothing I shall want.

2nd Reading EPH 5:8-14

Brothers and sisters: You were once darkness, but now you are light in the Lord. Live as children of light, for light produces every kind of goodness and righteousness and truth. Try to learn what is pleasing to the Lord. Take no part in the fruitless works of darkness; rather expose them, for it is shameful even to mention the things done by them in secret; but everything exposed by the light becomes visible, for everything that becomes visible is light.

Therefore, it says: "Awake, O sleeper, and arise from the dead, and Christ will give you light."

Gospel Acclamation: JN 8:12

I am the light of the world, says the Lord; whoever follows me will have the light of life.

Gospel JN 9:1-41

As Jesus passed by he saw a man blind from birth. His disciples asked him, "Rabbi, who sinned, this man or his parents, that he was born blind?"

Jesus answered, "Neither he nor his parents sinned; it is so that the works of God might be made visible through him. We have to do the works of the one who sent me while it is day. Night is coming when no one can work. While I am in the world, I am the light of the world." When he had said this, he spat on the ground and made clay with the saliva, and smeared the clay on his eyes, and said to him, "Go wash in the Pool of Siloam" —which means Sent—. So he went and washed, and came back able to see.

His neighbors and those who had seen him earlier as a beggar said, "Isn't this the one who used to sit and beg?" Some said, "It is, "but others said, "No, he just looks like him." He said, "I am." So they said to him, "How were your eyes opened?" He replied, "The man called Jesus made clay and anointed my eyes and told me, 'Go to Siloam and wash.' So I went there and washed and was able to see." And they said to him, "Where is he?" He said, "I don't know."

They brought the one who was once blind to the Pharisees. Now Jesus had made clay and opened his eyes on a Sabbath. So then the Pharisees also asked him how he was able to see. He said to them, "He put clay on my eyes, and I washed, and now I can see." So some of the Pharisees said, "This man is not from God, because he does not keep the Sabbath."

But others said, "How can a sinful man do such signs?" And there was a division among them. So they said to the blind man again, "What do you have to say about him, since he opened your eyes?" He said, "He is a prophet."

Now the Jews did not believe that he had been blind and gained his sight until they summoned the parents of the one who had gained his sight.

They asked them, "Is this your son, who you say was born blind?

How does he now see?" His parents answered and said, "We know that this is our son and that he was born blind. We do not know how he sees now, nor do we know who opened his eyes. Ask him, he is of age; he can speak for himself." His parents said this because they were afraid of the Jews, for the Jews had already agreed that if anyone acknowledged him as the Christ, he would be expelled from the synagogue. For this reason his parents said, "He is of age; question him." So a second time they called the man who had been blind and said to him, "Give God the praise! We know that this man is a sinner."

He replied, If he is a sinner, I do not know. One thing I do know is that I was blind and now I see." So they said to him, "What did he do to you? How did he open your eyes?" He answered them, "I told you already and you did not listen. Why do you want to hear it again?

Do you want to become his disciples, too?" They ridiculed him and said, "You are that man's disciple; we are disciples of Moses! We know that God spoke to Moses, but we do not know where this one is from." The man answered and said to them, "This is what is so amazing, that you do not know where he is from, yet he opened my eyes. We know that God does not listen to sinners, but if one is devout and does his will, he listens to him. It is unheard of that anyone ever opened the eyes of a person born blind. If this man were not from God, he would not be able to do anything."

They answered and said to him, "You were born totally in sin, and are you trying to teach us?" Then they threw him out. When Jesus heard that they had thrown him out, he found him and said, Do you believe in the Son of Man?"

He answered and said, "Who is he, sir, that I may believe in him?" Jesus said to him, "You have seen him, the one speaking with you is he." He said "I do believe, Lord," and he worshiped him. Then Jesus said, "I came into this world for judgment, so that those who do not see might see, and those who do see might become blind." Some of the Pharisees who were with him heard this and said to him, "Surely we are not also blind, are we?" Jesus said to them, "If you were blind, you would have no sin; but now you are saying, 'We see,' so your sin remains.

Or   JN 9:1, 6-9, 13-17, 34-38

As Jesus passed by he saw a man blind from birth. He spat on the ground and made clay with the saliva, and smeared the clay on his eyes, and said to him, "Go wash in the Pool of Siloam" — which means Sent —.

So he went and washed, and came back able to see. His neighbors and those who had seen him earlier as a beggar said, "Isn't this the one who used to sit and beg?" Some said, "It is, "but others said, "No, he just looks like him." He said, "I am."

They brought the one who was once blind to the Pharisees. Now Jesus had made clay and opened his eyes on a Sabbath. So then the Pharisees also asked him how he was able to see. He said to them, "He put clay on my eyes, and I washed, and now I can see." So some of the Pharisees said, "This man is not from God, because he does not keep the Sabbath." But others said, "How can a sinful man do such signs?" And there was a division among them. So they said to the blind man again, "What do you have to say about him, since he opened your eyes?"

He said, "He is a prophet."

They answered and said to him, "You were born totally in sin, and are you trying to teach us?" Then they threw him out. When Jesus heard that they had thrown him out, he found him and said, "Do you believe in the Son of Man?" He answered and said, "Who is he sir, that I may believe in him?" Jesus said to him, "You have seen him, and the one speaking with you is he."

He said, "I do believe, Lord," and he worshiped him.

138

Monday of the Fourth Week of Lent

1st Reading IS 65:17-21

Thus says the LORD: Lo, I am about to create new heavens and a new earth; The things of the past shall not be remembered or come to mind. Instead, there shall always be rejoicing and happiness in what I create; For I create Jerusalem to be a joy and its people to be a delight; I will rejoice in Jerusalem and exult in my people.

No longer shall the sound of weeping be heard there, or the sound of crying; No longer shall there be in it an infant who lives but a few days, or an old man who does not round out his full lifetime; He dies a mere youth who reaches but a hundred years, and he who fails of a hundred shall be thought accursed. They shall live in the houses they build, and eat the fruit of the vineyards they plant.

Responsorial Psalm PS 30:2 AND 4, 5-6, 11-12A AND 13B

R. (2a) I will praise you, Lord, for you have rescued me.

I will extol you, O LORD, for you drew me clear and did not let my enemies rejoice over me. O LORD, you brought me up from the nether world; you preserved me from among those going down into the pit.

R. I will praise you, Lord, for you have rescued me.

Sing praise to the LORD, you his faithful ones, and give thanks to his holy name. For his anger lasts but a moment; a lifetime, his good will. At nightfall, weeping enters in, but with the dawn, rejoicing.

R. I will praise you, Lord, for you have rescued me.

"Hear, O LORD, and have pity on me; O LORD, be my helper." You changed my mourning into dancing; O LORD, my God, forever will I give you thanks.

R. I will praise you, Lord, for you have rescued me.

Gospel Acclamation: **AM 5:14**

Seek good and not evil so that you may live, and the LORD will be with you.

At that time Jesus left [Samaria] for Galilee. For Jesus himself testified that a prophet has no honor in his native place. When he came into Galilee, the Galileans welcomed him, since they had seen all he had done in Jerusalem at the feast; for they themselves had gone to the feast.

Then he returned to Cana in Galilee, where he had made the water wine. Now there was a royal official whose son was ill in Capernaum. When he heard that Jesus had arrived in Galilee from Judea, he went to him and asked him to come down and heal his son, who was near death. Jesus said to him, "Unless you people see signs and wonders, you will not believe." The royal official said to him, "Sir, come down before my child dies." Jesus said to him, "You may go; your son will live."

The man believed what Jesus said to him and left. While the man was on his way back, his slaves met him and told him that his boy would live. He asked them when he began to recover. They told him, "The fever left him yesterday, about one in the afternoon." The father realized that just at that time Jesus had said to him, "Your son will live," and he and his whole household came to believe. Now this was the second sign Jesus did when he came to Galilee from Judea.

MARCH 16TH, 2021
Tuesday of the Fourth Week of Lent

1st Reading EZ 47:1-9, 12

The angel brought me, Ezekiel, back to the entrance of the temple of the LORD, and I saw water flowing out from beneath the threshold of the temple toward the east, for the façade of the temple was toward the east; the water flowed down from the right side of the temple, south of the altar. He led me outside by the north gate, and around to the outer gate facing the east, where I saw water trickling from the right side. Then when he had walked off to the east with a measuring cord in his hand, he measured off a thousand cubits and had me wade through the water, which was ankle-deep. He measured off another thousand and once more had me wade through the water, which was now knee-deep. Again he measured off a thousand and had me wade; the water was up to my waist. Once more he measured off a thousand, but there was now a river through which I could not wade; for the water had risen so high it had become a river that could not be crossed except by swimming.

He asked me, "Have you seen this, son of man?" Then he brought me to the bank of the river, where he had me sit. Along the bank of the river I saw very many trees on both sides. He said to me, "This water flows into the eastern district down upon the Arabah, and empties into the sea, the salt waters, which it makes fresh. Wherever the river flows, every sort of living creature that can multiply shall live, and there shall be abundant fish, for wherever this water comes the sea shall be made fresh. Along both banks of the river, fruit trees of every kind shall grow; their leaves shall not fade, nor their fruit fail. Every month they shall bear fresh fruit, for they shall be watered by the flow from the sanctuary. Their fruit shall serve for food, and their leaves for medicine."

Responsorial Psalm PS 46:2-3, 5-6, 8-9
R. (8) The Lord of hosts is with us; our stronghold is the God of Jacob.

God is our refuge and our strength, an ever-present help in distress. Therefore we fear not, though the earth be shaken and mountains plunge into the depths of the sea.

R... The Lord of hosts is with us; our stronghold is the God of Jacob.

There is a stream whose runlets gladden the city of God, the holy dwelling of the Most High. God is in its midst; it shall not be disturbed; God will help it at the break of dawn.

R... The Lord of hosts is with us; our stronghold is the God of Jacob.

The LORD of hosts is with us; our stronghold is the God of Jacob. Come! behold the deeds of the LORD, the astounding things he has wrought on earth.

R... The Lord of hosts is with us; our stronghold is the God of Jacob.

Gospel Acclamation: PS 51:12A, 14A

A clean heart create for me, O God; give me back the joy of your salvation.

Gospel JN 5:1-16
There was a feast of the Jews, and Jesus went up to Jerusalem. Now there is in Jerusalem at the Sheep Gate a pool called in Hebrew Bethesda, with five porticoes. In these lay a large number of ill, blind, lame, and crippled. One man was there who had been ill for thirty-eight years. When Jesus saw him lying there and knew that he had been ill for a long time, he said to him, "Do

141

you want to be well?" The sick man answered him, "Sir, I have no one to put me into the pool when the water is stirred up; while I am on my way, someone else gets down there before me." Jesus said to him, "Rise, take up your mat, and walk." Immediately the man became well, took up his mat, and walked.

Now that day was a Sabbath. So the Jews said to the man who was cured, "It is the Sabbath, and it is not lawful for you to carry your mat." He answered them, "The man who made me well told me, 'Take up your mat and walk.'" They asked him, "Who is the man who told you, 'Take it up and walk'?" The man who was healed did not know who it was, for Jesus had slipped away, since there was a crowd there.

After this Jesus found him in the temple area and said to him, "Look, you are well; do not sin any more, so that nothing worse may happen to you." The man went and told the Jews that Jesus was the one who had made him well. Therefore, the Jews began to persecute Jesus because he did this on a Sabbath.

MARCH 17TH, 2021
Wednesday of the Fourth Week of Lent

1st Reading IS 49:8-15

Thus says the LORD: In a time of favor I answer you, on the day of salvation I help you; and I have kept you and given you as a covenant to the people, To restore the land and allot the desolate heritages, Saying to the prisoners: Come out! To those in darkness: Show yourselves! Along the ways they shall find pasture, on every bare height shall their pastures be. They shall not hunger or thirst, nor shall the scorching wind or the sun strike them; For he who pities them leads them and guides them beside springs of water.

I will cut a road through all my mountains, and make my highways level. See, some shall come from afar, others from the north and the west, and some from the land of Syene. Sing out, O heavens, and rejoice, O earth, break forth into song, you mountains. For the LORD comforts his people and shows mercy to his afflicted. But Zion said, "The LORD has forsaken me; my Lord has forgotten me." Can a mother forget her infant, be without tenderness for the child of her womb? Even should she forget, I will never forget you.

R.. (8a) The Lord is gracious and merciful.

The LORD is gracious and merciful, slow to anger and of great kindness. The LORD is good to all and compassionate toward all his works.

R.. The Lord is gracious and merciful.

The LORD is faithful in all his words and holy in all his works. The LORD lifts up all who are falling and raises up all who are bowed down.

R.. The Lord is gracious and merciful.

The LORD is just in all his ways and holy in all his works. The LORD is near to all who call upon him, to all who call upon him in truth.

R. The Lord is gracious and merciful.

Gospel Acclamation: JN 11:25A, 26

I am the resurrection and the life, says the Lord; whoever believes in me will never die.

Gospel JN 5:17-30

Jesus answered the Jews: "My Father is at work until now, so I am at work." For this reason they tried all the more to kill him, because he not only broke the Sabbath but he also called God his own father, making himself equal to God.

Jesus answered and said to them, "Amen, amen, I say to you, the Son cannot do anything on his own, but only what he sees the Father doing; for what he does, the Son will do also. For the Father loves the Son and shows him everything that he himself does, and he will show him greater works than these, so that you may be amazed. For just as the Father raises the dead and gives life, so also does the Son give life to whomever he wishes. Nor does the Father judge anyone, but he has given all judgment to the Son, so that all may honor the Son just as they honor the Father.

Whoever does not honor the Son does not honor the Father who sent him. Amen, amen, I say to you, whoever hears my word and believes in the one who sent me has eternal life and will not come to condemnation, but has passed from death to life. Amen, amen, I say to you, the hour is coming and is now here when the dead will hear the voice of the Son of God, and those who hear will live. For just as the Father has life in himself, so also he gave to the Son the possession of life in himself.

And he gave him power to exercise judgment, because he is the Son of Man. Do not be amazed at this, because the hour is coming in which all who are in the tombs will hear his voice and will come out, those who have done good deeds to the resurrection of life, but those who have done wicked deeds to the resurrection of condemnation. "I cannot do anything on my own; I judge as I hear, and my judgment is just, because I do not seek my own will but the will of the one who sent me."

MARCH 18TH, 2021
Thursday of the Fourth Week of Lent

1st Reading EX 32:7-14

The LORD said to Moses, "Go down at once to your people whom you brought out of the land of Egypt, for they have become depraved. They have soon turned aside from the way I pointed out to them, making for themselves a molten calf and worshiping it, sacrificing to it and crying out, 'This is your God, O Israel, who brought you out of the land of Egypt!'

The LORD said to Moses, "I see how stiff-necked this people is. Let me alone, then, that my wrath may blaze up against them to consume them. Then I will make of you a great nation." But Moses implored the LORD, his God, saying, "Why, O LORD, should your wrath blaze up against your own people, whom you brought out of the land of Egypt with such great power and with so strong a hand?

Why should the Egyptians say, 'With evil intent he brought them out, that he might kill them in the mountains and exterminate them from the face of the earth'? Let your blazing wrath die down; relent in punishing your people.

Remember your servants Abraham, Isaac and Israel, and how you swore to them by your own self, saying, 'I will make your descendants as numerous as the stars in the sky; and all this land that I promised, I will give your descendants as their perpetual heritage.'" So the LORD relented in the punishment he had threatened to inflict on his people.

Responsorial Psalm PS 106:19-20, 21-22, 23

R... (4a) Remember us, O Lord, as you favor your people.

Our fathers made a calf in Horeb and adored a molten image; They exchanged their glory for the image of a grass-eating bullock.

R. Remember us, O Lord, as you favor your people.

They forgot the God who had saved them, who had done great deeds in Egypt, Wondrous deeds in the land of Ham, terrible things at the Red Sea.

R. Remember us, O Lord, as you favor your people.

Then he spoke of exterminating them, but Moses, his chosen one, withstood him in the breach to turn back his destructive wrath.

R. Remember us, O Lord, as you favor your people.

Gospel Acclamation: JN 3:16

God so loved the world that he gave his only-begotten Son, so that everyone who believes in him might have eternal life.

Gospel   JN 5:31-47

Jesus said to the Jews: "If I testify on my own behalf, my testimony is not true. But there is another who testifies on my behalf, and I know that the testimony he gives on my behalf is true. You sent emissaries to John, and he testified to the truth. I do not accept human testimony, but I say this so that you may be saved.

He was a burning and shining lamp, and for a while you were content to rejoice in his light. But I have testimony greater than John's. The works that the Father gave me to accomplish, these works that I perform testify on my behalf that the Father has sent me.

Moreover, the Father who sent me has testified on my behalf. But you have never heard his voice nor seen his form, and you do not have his word remaining in you, because you do not believe in the one whom he has sent. You search the Scriptures, because you think you have eternal life through them; even they testify on my behalf. But you do not want to come to me to have life.

"I do not accept human praise; moreover, I know that you do not have the love of God in you. I came in the name of my Father, but you do not accept me; yet if another comes in his own name, you will accept him. How can you believe, when you accept praise from one another and do not seek the praise

145

that comes from the only God? Do not think that I will accuse you before the Father: the one who will accuse you is Moses, in whom you have placed your hope.

For if you had believed Moses, you would have believed me, because he wrote about me. But if you do not believe his writings, how will you believe my words?"

MARCH 19TH, 2021
Solemnity of Saint Joseph, husband of the Blessed Virgin Mary

1st Reading 2 SM 7:4-5A, 12-14A, 16

The LORD spoke to Nathan and said: "Go, tell my servant David, 'When your time comes and you rest with your ancestors, I will raise up your heir after you, sprung from your loins, and I will make his kingdom firm. It is he who shall build a house for my name.

And I will make his royal throne firm forever. I will be a father to him, and he shall be a son to me. Your house and your kingdom shall endure forever before me; your throne shall stand firm forever.'"

Responsorial Psalm   PS 89:2-3, 4-5, 27 AND 29

R. The son of David will live for ever.

The promises of the LORD I will sing forever; through all generations my mouth shall proclaim your faithfulness, For you have said, "My kindness is established forever"; in heaven you have confirmed your faithfulness.

R. The son of David will live for ever.

"I have made a covenant with my chosen one, I have sworn to David my servant: Forever will I confirm your posterity and establish your throne for all generations."

R. The son of David will live for ever.

"He shall say of me, 'You are my father, my God, the Rock, my savior.' Forever I will maintain my kindness toward him, and my covenant with him stands firm."

R. The son of David will live for ever.

2nd Reading   ROM 4:13, 16-18, 22

Brothers and sisters: It was not through the law that the promise was made to Abraham and his descendants that he would inherit the world, but through the righteousness that comes from faith. For this reason, it depends on faith, so that it may be a gift, and the promise may be guaranteed to all his descendants, not to those who only adhere to the law but to those who follow the faith of Abraham, who is the father of all of us, as it is written, I have made you father of many nations.

He is our father in the sight of God, in whom he believed, who gives life to the dead and calls into being what does not exist. He believed, hoping against hope, that he would become the father of many nations, according to what was said, Thus shall your descendants be. That is why it was credited to him as righteousness.

Gospel Acclamation: PS 84:5

Blessed are those who dwell in your house, O Lord; they never cease to praise you.

Gospel MT 1:16, 18-21, 24A

Jacob was the father of Joseph, the husband of Mary. Of her was born Jesus who is called the Christ. Now this is how the birth of Jesus Christ came about. When his mother Mary was betrothed to Joseph, but before they lived together, she was found with child through the Holy Spirit. Joseph her husband, since he was a righteous man, yet unwilling to expose her to shame, decided to divorce her quietly. Such was his intention when, behold, the angel of the Lord appeared to him in a dream and said, "Joseph, son of David, do not be afraid to take Mary your wife into your home. For it is through the Holy Spirit that this child has been conceived in her. She will bear a son and you are to name him Jesus, because he will save his people from their sins." When Joseph awoke, he did as the angel of the Lord had commanded him and took his wife into his home.

Or   LK 2:41-51A

Each year Jesus' parents went to Jerusalem for the feast of Passover, and when he was twelve years old, they went up according to festival custom. After they had completed its days, as they were returning, the boy Jesus remained behind in Jerusalem, but his parents did not know it.

Thinking that he was in the caravan, they journeyed for a day and looked for him among their relatives and acquaintances, but not finding him, they returned to Jerusalem to look for him. After three days they found him in the temple, sitting in the midst of the teachers, listening to them and asking them questions, and all who heard him were astounded at his understanding and his answers. When his parents saw him, they were astonished, and his mother said to him, "Son, why have you done this to us? Your father and I have been looking for you with great anxiety."

And he said to them, "Why were you looking for me? Did you not know that I must be in my Father's house?" But they did not understand what he said to them. He went down with them and came to Nazareth, and was obedient to them

MARCH 20TH, 2021
Saturday of the Fourth Week of Lent

1st Reading JER 11:18-20
I knew their plot because the LORD informed me; at that time you, O LORD, showed me their doings. Yet I, like a trusting lamb led to slaughter, had not realized that they were hatching plots against me: "Let us destroy the tree in its vigor; let us cut him off from the land of the living, so that his name will be spoken no more." But, you, O LORD of hosts, O just Judge, searcher of mind and heart,

Let me witness the vengeance you take on them, for to you I have entrusted my cause!

Responsorial Psalm   PS 7:2-3, 9BC-10, 11-12
R. (2a) O Lord, my God, in you I take refuge.

O LORD, my God, in you I take refuge; save me from all my pursuers and rescue me, Lest I become like the lion's prey, to be torn to pieces, with no one to rescue me.

R. O Lord, my God, in you I take refuge.

Do me justice, O LORD, because I am just, and because of the innocence that is mine. Let the malice of the wicked come to an end, but sustain the just, O searcher of heart and soul, O just God.

R. O Lord, my God, in you I take refuge.

A shield before me is God, who saves the upright of heart; A just judge is God, a God who punishes day by day.

R. O Lord, my God, in you I take refuge.

Gospel Acclamation: LK 8:15

Blessed are they who have kept the word with a generous heart and yield a harvest through perseverance.

Gospel   JN 7:40-53

Some in the crowd who heard these words of Jesus said, "This is truly the Prophet." Others said, "This is the Christ." But others said, "The Christ will not come from Galilee, will he? Does not Scripture say that the Christ will be of David's family and come from Bethlehem, the village where David lived?" So a division occurred in the crowd because of him. Some of them even wanted to arrest him, but no one laid hands on him.

So the guards went to the chief priests and Pharisees, who asked them, "Why did you not bring him?" The guards answered, "Never before has anyone spoken like this man." So the Pharisees answered them, "Have you also been deceived? Have any of the authorities or the Pharisees believed in him? But this crowd, which does not know the law, is accursed." Nicodemus, one of their members who had come to him earlier, said to them, "Does our law condemn a man before it first hears him and finds out what he is doing?" They answered and said to him,

"You are not from Galilee also, are you? Look and see that no prophet arises from Galilee." Then each went to his own house.

MARCH 21ST, 2021
Fifth Sunday of Lent – Year B

1st Reading Jer 31:31-34

The days are coming, says the LORD, when I will make a new covenant with the house of Israel and the house of Judah.

It will not be like the covenant I made with their fathers the day I took them by the hand to lead them forth from the land of Egypt; for they broke my covenant, and I had to show myself their master, says the LORD.

149

But this is the covenant that I will make with the house of Israel after those days, says the LORD.

I will place my law within them and write it upon their hearts; I will be their God, and they shall be my people.

No longer will they have need to teach their friends and relatives how to know the LORD.

All, from least to greatest, shall know me, says the LORD, for I will forgive their evildoing and remember their sin no more.

Responsorial Psalm PS 51:3-4, 12-13, 14-15
R. (12a) Create a clean heart in me, O God.

Have mercy on me, O God, in your goodness; in the greatness of your compassion wipe out my offense.

Thoroughly wash me from my guilt and of my sin cleanse me.

R. Create a clean heart in me, O God.

A clean heart create for me, O God, and a steadfast spirit renew within me.

Cast me not out from your presence, and your Holy Spirit take not from me.

R. Create a clean heart in me, O God.

Give me back the joy of your salvation, and a willing spirit sustain in me.

I will teach transgressors your ways, and sinners shall return to you.

R. Create a clean heart in me, O God.

2nd Reading Heb 5:7-9
In the days when Christ Jesus was in the flesh, he offered prayers and supplications with loud cries and tears to the one who was able to save him from death, and he was heard because of his reverence.

Son though he was, he learned obedience from what he suffered; and when he was made perfect, he became the source of eternal salvation for all who obey him..

Gospel Acclamation: Jn 12:26

Whoever serves me must follow me, says the Lord; and where I am, there also will my servant be.

Some Greeks who had come to worship at the Passover Feast came to Philip, who was from Bethsaida in Galilee, and asked him, "Sir, we would like to see Jesus."

Philip went and told Andrew; then Andrew and Philip went and told Jesus.

Jesus answered them,

"The hour has come for the Son of Man to be glorified.

Amen, amen, I say to you, unless a grain of wheat falls to the ground and dies, it remains just a grain of wheat; but if it dies, it produces much fruit.

Whoever loves his life loses it, and whoever hates his life in this world will preserve it for eternal life.

Whoever serves me must follow me, and where I am, there also will my servant be. The Father will honor whoever serves me.

"I am troubled now. Yet what should I say?' Father, save me from this hour'?

But it was for this purpose that I came to this hour. Father, glorify your name."

Then a voice came from heaven, "I have glorified it and will glorify it again."

The crowd there heard it and said it was thunder; but others said, "An angel has spoken to him."

Jesus answered and said, "This voice did not come for my sake but for yours. Now is the time of judgment on this world; now the ruler of this world will be driven out.

And when I am lifted up from the earth,

I will draw everyone to myself."He said this indicating the kind of death he would die.

Monday of the Fifth Week of Lent

1st Reading DN 13:1-9, 15-17, 19-30, 33-62

In Babylon there lived a man named Joakim, who married a very beautiful and God-fearing woman, Susanna, the daughter of Hilkiah; her pious parents had trained their daughter according to the law of Moses. Joakim was very rich; he had a garden near his house, and the Jews had recourse to him often because he was the most respected of them all.

That year, two elders of the people were appointed judges, of whom the Lord said, "Wickedness has come out of Babylon: from the elders who were to govern the people as judges." These men, to whom all brought their cases, frequented the house of Joakim. When the people left at noon, Susanna used to enter her husband's garden for a walk. When the old men saw her enter every day for her walk, they began to lust for her. They suppressed their consciences; they would not allow their eyes to look to heaven, and did not keep in mind just judgments.

One day, while they were waiting for the right moment, she entered the garden as usual, with two maids only. She decided to bathe, for the weather was warm. Nobody else was there except the two elders, who had hidden themselves and were watching her. "Bring me oil and soap," she said to the maids, "and shut the garden doors while I bathe."

As soon as the maids had left, the two old men got up and hurried to her. "Look," they said, "the garden doors are shut, and no one can see us; give in to our desire, and lie with us. If you refuse, we will testify against you that you dismissed your maids because a young man was here with you."

"I am completely trapped," Susanna groaned. "If I yield, it will be my death; if I refuse, I cannot escape your power. Yet it is better for me to fall into your power without guilt than to sin before the Lord." Then Susanna shrieked, and the old men also shouted at her, as one of them ran to open the garden doors.

When the people in the house heard the cries from the garden, they rushed in by the side gate to see what had happened to her. At the accusations by the old men, the servants felt very much ashamed, for never had any such thing been said about Susanna.

When the people came to her husband Joakim the next day, the two wicked elders also came, fully determined to put Susanna to death. Before all the people they ordered: "Send for Susanna, the daughter of Hilkiah, the wife of Joakim." When she was sent for, she came with her parents, children and all her relatives. All her relatives and the onlookers were weeping.

In the midst of the people the two elders rose up and laid their hands on her head.

Through tears she looked up to heaven, for she trusted in the Lord wholeheartedly. The elders made this accusation: "As we were walking in the garden alone, this woman entered with two girls and shut the doors of the garden, dismissing the girls. A young man, who was hidden there, came and lay with her. When we, in a corner of the garden, saw this crime, we ran toward them.

We saw them lying together, but the man we could not hold, because he was stronger than we; he opened the doors and ran off. Then we seized her and asked who the young man was, but she refused to tell us. We testify to this." The assembly believed them, since they were elders and judges of the people, and they condemned her to death.

But Susanna cried aloud: "O eternal God, you know what is hidden and are aware of all things before they come to be: you know that they have testified falsely against me. Here I am about to die, though I have done none of the things with which these wicked men have charged me."

The Lord heard her prayer. As she was being led to execution, God stirred up the holy spirit of a young boy named Daniel, and he cried aloud: "I will have no part in the death of this woman." All the people turned and asked him, "What is this you are saying?" He stood in their midst and continued, "Are you such fools, O children of Israel! To condemn a woman of Israel without examination and without clear evidence? Return to court, for they have testified falsely against her."

Then all the people returned in haste. To Daniel the elders said, "Come, sit with us and inform us, since God has given you the prestige of old age." But he replied, "Separate these two far from each other that I may examine them."

After they were separated one from the other, he called one of them and said: "How you have grown evil with age! Now have your past sins come to term: passing unjust sentences, condemning the innocent, and freeing the guilty, although the Lord says, 'The innocent and the just you shall not put to death.'

Now, then, if you were a witness, tell me under what tree you saw them together." "Under a mastic tree," he answered. Daniel replied, "Your fine lie has cost you your head, for the angel of God shall receive the sentence from him and split you in two." Putting him to one side, he ordered the other one to be brought. Daniel said to him, "Offspring of Canaan, not of Judah, beauty has seduced you, lust has subverted your conscience. This is how you acted with the daughters of Israel, and in their fear they yielded to you; but a daughter of Judah did not tolerate your wickedness. Now, then, tell me under what tree you surprised them together." "Under an oak," he said. Daniel replied, "Your fine lie has cost you also your head, for the angel of God waits with a sword to cut you in two so as to make an end of you both."

The whole assembly cried aloud, blessing God who saves those who hope in him.

They rose up against the two elders, for by their own words Daniel had convicted them of perjury. According to the law of Moses, they inflicted on them the penalty they had plotted to impose on their neighbor: they put them to death. Thus was innocent blood spared that day.

Or DN 13:41C-62

The assembly condemned Susanna to death.

But Susanna cried aloud: "O eternal God, you know what is hidden and are aware of all things before they come to be: you know that they have testified falsely against me. Here I am about to die, though I have done none of the things with which these wicked men have charged me."

The Lord heard her prayer. As she was being led to execution, God stirred up the holy spirit of a young boy named Daniel, and he cried aloud: "I will have no part in the death of this woman." All the people turned and asked him, "What is this you are saying?" He stood in their midst and continued, "Are you such fools, O children of Israel! To condemn a woman of Israel without examination and without clear evidence? Return to court, for they have testified falsely against her."

Then all the people returned in haste. To Daniel the elders said, "Come, sit with us and inform us, since God has given you the prestige of old age." But he replied, "Separate these two far from each other that I may examine them."

After they were separated one from the other, he called one of them and said: "How you have grown evil with age! Now have your past sins come to term: passing unjust sentences, condemning the innocent, and freeing the guilty, although the Lord says, 'The innocent and the just you shall not put to death.'

Now, then, if you were a witness, tell me under what tree you saw them together." "Under a mastic tree," he answered. Daniel replied, "Your fine lie has cost you your head, for the angel of God shall receive the sentence from him and split you in two. "Putting him to one side, he ordered the other one to be brought. Daniel said to him, "Offspring of Canaan, not of Judah, beauty has seduced you, lust has subverted your conscience. This is how you acted with the daughters of Israel, and in their fear they yielded to you; but a daughter of Judah did not tolerate your wickedness. Now, then, tell me under what tree you surprised them together." "Under an oak," he said. Daniel replied, "Your fine lie has cost you also your head," for the angel of God waits with a sword to cut you in two so as to make an end of you both."

The whole assembly cried aloud, blessing God who saves those who hope in him.

They rose up against the two elders, for by their own words Daniel had convicted them of perjury. According to the law of Moses, they inflicted on them the penalty they had plotted to impose on their neighbor: they put them to death. Thus was innocent blood spared that day.

Responsorial Psalm PS 23:1-3A, 3B-4, 5, 6
R. (4ab) Even though I walk in the dark valley I fear no evil; for you are at my side.

The LORD is my shepherd; I shall not want. In verdant pastures he gives me repose; Beside restful waters he leads me; he refreshes my soul.

R. Even though I walk in the dark valley I fear no evil; for you are at my side.

He guides me in right paths for his name's sake. Even though I walk in the dark valley I fear no evil; for you are at my side With your rod and your staff that give me courage.

R. Even though I walk in the dark valley I fear no evil; for you are at my side.

You spread the table before me in the sight of my foes; You anoint my head with oil; my cup overflows.

R. Even though I walk in the dark valley I fear no evil; for you are at my side.

Only goodness and kindness follow me all the days of my life; And I shall dwell in the house of the LORD for years to come.

R. Even though I walk in the dark valley I fear no evil; for you are at my side.

Gospel Acclamation: EZ 33:11

I take no pleasure in the death of the wicked man, says the Lord, but rather in his conversion, that he may live.

Gospel Jn 8:1-11
Jesus went to the Mount of Olives.

But early in the morning he arrived again in the temple area, and all the people started coming to him, and he sat down and taught them.

Then the scribes and the Pharisees brought a woman who had been caught in adultery and made her stand in the middle.

They said to him,

"Teacher, this woman was caught in the very act of committing adultery.

Now in the law, Moses commanded us to stone such women. So what do you say?" They said this to test him, so that they could have some charge to bring against him.

Jesus bent down and began to write on the ground with his finger.

But when they continued asking him, he straightened up and said to them,

"Let the one among you who is without sin be the first to throw a stone at her." Again he bent down and wrote on the ground.

And in response, they went away one by one, beginning with the elders. So he was left alone with the woman before him.

Then Jesus straightened up and said to her, "Woman, where are they?

Has no one condemned you?"She replied, "No one, sir."Then Jesus said, "Neither do I condemn you.Go, and from now on do not sin any more."

MARCH 23RD, 2021
Tuesday of the Fifth Week of Lent

1st Reading NM 21:4-9

From Mount Hor the children of Israel set out on the Red Sea road, to bypass the land of Edom. But with their patience worn out by the journey, the people complained against God and Moses, "Why have you brought us up from Egypt to die in this desert, where there is no food or water? We are disgusted with this wretched food!"

In punishment the LORD sent among the people saraph serpents, which bit the people so that many of them died. Then the people came to Moses and said, "We have sinned in complaining against the LORD and you. Pray the LORD to take the serpents away from us." So Moses prayed for the people, and the LORD said to Moses, "Make a saraph and mount it on a pole, and whoever looks at it after being bitten will live." Moses accordingly made a bronze serpent and mounted it on a pole, and whenever anyone who had been bitten by a serpent looked at the bronze serpent, he lived.

Responsorial Psalm   PS 102:2-3, 16-18, 19-21

R. (2) O Lord, hear my prayer, and let my cry come to you.

O LORD, hear my prayer, and let my cry come to you. Hide not your face from me in the day of my distress. Incline your ear to me;   in the day when I call, answer me speedily.

R. O Lord, hear my prayer, and let my cry come to you.

The nations shall revere your name, O LORD, and all the kings of the earth your glory, When the LORD has rebuilt Zion and appeared in his glory;

When he has regarded the prayer of the destitute, and not despised their prayer.

R. O Lord, hear my prayer, and let my cry come to you.

Let this be written for the generation to come, and let his future creatures praise the LORD: "The LORD looked down from his holy height, from heaven he beheld the earth, To hear the groaning of the prisoners, to release those doomed to die."

R. O Lord, hear my prayer, and let my cry come to you.

Gospel Acclamation:

The seed is the word of God, Christ is the sower; all who come to him will live for ever.

Gospel JN 8:21-30

Jesus said to the Pharisees: "I am going away and you will look for me, but you will die in your sin. Where I am going you cannot come." So the Jews said,

"He is not going to kill himself, is he, because he said, 'Where I am going you cannot come'?" He said to them, "You belong to what is below, I belong to what is above. You belong to this world, but I do not belong to this world. That is why I told you that you will die in your sins. For if you do not believe that I AM, you will die in your sins." So they said to him, "Who are you?"

Jesus said to them, "What I told you from the beginning. I have much to say about you in condemnation. But the one who sent me is true, and what I heard from him I tell the world." They did not realize that he was speaking to them of the Father. So Jesus said to them, "When you lift up the Son of Man, then you will realize that I AM, and that I do nothing on my own, but I say only what the Father taught me. The one who sent me is with me. He has not left me alone, because I always do what is pleasing to him." Because he spoke this way, many came to believe in him.

MARCH 24TH, 2021
Wednesday of the Fifth Week of Lent

1st Reading   Dn 3:14-20, 91-92, 95

King Nebuchadnezzar said: "Is it true, Shadrach, Meshach, and Abednego, that you will not serve my god, or worship the golden statue that I set up? Be ready now to fall down and worship the statue I had made, whenever you hear the sound of the trumpet, flute, lyre, harp, psaltery, bagpipe, and all the other musical instruments; otherwise, you shall be instantly cast into the white-hot furnace; and who is the God who can deliver you out of my hands?" Shadrach, Meshach, and Abednego answered King Nebuchadnezzar, "There is no need for us to defend ourselves before you in this matter. If our God, whom we serve, can save us from the white-hot furnace and from your hands, O king, may he save us! But even if he will not, know, O king, that we will not serve your god or worship the golden statue that you set up."

King Nebuchadnezzar's face became livid with utter rage against Shadrach, Meshach, and Abednego. He ordered the furnace to be heated seven times more than usual and had some of the strongest men in his army bind Shadrach, Meshach, and Abednego and cast them into the white-hot furnace.

Nebuchadnezzar rose in haste and asked his nobles, "Did we not cast three men bound into the fire?" "Assuredly, O king," they answered. "But," he replied, "I see four men unfettered and unhurt, walking in the fire, and the fourth looks like a son of God." Nebuchadnezzar exclaimed, "Blessed be the God of Shadrach, Meshach, and Abednego, who sent his angel to deliver the servants who trusted in him; they disobeyed the royal command and yielded their bodies rather than serve or worship any god except their own God."

Responsorial Psalm   DANIEL 3:52, 53, 54, 55, 56
R. (52b) Glory and praise for ever!

"Blessed are you, O Lord, the God of our fathers, praiseworthy and exalted above all forever; And blessed is your holy and glorious name, praiseworthy and exalted above all for all ages."

R. Glory and praise for ever!

"Blessed are you in the temple of your holy glory, praiseworthy and exalted above all forever.

R. Glory and praise for ever!

"Blessed are you on the throne of your kingdom, praiseworthy and exalted above all forever."

R. Glory and praise for ever!

"Blessed are you who look into the depths from your throne upon the cherubim; praiseworthy and exalted above all forever."

R. Glory and praise for ever!

"Blessed are you in the firmament of heaven, praiseworthy and glorious forever."

R. Glory and praise for ever!

Gospel Acclamation: LK 8:15

Blessed are they who have kept the word with a generous heart and yield a harvest through perseverance.

Gospel   JN 8:31-42

Jesus said to those Jews who believed in him, "If you remain in my word, you will truly be my disciples, and you will know the truth, and the truth will set you free." They answered him, "We are descendants of Abraham and have never been enslaved to anyone. How can you say, 'You will become free'?" Jesus answered them, "Amen, amen, I say to you, everyone who commits sin is a slave of sin.

A slave does not remain in a household forever, but a son always remains. So if the Son frees you, then you will truly be free. I know that you are descendants of Abraham. But you are trying to kill me, because my word has no room among you. I tell you what I have seen in the Father's presence; then do what you have heard from the Father." They answered and said to him, "Our father is Abraham." Jesus said to them, "If you were Abraham's children, you would be doing the works of Abraham.

But now you are trying to kill me, a man who has told you the truth that I heard from God; Abraham did not do this. You are doing the works of your father!" So they said to him, "We were not born of fornication. We have one Father, God." Jesus said to them, "If God were your Father, you would love me, for I came from God and am here; I did not come on my own, but he sent me."

MARCH 25TH, 2021
Solemnity of the Annunciation of the Lord

1st Reading   IS 7:10-14; 8:10

The LORD spoke to Ahaz, saying: Ask for a sign from the LORD, your God; let it be deep as the nether world, or high as the sky! But Ahaz answered, "I will not ask! I will not tempt the LORD!" Then Isaiah said: Listen, O house of David! Is it not enough for you to weary people, must you also weary my God? Therefore the Lord himself will give you this sign: the virgin shall be with child, and bear a son, and shall name him Emmanuel, which means "God is with us!"

Responsorial Psalm   PS 40:7-8A, 8B-9, 10, 11
R. (8a and 9a) Here I am, Lord; I come to do your will.

Sacrifice or oblation you wished not, but ears open to obedience you gave me. Holocausts or sin-offerings you sought not; then said I, "Behold I come."

R. Here I am, Lord; I come to do your will. "In the written scroll it is prescribed for me, To do your will, O my God, is my delight, and your law is within my heart!"

R. Here I am, Lord; I come to do your will.

I announced your justice in the vast assembly; I did not restrain my lips, as you, O LORD, know.

R. Here I am, Lord; I come to do your will.

Your justice I kept not hid within my heart; your faithfulness and your salvation I have spoken of; I have made no secret of your kindness and your truth in the vast assembly.

R. Here I am, Lord; I come to do your will.

2nd Reading   HEB 10:4-10
Brothers and sisters: It is impossible that the blood of bulls and goats take away sins. For this reason, when Christ came into the world, he said:

"Sacrifice and offering you did not desire, but a body you prepared for me; in holocausts and sin offerings you took no delight. Then I said, 'As is written of me in the scroll, behold, I come to do your will, O God. "First he says, "Sacrifices and offerings, holocausts and sin offerings, you neither desired nor delighted in."

These are offered according to the law. Then he says, "Behold, I come to do your will." He takes away the first to establish the second. By this "will," we have been consecrated through the offering of the Body of Jesus Christ once for all.

Gospel Acclamation: JN 1:14AB

The Word of God became flesh and made his dwelling among us; and we saw his glory.

Gospel LK 1:26-38

The angel Gabriel was sent from God to a town of Galilee called Nazareth, to a virgin betrothed to a man named Joseph, of the house of David, and the virgin's name was Mary. And coming to her, he said, "Hail, full of grace! The Lord is with you." But she was greatly troubled at what was said and pondered what sort of greeting this might be.

Then the angel said to her, "Do not be afraid, Mary, for you have found favor with God. Behold, you will conceive in your womb and bear a son, and you shall name him Jesus. He will be great and will be called Son of the Most High, and the Lord God will give him the throne of David his father, and he will rule over the house of Jacob forever, and of his Kingdom there will be no end." But Mary said to the angel, "How can this be, since I have no relations with a man?" And the angel said to her in reply, "The Holy Spirit will come upon you, and the power of the Most High will overshadow you. Therefore the child to be born will be called holy, the Son of God.

And behold, Elizabeth, your relative, has also conceived a son in her old age, and this is the sixth month for her who was called barren; for nothing will be impossible for God." Mary said, "Behold, I am the handmaid of the Lord. May it be done to me according to your word."Then the angel departed from her.

MARCH 26TH, 2021
Friday of the Fifth Week of Lent

1st Reading JER 20:10-13

I hear the whisperings of many: "Terror on every side! Denounce! let us denounce him!" All those who were my friends are on the watch for any misstep of mine. "Perhaps he will be trapped; then we can prevail, and take our vengeance on him." But the LORD is with me, like a mighty champion:

my persecutors will stumble, they will not triumph. In their failure they will be put to utter shame, to lasting, unforgettable confusion. O LORD of hosts, you who test the just, who probe mind and heart, Let me witness the vengeance you take on them, for to you I have entrusted my cause. Sing to the LORD, praise the LORD,

For he has rescued the life of the poor from the power of the wicked!

Responsorial Psalm   PS 18:2-3A, 3BC-4, 5-6, 7
R. (see 7) In my distress I called upon the Lord, and he heard my voice.

I love you, O LORD, my strength, O LORD, my rock, my fortress, my deliverer.

R. In my distress I called upon the Lord, and he heard my voice.

My God, my rock of refuge, my shield, the horn of my salvation, my stronghold! Praised be the LORD, I exclaim, and I am safe from my enemies.

R. In my distress I called upon the Lord, and he heard my voice.

The breakers of death surged round about me, the destroying floods overwhelmed me; The cords of the nether world enmeshed me, the snares of death overtook me.

R. In my distress I called upon the Lord, and he heard my voice. In my distress I called upon the LORD and cried out to my God; From his temple he heard my voice, and my cry to him reached his ears.

R. In my distress I called upon the Lord, and he heard my voice.

Gospel Acclamation: JN 6:63C, 68C

Your words, Lord, are Spirit and life; you have the words of everlasting life.

Gospel   JN 10:31-42
The Jews picked up rocks to stone Jesus. Jesus answered them, "I have shown you many good works from my Father. For which of these are you trying to stone me?" The Jews answered him, "We are not stoning you for a good work but for blasphemy. You, a man, are making yourself God." Jesus answered them,

163

"Is it not written in your law, 'I said, 'You are gods'"? If it calls them gods to whom the word of God came, and Scripture cannot be set aside, can you say that the one whom the Father has consecrated and sent into the world blasphemes because I said, 'I am the Son of God'? If I do not perform my Father's works, do not believe me; but if I perform them, even if you do not believe me, believe the works, so that you may realize and understand that the Father is in me and I am in the Father." Then they tried again to arrest him; but he escaped from their power.

He went back across the Jordan to the place where John first baptized, and there he remained. Many came to him and said, "John performed no sign, but everything John said about this man was true." And many there began to believe in him.

MARCH 27TH, 2021
Saturday of the Fifth Week of Lent

1st Reading EZ 37:21-28
Thus says the Lord GOD: I will take the children of Israel from among the nations to which they have come, and gather them from all sides to bring them back to their land. I will make them one nation upon the land, in the mountains of Israel, and there shall be one prince for them all. Never again shall they be two nations, and never again shall they be divided into two kingdoms.

No longer shall they defile themselves with their idols, their abominations, and all their transgressions. I will deliver them from all their sins of apostasy, and cleanse them so that they may be my people and I may be their God. My servant David shall be prince over them, and there shall be one shepherd for them all; they shall live by my statutes and carefully observe my decrees. They shall live on the land that I gave to my servant Jacob, the land where their fathers lived; they shall live on it forever, they, and their children, and their children's children, with my servant David their prince forever.

I will make with them a covenant of peace; it shall be an everlasting covenant with them, and I will multiply them, and put my sanctuary among them forever. My dwelling shall be with them; I will be their God, and they shall be my people. Thus the nations shall know that it is I, the LORD, who make Israel holy, when my sanctuary shall be set up among them forever.

R. (see 10d) The Lord will guard us, as a shepherd guards his flock.

Hear the word of the LORD, O nations, proclaim it on distant isles, and say: He who scattered Israel, now gathers them together, he guards them as a shepherd his flock.

R... The Lord will guard us, as a shepherd guards his flock.

The LORD shall ransom Jacob, he shall redeem him from the hand of his conqueror. Shouting, they shall mount the heights of Zion, they shall come streaming to the LORD's blessings: The grain, the wine, and the oil, the sheep and the oxen.

R... The Lord will guard us, as a shepherd guards his flock.

Then the virgins shall make merry and dance, and young men and old as well. I will turn their mourning into joy, I will console and gladden them after their sorrows.

R... The Lord will guard us, as a shepherd guards his flock.

Gospel Acclamation: EZ 18:31

Cast away from you all the crimes you have committed, says the LORD, and make for yourselves a new heart and a new spirit.

Gospel   JN 11:45-56

Many of the Jews who had come to Mary and seen what Jesus had done began to believe in him. But some of them went to the Pharisees and told them what Jesus had done. So the chief priests and the Pharisees convened the Sanhedrin and said,

"What are we going to do? This man is performing many signs. If we leave him alone, all will believe in him, and the Romans will come and take away both our land and our nation." But one of them, Caiaphas, who was high priest that year, said to them, "You know nothing, nor do you consider that it is better for you that one man should die instead of the people, so that the whole nation may not perish." He did not say this on his own, but since he was high priest for that year, he prophesied that Jesus was going to die for the nation, and not only for the nation, but also to gather into one the dispersed children of God. So from that day on they planned to kill him.

So Jesus no longer walked about in public among the Jews, but he left for the region near the desert, to a town called Ephraim, and there he remained with his disciples.

Now the Passover of the Jews was near, and many went up from the country to Jerusalem before Passover to purify themselves. They looked for Jesus and said to one another as they were in the temple area, "What do you think? That he will not come to the feast?"

MARCH 28TH, 2021
Palm Sunday of the Lord's Passion

At the Procession with Palms - Gospel   Mk 11:1-10

When Jesus and his disciples drew near to Jerusalem, to Bethphage and Bethany at the Mount of Olives, he sent two of his disciples and said to them,

"Go into the village opposite you, and immediately on entering it, you will find a colt tethered on which no one has ever sat.

Untie it and bring it here. If anyone should say to you, 'Why are you doing this?' reply,

'The Master has need of it and will send it back here at once.'" So they went off and found a colt tethered at a gate outside on the street, and they untied it.

Some of the bystanders said to them, "What are you doing, untying the colt?" They answered them just as Jesus had told them to, and they permitted them to do it.

So they brought the colt to Jesus and put their cloaks over it.

And he sat on it. Many people spread their cloaks on the road, and others spread leafy branches that they had cut from the fields.

Those preceding him as well as those following kept crying out: "Hosanna!

Blessed is he who comes in the name of the Lord!

Blessed is the kingdom of our father David that is to come!

Hosanna in the highest!"

OR:

Jn 12:12-16

When the great crowd that had come to the feast heard that Jesus was coming to Jerusalem, they took palm branches and went out to meet him, and cried out:

"Hosanna!

"Blessed is he who comes in the name of the Lord, the king of Israel."

Jesus found an ass and sat upon it, as is written: Fear no more, O daughter Zion; see, your king comes, seated upon an ass's colt.

His disciples did not understand this at first, but when Jesus had been glorified they remembered that these things were written about him and that they had done this for him.

At The Mass –1st Reading Is 50:4-7
The Lord GOD has given me a well-trained tongue, that I might know how to speak to the weary a word that will rouse them.

Morning after morning he opens my ear that I may hear; and I have not rebelled, have not turned back.

I gave my back to those who beat me, my cheeks to those who plucked my beard; my face I did not shield from buffets and spitting.

The Lord GOD is my help; therefore I am not disgraced;

I have set my face like flint, knowing that I shall not be put to shame.my face like flint, knowing that I shall not be put to shame.

Responsorial Psalm   PS 22:8-9, 17-18, 19-20, 23-24.
R. (2a) My God, my God, why have you abandoned me?

All who see me scoff at me; they mock me with parted lips, they wag their heads: "He relied on the LORD; let him deliver him, let him rescue him, if he loves him."

R. My God, my God, why have you abandoned me?

Indeed, many dogs surround me, a pack of evildoers closes in upon me; They have pierced my hands and my feet; I can count all my bones.

R. My God, my God, why have you abandoned me?

They divide my garments among them, and for my vesture they cast lots. But you, O LORD, be not far from me; O my help, hasten to aid me.

R. My God, my God, why have you abandoned me?

I will proclaim your name to my brethren; in the midst of the assembly I will praise you: "You who fear the LORD, praise him; all you descendants of Jacob, give glory to him; revere him, all you descendants of Israel!"

R. My God, my God, why have you abandoned me?

2nd Reading PHIL 2:6-11

Christ Jesus, though he was in the form of God, did not regard equality with God something to be grasped. Rather, he emptied himself, taking the form of a slave, coming in human likeness; and found human in appearance, he humbled himself, becoming obedient to the point of death, even death on a cross. Because of this, God greatly exalted him and bestowed on him the name which is above every name, that at the name of Jesus every knee should bend, of those in heaven and on earth and under the earth, and every tongue confess that Jesus Christ is Lord, to the glory of God the Father.

Gospel Acclamation Phil 2:6-11

Christ became obedient to the point of death, even death on a cross because of this, God greatly exalted him and bestowed on him the name which is above every name.

Gospel   Mk 14:1—15:47

The Passover and the Feast of Unleavened Bread were to take place in two days' time.

So the chief priests and the scribes were seeking a way to arrest him by treachery and put him to death.

They said, "Not during the festival, for fear that there may be a riot among the people."

When he was in Bethany reclining at table in the house of Simon the leper, a woman came with an alabaster jar of perfumed oil, costly genuine spikenard. She broke the alabaster jar and poured it on his head.

There were some who were indignant. "Why has there been this waste of perfumed oil?

It could have been sold for more than three hundred days' wages and the money given to the poor." They were infuriated with her.

Jesus said, "Let her alone. Why do you make trouble for her? She has done a good thing for me.

The poor you will always have with you, and whenever you wish you can do good to them, but you will not always have me.

She has done what she could. She has anticipated anointing my body for burial.

Amen, I say to you, wherever the gospel is proclaimed to the whole world, what she has done will be told in memory of her."

Then Judas Iscariot, one of the Twelve, went off to the chief priests to hand him over to them.

When they heard him they were pleased and promised to pay him money.

Then he looked for an opportunity to hand him over.

On the first day of the Feast of Unleavened Bread, when they sacrificed the Passover lamb, his disciples said to him,

"Where do you want us to go and prepare for you to eat the Passover?"

He sent two of his disciples and said to them,

"Go into the city and a man will meet you, carrying a jar of water.

Follow him. Wherever he enters, say to the master of the house,

'The Teacher says, "Where is my guest room where I may eat the Passover with my disciples?"'

Then he will show you a large upper room furnished and ready. Make the preparations for us there."

The disciples then went off, entered the city, and found it just as he had told them; and they prepared the Passover.

When it was evening, he came with the Twelve. And as they reclined at table and were eating, Jesus said,

"Amen, I say to you, one of you will betray me, one who is eating with me." They began to be distressed and to say to him, one by one,

"Surely it is not I?"

He said to them," One of the Twelve, the one who dips with me into the dish.

For the Son of Man indeed goes, as it is written of him, but woe to that man by whom the Son of Man is betrayed.

It would be better for that man if he had never been born."

While they were eating, he took bread, said the blessing, broke it, and gave it to them, and said,

"Take it; this is my body."

Then he took a cup, gave thanks, and gave it to them, and they all drank from it.

He said to them,

"This is my blood of the covenant, which will be shed for many.

Amen, I say to you, I shall not drink again the fruit of the vine until the day when I drink it new in the kingdom of God."

Then, after singing a hymn, they went out to the Mount of Olives.

Then Jesus said to them, "All of you will have your faith shaken, for it is written:

I will strike the shepherd, and the sheep will be dispersed.

But after I have been raised up, I shall go before you to Galilee."

Peter said to him, "Even though all should have their faith shaken, mine will not be."

Then Jesus said to him, "Amen, I say to you, this very night before the cock crows twice you will deny me three times."

But he vehemently replied, "Even though I should have to die with you,

I will not deny you." And they all spoke similarly.

Then they came to a place named Gethsemane, and he said to his disciples, "Sit here while I pray."

He took with him Peter, James, and John, and began to be troubled and distressed.

Then he said to them, "My soul is sorrowful even to death.

Remain here and keep watch."

He advanced a little and fell to the ground and prayed that if it were possible the hour might pass by him; he said, "Abba, Father, all things are possible to you.

Take this cup away from me, but not what I will but what you will."

When he returned he found them asleep. He said to Peter, "Simon, are you asleep?

Could you not keep watch for one hour? Watch and pray that you may not undergo the test.

The spirit is willing but the flesh is weak." Withdrawing again, he prayed, saying the same thing.

Then he returned once more and found them asleep, for they could not keep their eyes open and did not know what to answer him.

He returned a third time and said to them,

"Are you still sleeping and taking your rest? It is enough. The hour has come.

Behold, the Son of Man is to be handed over to sinners. Get up, let us go. See, my betrayer is at hand."

Then, while he was still speaking,

Judas, one of the Twelve, arrived, accompanied by a crowd with swords and clubs who had come from the chief priests, the scribes, and the elders.

His betrayer had arranged a signal with them, saying,

"The man I shall kiss is the one; arrest him and lead him away securely."

He came and immediately went over to him and said," Rabbi." And he kissed him.

At this they laid hands on him and arrested him.

One of the bystanders drew his sword, struck the high priest's servant, and cut off his ear.

Jesus said to them in reply, "Have you come out as against a robber, with swords and clubs, to seize me?

Day after day I was with you teaching in the temple area, yet you did not arrest me; but that the Scriptures may be fulfilled."

And they all left him and fled.

Now a young man followed him wearing nothing but a linen cloth about his body.

They seized him, but he left the cloth behind and ran off naked.

They led Jesus away to the high priest, and all the chief priests and the elders and the scribes came together.

Peter followed him at a distance into the high priest's courtyard and was seated with the guards, warming himself at the fire.

The chief priests and the entire Sanhedrin kept trying to obtain testimony against Jesus in order to put him to death, but they found none.

Many gave false witness against him, but their testimony did not agree.

Some took the stand and testified falsely against him, alleging, "We heard him say,

'I will destroy this temple made with hands and within three days I will build another not made with hands.'"

Even so their testimony did not agree.

The high priest rose before the assembly and questioned Jesus, saying, "Have you no answer?

What are these men testifying against you?" But he was silent and answered nothing. Again the high priest asked him and said to him,

"Are you the Christ, the son of the Blessed One?" Then Jesus answered, "I am; and 'you will see the Son of Man seated at the right hand of the Power and coming with the clouds of heaven.'"

At that the high priest tore his garments and said, "hat further need have we of witnesses?

You have heard the blasphemy. What do you think?"

They all condemned him as deserving to die. Some began to spit on him.

They blindfolded him and struck him and said to him, "Prophesy!" And the guards greeted him with blows.

While Peter was below in the courtyard, one of the high priest's maids came along. Seeing Peter warming himself, she looked intently at him and said, "You too were with the Nazarene, Jesus."

But he denied it saying, "I neither know nor understand what you are talking about."

So he went out into the outer court. Then the cock crowed.

The maid saw him and began again to say to the bystanders, "This man is one of them." Once again he denied it.

A little later the bystanders said to Peter once more, "Surely you are one of them; for you too are a Galilean."

He began to curse and to swear, "I do not know this man about whom you are talking."

And immediately a cock crowed a second time. Then Peter remembered the word that Jesus had said to him,

"Before the cock crows twice you will deny me three times." He broke down and wept.

As soon as morning came, the chief priests with the elders and the scribes, that is, the whole Sanhedrin held a council.

They bound Jesus, led him away, and handed him over to Pilate.

Pilate questioned him, "Are you the king of the Jews?" He said to him in reply, "You say so." The chief priests accused him of many things. Again Pilate questioned him,

"Have you no answer? See how many things they accuse you of."

Jesus gave him no further answer, so that Pilate was amazed.

Now on the occasion of the feast he used to release to them one prisoner whom they requested.

A man called Barabbas was then in prison along with the rebels who had committed murder in a rebellion.

The crowd came forward and began to ask him to do for them as he was accustomed.

Pilate answered, "Do you want me to release to you the king of the Jews?"

For he knew that it was out of envy that the chief priests had handed him over. But the chief priests stirred up the crowd to have him release Barabbas for them instead.

Pilate again said to them in reply,

"Then what do you want me to do with the man you call the king of the Jews?"

They shouted again, "Crucify him."

Pilate said to them, "Why? What evil has he done?"

They only shouted the louder, "Crucify him."

So Pilate, wishing to satisfy the crowd, released Barabbas to them and, after he had Jesus scourged, handed him over to be crucified.

The soldiers led him away inside the palace, that is, the praetorium, and assembled the whole cohort.

They clothed him in purple and, weaving a crown of thorns, placed it on him.

They began to salute him with, "Hail, King of the Jews!" and kept striking his head with a reed and spitting upon him.

They knelt before him in homage. And when they had mocked him, they stripped him of the purple cloak, dressed him in his own clothes, and led him out to crucify him.

They pressed into service a passer-by, Simon, a Cyrenian, who was coming in from the country, the father of Alexander and Rufus, to carry his cross.

They brought him to the place of Golgotha which is translated Place of the Skull —,

They gave him wine drugged with myrrh, but he did not take it.

Then they crucified him and divided his garments by casting lots for them to see what each should take.

It was nine o'clock in the morning when they crucified him. The inscription of the charge against him read,

"The King of the Jews."

With him they crucified two revolutionaries, one on his right and one on his left.

Those passing by reviled him, shaking their heads and saying,

"Aha! You who would destroy the temple and rebuild it in three days, save yourself by coming down from the cross."

Likewise the chief priests, with the scribes, mocked him among themselves and said,

"He saved others; he cannot save himself.

Let the Christ, the King of Israel, come down now from the cross that we may see and believe."

Those who were crucified with him also kept abusing him.

At noon darkness came over the whole land until three in the afternoon.

And at three o'clock Jesus cried out in a loud voice,

"Eloi, Eloi, lema sabachthani?" which is translated,

"My God, my God, why have you forsaken me?" Some of the bystanders who heard it said,

"Look, he is calling Elijah."

One of them ran, soaked a sponge with wine, put it on a reed and gave it to him to drink saying, "Wait, let us see if Elijah comes to take him down."

Jesus gave a loud cry and breathed his last.

Here all kneel and pause for a short time.

The veil of the sanctuary was torn in two from top to bottom.

When the centurion who stood facing him saw how he breathed his last he said,

"Truly this man was the Son of God!" There were also women looking on from a distance.

Among them were Mary Magdalene, Mary the mother of the younger James and of Joses, and Salome.

These women had followed him when he was in Galilee and ministered to him.

There were also many other women who had come up with him to Jerusalem.

When it was already evening, since it was the day of preparation, the day before the sabbath, Joseph of Arimathea, a distinguished member of the council, who was himself awaiting the kingdom of God, came and courageously went to Pilate and asked for the body of Jesus.

Pilate was amazed that he was already dead.

He summoned the centurion and asked him if Jesus had already died.

And when he learned of it from the centurion, he gave the body to Joseph.

Having bought a linen cloth, he took him down, wrapped him in the linen cloth, and laid him in a tomb that had been hewn out of the rock.

Then he rolled a stone against the entrance to the tomb.

Mary Magdalene and Mary the mother of Joses watched where he was laid.

OR:

Mk 15:1-39

As soon as morning came, the chief priests with the elders and the scribes, that is, the whole Sanhedrin held a council.

They bound Jesus, led him away, and handed him over to Pilate.

Pilate questioned him,

"Are you the king of the Jews?"

He said to him in reply, "You say so." The chief priests accused him of many things. Again Pilate questioned him,

"Have you no answer? See how many things they accuse you of."

Jesus gave him no further answer, so that Pilate was amazed.

Now on the occasion of the feast he used to release to them one prisoner whom they requested.

A man called Barabbas was then in prison along with the rebels who had committed murder in a rebellion.

The crowd came forward and began to ask him to do for them as he was accustomed.

Pilate answered,

"Do you want me to release to you the king of the Jews?"

For he knew that it was out of envy that the chief priests had handed him over.

But the chief priests stirred up the crowd to have him release Barabbas for them instead. Pilate again said to them in reply,

"Then what do you want me to do with the man you call the king of the Jews?"

They shouted again, "Crucify him." Pilate said to them, "Why? What evil has he done?"

They only shouted the louder, "Crucify him."

So Pilate, wishing to satisfy the crowd, released Barabbas to them and, after he had Jesus scourged, handed him over to be crucified.

The soldiers led him away inside the palace, that is, the praetorium, and assembled the whole cohort.

They clothed him in purple and, weaving a crown of thorns, placed it on him.

They began to salute him with, "Hail, King of the Jews!" and kept striking his head with a reed and spitting upon him.

They knelt before him in homage. And when they had mocked him, they stripped him of the purple cloak, dressed him in his own clothes, and led him out to crucify him.

They pressed into service a passer-by, Simon, a Cyrenian, who was coming in from the country, the father of Alexander and Rufus, to carry his cross.

They brought him to the place of Golgotha

—which is translated Place of the Skull —

They gave him wine drugged with myrrh, but he did not take it.

Then they crucified him and divided his garments by casting lots for them to see what each should take. It was nine o'clock in the morning when they crucified him.

The inscription of the charge against him read,

"The King of the Jews."

With him they crucified two revolutionaries, one on his right and one on his left.

Those passing by reviled him, shaking their heads and saying,

"Aha! You who would destroy the temple and rebuild it in three days, save yourself by coming down from the cross."

Likewise the chief priests, with the scribes, mocked him among themselves and said,

"He saved others; he cannot save himself.

Let the Christ, the King of Israel, come down now from the cross that we may see and believe."

Those who were crucified with him also kept abusing him.

At noon darkness came over the whole land until three in the afternoon.

And at three o'clock Jesus cried out in a loud voice,

"Eloi, Eloi, lema sabachthani?" which is translated,

"My God, my God, why have you forsaken me?" Some of the bystanders who heard it said,

"Look, he is calling Elijah." One of them ran, soaked a sponge with wine, put it on a reed and gave it to him to drink saying,

"Wait, let us see if Elijah comes to take him down."

Jesus gave a loud cry and breathed his last.

Here all kneel and pause for a short time.

The veil of the sanctuary was torn in two from top to bottom.

When the centurion who stood facing him saw how he breathed his last he said,

"Truly this man was the Son of God!"

MARCH 29TH, 2021
Monday of Holy Week

1st Reading IS 42:1-7

Here is my servant whom I uphold, my chosen one with whom I am pleased, Upon whom I have put my Spirit; he shall bring forth justice to the nations, Not crying out, not shouting, not making his voice heard in the street. A bruised reed he shall not break, and a smoldering wick he shall not quench, Until he establishes justice on the earth; the coastlands will wait for his teaching.

Thus says God, the LORD, who created the heavens and stretched them out, who spreads out the earth with its crops, Who gives breath to its people and spirit to those who walk on it: I, the LORD, have called you for the victory of justice, I have grasped you by the hand; I formed you, and set you as a covenant of the people, a light for the nations, To open the eyes of the blind, to bring out prisoners from confinement, and from the dungeon, those who live in darkness.

Responsorial Psalm   PS 27:1, 2, 3, 13-14

R.. (1a) The Lord is my light and my salvation.

The LORD is my light and my salvation; whom should I fear? The LORD is my life's refuge; of whom should I be afraid?

R.. The Lord is my light and my salvation.

When evildoers come at me to devour my flesh, My foes and my enemies themselves stumble and fall.

R.. The Lord is my light and my salvation.

Though an army encamp against me, my heart will not fear; Though war be waged upon me, even then will I trust.

R.. The Lord is my light and my salvation.

I believe that I shall see the bounty of the LORD in the land of the living. Wait for the LORD with courage; be stouthearted, and wait for the LORD.

R... The Lord is my light and my salvation.

Gospel Acclamation:

Hail to you, our King; you alone are compassionate with our faults.

Gospel   JN 12:1-11

Six days before Passover Jesus came to Bethany, where Lazarus was, whom Jesus had raised from the dead. They gave a dinner for him there, and Martha served, while Lazarus was one of those reclining at table with him. Mary took a liter of costly perfumed oil made from genuine aromatic nard and anointed the feet of Jesus and dried them with her hair; the house was filled with the fragrance of the oil. Then Judas the Iscariot, one of his disciples, and the one who would betray him, said, "Why was this oil not sold for three hundred days' wages and given to the poor?" He said this not because he cared about the poor but because he was a thief and held the money bag and used to steal the contributions.

So Jesus said, "Leave her alone. Let her keep this for the day of my burial. You always have the poor with you, but you do not always have me."

The large crowd of the Jews found out that he was there and came, not only because of him, but also to see Lazarus, whom he had raised from the dead. And the chief priests plotted to kill Lazarus too, because many of the Jews were turning away and believing in Jesus because of him.

MARCH 30TH, 2021
Tuesday of Holy Week

1st Reading IS 49:1-6

Hear me, O islands, listen, O distant peoples. The LORD called me from birth; from my mother's womb he gave me my name. He made of me a sharp-edged sword and concealed me in the shadow of his arm. He made me a polished arrow, in his quiver he hid me. You are my servant, he said to me, Israel, through whom I show my glory.

Though I thought I had toiled in vain, and for nothing, uselessly, spent my strength, Yet my reward is with the LORD, my recompense is with my God. For now the LORD has spoken who formed me as his servant from the womb,

That Jacob may be brought back to him and Israel gathered to him; And I am made glorious in the sight of the LORD, and my God is now my strength! It is too little, he says, for you to be my servant, to raise up the tribes of Jacob, and restore the survivors of Israel; I will make you a light to the nations, that my salvation may reach to the ends of the earth.

Responsorial Psalm   PS 71:1-2, 3-4A, 5AB-6AB, 15 AND 17
R. (see 15ab) I will sing of your salvation.

In you, O LORD, I take refuge; let me never be put to shame. In your justice rescue me, and deliver me; incline your ear to me, and save me.

R. I will sing of your salvation.

Be my rock of refuge, a stronghold to give me safety, for you are my rock and my fortress. O my God, rescue me from the hand of the wicked.

R. I will sing of your salvation.

For you are my hope, O LORD; my trust, O God, from my youth. On you I depend from birth; from my mother's womb you are my strength.

R. I will sing of your salvation.

My mouth shall declare your justice, day by day your salvation. O God, you have taught me from my youth, and till the present I proclaim your wondrous deeds.

R. I will sing of your salvation.

Gospel Acclamation:

Hail to you, our King, obedient to the Father; you were led to your crucifixion like a gentle lamb to the slaughter.

Gospel   JN 13:21-33, 36-38
Reclining at table with his disciples, Jesus was deeply troubled and testified, "Amen, amen, I say to you, one of you will betray me." The disciples looked

at one another, at a loss as to whom he meant. One of his disciples, the one whom Jesus loved, was reclining at Jesus' side. So Simon Peter nodded to him to find out whom he meant. He leaned back against Jesus' chest and said to him,

"Master, who is it?" Jesus answered, "It is the one to whom I hand the morsel after I have dipped it." So he dipped the morsel and took it and handed it to Judas, son of Simon the Iscariot. After Judas took the morsel, Satan entered him. So Jesus said to him, "What you are going to do, do quickly." Now none of those reclining at table realized why he said this to him. Some thought that since Judas kept the money bag, Jesus had told him, "Buy what we need for the feast," or to give something to the poor. So Judas took the morsel and left at once. And it was night.

When he had left, Jesus said, "Now is the Son of Man glorified, and God is glorified in him. If God is glorified in him, God will also glorify him in himself, and he will glorify him at once. My children, I will be with you only a little while longer. You will look for me, and as I told the Jews, 'Where I go you cannot come,' so now I say it to you." Simon Peter said to him, "Master, where are you going?" Jesus answered him,

"Where I am going, you cannot follow me now, though you will follow later."

Peter said to him, "Master, why can I not follow you now? I will lay down my life for you." Jesus answered, "Will you lay down your life for me? Amen, amen, I say to you, the cock will not crow before you deny me three times."

MARCH 31TH, 2021
Wednesday of Holy Week

1st Reading IS 50:4-9A
The Lord GOD has given me a well-trained tongue,

That I might know how to speak to the weary a word that will rouse them. Morning after morning he opens my ear that I may hear; And I have not rebelled, have not turned back. I gave my back to those who beat me, my cheeks to those who plucked my beard; My face I did not shield from buffets and spitting.

The Lord GOD is my help, therefore I am not disgraced; I have set my face like flint, knowing that I shall not be put to shame. He is near who upholds my right; if anyone wishes to oppose me, let us appear together. Who disputes my right?

Let him confront me. See, the Lord GOD is my help; who will prove me wrong?

Responsorial Psalm PS 69:8-10, 21-22, 31 AND 33-34
R. (14c) Lord, in your great love, answers me.

For your sake I bear insult, and shame covers my face. I have become an outcast to my brothers, a stranger to my mother's sons, because zeal for your house consumes me, and the insults of those who blaspheme you fall upon me.

R. Lord, in your great love, answer me.

Insult has broken my heart, and I am weak, I looked for sympathy, but there was none; for consolers, not one could I find. Rather they put gall in my food, and in my thirst they gave me vinegar to drink.

R. Lord, in your great love, answer me.

I will praise the name of God in song, and I will glorify him with thanksgiving: "See, you lowly ones, and be glad; you who seek God, may your hearts revive! For the LORD hears the poor, and his own who are in bonds he spurns not."

R. Lord, in your great love, answer me.

Acclamation:

Hail to you, our King; you alone are compassionate with our errors.

Or

Hail to you, our King, obedient to the Father; you were led to your crucifixion like a gentle lamb to the slaughter.

Gospel MT 26:14-25
One of the Twelve, who was called Judas Iscariot, went to the chief priests and said, "What are you willing to give me if I hand him over to you?" They

paid him thirty pieces of silver, and from that time on he looked for an opportunity to hand him over.

On the first day of the Feast of Unleavened Bread, the disciples approached Jesus and said, "Where do you want us to prepare for you to eat the Passover?"

He said, "Go into the city to a certain man and tell him, 'The teacher says, My appointed time draws near; in your house I shall celebrate the Passover with my disciples." The disciples then did as Jesus had ordered, and prepared the Passover.

When it was evening, he reclined at table with the Twelve. And while they were eating, he said, "Amen, I say to you, one of you will betray me." Deeply distressed at this, they began to say to him one after another, "Surely it is not I, Lord?"

He said in reply, "He who has dipped his hand into the dish with me is the one who will betray me. The Son of Man indeed goes, as it is written of him, but woe to that man by whom the Son of Man is betrayed. It would be better for that man if he had never been born." Then Judas, his betrayer, said in reply,

"Surely it is not I, Rabbi?" He answered, "You have said so."

APRIL 1ST, 2021
Holy Thursday

Evening Mass of the Lord's Supper

1st Reading Ex 12:1-8, 11-14
The LORD said to Moses and Aaron in the land of Egypt,

"This month shall stand at the head of your calendar; you shall reckon it the first month of the year.

Tell the whole community of Israel:

On the tenth of this month every one of your families must procure for itself a lamb, one apiece for each household.

If a family is too small for a whole lamb, it shall join the nearest household in procuring one and shall share in the lamb in proportion to the number of persons who partake of it.

The lamb must be a year-old male and without blemish.

You may take it from either the sheep or the goats.

You shall keep it until the fourteenth day of this month, and then, with the whole assembly of Israel present, it shall be slaughtered during the evening twilight.

They shall take some of its blood and apply it to the two doorposts and the lintel of every house in which they partake of the lamb.

That same night they shall eat its roasted flesh with unleavened bread and bitter herbs.

"This is how you are to eat it: with your loins girt, sandals on your feet and your staff in hand, you shall eat like those who are in flight.

It is the Passover of the LORD.

For on this same night I will go through Egypt, striking down every firstborn of the land, both man and beast, and executing judgment on all the gods of Egypt—I, the LORD!

But the blood will mark the houses where you are. Seeing the blood, I will pass over you; thus, when I strike the land of Egypt, no destructive blow will come upon you.

"This day shall be a memorial feast for you, which all your generations shall celebrate with pilgrimage to the LORD, as a perpetual institution."

Responsorial Psalm   PS 116:12-13, 15-16bc, 17-18
R. (2) (cf. 1 Cor 10:16) Our blessing-cup is a communion with the Blood of Christ.

How shall I make a return to the LORD for all the good he has done for me?

The cup of salvation I will take up, and I will call upon the name of the LORD.

R. Our blessing-cup is a communion with the Blood of Christ.

Precious in the eyes of the LORD is the death of his faithful ones.

I am your servant, the son of your handmaid; you have loosed my bonds.

R. Our blessing-cup is a communion with the Blood of Christ.

To you will I offer sacrifice of thanksgiving, and I will call upon the name of the LORD.

My vows to the LORD I will pay in the presence of all his people.

R. Our blessing-cup is a communion with the Blood of Christ.

2nd Reading 1 Cor 11:23-26
Brothers and sisters:

I received from the Lord what I also handed on to you, that the Lord Jesus, on the night he was handed over, took bread, and, after he had given thanks, broke it and said, "This is my body that is for you.

Do this in remembrance of me." In the same way also the cup, after supper, saying,

"This cup is the new covenant in my blood. Do this, as often as you drink it, in remembrance of me."

For as often as you eat this bread and drink the cup, you proclaim the death of the Lord until he comes

Gospel Acclamation: Jn 13:34

I give you a new commandment, says the Lord: love one another as I have loved you..

Gospel Jn 13:1-15
Before the feast of Passover, Jesus knew that his hour had come to pass from this world to the Father.

He loved his own in the world and he loved them to the end.

The devil had already induced Judas, son of Simon the Iscariot, to hand him over. So, during supper, fully aware that the Father had put everything into his power and that he had come from God and was returning to God, he rose from supper and took off his outer garments.

He took a towel and tied it around his waist.

Then he poured water into a basin and began to wash the disciples' feet and dry them with the towel around his waist.

He came to Simon Peter, who said to him,

"Master, are you going to wash my feet?"

Jesus answered and said to him,

"What I am doing, you do not understand now, but you will understand later."

Peter said to him, "You will never wash my feet."

Jesus answered him, "Unless I wash you, you will have no inheritance with me." Simon Peter said to him,

"Master, then not only my feet, but my hands and head as well."

Jesus said to him, "Whoever has bathed has no need except to have his feet washed, for he is clean all over; so you are clean, but not all."

For he knew who would betray him; for this reason, he said, "Not all of you are clean."

So when he had washed their feet and put his garments back on and reclined at table again, he said to them, "Do you realize what I have done for you?

You call me 'teacher' and 'master,' and rightly so, for indeed I am.

If I, therefore, the master and teacher, have washed your feet, you ought to wash one another's feet.

I have given you a model to follow, so that as I have done for you, you should also do."

APRIL 2ND, 2021
Good Friday of the Lord's Passion

See, my servant shall prosper; he shall be raised high and greatly exalted. Even as many were amazed at him so marred was his look beyond human semblance and his appearance beyond that of the sons of man so shall he startle many nations, because of him kings shall stand speechless; for those who have not been told shall see, those who have not heard shall ponder it.

Who would believe what we have heard? To whom has the arm of the LORD been revealed? He grew up like a sapling before him, like a shoot from the parched earth; there was in him no stately bearing to make us look at him, nor appearance that would attract us to him. He was spurned and avoided by people, a man of suffering, accustomed to infirmity, one of those from whom people hide their faces, spurned, and we held him in no esteem.

Yet it was our infirmities that he bore, our sufferings that he endured, while we thought of him as stricken, as one smitten by God and afflicted. But he was pierced for our offenses, crushed for our sins; upon him was the chastisement that makes us whole, by his stripes we were healed. We had all gone astray like sheep, each following his own way; but the LORD laid upon him the guilt of us all.

Though he was harshly treated, he submitted and opened not his mouth; like a lamb led to the slaughter or a sheep before the shearers, he was silent and opened not his mouth. Oppressed and condemned, he was taken away, and who would have thought any more of his destiny? When he was cut off from the land of the living, and smitten for the sin of his people, a grave was assigned him among the wicked and a burial place with evildoers, though he had done no wrong nor spoken any falsehood. But the LORD was pleased to crush him in infirmity.

If he gives his life as an offering for sin, he shall see his descendants in a long life, and the will of the LORD shall be accomplished through him. Because of his affliction he shall see the light in fullness of days; through his suffering, my servant shall justify many, and their guilt he shall bear. Therefore I will give him his portion among the great, and he shall divide the spoils with the mighty, because he surrendered himself to death and was counted among the wicked; and he shall take away the sins of many, and win pardon for their offenses.

Responsorial Psalm PS 31:2, 6, 12-13, 15-16, 17, 25
R. (Lk 23:46) Father, into your hands I commend my spirit.

In you, O LORD, I take refuge; let me never be put to shame. In your justice rescue me. Into your hands I commend my spirit; you will redeem me, O LORD, O faithful God.

R. Father, into your hands I commend my spirit.

For all my foes I am an object of reproach, a laughingstock to my neighbors, and a dread to my friends; they who see me abroad flee from me. I am forgotten like the unremembered dead; I am like a dish that is broken.

R. Father, into your hands I commend my spirit.

But my trust is in you, O LORD; I say, "You are my God. In your hands is my destiny; rescue me from the clutches of my enemies and my persecutors."

R. Father, into your hands I commend my spirit.

Let your face shine upon your servant; save me in your kindness. Take courage and be stouthearted, all you who hope in the LORD.

R. Father, into your hands I commend my spirit.

2nd Reading HEB 4:14-16; 5:7-9

Brothers and sisters: Since we have a great high priest who has passed through the heavens, Jesus, the Son of God, let us hold fast to our confession. For we do not have a high priest who is unable to sympathize with our weaknesses, but one who has similarly been tested in every way, yet without sin. So let us confidently approach the throne of grace to receive mercy and to find grace for timely help.

In the days when Christ was in the flesh, he offered prayers and supplications with loud cries and tears to the one who was able to save him from death, and he was heard because of his reverence. Son though he was, he learned obedience from what he suffered; and when he was made perfect, he became the source of eternal salvation for all who obey him.

Gospel Acclamation: PHIL 2:8-9

Christ became obedient to the point of death, even death on a cross. Because of this, God greatly exalted him and bestowed on him the name which is above every other name.

Jesus went out with his disciples across the Kidron valley to where there was a garden, into which he and his disciples entered. Judas his betrayer also knew the place, because Jesus had often met there with his disciples. So Judas got a band of soldiers and guards from the chief priests and the Pharisees and went there with lanterns, torches, and weapons. Jesus, knowing everything that was going to happen to him, went out and said to them, "Whom are you looking for?"

They answered him, "Jesus the Nazorean." He said to them, "I AM." Judas his betrayer was also with them. When he said to them, "I AM," they turned away and fell to the ground. So he again asked them, "Whom are you looking for?"

They said, "Jesus the Nazorean." Jesus answered, "I told you that I AM. So if you are looking for me, let these men go." This was to fulfill what he had said, "I have not lost any of those you gave me."

Then Simon Peter, who had a sword, drew it, struck the high priest's slave, and cut off his right ear. The slave's name was Malchus. Jesus said to Peter, "Put your sword into its scabbard. Shall I not drink the cup that the Father gave me?"

So the band of soldiers, the tribune, and the Jewish guards seized Jesus, bound him, and brought him to Annas first. He was the father-in-law of Caiaphas, who was high priest that year. It was Caiaphas who had counseled the Jews that it was better that one man should die rather than the people.

Simon Peter and another disciple followed Jesus. Now the other disciple was known to the high priest, and he entered the courtyard of the high priest with Jesus. But Peter stood at the gate outside. So the other disciple, the acquaintance of the high priest, went out and spoke to the gatekeeper and brought Peter in.

Then the maid who was the gatekeeper said to Peter, "You are not one of this man's disciples, are you?" He said, "I am not." Now the slaves and the guards were standing around a charcoal fire that they had made, because it was cold, and were warming themselves. Peter was also standing there keeping warm. The high priest questioned Jesus about his disciples and about his doctrine.

Jesus answered him, "I have spoken publicly to the world. I have always taught in a synagogue or in the temple area where all the Jews gather, and in secret I have said nothing. Why ask me? Ask those who heard me what I said to them. They know what I said." When he had said this, one of the temple guards standing there struck Jesus and said, "Is this the way you answer the high priest?"

Jesus answered him, "If I have spoken wrongly, testify to the wrong; but if I have spoken rightly, why do you strike me?" Then Annas sent him bound to Caiaphas the high priest.

Now Simon Peter was standing there keeping warm. And they said to him, "You are not one of his disciples, are you?" He denied it and said, "I am not."

One of the slaves of the high priest, a relative of the one whose ear Peter had cut off, said, "Didn't I see you in the garden with him?" Again Peter denied it. And immediately the cock crowed.

Then they brought Jesus from Caiaphas to the praetorium. It was morning. And they themselves did not enter the praetorium, in order not to be defiled so that they could eat the Passover. So Pilate came out to them and said, "What charge do you bring against this man?" They answered and said to him, "If he were not a criminal, we would not have handed him over to you." At this, Pilate said to them,

"Take him yourselves, and judge him according to your law." The Jews answered him, "We do not have the right to execute anyone, " in order that the word of Jesus might be fulfilled that he said indicating the kind of death he would die.

So Pilate went back into the praetorium and summoned Jesus and said to him, "Are you the King of the Jews?" Jesus answered, "Do you say this on your own or have others told you about me?" Pilate answered, "I am not a Jew, am I? Your own nation and the chief priests handed you over to me. What have you done?"

Jesus answered, "My kingdom does not belong to this world. If my kingdom did belong to this world, my attendants would be fighting to keep me from being handed over to the Jews. But as it is, my kingdom is not here."

So Pilate said to him, "Then you are a king?" Jesus answered, "You say I am a king. For this I was born and for this I came into the world, to testify to the truth.

Everyone who belongs to the truth listens to my voice." Pilate said to him, "What is truth?"

When he had said this, he again went out to the Jews and said to them,

"I find no guilt in him. But you have a custom that I release one prisoner to you at Passover. Do you want me to release to you the King of the Jews?" They cried out again, "Not this one but Barabbas!" Now Barabbas was a revolutionary.

Then Pilate took Jesus and had him scourged. And the soldiers wove a crown out of thorns and placed it on his head, and clothed him in a purple cloak, and they came to him and said, "Hail, King of the Jews!" And they struck him repeatedly.

Once more Pilate went out and said to them, "Look, I am bringing him out to you, so that you may know that I find no guilt in him." So Jesus came out, wearing the crown of thorns and the purple cloak. And he said to them, "Behold, the man!"

When the chief priests and the guards saw him they cried out, "Crucify him, crucify him!" Pilate said to them, "Take him yourselves and crucify him. I find no guilt in him."

The Jews answered, "We have a law, and according to that law he ought to die, because he made himself the Son of God." Now when Pilate heard this statement, he became even more afraid, and went back into the praetorium and said to Jesus, "Where are you from?" Jesus did not answer him. So Pilate said to him,

"Do you not speak to me? Do you not know that I have power to release you and I have power to crucify you?" Jesus answered him, "You would have no power over me if it had not been given to you from above. For this reason the one who handed me over to you has the greater sin." Consequently, Pilate tried to release him; but the Jews cried out, "If you release him, you are not a Friend of Caesar.

Everyone who makes himself a king opposes Caesar." When Pilate heard these words he brought Jesus out and seated him on the judge's bench in the place called Stone Pavement, in Hebrew, Gabbatha.

It was preparation day for Passover, and it was about noon. And he said to the Jews, "Behold, your king!" They cried out, "Take him away, take him away! Crucify him!" Pilate said to them, "Shall I crucify your king?" The chief priests answered,

"We have no king but Caesar." Then he handed him over to them to be crucified.

So they took Jesus, and, carrying the cross himself, he went out to what is called the Place of the Skull, in Hebrew, Golgotha. There they crucified him, and with him two others, one on either side, with Jesus in the middle. Pilate also had an inscription written and put on the cross. It read, "Jesus the Nazorean, the King of the Jews." Now many of the Jews read this inscription, because the place where Jesus was crucified was near the city; and it was written in Hebrew, Latin, and Greek. So the chief priests of the Jews said to Pilate, "Do not write 'The King of the Jews,' but that he said, 'I am the King of the Jews'." Pilate answered, "What I have written, I have written."

When the soldiers had crucified Jesus, they took his clothes and divided them into four shares, a share for each soldier. They also took his tunic, but the tunic was seamless, woven in one piece from the top down. So they said to one another,

"Let's not tear it, but cast lots for it to see whose it will be, " in order that the passage of Scripture might be fulfilled that says: They divided my garments among them, and for my vesture they cast lots. This is what the soldiers did. Standing by the cross of Jesus were his mother and his mother's sister, Mary the wife of Clopas, and Mary of Magdala. When Jesus saw his mother and the disciple there whom he loved he said to his mother, "Woman, behold, your son." Then he said to the disciple, "Behold, your mother." And from that hour the disciple took her into his home.

After this, aware that everything was now finished, in order that the Scripture might be fulfilled, Jesus said, "I thirst." There was a vessel filled with common wine. So they put a sponge soaked in wine on a sprig of hyssop and put it up to his mouth. When Jesus had taken the wine, he said, "It is finished." And bowing his head, he handed over the spirit.

Here all kneel and pause for a short time.

Now since it was preparation day, in order that the bodies might not remain on the cross on the Sabbath, for the Sabbath day of that week was a solemn one, the Jews asked Pilate that their legs be broken and that they be taken down.

So the soldiers came and broke the legs of the first and then of the other one who was crucified with Jesus. But when they came to Jesus and saw that he was already dead, they did not break his legs, but one soldier thrust his lance into his side, and immediately blood and water flowed out. An eyewitness has testified, and his testimony is true; he knows that he is speaking the truth, so that you also may come to believe. For this happened so that the Scripture passage might be fulfilled:

Not a bone of it will be broken. And again another passage says: They will look upon him whom they have pierced.

After this, Joseph of Arimathea, secretly a disciple of Jesus for fear of the Jews, asked Pilate if he could remove the body of Jesus. And Pilate permitted it.

So he came and took his body. Nicodemus, the one who had first come to him at night, also came bringing a mixture of myrrh and aloes weighing about one hundred pounds. They took the body of Jesus and bound it with burial cloths along with the spices, according to the Jewish burial custom. Now in the place where he had been crucified there was a garden, and in the garden a new tomb, in which no one had yet been buried. So they laid Jesus there because of the Jewish preparation day; for the tomb was close by.

APRIL 3RD, 2021
Holy Saturday

At the Easter Vigil in the Holy Night of Easter

1st Reading Gn 1:1—2:2
In the beginning, when God created the heavens and the earth, the earth was a formless wasteland, and darkness covered the abyss, while a mighty wind swept over the waters.

Then God said, "Let there be light," and there was light. God saw how good the light was. God then separated the light from the darkness. God called the light "day," and the darkness he called "night." Thus evening came, and morning followed—the first day.

Then God said, "Let there be a dome in the middle of the waters, to separate one body of water from the other." And so it happened:

God made the dome, and it separated the water above the dome from the water below it. God called the dome "the sky." Evening came, and morning followed—the second day.

Then God said, "Let the water under the sky be gathered into a single basin, so that the dry land may appear." And so it happened: the water under the sky was gathered into its basin, and the dry land appeared. God called the dry land "the earth, " and the basin of the water he called "the sea." God saw how good it was. Then God said, "Let the earth bring forth vegetation: every kind of plant that bears seed and every kind of fruit tree on earth that bears fruit with its seed in it."

And so it happened: the earth brought forth every kind of plant that bears seed and every kind of fruit tree on earth that bears fruit with its seed in it. God saw how good it was. Evening came, and morning followed—the third day.

Then God said: "Let there be lights in the dome of the sky, to separate day from night. Let them mark the fixed times, the days and the years, and serve as luminaries in the dome of the sky, to shed light upon the earth." And so it happened: God made the two great lights, the greater one to govern the day, and the lesser one to govern the night; and he made the stars. God set them in the dome of the sky, to shed light upon the earth, to govern the day and the night, and to separate the light from the darkness. God saw how good it was.

Evening came, and morning followed—the fourth day.

Then God said, "Let the water teem with an abundance of living creatures, and on the earth let birds fly beneath the dome of the sky." And so it happened:

God created the great sea monsters and all kinds of swimming creatures with which the water teems, and all kinds of winged birds. God saw how good it was, and God blessed them, saying, "Be fertile, multiply, and fill the water of the seas; and let the birds multiply on the earth." Evening came, and morning followed—the fifth day.

Then God said, "Let the earth bring forth all kinds of living creatures: cattle, creeping things, and wild animals of all kinds." And so it happened: God made all kinds of wild animals, all kinds of cattle, and all kinds of creeping things of the earth. God saw how good it was. Then God said: "Let us make man in our image, after our likeness. Let them have dominion over the fish of the sea, the birds of the air, and the cattle, and over all the wild animals and all the creatures that crawl on the ground." God created man in his image; in the image of God he created him; male and female he created them. God blessed them, saying:

"Be fertile and multiply; fill the earth and subdue it. Have dominion over the fish of the sea, the birds of the air, and all the living things that move on the earth."

God also said: "See, I give you every seed-bearing plant all over the earth and every tree that has seed-bearing fruit on it to be your food; and to all the animals of the land, all the birds of the air, and all the living creatures that crawl on the ground, I give all the green plants for food." And so it happened. God looked at everything he had made, and he found it very good. Evening came, and morning followed—the sixth day. Thus the heavens and the earth and all their array were completed. Since on the seventh day God was finished with the work he had been doing, he rested on the seventh day from all the work he had undertaken.

Or GN 1:1, 26-31A

In the beginning, when God created the heavens and the earth, God said: "Let us make man in our image, after our likeness. Let them have dominion over the fish of the sea, the birds of the air, and the cattle, and over all the wild animals and all the creatures that crawl on the ground." God created man in his image; in the image of God he created him; male and female he created them. God blessed them, saying: "Be fertile and multiply; fill the earth and subdue it.

Have dominion over the fish of the sea, the birds of the air, and all the living things that move on the earth." God also said: "See, I give you every seed-bearing plant all over the earth and every tree that has seed-bearing fruit on it to be your food; and to all the animals of the land, all the birds of the air, and all the living creatures that crawl on the ground, I give all the green plants for food." And so it happened. God looked at everything he had made, and found it very good.

Responsorial Psalm PS 104:1-2, 5-6, 10, 12, 13-14, 24, 35
R. (30) Lord, send out your Spirit, and renew the face of the earth.

Bless the LORD, O my soul! O LORD, my God, you are great indeed! You are clothed with majesty and glory, robed in light as with a cloak.

R. Lord, send out your Spirit, and renew the face of the earth.

You fixed the earth upon its foundation, not to be moved forever; with the ocean, as with a garment, you covered it; above the mountains the waters stood.

R. Lord, send out your Spirit, and renew the face of the earth.

You send forth springs into the watercourses that wind among the mountains. Beside them the birds of heaven dwell; from among the branches they send forth their song.

R. Lord, send out your Spirit, and renew the face of the earth.

You water the mountains from your palace; the earth is replete with the fruit of your works. You raise grass for the cattle, and vegetation for man's use, Producing bread from the earth.

R. Lord, send out your Spirit, and renew the face of the earth.

How manifold are your works, O LORD! In wisdom you have wrought them all— the earth is full of your creatures. Bless the LORD, O my soul! Alleluia.

R. Lord, send out your Spirit, and renew the face of the earth.

Or   PS 33:4-5, 6-7, 12-13, 20 AND 22

R... (5b) The earth is full of the goodness of the Lord.

Upright is the word of the LORD, and all his works are trustworthy. He loves justice and right; of the kindness of the LORD the earth is full.

R. The earth is full of the goodness of the Lord.

By the word of the LORD the heavens were made; by the breath of his mouth all their host. He gathers the waters of the sea as in a flask; in cellars he confines the deep.

R. The earth is full of the goodness of the Lord.

Blessed the nation whose God is the LORD, the people he has chosen for his own inheritance. From heaven the LORD looks down; he sees all mankind.

R. The earth is full of the goodness of the Lord.

Our soul waits for the LORD, who is our help and our shield. May your kindness, O LORD, be upon us who have put our hope in you.

R. The earth is full of the goodness of the Lord.

2nd Reading GN 22:1-18

God put Abraham to the test. He called to him, "Abraham!" "Here I am, " he replied. Then God said: "Take your son Isaac, your only one, whom you love, and go to the land of Moriah. There you shall offer him up as a holocaust on a height that I will point out to you." Early the next morning Abraham saddled his donkey, took with him his son Isaac and two of his servants as well, and with the wood that he had cut for the holocaust, set out for the place of which God had told him.

On the third day Abraham got sight of the place from afar. Then he said to his servants: "Both of you stay here with the donkey, while the boy and I go on over yonder. We will worship and then come back to you." Thereupon Abraham took the wood for the holocaust and laid it on his son Isaac's shoulders, while he himself carried the fire and the knife. As the two walked on together, Isaac spoke to his father Abraham: "Father!" Isaac said. "Yes, son, " he replied. Isaac continued, "Here are the fire and the wood, but where is the sheep for the holocaust?" "Son," Abraham answered, "God himself will provide the sheep for the holocaust." Then the two continued going forward. When they came to the place of which God had told him, Abraham built an altar there and arranged the wood on it. Next he tied up his son Isaac, and put him on top of the wood on the altar. Then he reached out and took the knife to slaughter his son. But the LORD's messenger called to him from heaven, "Abraham, Abraham!" "Here I am!" he answered. "Do not lay your hand on the boy," said the messenger. "Do not do the least thing to him. I know now how devoted you are to God, since you did not withhold from me your own beloved son." As Abraham looked about, he spied a ram caught by its horns in the thicket. So he went and took the ram and offered it up as a holocaust in place of his son. Abraham named the site Yahweh-yireh; hence people now say, On the mountain the LORD will see."

Again the LORD's messenger called to Abraham from heaven and said:

"I swear by myself, declares the LORD, that because you acted as you did in not withholding from me your beloved son, I will bless you abundantly and make your descendants as countless as the stars of the sky and the sands of the seashore; your descendants shall take possession of the gates of their enemies, and in your descendants all the nations of the earth shall find blessing all this because you obeyed my command."

Or GN 22:1-2, 9A, 10-13, 15-18

God put Abraham to the test. He called to him, "Abraham!" "Here I am, " he replied. Then God said: "Take your son Isaac, your only one, whom you love, and go to the land of Moriah. There you shall offer him up as a holocaust on a height that I will point out to you."

When they came to the place of which God had told him, Abraham built an altar there and arranged the wood on it. Then he reached out and took the knife to slaughter his son. But the LORD's messenger called to him from heaven,

"Abraham, Abraham!" "Here I am, " he answered. "Do not lay your hand on the boy, " said the messenger. "Do not do the least thing to him. I know now how devoted you are to God, since you did not withhold from me your own beloved son." As Abraham looked about, he spied a ram caught by its horns in the thicket.

So he went and took the ram and offered it up as a holocaust in place of his son.

Again the LORD's messenger called to Abraham from heaven and said: "I swear by myself, declares the LORD, that because you acted as you did in not withholding from me your beloved son, I will bless you abundantly and make your descendants as countless as the stars of the sky and the sands of the seashore; your descendants shall take possession of the gates of their enemies, and in your descendants all the nations of the earth shall find blessing all this because you obeyed my command."

R. (1) You are my inheritance, O Lord.

O LORD, my allotted portion and my cup, you it is who hold fast my lot. I set the LORD ever before me; with him at my right hand I shall not be disturbed.

R. You are my inheritance, O Lord.

Therefore my heart is glad and my soul rejoices, my body, too, abides in confidence; because you will not abandon my soul to the netherworld, nor will you suffer your faithful one to undergo corruption.

R. You are my inheritance, O Lord.

You will show me the path to life, fullness of joys in your presence, the delights at your right hand forever.

R. You are my inheritance, O Lord.

3rd Reading EX 14:15—15:1

The LORD said to Moses, "Why are you crying out to me? Tell the Israelites to go forward. And you, lift up your staff and, with hand outstretched over the sea, split the sea in two, that the Israelites may pass through it on dry land.

But I will make the Egyptians so obstinate that they will go in after them.

Then I will receive glory through Pharaoh and all his army, his chariots and charioteers. The Egyptians shall know that I am the LORD, when I receive glory through Pharaoh and his chariots and charioteers."

The angel of God, who had been leading Israel's camp, now moved and went around behind them. The column of cloud also, leaving the front, took up its place behind them, so that it came between the camp of the Egyptians and that of Israel. But the cloud now became dark, and thus the night passed without the rival camps coming any closer together all night long. Then Moses stretched out his hand over the sea, and the LORD swept the sea with a strong east wind throughout the night and so turned it into dry land.

When the water was thus divided, the Israelites marched into the midst of the sea on dry land, with the water like a wall to their right and to their left.

The Egyptians followed in pursuit; all Pharaoh's horses and chariots and charioteers went after them right into the midst of the sea.

In the night watch just before dawn the LORD cast through the column of the fiery cloud upon the Egyptian force a glance that threw it into a panic; and he so clogged their chariot wheels that they could hardly drive. With that the Egyptians sounded the retreat before Israel, because the LORD was fighting for them against the Egyptians.

Then the LORD told Moses, Stretch out your hand over the sea, that the water may flow back upon the Egyptians, upon their chariots and their charioteers."

So Moses stretched out his hand over the sea, and at dawn the sea flowed back to its normal depth. The Egyptians were fleeing head on toward the sea, when the LORD hurled them into its midst. As the water flowed back, it covered the chariots and the charioteers of Pharaoh's whole army which had followed the Israelites into the sea. Not a single one of them escaped. But the Israelites had marched on dry land through the midst of the sea, with the water like a wall to their right and to their left. Thus the LORD saved Israel on that day from the power of the Egyptians. When Israel saw the Egyptians lying dead on the seashore and beheld the great power that the LORD had shown against the Egyptians, they feared the LORD and believed in him and in his servant Moses.

Then Moses and the Israelites sang this song to the LORD: I will sing to the LORD, for he is gloriously triumphant; horse and chariot he has cast into the sea.

Responsorial Psalm EX 15:1-2, 3-4, 5-6, 17-18
R. (1b) Let us sing to the Lord; he has covered himself in glory.

I will sing to the LORD, for he is gloriously triumphant; horse and chariot he has cast into the sea. My strength and my courage is the LORD, and he has been my savior. He is my God, I praise him; the God of my father, I extol him.

R. Let us sing to the Lord; he has covered himself in glory.

The LORD is a warrior, LORD is his name! Pharaoh's chariots and army he hurled into the sea; the elite of his officers were submerged in the Red Sea.

R. Let us sing to the Lord; he has covered himself in glory.

The flood waters covered them, they sank into the depths like a stone. Your right hand, O LORD, magnificent in power, your right hand, O LORD, has shattered the enemy.

R. Let us sing to the Lord; he has covered himself in glory.

You brought in the people you redeemed and planted them on the mountain of your inheritance the place where you made your seat, O LORD, the sanctuary, LORD, which your hands established. The LORD shall reign forever and ever.

R. Let us sing to the Lord; he has covered himself in glory.

4th Reading IS 54:5-14

The One who has become your husband is your Maker; his name is the LORD of hosts; your redeemer is the Holy One of Israel, called God of all the earth.

The LORD calls you back, like a wife forsaken and grieved in spirit, a wife married in youth and then cast off, says your God. For a brief moment I abandoned you, but with great tenderness I will take you back. In an outburst of wrath, for a moment I hid my face from you; but with enduring love I take pity on you, says the LORD, your redeemer. This is for me like the days of Noah, when I swore that the waters of Noah should never again deluge the earth; so I have sworn not to be angry with you, or to rebuke you. Though the mountains leave their place and the hills be shaken, my love shall never leave you nor my covenant of peace be shaken, says the LORD, who has mercy on you. O afflicted one, storm-battered and unconsoled, I lay your pavements in carnelians, and your foundations in sapphires; I will make your battlements of rubies, your gates of carbuncles, and all your walls of precious stones. All your children shall be taught by the LORD, and great shall be the peace of your children. In justice shall you be established, far from the fear of oppression, where destruction cannot come near you.

Responsorial Psalm PS 30:2, 4, 5-6, 11-12, 13

R. (2a) I will praise you, Lord, for you have rescued me.

I will extol you, O LORD, for you drew me clear and did not let my enemies rejoice over me. O LORD, you brought me up from the netherworld; you preserved me from among those going down into the pit.

R. I will praise you, Lord, for you have rescued me.

Sing praise to the LORD, you his faithful ones, and give thanks to his holy name. For his anger lasts but a moment; a lifetime, his good will. At nightfall, weeping enters in, but with the dawn, rejoicing.

R. I will praise you, Lord, for you have rescued me.

Hear, O LORD, and have pity on me; O LORD, be my helper. You changed my mourning into dancing; O LORD, my God, forever will I give you thanks.

R. I will praise you, Lord, for you have rescued me.

5th Reading   IS 55:1-11

Thus says the LORD: All you who are thirsty, come to the water! You who have no money, come, receive grain and eat; come, without paying and without cost, drink wine and milk! Why spend your money for what is not bread, your wages for what fails to satisfy? Heed me, and you shall eat well, you shall delight in rich fare. Come to me heedfully, listen, that you may have life. I will renew with you the everlasting covenant, the benefits assured to David. As I made him a witness to the peoples, a leader and commander of nations, so shall you summon a nation you knew not, and nations that knew you not shall run to you, because of the LORD, your God, the Holy One of Israel, who has glorified you.

Seek the LORD while he may be found, call him while he is near. Let the scoundrel forsake his way, and the wicked man his thoughts; let him turn to the LORD for mercy; to our God, who is generous in forgiving. For my thoughts are not your thoughts, nor are your ways my ways, says the LORD. As high as the heavens are above the earth, so high are my ways above your ways and my thoughts above your thoughts.

For just as from the heavens the rain and snow come down and do not return there till they have watered the earth, making it fertile and fruitful, giving seed to the one who sows and bread to the one who eats, so shall my word be that goes forth from my mouth; my word shall not return to me void, but shall do my will, achieving the end for which I sent it.

Responsorial Psalm IS 12:2-3, 4, 5-6

R. (3) You will draw water joyfully from the springs of salvation.

God indeed is my savior; I am confident and unafraid. My strength and my courage is the LORD, and he has been my savior. With joy you will draw water at the fountain of salvation.

R. You will draw water joyfully from the springs of salvation.

Give thanks to the LORD, acclaim his name; among the nations make known his deeds, proclaim how exalted is his name.

R. You will draw water joyfully from the springs of salvation.

Sing praise to the LORD for his glorious achievement; let this be known throughout all the earth. Shout with exultation, O city of Zion, for great in your midst is the Holy One of Israel!

R. You will draw water joyfully from the springs of salvation.

6th Reading BAR 3:9-15, 32C4:4
Hear, O Israel, the commandments of life: listen, and know prudence!

How is it, Israel, that you are in the land of your foes, grown old in a foreign land, defiled with the dead, accounted with those destined for the netherworld?

You have forsaken the fountain of wisdom! Had you walked in the way of God, you would have dwelt in enduring peace. Learn where prudence is, where strength, where understanding; that you may know also where are length of days, and life, where light of the eyes, and peace. Who has found the place of wisdom, who has entered into her treasuries? The One who knows all things knows her; he has probed her by his knowledge

The One who established the earth for all time, and filled it with four-footed beasts; he who dismisses the light, and it departs, calls it, and it obeys him trembling; before whom the stars at their posts shine and rejoice; when he calls them, they answer, "Here we are!" shining with joy for their Maker. Such is our God; no other is to be compared to him: he has traced out the whole way of understanding, and has given her to Jacob, his servant, to Israel, his beloved son.

Since then she has appeared on earth, and moved among people. She is the book of the precepts of God, the law that endures forever; all who cling to her will live, but those will die who forsake her. Turn, O Jacob, and receive her: walk by her light toward splendor. Give not your glory to another, your privileges to an alien race. Blessed are we, O Israel; for what pleases God is known to us!

R. (John 6:68c) Lord, you have the words of everlasting life.

The law of the LORD is perfect, refreshing the soul; the decree of the LORD is trustworthy, giving wisdom to the simple.

R. Lord, you have the words of everlasting life.

The precepts of the LORD are right, rejoicing the heart; the command of the LORD is clear, enlightening the eye.

R. Lord, you have the words of everlasting life.

The fear of the LORD is pure, enduring forever; the ordinances of the LORD are true, all of them just.

R. Lord, you have the words of everlasting life.

They are more precious than gold, than a heap of purest gold; sweeter also than syrup or honey from the comb.

R. Lord, you have the words of everlasting life.

7th Reading EZ 36:16-17A, 18-28
The word of the LORD came to me, saying: Son of man, when the house of Israel lived in their land, they defiled it by their conduct and deeds. Therefore I poured out my fury upon them because of the blood that they poured out on the ground, and because they defiled it with idols. I scattered them among the nations, dispersing them over foreign lands; according to their conduct and deeds I judged them. But when they came among the nations wherever they came, they served to profane my holy name, because it was said of them: "These are the people of the LORD, yet they had to leave their land." So I have relented because of my holy name which the house of Israel profaned among the nations where they came.

Therefore say to the house of Israel: Thus says the Lord GOD: Not for your sakes do I act, house of Israel, but for the sake of my holy name, which you profaned among the nations to which you came. I will prove the holiness of my great name, profaned among the nations, in whose midst you have profaned it.

Thus the nations shall know that I am the LORD, says the Lord GOD, when in their sight I prove my holiness through you. For I will take you away from among the nations, gather you from all the foreign lands, and bring you back to your own land. I will sprinkle clean water upon you to cleanse you from all your impurities, and from all your idols I will cleanse you. I will give you a new heart and place a new spirit within you, taking from your bodies your stony hearts and giving you natural hearts. I will put my spirit within you and make you live by my statutes, careful to observe my decrees. You shall live in the land I gave your fathers; you shall be my people, and I will be your God.

Responsorial Psalm PS 42:3, 5; 43:3, 4
When baptism is celebrated.

R... (42:2) Like a deer that longs for running streams, my soul longs for you, my God.

Athirst is my soul for God, the living God. When shall I go and behold the face of God?

R. Like a deer that longs for running streams, my soul longs for you, my God.

I went with the throng and led them in procession to the house of God, Amid loud cries of joy and thanksgiving, with the multitude keeping festival.

R. Like a deer that longs for running streams, my soul longs for you, my God.

Send forth your light and your fidelity; they shall lead me on And bring me to your holy mountain, to your dwelling-place.

R. Like a deer that longs for running streams, my soul longs for you, my God.

Then will I go in to the altar of God, the God of my gladness and joy; then will I give you thanks upon the harp, O God, my God!

R. Like a deer that longs for running streams, my soul longs for you, my God.

Or   IS 12:2-3, 4BCD, 5-6

When baptism is not celebrated.

R. (3) You will draw water joyfully from the springs of salvation.

God indeed is my savior; I am confident and unafraid. My strength and my courage is the LORD, and he has been my savior. With joy you will draw water at the fountain of salvation.

R. You will draw water joyfully from the springs of salvation.

Give thanks to the LORD, acclaim his name; among the nations make known his deeds, proclaim how exalted is his name.

R. You will draw water joyfully from the springs of salvation.

Sing praise to the LORD for his glorious achievement; let this be known throughout all the earth. Shout with exultation, O city of Zion, for great in your midst is the Holy One of Israel!

R. You will draw water joyfully from the springs of salvation.

Or PS 51:12-13, 14-15, 18-19

When baptism is not celebrated

R. (12a) Create a clean heart in me, O God.

A clean heart create for me, O God, and a steadfast spirit renew within me. Cast me not out from your presence, and your Holy Spirit take not from me.

R. Create a clean heart in me, O God. Give me back the joy of your salvation, and a willing spirit sustain in me. I will teach transgressors your ways, and sinners shall return to you.

R. Create a clean heart in me, O God.

For you are not pleased with sacrifices; should I offer a holocaust, you would not accept it. My sacrifice, O God, is a contrite spirit; a heart contrite and humbled, O God, you will not spurn.

R. Create a clean heart in me, O God.

Epistle   ROM 6:3-11

Brothers and sisters: Are you unaware that we who were baptized into Christ Jesus were baptized into his death? We were indeed buried with him through baptism into death, so that, just as Christ was raised from the dead by the glory of the Father, we too might live in newness of life.

For if we have grown into union with him through a death like his, we shall also be united with him in the resurrection. We know that our old self was crucified with him, so that our sinful body might be done away with, that we might no longer be in slavery to sin. For a dead person has been absolved from sin. If, then, we have died with Christ, we believe that we shall also live with him. We know that Christ, raised from the dead, dies no more; death no longer has power over him. As to his death, he died to sin once and for all; as to his life, he lives for God. Consequently, you too must think of yourselves as being dead to sin and living for God in Christ Jesus.

Responsorial Psalm Ps 118:1-2, 16-17, 22-23

R. Alleluia, alleluia, alleluia.

Give thanks to the LORD, for he is good, for his mercy endures forever.

Let the house of Israel say, "His mercy endures forever."

R. Alleluia, alleluia, alleluia.

The right hand of the LORD has struck with power; the right hand of the LORD is exalted.

I shall not die, but live, and declare the works of the LORD.

R. Alleluia, alleluia, alleluia.

The stone the builders rejected has become the cornerstone.

By the LORD has this been done; it is wonderful in our eyes.

R. Alleluia, alleluia, alleluia.

Gospel   Mark 16:1-7

When the sabbath was over,

Mary Magdalene, Mary, the mother of James, and Salome bought spices so that they might go and anoint him.

Very early when the sun had risen, on the first day of the week, they came to the tomb.

They were saying to one another,

"Who will roll back the stone for us from the entrance to the tomb?"

When they looked up, they saw that the stone had been rolled back; it was very large.

On entering the tomb they saw a young man sitting on the right side, clothed in a white robe, and they were utterly amazed.

He said to them, "Do not be amazed! You seek Jesus of Nazareth, the crucified.

He has been raised; he is not here. Behold the place where they laid him.

But go and tell his disciples and Peter, 'He is going before you to Galilee; there you will see him, as he told you.'"

APRIL 4TH, 2021

Easter Sunday
The Resurrection of the Lord

The Mass of Easter Day

1st Reading   ACTS 10:34A, 37-43
Peter proceeded to speak and said: "You know what has happened all over Judea, beginning in Galilee after the baptism that John preached, how God anointed Jesus of Nazareth with the Holy Spirit and power. He went about doing good and healing all those oppressed by the devil, for God was with him. We are witnesses of all that he did both in the country of the Jews and in Jerusalem.

They put him to death by hanging him on a tree. This man God raised on the third day and granted that he be visible, not to all the people, but to us, the witnesses chosen by God in advance, who ate and drank with him after he rose from the dead. He commissioned us to preach to the people and testify that he is the one appointed by God as judge of the living and the dead. To him all the prophets bear witness, that everyone who believes in him will receive forgiveness of sins through his name."

Responsorial Psalm   PS 118:1-2, 16-17, 22-23.
R. (24) This is the day the Lord has made; let us rejoice and be glad.

or:

R. Alleluia.

Give thanks to the LORD, for he is good, for his mercy endures forever. Let the house of Israel say, "His mercy endures forever."

R. This is the day the Lord has made; let us rejoice and be glad.

or:

R. Alleluia.

"The right hand of the LORD has struck with power; the right hand of the LORD is exalted. I shall not die, but live, and declare the works of the LORD."

R. This is the day the Lord has made; let us rejoice and be glad.

or:

R. Alleluia.

The stone which the builders rejected has become the cornerstone. By the LORD has this been done; it is wonderful in our eyes.

R. This is the day the Lord has made; let us rejoice and be glad.

or:

R. Alleluia.

2nd Reading   COL 3:1-4
Brothers and sisters: If then you were raised with Christ, seek what is above, where Christ is seated at the right hand of God. Think of what is above, not of what is on earth. For you have died, and your life is hidden with Christ in God.

When Christ your life appears, then you too will appear with him in glory.

Or   I COR 5:6B-8

Brothers and sisters: Do you not know that a little yeast leavens all the dough?

Clear out the old yeast, so that you may become a fresh batch of dough, inasmuch as you are unleavened. For our paschal lamb, Christ, has been sacrificed. Therefore, let us celebrate the feast, not with the old yeast, the yeast of malice and wickedness, but with the unleavened bread of sincerity and truth.

Sequence Victimae Paschali Laudes

Christians, to the Paschal Victim

 Offer your thankful praises!

A Lamb the sheep redeems;

Christ, who only is sinless,

Reconciles sinners to the Father.

Death and life have contended in that combat stupendous:

The Prince of life, who died, reigns immortal.

Speak, Mary, declaring

What you saw, wayfaring.

"The tomb of Christ, who is living,

The glory of Jesus' resurrection; bright angels attesting,

The shroud and napkin resting.

Yes, Christ my hope is arisen; to Galilee he goes before you."

Christ indeed from death is risen, our new life obtaining.

Have mercy, victor King, ever reigning!

 Amen. Alleluia.

Alleluia CF. 1 COR 5:7B-8A

R. Alleluia, alleluia.

Christ, our paschal lamb, has been sacrificed; let us then feast with joy in the Lord.

R. Alleluia, alleluia.

Gospel JN 20:1-9
On the first day of the week, Mary of Magdala came to the tomb early in the morning, while it was still dark, and saw the stone removed from the tomb.

So she ran and went to Simon Peter and to the other disciple whom Jesus loved, and told them, "They have taken the Lord from the tomb, and we don't know where they put him." So Peter and the other disciple went out and came to the tomb. They both ran, but the other disciple ran faster than Peter and arrived at the tomb first; he bent down and saw the burial cloths there, but did not go in.

When Simon Peter arrived after him, he went into the tomb and saw the burial cloths there, and the cloth that had covered his head, not with the burial cloths but rolled up in a separate place. Then the other disciple also went in, the one who had arrived at the tomb first, and he saw and believed. For they did not yet understand the Scripture that he had to rise from the dead.

APRIL 5TH, 2021
Monday in the Octave of Easter

1st Reading ACTS 2:14, 22-33
On the day of Pentecost, Peter stood up with the Eleven, raised his voice, and proclaimed: "You who are Jews, indeed all of you staying in Jerusalem. Let this be known to you, and listen to my words.

"You who are children of Israel, hear these words. Jesus the Nazorean was a man commended to you by God with mighty deeds, wonders, and signs, which God worked through him in your midst, as you yourselves know. This man, delivered up by the set plan and foreknowledge of God, you killed, using lawless men to crucify him. But God raised him up, releasing him from the throes of death, because it was impossible for him to be held by it. For David says of him:

I saw the Lord ever before me, with him at my right hand I shall not be disturbed. Therefore my heart has been glad and my tongue has exulted; my flesh, too, will dwell in hope, because you will not abandon my soul to the nether world, nor will you suffer your holy one to see corruption. You have made known to me the paths of life; you will fill me with joy in your presence.

My brothers, one can confidently say to you about the patriarch David that he died and was buried, and his tomb is in our midst to this day. But since he was a prophet and knew that God had sworn an oath to him that he would set one of his descendants upon his throne, he foresaw and spoke of the resurrection of the Christ, that neither was he abandoned to the netherworld nor did his flesh see corruption. God raised this Jesus; of this we are all witnesses. Exalted at the right hand of God, he poured forth the promise of the Holy Spirit that he received from the Father, as you both see and hear."

Responsorial Psalm   PS 16:1-2A AND 5, 7-8, 9-10, 11
R. (1) Keep me safe, O God; you are my hope.

or:

R. Alleluia.

Keep me, O God, for in you I take refuge; I say to the LORD, "My Lord are you." O LORD, my allotted portion and my cup, you it is who hold fast my lot.

R. Keep me safe, O God; you are my hope.

or:

R. Alleluia.

I bless the LORD who counsels me; even in the night my heart exhorts me. I set the LORD ever before me; with him at my right hand I shall not be disturbed.

R. Keep me safe, O God; you are my hope.

or:

214

R. Alleluia.

Therefore my heart is glad and my soul rejoices, my body, too, abides in confidence; Because you will not abandon my soul to the nether world, nor will you suffer your faithful one to undergo corruption.

R. Keep me safe, O God; you are my hope.

or:

R. Alleluia.

You will show me the path to life, fullness of joys in your presence, the delights at your right hand forever.

R. Keep me safe, O God; you are my hope.

or:

R. Alleluia.

Alleluia PS 118:24

R. Alleluia, alleluia.

This is the day the LORD has made; let us be glad and rejoice in it.

R. Alleluia, alleluia.

Gospel MT 28:8-15

Mary Magdalene and the other Mary went away quickly from the tomb, fearful yet overjoyed, and ran to announce the news to his disciples. And behold, Jesus met them on their way and greeted them. They approached, embraced his feet, and did him homage. Then Jesus said to them, "Do not be afraid. Go tell my brothers to go to Galilee, and there they will see me."

While they were going, some of the guard went into the city and told the chief priests all that had happened. The chief priests assembled with the elders and took counsel; then they gave a large sum of money to the soldiers, telling them, "You are to say, 'His disciples came by night and stole him while we were asleep.' And if this gets to the ears of the governor, we will satisfy him and keep you out of trouble." The soldiers took the money and did as they were instructed. And this story has circulated among the Jews to the present day.

APRIL 6TH, 2021

Tuesday in the Octave of Easter

1st Reading ACTS 2:36-41

On the day of Pentecost, Peter said to the Jewish people, "Let the whole house of Israel know for certain that God has made him both Lord and Christ, this Jesus whom you crucified."

Now when they heard this, they were cut to the heart, and they asked Peter and the other Apostles, "What are we to do, my brothers?" Peter said to them, "Repent and be baptized, every one of you, in the name of Jesus Christ, for the forgiveness of your sins; and you will receive the gift of the Holy Spirit.

For the promise is made to you and to your children and to all those far off, whomever the Lord our God will call." He testified with many other arguments, and was exhorting them, "Save yourselves from this corrupt generation."

Those who accepted his message were baptized, and about three thousand persons were added that day.

R...(5b) The earth is full of the goodness of the Lord.

or:

R. Alleluia.

Upright is the word of the LORD, and all his works are trustworthy. He loves justice and right; of the kindness of the LORD the earth is full.

R. The earth is full of the goodness of the Lord.

or:

R. Alleluia.

See, the eyes of the LORD are upon those who fear him, upon those who hope for his kindness, To deliver them from death and preserve them in spite of famine.

R. The earth is full of the goodness of the Lord.

or:

R. Alleluia.

Our soul waits for the LORD, who is our help and our shield. May your kindness, O LORD, be upon us who have put our hope in you.

R. The earth is full of the goodness of the Lord.

or:

R. Alleluia.

Alleluia   PS 118:24

R. Alleluia, alleluia.

This is the day the LORD has made; let us be glad and rejoice in it.

R. Alleluia, alleluia.

Gospel   JN 20:11-18

Mary Magdalene stayed outside the tomb weeping. And as she wept, she bent over into the tomb and saw two angels in white sitting there, one at the head and one at the feet where the Body of Jesus had been. And they said to her, "Woman, why are you weeping?" She said to them, "They have taken my Lord, and I don't know where they laid him." When she had said this, she turned around and saw Jesus there, but did not know it was Jesus. Jesus said to her, "Woman, why are you weeping? Whom are you looking for?" She thought it was the gardener and said to him, "Sir, if you carried him away, tell me where you laid him, and I will take him." Jesus said to her, "Mary!" She turned and said to him in Hebrew, "Rabbouni," which means Teacher.

Jesus said to her, "Stop holding on to me, for I have not yet ascended to the Father. But go to my brothers and tell them, 'I am going to my Father and your Father, to my God and your God.'" Mary went and announced to the disciples,

"I have seen the Lord," and then reported what he had told her.

APRIL 7TH, 2021
Wednesday in the Octave of Easter

Peter and John were going up to the temple area for the three o'clock hour of prayer. And a man crippled from birth was carried and placed at the gate of the temple called "the Beautiful Gate" every day to beg for alms from the people who entered the temple. When he saw Peter and John about to go into the temple,he asked for alms. But Peter looked intently at him, as did John, and said, "Look at us." He paid attention to them, expecting to receive something from them.

Peter said, "I have neither silver nor gold, but what I do have I give you: in the name of Jesus Christ the Nazorean, rise and walk." Then Peter took him by the right hand and raised him up, and immediately his feet and ankles grew strong. He leaped up, stood, and walked around, and went into the temple with them, walking and jumping and praising God. When all the people saw him walking and praising God, they recognized him as the one who used to sit begging at the Beautiful Gate of the temple, and they were filled with amazement and astonishment at what had happened to him.

Responsorial Psalm PS 105:1-2, 3-4, 6-7, 8-9
R.(3b) Rejoice, O hearts that seek the Lord.

or:

R. Alleluia.

Give thanks to the LORD, invoke his name; make known among the nations his deeds. Sing to him, sing his praise, proclaim all his wondrous deeds.

R. Rejoice, O hearts that seek the Lord.

or:

R. Alleluia.

Glory in his holy name; rejoice, O hearts that seek the LORD! Look to the LORD in his strength; seek to serve him constantly.

R. Rejoice, O hearts that seek the Lord.

or:

R. Alleluia.

You descendants of Abraham, his servants, sons of Jacob, his chosen ones! He, the LORD, is our God; throughout the earth his judgments prevail.

R. Rejoice, O hearts that seek the Lord.

or:

R. Alleluia.

He remembers forever his covenant which he made binding for a thousand generations Which he entered into with Abraham and by his oath to Isaac.

R. Rejoice, O hearts that seek the Lord.

or:

R. Alleluia.

Alleluia PS 118:24

R. Alleluia, alleluia.

This is the day the LORD has made; let us be glad and rejoice in it.

R. Alleluia, alleluia.

Gospel LK 24:13-35

That very day, the first day of the week, two of Jesus' disciples were going to a village seven miles from Jerusalem called Emmaus, and they were conversing about all the things that had occurred. And it happened that while they were conversing and debating, Jesus himself drew near and walked with them, but their eyes were prevented from recognizing him. He asked them, "What are you discussing as you walk along?" They stopped, looking downcast. One of them, named Cleopas, said to him in reply, "Are you the only visitor to Jerusalem who does not know of the things that have taken place there in these days?"

And he replied to them, "What sort of things?"

They said to him, "The things that happened to Jesus the Nazarene, who was a prophet mighty in deed and word before God and all the people, how our chief priests and rulers both handed him over to a sentence of death and crucified him. But we were hoping that he would be the one to redeem Israel; and besides all this, it is now the third day since this took place. Some

219

women from our group, however, have astounded us: they were at the tomb early in the morning and did not find his Body; they came back and reported that they had indeed seen a vision of angels who announced that he was alive. Then some of those with us went to the tomb and found things just as the women had described, but him they did not see." And he said to them, "Oh, how foolish you are! How slow of heart to believe all that the prophets spoke! Was it not necessary that the Christ should suffer these things and enter into his glory?"

Then beginning with Moses and all the prophets, he interpreted to them what referred to him in all the Scriptures. As they approached the village to which they were going, he gave the impression that he was going on farther. But they urged him, "Stay with us, for it is nearly evening and the day is almost over." So he went in to stay with them. And it happened that, while he was with them at table, he took bread, said the blessing, broke it, and gave it to them. With that their eyes were opened and they recognized him, but he vanished from their sight.

Then they said to each other, "Were not our hearts burning within us while he spoke to us on the way and opened the Scriptures to us?" So they set out at once and returned to Jerusalem where they found gathered together the Eleven and those with them who were saying, "The Lord has truly been raised and has appeared to Simon!"

Then the two recounted what had taken place on the way and how he was made known to them in the breaking of the bread.

APRIL 8TH, 2021
Thursday in the Octave of Easter

1st Reading ACTS 3:11-26
As the crippled man who had been cured clung to Peter and John, all the people hurried in amazement toward them in the portico called "Solomon's Portico."

When Peter saw this, he addressed the people, "You children of Israel, why are you amazed at this, and why do you look so intently at us as if we had made him walk by our own power or piety? The God of Abraham, the God of Isaac, and the God of Jacob, the God of our fathers, has glorified his servant Jesus whom you handed over and denied in Pilate's presence, when he had decided to release him.

You denied the Holy and Righteous One and asked that a murderer be released to you. The author of life you put to death, but God raised him from the dead; of this we are witnesses. And by faith in his name, this man, whom you see and know, his name has made strong, and the faith that comes through it has given him this perfect health, in the presence of all of you. Now I know, brothers and sisters, that you acted out of ignorance, just as your leaders did; but God has thus brought to fulfillment what he had announced beforehand through the mouth of all the prophets, that his Christ would suffer. Repent, therefore, and be converted, that your sins may be wiped away, and that the Lord may grant you times of refreshment and send you the Christ already appointed for you, Jesus, whom heaven must receive until the times of universal restoration of which God spoke through the mouth of his holy prophets from of old. For Moses said:

A prophet like me will the Lord, your God, raise up for you from among your own kin; to him you shall listen in all that he may say to you. Everyone who does not listen to that prophet will be cut off from the people.

"Moreover, all the prophets who spoke, from Samuel and those afterwards, also announced these days. You are the children of the prophets and of the covenant that God made with your ancestors when he said to Abraham, In your offspring all the families of the earth shall be blessed. For you first, God raised up his servant and sent him to bless you by turning each of you from your evil ways."

Responsorial Psalm   PS 8:2AB AND 5, 6-7, 8-9
R.(2ab) O Lord, our God, how wonderful your name in all the earth!

or:

R. Alleluia.

O LORD, our Lord, how glorious is your name over all the earth! What is man that you should be mindful of him, or the son of man that you should care for him?

R. O Lord, our God, how wonderful your name in all the earth!

or:

R. Alleluia.

You have made him little less than the angels, and crowned him with glory and honor. You have given him rule over the works of your hands, putting all things under his feet.

R. O Lord, our God, how wonderful your name in all the earth!

or:

R. Alleluia.

All sheep and oxen, yes, and the beasts of the field, The birds of the air, the fishes of the sea, and whatever swims the paths of the seas.

R. O Lord, our God, how wonderful your name in all the earth!

or:

R. Alleluia.

Alleluia   PS 118:24

R. Alleluia, alleluia.

This is the day the LORD has made; let us be glad and rejoice in it.

R. Alleluia, alleluia.

Gospel   LK 24:35-48
The disciples of Jesus recounted what had taken place along the way, and how they had come to recognize him in the breaking of bread.

While they were still speaking about this, he stood in their midst and said to them, "Peace be with you." But they were startled and terrified and thought that they were seeing a ghost. Then he said to them, "Why are you troubled?

And why do questions arise in your hearts? Look at my hands and my feet, that it is I myself. Touch me and see, because a ghost does not have flesh and bones as you can see I have." And as he said this, he showed them his hands and his feet. While they were still incredulous for joy and were amazed, he asked them, "Have you anything here to eat?" They gave him a piece of baked fish; he took it and ate it in front of them.

He said to them, "These are my words that I spoke to you while I was still with you, that everything written about me in the law of Moses and in the prophets and psalms must be fulfilled." Then he opened their minds to understand the Scriptures. And he said to them, "Thus it is written that the Christ would suffer and rise from the dead on the third day and that repentance, for the forgiveness of sins, would be preached in his name to all the nations, beginning from Jerusalem. You are witnesses of these things."

APRIL 9TH, 2021
Friday in the Octave of Easter

1st Reading   ACTS 4:1-12
After the crippled man had been cured, while Peter and John were still speaking to the people, the priests, the captain of the temple guard, and the Sadducees confronted them, disturbed that they were teaching the people and proclaiming in Jesus the resurrection of the dead. They laid hands on Peter and John and put them in custody until the next day, since it was already evening. But many of those who heard the word came to believe and the number of men grew to about five thousand.

On the next day, their leaders, elders, and scribes were assembled in Jerusalem, with Annas the high priest, Caiaphas, John, Alexander, and all who were of the high-priestly class. They brought them into their presence and questioned them,

"By what power or by what name have you done this?" Then Peter, filled with the Holy Spirit, answered them, "Leaders of the people and elders: If we are being examined today about a good deed done to a cripple, namely, by what means he was saved, then all of you and all the people of Israel should know that it was in the name of Jesus Christ the Nazorean whom you crucified, whom God raised from the dead; in his name this man stands before you healed. He is the stone rejected by you, the builders, which has become the cornerstone. There is no salvation through anyone else, nor is there any other name under heaven given to the human race by which we are to be saved."

Responsorial Psalm   PS 118:1-2 AND 4, 22-24, 25-27A
R...(22) The stone rejected by the builders has become the cornerstone.

or:

R. Alleluia.

Give thanks to the LORD, for he is good, for his mercy endures forever. Let the house of Israel say, "His mercy endures forever." Let those who fear the LORD say, "His mercy endures forever."

R. The stone rejected by the builders has become the cornerstone.

or:

R. Alleluia.

The stone which the builders rejected has become the cornerstone. By the LORD has this been done; it is wonderful in our eyes. This is the day the LORD has made; let us be glad and rejoice in it.

R. The stone rejected by the builders has become the cornerstone.

or:

R. Alleluia.

O LORD, grant salvation! O LORD, grant prosperity! Blessed is he who comes in the name of the LORD; we bless you from the house of the LORD. The LORD is God, and he has given us light.

R. The stone rejected by the builders has become the cornerstone.

or:

R. Alleluia.

Alleluia   PS 118:24

R. Alleluia, alleluia.

This is the day the LORD has made; let us be glad and rejoice in it.

R. Alleluia, alleluia.

Gospel JN 21:1-14

Jesus revealed himself again to his disciples at the Sea of Tiberias.

He revealed himself in this way. Together were Simon Peter, Thomas called Didymus, Nathanael from Cana in Galilee, Zebedee's sons, and two others of his disciples. Simon Peter said to them, "I am going fishing." They said to

224

him, "We also will come with you." So they went out and got into the boat, but that night they caught nothing. When it was already dawn, Jesus was standing on the shore; but the disciples did not realize that it was Jesus. Jesus said to them, "Children, have you caught anything to eat?" They answered him, "No." So he said to them, "Cast the net over the right side of the boat and you will find something."

So they cast it, and were not able to pull it in because of the number of fish. So the disciple whom Jesus loved said to Peter, "It is the Lord."

When Simon Peter heard that it was the Lord, he tucked in his garment, for he was lightly clad, and jumped into the sea. The other disciples came in the boat, for they were not far from shore, only about a hundred yards, dragging the net with the fish. When they climbed out on shore, they saw a charcoal fire with fish on it and bread. Jesus said to them, "Bring some of the fish you just caught."

So Simon Peter went over and dragged the net ashore full of one hundred fifty-three large fish. Even though there were so many, the net was not torn.

Jesus said to them, "Come, have breakfast." And none of the disciples dared to ask him, "Who are you?" because they realized it was the Lord. Jesus came over and took the bread and gave it to them, and in like manner the fish. This was now the third time Jesus was revealed to his disciples after being raised from the dead.

APRIL 10TH, 2021
Saturday in the Octave of Easter

1st Reading ACTS 4:13-21

Observing the boldness of Peter and John and perceiving them to be uneducated, ordinary men, the leaders, elders, and scribes were amazed, and they recognized them as the companions of Jesus. Then when they saw the man who had been cured standing there with them, they could say nothing in reply. So they ordered them to leave the Sanhedrin, and conferred with one another, saying,

"What are we to do with these men? Everyone living in Jerusalem knows that a remarkable sign was done through them, and we cannot deny it. But so that it may not be spread any further among the people, let us give them a stern warning never again to speak to anyone in this name."

So they called them back and ordered them not to speak or teach at all in the name of Jesus. Peter and John, however, said to them in reply, "Whether it is right in the sight of God for us to obey you rather than God, you be the judges. It is impossible for us not to speak about what we have seen and heard."

After threatening them further, they released them, finding no way to punish them, on account of the people who were all praising God for what had happened.

Responsorial Psalm   PS 118:1 AND 14-15AB, 16-18, 19-21
R...(21a) I will give thanks to you, for you have answered me.

or:

R. Alleluia.

Give thanks to the LORD, for he is good, for his mercy endures forever. My strength and my courage is the LORD, and he has been my savior.

The joyful shout of victory in the tents of the just.

R. I will give thanks to you, for you have answered me.

or:

R. Alleluia.

"The right hand of the LORD is exalted; the right hand of the LORD has struck with power." I shall not die, but live, and declare the works of the LORD. Though the LORD has indeed chastised me, yet he has not delivered me to death.

R. I will give thanks to you, for you have answered me.

or:

R. Alleluia.

Open to me the gates of justice; I will enter them and give thanks to the LORD. This is the gate of the LORD; the just shall enter it. I will give thanks to you, for you have answered me and have been my savior.

R. I will give thanks to you, for you have answered me.

or:

R. Alleluia.

Alleluia PS 118:24

R. Alleluia, alleluia.

This is the day the LORD has made; let us be glad and rejoice in it.

R. Alleluia, alleluia.

Gospel MK 16:9-15

When Jesus had risen, early on the first day of the week, he appeared first to Mary Magdalene, out of whom he had driven seven demons. She went and told his companions who were mourning and weeping. When they heard that he was alive and had been seen by her, they did not believe.

After this he appeared in another form to two of them walking along on their way to the country. They returned and told the others; but they did not believe them either.

But later, as the Eleven were at table, he appeared to them and rebuked them for their unbelief and hardness of heart because they had not believed those who saw him after he had been raised. He said to them, "Go into the whole world and proclaim the Gospel to every creature."

APRIL 11TH, 2021
Second Sunday of Easter

1st Reading Acts 4:32-35

The community of believers was of one heart and mind, and no one claimed that any of his possessions was his own, but they had everything in common.

With great power the apostles bore witness to the resurrection of the Lord Jesus, and great favor was accorded them all.

There was no needy person among them, for those who owned property or houses would sell them, bring the proceeds of the sale, and put them at the feet of the apostles, and they were distributed to each according to need.

R. (1) Give thanks to the Lord for he is good, his love is everlasting.

or:

R. Alleluia.

Let the house of Israel say, "His mercy endures forever." Let the house of Aaron say, "His mercy endures forever." Let those who fear the LORD say, "His mercy endures forever."

R. Give thanks to the Lord for he is good, his love is everlasting.

or:

R. Alleluia.

I was hard pressed and was falling, but the LORD helped me. My strength and my courage is the LORD, and he has been my savior. The joyful shout of victory in the tents of the just:

R. Give thanks to the Lord for he is good, his love is everlasting.

or:

R. Alleluia.

The stone which the builders rejected has become the cornerstone. By the LORD has this been done; it is wonderful in our eyes. This is the day the LORD has made; let us be glad and rejoice in it.

R. Give thanks to the Lord for he is good, his love is everlasting.

or:

R. Alleluia.

2nd Reading 1 Jn 5:1-6
Beloved:

Everyone who believes that Jesus is the Christ is begotten by God, and everyone who loves the Father loves also the one begotten by him.

In this way we know that we love the children of God when we love God and obey his commandments. For the love of God is this, that we keep his commandments.

And his commandments are not burdensome, for whoever is begotten by God conquers the world.

And the victory that conquers the world is our faith. Who indeed is the victor over the world but the one who believes that Jesus is the Son of God?

This is the one who came through water and blood, Jesus Christ, not by water alone, but by water and blood.

The Spirit is the one that testifies, and the Spirit is truth.

Alleluia JN 20:29

R. Alleluia, alleluia.

You believe in me, Thomas, because you have seen me, says the Lord; blessed are those who have not seen me, but still believe!

R. Alleluia, alleluia.

Gospel JN 20:19-31

On the evening of that first day of the week, when the doors were locked, where the disciples were, for fear of the Jews, Jesus came and stood in their midst and said to them, "Peace be with you." When he had said this, he showed them his hands and his side. The disciples rejoiced when they saw the Lord. Jesus said to them again, "Peace be with you. As the Father has sent me, so I send you."

And when he had said this, he breathed on them and said to them, "Receive the Holy Spirit. Whose sins you forgive are forgiven them, and whose sins you retain are retained." Thomas, called Didymus, one of the Twelve, was not with them when Jesus came.

So the other disciples said to him, "We have seen the Lord." But he said to them, "Unless I see the mark of the nails in his hands and put my finger into the nailmarks and put my hand into his side, I will not believe."

Now a week later his disciples were again inside and Thomas was with them. Jesus came, although the doors were locked, and stood in their midst and said, "Peace be with you." Then he said to Thomas, "Put your finger here and see my hands, and bring your hand and put it into my side, and do not be unbelieving, but believe." Thomas answered and said to him, "My Lord and my God!"

Jesus said to him, "Have you come to believe because you have seen me? Blessed are those who have not seen and have believed." Now Jesus did many other signs in the presence of his disciples that are not written in this book. But these are written that you may come to believe that Jesus is the Christ, the Son of God, and that through this belief you may have life in his name.

APRIL 12TH, 2021
Monday of the Second Week of Easter

1st Reading ACTS 4:23-31

After their release Peter and John went back to their own people and reported what the chief priests and elders had told them. And when they heard it, they raised their voices to God with one accord and said, "Sovereign Lord, maker of heaven and earth and the sea and all that is in them, you said by the Holy Spirit through the mouth of our father David, your servant:

Why did the Gentiles rage and the peoples entertain folly? The kings of the earth took their stand and the princes gathered together against the Lord and against his anointed. Indeed they gathered in this city against your holy servant Jesus whom you anointed, Herod and Pontius Pilate, together with the Gentiles and the peoples of Israel, to do what your hand and your will had long ago planned to take place.

And now, Lord, take note of their threats, and enable your servants to speak your word with all boldness, as you stretch forth your hand to heal, and signs and wonders are done through the name of your holy servant Jesus." As they prayed, the place where they were gathered shook, and they were all filled with the Holy Spirit and continued to speak the word of God with boldness.

Responsorial Psalm PS 2:1-3, 4-7A, 7B-9

R. (see 11d) Blessed are all who take refuge in the Lord.

or:

R. Alleluia.

Why do the nations rage and the peoples utter folly? The kings of the earth rise up, and the princes conspire together against the LORD and against his anointed: "Let us break their fetters and cast their bonds from us!"

R. Blessed are all who take refuge in the Lord.

or:

R. Alleluia.

He who is enthroned in heaven laughs; the LORD derides them. Then in anger he speaks to them; he terrifies them in his wrath: "I myself have set up my king on Zion, my holy mountain." I will proclaim the decree of the LORD.

R. Blessed are all who take refuge in the Lord.

or:

R. Alleluia.

The LORD said to me, "You are my Son; this day I have begotten you. Ask of me and I will give you the nations for an inheritance and the ends of the earth for your possession. You shall rule them with an iron rod; you shall shatter them like an earthen dish."

R. Blessed are all who take refuge in the Lord.

or:

R. Alleluia.

Alleluia COL 3:1

R. Alleluia, alleluia.

If then you were raised with Christ, seek what is above, where Christ is seated at the right hand of God.

R. Alleluia, alleluia.

Gospel JN 3:1-8

There was a Pharisee named Nicodemus, a ruler of the Jews.

He came to Jesus at night and said to him, "Rabbi, we know that you are a teacher who has come from God, for no one can do these signs that you are doing unless God is with him." Jesus answered and said to him,

"Amen, amen, I say to you, unless one is born from above, he cannot see the Kingdom of God." Nicodemus said to him, "How can a man once grown old be born again? Surely he cannot reenter his mother's womb and be born again, can he?" Jesus answered, "Amen, amen, I say to you, unless one is born of water and Spirit he cannot enter the Kingdom of God. What is born of flesh is flesh and what is born of spirit is spirit. Do not be amazed that I told you, 'You must be born from above.' The wind blows where it wills, and you can hear the sound it makes, but you do not know where it comes from or where it goes; so it is with everyone who is born of the Spirit."

APRIL 13 TH, 2021
Tuesday of the Second Week of Easter

1st Reading ACTS 4:32-37
The community of believers was of one heart and mind, and no one claimed that any of his possessions was his own, but they had everything in common.

With great power the Apostles bore witness to the resurrection of the Lord Jesus, and great favor was accorded them all. There was no needy person among them, for those who owned property or houses would sell them, bring the proceeds of the sale, and put them at the feet of the Apostles, and they were distributed to each according to need.

Thus Joseph, also named by the Apostles Barnabas (which is translated A son of encouragement"), a Levite, a Cypriot by birth, sold a piece of property that he owned, then brought the money and put it at the feet of the Apostles.

Responsorial Psalm PS 93:1AB, 1CD-2, 5
R.(1a) The Lord is king; he is robed in majesty.

or:

R. Alleluia.

The LORD is king, in splendor robed; robed is the LORD and girt about with strength.

R... The Lord is king; he is robed in majesty.

or:

R. Alleluia.

And he has made the world firm, not to be moved. Your throne stands firm from of old; from everlasting you are, O LORD.

R... The Lord is king; he is robed in majesty.

or:

R. Alleluia.

Your decrees are worthy of trust indeed: holiness befits your house, O LORD, for length of days.

R... The Lord is king; he is robed in majesty.

or:

R. Alleluia.

Alleluia JN 3:14-15

R. Alleluia, alleluia.

The Son of Man must be lifted up, so that everyone who believes in him may have eternal life.

R. Alleluia, alleluia.

Gospel JN 3:7B-15
Jesus said to Nicodemus: "'You must be born from above.'

The wind blows where it wills, and you can hear the sound it makes, but you do not know where it comes from or where it goes; so it is with everyone who is born of the Spirit." Nicodemus answered and said to him,

'How can this happen?" Jesus answered and said to him, "You are the teacher of Israel and you do not understand this? Amen, amen, I say to you, we speak of what we know and we testify to what we have seen, but you people do not accept our testimony. If I tell you about earthly things and you do not believe, how will you believe if I tell you about heavenly things? No one has gone up to heaven except the one who has come down from heaven, the Son of Man.

And just as Moses lifted up the serpent in the desert, so must the Son of Man be lifted up, so that everyone who believes in him may have eternal life."

APRIL 14TH, 2021
Wednesday of the Second Week of Easter

1ST Reading ACTS 5:17-26
The high priest rose up and all his companions, that is, the party of the Sadducees, and, filled with jealousy, laid hands upon the Apostles and put them in the public jail. But during the night, the angel of the Lord opened the doors of the prison, led them out, and said, "Go and take your place in the temple area, and tell the people everything about this life."

When they heard this, they went to the temple early in the morning and taught.

When the high priest and his companions arrived, they convened the Sanhedrin, the full senate of the children of Israel, and sent to the jail to have them brought in. But the court officers who went did not find them in the prison, so they came back and reported, "We found the jail securely locked and the guards stationed outside the doors, but when we opened them, we found no one inside."

When the captain of the temple guard and the chief priests heard this report, they were at a loss about them, as to what this would come to. Then someone came in and reported to them, "The men whom you put in prison are in the temple area and are teaching the people." Then the captain and the court officers went and brought them, but without force, because they were afraid of being stoned by the people.

Responsorial Psalm PS 34:2-3, 4-5, 6-7, 8-9
R...(7a) The Lord hears the cry of the poor.

or:

R. Alleluia.

I will bless the LORD at all times; his praise shall be ever in my mouth. Let my soul glory in the LORD; the lowly will hear me and be glad.

R...The Lord hears the cry of the poor.

or:

R. Alleluia.

Glorify the LORD with me, let us together extol his name. I sought the LORD, and he answered me and delivered me from all my fears.

R... The Lord hears the cry of the poor.

or:

R. Alleluia.

Look to him that you may be radiant with joy, and your faces may not blush with shame. When the poor one called out, the LORD heard, and from all his distress he saved him.

R... The Lord hears the cry of the poor.

or:

R. Alleluia.

The angel of the LORD encamps around those who fear him, and delivers them. Taste and see how good the LORD is; blessed the man who takes refuge in him.

R... The Lord hears the cry of the poor.

or:

R. Alleluia.

Alleluia JN 3:16

R. Alleluia, alleluia.

God so love the world that he gave his only-begotten Son, so that everyone who believes in him might have eternal life.

R. Alleluia, alleluia.

Gospel JN 3:16-21
God so loved the world that he gave his only begotten Son, so that everyone who believes in him might not perish but might have eternal life. For God did not send his Son into the world to condemn the world, but that the world might be saved through him.

Whoever believes in him will not be condemned, but whoever does not believe has already been condemned, because he has not believed in the name of the only-begotten Son of God. And this is the verdict, that the light came into the world, but people preferred darkness to light, because their works were evil.

For everyone who does wicked things hates the light and does not come toward the light, so that his works might not be exposed. But whoever lives the truth comes to the light, so that his works may be clearly seen as done in God.

APRIL 15TH, 2021
Thursday of the Second Week of Easter

1ST Reading ACTS 5:27-33
When the court officers had brought the Apostles in and made them stand before the Sanhedrin, the high priest questioned them, "We gave you strict orders did we not, to stop teaching in that name. Yet you have filled Jerusalem with your teaching and want to bring this man's blood upon us." But Peter and the Apostles said in reply, "We must obey God rather than men.

The God of our ancestors raised Jesus, though you had him killed by hanging him on a tree.

God exalted him at his right hand as leader and savior to grant Israel repentance and forgiveness of sins.

We are witnesses of these things, as is the Holy Spirit whom God has given to those who obey him. "When they heard this, they became infuriated and wanted to put them to death.

R...(7a) The Lord hears the cry of the poor.

or:

R. Alleluia.

I will bless the LORD at all times; his praise shall be ever in my mouth. Taste and see how good the LORD is; blessed the man who takes refuge in him.

R... The Lord hears the cry of the poor.

or:

R. Alleluia.

The LORD confronts the evildoers, to destroy remembrance of them from the earth. When the just cry out, the LORD hears them, and from all their distress he rescues them.

R... The Lord hears the cry of the poor.

or:

R. Alleluia.

The LORD is close to the brokenhearted; and those who are crushed in spirit he saves. Many are the troubles of the just man, but out of them all the LORD delivers him.

R... The Lord hears the cry of the poor.

or:

R. Alleluia.

Alleluia JN 20:29

R. Alleluia, alleluia.

You believe in me, Thomas, because you have seen me, says the Lord; blessed are those who have not seen, but still believe!

R. Alleluia, alleluia.

The one who comes from above is above all.

The one who is of the earth is earthly and speaks of earthly things. But the one who comes from heaven is above all. He testifies to what he has seen and heard, but no one accepts his testimony.

Whoever does accept his testimony certifies that God is trustworthy. For the one whom God sent speaks the words of God. He does not ration his gift of the Spirit.

The Father loves the Son and has given everything over to him. Whoever believes in the Son has eternal life, but whoever disobeys the Son will not see life, but the wrath of God remains upon him.

APRIL 16TH, 2021

Feast of Saints Philip and James, Apostles

1ST Reading Acts 5:34-42

A Pharisee in the Sanhedrin named Gamaliel, a teacher of the law, respected by all the people, stood up, ordered the Apostles to be put outside for a short time, and said to the Sanhedrin, "Fellow children of Israel, be careful what you are about to do to these men.

Some time ago, Theudas appeared, claiming to be someone important, and about four hundred men joined him, but he was killed, and all those who were loyal to him were disbanded and came to nothing.

After him came Judas the Galilean at the time of the census.

He also drew people after him, but he too perished and all who were loyal to him were scattered.

So now I tell you, have nothing to do with these men, and let them go.

For if this endeavor or this activity is of human origin, it will destroy itself.

But if it comes from God, you will not be able to destroy them; you may even find yourselves fighting against God."

They were persuaded by him.

After recalling the Apostles, they had them flogged, ordered them to stop speaking in the name of Jesus, and dismissed them.

So they left the presence of the Sanhedrin, rejoicing that they had been found worthy to suffer dishonor for the sake of the name.

And all day long, both at the temple and in their homes, they did not stop teaching and proclaiming the Christ, Jesus.

Responsorial Psalm PS 27:1, 4, 13-14
R (see 4abc) One thing I seek: to dwell in the house of the Lord.

or:

R. Alleluia.

The LORD is my light and my salvation; whom should I fear?

The LORD is my life's refuge; of whom should I be afraid?

R. One thing I seek: to dwell in the house of the Lord.

or:

R. Alleluia.

One thing I ask of the LORD this I seek:

To dwell in the house of the LORD all the days of my life,

That I may gaze on the loveliness of the LORD and contemplate his temple.

R. One thing I seek: to dwell in the house of the Lord.

or:

R.   Alleluia.

I believe that I shall see the bounty of the LORD in the land of the living.

Wait for the LORD with courage; be stouthearted, and wait for the LORD.

R. One thing I seek: to dwell in the house of the Lord.

or:

R. Alleluia.

Alleluia   Mt 4:4b

R. Alleluia, alleluia.

One does not live on bread alone, but on every word that comes forth from the mouth of God.

R. Alleluia, alleluia.

Gospel Jn 6:1-15

Jesus went across the Sea of Galilee.

A large crowd followed him, because they saw the signs he was performing on the sick.

Jesus went up on the mountain, and there he sat down with his disciples. The Jewish feast of Passover was near.

When Jesus raised his eyes and saw that a large crowd was coming to him, he said to Philip, "Where can we buy enough food for them to eat?"

He said this to test him, because he himself knew what he was going to do.

Philip answered him,

"Two hundred days' wages worth of food would not be enough for each of them to have a little."

One of his disciples, Andrew, the brother of Simon Peter, said to him,

"There is a boy here who has five barley loaves and two fish; but what good are these for so many?"

Jesus said, "Have the people recline." Now there was a great deal of grass in that place.

So the men reclined, about five thousand in number.

Then Jesus took the loaves, gave thanks, and distributed them to those who were reclining, and also as much of the fish as they wanted.

When they had had their fill, he said to his disciples, "Gather the fragments left over, so that nothing will be wasted."

So they collected them, and filled twelve wicker baskets with fragments from the five barley loaves that had been more than they could eat.

When the people saw the sign he had done, they said,

"This is truly the Prophet, the one who is to come into the world."

Since Jesus knew that they were going to come and carry him off to make him king, he withdrew again to the mountain alone.

APRIL 17TH, 2021
Saturday of the Second Week of Easter

1ST Reading   ACTS 6:1-7
As the number of disciples continued to grow, the Hellenists complained against the Hebrews because their widows were being neglected in the daily distribution. So the Twelve called together the community of the disciples and said, "It is not right for us to neglect the word of God to serve at table.

Brothers, select from among you seven reputable men, filled with the Spirit and wisdom, whom we shall appoint to this task, whereas we shall devote ourselves to prayer and to the ministry of the word."

The proposal was acceptable to the whole community, so they chose Stephen, a man filled with faith and the Holy Spirit, also Philip, Prochorus, Nicanor, Timon, Parmenas, and Nicholas of Antioch, a convert to Judaism. They presented these men to the Apostles who prayed and laid hands on them. The word of God continued to spread, and the number of the disciples in Jerusalem increased greatly; even a large group of priests were becoming obedient to the faith.

Responsorial Psalm   PS 33:1-2, 4-5, 18-19
R.(22) Lord, let your mercy be on us, as we place our trust in you.

or:

R. Alleluia.

Exult, you just, in the LORD; praise from the upright is fitting. Give thanks to the LORD on the harp; with the ten-stringed lyre chant his praises.

R. Lord, let your mercy be on us, as we place our trust in you.

or:

R. Alleluia.

Upright is the word of the LORD, and all his works are trustworthy. He loves justice and right; of the kindness of the LORD the earth is full.

R. Lord, let your mercy be on us, as we place our trust in you.

or:

R. Alleluia.

See, the eyes of the LORD are upon those who fear him, upon those who hope for his kindness, To deliver them from death and preserve them in spite of famine.

R. Lord, let your mercy be on us, as we place our trust in you.

or:

R. Alleluia.

Alleluia

R. Alleluia, alleluia.

Christ is risen, who made all things; he has shown mercy on all people.

R. Alleluia, alleluia.

Gospel JN 6:16-21
When it was evening, the disciples of Jesus went down to the sea, embarked in a boat, and went across the sea to Capernaum. It had already grown dark, and Jesus had not yet come to them.

The sea was stirred up because a strong wind was blowing.

When they had rowed about three or four miles, they saw Jesus walking on the sea and coming near the boat, and they began to be afraid. But he said to them, "It is I. Do not be afraid." They wanted to take him into the boat, but the boat immediately arrived at the shore to which they were heading.

APRIL 18TH, 2021
Third Sunday of Easter

1ST Reading Acts 3:13-15, 17-19
Peter said to the people:

"The God of Abraham, the God of Isaac, and the God of Jacob, the God of our fathers, has glorified his servant Jesus, whom you handed over and denied in Pilate's presence when he had decided to release him.

You denied the Holy and Righteous One and asked that a murderer be released to you.

The author of life you put to death, but God raised him from the dead; of this we are witnesses.

Now I know, brothers, that you acted out of ignorance, just as your leaders did; but God has thus brought to fulfillment what he had announced beforehand through the mouth of all the prophets, that his Christ would suffer.

Repent, therefore, and be converted, that your sins may be wiped away."

Responsorial Psalm PS 4:2, 4, 7-8, 9
R. (7a) Lord, let your face shine on us.

or:

R. Alleluia.

When I call, answer me, O my just God, you who relieve me when I am in distress; have pity on me, and hear my prayer!

R. Lord, let your face shine on us.

or:

R. Alleluia.

Know that the LORD does wonders for his faithful one; the LORD will hear me when I call upon him.

R. Lord, let your face shine on us.

or:

R. Alleluia.

O LORD, let the light of your countenance shine upon us! You put gladness into my heart.

R. Lord, let your face shine on us.

or:

R. Alleluia.

As soon as I lie down, I fall peacefully asleep, for you alone, O LORD, bring security to my dwelling.

R. Lord, let your face shine on us.

or:

R. Alleluia

2ND Reading 1 Jn 2:1-5a

My children, I am writing this to you so that you may not commit sin.

But if anyone does sin, we have an Advocate with the Father,

Jesus Christ the righteous one.

He is expiation for our sins and not for our sins only but for those of the whole world.

The way we may be sure that we know him is to keep his commandments.

Those who say, "I know him," but do not keep his commandments are liars, and the truth is not in them.

But whoever keeps his word, the love of God is truly perfected in him.

Alleluia Cf. Lk 24:32

R. Alleluia, alleluia.

Lord Jesus, open the Scriptures to us; make our hearts burn while you speak to us.

R. Alleluia, alleluia.

Gospel Lk 24:35-48

The two disciples recounted what had taken place on the way, and how Jesus was made known to them in the breaking of bread.

While they were still speaking about this, he stood in their midst and said to them,

"Peace be with you."

But they were startled and terrified and thought that they were seeing a ghost.

Then he said to them, "Why are you troubled?

And why do questions arise in your hearts? Look at my hands and my feet, that it is I myself.

Touch me and see, because a ghost does not have flesh and bones as you can see I have." And as he said this, he showed them his hands and his feet.

While they were still incredulous for joy and were amazed, he asked them, "Have you anything here to eat?"

They gave him a piece of baked fish; he took it and ate it in front of them.

He said to them,

"These are my words that I spoke to you while I was still with you, that everything written about me in the law of Moses and in the prophets and psalms must be fulfilled."

Then he opened their minds to understand the Scriptures. And he said to them,

"Thus it is written that the Christ would suffer and rise from the dead on the third day and that repentance, for the forgiveness of sins, would be preached in his name to all the nations, beginning from Jerusalem.

245

You are witnesses of these things."

APRIL 19TH, 2021
Monday of the Third Week of Easter

1ST Reading ACTS 6:8-15

Stephen, filled with grace and power, was working great wonders and signs among the people. Certain members of the so-called Synagogue of Freedmen, Cyreneans, and Alexandrians, and people from Cilicia and Asia, came forward and debated with Stephen, but they could not withstand the wisdom and the Spirit with which he spoke. Then they instigated some men to say, "We have heard him speaking blasphemous words against Moses and God."

They stirred up the people, the elders, and the scribes, accosted him, seized him, and brought him before the Sanhedrin. They presented false witnesses who testified, "This man never stops saying things against this holy place and the law. For we have heard him claim that this Jesus the Nazorean will destroy this place and change the customs that Moses handed down to us."

All those who sat in the Sanhedrin looked intently at him and saw that his face was like the face of an angel.

Responsorial Psalm   PS 119:23-24, 26-27, 29-30

R...(1ab) Blessed are they who follow the law of the Lord!

or:

R. Alleluia.

Though princes meet and talk against me, your servant meditates on your statutes. Yes, your decrees are my delight; they are my counselors.

R. Blessed are they who follow the law of the Lord!

or:

R. Alleluia.

I declared my ways, and you answered me; teach me your statutes. Make me understand the way of your precepts, and I will meditate on your wondrous deeds.

R. Blessed are they who follow the law of the Lord!

or:

R. Alleluia.

Remove from me the way of falsehood, and favor me with your law. The way of truth I have chosen; I have set your ordinances before me.

R. Blessed are they who follow the law of the Lord!

or:

R. Alleluia.

Alleluia MT 4:4B

R. Alleluia, alleluia.

One does not live on bread alone but on every word that comes forth from the mouth of God.

R. Alleluia, alleluia.

Gospel JN 6:22-29

[After Jesus had fed the five thousand men, his disciples saw him walking on the sea.]

The next day, the crowd that remained across the sea saw that there had been only one boat there, and that Jesus had not gone along with his disciples in the boat, but only his disciples had left. Other boats came from Tiberias near the place where they had eaten the bread when the Lord gave thanks.

When the crowd saw that neither Jesus nor his disciples were there, they themselves got into boats and came to Capernaum looking for Jesus. And when they found him across the sea they said to him, "Rabbi, when did you get here?" Jesus answered them and said, "Amen, amen, I say to you, you are looking for me not because you saw signs but because you ate the loaves and were filled. Do not work for food that perishes but for the food that endures for eternal life, which the Son of Man will give you.

For on him the Father, God, has set his seal."

So they said to him, "What can we do to accomplish the works of God?" Jesus answered and said to them, "This is the work of God, that you believe in the one he sent."

APRIL 20TH, 2021
Tuesday of the Third Week of Easter

1ST Reading ACTS 7:51—8:1A
Stephen said to the people, the elders, and the scribes: "You stiff-necked people, uncircumcised in heart and ears, you always oppose the Holy Spirit; you are just like your ancestors. Which of the prophets did your ancestors not persecute?

They put to death those who foretold the coming of the righteous one, whose betrayers and murderers you have now become. You received the law as transmitted by angels, but you did not observe it."

When they heard this, they were infuriated, and they ground their teeth at him. But Stephen, filled with the Holy Spirit, looked up intently to heaven and saw the glory of God and Jesus standing at the right hand of God, and Stephen said, "Behold, I see the heavens opened and the Son of Man standing at the right hand of God." But they cried out in a loud voice, covered their ears, and rushed upon him together. They threw him out of the city, and began to stone him. The witnesses laid down their cloaks at the feet of a young man named Saul. As they were stoning Stephen, he called out, "Lord Jesus, receive my spirit."

Then he fell to his knees and cried out in a loud voice, "Lord, do not hold this sin against them"; and when he said this, he fell asleep. Now Saul was consenting to his execution.

Responsorial Psalm PS 31:3CD-4, 6 AND 7B AND 8A, 17 AND 21AB
R.. (6a) Into your hands, O Lord, I commend my spirit.

or:

R. Alleluia.

Be my rock of refuge, a stronghold to give me safety. You are my rock and my fortress; for your name's sake you will lead and guide me.

R. Into your hands, O Lord, I commend my spirit.

or:

R. Alleluia.

Into your hands I commend my spirit; you will redeem me, O LORD, O faithful God. My trust is in the LORD; I will rejoice and be glad of your mercy.

R. Into your hands, O Lord, I commend my spirit.

or:

R. Alleluia.

Let your face shine upon your servant; save me in your kindness. You hide them in the shelter of your presence from the plottings of men.

R. Into your hands, O Lord, I commend my spirit.

or:

R. Alleluia.

Alleluia   JN 6:35AB

R. Alleluia, alleluia.

I am the bread of life, says the Lord; whoever comes to me will never hunger.

R. Alleluia, alleluia.

Gospel JN 6:30-35
The crowd said to Jesus:

"What sign can you do, that we may see and believe in you? What can you do? Our ancestors ate manna in the desert, as it is written:

He gave them bread from heaven to eat." So Jesus said to them, "Amen, amen, I say to you, it was not Moses who gave the bread from heaven; my Father gives you the true bread from heaven. For the bread of God is that which comes down from heaven and gives life to the world."

So they said to Jesus, "Sir, give us this bread always."

Jesus said to them, "I am the bread of life; whoever comes to me will never hunger, and whoever believes in me will never thirst."

APRIL 21ST, 2021
Wednesday of the Third Week of Easter

1ST Reading   ACTS 8:1B-8

There broke out a severe persecution of the Church in Jerusalem, and all were scattered throughout the countryside of Judea and Samaria, except the Apostles. Devout men buried Stephen and made a loud lament over him.

Saul, meanwhile, was trying to destroy the Church; entering house after house and dragging out men and women, he handed them over for imprisonment.

Now those who had been scattered went about preaching the word. Thus Philip went down to the city of Samaria and proclaimed the Christ to them.

With one accord, the crowds paid attention to what was said by Philip when they heard it and saw the signs he was doing. For unclean spirits, crying out in a loud voice, came out of many possessed people, and many paralyzed and crippled people were cured. There was great joy in that city.

Responsorial Psalm   PS 66:1-3A, 4-5, 6-7A
R... (1) Let all the earth cry out to God with joy.

or:

R. Alleluia.

Shout joyfully to God, all the earth, sing praise to the glory of his name; proclaim his glorious praise. Say to God, "How tremendous are your deeds!"

R... Let all the earth cry out to God with joy.

or:

R. Alleluia.

"Let all on earth worship and sing praise to you, sing praise to your name!" Come and see the works of God, his tremendous deeds among the children of Adam.

R. Let all the earth cry out to God with joy.

or:

R. Alleluia.

He has changed the sea into dry land; through the river they passed on foot; therefore let us rejoice in him.

He rules by his might forever.

R. Let all the earth cry out to God with joy.

or:

R. Alleluia.

Alleluia See JN 6:40

R. Alleluia, alleluia.

Everyone who believes in the Son has eternal life, and I shall raise him up on the last day, says the Lord.

R. Alleluia, alleluia.

Gospel JN 6:35-40
Jesus said to the crowds,

"I am the bread of life; whoever comes to me will never hunger, and whoever believes in me will never thirst. But I told you that although you have seen me, you do not believe. Everything that the Father gives me will come to me, and I will not reject anyone who comes to me, because I came down from heaven not to do my own will but the will of the one who sent me. And this is the will of the one who sent me, that I should not lose anything of what he gave me, but that I should raise it on the last day. For this is the will of my Father, that everyone who sees the Son and believes in him may have eternal life, and I shall raise him on the last day."

APRIL 22ND,2021
Thursday of the Third Week of Easter

1ST Reading ACTS 8:26-40

The angel of the Lord spoke to Philip, "Get up and head south on the road that goes down from Jerusalem to Gaza, the desert route." So he got up and set out. Now there was an Ethiopian eunuch, a court official of the Candace, that is, the queen of the Ethiopians, in charge of her entire treasury, who had come to Jerusalem to worship, and was returning home. Seated in his chariot, he was reading the prophet Isaiah.

The Spirit said to Philip, "Go and join up with that chariot." Philip ran up and heard him reading Isaiah the prophet and said, "Do you understand what you are reading?" He replied, "How can I, unless someone instructs me?" So he invited Philip to get in and sit with him. This was the Scripture passage he was reading:

Like a sheep he was led to the slaughter, and as a lamb before its shearer is silent, so he opened not his mouth. In his humiliation justice was denied him.

Who will tell of his posterity? For his life is taken from the earth.

Then the eunuch said to Philip in reply, "I beg you, about whom is the prophet saying this? About himself, or about someone else?" Then Philip opened his mouth and, beginning with this Scripture passage, he proclaimed Jesus to him. As they traveled along the road they came to some water, and the eunuch said, "Look, there is water.

What is to prevent my being baptized?" Then he ordered the chariot to stop, and Philip and the eunuch both went down into the water, and he baptized him. When they came out of the water, the Spirit of the Lord snatched Philip away, and the eunuch saw him no more, but continued on his way rejoicing. Philip came to Azotus, and went about proclaiming the good news to all the towns until he reached Caesarea.

Responsorial Psalm PS 66:8-9, 16-17, 20

R...(1) Let all the earth cry out to God with joy.

or:

R. Alleluia.

Bless our God, you peoples, loudly sound his praise; He has given life to our souls, and has not let our feet slip.

R. Let all the earth cry out to God with joy.

or:

R. Alleluia.

Hear now, all you who fear God, while I declare what he has done for me. When I appealed to him in words, praise was on the tip of my tongue.

R. Let all the earth cry out to God with joy.

or:

R. Alleluia.

Blessed be God who refused me not my prayer or his kindness!

R. Let all the earth cry out to God with joy.

or:

R. Alleluia.

Alleluia JN 6:51

R. Alleluia, alleluia.

I am the living bread that came down from heaven, says the Lord; whoever eats this bread will live forever.

R. Alleluia, alleluia.

Gospel JN 6:44-51
Jesus said to the crowds:

"No one can come to me unless the Father who sent me draw him, and I will raise him on the last day. It is written in the prophets:

They shall all be taught by God.

Everyone who listens to my Father and learns from him comes to me. Not that anyone has seen the Father except the one who is from God; he has seen the Father. Amen, amen, I say to you, whoever believes has eternal life. I am the bread of life.

Your ancestors ate the manna in the desert, but they died; this is the bread that comes down from heaven so that one may eat it and not die.

I am the living bread that came down from heaven; whoever eats this bread will live forever; and the bread that I will give is my Flesh for the life of the world."

APRIL 23RD, 2021
Friday of the Third Week of Easter

1ST Reading   ACTS 9:1-20

Saul, still breathing murderous threats against the disciples of the Lord, went to the high priest and asked him for letters to the synagogues in Damascus, that, if he should find any men or women who belonged to the Way, he might bring them back to Jerusalem in chains.

On his journey, as he was nearing Damascus, a light from the sky suddenly flashed around him. He fell to the ground and heard a voice saying to him, "Saul, Saul, why are you persecuting me?" He said, "Who are you, sir?" The reply came, "I am Jesus, whom you are persecuting. Now get up and go into the city and you will be told what you must do." The men who were traveling with him stood speechless, for they heard the voice but could see no one. Saul got up from the ground, but when he opened his eyes he could see nothing; so they led him by the hand and brought him to Damascus. For three days he was unable to see, and he neither ate nor drank.

There was a disciple in Damascus named Ananias, and the Lord said to him in a vision, "Ananias." He answered, "Here I am, Lord." The Lord said to him, "Get up and go to the street called Straight and ask at the house of Judas for a man from Tarsus named Saul. He is there praying, and in a vision he has seen a man named Ananias come in and lay his hands on him, that he may regain his sight." But Ananias replied, "Lord, I have heard from many sources about this man, what evil things he has done to your holy ones in Jerusalem.

And here he has authority from the chief priests to imprison all who call upon your name." But the Lord said to him, "Go, for this man is a chosen instrument of mine to carry my name before Gentiles, kings, and children of Israel, and I will show him what he will have to suffer for my name."

So Ananias went and entered the house; laying his hands on him, he said, "Saul, my brother, the Lord has sent me, Jesus who appeared to you on the way by which you came, that you may regain your sight and be filled with the

Holy Spirit." Immediately things like scales fell from his eyes and he regained his sight.

He got up and was baptized, and when he had eaten, he recovered his strength. He stayed some days with the disciples in Damascus, and he began at once to proclaim Jesus in the synagogues, that he is the Son of God.

Responsorial Psalm   PS 117:1BC, 2
R... (Mark 16:15) Go out to all the world and tell the Good News.

or:

R. Alleluia.

Praise the LORD, all you nations; glorify him, all you peoples!

R... Go out to all the world and tell the Good News.

or:

R. Alleluia.

For steadfast is his kindness toward us, and the fidelity of the LORD endures forever.

R. Go out to all the world and tell the Good News.

or:

R. Alleluia.

Alleluia   JN 6:56

R. Alleluia, alleluia.

Whoever eats my Flesh and drinks my Blood, remains in me and I in him, says the Lord.

R. Alleluia, alleluia.

Gospel   JN 6:52-59
The Jews quarreled among themselves, saying, "How can this man give us his Flesh to eat?" Jesus said to them, "Amen, amen, I say to you, unless you eat the Flesh of the Son of Man and drink his Blood, you do not have life

within you. Whoever eats my Flesh and drinks my Blood has eternal life, and I will raise him on the last day. For my Flesh is true food, and my Blood is true drink.

Whoever eats my Flesh and drinks my Blood remains in me and I in him. Just as the living Father sent me and I have life because of the Father, so also the one who feeds on me will have life because of me. This is the bread that came down from heaven. Unlike your ancestors who ate and still died, whoever eats this bread will live forever." These things he said while teaching in the synagogue in Capernaum.

APRIL 24TH, 2021
Saturday of the Third Week of Easter

1ST Reading ACTS 9:31-42

The Church throughout all Judea, Galilee, and Samaria was at peace. She was being built up and walked in the fear of the Lord, and with the consolation of the Holy Spirit she grew in numbers.

As Peter was passing through every region, he went down to the holy ones living in Lydda. There he found a man named Aeneas, who had been confined to bed for eight years, for he was paralyzed.

Peter said to him, "Aeneas, Jesus Christ heals you. Get up and make your bed." He got up at once. And all the inhabitants of Lydda and Sharon saw him, and they turned to the Lord. Now in Joppa there was a disciple named Tabitha (which translated is Dorcas). She was completely occupied with good deeds and almsgiving. Now during those days she fell sick and died, so after washing her, they laid her out in a room upstairs. Since Lydda was near Joppa, the disciples, hearing that Peter was there, sent two men to him with the request, "Please come to us without delay."

So Peter got up and went with them. When he arrived, they took him to the room upstairs where all the widows came to him weeping and showing him the tunics and cloaks that Dorcas had made while she was with them. Peter sent them all out and knelt down and prayed. Then he turned to her body and said, "Tabitha, rise up." She opened her eyes, saw Peter, and sat up. He gave her his hand and raised her up, and when he had called the holy ones and the widows, he presented her alive. This became known all over Joppa, and many came to believe in the Lord.

R...(12) How shall I make a return to the Lord for all the good he has done for me?

or:

R. Alleluia.

How shall I make a return to the LORD for all the good he has done for me? The cup of salvation I will take up, and I will call upon the name of the LORD

R. How shall I make a return to the Lord for all the good he has done for me?

or:

R. Alleluia.

My vows to the LORD I will pay in the presence of all his people. Precious in the eyes of the LORD is the death of his faithful ones.

R. How shall I make a return to the Lord for all the good he has done for me?

or:

R. Alleluia.

O LORD, I am your servant;

I am your servant, the son of your handmaid; you have loosed my bonds. To you will I offer sacrifice of thanksgiving, and I will call upon the name of the LORD.

R. How shall I make a return to the Lord for all the good he has done for me?

or:

R. Alleluia.

Alleluia See JN 6:63C, 68C

R. Alleluia, alleluia.

Your words, Lord, are Spirit and life; you have the words of everlasting life.

R. Alleluia, alleluia.

Gospel JN 6:60-69

Many of the disciples of Jesus who were listening said, "This saying is hard; who can accept it?" Since Jesus knew that his disciples were murmuring about this, he said to them, "Does this shock you? What if you were to see the Son of Man ascending to where he was before? It is the Spirit that gives life, while the flesh is of no avail.

The words I have spoken to you are Spirit and life. But there are some of you who do not believe." Jesus knew from the beginning the ones who would not believe and the one who would betray him. And he said, "For this reason I have told you that no one can come to me unless it is granted him by my Father."

As a result of this, many of his disciples returned to their former way of life and no longer walked with him. Jesus then said to the Twelve, "Do you also want to leave?" Simon Peter answered him, "Master, to whom shall we go? You have the words of eternal life. We have come to believe and are convinced that you are the Holy One of God."

APRIL 25TH, 2021
Fourth Sunday of Easter

1ST Reading Acts 4:8-12

Peter, filled with the Holy Spirit, said:

"Leaders of the people and elders:

If we are being examined today about a good deed done to a cripple, namely, by what means he was saved, then all of you and all the people of Israel should know that it was in the name of Jesus Christ the Nazorean whom you crucified, whom God raised from the dead; in his name this man stands before you healed.

He is the stone rejected by you, the builders, which has become the cornerstone.

There is no salvation through anyone else, nor is there any other name under heaven given to the human race by which we are to be saved."

Responsorial Psalm   PS 118:1, 8-9, 21-23, 26, 28, 29

R.. (22) The stone rejected by the builders has become the cornerstone.

or:

R. Alleluia.

Give thanks to the LORD, for he is good, for his mercy endures forever.

It is better to take refuge in the LORD than to trust in man.

It is better to take refuge in the LORD than to trust in princes.

R. The stone rejected by the builders has become the cornerstone.

or:

R. Alleluia.

I will give thanks to you, for you have answered me and have been my savior.

The stone which the builders rejected has become the cornerstone.

By the LORD has this been done; it is wonderful in our eyes.

R. The stone rejected by the builders has become the cornerstone.

or:

R. Alleluia.

Blessed is he who comes in the name of the LORD; we bless you from the house of the LORD.

I will give thanks to you, for you have answered me and have been my savior.

Give thanks to the LORD, for he is good; for his kindness endures forever.

R. The stone rejected by the builders has become the cornerstone.

or:

R. Alleluia.

2ND Reading 1 Jn 3:1-2
Beloved:

See what love the Father has bestowed on us that we may be called the children of God.

Yet so we are. The reason the world does not know us is that it did not know him.

Beloved, we are God's children now; what we shall be has not yet been revealed.

We do know that when it is revealed we shall be like him, for we shall see him as he is.

Alleluia   JN 10:14

R. Alleluia, alleluia.

I am the good shepherd, says the Lord; I know my sheep, and mine know me.

R. Alleluia, alleluia.

Gospel Jn 10:11-18
Jesus said:

"I am the good shepherd.

A good shepherd lays down his life for the sheep.

A hired man, who is not a shepherd and whose sheep are not his own, sees a wolf coming and leaves the sheep and runs away, and the wolf catches and scatters them.

This is because he works for pay and has no concern for the sheep. I am the good shepherd, and I know mine and mine know me, just as the Father knows me and I know the Father; and I will lay down my life for the sheep.

I have other sheep that do not belong to this fold.

These also I must lead, and they will hear my voice, and there will be one flock, one shepherd.

This is why the Father loves me, because I lay down my life in order to take it up again. No one takes it from me, but I lay it down on my own.

I have power to lay it down, and power to take it up again.

This command I have received from my Father."

APRIL 26TH, 2021
Monday of the Fourth Week of Easter

1ST Reading ACTS 11:1-18

The Apostles and the brothers who were in Judea heard that the Gentiles too had accepted the word of God. So when Peter went up to Jerusalem the circumcised believers confronted him, saying, 'You entered the house of uncircumcised people and ate with them." Peter began and explained it to them step by step, saying, "I was at prayer in the city of Joppa when in a trance I had a vision, something resembling a large sheet coming down, lowered from the sky by its four corners, and it came to me. Looking intently into it, I observed and saw the four-legged animals of the earth, the wild beasts, the reptiles, and the birds of the sky. I also heard a voice say to me, 'Get up, Peter. Slaughter and eat.' But I said, 'Certainly not, sir, because nothing profane or unclean has ever entered my mouth.' But a second time a voice from heaven answered, 'What God has made clean, you are not to call profane.'

This happened three times, and then everything was drawn up again into the sky. Just then three men appeared at the house where we were, who had been sent to me from Caesarea. The Spirit told me to accompany them without discriminating. These six brothers also went with me, and we entered the man's house.

He related to us how he had seen the angel standing in his house, saying, 'Send someone to Joppa and summon Simon, who is called Peter, who will speak words to you by which you and all your household will be saved.'

As I began to speak, the Holy Spirit fell upon them as it had upon us at the beginning, and I remembered the word of the Lord, how he had said, 'John baptized with water but you will be baptized with the Holy Spirit.' If then

261

God gave them the same gift he gave to us when we came to believe in the Lord Jesus Christ, who was I to be able to hinder God?" When they heard this, they stopped objecting and glorified God, saying, "God has then granted life-giving repentance to the Gentiles too."

Responsorial Psalm PS 42:2-3; 43:3, 4
R....(see 3a) Athirst is my soul for the living God.

or:

R. Alleluia.

As the hind longs for the running waters, so my soul longs for you, O God. Athirst is my soul for God, the living God. When shall I go and behold the face of God?

R. Athirst is my soul for the living God.

or:

R. Alleluia.

Send forth your light and your fidelity; they shall lead me on And bring me to your holy mountain, to your dwelling-place.

R. Athirst is my soul for the living God.

or:

R. Alleluia.

Then will I go in to the altar of God, the God of my gladness and joy; Then will I give you thanks upon the harp, O God, my God!

R. Athirst is my soul for the living God.

or:

R. Alleluia.

Alleluia JN 10:14

R. Alleluia, alleluia.

I am the good shepherd, says the Lord; I know my sheep, and mine know me.

R. Alleluia, alleluia.

Gospel JN 10:1-10
Jesus said:

"Amen, amen, I say to you, whoever does not enter a sheepfold through the gate but climbs over elsewhere is a thief and a robber.

But whoever enters through the gate is the shepherd of the sheep. The gatekeeper opens it for him, and the sheep hear his voice, as he calls his own sheep by name and leads them out. When he has driven out all his own, he walks ahead of them, and the sheep follow him, because they recognize his voice. But they will not follow a stranger; they will run away from him, because they do not recognize the voice of strangers." Although Jesus used this figure of speech, they did not realize what he was trying to tell them.

So Jesus said again, "Amen, amen, I say to you, I am the gate for the sheep. All who came before me are thieves and robbers, but the sheep did not listen to them. I am the gate. Whoever enters through me will be saved, and will come in and go out and find pasture. A thief comes only to steal and slaughter and destroy; I came so that they might have life and have it more abundantly."

APRIL 27TH, 2021
Tuesday of the Fourth Week of Easter

1ST Reading Acts 11:19-26
Those who had been scattered by the persecution that arose because of Stephen went as far as Phoenicia, Cyprus, and Antioch, preaching the word to no one but Jews.

There were some Cypriots and Cyrenians among them, however, who came to Antioch and began to speak to the Greeks as well, proclaiming the Lord Jesus.

The hand of the Lord was with them and a great number who believed turned to the Lord.

The news about them reached the ears of the Church in Jerusalem, and they sent Barnabas to go to Antioch.

When he arrived and saw the grace of God, he rejoiced and encouraged them all to remain faithful to the Lord in firmness of heart, for he was a good man, filled with the Holy Spirit and faith.

And a large number of people was added to the Lord.

Then he went to Tarsus to look for Saul, and when he had found him he brought him to Antioch.

For a whole year they met with the Church and taught a large number of people, and it was in Antioch that the disciples were first called Christians..

Responsorial Psalm PS 87:1b-3, 4-5, 6-7
R... (117:1a) All you nations, praise the Lord.

or:

R. Alleluia.

His foundation upon the holy mountains the LORD loves:

The gates of Zion, more than any dwelling of Jacob.

Glorious things are said of you, O city of God!

R.   All you nations, praise the Lord.

or:

R. Alleluia.

I tell of Egypt and Babylon among those who know the LORD;

Of Philistia, Tyre, Ethiopia: "This man was born there."

And of Zion they shall say: "One and all were born in her;

And he who has established her is the Most High LORD."

R. All you nations, praise the Lord.

or:

R. Alleluia.

They shall note, when the peoples are enrolled: "This man was born there."

And all shall sing, in their festive dance: "My home is within you."

R. All you nations, praise the Lord.

Alleluia Jn 10:27

R. Alleluia, alleluia.

My sheep hear my voice, says the Lord; I know them, and they follow me.

R. Alleluia, alleluia.

Gospel JN 15:9-17
Jesus said to his disciples:

"As the Father loves me, so I also love you. Remain in my love. If you keep my commandments, you will remain in my love, just as I have kept my Father's commandments and remain in his love.

"I have told you this so that my joy might be in you and your joy might be complete. This is my commandment: love one another as I love you.

No one has greater love than this, to lay down one's life for one's friends. You are my friends if you do what I command you. I no longer call you slaves, because a slave does not know what his master is doing. I have called you friends, because I have told you everything I have heard from my Father.

It was not you who chose me, but I who chose you and appointed you to go and bear fruit that will remain, so that whatever you ask the Father in my name he may give you. This I command you: love one another."

APRIL 28TH, 2021
Wednesday of the Fourth Week of Easter

1ST Reading ACTS 12:24—13:5A
The word of God continued to spread and grow.

After Barnabas and Saul completed their relief mission, they returned to Jerusalem, taking with them John, who is called Mark.

Now there were in the Church at Antioch prophets and teachers: Barnabas, Symeon who was called Niger, Lucius of Cyrene, Manaen who was a close friend of Herod the tetrarch, and Saul. While they were worshiping the Lord and fasting, the Holy Spirit said, "Set apart for me Barnabas and Saul for the work to which I have called them." Then, completing their fasting and prayer, they laid hands on them and sent them off.

So they, sent forth by the Holy Spirit, went down to Seleucia and from there sailed to Cyprus. When they arrived in Salamis, they proclaimed the word of God in the Jewish synagogues.

Responsorial Psalm   PS 67:2-3, 5, 6 AND 8
R...(4) O God, let all the nations praise you!

or:

R. Alleluia.

May God have pity on us and bless us; may he let his face shine upon us. So may your way be known upon earth; among all nations, your salvation.

R. O God, let all the nations praise you!

or:

R. Alleluia.

May the nations be glad and exult because you rule the peoples in equity; the nations on the earth you guide.

R. O God, let all the nations praise you!

or:

R. Alleluia.

May the peoples praise you, O God; may all the peoples praise you! May God bless us, and may all the ends of the earth fear him!

R... O God let all the nations praise you!

or:

R. Alleluia.

Alleluia JN 8:12

R. Alleluia, alleluia.

I am the light of the world, says the Lord; whoever follows me will have the light of life.

R. Alleluia, alleluia.

Gospel JN 12:44-50

Jesus cried out and said, "Whoever believes in me believes not only in me but also in the one who sent me, and whoever sees me sees the one who sent me.

I came into the world as light, so that everyone who believes in me might not remain in darkness.

And if anyone hears my words and does not observe them, I do not condemn him, for I did not come to condemn the world but to save the world.

Whoever rejects me and does not accept my words has something to judge him: the word that I spoke, it will condemn him on the last day, because I did not speak on my own, but the Father who sent me commanded me what to say and speak. And I know that his commandment is eternal life. So what I say, I say as the Father told me."

APRIL 29TH, 2021
Memorial of Saint Catherine of Siena, Virgin and Doctor of the Church

1ST Reading ACTS 13:13-25

From Paphos, Paul and his companions set sail and arrived at Perga in Pamphylia. But John left them and returned to Jerusalem. They continued on from Perga and reached Antioch in Pisidia. On the sabbath they entered into the synagogue and took their seats. After the reading of the law and the prophets, the synagogue officials sent word to them, "My brothers, if one of you has a word of exhortation for the people, please speak."

So Paul got up, motioned with his hand, and said, "Fellow children of Israel and you others who are God-fearing, listen. The God of this people Israel chose our ancestors and exalted the people during their sojourn in the land of Egypt. With uplifted arm he led them out, and for about forty years he put up with them in the desert. When he had destroyed seven nations in the land of Canaan, he gave them their land as an inheritance at the end of about four hundred and fifty years. After these things he provided judges up to Samuel the prophet.

Then they asked for a king. God gave them Saul, son of Kish, a man from the tribe of Benjamin, for forty years. Then he removed him and raised up David as their king; of him he testified, I have found David, son of Jesse, a man after my own heart; he will carry out my every wish.

From this man's descendants God, according to his promise, has brought to Israel a savior, Jesus.

John heralded his coming by proclaiming a baptism of repentance to all the people of Israel; and as John was completing his course, he would say, 'What do you suppose that I am? I am not he. Behold, one is coming after me; I am not worthy to unfasten the sandals of his feet.'"

Responsorial Psalm PS 89:2-3, 21-22, 25 AND 27
R...(2) For ever I will sing the goodness of the Lord.

or:

R. Alleluia.

The favors of the LORD I will sing forever; through all generations my mouth shall proclaim your faithfulness. For you have said, "My kindness is established forever"; in heaven you have confirmed your faithfulness.

R. For ever I will sing the goodness of the Lord.

or:

R. Alleluia.

"I have found David, my servant; with my holy oil I have anointed him, That my hand may be always with him, and that my arm may make him strong."

R. For ever I will sing the goodness of the Lord.

or:

R. Alleluia.

"My faithfulness and my mercy shall be with him, and through my name shall his horn be exalted. He shall say of me, 'You are my father, my God, the Rock, my savior.'"

R. For ever I will sing the goodness of the Lord.

or:

R. Alleluia.

Alleluia SEE RV 1:5AB

R. Alleluia, alleluia.

Jesus Christ, you are the faithful witness, the firstborn of the dead, you have loved us and freed us from our sins by your Blood.

R. Alleluia, alleluia

Gospel JN 13:16-20
When Jesus had washed the disciples' feet, he said to them: "Amen, amen, I say to you, no slave is greater than his master nor any messenger greater than the one who sent him. If you understand this, blessed are you if you do it.

I am not speaking of all of you. I know those whom I have chosen. But so that the Scripture might be fulfilled, The one who ate my food has raised his heel against me. From now on I am telling you before it happen, so that when it happens you may believe that I AM.

Amen, amen, I say to you, whoever receives the one I send receives me, and whoever receives me receives the one who sent me.

APRIL 30TH, 2021
Friday of the Fourth Week of Easter

1ST Reading   ACTS 13:26-33
When Paul came to Antioch in Pisidia, he said in the synagogue: "My brothers, children of the family of Abraham, and those others among you who are God-fearing, to us this word of salvation has been sent.

The inhabitants of Jerusalem and their leaders failed to recognize him, and by condemning him they fulfilled the oracles of the prophets that are read sabbath after sabbath.

For even though they found no grounds for a death sentence, they asked Pilate to have him put to death, and when they had accomplished all that was written about him, they took him down from the tree and placed him in a tomb. But God raised him from the dead, and for many days he appeared to those who had come up with him from Galilee to Jerusalem.

These are now his witnesses before the people. We ourselves are proclaiming this good news to you that what God promised our fathers he has brought to fulfillment for us, their children, by raising up Jesus, as it is written in the second psalm, You are my Son; this day I have begotten you."

Responsorial Psalm PS 2:6-7, 8-9, 10-11AB
R.. .(7bc) You are my Son; this day I have begotten you.

or:

R. Alleluia.

"I myself have set up my king on Zion, my holy mountain." I will proclaim the decree of the LORD: The LORD said to me, "You are my Son; this day I have begotten you."

R. You are my Son; this day I have begotten you.

or:

R. Alleluia.

"Ask of me and I will give you the nations for an inheritance and the ends of the earth for your possession. You shall rule them with an iron rod; you shall shatter them like an earthen dish."

R. You are my Son; this day I have begotten you.

or:

R. Alleluia.

And now, O kings, give heed; take warning, you rulers of the earth. Serve the LORD with fear, and rejoice before him; with trembling rejoice.

R. You are my Son; this day I have begotten you.

or:

R. Alleluia.

Alleluia JN 14:6

R. Alleluia, alleluia.

I am the way and the truth and the life, says the Lord; no one comes to the Father except through me.

R. Alleluia, alleluia.

Gospel JN 14:1-6
Jesus said to his disciples:

"Do not let your hearts be troubled. You have faith in God; have faith also in me. In my Father's house there are many dwelling places. If there were not, would I have told you that I am going to prepare a place for you? And if I go and prepare a place for you,

I will come back again and take you to myself, so that where I am you also may be. Where I am going you know the way." Thomas said to him, "Master, we do not know where you are going; how can we know the way?" Jesus said to him, "I am the way and the truth and the life. No one comes to the Father except through me."

MAY 1ST, 2021
Saturday of the Fourth Week of Easter

1ST Reading ACTS 13:44-52
On the following Sabbath almost the whole city gathered to hear the word of the Lord. When the Jews saw the crowds, they were filled with jealousy and with violent abuse contradicted what Paul said. Both Paul and Barnabas spoke out boldly and said, "It was necessary that the word of God be spoken to you first, but since you reject it and condemn yourselves as unworthy of eternal life, we now turn to the Gentiles.

For so the Lord has commanded us, I have made you a light to the Gentiles, that you may be an instrument of salvation to the ends of the earth." The

Gentiles were delighted when they heard this and glorified the word of the Lord. All who were destined for eternal life came to believe, and the word of the Lord continued to spread through the whole region.

The Jews, however, incited the women of prominence who were worshipers and the leading men of the city, stirred up a persecution against Paul and Barnabas, and expelled them from their territory. So they shook the dust from their feet in protest against them and went to Iconium. The disciples were filled with joy and the Holy Spirit.

Responsorial Psalm PS 98:1, 2-3AB, 3CD-4
R.... (3cd) All the ends of the earth have seen the saving power of God.

or:

R. Alleluia.

Sing to the LORD a new song, for he has done wondrous deeds; His right hand has won victory for him, his holy arm.

R. All the ends of the earth have seen the saving power of God.

or:

R. Alleluia.

The LORD has made his salvation known: in the sight of the nations he has revealed his justice. He has remembered his kindness and his faithfulness toward the house of Israel.

R. All the ends of the earth have seen the saving power of God.

or:

R. Alleluia.

All the ends of the earth have seen the salvation by our God. Sing joyfully to the LORD, all you lands; break into song; sing praise.

R. All the ends of the earth have seen the saving power of God.

or:

R. Alleluia.

Alleluia JN 8:31B-32

R. Alleluia, alleluia.

If you remain in my word, you will truly be my disciples, and you will know the truth, says the Lord.

R. Alleluia, alleluia.

Jesus said to his disciples:

"If you know me, then you will also know my Father. From now on you do know him and have seen him." Philip said to Jesus, "Master, show us the Father, and that will be enough for us." Jesus said to him, "Have I been with you for so long a time and you still do not know me, Philip?

Whoever has seen me has seen the Father.

How can you say, 'Show us the Father'? Do you not believe that I am in the Father and the Father is in me? The words that I speak to you I do not speak on my own. The Father who dwells in me is doing his works. Believe me that I am in the Father and the Father is in me, or else, believe because of the works themselves.

Amen, amen, I say to you, whoever believes in me will do the works that I do, and will do greater ones than these, because I am going to the Father. And whatever you ask in my name, I will do, so that the Father may be glorified in the Son. If you ask anything of me in my name, I will do it."

MAY 2ND, 2021
Fifth Sunday of Easter

1ST Reading Acts 9:26-31
When Saul arrived in Jerusalem he tried to join the disciples, but they were all afraid of him, not believing that he was a disciple.

Then Barnabas took charge of him and brought him to the apostles, and he reported to them how he had seen the Lord, and that he had spoken to him, and how in Damascus he had spoken out boldly in the name of Jesus.

He moved about freely with them in Jerusalem, and spoke out boldly in the name of the Lord.

He also spoke and debated with the Hellenists, but they tried to kill him.

And when the brothers learned of this, they took him down to Caesarea and sent him on his way to Tarsus.

The church throughout all Judea, Galilee, and Samaria was at peace.

It was being built up and walked in the fear of the Lord, and with the consolation of the Holy Spirit it grew in numbers.

Responsorial Psalm PS 22:26-27, 28, 30, 31-32
R. (26a) I will praise you, Lord, in the assembly of your people.

or:

R. Alleluia.

I will fulfill my vows before those who fear the LORD. The lowly shall eat their fill; they who seek the LORD shall praise him: "May your hearts live forever!"

R. I will praise you, Lord, in the assembly of your people.

or:

R. Alleluia.

All the ends of the earth shall remember and turn to the LORD; all the families of the nations shall bow down before him.

R. I will praise you, Lord, in the assembly of your people.

or:

R. Alleluia.

To him alone shall bow down all who sleep in the earth; before him shall bend all who go down into the dust.

R. I will praise you, Lord, in the assembly of your people.

or:

R. Alleluia.

And to him my soul shall live; my descendants shall serve him.

Let the coming generation be told of the LORD that they may proclaim to a people yet to be born the justice he has shown.

R. I will praise you, Lord, in the assembly of your people.

or:

R. Alleluia.

2ND Reading 1 Jn 3:18-24

Children, let us love not in word or speech but indeed and truth.

Now this is how we shall know that we belong to the truth and reassure our hearts before him in whatever our hearts condemn, for God is greater than our hearts and knows everything.

Beloved, if our hearts do not condemn us, we have confidence in God and receive from him whatever we ask, because we keep his commandments and do what pleases him.

And his commandment is this: we should believe in the name of his Son, Jesus Christ, and love one another just as he commanded us.

Those who keep his commandments remain in him, and he in them, and the way we know that he remains in us is from the Spirit he gave us.

Alleluia Jn 15:4a, 5b

R. Alleluia, alleluia.

Remain in me as I remain in you, says the Lord. Whoever remains in me will bear much fruit..

R. Alleluia, alleluia.

Gospel Jn 15:1-8

Jesus said to his disciples:

"I am the true vine, and my Father is the vine grower.

He takes away every branch in me that does not bear fruit, and every one that does he prunes so that it bears more fruit.

You are already pruned because of the word that I spoke to you. Remain in me, as I remain in you.

Just as a branch cannot bear fruit on its own unless it remains on the vine, so neither can you unless you remain in me.

I am the vine, you are the branches.

Whoever remains in me and I in him will bear much fruit, because without me you can do nothing.

Anyone who does not remain in me will be thrown out like a branch and wither; people will gather them and throw them into a fire and they will be burned.

If you remain in me and my words remain in you, ask for whatever you want and it will be done for you.

By this is my Father glorified, that you bear much fruit and become my disciples.".".

MAY 3RD, 2021
Feast of Saints Philip and James, Apostles

1ST Reading 1 Cor 15:1-8
I am reminding you, brothers and sisters, of the Gospel I preached to you, which you indeed received and in which you also stand.

Through it you are also being saved, if you hold fast to the word I preached to you, unless you believed in vain.

For I handed on to you as of first importance what I also received: that Christ died for our sins in accordance with the Scriptures; that he was buried; that he was raised on the third day in accordance with the Scriptures; that he appeared to Cephas, then to the Twelve.

After that, he appeared to more than five hundred brothers and sisters at once, most of whom are still living, though some have fallen asleep.

After that he appeared to James, then to all the Apostles.

Last of all, as to one born abnormally, he appeared to me.

Responsorial Psalm PS 19:2-3, 4-5
R (5) Their message goes out through all the earth.

or:

R. Alleluia.

The heavens declare the glory of God; and the firmament proclaims his handiwork.

Day pours out the word to day; and night to night imparts knowledge.

R. Their message goes out through all the earth.

or:

R. Alleluia.

Not a word nor a discourse whose voice is not heard;

Through all the earth their voice resounds, and to the ends of the world, their message.

R. Their message goes out through all the earth.

or:

R. Alleluia.

Alleluia Jn 14:6b, 9c

R. Alleluia, alleluia.

I am the way, the truth, and the life, says the Lord; Philip, whoever has seen me has seen the Father..

R. Alleluia, alleluia.

Gospel Jn 14:6-14
Jesus said to Thomas, "I am the way and the truth and the life. No one comes to the Father except through me. If you know me, then you will also

know my Father. From now on you do know him and have seen him." Philip said to him,

"Master, show us the Father, and that will be enough for us. "Jesus said to him, "Have I been with you for so long a time and you still do not know me, Philip?

Whoever has seen me has seen the Father. How can you say, 'Show us the Father'? Do you not believe that I am in the Father and the Father is in me? The words that I speak to you I do not speak on my own.

The Father who dwells in me is doing his works.

Believe me that I am in the Father and the Father is in me, or else, believe because of the works themselves.

Amen, amen, I say to you, whoever believes in me will do the works that I do, and will do greater ones than these, because I am going to the Father.

And whatever you ask in my name, I will do, so that the Father may be glorified in the Son. If you ask anything of me in my name, I will do it."

MAY 4TH, 2021
Tuesday of Fifth Week of Easter

1ST Reading ACTS 14:19-28

In those days, some Jews from Antioch and Iconium arrived and won over the crowds. They stoned Paul and dragged him out of the city, supposing that he was dead. But when the disciples gathered around him, he got up and entered the city. On the following day he left with Barnabas for Derbe.

After they had proclaimed the good news to that city and made a considerable number of disciples, they returned to Lystra and to Iconium and to Antioch.

They strengthened the spirits of the disciples and exhorted them to persevere in the faith, saying, "It is necessary for us to undergo many hardships to enter the Kingdom of God." They appointed presbyters for them in each Church and, with prayer and fasting, commended them to the Lord in whom they had put their faith. Then they traveled through Pisidia and reached Pamphylia.

After proclaiming the word at Perga they went down to Attalia. From there they sailed to Antioch, where they had been commended to the grace of God for the work they had now accomplished.

And when they arrived, they called the Church together and reported what God had done with them and how he had opened the door of faith to the Gentiles. Then they spent no little time with the disciples.

Responsorial Psalm PS 145:10-11, 12-13AB, 21
R... (See 12) Your friends make known, O Lord, the glorious splendor of your kingdom.

or:

R. Alleluia.

Let all your works give you thanks, O LORD, and let your faithful ones bless you. Let them discourse of the glory of your kingdom and speak of your might.

R. Your friends make known, O Lord, the glorious splendor of your kingdom.

or:

R. Alleluia.

Making known to men your might and the glorious splendor of your kingdom. Your kingdom is a kingdom for all ages, and your dominion endures through all generations.

R. Your friends make known, O Lord, the glorious splendor of your kingdom.

or:

R. Alleluia.

May my mouth speak the praise of the LORD, and may all flesh bless his holy name forever and ever.

R. Your friends make known, O Lord, the glorious splendor of your kingdom.

or:

R. Alleluia.

Alleluia. SEE LK 24:46, 26

R. Alleluia, alleluia.

Christ had to suffer and to rise from the dead, and so enter into his glory.

R. Alleluia, alleluia.

Gospel   JN 14:27-31A
Jesus said to his disciples:

"Peace I leave with you; my peace I give to you.

Not as the world gives do I give it to you. Do not let your hearts be troubled or afraid. You heard me tell you, 'I am going away and I will come back to you.'

If you loved me, you would rejoice that I am going to the Father; for the Father is greater than I. And now I have told you this before it happens, so that when it happens you may believe. I will no longer speak much with you, for the ruler of the world is coming. He has no power over me, but the world must know that I love the Father and that I do just as the Father has commanded me."

MAY 5TH, 2021
Wednesday of the Fifth Week of Easter

1ST Reading ACTS 15:1-6
Some who had come down from Judea were instructing the brothers, "Unless you are circumcised according to the Mosaic practice, you cannot be saved." Because there arose no little dissension and debate by Paul and Barnabas with them, it was decided that Paul, Barnabas, and some of the others should go up to Jerusalem to the Apostles and presbyters about this question. They were sent on their journey by the Church, and passed through Phoenicia and Samaria telling of the conversion of the Gentiles, and brought great joy to all the brethren.

When they arrived in Jerusalem, they were welcomed by the Church, as well as by the Apostles and the presbyters, and they reported what God had done with them. But some from the party of the Pharisees who had become believers stood up and said, "It is necessary to circumcise them and direct them to observe the Mosaic law."

The Apostles and the presbyters met together to see about this matter.

Responsorial Psalm   PS 122:1-2, 3-4AB, 4CD-5
R... (see 1) Let us go rejoicing to the house of the Lord.

or:

R. Alleluia.

I rejoiced because they said to me, "We will go up to the house of the LORD." And now we have set foot within your gates, O Jerusalem.

R. Let us go rejoicing to the house of the Lord.

or:

R. Alleluia.

Jerusalem, built as a city with compact unity. To it the tribes go up, the tribes of the LORD.

R. Let us go rejoicing to the house of the Lord.

or:

R. Alleluia.

According to the decree for Israel, to give thanks to the name of the LORD. In it are set up judgment seats, seats for the house of David.

R. Let us go rejoicing to the house of the Lord.

or:

R. Alleluia.

Alleluia   JN 15:4A, 5B

R. Alleluia, alleluia.

Remain in me, as I remain in you, says the Lord; whoever remains in me will bear much fruit.

R. Alleluia, alleluia.

Gospel JN 15:1-8
Jesus said to his disciples:

"I am the true vine, and my Father is the vine grower. He takes away every branch in me that does not bear fruit, and everyone that does he prunes so that it bears more fruit. You are already pruned because of the word that I spoke to you. Remain in me, as I remain in you. Just as a branch cannot bear fruit on its own unless it remains on the vine, so neither can you unless you remain in me. I am the vine, you are the branches.

Whoever remains in me and I in him will bear much fruit, because without me you can do nothing. Anyone who does not remain in me will be thrown out like a branch and wither; people will gather them and throw them into a fire and they will be burned. If you remain in me and my words remain in you, ask for whatever you want and it will be done for you. By this is my Father glorified, that you bear much fruit and become my disciples."

MAY 6TH, 2021
Thursday of the Fifth Week of Easter

1ST Reading ACTS 15:7-21
After much debate had taken place, Peter got up and said to the Apostles and the presbyters, "My brothers, you are well aware that from early days

God made his choice among you that through my mouth the Gentiles would hear the word of the Gospel and believe. And God, who knows the heart, bore witness by granting them the Holy Spirit just as he did us.

He made no distinction between us and them, for by faith he purified their hearts. Why, then, are you now putting God to the test by placing on the shoulders of the disciples a yoke that neither our ancestors nor we have been able to bear? On the contrary, we believe that we are saved through the grace of the Lord Jesus, in the same way as they."

The whole assembly fell silent, and they listened while Paul and Barnabas described the signs and wonders God had worked among the Gentiles through them.

After they had fallen silent, James responded, "My brothers, listen to me. Symeon has described how God first concerned himself with acquiring from among the Gentiles a people for his name. The words of the prophets agree with this, as is written:

After this I shall return and rebuild the fallen hut of David; from its ruins I shall rebuild it and raise it up again, so that the rest of humanity may seek out the Lord, even all the Gentiles on whom my name is invoked. Thus says the Lord who accomplishes these things, known from of old.

It is my judgment, therefore, that we ought to stop troubling the Gentiles who turn to God, but tell them by letter to avoid pollution from idols, unlawful marriage, the meat of strangled animals, and blood. For Moses, for generations now, has had those who proclaim him in every town, as he has been read in the synagogues every sabbath."

Responsorial Psalm   PS 96:1-2A, 2B-3, 10
R.. (3) Proclaim God's marvelous deeds to all the nations.

or:

R. Alleluia.

Sing to the LORD a new song; sing to the LORD, all you lands. Sing to the LORD; bless his name.

R.. Proclaim God's marvelous deeds to all the nations.

or:

R. Alleluia.

Announce his salvation, day after day. Tell his glory among the nations; among all peoples, his wondrous deeds.

R.. Proclaim God's marvelous deeds to all the nations.

or:

R. Alleluia.

Say among the nations: The LORD is king. He has made the world firm, not to be moved; he governs the peoples with equity.

R... Proclaim God's marvelous deeds to all the nations.

or:

R. Alleluia.

Alleluia JN 10:27

R. Alleluia, alleluia.

My sheep hear my voice, says the Lord; I know them, and they follow me.

R. Alleluia, alleluia.

Gospel JN 15:9-11
Jesus said to his disciples:

"As the Father loves me, so I also love you. Remain in my love. If you keep my commandments, you will remain in my love, just as I have kept my Father's commandments and remain in his love.

"I have told you this so that my joy might be in you and your joy might be complete."

MAY 7TH, 2021
Friday of the Fifth Week of Easter

1ST Reading ACTS 15:22-31
The Apostles and presbyters, in agreement with the whole Church, decided to choose representatives and to send them to Antioch with Paul and Barnabas. The ones chosen were Judas, who was called Barsabbas, and Silas, leaders among the brothers. This is the letter delivered by them: "The Apostles and the presbyters, your brothers, to the brothers in Antioch, Syria, and Cilicia of Gentile origin: greetings. Since we have heard that some of our number who went out without any mandate from us have upset you with their teachings and disturbed your peace of mind, we have with one accord decided to choose representatives and to send them to you along with our beloved Barnabas and Paul, who have dedicated their lives to the name of our Lord Jesus Christ.

So we are sending Judas and Silas who will also convey this same message by word of mouth:

'It is the decision of the Holy Spirit and of us not to place on you any burden beyond these necessities, namely, to abstain from meat sacrificed to idols, from blood, from meats of strangled animals, and from unlawful marriage. If you keep free of these, you will be doing what is right. Farewell.'" And so they were sent on their journey. Upon their arrival in Antioch they called the assembly together and delivered the letter. When the people read it, they were delighted with the exhortation.

Responsorial Psalm   PS 57:8-9, 10 AND 12
R. (10a) I will give you thanks among the peoples, O Lord.

or:

R. Alleluia.

My heart is steadfast, O God; my heart is steadfast; I will sing and chant praise. Awake, O my soul; awake, lyre and harp! I will wake the dawn.

R. I will give you thanks among the peoples, O Lord.

or:

R. Alleluia.

I will give thanks to you among the peoples, O LORD, I will chant your praise among the nations. For your mercy towers to the heavens, and your faithfulness to the skies. Be exalted above the heavens, O God; above all the earth be your glory!

R. I will give you thanks among the peoples, O Lord.

or:

R. Alleluia.

Alleluia   JN 15:15B

R. Alleluia, alleluia.

I call you my friends, says the Lord, for I have made known to you all that the Father has told me.

R. Alleluia, alleluia.

Gospel JN 15:12-17
Jesus said to his disciples:

"This is my commandment: love one another as I love you. No one has
greater love than this, to lay down one's life for one's friends. You are my
friends if you do what I command you. I no longer call you slaves, because a
slave does not know what his master is doing.

I have called you friends, because I have told you everything I have heard
from my Father. It was not you who chose me, but I who chose you and
appointed you to go and bear fruit that will remain, so that whatever you ask
the Father in my name he may give you. This I command you: love one
another."

MAY 8TH, 2021
Saturday of the Fifth Week of Easter

1ST Reading ACTS 16:1-10
Paul reached also Derbe and Lystra where there was a disciple named
Timothy, the son of a Jewish woman who was a believer, but his father was a
Greek.

The brothers in Lystra and Iconium spoke highly of him, and Paul wanted
him to come along with him.

On account of the Jews of that region, Paul had him circumcised, for they all
knew that his father was a Greek. As they traveled from city to city, they
handed on to the people for observance the decisions reached by the
Apostles and presbyters in Jerusalem. Day after day the churches grew
stronger in faith and increased in number.

They traveled through the Phrygian and Galatian territory because they had
been prevented by the Holy Spirit from preaching the message in the
province of Asia.

When they came to Mysia, they tried to go on into Bithynia, but the Spirit of
Jesus did not allow them, so they crossed through Mysia and came down to
Troas. During the night Paul had a vision. A Macedonian stood before him
and implored him with these words, "Come over to Macedonia and help us."

When he had seen the vision, we sought passage to Macedonia at once, concluding that God had called us to proclaim the Good News to them.

Responsorial Psalm   PS 100:1B-2, 3, 5
R. (2a) Let all the earth cry out to God with joy.

or:

R. Alleluia.

Sing joyfully to the LORD, all you lands; serve the LORD with gladness; come before him with joyful song.

R. Let all the earth cry out to God with joy.

or:

R. Alleluia.

Know that the LORD is God; he made us, his we are; his people, the flock he tends.

R. Let all the earth cry out to God with joy.

or:

R. Alleluia.

The LORD is good his kindness endures forever, and his faithfulness, to all generations.

R. Let all the earth cry out to God with joy.

or:

R. Alleluia.

Alleluia   COL 3:1

R. Alleluia, alleluia.

If then you were raised with Christ, seek what is above, where Christ is seated at the right hand of God.

R. Alleluia, alleluia.

Jesus said to his disciples:

"If the world hates you, realize that it hated me first. If you belonged to the world, the world would love its own; but because you do not belong to the world, and I have chosen you out of the world, the world hates you.

Remember the word I spoke to you, 'No slave is greater than his master.' If they persecuted me, they will also persecute you. If they kept my word, they will also keep yours. And they will do all these things to you on account of my name, because they do not know the one who sent me."

MAY 9TH, 2021
Sixth Sunday of Easter

1ST Reading Acts 10:25-26, 34-35, 44-48

When Peter entered, Cornelius met him and, falling at his feet, paid him homage. Peter, however, raised him up, saying,

"Get up. I myself am also a human being."

Then Peter proceeded to speak and said, "In truth, I see that God shows no partiality. Rather, in every nation whoever fears him and acts uprightly is acceptable to him."

While Peter was still speaking these things, the Holy Spirit fell upon all who were listening to the word.

The circumcised believers who had accompanied Peter were astounded that the gift of the Holy Spirit should have been poured out on the Gentiles also, for they could hear them speaking in tongues and glorifying God.

Then Peter responded,

"Can anyone withhold the water for baptizing these people, who have received the Holy Spirit even as we have?" He ordered them to be baptized in the name of Jesus Christ.

Responsorial Psalm PS 98:1, 2-3, 3-4

R. (cf. 2b) The Lord has revealed to the nations his saving power.

or:

R. Alleluia.

Sing to the LORD a new song, for he has done wondrous deeds;

His right hand has won victory for him, his holy arm.

R. The Lord has revealed to the nations his saving power.

or:

R. Alleluia.

The LORD has made his salvation known: in the sight of the nations he has revealed his justice.

He has remembered his kindness and his faithfulness toward the house of Israel.

R. The Lord has revealed to the nations his saving power.

or:

R. Alleluia.

All the ends of the earth have see the salvation by our God.

Sing joyfully to the LORD, all you lands; break into song; sing praise.

R. The Lord has revealed to the nations his saving power.

or:

R. Alleluia.

2ND Reading 1 Jn 4:7-10

Beloved, let us love one another, because love is of God; everyone who loves is begotten by God and knows God.

Whoever is without love does not know God, for God is love. In this way the love of God was revealed to us:

God sent his only Son into the world so that we might have life through him.

In this is love: not that we have loved God, but that he loved us and sent his Son as expiation for our sins..

Alleluia Jn 14:23

R. Alleluia, alleluia.

Whoever loves me will keep my word, says the Lord, and my Father will love him and we will come to him.

R. Alleluia, alleluia.

Gospel Jn 15:9-17
Jesus said to his disciples:

"As the Father loves me, so I also love you.

Remain in my love. If you keep my commandments, you will remain in my love, just as I have kept my Father's commandments and remain in his love.

"I have told you this so that my joy may be in you and your joy might be complete.

This is my commandment: love one another as I love you.

No one has greater love than this, to lay down one's life for one's friends. You are my friends if you do what I command you. I no longer call you slaves, because a slave does not know what his master is doing. I have called you friends, because I have told you everything I have heard from my Father.

It was not you who chose me, but I who chose you and appointed you to go and bear fruit that will remain, so that whatever you ask the Father in my name he may give you.

This I command you: love one another."

MAY 10TH, 2021
Monday of the Sixth Week of Easter

1ST Reading ACTS 16:11-15
We set sail from Troas, making a straight run for Samothrace, and on the next day to Neapolis, and from there to Philippi, a leading city in that district of Macedonia and a Roman colony. We spent some time in that city. On the sabbath we went outside the city gate along the river where we thought there would be a place of prayer.

We sat and spoke with the women who had gathered there. One of them, a woman named Lydia, a dealer in purple cloth, from the city of Thyatira, a worshiper of God, listened, and the Lord opened her heart to pay attention to what Paul was saying. After she and her household had been baptized, she offered us an invitation, "If you consider me a believer in the Lord, come and stay at my home," and she prevailed on us.

Responsorial Psalm   PS 149:1B-2, 3-4, 5-6A AND 9B
R. (see 4a) The Lord takes delight in his people.

or:

R. Alleluia.

Sing to the LORD a new song of praise in the assembly of the faithful. Let Israel be glad in their maker, let the children of Zion rejoice in their king.

R... The Lord takes delight in his people.

or:

R. Alleluia.

Let them praise his name in the festive dance, let them sing praise to him with timbrel and harp. For the LORD loves his people, and he adorns the lowly with victory.

R... The Lord takes delight in his people.

or:

R. Alleluia.

Let the faithful exult in glory; let them sing for joy upon their couches. Let the high praises of God be in their throats. This is the glory of all his faithful. Alleluia.

R... The Lord takes delight in his people.

or:

R. Alleluia.

Alleluia JN 15:26B, 27A

R. Alleluia, alleluia.

The Spirit of truth will testify to me, says the Lord, and you also will testify.

R. Alleluia, alleluia.

Gospel JN 15:26—16:4A
Jesus said to his disciples:

"When the Advocate comes whom I will send you from the Father, the Spirit of truth who proceeds from the Father, he will testify to me. And you also testify, because you have been with me from the beginning.

"I have told you this so that you may not fall away. They will expel you from the synagogues; in fact, the hour is coming when everyone who kills you will think he is offering worship to God. They will do this because they have not known either the Father or me. I have told you this so that when their hour comes you may remember that I told you."

MAY 11TH, 2021
Tuesday of the Sixth Week of Easter

1ST Reading ACTS 16:22-34
The crowd in Philippi joined in the attack on Paul and Silas, and the magistrates had them stripped and ordered them to be beaten with rods. After inflicting many blows on them, they threw them into prison and instructed the jailer to guard them securely. When he received these instructions, he put them in the innermost cell and secured their feet to a stake. About midnight, while Paul and Silas were praying and singing hymns to God as the prisoners listened, there was suddenly such a severe earthquake that the foundations of the jail shook; all the doors flew open, and the chains of all were pulled loose.

When the jailer woke up and saw the prison doors wide open, he drew his sword and was about to kill himself, thinking that the prisoners had escaped. But Paul shouted out in a loud voice, "Do no harm to yourself; we are all here."

He asked for a light and rushed in and, trembling with fear, he fell down before Paul and Silas. Then he brought them out and said, "Sirs, what must I do to be saved?" And they said, "Believe in the Lord Jesus and you and your household will be saved." So they spoke the word of the Lord to him and to everyone in his house. He took them in at that hour of the night and bathed their wounds; then he and all his family were baptized at once. He brought them up into his house and provided a meal and with his household rejoiced at having come to faith in God.

Responsorial Psalm PS 138:1-2AB, 2CDE-3, 7C-8
R. (7c) Your right hand saves me, O Lord.

or:

R. Alleluia.

I will give thanks to you, O LORD, with all my heart, for you have heard the words of my mouth; in the presence of the angels I will sing your praise; I will worship at your holy temple, and give thanks to your name.

R. Your right hand saves me, O Lord.

or:

R. Alleluia.

Because of your kindness and your truth, you have made great above all things your name and your promise. When I called, you answered me; you built up strength within me.

R. Your right hand saves me, O Lord.

or:

R. Alleluia.

Your right hand saves me. The LORD will complete what he has done for me; your kindness, O LORD, endures forever; forsake not the work of your hands.

R. Your right hand saves me, O Lord.

or:

R. Alleluia.

Alleluia SEE JN 16:7, 13

R. Alleluia, alleluia.

I will send to you the Spirit of truth, says the Lord; he will guide you to all truth.

R. Alleluia, alleluia.

Jesus said to his disciples:

"Now I am going to the one who sent me, and not one of you asks me, 'Where are you going?' But because I told you this, grief has filled your hearts.

But I tell you the truth, it is better for you that I go. For if I do not go, the Advocate will not come to you. But if I go, I will send him to you. And when he comes he will convict the world in regard to sin and righteousness and condemnation: sin, because they do not believe in me; righteousness, because I am going to the Father and you will no longer see me; condemnation, because the ruler of this world has been condemned."

MAY 12TH, 2021
Wednesday of the Sixth Week of Easter

1ST Reading ACTS 17:15, 22—18:1
After Paul's escorts had taken him to Athens, they came away with instructions for Silas and Timothy to join him as soon as possible.

Then Paul stood up at the Areopagus and said: "You Athenians, I see that in every respect you are very religious. For as I walked around looking carefully at your shrines, I even discovered an altar inscribed, 'To an Unknown God.' What therefore you unknowingly worship, I proclaim to you. The God who made the world and all that is in it, the Lord of heaven and earth, does not dwell in sanctuaries made by human hands, nor is he served by human hands because he needs anything.

Rather it is he who gives to everyone life and breath and everything. He made from one the whole human race to dwell on the entire surface of the earth, and he fixed the ordered seasons and the boundaries of their regions, so that people might seek God, even perhaps grope for him and find him, though indeed he is not far from any one of us. For 'In him we live and move and have our being,' as even some of your poets have said, 'For we too are his offspring.'

Since therefore we are the offspring of God, we ought not to think that the divinity is like an image fashioned from gold, silver, or stone by human art and imagination. God has overlooked the times of ignorance, but now he demands that all people everywhere repent because he has established a day on which he will 'judge the world with justice' through a man he has appointed, and he has provided confirmation for all by raising him from the dead."

When they heard about resurrection of the dead, some began to scoff, but others said, "We should like to hear you on this some other time." And so Paul left them. But some did join him, and became believers. Among them were Dionysius, a member of the Court of the Areopagus, a woman named Damaris, and others with them. After this he left Athens and went to Corinth.

Responsorial Psalm   PS 148:1-2, 11-12, 13, 14
R. Heaven and earth are full of your glory.

or:

R. Alleluia.

Praise the LORD from the heavens; praise him in the heights. Praise him, all you his angels; praise him, all you his hosts.

R. Heaven and earth are full of your glory.

or:

R. Alleluia.

Let the kings of the earth and all peoples, the princes and all the judges of the earth, Young men too, and maidens, old men and boys.

R. Heaven and earth are full of your glory.

or:

R. Alleluia.

Praise the name of the LORD, for his name alone is exalted; His majesty is above earth and heaven.

R. Heaven and earth are full of your glory.

or:

R. Alleluia.

He has lifted up the horn of his people; Be this his praise from all his faithful ones, from the children of Israel, the people close to him.

Alleluia.

R. Heaven and earth are full of your glory.

or:

R. Alleluia.

Alleluia JN 14:16

R. Alleluia, alleluia.

I will ask the Father and he will give you another Advocate to be with you always.

R. Alleluia, alleluia.

Gospel JN 16:12-15

Jesus said to his disciples:

"I have much more to tell you, but you cannot bear it now. But when he comes, the Spirit of truth, he will guide you to all truth. He will not speak on his own, but he will speak what he hears, and will declare to you the things that are coming.

He will glorify me, because he will take from what is mine and declare it to you.

Everything that the Father has is mine; for this reason I told you that he will take from what is mine and declare it to you."

1ST Reading Acts 18:1-8

Paul left Athens and went to Corinth.

There he met a Jew named Aquila, a native of Pontus, because Claudius had ordered all the Jews to leave Rome.

He went to visit them and, because he practiced the same trade, stayed with them and worked, for they were tentmakers by trade.

Every sabbath, he entered into discussions in the synagogue, attempting to convince both Jews and Greeks.

When Silas and Timothy came down from Macedonia, Paul began to occupy himself totally with preaching the word, testifying to the Jews that the Christ was Jesus.

When they opposed him and reviled him, he shook out his garments and said to them, "Your blood be on your heads!

I am clear of responsibility. From now on I will go to the Gentiles."

So he left there and went to a house belonging to a man named Titus Justus, a worshiper of God; his house was next to a synagogue. Crispus, the synagogue official, came to believe in the Lord along with his entire household, and many of the Corinthians who heard believed and were baptized.

Responsorial Psalm PS 98:1, 2-3ab, 3cd-4

R. (see 2b) The Lord has revealed to the nations his saving power.

or:

R. Alleluia.

Sing to the LORD a new song, for he has done wondrous deeds;

His right hand has won victory for him, his holy arm.

R. The Lord has revealed to the nations his saving power.

or:

R. Alleluia.

The LORD has made his salvation known: in the sight of the nations he has revealed his justice.

He has remembered his kindness and his faithfulness toward the house of Israel.

R. The Lord has revealed to the nations his saving power.

or:

R. Alleluia.

All the ends of the earth have seen the salvation by our God.

Sing joyfully to the LORD, all you lands; break into song; sing praise.

R. The Lord has revealed to the nations his saving power.

or:

R. Alleluia.

Alleluia Jn 14:18

R. Alleluia, alleluia.

I will not leave you orphans, says the Lord; I will come back to you, and your hearts will rejoice.

R. Alleluia, alleluia.

Gospel Jn 16:16-20
Jesus said to his disciples:

"A little while and you will no longer see me, and again a little while later and you will see me."

So some of his disciples said to one another, "What does this mean that he is saying to us, 'A little while and you will not see me, and again a little while and you will see me,' and 'Because I am going to the Father'?"

So they said, "What is this 'little while' of which he speaks? We do not know what he means." Jesus knew that they wanted to ask him, so he said to them,

"Are you discussing with one another what I said, 'A little while and you will not see me, and again a little while and you will see me'?

Amen, amen, I say to you, you will weep and mourn, while the world rejoices; you will grieve, but your grief will become joy.".

MAY 14Th, 2021
Feast of Saint Matthias, Apostle

1ST Reading Acts 1:15-17, 20-26
Peter stood up in the midst of the brothers and sisters (there was a group of about one hundred and twenty persons in the one place).

He said, "My brothers and sisters, the Scripture had to be fulfilled which the Holy Spirit spoke beforehand through the mouth of David, concerning Judas, who was the guide for those who arrested Jesus.

Judas was numbered among us and was allotted a share in this ministry.

For it is written in the Book of Psalms:

Let his encampment become desolate, and may no one dwell in it. and: May another take his office.

Therefore, it is necessary that one of the men who accompanied us the whole time the Lord Jesus came and went among us, beginning from the baptism of John until the day on which he was taken up from us, become with us a witness to his resurrection."

So they proposed two, Joseph called Barsabbas, who was also known as Justus, and Matthias.

Then they prayed, "You, Lord, who know the hearts of all, show which one of these two you have chosen to take the place in this apostolic ministry from which Judas turned away to go to his own place."

Then they gave lots to them, and the lot fell upon Matthias, and he was counted with the Eleven Apostles..

R (8) The Lord will give him a seat with the leaders of his people.

or:

R. Alleluia.

Praise, you servants of the LORD, praise the name of the LORD.

Blessed be the name of the LORD both now and forever.

R. The Lord will give him a seat with the leaders of his people.

or:

R. Alleluia.

From the rising to the setting of the sun is the name of the LORD to be praised.

High above all nations is the LORD; above the heavens is his glory.

R. The Lord will give him a seat with the leaders of his people.

or:

R. Alleluia.

Who is like the LORD, our God, who is enthroned on high and looks upon the heavens and the earth below?

R. The Lord will give him a seat with the leaders of his people.

or:

R. Alleluia.

He raises up the lowly from the dust; from the dunghill he lifts up the poor

To seat them with princes, with the princes of his own people.

R. The Lord will give him a seat with the leaders of his people.

or:

R. Alleluia..

Alleluia See Jn 15:16

R. Alleluia, alleluia.

I chose you from the world, to go and bear fruit that will last, says the Lord.

R. Alleluia, alleluia.

Gospel Jn 15:9-17
Jesus said to his disciples:

"As the Father loves me, so I also love you. Remain in my love.

If you keep my commandments, you will remain in my love, just as I have kept my Father's commandments and remain in his love.

"I have told you this so that my joy might be in you and your joy might be complete.

This is my commandment: love one another as I love you. No one has greater love than this, to lay down one's life for one's friends.

You are my friends if you do what I command you.

I no longer call you slaves, because a slave does not know what his master is doing.

I have called you friends, because I have told you everything I have heard from my Father.

It was not you who chose me, but I who chose you and appointed you to go and bear fruit that will remain, so that whatever you ask the Father in my name he may give you.

This I command you: love one another."

MAY 15TH, 2021
Saturday of the Sixth Week of Easter

301

After staying in Antioch some time, Paul left and traveled in orderly sequence through the Galatian country and Phrygia, bringing strength to all the disciples.

A Jew named Apollos, a native of Alexandria, an eloquent speaker, arrived in Ephesus. He was an authority on the Scriptures. He had been instructed in the Way of the Lord and, with ardent spirit, spoke and taught accurately about Jesus, although he knew only the baptism of John.

He began to speak boldly in the synagogue; but when Priscilla and Aquila heard him, they took him aside and explained to him the Way of God more accurately.

And when he wanted to cross to Achaia, the brothers encouraged him and wrote to the disciples there to welcome him. After his arrival he gave great assistance to those who had come to believe through grace. He vigorously refuted the Jews in public, establishing from the Scriptures that the Christ is Jesus.

Responsorial Psalm PS 47:2-3, 8-9, 10
R... (8a) God is king of all the earth.

or:

R. Alleluia.

All you peoples, clap your hands; shout to God with cries of gladness. For the LORD, the Most High, the awesome, is the great king over all the earth.

R. God is king of all the earth.

or:

R. Alleluia.

For king of all the earth is God; sing hymns of praise. God reigns over the nations, God sits upon his holy throne.

R. God is king of all the earth.

or:

R. Alleluia.

The princes of the peoples are gathered together with the people of the God of Abraham. For God's are the guardians of the earth; he is supreme.

R. God is king of all the earth.

or:

R. Alleluia.

Alleluia JN 16:28

R. Alleluia, alleluia.

I came from the Father and have come into the world;now I am leaving the world and going back to the Father.

R. Alleluia, alleluia.

Gospel JN 16:23B-28
Jesus said to his disciples:

"Amen, amen, I say to you, whatever you ask the Father in my name he will give you. Until now you have not asked anything in my name; ask and you will receive, so that your joy may be complete.

"I have told you this in figures of speech. The hour is coming when I will no longer speak to you in figures but I will tell you clearly about the Father. On that day you will ask in my name, and I do not tell you that I will ask the Father for you. For the Father himself loves you, because you have loved me and have come to believe that I came from God. I came from the Father and have come into the world. Now I am leaving the world and going back to the Father."

MAY 16TH, 2021
Seventh Sunday of Easter

1ST Reading Acts 1:15-17, 20a, 20c-26
Peter stood up in the midst of the brothers there was a group of about one hundred and twenty persons in the one place —.

He said, "My brothers, the Scripture had to be fulfilled which the Holy Spirit spoke beforehand through the mouth of David, concerning Judas, who was the guide for those who arrested Jesus.

He was numbered among us and was allotted a share in this ministry.

"For it is written in the Book of Psalms: May another take his office. "Therefore, it is necessary that one of the men who accompanied us the whole time the Lord Jesus came and went among us, beginning from the baptism of John until the day on which he was taken up from us, become with us a witness to his resurrection."

So they proposed two, Judas called Barsabbas, who was also known as Justus, and Matthias.

Then they prayed,

"You, Lord, who know the hearts of all, show which one of these two you have chosen to take the place in this apostolic ministry from which Judas turned away to go to his own place."

Then they gave lots to them, and the lot fell upon Matthias, and he was counted with the eleven apostles.

Responsorial Psalm PS 103:1-2, 11-12, 19-20
R.. (19a) The Lord has set his throne in heaven.

or:

R. Alleluia.

Bless the LORD, O my soul, and all my being, bless his holy name.

Bless the LORD, O my soul, and forget not all his benefits.

R. The Lord has set his throne in heaven.

or:

R. Alleluia.

For as the heavens are high above the earth, so surpassing is his kindness toward those who fear him.

As far as the east is from the west, so far has he put our transgressions from us.

R. The Lord has set his throne in heaven.

or:

R. Alleluia.

The LORD has established his throne in heaven, and his kingdom rules over all.

Bless the LORD, all you his angels, you mighty in strength, who do his bidding.

R. The Lord has set his throne in heaven.

or:

R. Alleluia.

2ND Reading 1 Jn 4:11-16
Beloved, if God so loved us, we also must love one another.

No one has ever seen God.

Yet, if we love one another, God remains in us, and his love is brought to perfection in us

This is how we know that we remain in him and he in us, that he has given us of his Spirit.

Moreover, we have seen and testify that the Father sent his Son as savior of the world.

Whoever acknowledges that Jesus is the Son of God, God remains in him and he in God.

We have come to know and to believe in the love God has for us. God is love, and whoever remains in love remains in God and God in him.

Alleluia   Cf. Jn 14:18

R. Alleluia, alleluia.

305

I will not leave you orphans, says the Lord. I will come back to you, and your hearts will rejoice..

R. Alleluia, alleluia.

Lifting up his eyes to heaven, Jesus prayed saying:

"Holy Father, keep them in your name that you have given me, so that they may be one just as we are one.

When I was with them I protected them in your name that you gave me, and I guarded them, and none of them was lost except the son of destruction, in order that the Scripture might be fulfilled.

But now I am coming to you.

I speak this in the world so that they may share my joy completely. I gave them your word, and the world hated them, because they do not belong to the world any more than I belong to the world.

I do not ask that you take them out of the world but that you keep them from the evil one.

They do not belong to the world any more than I belong to the world.

Consecrate them in the truth. Your word is truth.

As you sent me into the world, so I sent them into the world. And I consecrate myself for them, so that they also may be consecrated in truth."

MAY 17TH, 2021
Monday of the Seventh Week of Easter

1ST Reading   ACTS 19:1-8
While Apollos was in Corinth, Paul traveled through the interior of the country and down to Ephesus where he found some disciples.

He said to them, "Did you receive the Holy Spirit when you became believers?" They answered him, "We have never even heard that there is a Holy Spirit." He said, "How were you baptized?" They replied, "With the baptism of John."

306

Paul then said, "John baptized with a baptism of repentance, telling the people to believe in the one who was to come after him, that is, in Jesus." When they heard this, they were baptized in the name of the Lord Jesus.

And when Paul laid his hands on them, the Holy Spirit came upon them, and they spoke in tongues and prophesied. Altogether there were about twelve men. He entered the synagogue, and for three months debated boldly with persuasive arguments about the Kingdom of God.

Responsorial Psalm PS 68:2-3AB, 4-5ACD, 6-7AB
R. (33a) Sing to God, O kingdoms of the earth.

or:

R. Alleluia.

God arises; his enemies are scattered, and those who hate him flee before him. As smoke is driven away, so are they driven; as wax melts before the fire.

R. Sing to God, O kingdoms of the earth.

or:

R. Alleluia.

But the just rejoice and exult before God; they are glad and rejoice. Sing to God, chant praise to his name; whose name is the LORD.

R. Sing to God, O kingdoms of the earth.

or:

R. Alleluia.

The father of orphans and the defender of widows is God in his holy dwelling. God gives a home to the forsaken; he leads forth prisoners to prosperity.

R. Sing to God, O kingdoms of the earth.

or:

R. Alleluia.

R. Alleluia, alleluia.

If then you were raised with Christ, seek what is above, where Christ is seated at the right hand of God.

R. Alleluia, alleluia.

Gospel JN 16:29-33
The disciples said to Jesus,

"Now you are talking plainly, and not in any figure of speech.

Now we realize that you know everything and that you do not need to have anyone question you. Because of this we believe that you came from God."

Jesus answered them, "Do you believe now? Behold, the hour is coming and has arrived when each of you will be scattered to his own home and you will leave me alone. But I am not alone, because the Father is with me. I have told you this so that you might have peace in me. In the world you will have trouble, but take courage, I have conquered the world.

MAY 18TH, 2021
Tuesday of the Seventh Week of Easter

1ST Reading ACTS 20:17-27
From Miletus Paul had the presbyters of the Church at Ephesus summoned.

When they came to him, he addressed them, "You know how I lived among you the whole time from the day I first came to the province of Asia.

I served the Lord with all humility and with the tears and trials that came to me because of the plots of the Jews, and I did not at all shrink from telling you what was for your benefit, or from teaching you in public or in your homes.

I earnestly bore witness for both Jews and Greeks to repentance before God and to faith in our Lord Jesus. But now, compelled by the Spirit, I am going to Jerusalem. What will happen to me there I do not know, except that in one city after another the Holy Spirit has been warning me that imprisonment and hardships await me. Yet I consider life of no importance to me, if only I may finish my course and the ministry that I received from the Lord Jesus, to bear witness to the Gospel of God's grace.

"But now I know that none of you to whom I preached the kingdom during my travels will ever see my face again. And so I solemnly declare to you this day that I am not responsible for the blood of any of you, for I did not shrink from proclaiming to you the entire plan of God."

Responsorial Psalm PS 68:10-11, 20-21
R.. (33a) Sing to God, O kingdoms of the earth.

or:

R. Alleluia.

A bountiful rain you showered down, O God, upon your inheritance; you restored the land when it languished; Your flock settled in it; in your goodness, O God, you provided it for the needy.

R. Sing to God, O kingdoms of the earth.

or:

R. Alleluia.

Blessed day by day be the Lord, who bears our burdens; God, who is our salvation. God is a saving God for us; the LORD, my Lord, controls the passageways of death.

R. Sing to God, O kingdoms of the earth.

or:

R. Alleluia.

Alleluia JN 14:16

R. Alleluia, alleluia.

I will ask the father and he will give you another Advocate to be with you always.

R. Alleluia, alleluia.

Jesus raised his eyes to heaven and said,

"Father, the hour has come. Give glory to your son, so that your son may glorify you, just as you gave him authority over all people, so that your son may give eternal life to all you gave him. Now this is eternal life, that they should know you, the only true God, and the one whom you sent, Jesus Christ. I glorified you on earth by accomplishing the work that you gave me to do. Now glorify me, Father, with you, with the glory that I had with you before the world began.

"I revealed your name to those whom you gave me out of the world.

They belonged to you, and you gave them to me, and they have kept your word. Now they know that everything you gave me is from you, because the words you gave to me I have given to them, and they accepted them and truly understood that I came from you, and they have believed that you sent me.

I pray for them. I do not pray for the world but for the ones you have given me, because they are yours, and everything of mine is yours and everything of yours is mine, and I have been glorified in them. And now I will no longer be in the world, but they are in the world, while I am coming to you."

MAY 19TH, 2021
Wednesday of the Seventh Week of Easter

1ST Reading ACTS 20:28-38
At Miletus, Paul spoke to the presbyters of the Church of Ephesus:

"Keep watch over yourselves and over the whole flock of which the Holy Spirit has appointed you overseers, in which you tend the Church of God that he acquired with his own Blood. I know that after my departure savage wolves will come among you, and they will not spare the flock.

And from your own group, men will come forward perverting the truth to draw the disciples away after them. So be vigilant and remember that for three years, night and day, I unceasingly admonished each of you with tears.

And now I commend you to God and to that gracious word of his that can build you up and give you the inheritance among all who are consecrated. I have never wanted anyone's silver or gold or clothing. You know well that these very hands have served my needs and my companions. In every way I have shown you that by hard work of that sort we must help the weak, and keep in mind the words of the Lord Jesus who himself said, 'It is more blessed to give than to receive.'"

When he had finished speaking he knelt down and prayed with them all. They were all weeping loudly as they threw their arms around Paul and kissed him, for they were deeply distressed that he had said that they would never see his face again. Then they escorted him to the ship.

Responsorial Psalm   PS 68:29-30, 33-35A, 35BC-36AB
R...(33a) Sing to God, O kingdoms of the earth.

or:

R. Alleluia.

Show forth, O God, your power, the power, O God, with which you took our part; For your temple in Jerusalem let the kings bring you gifts.

R. Sing to God, O Kingdoms of the earth.

or:

R. Alleluia.

You kingdoms of the earth, sing to God, chant praise to the Lord who rides on the heights of the ancient heavens. Behold, his voice resounds, the voice of power: "Confess the power of God!"

R. Sing to God, O kingdoms of the earth.

or:

R. Alleluia.

Over Israel is his majesty; his power is in the skies. Awesome in his sanctuary is God, the God of Israel; he gives power and strength to his people.

R. Sing to God, O kingdoms of the earth.

or:

R. Alleluia.

Alleluia SEE JN 17:17B, 17A

R. Alleluia, alleluia.

Your word, O Lord, is truth; consecrate us in the truth.

R. Alleluia, alleluia.

Gospel JN 17:11B-19
Lifting up his eyes to heaven, Jesus prayed, saying:

"Holy Father, keep them in your name so that they may be one just as we are one.

When I was with them I protected them in your name that you gave me, and I guarded them, and none of them was lost except the son of destruction, in order that the Scripture might be fulfilled. But now I am coming to you.

I speak this in the world so that they may share my joy completely. I gave them your word, and the world hated them, because they do not belong to the world any more than I belong to the world. I do not ask that you take them out of the world but that you keep them from the Evil One. They do not belong to the world any more than I belong to the world. Consecrate them in the truth. Your word is truth.

As you sent me into the world, so I sent them into the world. And I consecrate myself for them, so that they also may be consecrated in truth."

MAY 20TH, 2021
Thursday of the Seventh Week of Easter

1ST Reading ACTS 22:30; 23:6-11
Wishing to determine the truth about why Paul was being accused by the Jews, the commander freed him and ordered the chief priests and the whole Sanhedrin to convene.

Then he brought Paul down and made him stand before them.

Paul was aware that some were Sadducees and some Pharisees, so he called out before the Sanhedrin, "My brothers, I am a Pharisee, the son of Pharisees;

I am on trial for hope in the resurrection of the dead." When he said this, a dispute broke out between the Pharisees and Sadducees, and the group became divided.

For the Sadducees say that there is no resurrection or angels or spirits, while the Pharisees acknowledge all three. A great uproar occurred, and some scribes belonging to the Pharisee party stood up and sharply argued, "We find nothing wrong with this man.

Suppose a spirit or an angel has spoken to him?" The dispute was so serious that the commander, afraid that Paul would be torn to pieces by them, ordered his troops to go down and rescue Paul from their midst and take him into the compound. The following night the Lord stood by him and said, "Take courage. For just as you have borne witness to my cause in Jerusalem, so you must also bear witness in Rome."

Responsorial Psalm PS 16:1-2A AND 5, 7-8, 9-10, 11
R... (1) Keep me safe, O God; you are my hope.

or:

R. Alleluia.

Keep me, O God, for in you I take refuge; I say to the LORD, "My Lord are you." O LORD, my allotted portion and my cup, you it is who hold fast my lot.

R. Keep me safe, O God; you are my hope.

or:

R. Alleluia.

I bless the LORD who counsels me; even in the night my heart exhorts me. I set the LORD ever before me; with him at my right hand I shall not be disturbed.

R. Keep me safe, O God; you are my hope.

or:

R. Alleluia.

Therefore my heart is glad and my soul rejoices, my body, too, abides in confidence; Because you will not abandon my soul to the nether world, nor will you suffer your faithful one to undergo corruption.

R. Keep me safe, O God; you are my hope.

or:

R. Alleluia.

You will show me the path to life, fullness of joys in your presence, the delights at your right hand forever.

R. Keep me safe, O God; you are my hope.

or:

R. Alleluia.

Alleluia   JN 17:21

R. Alleluia, alleluia.

May they all be one as you, Father, are in me and I in you, that the world may believe that you sent me, says the Lord.

R. Alleluia, alleluia.

Gospel JN 17:20-26
Lifting up his eyes to heaven, Jesus prayed saying:

"I pray not only for these, but also for those who will believe in me through their word, so that they may all be one, as you, Father, are in me and I in you, that they also may be in us, that the world may believe that you sent me.

And I have given them the glory you gave me, so that they may be one, as we are one, I in them and you in me, that they may be brought to perfection as one, that the world may know that you sent me, and that you loved them even as you loved me.

314

Father, they are your gift to me. I wish that where I am they also may be with me, that they may see my glory that you gave me, because you loved me before the foundation of the world. Righteous Father, the world also does not know you, but I know you, and they know that you sent me. I made known to them your name and I will make it known, that the love with which you loved me may be in them and I in them."

MAY 21ST, 2021
Friday of the Seventh Week of Easter

1ST Reading ACTS 25:13B-21
King Agrippa and Bernice arrived in Caesarea on a visit to Festus.

Since they spent several days there, Festus referred Paul's case to the king, saying, "There is a man here left in custody by Felix. When I was in Jerusalem the chief priests and the elders of the Jews brought charges against him and demanded his condemnation. I answered them that it was not Roman practice to hand over an accused person before he has faced his accusers and had the opportunity to defend himself against their charge.

So when they came together here, I made no delay; the next day I took my seat on the tribunal and ordered the man to be brought in. His accusers stood around him, but did not charge him with any of the crimes I suspected.

Instead they had some issues with him about their own religion and about a certain Jesus who had died but who Paul claimed was alive. Since I was at a loss how to investigate this controversy, I asked if he were willing to go to Jerusalem and there stand trial on these charges. And when Paul appealed that he be held in custody for the Emperor's decision, I ordered him held until I could send him to Caesar."

Responsorial Psalm PS 103:1-2, 11-12, 19-20AB
R... (19a) The Lord has established his throne in heaven.

or:

R. Alleluia.

Bless the LORD, O my soul; and all my being, bless his holy name. Bless the LORD, O my soul, and forget not all his benefits.

R... The Lord has established his throne in heaven.

or:

R. Alleluia.

For as the heavens are high above the earth, so surpassing is his kindness toward those who fear him. As far as the east is from the west, so far has he put our transgressions from us.

R... The Lord has established his throne in heaven.

or:

R. Alleluia.

The LORD has established his throne in heaven, and his kingdom rules over all. Bless the LORD, all you his angels, you mighty in strength, who do his bidding.

R... The Lord has established his throne in heaven.

or:

R. Alleluia.

Alleluia   JN 14:26

R. Alleluia, alleluia.

The Holy Spirit will teach you everything and remind you of all I told you.

R. Alleluia, alleluia.

Gospel JN 21:15-19

After Jesus had revealed himself to his disciples and eaten breakfast with them, he said to Simon Peter, "Simon, son of John, do you love me more than these?"

Simon Peter answered him, "Yes, Lord, you know that I love you."

Jesus said to him, "Feed my lambs." He then said to Simon Peter a second time, "Simon, son of John, do you love me?" Simon Peter answered him, "Yes, Lord, you know that I love you." He said to him, "Tend my sheep."

He said to him the third time, "Simon, son of John, do you love me?" Peter was distressed that he had said to him a third time, "Do you love me?" and he said to him, "Lord, you know everything; you know that I love you."

Jesus said to him, "Feed my sheep.

Amen, amen, I say to you, when you were younger, you used to dress yourself and go where you wanted; but when you grow old, you will stretch out your hands, and someone else will dress you and lead you where you do not want to go." He said this signifying by what kind of death he would glorify God. And when he had said this, he said to him, "Follow me."

MAY 22ND, 2021
Saturday of the Seventh Week of Easter - Mass in the Morning

1ST Reading ACTS 28:16-20, 30-31
When he entered Rome, Paul was allowed to live by himself, with the soldier who was guarding him.

Three days later he called together the leaders of the Jews.

When they had gathered he said to them, "My brothers, although I had done nothing against our people or our ancestral customs, I was handed over to the Romans as a prisoner from Jerusalem.

After trying my case the Romans wanted to release me, because they found nothing against me deserving the death penalty. But when the Jews objected, I was obliged to appeal to Caesar, even though I had no accusation to make against my own nation. This is the reason, then, I have requested to see you and to speak with you, for it is on account of the hope of Israel that I wear these chains."

He remained for two full years in his lodgings. He received all who came to him, and with complete assurance and without hindrance he proclaimed the Kingdom of God and taught about the Lord Jesus Christ.

Responsorial Psalm PS 11:4, 5 AND 7
R. (see 7b) The just will gaze on your face, O Lord.

or:

R. Alleluia.

The LORD is in his holy temple; the LORD's throne is in heaven. His eyes behold, his searching glance is on mankind.

R. The just will gaze on your face, O Lord.

or:

R. Alleluia.

The LORD searches the just and the wicked; the lover of violence he hates. For the LORD is just, he loves just deeds; the upright shall see his face.

R. The just will gaze on your face, O Lord.

or:

R. Alleluia.

Alleluia JN 16:7, 13

R. Alleluia, alleluia.

I will send to you the Spirit of truth, says the Lord; he will guide you to all truth.

R. Alleluia, alleluia.

Gospel JN 21:20-25

Peter turned and saw the disciple following whom Jesus loved, the one who had also reclined upon his chest during the supper and had said, "Master, who is the one who will betray you?" When Peter saw him, he said to Jesus, "Lord, what about him?" Jesus said to him, "What if I want him to remain until I come? What concern is it of yours? You follow me." So the word spread among the brothers that that disciple would not die. But Jesus had not told him that he would not die, just "What if I want him to remain until I come? What concern is it of yours?"

It is this disciple who testifies to these things and has written them, and we know that his testimony is true. There are also many other things that Jesus did, but if these were to be described individually, I do not think the whole world would contain the books that would be written.

MAY 23RD, 2021

Pentecost Sunday - Mass during the Day

1ST Reading ACTS 2:1-11

When the time for Pentecost was fulfilled, they were all in one place together.

And suddenly there came from the sky a noise like a strong driving wind, and it filled the entire house in which they were. Then there appeared to them tongues as of fire, which parted and came to rest on each one of them. And they were all filled with the Holy Spirit and began to speak in different tongues, as the Spirit enabled them to proclaim.

Now there were devout Jews from every nation under heaven staying in Jerusalem.

At this sound, they gathered in a large crowd, but they were confused because each one heard them speaking in his own language. They were astounded, and in amazement they asked, "Are not all these people who are speaking Galileans?

Then how does each of us hear them in his native language? We are Parthians, Medes, and Elamites, inhabitants of Mesopotamia, Judea and Cappadocia, Pontus and Asia, Phrygia and Pamphylia, Egypt and the districts of Libya near Cyrene, as well as travelers from Rome, both Jews and converts to Judaism, Cretans and Arabs, yet we hear them speaking in our own tongues of the mighty acts of God."

Responsorial Psalm   PS 104:1, 24, 29-30, 31, 34

R. (cf. 30) Lord, send out your Spirit, and renew the face of the earth.

or:

R. Alleluia.

Bless the LORD, O my soul! O LORD, my God, you are great indeed! How manifold are your works, O LORD! the earth is full of your creatures;

R. Lord, send out your Spirit, and renew the face of the earth.

or:

R. Alleluia.

May the glory of the LORD endure forever; may the LORD be glad in his works! Pleasing to him be my theme; I will be glad in the LORD.

R. Lord, send out your Spirit, and renew the face of the earth.

or:

R. Alleluia.

If you take away their breath, they perish and return to their dust. When you send forth your spirit, they are created, and you renew the face of the earth.

R. Lord, send out your Spirit, and renew the face of the earth.

or:

R. Alleluia.

2ND Reading 1 COR 12:3B-7, 12-13
Brothers and sisters:

No one can say, "Jesus is Lord," except by the Holy Spirit. There are different kinds of spiritual gifts but the same Spirit; there are different forms of service but the same Lord; there are different workings but the same God who produces all of them in everyone.

To each individual the manifestation of the Spirit is given for some benefit. As a body is one though it has many parts, and all the parts of the body, though many, are one body, so also Christ. For in one Spirit we were all baptized into one body, whether Jews or Greeks, slaves or free persons, and we were all given to drink of one Spirit.

Or: ROM 8:8-17

Brothers and sisters:

Those who are in the flesh cannot please God. But you are not in the flesh; on the contrary, you are in the spirit, if only the Spirit of God dwells in you.

Whoever does not have the Spirit of Christ does not belong to him. But if Christ is in you, although the body is dead because of sin, the spirit is alive because of righteousness. If the Spirit of the one who raised Jesus from the dead dwells in you, the one who raised Christ from the dead will give life to your mortal bodies also, through his Spirit that dwells in you. Consequently,

320

brothers and sisters, we are not debtors to the flesh, to live according to the flesh.

For if you live according to the flesh, you will die, but if by the Spirit you put to death the deeds of the body, you will live.

For those who are led by the Spirit of God are sons of God. For you did not receive a spirit of slavery to fall back into fear, but you received a Spirit of adoption, through whom we cry, "Abba, Father!" The Spirit himself bears witness with our spirit that we are children of God, and if children, then heirs, heirs of God and joint heirs with Christ, if only we suffer with him so that we may also be glorified with him.

Sequence Veni, Sancte Spiritus

Come, Holy Spirit, come!

And from your celestial home

Shed a ray of light divine!

Come, Father of the poor!

Come, source of all our store!

Come, within our bosoms shine.

You, of comforters the best;

You, the soul's most welcome guest;

Sweet refreshment here below;

In our labor, rest most sweet;

Grateful coolness in the heat;

Solace in the midst of woe.

O most blessed Light divine,

Shine within these hearts of yours,

 And our inmost being fill!

Where you are not, we have naught,

Nothing good in deed or thought,

Nothing free from taint of ill.

Heal our wounds, our strength renew;

On our dryness pour your dew;

Wash the stains of guilt away:

Bend the stubborn heart and will;

Melt the frozen, warm the chill;

Guide the steps that go astray.

On the faithful, who adore

And confess you, evermore

In your sevenfold gift descend;

Give them virtue's sure reward;

Give them your salvation, Lord;

Give them joys that never end. Amen.

Alleluia.

Alleluia

R. Alleluia, alleluia.

Come, Holy Spirit, fill the hearts of your faithful and kindle in them the fire
of your love.

R. Alleluia, alleluia.

Gospel JN 20:19-23
On the evening of that first day of the week, when the doors were locked,
where the disciples were, for fear of the Jews, Jesus came and stood in their
midst and said to them, "Peace be with you."

When he had said this, he showed them his hands and his side. The disciples rejoiced when they saw the Lord. Jesus said to them again, "Peace be with you. As the Father has sent me, so I send you." And when he had said this, he breathed on them and said to them, "Receive the Holy Spirit. Whose sins you forgive are forgiven them, and whose sins you retain are retained."

Jn 15:26-27; 16:12-15

Jesus said to his disciples:

"When the Advocate comes whom I will send you from the Father, the Spirit of truth that proceeds from the Father, he will testify to me.

And you also testify, because you have been with me from the beginning.

"I have much more to tell you, but you cannot bear it now.

But when he comes, the Spirit of truth, he will guide you to all truth. He will not speak on his own, but he will speak what he hears, and will declare to you the things that are coming.

He will glorify me, because he will take from what is mine and declare it to you.

Everything that the Father has is mine; for this reason I told you that he will take from what is mine and declare it to you."

MAY 24TH, 2021
Memorial of the Blessed Virgin Mary, Mother of the Church

1ST Reading GN 3:9-15, 20
After Adam had eaten of the tree, the LORD God called to him and asked him, "Where are you?"

He answered, "I heard you in the garden; but I was afraid, because I was naked, so I hid myself." Then he asked, "Who told you that you were naked? You have eaten, then, from the tree of which I had forbidden you to eat!"

The man replied, "The woman whom you put here with me— she gave me fruit from the tree, and so I ate it." The LORD God then asked the woman, "Why did you do such a thing?"

The woman answered, "The serpent tricked me into it, so I ate it." Then the LORD God said to the serpent: "Because you have done this, you shall be banned from all the animals and from all the wild creatures; On your belly shall you crawl, and dirt shall you eat all the days of your life.

I will put enmity between you and the woman, and between your offspring and hers; He will strike at your head, while you strike at his heel." The man called his wife Eve, because she became the mother of all the living.

Or ACTS 1:12-14

After Jesus had been taken up to heaven, the Apostles returned to Jerusalem from the mount called Olivet, which is near Jerusalem, a sabbath day's journey away.

When they entered the city they went to the upper room where they were staying, Peter and John and James and Andrew, Philip and Thomas, Bartholomew and Matthew, James son of Alphaeus, Simon the Zealot, and Judas son of James.

All these devoted themselves with one accord to prayer, together with some women, and Mary the mother of Jesus, and his brothers.

Responsorial Psalm PS 87:1-2, 3 AND 5, 6-7
R. (3) Glorious things are told of you, O city of God.

His foundation upon the holy mountains the LORD loves: The gates of Zion, more than any dwelling of Jacob.

R. Glorious things are told of you, O city of God.

Glorious things are said of you,

O city of God! And of Zion they shall say: "One and all were born in her; And he who has established her is the Most High LORD."

R. Glorious things are told of you, O city of God.

They shall note, when the peoples are enrolled: "This man was born there." And all shall sing, in their festive dance: "My home is within you."

R. Glorious things are told of you, O city of God.

Alleluia

R. Alleluia, alleluia.

O happy Virgin, you gave birth to the Lord; O blessed mother of the Church, you warm our hearts with the Spirit of your Son Jesus Christ.

R. Alleluia, alleluia.

Gospel JN 19:25-34
Standing by the cross of Jesus were his mother and his mother's sister, Mary the wife of Clopas, and Mary of Magdala.

When Jesus saw his mother and the disciple there whom he loved, he said to his mother, "Woman, behold, your son." Then he said to the disciple, "Behold, your mother." And from that hour the disciple took her into his home. After this, aware that everything was now finished, in order that the Scripture might be fulfilled,

Jesus said, "I thirst."

There was a vessel filled with common wine. So they put a sponge soaked in wine on a sprig of hyssop and put it up to his mouth. When Jesus had taken the wine, he said, "It is finished." And bowing his head, he handed over the spirit. Now since it was preparation day, in order that the bodies might not remain on the cross on the sabbath, for the sabbath day of that week was a solemn one, the Jews asked Pilate that their legs be broken and they be taken down.

So the soldiers came and broke the legs of the first and then of the other one who was crucified with Jesus.

But when they came to Jesus and saw that he was already dead, they did not break his legs, but one soldier thrust his lance into his side, and immediately Blood and water flowed out.

MAY 25TH, 2021
Tuesday of the Eighth Week in Ordinary Time

1ST Reading Sir 35:1-12
To keep the law is a great oblation, and he who observes the commandments sacrifices a peace offering.

In works of charity one offers fine flour, and when he gives alms he presents his sacrifice of praise.

To refrain from evil pleases the LORD, and to avoid injustice is atonement.

Appear not before the LORD empty-handed, for all that you offer is in fulfillment of the precepts.

The just one's offering enriches the altar and rises as a sweet odor before the Most High.

The just one's sacrifice is most pleasing, nor will it ever be forgotten.

In a generous spirit pay homage to the LORD, be not sparing of freewill gifts.

With each contribution show a cheerful countenance, and pay your tithes in a spirit of joy.

Give to the Most High as he has given to you, generously, according to your means. For the LORD is one who always repays, and he will give back to you sevenfold.

But offer no bribes, these he does not accept! Trust not in sacrifice of the fruits of extortion.

For he is a God of justice, who knows no favorites.

Responsorial Psalm PS 50:5-6, 7-8, 14 and 23
R.(23b) To the upright I will show the saving power of God.

"Gather my faithful ones before me, those who have made a covenant with me by sacrifice."

And the heavens proclaim his justice; for God himself is the judge.

R. To the upright I will show the saving power of God.

"Hear, my people, and I will speak; Israel, I will testify against you; God, your God, am I.

Not for your sacrifices do I rebuke you, for your burnt offerings are before me always."

R. To the upright I will show the saving power of God.

"Offer to God praise as your sacrifice and fulfill your vows to the Most High.

He that offers praise as a sacrifice glorifies me; and to him that goes the right way I will show the salvation of God."

R. To the upright I will show the saving power of God.

Alleluia   See Mt 11:25

R. Alleluia, alleluia.

Blessed are you, Father, Lord of heaven and earth; you have revealed to little ones the mysteries of the Kingdom..

R. Alleluia, alleluia.

Gospel Mk 10:28-31
Peter began to say to Jesus,

'We have given up everything and followed you."

Jesus said, "Amen, I say to you, there is no one who has given up house or brothers or sisters or mother or father or children or lands for my sake and for the sake of the Gospel who will not receive a hundred times more now in this present age: houses and brothers and sisters and mothers and children and lands, with persecutions, and eternal life in the age to come.

But many that are first will be last, and the last will be first.""

MAY 26TH, 2021
Memorial of Saint Philip Neri, Priest

1ST Reading Sir 36:1, 4-5a, 10-17
Come to our aid, O God of the universe, look upon us, show us the light of your mercies, and put all the nations in dread of you!

Thus they will know, as we know, that there is no God but you, O Lord.

Give new signs and work new wonders.

Gather all the tribes of Jacob, that they may inherit the land as of old,

Show mercy to the people called by your name; Israel, whom you named your firstborn.

Take pity on your holy city, Jerusalem, your dwelling place.

Fill Zion with your majesty, your temple with your glory.

Give evidence of your deeds of old; fulfill the prophecies spoken in your name. Reward those who have hoped in you, and let your prophets be proved true.

Hear the prayer of your servants, for you are ever gracious to your people; and lead us in the way of justice.

Thus it will be known to the very ends of the earth that you are the eternal God.

Responsorial Psalm PS 79:8, 9, 11 and 13
R. (Sirach 36:1b) Show us, O Lord, the light of your kindness.

Remember not against us the iniquities of the past; may your compassion quickly come to us, for we are brought very low.

R. Show us, O Lord, the light of your kindness.

Help us, O God our savior, because of the glory of your name;

Deliver us and pardon our sins for your name's sake.

R. Show us, O Lord, the light of your kindness.

Let the prisoners' sighing come before you; with your great power free those doomed to death.

Then we, your people and the sheep of your pasture, will give thanks to you forever; through all generations we will declare your praise.

R. Show us, O Lord, the light of your kindness..

Alleluia Mk 10:45

R. Alleluia, alleluia.

The Son of Man came to serve, and to give his life as a ransom for many

R. Alleluia, alleluia.

The disciples were on the way, going up to Jerusalem, and Jesus went ahead of them.

They were amazed, and those who followed were afraid.

Taking the Twelve aside again, he began to tell them what was going to happen to him.

"Behold, we are going up to Jerusalem, and the Son of Man will be handed over to the chief priests and the scribes, and they will condemn him to death and hand him over to the Gentiles who will mock him, spit upon him, scourge him, and put him to death, but after three days he will rise."

Then James and John, the sons of Zebedee, came to Jesus and said to him, 'Teacher, we want you to do for us whatever we ask of you."

He replied, 'What do you wish me to do for you?" They answered him,

"Grant that in your glory we may sit one at your right and the other at your left."

Jesus said to them, "You do not know what you are asking.

Can you drink the chalice that I drink or be baptized with the baptism with which I am baptized?"

They said to him, 'We can." Jesus said to them, "The chalice that I drink, you will drink, and with the baptism with which I am baptized, you will be baptized; but to sit at my right or at my left is not mine to give but is for those for whom it has been prepared."

When the ten heard this, they became indignant at James and John.

Jesus summoned them and said to them, "You know that those who are recognized as rulers over the Gentiles lord it over them, and their great ones make their authority over them felt.

But it shall not be so among you.

Rather, whoever wishes to be great among you will be your servant; whoever wishes to be first among you will be the slave of all.

For the Son of Man did not come to be served but to serve and to give his life as a ransom for many."

MAY 27TH, 2021
Thursday of the Eighth Week in Ordinary Time

1ST Reading Sir 42:15-25
Now will I recall God's works; what I have seen, I will describe.

At God's word were his works brought into being; they do his will as he has ordained for them.

As the rising sun is clear to all, so the glory of the LORD fills all his works;

Yet even God's holy ones must fail in recounting the wonders of the LORD,

Though God has given these, his hosts, the strength to stand firm before his glory. He plumbs the depths and penetrates the heart; their innermost being he understands.

The Most High possesses all knowledge, and sees from of old the things that are to come:

He makes known the past and the future, and reveals the deepest secrets.

No understanding does he lack; no single thing escapes him.

Perennial is his almighty wisdom; he is from all eternity one and the same,

With nothing added, nothing taken away; no need of a counselor for him!

How beautiful are all his works! even to the spark and fleeting vision!

The universe lives and abides forever; to meet each need, each creature is preserved.

All of them differ, one from another, yet none of them has he made in vain,

For each in turn, as it comes, is good; can one ever see enough of their splendor?

R.(6a) By the word of the Lord the heavens were made.

Give thanks to the LORD on the harp; with the ten-stringed lyre chant his praises.

Sing to him a new song; pluck the strings skillfully, with shouts of gladness.

R. By the word of the Lord the heavens were made.

For upright is the word of the LORD and all his works are trustworthy.

He loves justice and right; of the kindness of the LORD the earth is full.

R. By the word of the Lord the heavens were made.

By the word of the Lord the heavens were made; by the breath of his mouth all their host.

He gathers the waters of the sea as in a flask; in cellars he confines the deep.

R. By the word of the Lord the heavens were made.

Let all the earth fear the Lord; let all who dwell in the world revere him.

For he spoke and it was made; he commanded, and it stood forth.

R. By the word of the Lord the heavens were made.

Alleluia Jn 8:12

R. Alleluia, alleluia.

I am the light of the world, says the Lord; whoever follows me will have the light of life.

R. Alleluia, alleluia.

Gospel Mk 10:46-52
As Jesus was leaving Jericho with his disciples and a sizable crowd,

Bartimaeus, a blind man, the son of Timaeus, sat by the roadside begging.

On hearing that it was Jesus of Nazareth, he began to cry out and say,

"Jesus, son of David, have pity on me." And many rebuked him, telling him to be silent.

But he kept calling out all the more, "Son of David, have pity on me."

Jesus stopped and said, "Call him." So they called the blind man, saying to him,

"Take courage; get up, Jesus is calling you." He threw aside his cloak, sprang up, and came to Jesus.

Jesus said to him in reply, "What do you want me to do for you?" The blind man replied to him, "Master, I want to see." Jesus told him, 'Go your way; your faith has saved you."

Immediately he received his sight and followed him on the way.

MAY 28TH, 2021
Friday of the Eighth Week in Ordinary Time

1ST Reading Sir 44:1, 9-13
Now will I praise those godly men, our ancestors, each in his own time.

But of others there is no memory, for when they ceased, they ceased. And they are as though they had not lived, they and their children after them.

Yet these also were godly men whose virtues have not been forgotten;

Their wealth remains in their families, their heritage with their descendants;

Through God's covenant with them their family endures, their posterity, for their sake. And for all time their progeny will endure, their glory will never be blotted out.

Responsorial Psalm PS 149:1b-2, 3-4, 5-6a and 9b
R. (see 4a) The Lord takes delight in his people.

or:

R. Alleluia.

Sing to the LORD a new song of praise in the assembly of the faithful.

Let Israel be glad in their maker, let the children of Zion rejoice in their king.

R. The Lord takes delight in his people.

or:

R. Alleluia.

Let them praise his name in the festive dance, et them sing praise to him with timbrel and harp.

For the LORD loves his people, and he adorns the lowly with victory.

R. The Lord takes delight in his people.

or:

R. Alleluia.

Let the faithful exult in glory; let them sing for joy upon their couches;

Let the high praises of God be in their throats. This is the glory of all his faithful. Alleluia.

R. The Lord takes delight in his people.

or:

R. Alleluia.

Alleluia See Jn 15:16

R. Alleluia, alleluia.

I chose you from the world, to go and bear fruit that will last, says the Lord.

R. Alleluia, alleluia.

Gospel Mk 11:11-26

Jesus entered Jerusalem and went into the temple area.

He looked around at everything and, since it was already late, went out to Bethany with the Twelve.

The next day as they were leaving Bethany he was hungry. Seeing from a distance a fig tree in leaf, he went over to see if he could find anything on it. When he reached it he found nothing but leaves; it was not the time for figs.

And he said to it in reply, "May no one ever eat of your fruit again!"

And his disciples heard it.

They came to Jerusalem, and on entering the temple area he began to drive out those selling and buying there.

He overturned the tables of the money changers and the seats of those who were selling doves. He did not permit anyone to carry anything through the temple area.

Then he taught them saying, "Is it not written: My house shall be called a house of prayer for all peoples? But you have made it a den of thieves."

The chief priests and the scribes came to hear of it and were seeking a way to put him to death, yet they feared him because the whole crowd was astonished at his teaching.

When evening came, they went out of the city.

Early in the morning, as they were walking along, they saw the fig tree withered to its roots.

Peter remembered and said to him, "Rabbi, look! The fig tree that you cursed has withered."

Jesus said to them in reply, "Have faith in God. Amen, I say to you, whoever says to this mountain,

'Be lifted up and thrown into the sea,' and does not doubt in his heart but believes that what he says will happen; it shall be done for him.

Therefore I tell you, all that you ask for in prayer, believe that you will receive it and it shall be yours.

When you stand to pray, forgive anyone against whom you have a grievance, so that your heavenly Father may in turn forgive you your transgressions."

1ST Reading Sir 51:12cd-20

I thank the LORD and I praise him; I bless the name of the LORD.

When I was young and innocent, I sought wisdom openly in my prayer

I prayed for her before the temple, and I will seek her until the end, and she flourished as a grape soon ripe.

My heart delighted in her. My feet kept to the level path because from earliest youth I was familiar with her.

In the short time I paid heed, I met with great instruction.

Since in this way I have profited, I will give my teacher grateful praise.

I became resolutely devoted to her the good I persistently strove for.

My soul was tormented in seeking her,

My hand opened her gate and I came to know her secrets.

I directed my soul to her, and in cleanness I attained to her.

Responsorial Psalm PS 19:8, 9, 10, 11

R. (9ab) The precepts of the Lord give joy to the heart.

The law of the LORD is perfect, refreshing the soul.

The decree of the LORD is trustworthy, giving wisdom to the simple.

R. The precepts of the Lord give joy to the heart.

The precepts of the LORD are right, rejoicing the heart.

The command of the LORD is clear, enlightening the eye.

R. The precepts of the Lord give joy to the heart.

The fear of the LORD is pure, enduring forever;

The ordinances of the LORD are true, all of them just.

R. The precepts of the Lord give joy to the heart.

They are more precious than gold, than a heap of purest gold;

Sweeter also than syrup or honey from the comb.

R. The precepts of the Lord give joy to the heart.

Alleluia See Col 3:16a, 17c

R. Alleluia, alleluia.

Let the word of Christ dwell in you richly; giving thanks to God the Father through him.

R. Alleluia, alleluia.

Gospel Mk 11:27-33

Jesus and his disciples returned once more to Jerusalem.

As he was walking in the temple area, the chief priests, the scribes, and the elders approached him and said to him,

"By what authority are you doing these things? Or who gave you this authority to do them?"

Jesus said to them, "I shall ask you one question.

Answer me, and I will tell you by what authority I do these things.

Was John's baptism of heavenly or of human origin? Answer me." They discussed this among themselves and said,

"If we say, 'Of heavenly origin,' he will say, 'Then why did you not believe him?'

But shall we say, 'Of human origin'?"– they feared the crowd, for they all thought John really was a prophet. So they said to Jesus in reply, "We do not know." Then Jesus said to them,

"Neither shall I tell you by what authority I do these things.""

1ST Reading Dt 4:32-34, 39-40
Moses said to the people:

"Ask now of the days of old, before your time, ever since God created man upon the earth; ask from one end of the sky to the other:

Did anything so great ever happen before?

Was it ever heard of?

Did a people ever hear the voice of God speaking from the midst of fire, as you did, and live? Or did any god venture to go and take a nation for himself from the midst of another nation, by testings, by signs and wonders, by war, with strong hand and outstretched arm, and by great terrors, all of which the LORD, your God, did for you in Egypt before your very eyes?

This is why you must now know, and fix in your heart, that the LORD is God in the heavens above and on earth below, and that there is no other.

You must keep his statutes and commandments that I enjoin on you today, that you and your children after you may prosper, and that you may have long life on the land which the LORD, your God, is giving you forever."

Responsorial Psalm   PS 33:4-5, 6, 9, 18-19, 20, 22
R. (12b) Blessed the people the Lord has chosen to be his own.

Upright is the word of the LORD, and all his works are trustworthy.

He loves justice and right; of the kindness of the Lord the earth is full.

R. Blessed the people the Lord has chosen to be his own.

By the word of the LORD the heavens were made; by the breath of his mouth all their host.

For he spoke, and it was made; he commanded, and it stood forth.

R. Blessed the people the Lord has chosen to be his own.

See, the eyes of the LORD are upon those who fear him, upon those who hope for his kindness,

To deliver them from death and preserve them in spite of famine.

R. Blessed the people the Lord has chosen to be his own.

Our soul waits for the LORD, who is our help and our shield.

May your kindness, O LORD, be upon us who have put our hope in you.

R. Blessed the people the Lord has chosen to be his own.

2ND Reading Rom 8:14-17
Brothers and sisters:

For those who are led by the Spirit of God are sons of God.

For you did not receive a spirit of slavery to fall back into fear, but you received a Spirit of adoption, through whom we cry, "Abba, Father!"

The Spirit himself bears witness with our spirit that we are children of God, and if children, then heirs, heirs of God and joint heirs with Christ, if only we suffer with him so that we may also be glorified with him.

Alleluia Rv 1:8

R. Alleluia, alleluia.

Glory to the Father, the Son, and the Holy Spirit; to God who is, who was, and who is to come.

R. Alleluia, alleluia.

Gospel Mt 28:16-20
The eleven disciples went to Galilee, to the mountain to which Jesus had ordered them.

When they all saw him, they worshiped, but they doubted. Then Jesus approached and said to them,

"All power in heaven and on earth has been given to me.

Go, therefore, and make disciples of all nations, baptizing them in the name of the Father, and of the Son, and of the Holy Spirit, teaching them to observe all that I have commanded you.

And behold, I am with you always, until the end of the age."

MAY 31TH, 2021
Feast of the Visitation of the Blessed Virgin Mary

1ST Reading Zep 3:14-18a

Shout for joy, O daughter Zion! Sing joyfully, O Israel!

Be glad and exult with all your heart, O daughter Jerusalem!

The LORD has removed the judgment against you, he has turned away your enemies;

The King of Israel, the LORD, is in your midst, you have no further misfortune to fear.

On that day, it shall be said to Jerusalem: Fear not, O Zion, be not discouraged!

The LORD, your God, is in your midst, a mighty savior;

He will rejoice over you with gladness, and renew you in his love,

He will sing joyfully because of you, as one sings at festivals.

OR:

Rom 12:9-16

Brothers and sisters:

Let love be sincere; hate what is evil, hold on to what is good; love one another with mutual affection; anticipate one another in showing honor.

Do not grow slack in zeal, be fervent in spirit, serve the Lord.

Rejoice in hope, endure in affliction, persevere in prayer.

Contribute to the needs of the holy ones, exercise hospitality.

Bless those who persecute you, bless and do not curse them.

Rejoice with those who rejoice, weep with those who weep.

Have the same regard for one another; do not be haughty but associate with the lowly; do not be wise in your own estimation..

Isaiah 12:2-3, 4bcd, 5-6
R. (6) Among you is the great and Holy One of Israel.

God indeed is my savior; I am confident and unafraid.

My strength and my courage is the LORD, and he has been my savior.

With joy you will draw water at the fountain of salvation.

R. Among you is the great and Holy One of Israel.

Give thanks to the LORD, acclaim his name among the nations make known his deeds, proclaim how exalted is his name.

R. Among you is the great and Holy One of Israel.

Sing praise to the LORD for his glorious achievement; let this be known throughout all the earth.

Shout with exultation, O city of Zion, for great in your midst is the Holy One of Israel!

R. Among you is the great and Holy One of Israel.

Alleluia   See Lk 1:45

R. Alleluia, alleluia.

Blessed are you, O Virgin Mary, who believed that what was spoken to you by the Lord would be fulfilled

R. Alleluia, alleluia.

Gospel Lk 1:39-56
Mary set out and traveled to the hill country in haste to a town of Judah, where she entered the house of Zechariah and greeted Elizabeth.

When Elizabeth heard Mary's greeting, the infant leaped in her womb, and Elizabeth, filled with the Holy Spirit, cried out in a loud voice and said,

"Most blessed are you among women, and blessed is the fruit of your womb.

And how does this happen to me, that the mother of my Lord should come to me?

For at the moment the sound of your greeting reached my ears, the infant in my womb leaped for joy.

Blessed are you who believed that what was spoken to you by the Lord would be fulfilled."

And Mary said:

"My soul proclaims the greatness of the Lord; my spirit rejoices in God my Savior, for he has looked with favor on his lowly servant.

From this day all generations will call me blessed: the Almighty has done great things for me, and holy is his Name.

He has mercy on those who fear him in every generation.

He has shown the strength of his arm, he has scattered the proud in their conceit.

He has cast down the mighty from their thrones, and has lifted up the lowly.

He has filled the hungry with good things, and the rich he has sent away empty.

He has come to the help of his servant Israel for he has remembered his promise of mercy, the promise he made to our fathers, to Abraham and his children for ever."

Mary remained with her about three months and then returned to her home.

JUNE 1ST, 2021
Memorial of Saint Justin, Martyr

1ST Reading Tb 2:9-14

On the night of Pentecost, after I had buried the dead, I, Tobit, went into my courtyard to sleep next to the courtyard wall. My face was uncovered because of the heat. I did not know there were birds perched on the wall above me, till their warm droppings settled in my eyes, causing cataracts. I went to see some doctors for a cure but the more they anointed my eyes with various salves, the worse the cataracts became, until I could see no more. For four years I was deprived of eyesight, and all my kinsmen were grieved at my condition. Ahiqar, however, took care of me for two years, until he left for Elymais. At that time, my wife Anna worked for hire at weaving cloth, the kind of work women do. When she sent back the goods to their owners, they would pay her. Late in winter on the seventh of Dystrus, she finished the cloth and sent it back to the owners. They paid her the full salary and also gave her a young goat for the table. On entering my house the goat began to bleat. I called to my wife and said: "Where did this goat come from? Perhaps it was stolen! Give it back to its owners; we have no right to eat stolen food!" She said to me, "It was given to me as a bonus over and above my wages." Yet I would not believe her, and told her to give it back to its owners. I became very angry with her over this. So she retorted: "Where are your charitable deeds now? Where are your virtuous acts? See! Your true character is finally showing itself!"

Responsorial Psalm   PS 112:1-2, 7-8, 9
R. (see 7c) The heart of the just one is firm, trusting in the Lord.

or:

R. Alleluia.

Blessed the man who fears the LORD, who greatly delights in his commands. His posterity shall be mighty upon the earth; the upright generation shall be blessed.

R. The heart of the just one is firm, trusting in the Lord.

or:

R. Alleluia.

An evil report he shall not fear; his heart is firm, trusting in the LORD.

His heart is steadfast; he shall not fear till he looks down upon his foes.

R. The heart of the just one is firm, trusting in the Lord.

or:

R. Alleluia.

Lavishly he gives to the poor; his generosity shall endure forever; his horn shall be exalted in glory.

R. The heart of the just one is firm, trusting in the Lord.

or:

R. Alleluia.

Alleluia Eph 1:17-18

R. Alleluia, alleluia.

May the Father of our Lord Jesus Christ enlighten the eyes of our hearts, that we may know what is the hope that belongs to his call.

R. Alleluia, alleluia.

Gospel MT 12:13-17

Some Pharisees and Herodians were sent to Jesus to ensnare him in his speech. They came and said to him, "Teacher, we know that you are a truthful man and that you are not concerned with anyone's opinion. You do not regard a person's status but teach the way of God in accordance with the truth. Is it lawful to pay the census tax to Caesar or not? Should we pay or should we not pay?" Knowing their hypocrisy he said to them, "Why are you testing me? Bring me a denarius to look at." They brought one to him and he said to them, "Whose image and inscription is this?" They replied to him, "Caesar's." So Jesus said to them, "Repay to Caesar what belongs to Caesar and to God what belongs to God." They were utterly amazed at him.

JUNE 2ND, 2021
Wednesday of the Ninth Week in Ordinary Time

1ST Reading Tb 3:1-11a, 16-17a
Grief-stricken in spirit, I, Tobit, groaned and wept aloud.

Then with sobs I began to pray: "You are righteous, O Lord, and all your deeds are just;All your ways are mercy and truth; you are the judge of the world. And now, O Lord, may you be mindful of me, and look with favor upon me. Punish me not for my sins, nor for my inadvertent offenses, nor for those of my ancestors. "We sinned against you, and disobeyed your commandments. So you handed us over to plundering, exile, and death, till you made us the talk and reproach of all the nations among whom you had dispersed us. "Yes, your judgments are many and true in dealing with me as my sins and those of my ancestors deserve.

For we have not kept your commandments, nor have we trodden the paths of truth before you. "So now, deal with me as you please, and command my life breath to be taken from me, that I may go from the face of the earth into dust.It is better for me to die than to live, because I have heard insulting calumnies, and I am overwhelmed with grief.

"Lord, command me to be delivered from such anguish; let me go to the everlasting abode; Lord, refuse me not. For it is better for me to die than to endure so much misery in life, and to hear these insults! "On the same day, at Ecbatana in Media, it so happened that Raguel's daughter Sarah also had to listen to abuse, from one of her father's maids. For she had been married to seven husbands, but the wicked demon Asmodeus killed them off before they could have intercourse with her, as it is prescribed for wives.

So the maid said to her: "You are the one who strangles your husbands! Look at you! You have already been married seven times, but you have had no joy with any one of your husbands.

Why do you beat us? Is it on account of your seven husbands, because they are dead? May we never see a son or daughter of yours!" The girl was deeply saddened that day, and she went into an upper chamber of her house, where she planned to hang herself. But she reconsidered, saying to herself: "No! People would level this insult against my father: 'You had only one beloved daughter, but she hanged herself because of ill fortune!' And thus would I cause my father in his old age to go down to the nether world laden with sorrow.

It is far better for me not to hang myself, but to beg the Lord to have me die, so that I need no longer live to hear such insults." At that time, then, she spread out her hands, and facing the window, poured out her prayer: "Blessed are you, O Lord, merciful God, and blessed is your holy and honorable name.

Blessed are you in all your works for ever!" At that very time, the prayer of these two suppliants was heard in the glorious presence of Almighty God. So Raphael was sent to heal them both: to remove the cataracts from Tobit's eyes, so that he might again see God's sunlight; and to marry Raguel's daughter Sarah to Tobit's son Tobiah, and then drive the wicked demon Asmodeus from her.

You are being enriched in every way for all generosity, which through us produces thanksgiving to God.

Responsorial Psalm PS 25:2-3, 4-5ab, 6 and 7bc, 8-9
R. (1) To you, O Lord, I lift my soul.

In you I trust; let me not be put to shame; let not my enemies exult over me.

No one who waits for you shall be put to shame; those shall be put to shame who heedlessly break faith.

R. To you, O Lord, I lift my soul.

Your ways, O LORD, make known to me; teach me your paths,

Guide me in your truth and teach me, for you are God my savior.

R. To you, O Lord, I lift my soul.

Remember that your compassion, O LORD, and your kindness are from of old.

In your kindness remember me, because of your goodness, O LORD.

R. To you, O Lord, I lift my soul.

Good and upright is the LORD; thus he shows sinners the way.

He guides the humble to justice, he teaches the humble his way.

R. To you, O Lord, I lift my soul.

or:

R. Alleluia. Alleluia: JN 11:25a, 26

R. Alleluia, alleluia.

I am the resurrection and the life, says the Lord; whoever believes in me will never die.

R. Alleluia, alleluia.

Some Sadducees, who say there is no resurrection, came to Jesus and put this question to him, saying, "Teacher, Moses wrote for us, 'If someone's brother dies, leaving a wife but no child, his brother must take the wife and raise up descendants for his brother.' Now there were seven brothers.

The first married a woman and died, leaving no descendants. So the second brother married her and died, leaving no descendants and the third likewise. And the seven left no descendants. Last of all the woman also died. At the resurrection when they arise whose wife will she be? For all seven had been married to her." Jesus said to them, "Are you not misled because you do not know the Scriptures or the power of God?

When they rise from the dead, they neither marry nor are given in marriage, but they are like the angels in heaven. As for the dead being raised, have you not read in the Book of Moses, in the passage about the bush, how God told him, I am the God of Abraham, the God of Isaac, and the God of Jacob? He is not God of the dead but of the living. You are greatly misled."

JUNE 3RD, 2021
Memorial of Saint Charles Lwanga and Companions, Martyrs

1ST Reading Tb 6:10-11; 7:1bcde, 9-17; 8:4-9a

When the angel Raphael and Tobiah had entered Media and were getting close to Ecbatana, Raphael said to the boy, "Tobiah, my brother!" He replied: "Here I am!" He said: "Tonight we must stay with Raguel, who is a relative of yours. He has a daughter named Sarah." So he brought him to the house of Raguel, whom they found seated by his courtyard gate.

They greeted him first. He said to them, "Greetings to you too, brothers! Good health to you, and welcome!" And he brought them into his home. Raguel slaughtered a ram from the flock and gave them a cordial reception.

When they had bathed and reclined to eat, Tobiah said to Raphael, "Brother Azariah, ask Raguel to let me marry my kinswoman Sarah." Raguel overheard the words; so he said to the boy: "Eat and drink and be merry tonight, for no man is more entitled to marry my daughter Sarah than you, brother. Besides, not even I have the right to give her to anyone but you, because you are my closest relative.

But I will explain the situation to you very frankly. I have given her in marriage to seven men, all of whom were kinsmen of ours, and all died on the very night they approached her. But now, son, eat and drink.

I am sure the Lord will look after you both." Tobiah answered, "I will eat or drink nothing until you set aside what belongs to me." Raguel said to him: "I will do it. She is yours according to the decree of the Book of Moses. Your marriage to her has been decided in heaven! Take your kinswoman; from now on you are her love, and she is your beloved. She is yours today and ever after. And tonight, son, may the Lord of heaven prosper you both. May he grant you mercy and peace."

Then Raguel called his daughter Sarah, and she came to him. He took her by the hand and gave her to Tobiah with the words: "Take her according to the law. According to the decree written in the Book of Moses she is your wife. Take her and bring her back safely to your father. And may the God of heaven grant both of you peace and prosperity." Raguel then called Sarah's mother and told her to bring a scroll, so that he might draw up a marriage contract stating that he gave Sarah to Tobiah as his wife according to the decree of the Mosaic law.

Her mother brought the scroll, and Raguel drew up the contract, to which they affixed their seals. Afterward they began to eat and drink.

Later Raguel called his wife Edna and said, "My love, prepare the other bedroom and bring the girl there." She went and made the bed in the room, as she was told, and brought the girl there. After she had cried over her, she wiped away the tears and said: "Be brave, my daughter. May the Lord grant you joy in place of your grief.

Courage, my daughter." Then she left. When the girl's parents left the bedroom and closed the door behind them, Tobiah arose from bed and said to his wife, "My love, get up. Let us pray and beg our Lord to have mercy on us and to grant us deliverance." She got up, and they started to pray and beg that deliverance might be theirs. And they began to say: "Blessed are you, O God of our fathers, praised be your name forever and ever.

Let the heavens and all your creation praise you forever. You made Adam and you gave him his wife Eve to be his help and support; and from these two the human race descended. You said, 'It is not good for the man to be alone; let us make him a partner like himself.' Now, Lord, you know that I take this wife of mine not because of lust, but for a noble purpose. Call down

347

your mercy on me and on her, and allow us to live together to a happy old age. "They said together, "Amen, amen," and went to bed for the night!

Responsorial Psalm PS 128:1-2, 3, 4-5
R. (see 1a) Blessed are those who fear the Lord.

Blessed are you who fear the LORD, who walk in his ways!

For you shall eat the fruit of your handiwork; Blessed shall you be, and favored.

R. Blessed are those who fear the Lord.

Your wife shall be like a fruitful vine in the recesses of your home;

Your children like olive plants around your table.

R. Blessed are those who fear the Lord.

Behold, thus is the man blessed who fears the LORD.

The LORD bless you from Zion: may you see the prosperity of Jerusalem all the days of your life.

R. Blessed are those who fear the Lord

Alleluia   2 Tm 1:10

R. Alleluia, alleluia.

Our Savior Jesus Christ has destroyed deathand brought life to light through the Gospel.

R. Alleluia, alleluia.

Gospel MT 12:28-34
One of the scribes came to Jesus and asked him, "Which is the first of all the commandments?"

Jesus replied, "The first is this: Hear, O Israel! The Lord our God is Lord alone! You shall love the Lord your God with all your heart, with all your soul, with all your mind, and with all your strength. The second is this:

You shall love your neighbor as yourself. There is no other commandment greater than these." The scribe said to him, "Well said, teacher. You are right in saying,

He is one and there is no other than he. And to love him with all your heart, with all your understanding, with all your strength, and to love your neighbor as yourself is worth more than all burnt offerings and sacrifices." And when Jesus saw that he answered with understanding, he said to him, "You are not far from the Kingdom of God." And no one dared to ask him any more questions"

JUNE 4TH, 2021
Friday of the Ninth Week in Ordinary Time

1ST Reading Tb 11:5-17
Anna sat watching the road by which her son was to come.

When she saw him coming, she exclaimed to his father, "Tobit, your son is coming, and the man who traveled with him!" Raphael said to Tobiah before he reached his father: "I am certain that his eyes will be opened. Smear the fish gall on them.

This medicine will make the cataracts shrink and peel off from his eyes; then your father will again be able to see the light of day." Then Anna ran up to her son, threw her arms around him, and said to him, "Now that I have seen you again, son, I am ready to die!"

And she sobbed aloud. Tobit got up and stumbled out through the courtyard gate. Tobiah went up to him with the fish gall in his hand, and holding him firmly, blew into his eyes. "Courage, father," he said. Next he smeared the medicine on his eyes, and it made them smart.

Then, beginning at the corners of Tobit's eyes, Tobiah used both hands to peel off the cataracts. When Tobit saw his son, he threw his arms around him and wept. He exclaimed, "I can see you, son, the light of my eyes!" Then he said: "Blessed be God, and praised be his great name, and blessed be all his holy angels. May his holy name be praised throughout all the ages, because it was he who scourged me, and it is he who has had mercy on me.

Behold, I now see my son Tobiah!"Then Tobit went back in, rejoicing and praising God with full voice for everything that had happened. Tobiah told his father that the

Lord God had granted him a successful journey; that he had brought back the money; and that he had married Raguel's daughter Sarah, who would arrive shortly, for she was approaching the gate of Nineveh. Tobit and Anna rejoiced and went out to the gate of Nineveh to meet their daughter-in-law.

When the people of Nineveh saw Tobit walking along briskly, with no one leading him by the hand, they were amazed. Before them all Tobit proclaimed how God had mercifully restored sight to his eyes.

When Tobit reached Sarah, the wife of his son Tobiah, he greeted her: "Welcome, my daughter! Blessed be your God for bringing you to us, daughter! Blessed is your father, and blessed is my son Tobiah, and blessed are you, daughter!

Welcome to your home with blessing and joy. Come in, daughter!" That day there was joy for all the Jews who lived in Nineveh..

Responsorial Psalm PS 146:1b-2, 6c-7, 8-9a, 9bc-10
R. (1b) Praise the Lord, my soul!

or:

R. Alleluia.

Praise the LORD, O my soul; I will praise the LORD all my life; I will sing praise to my God while I live.

R. Praise the Lord, my soul!

or:

R. Alleluia.

The LORD keeps faith forever, secures justice for the oppressed, gives food to the hungry.

The LORD sets captives free.

R. Praise the Lord, my soul!

or:

R. Alleluia.

The LORD gives sight to the blind.

The LORD raises up those who are bowed down; the LORD loves the just.
The LORD protects strangers.

R. Praise the Lord, my soul!

or:

R. Alleluia.

The fatherless and the widow he sustains, but the way of the wicked he
thwarts

The LORD shall reign forever, your God, O Zion, through all generations!
Alleluia.

R. Praise the Lord, my soul!

or:

R. Alleluia Jn 14:23

R. Alleluia, alleluia.

Whoever loves me will keep my word, and my Father will love him and we
will come to him

R. Alleluia, alleluia.

Gospel Mk 12:35-37

As Jesus was teaching in the temple area he said, "How do the scribes claim
that the Christ is the son of David? David himself, inspired by the Holy
Spirit, said:

The Lord said to my lord, 'Sit at my right hand until I place your enemies
under your feet.' David himself calls him 'lord'; so how is he his son?"

The great crowd heard this with delight."

JUNE 5TH, 2021
Memorial of Saint Boniface, Bishop and Martyr

1ST Reading Tb 12:1, 5-15, 20

Tobit called his son Tobiah and said to him,

"Son, see to it that you give what is due to the man

who made the journey with you; give him a bonus too."So he called Raphael and said,

"Take as your wages half of all that you have brought back,

and go in peace." Raphael called the two men aside privately and said to them:

"Thank God! Give him the praise and the glory. Before all the living, acknowledge the many good things he has done for you, by blessing and extolling his name in song.

Honor and proclaim God's deeds, and do not be slack in praising him.

A king's secret it is prudent to keep, but the works of God are to be declared and made known.

Praise them with due honor. Do good, and evil will not find its way to you.

Prayer and fasting are good, but better than either is almsgiving accompanied by righteousness.

A little with righteousness is better than abundance with wickedness.

It is better to give alms than to store up gold; for almsgiving saves one from death and expiates every sin.

Those who regularly give alms shall enjoy a full life; but those habitually guilty of sin are their own worst enemies.

"I will now tell you the whole truth; I will conceal nothing at all from you. I have already said to you,

'A king's secret it is prudent to keep, but the works of God are to be made known with due honor.'

I can now tell you that when you, Tobit, and Sarah prayed, it was I who presented and read the record of your prayer before the Glory of the Lord; and I did the same thing when you used to bury the dead.

When you did not hesitate to get up and leave your dinner in order to go and bury the dead,

I was sent to put you to the test. At the same time, however,

God commissioned me to heal you and your daughter-in-law Sarah.

I am Raphael, one of the seven angels who enter and serve before the Glory of the Lord."

"So now get up from the ground and praise God.

Behold, I am about to ascend to him who sent me; write down all these things that have happened to you

Responsorial Psalm Tobit 13:2, 6efgh, 7, 8
R. (1b) Blessed be God, who lives for ever.

He scourges and then has mercy; he casts down to the depths of the nether world, and he brings up from the great abyss.

No one can escape his hand.

R. Blessed be God, who lives for ever.

So now consider what he has done for you, and praise him with full voice.

Bless the Lord of righteousness, and exalt the King of ages.

R. Blessed be God, who lives for ever.

In the land of my exile I praise him and show his power and majesty to a sinful nation.

R. Blessed be God, who lives for ever.

Bless the Lord, all you his chosen ones, and may all of you praise his majesty.

Celebrate days of gladness, and give him praise.

R. Blessed be God, who lives for ever..

353

Alleluia Mt 5:3

R. Alleluia, alleluia.

Blessed are the poor in spirit for theirs is the Kingdom of heaven..

R. Alleluia, alleluia.

Gospel   Mk 12:38-44
In the course of his teaching Jesus said,

"Beware of the scribes, who like to go around in long robes and accept greetings in the marketplaces, seats of honor in synagogues, and places of honor at banquets.

They devour the houses of widows and, as a pretext, recite lengthy prayers.

They will receive a very severe condemnation."

He sat down opposite the treasury and observed how the crowd put money into the treasury. Many rich people put in large sums.

A poor widow also came and put in two small coins worth a few cents. Calling his disciples to himself, he said to them, "Amen, I say to you, this poor widow put in more than all the other contributors to the treasury.

For they have all contributed from their surplus wealth, but she, from her poverty, has contributed all she had, her whole livelihood."

JUNE 6TH, 2021
The Solemnity of the Most Holy Body and Blood of Christ

1ST Reading Ex 24:3-8
When Moses came to the people and related all the words and ordinances of the LORD, they all answered with one voice,

"We will do everything that the LORD has told us." Moses then wrote down all the words of the LORD and, rising early the next day, he erected at the foot of the mountain an altar and twelve pillars for the twelve tribes of Israel.

Then, having sent certain young men of the Israelites to offer holocausts and sacrifice young bulls as peace offerings to the LORD, Moses took half of the blood and put it in large bowls; the other half he splashed on the altar. Taking the book of the covenant, he read it aloud to the people, who answered, "All that the LORD has said, we will heed and do." Then he took the blood and sprinkled it on the people, saying, "This is the blood of the covenant that the LORD has made with you in accordance with all these words of his."

Responsorial Psalm 116:12-13, 15-16, 17-18
R. (13)   I will take the cup of salvation, and call on the name of the Lord.

or:

R. Alleluia.

How shall I make a return to the LORD for all the good he has done for me?

The cup of salvation I will take up, and I will call upon the name of the LORD.

R. I will take the cup of salvation, and call on the name of the Lord.

or:

R. Alleluia.

Precious in the eyes of the LORD is the death of his faithful ones.

I am your servant, the son of your handmaid; you have loosed my bonds.

R. I will take the cup of salvation, and call on the name of the Lord.

or:

R. Alleluia.

To you will I offer sacrifice of thanksgiving, and I will call upon the name of the LORD.

My vows to the LORD I will pay in the presence of all his people.

R. I will take the cup of salvation, and call on the name of the Lord.

or:

R. Alleluia.

2ND Reading Heb 9:11-15
Brothers and sisters:

When Christ came as high priest of the good things that have come to be, passing through the greater and more perfect tabernacle not made by hands, that is, not belonging to this creation, he entered once for all into the sanctuary, not with the blood of goats and calves but with his own blood, thus obtaining eternal redemption. For if the blood of goats and bulls and the sprinkling of a heifer's ashes can sanctify those who are defiled so that their flesh is cleansed, how much more will the blood of Christ, who through the eternal Spirit offered himself unblemished to God, cleanse our consciences from dead works to worship the living God. For this reason he is mediator of a new covenant: since a death has taken place for deliverance from transgressions under the first covenant, those who are called may receive the promised eternal inheritance.

Sequence

Lauda Sion Laud,

O Zion, your salvation, Laud with hymns of exultation, Christ, your king and shepherd true:

Bring him all the praise you know, He is more than you bestow. Never can you reach his due.

Special theme for glad thanksgiving Is the quick'ning and the living Bread today before you set:

From his hands of old partaken, as we know, by faith unshaken, Where the Twelve at supper met.

Full and clear ring out your chanting, Joy nor sweetest grace be wanting, from your heart let praises burst: For today the feast is holden, When the institution olden of that supper was rehearsed.

Here the new law's new oblation, by the new king's revelation, Ends the form of ancient rite: Now the new the old effaces,

Truth away the shadow chases, Light dispels the gloom of night. What he did at supper seated, Christ ordained to be repeated, His memorial ne'er to cease: And his rule for guidance taking,

Bread and wine we hallow, making thus our sacrifice of peace. This the truth each Christian learns,

Bread into his flesh he turns, to his precious blood the wine: Sight has fail'd, nor thought conceives, But a dauntless faith believes,

Resting on a pow'r divine. Here beneath these signs are hidden Priceless things to sense forbidden; Signs, not things are all we see: Blood is poured and flesh is broken,

Yet in either wondrous token Christ entire we know to be. Whoso of this food partakes does not rend the Lord nor breaks; Christ is whole to all that taste:

Thousands are, as one, receivers, one, as thousands of believers, Eats of him who cannot waste.

Bad and good the feast are sharing, of what divers' dooms preparing, Endless death, or endless life.

Life to these, to those damnation, See how like participation Is with unlike issues rife. When the sacrament is broken,

Doubt not, but believe 'tis spoken, That each sever'd outward token doth the very whole contain. Nought the precious gifts divide,

Breaking but the sign betides Jesus still the same abides, still unbroken does remain. The shorter form of the sequence begins here. Lo! the angel's food is given

To the pilgrim who has striven; see the children's bread from heaven, which on dogs may not be spent. Truth the ancient types fulfilling, Isaac bound, a victim willing, Paschal lamb, its lifeblood spilling, manna to the fathers sent.

Very bread, good shepherd, tend us, Jesu, of your love befriend us, You refresh us, you defend us, Your eternal goodness send usIn the land of life to see.

You who all things can and know, who on earth such food bestow, Grant us with your saints, though lowest,

Where the heav'nly feast you show, Fellow heirs and guests to be. Amen.

Alleluia.

Alleluia Jn 6:51

R. Alleluia, alleluia.

I am the living bread that came down from heaven, says the Lord; whoever eats this bread will live forever.

R. Alleluia, alleluia.

Gospel Mk 14:12-16, 22-26
On the first day of the Feast of Unleavened Bread, when they sacrificed the Passover lamb, Jesus' disciples said to him, "Where do you want us to go and prepare for you to eat the Passover?" He sent two of his disciples and said to them, "Go into the city and a man will meet you, carrying a jar of water. Follow him. Wherever he enters, say to the master of the house, 'The Teacher says, "Where is my guest room where I may eat the Passover with my disciples? "Then he will show you a large upper room furnished and ready. Make the preparations for us there." The disciples then went off, entered the city, and found it just as he had told them; and they prepared the Passover. While they were eating, he took bread, said the blessing, broke it, gave it to them, and said, "Take it; this is my body." Then he took a cup, gave thanks, and gave it to them, and they all drank from it. He said to them, "This is my blood of the covenant, which will be shed for many. Amen, I say to you, I shall not drink again the fruit of the vine until the day when I drink it new in the kingdom of God." Then, after singing a hymn, they went out to the Mount of Olives.

JUNE 7TH, 2021
Monday of the Tenth Week in Ordinary Time

1ST Reading 2 Cor1:1-7
Paul, an Apostle of Christ Jesus by the will of God, and Timothy our brother, to the Church of God that is at Corinth, with all the holy ones throughout Achaia: grace to you and peace from God our Father and the

Lord Jesus Christ. Blessed be the God and Father of our Lord Jesus Christ, the Father of compassion and the God of all encouragement, who encourages us in our every affliction, so that we may be able to encourage those who are in any affliction with the encouragement with which we ourselves are encouraged by God. For as Christ's sufferings overflow to us, so through Christ does our encouragement also overflow. If we are afflicted, it is for your encouragement and salvation; if we are encouraged, it is for your encouragement, which enables you to endure the same sufferings that we suffer. Our hope for you is firm, for we know that as you share in the sufferings, you also share in the encouragement.

Responsorial Psalm 34:2-3, 4-5, 6-7, 8-9
R. (9a) Taste and see the goodness of the Lord.

I will bless the LORD at all times; his praise shall be ever in my mouth.

Let my soul glory in the LORD; the lowly will hear me and be glad.

R. Taste and see the goodness of the Lord.

Glorify the LORD with me, let us together extol his name.

I sought the LORD, and he answered me and delivered me from all my fears.

R. Taste and see the goodness of the Lord.

Look to him that you may be radiant with joy, and your faces may not blush with shame.

When the poor one called out, the LORD heard, and from all his distress he saved him.

R. Taste and see the goodness of the Lord.

The angel of the LORD encamps around those who fear him, and delivers them.

Taste and see how good the LORD is; blessed the man who takes refuge in him.

R. Taste and see the goodness of the Lord.

Alleluia Mt 5:12a

R. Alleluia, alleluia.

Rejoice and be glad; for your reward will be great in heaven.

R. Alleluia, alleluia.

When Jesus saw the crowds, he went up the mountain, and after he had sat down, his disciples came to him. He began to teach them, saying: "Blessed are the poor in spirit, for theirs is the Kingdom of heaven. Blessed are they who mourn, for they will be comforted. Blessed are the meek, for they will inherit the land. Blessed are they who hunger and thirst for righteousness, for they will be satisfied. Blessed are the merciful, for they will be shown mercy. Blessed are the clean of heart, for they will see God. Blessed are the peacemakers, for they will be called children of God. Blessed are they who are persecuted for the sake of righteousness, for theirs is the Kingdom of heaven. Blessed are you when they insult you and persecute you and utter every kind of evil against you falsely because of me. Rejoice and be glad, for your reward will be great in heaven. Thus they persecuted the prophets who were before you."

JUNE 8TH, 2021
Tuesday of the Tenth Week in Ordinary Time

1ST Reading 2 Cor 1:18-22
Brothers and sisters:

As God is faithful, our word to you is not "yes" and "no." For the Son of God, Jesus Christ, who was proclaimed to you by us, Silvanus and Timothy and me, was not "yes" and "no," but "yes" has been in him. For however many are the promises of God, their Yes is in him; therefore, the Amen from us also goes through him to God for glory. But the one who gives us security with you in Christ and who anointed us is God; he has also put his seal upon us and given the Spirit in our hearts as a first installment.

Responsorial Psalm 119:129, 130, 131, 132, 133, 135
R. (135a) Lord, let your face shine on me.

Wonderful are your decrees; therefore I observe them.

R. Lord, let your face shine on me.

The revelation of your words sheds light, gives understanding to the simple.

R. Lord, let your face shine on me.

I gasp with open mouth in my yearning for your commands.

R. Lord, let your face shine on me.

Turn to me in pity as you turn to those who love your name.

R. Lord, let your face shine on me.

Steady my footsteps according to your promise, and let no iniquity rule over me.

R. Lord, let your face shine on me.

Let your countenance shine upon your servant, and teach me your statutes.

R. Lord, let your face shine on me.

Alleluia Mt 5:16

R. Alleluia, alleluia.

Let your light shine before others that they may see your good deeds and glorify your heavenly Father.

R. Alleluia, alleluia.

Gospel Mt 5:13-16

Jesus said to his disciples: "You are the salt of the earth. But if salt loses its taste, with what can it be seasoned? It is no longer good for anything but to be thrown out and trampled underfoot. You are the light of the world. A city set on a mountain cannot be hidden. Nor do they light a lamp and then put it under a bushel basket; it is set on a lampstand, where it gives light to all in the house. Just so, your light must shine before others, that they may see your good deeds and glorify your heavenly Father."

JUNE 9TH, 2021
Wednesday of the Tenth Week in Ordinary Time

Brothers and sisters:

Such confidence we have through Christ toward God. Not that of ourselves we are qualified to take credit for anything as coming from us; rather, our qualification comes from God, who has indeed qualified us as ministers of a new covenant, not of letter but of spirit; for the letter brings death, but the Spirit gives life. Now if the ministry of death, carved in letters on stone, was so glorious that the children of Israel could not look intently at the face of Moses because of its glory that was going to fade, how much more will the ministry of the Spirit be glorious? For if the ministry of condemnation was glorious, the ministry of righteousness will abound much more in glory. Indeed, what was endowed with glory has come to have no glory in this respect because of the glory that surpasses it. For if what was going to fade was glorious, how much more will what endures be glorious.

Responsorial Psalm 99:5, 6, 7, 8, 9

R. (see 9c) Holy is the Lord our God.

Extol the LORD, our God, and worship at his footstool; holy is he!

R. Holy is the Lord our God.

Moses and Aaron were among his priests, and Samuel, among those who called upon his name; they called upon the LORD, and he answered them.

R. Holy is the Lord our God.

From the pillar of cloud he spoke to them; they heard his decrees and the law he gave them.

R. Holy is the Lord our God.

O LORD, our God, you answered them; a forgiving God you were to them, though requiting their misdeeds.

R. Holy is the Lord our God.

Extol the LORD, our God, and worship at his holy mountain; for holy is the LORD, our God.

R. Holy is the Lord our God.

R. Alleluia, alleluia.

Teach me your paths, my God, and guide me in your truth.

R. Alleluia, alleluia.

Gospel Mt 5:17-19
Jesus said to his disciples:

"Do not think that I have come to abolish the law or the prophets. I have come not to abolish but to fulfill. Amen, I say to you, until heaven and earth pass away, not the smallest letter or the smallest part of a letter will pass from the law, until all things have taken place. Therefore, whoever breaks one of the least of these commandments and teaches others to do so will be called least in the Kingdom of heaven. But whoever obeys and teaches these commandments will be called greatest in the Kingdom of heaven."

June 10TH, 2021
Thursday of the Tenth Week in Ordinary Time

1ST Reading 2 Cor 3:15—4:1, 3-6
Brothers and sisters:

To this day, whenever Moses is read, a veil lies over the hearts of the children of Israel, but whenever a person turns to the Lord the veil is removed. Now the Lord is the Spirit and where the Spirit of the Lord is, there is freedom. All of us, gazing with unveiled face on the glory of the Lord, are being transformed into the same image from glory to glory, as from the Lord who is the Spirit. Therefore, since we have this ministry through the mercy shown us, we are not discouraged. And even though our Gospel is veiled, it is veiled for those who are perishing, in whose case the god of this age has blinded the minds of the unbelievers, so that they may not see the light of the Gospel of the glory of Christ, who is the image of God. For we do not preach ourselves but Jesus Christ as Lord, and ourselves as your slaves for the sake of Jesus. For God who said, Let light shine out of darkness, has shone in our hearts to bring to light the knowledge of the glory of God on the face of Jesus Christ.

R. (see 10b) The glory of the Lord will dwell in our land.

I will hear what God proclaims; the LORD—for he proclaims peace to his people.

Near indeed is his salvation to those who fear him, glory dwelling in our land.

R. The glory of the Lord will dwell in our land.

Kindness and truth shall meet; justice and peace shall kiss.

Truth shall spring out of the earth, and justice shall look down from heaven.

R. The glory of the Lord will dwell in our land.

The LORD himself will give his benefits; our land shall yield its increase.

Justice shall walk before him, and salvation, along the way of his steps.

R. The glory of the Lord will dwell in our land.

Alleluia Jn 13:34

R. Alleluia, alleluia.

I give you a new commandment: love one another as I have loved you.

R. Alleluia, alleluia.

Gospel Mt 5:20-26
Jesus said to his disciples:

"I tell you, unless your righteousness surpasses that of the scribes and Pharisees, you will not enter into the Kingdom of heaven. "You have heard that it was said to your ancestors, you shall not kill; and whoever kills will be liable to judgment. But I say to you, whoever is angry with his brother will be liable to judgment, and whoever says to his brother, Raqa, will be answerable to the Sanhedrin, and whoever says, 'You fool,' will be liable to fiery Gehenna. Therefore, if you bring your gift to the altar, and there recall that your brother has anything against you, leave your gift there at the altar, go first and be reconciled with your brother, and then come and offer your gift. Settle with your opponent quickly while on the way to court with him.

Otherwise your opponent will hand you over to the judge, and the judge will hand you over to the guard, and you will be thrown into prison. Amen, I say to you, you will not be released until you have paid the last penny."

June 11TH, 2021
Solemnity of Most Sacred Heart of Jesus

1ST Reading Hos 11:1, 3-4, 8c-9
Thus says the LORD:

When Israel was a child I loved him, out of Egypt I called my son. Yet it was I who taught Ephraim to walk, who took them in my arms; I drew them with human cords, with bands of love; I fostered them like one who raises an infant to his cheeks; yet, though I stooped to feed my child, they did not know that I was their healer. My heart is overwhelmed, my pity is stirred. I will not give vent to my blazing anger, I will not destroy Ephraim again; For I am God and not a man, the Holy One present among you; I will not let the flames consume you.

Responsorial Psalm Is 12:2-3, 4, 5-6.
R. (3) You will draw water joyfully from the springs of salvation.

God indeed is my savior; I am confident and unafraid.

My strength and my courage is the LORD, and he has been my savior.

With joy you will draw water at the fountain of salvation.

R. You will draw water joyfully from the springs of salvation.

Give thanks to the LORD, acclaim his name; among the nations make known his deeds, proclaim how exalted is his name.

R. You will draw water joyfully from the springs of salvation.

Sing praise to the LORD for his glorious achievement; let this be known throughout all the earth.

Shout with exultation, O city of Zion, for great in your midst is the Holy One of Israel!

R. You will draw water joyfully from the springs of salvation.

Brothers and sisters:

To me, the very least of all the holy ones, this grace was given, to preach to
the Gentiles the inscrutable riches of Christ, and to bring to light for all what
is the plan of the mystery hidden from ages past in God who created all
things, so that the manifold wisdom of God might now be made known
through the church to the principalities and authorities in the heavens. This
was according to the eternal purpose that he accomplished in Christ Jesus
our Lord, in whom we have boldness of speech and confidence of access
through faith in him. For this reason I kneel before the Father, from whom
every family in heaven and on earth is named, that he may grant you in
accord with the riches of his glory to be strengthened with power through his
Spirit in the inner self, and that Christ may dwell in your hearts through faith;
that you, rooted and grounded in love, may have strength to comprehend
with all the holy ones what is the breadth and length and height and depth,
and to know the love of Christ which surpasses knowledge, so that you may
be filled with all the fullness of God.

AlleluiaMt 11:29ab

R. Alleluia, alleluia.

Take my yoke upon you, says the Lord; and learn from me, for I am meek
and gentle of heart.

R. Alleluia, alleluia.

OR:

1 Jn 4:10b

R. Alleluia, alleluia.

God first loved usand sent his Son as expiation for our sins.

R. Alleluia, alleluia.

Gospel Jn 19:31-37
Since it was preparation day, in order that the bodies might not remain on
the cross on the Sabbath, for the sabbath day of that week was a solemn one,
the Jews asked Pilate that their legs be broken and they be taken down. So
the soldiers came and broke the legs of the first and then of the other one

who was crucified with Jesus. But when they came to Jesus and saw that he was already dead, they did not break his legs, but one soldier thrust his lance into his side, and immediately blood and water flowed out. An eyewitness has testified, and his testimony is true; he knows that he is speaking the truth, so that you also may come to believe. For this happened so that the Scripture passage might be fulfilled: Not a bone of it will be broken. And again another passage says: They will look upon him whom they have pierced.

June 12TH, 2021
Memorial of the Immaculate Heart of Mary

1ST Reading 2 Cor 5:14-21

Brothers and sisters: The love of Christ impels us, once we have come to the conviction that one died for all; therefore, all have died. He indeed died for all, so that those who live might no longer live for themselves but for him who for their sake died and was raised. Consequently, from now on we regard no one according to the flesh; even if we once knew Christ according to the flesh, yet now we know him so no longer. So whoever is in Christ is a new creation: the old things have passed away; behold new things have come. And all this is from God, who has reconciled us to himself through Christ and given us the ministry of reconciliation, namely, God was reconciling the world to himself in Christ, not counting their trespasses against them and entrusting to us the message of reconciliation. So we are ambassadors for Christ, as if God were appealing through us. We implore you on behalf of Christ, be reconciled to God. For our sake he made him to be sin who did not know sin, so that we might become the righteousness of God in him.

Responsorial Psalm 103:1-2, 3-4, 9-10, 11-12

R. (8a) The Lord is kind and merciful.

Bless the LORD, O my soul; and all my being, bless his holy name.

Bless the LORD, O my soul, and forget not all his benefits.

R. The Lord is kind and merciful.

He pardons all your iniquities; he heals all your ills.

He redeems your life from destruction; he crowns you with kindness and compassion.

R. The Lord is kind and merciful.

He will not always chide, nor does he keep his wrath forever.

Not according to our sins does he deal with us, nor does he requite us according to our crimes.

R. The Lord is kind and merciful.

For as the heavens are high above the earth, so surpassing is his kindness toward those who fear him.

As far as the east is from the west, so far has he put our transgressions from us.

R. The Lord is kind and merciful.

Alleluia Lk 2:19

R. Alleluia, alleluia.

Blessed is the Virgin Mary who kept the word of God and pondered it in her heart.

R. Alleluia, alleluia.

Gospel Lk 2:41-51

Each year Jesus' parents went to Jerusalem for the feast of Passover, and when he was twelve years old, they went up according to festival custom. After they had completed its days, as they were returning, the boy Jesus remained behind in Jerusalem, but his parents did not know it. Thinking that he was in the caravan, they journeyed for a day and looked for him among their relatives and acquaintances, but not finding him, they returned to Jerusalem to look for him. After three days they found him in the temple, sitting in the midst of the teachers, listening to them and asking them questions, and all who heard him were astounded at his understanding and his answers. When his parents saw him, they were astonished, and his mother said to him, "Son, why have you done this to us? Your father and I have been looking for you with great anxiety." And he said to them, "Why were you looking for me? Did you not know that I must be in my Father's house?" But they did not understand what he said to them. He went down with them and came to Nazareth, and was obedient to them; and his mother kept all these things in her heart.

JUNE 13TH, 2021
Eleventh Sunday in Ordinary Time

1ST Reading Ez 17:22-24

Thus says the Lord GOD: I, too, will take from the crest of the cedar, from its topmost branches tear off a tender shoot, and plant it on a high and lofty mountain; on the mountain heights of Israel I will plant it. It shall put forth branches and bear fruit, and become a majestic cedar. Birds of every kind shall dwell beneath it, every winged thing in the shade of its boughs. And all the trees of the field shall know that I, the LORD, bring low the high tree, lift high the lowly tree, wither up the green tree, and make the withered tree bloom. As I, the LORD, have spoken, so will I do.

Responsorial Psalm92:2-3, 13-14, 15-16

R. (cf. 2a) Lord, it is good to give thanks to you.

It is good to give thanks to the LORD, to sing praise to your name, Most High,

To proclaim your kindness at dawn and your faithfulness throughout the night.

R. Lord, it is good to give thanks to you.

The just one shall flourish like the palm tree, like a cedar of Lebanon shall he grow.

They that are planted in the house of the LORD shall flourish in the courts of our God.

R. Lord, it is good to give thanks to you.

They shall bear fruit even in old age; vigorous and sturdy shall they be,

Declaring how just is the LORD, my rock, in whom there is no wrong.

R. Lord, it is good to give thanks to you.

2ND Reading 2 Cor 5:6-10

Brothers and sisters:

We are always courageous, although we know that while we are at home in the body we are away from the Lord, for we walk by faith, not by sight. Yet

369

we are courageous, and we would rather leave the body and go home to the Lord. Therefore, we aspire to please him, whether we are at home or away. For we must all appear before the judgment seat of Christ, so that each may receive recompense, according to what he did in the body, whether good or evil.

R. Alleluia, alleluia.

The seed is the word of God, Christ is the sower. All who come to him will live forever.

R. Alleluia, alleluia.

Gospel Mk 4:26-34
Jesus said to the crowds:

"This is how it is with the kingdom of God; it is as if a man was to scatter seed on the land and would sleep and rise night and day and through it all the seed would sprout and grow, he knows not how. Of its own accord the land yields fruit, first the blade, then the ear, then the full grain in the ear. And when the grain is ripe, he wields the sickle at once, for the harvest has come." He said, "To what shall we compare the kingdom of God, or what parable can we use for it? It is like a mustard seed that, when it is sown in the ground, is the smallest of all the seeds on the earth. But once it is sown, it springs up and becomes the largest of plants and puts forth large branches, so that the birds of the sky can dwell in its shade." With many such parables he spoke the word to them as they were able to understand it. Without parables he did not speak to them, but to his own disciples he explained everything in private.

JUNE 14TH, 2021
Monday of the Eleventh Week in Ordinary Time

1ST Reading 2 Cor 6:1-10
Brothers and sisters:

As your fellow workers, we appeal to you not to receive the grace of God in vain. For he says: In an acceptable time I heard you, and on the day of salvation I helped you. Behold, now is a very acceptable time; behold, now is the day of salvation. We cause no one to stumble in anything, in order that no fault may be found with our ministry; on the contrary, in everything we commend ourselves as ministers of God, through much endurance, in afflictions, hardships, constraints, beatings, imprisonments, riots, labors, vigils, fasts; by purity, knowledge, patience, kindness, in the Holy Spirit, in unfeigned love, in truthful speech, in the power of God; with weapons of righteousness at the right and at the left; through glory and dishonor, insult and praise.

We are treated as deceivers and yet are truthful; as unrecognized and yet acknowledged; as dying and behold we live; as chastised and yet not put to death; as sorrowful yet always rejoicing; as poor yet enriching many; as having nothing and yet possessing all things.

Responsorial Psalm 98:1, 2b, 3ab, 3cd-4

R. (2a) The Lord has made known his salvation.

Sing to the LORD a new song, for he has done wondrous deeds;

His right hand has won victory for him, his holy arm.

R. The Lord has made known his salvation.

In the sight of the nations he has revealed his justice.

He has remembered his kindness and his faithfulness toward the house of Israel.

R. The Lord has made known his salvation.

All the ends of the earth have seen the salvation by our God.

Sing joyfully to the LORD, all you lands; break into song; sing praise.

R. The Lord has made known his salvation.

Alleluia Ps 119:105

R. Alleluia, alleluia.

A lamp to my feet is your word, a light to my path.

R. Alleluia, alleluia.

Jesus said to his disciples: "You have heard that it was said, an eye for an eye and a tooth for a tooth. But I say to you, offer no resistance to one who is evil. When someone strikes you on your right cheek, turn the other one to him as well. If anyone wants to go to law with you over your tunic, hand him your cloak as well. Should anyone press you into service for one mile, go with him for two miles. Give to the one who asks of you, and do not turn your back on one who wants to borrow."

JUNE 15TH, 2021
Tuesday of the Eleventh Week in Ordinary Time

1ST Reading 2 Cor 8:1-9

We want you to know, brothers and sisters, of the grace of God that has been given to the churches of Macedonia, for in a severe test of affliction, the abundance of their joy and their profound poverty overflowed in a wealth of generosity on their part.

For according to their means, I can testify, and beyond their means, spontaneously, they begged us insistently for the favor of taking part in the service to the holy ones, and this, not as we expected, but they gave themselves first to the Lord and to us through the will of God, so that we urged Titus that, as he had already begun, he should also complete for you this gracious act also. Now as you excel in every respect, in faith, discourse, knowledge, all earnestness, and in the love we have for you, may you excel in this gracious act also.

I say this not by way of command, but to test the genuineness of your love by your concern for others. For you know the gracious act of our Lord Jesus Christ, that for your sake he became poor although he was rich, so that by his poverty you might become rich.

Responsorial Psalm 146:2, 5-6ab, 6c- 7, 8-9a
R. (1b) Praise the Lord, my soul!

or:

R. Alleluia.

Praise the LORD, my soul!

I will praise the LORD all my life; I will sing praise to my God while I live.

R. Praise the Lord, my soul!

or:

R. Alleluia.

Blessed he whose help is the God of Jacob, whose hope is in the LORD, his God,

Who made heaven and earth, the sea and all that is in them.

R. Praise the Lord, my soul!

or:

R. Alleluia.

Who keeps faith forever, secures justice for the oppressed, gives food to the hungry.

The LORD sets captives free.

R. Praise the Lord, my soul!

or:

R. Alleluia.

The LORD gives sight to the blind.

The LORD raises up those who were bowed down; the LORD loves the just. The LORD protects strangers.

R. Praise the Lord, my soul!

or:

R. Alleluia.

Alleluia Jn 13:34

R. Alleluia, alleluia.

I give you a new commandment: love one another as I have loved you.

R. Alleluia, alleluia.

Gospel Mt 5:43-48
Jesus said to his disciples:

"You have heard that it was said, you shall love your neighbor and hate your enemy. But I say to you, love your enemies and pray for those who persecute you, that you may be children of your heavenly Father, for he makes his sun rise on the bad and the good, and causes rain to fall on the just and the unjust. For if you love those who love you, what recompense will you have? Do not the tax collectors do the same? And if you greet your brothers only, what is unusual about that?

Do not the pagans do the same? So be perfect, just as your heavenly Father is perfect."

JUNE 16TH, 2021
Wednesday of the Eleventh Week in Ordinary Time

1ST Reading 2 Cor 9:6-11
Brothers and sisters, consider this: whoever sows sparingly will also reap sparingly, and whoever sows bountifully will also reap bountifully. Each must do as already determined, without sadness or compulsion, for God loves a cheerful giver. Moreover, God is able to make every grace abundant for you, so that in all things, always having all you need, you may have abundance for every good work. As it is written: He scatters abroad, he gives to the poor; his righteousness endures forever. The one who supplies seed to the sower and bread for food will supply and multiply your seed and increase the harvest of your righteousness. You are being enriched in every way for all generosity, which through us produces thanksgiving to God.

Responsorial Psalm 112:1bc-2, 3-4, 9
R. (1b) Blessed the man who fears the Lord.

or:

R. Alleluia.

Blessed the man who fears the LORD, who greatly delights in his commands.

His posterity shall be mighty upon the earth; the upright generation shall be blessed.

R. Blessed the man who fears the Lord.

or:

R. Alleluia.

Wealth and riches shall be in his house; his generosity shall endure forever.

Light shines through the darkness for the upright; he is gracious and merciful and just.

R. Blessed the man who fears the Lord.

or:

R. Alleluia.

Lavishly he gives to the poor; his generosity shall endure forever; his horn shall be exalted in glory.

R. Blessed the man who fears the Lord.

or:

R. Alleluia.

Alleluia Jn 14:23

R. Alleluia, alleluia.

Whoever loves me will keep my word, and my Father will love him and we will come to him.

R. Alleluia, alleluia.

Gospel Mt 6:1-6, 16-18
Jesus said to his disciples:

"Take care not to perform righteous deeds in order that people may see them; otherwise, you will have no recompense from your heavenly Father. When you give alms, do not blow a trumpet before you, as the hypocrites do in the synagogues and in the streets to win the praise of others. Amen, I say to you, they have received their reward. But when you give alms, do not let your left hand know what your right is doing, so that your almsgiving may be secret. And your Father who sees in secret will repay you. "When you pray, do not be like the hypocrites, who love to stand and pray in the synagogues and on street corners so that others may see them. Amen, I say to you, they have received their reward. But when you pray, go to your inner room, close the door, and pray to your Father in secret. And your Father who sees in secret will repay you. "When you fast, do not look gloomy like the hypocrites. They neglect their appearance, so that they may appear to others to be fasting. Amen, I say to you, they have received their reward. But when you fast, anoint your head and wash your face, so that you may not appear to others to be fasting, except to your Father who is hidden. And your Father who sees what is hidden will repay you."

JUNE 17TH, 2021
Thursday of the Eleventh Week in Ordinary Time

1ST Reading 2 Cor 11:1-11
Brothers and sisters:

If only you would put up with a little foolishness from me! Please put up with me. For I am jealous of you with the jealousy of God, since I betrothed you to one husband to present you as a chaste virgin to Christ. But I am afraid that, as the serpent deceived Eve by his cunning, your thoughts may be corrupted from a sincere and pure commitment to Christ. For if someone comes and preaches another Jesus than the one we preached, or if you receive a different spirit from the one you received or a different gospel from the one you accepted, you put up with it well enough. For I think that I am not in any way inferior to these "super apostles." Even if I am untrained in speaking, I am not so in knowledge; in every way we have made this plain to you in all things. Did I make a mistake when I humbled myself so that you might be exalted, because I preached the Gospel of God to you without charge? I plundered other churches by accepting from them in order to minister to you. And when I was with you and in need, I did not burden anyone, for the brothers who came from Macedonia supplied my needs. So I refrained and will refrain from burdening you in any way. By the truth of Christ in me, this boast of mine shall not be silenced in the regions of Achaia. And why? Because I do not love you? God knows I do!

376

R. (7a) Your works, O Lord, are justice and truth.

or:

R. Alleluia.

I will give thanks to the LORD with all my heart in the company and assembly of the just.

Great are the works of the LORD, exquisite in all their delights.

R. Your works, O Lord, are justice and truth.

or:

R. Alleluia.

Majesty and glory are his work, and his justice endures forever.

He has won renown for his wondrous deeds; gracious and merciful is the LORD.

R. Your works, O Lord, are justice and truth.

or:

R. Alleluia.

The works of his hands are faithful and just; sure are all his precepts,

Reliable forever and ever, wrought in truth and equity.

R. Your works, O Lord, are justice and truth.

or:

R. Alleluia.

Alleluia Rom 8:15bc

R. Alleluia, alleluia.

You have received a spirit of adoption as sons through which we cry: Abba! Father!

R. Alleluia, alleluia.

Gospel Mt 6:7-15
Jesus said to his disciples:

"In praying, do not babble like the pagans, who think that they will be heard because of their many words. Do not be like them. Your Father knows what you need before you ask him. "This is how you are to pray: 'Our Father who art in heaven, hallowed be thy name, thy Kingdom come, thy will be done, on earth as it is in heaven. Give us this day our daily bread; and forgive us our trespasses, as we forgive those who trespass against us; and lead us not into temptation, but deliver us from evil."If you forgive others their transgressions, your heavenly Father will forgive you. But if you do not forgive others, neither will your Father forgive your transgressions."

JUNE 18TH, 2021
Friday of the Eleventh Week in Ordinary Time

1ST Reading 2 Cor 11:18, 21-30
Brothers and sisters:

Since many boast according to the flesh, I too will boast. To my shame I say that we were too weak! But what anyone dares to boast of (I am speaking in foolishness) I also dare. Are they Hebrews? So am I. Are they children of Israel? So am I. Are they descendants of Abraham? So am I. Are they ministers of Christ? (I am talking like an insane person). I am still more, with far greater labors, far more imprisonments, far worse beatings, and numerous brushes with death. Five times at the hands of the Jews I received forty lashes minus one. Three times I was beaten with rods, once I was stoned, three times I was shipwrecked, I passed a night and a day on the deep; on frequent journeys, in dangers from rivers, dangers from robbers, dangers from my own race, dangers from Gentiles, dangers in the city, dangers in the wilderness, dangers at sea, dangers among false brothers; in toil and hardship, through many sleepless nights, through hunger and thirst, through frequent fasting, through cold and exposure.

And apart from these things, there is the daily pressure upon me of my anxiety for all the churches. Who is weak, and I am not weak? Who is led to sin, and I am not indignant? If I must boast, I will boast of the things that show my weakness.

R. (see 18b) From all their distress God rescues the just.

I will bless the LORD at all times; his praise shall be ever in my mouth.

Let my soul glory in the LORD; the lowly will hear me and be glad.

R. From all their distress God rescues the just.

Glorify the LORD with me, let us together extol his name.

I sought the LORD, and he answered meand delivered me from all my fears.

R. From all their distress God rescues the just.

Look to him that you may be radiant with joy, and your faces may not blush with shame.

When the poor one called out, the LORD heard, and from all his distress he saved him.

R. From all their distress God rescues the just.

Alleluia Mt 5:3

R. Alleluia, alleluia.

Blessed are the poor in spirit; for theirs is the Kingdom of heaven.

R. Alleluia, alleluia.

Gospel Mt 6:19-23

Jesus said to his disciples:

"Do not store up for yourselves treasures on earth, where moth and decay destroy, and thieves break in and steal. But store up treasures in heaven, where neither moth nor decay destroys, nor thieves break in and steal. For where your treasure is, there also will your heart be. "The lamp of the body is the eye. If your eye is sound, your whole body will be filled with light; but if your eye is bad, your whole body will be in darkness. And if the light in you is darkness, how great will the darkness be."

JUNE 19TH, 2021
Saturday of the Eleventh Week in Ordinary

1ST Reading 2 Cor 12:1-10
Brothers and sisters:

I must boast; not that it is profitable, but I will go on to visions and revelations of the Lord. I know a man in Christ who, fourteen years ago (whether in the body or out of the body I do not know, God knows), was caught up to the third heaven. And I know that this man(whether in the body or out of the body I do not know, God knows) was caught up into Paradise and heard ineffable things, which no one may utter. About this man I will boast, but about myself I will not boast, except about my weaknesses.

Although if I should wish to boast, I would not be foolish, for I would be telling the truth. But I refrain, so that no one may think more of me than what he sees in me or hears from me because of the abundance of the revelations. Therefore, that I might not become too elated, a thorn in the flesh was given to me, an angel of Satan, to beat me, to keep me from being too elated. Three times I begged the Lord about this that it might leave me, but he said to me, "My grace is sufficient for you, for power is made perfect in weakness." I will rather boast most gladly of my weaknesses, in order that the power of Christ may dwell with me. Therefore, I am content with weaknesses, insults, hardships, persecutions, and constraints, for the sake of Christ; for when I am weak, then I am strong.

Responsorial Psalm 34:8-9, 10-11, 12-13
R. (9a) Taste and see the goodness of the Lord.

The angel of the LORD encamps around those who fear him, and delivers them.

Taste and see how good the LORD is; blessed the man who takes refuge in him.

R. Taste and see the goodness of the Lord.

Fear the LORD, you his holy ones, for nought is lacking to those who fear him.

The great grow poor and hungry; but those who seek the LORD want for no good thing.

R. Taste and see the goodness of the Lord.

Come, children, hear me; I will teach you the fear of the LORD.

Which of you desires life, and takes delight in prosperous days?

R. Taste and see the goodness of the Lord.

Alleluia 2 Cor 8:9

R. Alleluia, alleluia.

Jesus Christ became poor although he was rich, so that by his poverty you might become rich.

R. Alleluia, alleluia.

Gospel Mt 6:24-34
Jesus said to his disciples:

"No one can serve two masters. He will either hate one and love the other, or be devoted to one and despise the other. You cannot serve God and mammon. "Therefore I tell you, do not worry about your life, what you will eat or drink, or about your body, what you will wear. Is not life more than food and the body more than clothing? Look at the birds in the sky; they do not sow or reap, they gather nothing into barns, yet your heavenly Father feeds them. Are not you more important than they? Can any of you by worrying add a single moment to your life-span? Why are you anxious about clothes? Learn from the way the wild flowers grow. They do not work or spin. But I tell you that not even Solomon in all his splendor was clothed like one of them. If God so clothes the grass of the field, which grows today and is thrown into the oven tomorrow, will he not much more provide for you, O you of little faith? So do not worry and say, 'What are we to eat?' or 'What are we to drink?' or 'What are we to wear?' All these things the pagans seek. Your heavenly Father knows that you need them all. But seek first the Kingdom of God and his righteousness, and all these things will be given you besides. Do not worry about tomorrow; tomorrow will take care of itself. Sufficient for a day is its own evil."

JUNE 20TH, 2021
Twelfth Sunday in Ordinary Time

The Lord addressed Job out of the storm and said: Who shut within doors the sea, when it burst forth from the womb; when I made the clouds its garment and thick darkness its swaddling bands? When I set limits for it and fastened the bar of its door, and said: Thus far shall you come but no farther, and here shall your proud waves be stilled!

Responsorial Psalm 107:23-24, 25-26, 28-29, 30-31

R. (1b) Give thanks to the Lord, his love is everlasting.

or:

R. Alleluia.

They who sailed the sea in ships, trading on the deep waters,

These saw the works of the LORD and his wonders in the abyss.

R. Give thanks to the Lord, his love is everlasting.

or:

R. Alleluia.

His command raised up a storm wind which tossed its waves on high.

They mounted up to heaven; they sank to the depths; their hearts melted away in their plight.

R. Give thanks to the Lord, his love is everlasting.

or:

R. Alleluia.

They cried to the LORD in their distress; from their straits he rescued them,

He hushed the storm to a gentle breeze, and the billows of the sea were stilled.

R. Give thanks to the Lord, his love is everlasting.

or:

R. Alleluia.

They rejoiced that they were calmed, and he brought them to their desired haven.

Let them give thanks to the LORD for his kindness and his wondrous deeds to the children of men.

R. Give thanks to the Lord, his love is everlasting.

or:

R. Alleluia.

2ND Reading 2 Cor 5:14-17
Brothers and sisters:

The love of Christ impels us, once we have come to the conviction that one died for all; therefore, all have died. He indeed died for all, so that those who live might no longer live for themselves but for him who for their sake died and was raised. Consequently, from now on we regard no one according to the flesh; even if we once knew Christ according to the flesh, yet now we know him so no longer. So whoever is in Christ is a new creation: the old things have passed away; behold new things have come.

Alleluia Lk 7:16

R. Alleluia, alleluia.

A great prophet has risen in our midst God has visited his people.

R. Alleluia, alleluia.

Gospel Mk 4:35-41
On that day, as evening drew on, Jesus said to his disciples: "Let us cross to the other side." Leaving the crowd, they took Jesus with them in the boat just as he was. And other boats were with him. A violent squall came up and waves were breaking over the boat, so that it was already filling up. Jesus was in the stern, asleep on a cushion. They woke him and said to him, "Teacher, do you not care that we are perishing?" He woke up, rebuked the wind, and said to the sea, "Quiet! Be still!" The wind ceased and there was great calm. Then he asked them, "Why are you terrified? Do you not yet have faith?" They were filled with great awe and said to one another, "Who then is this whom even wind and sea obey?"

1ST Reading Gn 12:1-9

The LORD said to Abram:

"Go forth from the land of your kinsfolk and from your father's house to a land that I will show you. "I will make of you a great nation, and I will bless you; I will make your name great, so that you will be a blessing. I will bless those who bless you and curse those who curse you. All the communities of the earth shall find blessing in you." Abram went as the LORD directed him, and Lot went with him.

Abram was seventy-five years old when he left Haran. Abram took his wife, Sarai, his brother's son Lot, all the possessions that they had accumulated, and the persons they had acquired in Haran, and they set out for the land of Canaan. When they came to the land of Canaan, Abram passed through the land as far as the sacred place at Shechem, by the terebinth of Moreh. (The Canaanites were then in the land.) The LORD appeared to Abram and said, "To your descendants I will give this land." So Abram built an altar there to the LORD who had appeared to him. From there he moved on to the hill country east of Bethel, pitching his tent with Bethel to the west and Ai to the east. He built an altar there to the LORD and invoked the LORD by name. Then Abram journeyed on by stages to the Negeb.

Responsorial Psalm 33:12-13, 18-19, 20 and 22

R. (12) Blessed the people the Lord has chosen to be his own.

Blessed the nation whose God is the LORD, the people he has chosen for his own inheritance.

From heaven the LORD looks down; he sees all mankind.

R. Blessed the people the Lord has chosen to be his own.

See, the eyes of the LORD are upon those who fear him, upon those who hope for his kindness,

To deliver them from death and preserve them in spite of famine.

R. Blessed the people the Lord has chosen to be his own.

Our soul waits for the LORD, who is our help and our shield.

May your kindness, O LORD, be upon us who have put our hope in you.

R. Blessed the people the Lord has chosen to be his own.

Alleluia Heb 4:12

R. Alleluia, alleluia.

The word of God is living and effective, able to discern reflections and thoughts of the heart.

R. Alleluia, alleluia.

Gospel Mt 7:1-5
Jesus said to his disciples:

"Stop judging, that you may not be judged. For as you judge, so will you be judged, and the measure with which you measure will be measured out to you. Why do you notice the splinter in your brother's eye, but do not perceive the wooden beam in your own eye? How can you say to your brother, 'Let me remove that splinter from your eye,' while the wooden beam is in your eye? You hypocrite, remove the wooden beam from your eye first; then you will see clearly to remove the splinter from your brother's eye."

JUNE 22ND, 2021
Tuesday of the Twelfth Week in Ordinary Time

1ST Reading Gn 13:2, 5-18
Abram was very rich in livestock, silver, and gold. Lot, who went with Abram, also had flocks and herds and tents, so that the land could not support them if they stayed together; their possessions were so great that they could not dwell together. There were quarrels between the herdsmen of Abram's livestock and those of Lot's. (At this time the Canaanites and the Perizzites were occupying the land.) So Abram said to Lot: "Let there be no strife between you and me, or between your herdsmen and mine, for we are kinsmen. Is not the whole land at your disposal? Please separate from me. If you prefer the left, I will go to the right; if you prefer the right, I will go to the left." Lot looked about and saw how well watered the whole Jordan Plain was as far as Zoar, like the LORD's own garden, or like Egypt. (This was

before the LORD had destroyed Sodom and Gomorrah.)Lot, therefore, chose for himself the whole Jordan Plain and set out eastward.

Thus they separated from each other; Abram stayed in the land of Canaan, while Lot settled among the cities of the Plain, pitching his tents near Sodom. Now the inhabitants of Sodom were very wicked in the sins they committed against the LORD. After Lot had left, the LORD said to Abram: "Look about you, and from where you are, gaze to the north and south, east and west; all the land that you see I will give to you and your descendants forever.

I will make your descendants like the dust of the earth; if anyone could count the dust of the earth, your descendants too might be counted. Set forth and walk about in the land, through its length and breadth, for to you I will give it."Abram moved his tents and went on to settle near the terebinth of Mamre, which is at Hebron. There he built an altar to the LORD.

Responsorial Psalm 15:2-3a, 3bc-4ab, 5
R. (1b) He who does justice will live in the presence of the Lord.

He who walks blamelessly and does justice; who thinks the truth in his heart and slanders not with his tongue.

R. He who does justice will live in the presence of the Lord.

Who harms not his fellow man, nor takes up a reproach against his neighbor;

By whom the reprobate is despised, while he honors those who fear the LORD.

R. He who does justice will live in the presence of the Lord.

Who lends not his money at usury and accepts no bribe against the innocent.

He who does these things shall never be disturbed.

R. He who does justice will live in the presence of the Lord.

Alleluia Jn 8:12

R. Alleluia, alleluia.

I am the light of the world, says the Lord; whoever follows me will have the light of life.

R. Alleluia, alleluia.

Gospel Mt 7:6, 12-14
Jesus said to his disciples:

"Do not give what is holy to dogs, or throw your pearls before swine, lest they trample them underfoot, and turn and tear you to pieces. "Do to others whatever you would have them do to you. This is the Law and the Prophets. "Enter through the narrow gate; for the gate is wide and the road broad that leads to destruction and those who enter through it are many. How narrow the gate and constricted the road that leads to life. And those who find it are few."

JUNE 23RD, 2021
Wednesday of the Twelfth Week in Ordinary Time

1ST Reading Gn 15:1-12, 17-18
The word of the LORD came to Abram in a vision:

"Fear not, Abram! I am your shield; I will make your reward very great." But Abram said, "O Lord GOD, what good will your gifts be, if I keep on being childless and have as my heir the steward of my house, Eliezer?" Abram continued, "See, you have given me no offspring, and so one of my servants will be my heir." Then the word of the LORD came to him: "No, that one shall not be your heir; your own issue shall be your heir."

He took him outside and said: "Look up at the sky and count the stars, if you can. Just so," he added, "shall your descendants be." Abram put his faith in the LORD, who credited it to him as an act of righteousness. He then said to him, "I am the LORD who brought you from Ur of the Chaldeans to give you this land as a possession." "O Lord GOD," he asked, "how am I to know that I shall possess it?" He answered him, "Bring me a three-year-old heifer, a three-year-old she-goat, a three-year-old ram, a turtledove, and a young pigeon." Abram brought him all these, split them in two, and placed each half opposite the other; but the birds he did not cut up.

Birds of prey swooped down on the carcasses, but Abram stayed with them. As the sun was about to set, a trance fell upon Abram, and a deep, terrifying darkness enveloped him. When the sun had set and it was dark, there appeared a smoking fire pot and a flaming torch, which passed between those pieces. It was on that occasion that the LORD made a covenant with

Abram, saying: "To your descendants I give this land, from the Wadi of Egypt to the Great River the Euphrates."

Responsorial Psalm 105:1-2, 3-4, 6-7, 8-9

R. (8a) The Lord remembers his covenant for ever.

or:

R.   Alleluia.

Give thanks to the LORD, invoke his name; make known among the nations his deeds.

Sing to him, sing his praise, proclaim all his wondrous deeds.

R. The Lord remembers his covenant for ever.

or:

R. Alleluia.

Glory in his holy name; rejoice, O hearts that seek the LORD!

Look to the LORD in his strength; seek to serve him constantly.

R. The Lord remembers his covenant for ever.

or:

R. Alleluia.

You descendants of Abraham, his servants, sons of Jacob, his chosen ones!

He, the LORD, is our God; throughout the earth his judgments prevail.

R. The Lord remembers his covenant for ever.

or:

R. Alleluia.

He remembers forever his covenant which he made binding for a thousand generations—

Which he entered into with Abraham and by his oath to Isaac.

R. The Lord remembers his covenant for ever.

or:

R. Alleluia.

Alleluia Jn 15:4a, 5b

R. Alleluia, alleluia.

Remain in me, as I remain in you, says the Lord; whoever remains in me will bear much fruit.

R. Alleluia, alleluia.

Gospel Mt 7:15-20
Jesus said to his disciples:

"Beware of false prophets, who come to you in sheep's clothing, but underneath are ravenous wolves. By their fruits you will know them. Do people pick grapes from thorn bushes, or figs from thistles? Just so, every good tree bears good fruit, and a rotten tree bears bad fruit.

A good tree cannot bear bad fruit, nor can a rotten tree bear good fruit. Every tree that does not bear good fruit will be cut down and thrown into the fire. So by their fruits you will know them."

JUNE 24TH, 2021
Solemnity of the Nativity of Saint John the Baptist
Vigil

1ST Reading Jer 1:4-10
In the days of King Josiah, the word of the LORD came to me, saying: Before I formed you in the womb I knew you, before you were born I dedicated you, a prophet to the nations I appointed you. "Ah, Lord GOD!" I said, "I know not how to speak; I am too young." But the LORD answered me, Say not, "I am too young." To whomever I send you, you shall go; whatever I command you, you shall speak. Have no fear before them, because I am with you to deliver you, says the LORD Then the LORD extended his hand and touched my mouth, saying, See, I place my words in your mouth! This day I set you over nations and over kingdoms, to root up and to tear down, to destroy and to demolish, to build and to plant.

R. (6) Since my mother's womb, you have been my strength.

In you, O LORD, I take refuge; let me never be put to shame.

In your justice rescue me, and deliver me; incline your ear to me, and save me.

R. Since my mother's womb, you have been my strength.

Be my rock of refuge, a stronghold to give me safety, for you are my rock and my fortress.

O my God, rescues me from the hand of the wicked.

R. Since my mother's womb, you have been my strength.

For you are my hope, O Lord; my trust, O LORD, from my youth.

On you I depend from birth; from my mother's womb you are my strength.

R. Since my mother's womb, you have been my strength.

My mouth shall declare your justice, day by day your salvation.

O God, you have taught me from my youth, and till the present I proclaim your wondrous deeds.

R. Since my mother's womb, you have been my strength.

2ND Reading 1 Pt 1:8-12
Beloved:

Although you have not seen Jesus Christ you love him; even though you do not see him now yet believe in him, you rejoice with an indescribable and glorious joy, as you attain the goal of your faith, the salvation of your souls. Concerning this salvation, prophets who prophesied about the grace that was to be yours searched and investigated it, investigating the time and circumstances that the Spirit of Christ within them indicated when he testified in advance to the sufferings destined for Christ and the glories to follow them. It was revealed to them that they were serving not themselves but you with regard to the things that have now been announced to you by those who preached the Good News to you through the Holy Spirit sent from heaven, things into which angels longed to look.

R. Alleluia, alleluia.

He came to testify to the light, to prepare a people fit for the Lord.

R. Alleluia, alleluia.

Gospel Lk 1:5-17

In the days of Herod, King of Judea, there was a priest named Zechariah of the priestly division of Abijah; his wife was from the daughters of Aaron, and her name was Elizabeth. Both were righteous in the eyes of God, observing all the commandments and ordinances of the Lord blamelessly. But they had no child, because Elizabeth was barren and both were advanced in years. Once when he was serving as priest in his division's turn before God, according to the practice of the priestly service, he was chosen by lot to enter the sanctuary of the Lord to burn incense.

Then, when the whole assembly of the people was praying outside at the hour of the incense offering, the angel of the Lord appeared to him, standing at the right of the altar of incense. Zechariah was troubled by what he saw, and fear came upon him. But the angel said to him, "Do not be afraid, Zechariah, because your prayer has been heard. Your wife Elizabeth will bear you a son, and you shall name him John. And you will have joy and gladness, and many will rejoice at his birth, for he will be great in the sight of the Lord. John will drink neither wine nor strong drink. He will be filled with the Holy Spirit even from his mother's womb, and he will turn many of the children of Israel to the Lord their God. He will go before him in the spirit and power of Elijah to turn their hearts toward their children and the disobedient to the understanding of the righteous, to prepare a people fit for the Lord."

Mass during the Day

1ST Reading Is 49:1-6

Hear me, O coastlands, listen, O distant peoples. The LORD called me from birth; from my mother's womb he gave me my name. He made of me a sharp-edged sword and concealed me in the shadow of his arm. He made me a polished arrow; in his quiver he hid me. You are my servant, he said to me, Israel, through whom I show my glory.

Though I thought I had toiled in vain, and for nothing, uselessly, spent my strength, yet my reward is with the LORD, my recompense is with my God.

For now the LORD has spoken who formed me as his servant from the womb, that Jacob may be brought back to him and Israel gathered to him; and I am made glorious in the sight of the LORD, and my God is now my strength! It is too little, he says, for you to be my servant, to raise up the tribes of Jacob, and restore the survivors of Israel;

I will make you a light to the nations that my salvation may reach to the ends of the earth.

Responsorial Psalm 139:1b-3, 13-14ab, 14c-15
R. (14) I praise you, for I am wonderfully made.

O LORD, you have probed me, you know me: you know when I sit and when I stand; you understand my thoughts from afar.

My journeys and my rest you scrutinize, with all my ways you are familiar.

R. I praise you for I am wonderfully made.

Truly you have formed my inmost being; you knit me in my mother's womb.

I give you thanks that I am fearfully, wonderfully made; wonderful are your works.

R. I praise you, for I am wonderfully made.

My soul also you knew full well; nor was my frame unknown to you

When I was made in secret, when I was fashioned in the depths of the earth.

R. I praise you, for I am wonderfully made.

2ND Reading Acts 13:22-26
In those days, Paul said: "God raised up David as king; of him God testified, I have found David, son of Jesse, a man after my own heart; he will carry out my every wish. From this man's descendants God, according to his promise, has brought to Israel a savior, Jesus. John heralded his coming by proclaiming a baptism of repentance to all the people of Israel; and as John was completing his course, he would say, 'What do you suppose that I am? I am not he. Behold, one is coming after me; I am not worthy to unfasten the sandals of his feet.' "My brothers, sons of the family of Abraham, and those others among you who are God-fearing, to us this word of salvation has been sent."

R. Alleluia, alleluia.

You, child, will be called prophet of the Most High, for you will go before the Lord to prepare his way.

R. Alleluia, alleluia.

Gospel Lk 1:57-66, 80

When the time arrived for Elizabeth to have her child she gave birth to a son. Her neighbors and relatives heard that the Lord had shown his great mercy toward her, and they rejoiced with her. When they came on the eighth day to circumcise the child, they were going to call him Zechariah after his father, but his mother said in reply, "No. He will be called John. "But they answered her, "There is no one among your relatives who has this name. "So they made signs, asking his father what he wished him to be called. He asked for a tablet and wrote, "John is his name," and all were amazed. Immediately his mouth was opened, his tongue freed, and he spoke blessing God. Then fear came upon all their neighbors, and all these matters were discussed throughout the hill country of Judea. All who heard these things took them to heart, saying, "What, then, will this child be?" For surely the hand of the Lord was with him. The child grew and became strong in spirit, and he was in the desert until the day of his manifestation to Israel.

JUNE 25TH, 2021
Friday of the Twelfth Week in Ordinary Time

1ST Reading Gn 17:1, 9-10, 15-22

When Abram was ninety-nine years old, the LORD appeared to him and said: "I am God the Almighty. Walk in my presence and be blameless." God also said to Abraham: "On your part, you and your descendants after you must keep my covenant throughout the ages. This is my covenant with you and your descendants after you that you must keep: every male among you shall be circumcised." God further said to Abraham: "As for your wife Sarai, do not call her Sarai; her name shall be Sarah. I will bless her, and I will give you a son by her. Him also will I bless; he shall give rise to nations, and rulers of peoples shall issue from him." Abraham prostrated himself and laughed as he said to himself, "Can a child be born to a man who is a hundred years old? Or can Sarah give birth at ninety?"

Then Abraham said to God, "Let but Ishmael live on by your favor!" God replied: "Nevertheless, your wife Sarah is to bear you a son, and you shall call him Isaac. I will maintain my covenant with him as an everlasting pact, to be his God and the God of his descendants after him. As for Ishmael, I am heeding you: I hereby bless him. I will make him fertile and will multiply him exceedingly. He shall become the father of twelve chieftains, and I will make of him a great nation. But my covenant I will maintain with Isaac, whom Sarah shall bear to you by this time next year." When he had finished speaking with him, God departed from Abraham.

Responsorial Psalm 128:1-2, 3, 4-5
R. (4) See how the Lord blesses those who fear him.

Blessed are you who fear the LORD, who walk in his ways!

For you shall eat the fruit of your handiwork; blessed shall you be, and favored.

R. See how the Lord blesses those who fear him.

Your wife shall be like a fruitful vine in the recesses of your home;

Your children like olive plants around your table.

R. See how the Lord blesses those who fear him.

Behold, thus is the man blessed who fears the LORD.

The LORD bless you from Zion: may you see the prosperity of Jerusalem all the days of your life.

R. See how the Lord blesses those who fear him.

Alleluia Mt 8:17

R. Alleluia, alleluia.

Christ took away our infirmitiesand bore our diseases.

R. Alleluia, alleluia.

Gospel Mt 8:1-4
When Jesus came down from the mountain, great crowds followed him. And then a leper approached, did him homage, and said, "Lord, if you wish, you

can make me clean." He stretched out his hand, touched him, and said, "I will do it. Be made clean." His leprosy was cleansed immediately. Then Jesus said to him, "See that you tell no one, but go show yourself to the priest, and offer the gift that Moses prescribed; that will be proof for them."

JUNE 26TH, 2021
Saturday of the Twelfth Week in Ordinary Time

1ST Reading Gn 8:1-15

The LORD appeared to Abraham by the Terebinth of Mamre, as Abraham sat in the entrance of his tent, while the day was growing hot. Looking up, he saw three men standing nearby. When he saw them, he ran from the entrance of the tent to greet them; and bowing to the ground, he said: "Sir, if I may ask you this favor, please do not go on past your servant. Let some water be brought, that you may bathe your feet, and then rest yourselves under the tree. Now that you have come this close to your servant, let me bring you a little food that you may refresh yourselves; and afterward you may go on your way." The men replied, "Very well, do as you have said." Abraham hastened into the tent and told Sarah, "Quick, three measures of fine flour! Knead it and make rolls." He ran to the herd, picked out a tender, choice steer, and gave it to a servant, who quickly prepared it.

Then Abraham got some curds and milk, as well as the steer that had been prepared, and set these before them; and he waited on them under the tree while they ate. They asked him, "Where is your wife Sarah?" He replied, "There in the tent." One of them said, "I will surely return to you about this time next year, and Sarah will then have a son." Sarah was listening at the entrance of the tent, just behind him.

Now Abraham and Sarah were old, advanced in years, and Sarah had stopped having her womanly periods. So Sarah laughed to herself and said, "Now that I am so withered and my husband is so old, am I still to have sexual pleasure?" But the LORD said to Abraham: "Why did Sarah laugh and say, 'Shall I really bear a child, old as I am?' Is anything too marvelous for the LORD to do? At the appointed time, about this time next year, I will return to you, and Sarah will have a son." Because she was afraid, Sarah dissembled, saying, "I didn't laugh." But he replied, "Yes you did."

Responsorial Psalm Luke 1:46-47, 48-49, 50 and 53, 54-55
R. (see 54b) The Lord has remembered his mercy.

"My soul proclaims the greatness of the Lord, my spirit rejoices in God my Savior."

R. The Lord has remembered his mercy.

"For he has looked with favor on his lowly servant.

From this day all generations will call me blessed: the Almighty has done great things for me, and holy is his Name."

R. The Lord has remembered his mercy.

"He has mercy on those who fear him in every generation.

He has filled the hungry with good things, and the rich he has sent away empty."

R. The Lord has remembered his mercy.

"He has come to the help of his servant Israel for he has remembered his promise of mercy,

The promise he made to our fathers, to Abraham and his children for ever."

R. The Lord has remembered his mercy.

Alleluia Mt 8:17

R. Alleluia, alleluia.

Christ took away our infirmities and bore our diseases.

R. Alleluia, alleluia.

Gospel Mt 8:5-17

When Jesus entered Capernaum, a centurion approached him and appealed to him, saying, "Lord, my servant is lying at home paralyzed, suffering dreadfully." He said to him, "I will come and cure him." The centurion said in reply, "Lord, I am not worthy to have you enter under my roof; only say the word and my servant will be healed. For I too am a man subject to authority, with soldiers subject to me. And I say to one, 'Go,' and he goes; and to another, 'Come here,' and he comes; and to my slave, 'Do this,' and he does it."

When Jesus heard this, he was amazed and said to those following him, "Amen, I say to you, in no one in Israel have I found such faith. I say to you, many will come from the east and the west, and will recline with Abraham, Isaac, and Jacob at the banquet in the Kingdom of heaven, but the children of the Kingdom will be driven out into the outer darkness, where there will be wailing and grinding of teeth." And Jesus said to the centurion, "You may go; as you have believed, let it be done for you." And at that very hour his servant was healed. Jesus entered the house of Peter, and saw his mother-in-law lying in bed with a fever. He touched her hand, the fever left her, and she rose and waited on him. When it was evening, they brought him many who were possessed by demons, and he drove out the spirits by a word and cured all the sick, to fulfill what had been said by Isaiah the prophet: He took away our infirmities and bore our diseases.

JUNE 27TH, 2021
Thirteenth Sunday in Ordinary Time

1ST Reading Wis 1:13-15; 2:23-24

God did not make death, nor does he rejoice in the destruction of the living. For he fashioned all things that they might have being; and the creatures of the world are wholesome, and there is not a destructive drug among them nor any domain of the netherworld on earth, for justice is undying. For God formed man to be imperishable; the image of his own nature he made him. But by the envy of the devil, death entered the world, and they who belong to his company experience it.

Responsorial Psalm 30:2, 4, 5-6, 11, 12, 13

R. (2a) I will praise you, Lord, for you have rescued me.

I will extol you, O LORD, for you drew me clear and did not let my enemies rejoice over me.

O LORD, you brought me up from the netherworld; you preserved me from among those going down into the pit.

R. I will praise you, Lord, for you have rescued me.

Sing praise to the LORD, you his faithful ones, and give thanks to his holy name.

For his anger lasts but a moment; a lifetime, his good will.

At nightfall, weeping enters in, but with the dawn, rejoicing.

R. I will praise you, Lord, for you have rescued me.

Hear, O LORD, and have pity on me; O LORD, be my helper.

You changed my mourning into dancing; O LORD, my God, forever will I give you thanks.

R. I will praise you, Lord, for you have rescued me.

2ND Reading 2 Cor 8:7, 9, 13-15
Brothers and sisters:

As you excel in every respect, in faith, discourse, knowledge, all earnestness, and in the love we have for you, may you excel in this gracious act also. For you know the gracious act of our Lord Jesus Christ, that though he was rich, for your sake he became poor, so that by his poverty you might become rich. Not that others should have relief while you are burdened, but that as a matter of equality your abundance at the present time should supply their needs, so that their abundance may also supply your needs, that there may be equality. As it is written: Whoever had much did not have more, and whoever had little did not have less.

Alleluia Cf. 2 Tm 1:10

R. Alleluia, alleluia.

Our Savior Jesus Christ destroyed death and brought life to light through the Gospel.

R. Alleluia, alleluia.

Gospel Mk 5:21-43 or 5:21-24, 35b-43
When Jesus had crossed again in the boat to the other side, a large crowd gathered around him, and he stayed close to the sea. One of the synagogue officials, named Jairus, came forward. Seeing him he fell at his feet and pleaded earnestly with him, saying, "My daughter is at the point of death. Please, come lay your hands on her that she may get well and live."

He went off with him, and a large crowd followed him and pressed upon him. There was a woman afflicted with hemorrhages for twelve years. She had suffered greatly at the hands of many doctors and had spent all that she had. Yet she was not helped but only grew worse. She had heard about Jesus and came up behind him in the crowd and touched his cloak. She said, "If I but touch his clothes,

I shall be cured." Immediately her flow of blood dried up. She felt in her body that she was healed of her affliction. Jesus, aware at once that power had gone out from him, turned around in the crowd and asked, "Who has touched my clothes?" But his disciples said to Jesus, "You see how the crowd is pressing upon you, and yet you ask, 'Who touched me?'"

And he looked around to see who had done it. The woman, realizing what had happened to her, approached in fear and trembling. She fell down before Jesus and told him the whole truth. He said to her, "Daughter, your faith has saved you. Go in peace and be cured of your affliction." While he was still speaking, people from the synagogue official's house arrived and said, "Your daughter has died; why trouble the teacher any longer?" Disregarding the message that was reported, Jesus said to the synagogue official, "Do not be afraid; just have faith. "He did not allow anyone to accompany him inside except Peter, James, and John, the brother of James. When they arrived at the house of the synagogue official, he caught sight of a commotion, people weeping and wailing loudly. So he went in and said to them, "Why this commotion and weeping? The child is not dead but asleep." And they ridiculed him. Then he put them all out. He took along the child's father and mother and those who were with him and entered the room where the child was. He took the child by the hand and said to her, "Talitha koum," which means, "Little girl, I say to you, arise!" The girl, a child of twelve, arose immediately and walked around. At that they were utterly astounded. He gave strict orders that no one should know this and said that she should be given something to eat.

OR:

When Jesus had crossed again in the boat to the other side, a large crowd gathered around him, and he stayed close to the sea. One of the synagogue officials, named Jairus, came forward. Seeing him he fell at his feet and pleaded earnestly with him, saying, "My daughter is at the point of death. Please, come lay your hands on her that she may get well and live." He went off with him, and a large crowd followed him and pressed upon him.

While he was still speaking, people from the synagogue official's house arrived and said, "Your daughter has died; why trouble the teacher any longer?" Disregarding the message that was reported, Jesus said to the synagogue official, "Do not be afraid; just have faith." He did not allow anyone to accompany him inside except Peter, James, and John, the brother of James. When they arrived at the house of the synagogue official, he caught sight of a commotion, people weeping and wailing loudly. So he went in and said to them, "Why this commotion and weeping? The child is not dead but asleep." And they ridiculed him. Then he put them all out. He took along the child's father and mother and those who were with him and entered the room where the child was. He took the child by the hand and said to her, "Talitha koum," which means, "Little girl, I say to you, arise!" The girl, a child of twelve, arose immediately and walked around. At that they were utterly astounded. He gave strict orders that no one should know this and said that she should be given something to eat.

JUNE 28TH, 2021
Memorial of Saint Irenaeus, Bishop and Martyr

1ST Reading Gn 18:16-33

Abraham and the men who had visited him by the Terebinth of Mamre set out from there and looked down toward Sodom; Abraham was walking with them, to see them on their way. The LORD reflected: "Shall I hide from Abraham what I am about to do, now that he is to become a great and populous nation, and all the nations of the earth are to find blessing in him? Indeed, I have singled him out that he may direct his children and his household after him to keep the way of the LORD by doing what is right and just, so that the LORD may carry into effect for Abraham the promises he made about him." Then the LORD said: "The outcry against Sodom and Gomorrah is so great, and their sin so grave, that I must go down and see whether or not their actions fully correspond to the cry against them that comes to me. I mean to find out." While the two men walked on farther toward Sodom, the LORD remained standing before Abraham. Then Abraham drew nearer to him and said: "Will you sweep away the innocent with the guilty? Suppose there were fifty innocent people in the city; would you wipe out the place, rather than spare it for the sake of the fifty innocent people within it? Far be it from you to do such a thing, to make the innocent die with the guilty, so that the innocent and the guilty would be treated alike! Should not the judge of all the world act with justice?"

The LORD replied, "If I find fifty innocent people in the city of Sodom, I will spare the whole place for their sake." Abraham spoke up again: "See how I am presuming to speak to my Lord, though I am but dust and ashes! What if there are five less than fifty innocent people?

Will you destroy the whole city because of those five?" He answered, "I will not destroy it if I find forty-five there." But Abraham persisted, saying, "What if only forty are found there?" He replied, "I will forbear doing it for the sake of forty." Then Abraham said, "Let not my Lord grow impatient if I go on.

What if only thirty are found there?" He replied, "I will forbear doing it if I can find but thirty there." Still Abraham went on, "Since I have thus dared to speak to my Lord, what if there are no more than twenty?" He answered, "I will not destroy it for the sake of the twenty." But he still persisted: "Please, let not my Lord grow angry if I speak up this last time. What if there are at least ten there?" He replied, "For the sake of those ten, I will not destroy it." The LORD departed as soon as he had finished speaking with Abraham, and Abraham returned home.

Responsorial Psalm 103:1b-2, 3-4, 8-9, 10-11
R. (8a) The Lord is kind and merciful.

Bless the LORD, O my soul; and all my being, bless his holy name.

Bless the LORD, O my soul, and forget not all his benefits.

R. The Lord is kind and merciful.

He pardons all your iniquities; he heals all your ills.

He redeems your life from destruction; he crowns you with kindness and compassion.

R. The Lord is kind and merciful.

Merciful and gracious is the LORD, slow to anger and abounding in kindness.

He will not always chide, nor does he keep his wrath forever.

R. The Lord is kind and merciful.

Not according to our sins does he deal with us, nor does he requite us according to our crimes.

For as the heavens are high above the earth, so surpassing is his kindness
toward those who fear him.

R. The Lord is kind and merciful.

Alleluia Ps 95:8

R. Alleluia, alleluia.

If today you hear his voice, harden not your hearts.

R. Alleluia, alleluia.

Gospel Mt 8:18-22

When Jesus saw a crowd around him, he gave orders to cross to the other
shore. A scribe approached and said to him, "Teacher, I will follow you
wherever you go." Jesus answered him, "Foxes have dens and birds of the
sky have nests, but the Son of Man has nowhere to rest his head." Another
of his disciples said to him, "Lord, let me go first and bury my father." But
Jesus answered him, "Follow me, and let the dead bury their dead."

JUNE 29TH, 2021
Solemnity of Saints Peter and Paul, Apostles
Vigil

1ST Reading Acts 3:1-10

Peter and John were going up to the temple area for the three o'clock hour
of prayer. And a man crippled from birth was carried and placed at the gate
of the temple called "the Beautiful Gate" every day to beg for alms from the
people who entered the temple. When he saw Peter and John about to go
into the temple, he asked for alms. But Peter looked intently at him, as did
John, and said, "Look at us." He paid attention to them, expecting to receive
something from them. Peter said, "I have neither silver nor gold, but what I
do have I give you: in the name of Jesus Christ the Nazorean, rise and walk."
Then Peter took him by the right hand and raised him up, and immediately
his feet and ankles grew strong. He leaped up, stood, and walked around, and
went into the temple with them, walking and jumping and praising God.
When all the people saw the man walking and praising God, they recognized
him as the one who used to sit begging at the Beautiful Gate of the temple,
and they were filled with amazement and astonishment at what had
happened to him.

R. (5) Their message goes out through all the earth.

The heavens declare the glory of God; and the firmament proclaims his handiwork.

Day pours out the word to day; and night to night imparts knowledge.

R. Their message goes out through all the earth.

Not a word or a discourse whose voice is not heard; through all the earth their voice resounds, and to the ends of the world, their message.

R. Their message goes out through all the earth.

2ND Reading Gal 1:11-20

I want you to know, brothers and sisters, that the Gospel preached by me is not of human origin. For I did not receive it from a human being, nor was I taught it, but it came through a revelation of Jesus Christ. For you heard of my former way of life in Judaism, how I persecuted the Church of God beyond measure and tried to destroy it, and progressed in Judaism beyond many of my contemporaries among my race, since I was even more a zealot for my ancestral traditions. But when God, who from my mother's womb had set me apart and called me through his grace, was pleased to reveal his Son to me, so that I might proclaim him to the Gentiles, I did not immediately consult flesh and blood, nor did I go up to Jerusalem to those who were Apostles before me; rather, I went into Arabia and then returned to Damascus. Then after three years I went up to Jerusalem to confer with Cephas and remained with him for fifteen days. But I did not see any other of the Apostles, only James the brother of the Lord.--As to what I am writing to you, behold, before God, I am not lying.

AlleluiaJn 21:17

R. Alleluia, alleluia.

Lord, you know everything:you know that I love you.

R. Alleluia, alleluia.

Gospel Jn 21:15-19

Jesus had revealed himself to his disciples and, when they had finished breakfast, said to Simon Peter, "Simon, son of John, do you love me more than these? "Simon Peter answered him, "Yes, Lord, you know that I love you. "Jesus said to him, "Feed my lambs. "He then said to Simon Peter a second time, "Simon, son of John, do you love me? "Simon Peter answered him, "Yes, Lord, you know that I love you. "He said to him, "Tend my sheep. "He said to him the third time, "Simon, son of John, do you love me? "Peter was distressed that he had said to him a third time, "Do you love me?" and he said to him, "Lord, you know everything; you know that I love you. "Jesus said to him, "Feed my sheep. Amen, amen, I say to you, when you were younger, you used to dress yourself and go where you wanted; but when you grow old, you will stretch out your hands, and someone else will dress you and lead you where you do not want to go. "He said this signifying by what kind of death he would glorify God. And when he had said this, he said to him, "Follow me."

Mass during the Day

1ST Reading Acts 12:1-11

In those days, King Herod laid hands upon some members of the Church to harm them. He had James, the brother of John, killed by the sword, and when he saw that this was pleasing to the Jews he proceeded to arrest Peter also. –It was the feast of Unleavened Bread. – He had him taken into custody and put in prison under the guard of four squads of four soldiers each.

He intended to bring him before the people after Passover. Peter thus was being kept in prison, but prayer by the Church was fervently being made to God on his behalf. On the very night before Herod was to bring him to trial, Peter, secured by double chains, was sleeping between two soldiers, while outside the door guards kept watch on the prison. Suddenly the angel of the Lord stood by him and a light shone in the cell. He tapped Peter on the side and awakened him, saying, "Get up quickly." The chains fell from his wrists. The angel said to him, "Put on your belt and your sandals." He did so. Then he said to him, "Put on your cloak and follow me." So he followed him out, not realizing that what was happening through the angel was real; he thought he was seeing a vision. They passed the first guard, then the second, and came to the Iron Gate leading out to the city, which opened for them by itself. They emerged and made their way down an alley, and suddenly the angel left him.

Then Peter recovered his senses and said, "Now I know for certain that the Lord sent his angel and rescued me from the hand of Herod and from all that the Jewish people had been expecting."

R. (5) The angel of the Lord will rescue those who fear him.

I will bless the LORD at all times; his praise shall be ever in my mouth.

Let my soul glory in the LORD; the lowly will hear me and be glad.

R. The angel of the Lord will rescue those who fear him.

Glorify the LORD with me, let us together extol his name.

I sought the LORD, and he answered me and delivered me from all my fears.

R. The angel of the Lord will rescue those who fear him.

Look to him that you may be radiant with joy, and your faces may not blush with shame.

When the poor one called out, the LORD heard, and from all his distress he saved him.

R. The angel of the Lord will rescue those who fear him.

The angel of the LORD encamps around those who fear him, and delivers them.

Taste and see how good the LORD is; blessed the man who takes refuge in him.

R. The angel of the Lord will rescue those who fear him.

2ND Reading Tm 4:6-8, 17-18

I, Paul, am already being poured out like a libation, and the time of my departure is at hand. I have competed well; I have finished the race; I have kept the faith. From now on the crown of righteousness awaits me, which the Lord, the just judge, will award to me on that day, and not only to me, but to all who have longed for his appearance. The Lord stood by me and gave me strength, so that through me the proclamation might be completed and all the Gentiles might hear it. And I was rescued from the lion's mouth. The Lord will rescue me from every evil threat and will bring me safe to his heavenly Kingdom. To him be glory forever and ever. Amen.

Alleluia Mt 16:18

R. Alleluia, alleluia.

You are Peter and upon this rock I will build my Church, and the gates of
the netherworld shall not prevail against it.

R. Alleluia, alleluia.

Gospel Mt 16:13-19
When Jesus went into the region of Caesarea Philippi he asked his disciples,
"Who do people say that the Son of Man is?" They replied, "Some say John
the Baptist, others Elijah, still others Jeremiah or one of the prophets." He
said to them, "But who do you say that I am?" Simon Peter said in reply,
"You are the Christ, the Son of the living God. "Jesus said to him in reply,
"Blessed are you, Simon son of Jonah. For flesh and blood has not revealed
this to you, but my heavenly Father. And so I say to you, you are Peter, and
upon this rock I will build my Church, and the gates of the netherworld shall
not prevail against it. I will give you the keys to the Kingdom of heaven.
Whatever you bind on earth shall be bound in heaven; and whatever you
loose on earth shall be loosed in heaven."

JUNE 30TH, 2021
Wednesday of the Thirteenth Week in Ordinary Time

1ST Reading Gn 21:5, 8-20a
Abraham was a hundred years old when his son Isaac was born to him. Isaac
grew, and on the day of the child's weaning Abraham held a great feast.
Sarah noticed the son whom Hagar the Egyptian had borne to Abraham
playing with her son Isaac; so she demanded of Abraham: "Drive out that
slave and her son! No son of that slave is going to share the inheritance with
my son Isaac!" Abraham was greatly distressed, especially on account of his
son Ishmael. But God said to Abraham: "Do not be distressed about the boy
or about your slave woman.

Heed the demands of Sarah, no matter what she is asking of you; for it is
through Isaac that descendants shall bear your name. As for the son of the
slave woman, I will make a great nation of him also, since he too is your
offspring." Early the next morning Abraham got some bread and a skin of
water and gave them to Hagar. Then, placing the child on her back, he sent
her away. As she roamed aimlessly in the wilderness of Beer-sheba, the water
in the skin was used up. So she put the child down under a shrub, and then
went and sat down opposite him, about a bowshot away; for she said to

herself, "Let me not watch to see the child die." As she sat opposite Ishmael, he began to cry.

God heard the boy's cry, and God's messenger called to Hagar from heaven: "What is the matter, Hagar? Don't be afraid; God has heard the boy's cry in this plight of his. Arise, lift up the boy and hold him by the hand; for I will make of him a great nation." Then God opened her eyes, and she saw a well of water. She went and filled the skin with water, and then let the boy drink. God was with the boy as he grew up.

Responsorial Psalm 34:7-8, 10-11, 12-13
R. (7a) The Lord hears the cry of the poor.

When the poor one called out, the LORD heard, and from all his distress he saved him. The angel of the LORD encamps around those who fear him, and delivers them.

R. The Lord hears the cry of the poor.

Fear the LORD, you his holy ones, for nought is lacking to those who fear him. The great grow poor and hungry; but those who seek the LORD want for no good thing.

R. The Lord hears the cry of the poor.

Come, children, hear me; I will teach you the fear of the LORD.

Which of you desires life, and takes delight in prosperous days?

R. The Lord hears the cry of the poor.

Alleluia Jas 1:18

R. Alleluia, alleluia.

The Father willed to give us birth by the word of truth that we may be a kind of first fruits of his creatures.

R. Alleluia, alleluia.

Gospel Mt 8:28-34
When Jesus came to the territory of the Gadarenes, two demoniacs who were coming from the tombs met him. They were so savage that no one could travel by that road. They cried out, "What have you to do with us, Son

of God? Have you come here to torment us before the appointed time?" Some distance away a herd of many swine was feeding.

The demons pleaded with him, "If you drive us out, send us into the herd of swine." And he said to them, "Go then!" They came out and entered the swine, and the whole herd rushed down the steep bank into the sea where they drowned. The swineherds ran away, and when they came to the town they reported everything, including what had happened to the demoniacs. Thereupon the whole town came out to meet Jesus, and when they saw him they begged him to leave their district.

JULY 1ST, 2021
Thursday of the Thirteenth Week in Ordinary Time

1ST Reading Gn 22:1b-19

God put Abraham to the test. He called to him, "Abraham!" "Here I am," he replied. Then God said: "Take your son Isaac, your only one, whom you love, and go to the land of Moriah. There you shall offer him up as a burnt offering on a height that I will point out to you." Early the next morning Abraham saddled his donkey, took with him his son Isaac, and two of his servants as well, and with the wood that he had cut for the burnt offering, set out for the place of which God had told him.

On the third day Abraham got sight of the place from afar. Then he said to his servants: "Both of you stay here with the donkey, while the boy and I go on over yonder. We will worship and then come back to you."

Thereupon Abraham took the wood for the burnt offering and laid it on his son Isaac's shoulders, while he himself carried the fire and the knife.

As the two walked on together, Isaac spoke to his father Abraham: "Father!" he said. "Yes, son," he replied. Isaac continued, "Here are the fire and the wood, but where is the sheep for the burnt offering?" "Son," Abraham answered, "God himself will provide the sheep for the burnt offering." Then the two continued going forward.

When they came to the place of which God had told him, Abraham built an altar there and arranged the wood on it. Next he tied up his son Isaac, and put him on top of the wood on the altar.

Then he reached out and took the knife to slaughter his son. But the LORD's messenger called to him from heaven, "Abraham, Abraham!" "Here I am," he answered. "Do not lay your hand on the boy," said the messenger. "Do not do the least thing to him. I know now how devoted you are to God, since you did not withhold from me your own beloved son." As Abraham looked about, he spied a ram caught by its horns in the thicket. So he went and took the ram and offered it up as a burnt offering in place of his son.

Abraham named the site Yahweh-yireh; hence people now say, "On the mountain the LORD will see." Again the LORD's messenger called to Abraham from heaven and said: "I swear by myself, declares the LORD, that because you acted as you did in not withholding from me your beloved son, I will bless you abundantly and make your descendants as countless as the stars of the sky and the sands of the seashore; your descendants shall take possession of the gates of their enemies, and in your descendants all the nations of the earth shall find blessing all this because you obeyed my command." Abraham then returned to his servants, and they set out together for Beer-sheba, where Abraham made his home.

Responsorial Psalm 115:1-2, 3-4, 5-6, 8-9
R. (9) I will walk in the presence of the Lord, in the land of the living.

or:

R. Alleluia.

Not to us, O LORD, not to us but to your name give glory because of your kindness, because of your truth.

Why should the pagans say, "Where is their God?"

R. I will walk in the presence of the Lord, in the land of the living.

or:

R. Alleluia.

Our God is in heaven; whatever he wills, he does.

Their idols are silver and gold, the handiwork of men.

R. I will walk in the presence of the Lord, in the land of the living.

or:

R. Alleluia.

They have mouths but speak not; they have eyes but see not;

They have ears but hear not; they have noses but smell not.

R. I will walk in the presence of the Lord, in the land of the living.

or:

R. Alleluia.

Their makers shall be like them, everyone who trusts in them.

The house of Israel trusts in the LORD; he is their help and their shield.

R. I will walk in the presence of the Lord, in the land of the living.

or:

R. Alleluia.

Alleluia 2 Cor 5:19

R. Alleluia, alleluia.

God was reconciling the world to himself in Christ and entrusting to us the message of reconciliation.

R. Alleluia, alleluia.

Gospel Mt 9:1-8

After entering a boat, Jesus made the crossing, and came into his own town. And there people brought to him a paralytic lying on a stretcher.

When Jesus saw their faith, he said to the paralytic, "Courage, child, your sins are forgiven." At that, some of the scribes said to themselves, "This man is blaspheming." Jesus knew what they were thinking, and said, "Why do you harbor evil thoughts? Which is easier, to say, 'Your sins are forgiven,' or to say, 'Rise and walk'? But that you may know that the Son of Man has authority on earth to forgive sins"– he then said to the paralytic, "Rise, pick up your stretcher, and go home." He rose and went home.

When the crowds saw this they were struck with awe and glorified God who had given such authority to men.

JULY 2ND, 2021
Friday of the Thirteenth Week in Ordinary Time

First Reading Gn 23:1-4, 19; 24:1-8, 62-67

The span of Sarah's life was one hundred and twenty-seven years. She died in Kiriatharba (that is, Hebron) in the land of Canaan, and Abraham performed the customary mourning rites for her.

Then he left the side of his dead one and addressed the Hittites: "Although I am a resident alien among you, sell me from your holdings a piece of property for a burial ground, that I may bury my dead wife." After the transaction, Abraham buried his wife Sarah in the cave of the field of Machpelah, facing Mamre (that is, Hebron) in the land of Canaan.

Abraham had now reached a ripe old age, and the LORD had blessed him in every way. Abraham said to the senior servant of his household, who had charge of all his possessions: "Put your hand under my thigh, and I will make you swear by the LORD, the God of heaven and the God of earth, that you will not procure a wife for my son from the daughters of the Canaanites among whom I live, but that you will go to my own land and to my kindred to get a wife for my son Isaac."

The servant asked him: "What if the woman is unwilling to follow me to this land? Should I then take your son back to the land from which you migrated?" "Never take my son back there for any reason," Abraham told him. "The LORD, the God of heaven, who took me from my father's house and the land of my kin, and who confirmed by oath the promise he then made to me, 'I will give this land to your descendants'– he will send his messenger before you, and you will obtain a wife for my son there. If the woman is unwilling to follow you, you will be released from this oath. But never take my son back there! "A long time later, Isaac went to live in the region of the Negeb.

One day toward evening he went out . . . in the field, and as he looked around, he noticed that camels were approaching. Rebekah, too, was looking about, and when she saw him, she alighted from her camel and asked the servant, "Who is the man out there, walking through the fields toward us?" "That is my master," replied the servant.

Then she covered herself with her veil. The servant recounted to Isaac all the things he had done. Then Isaac took Rebekah into his tent; he married her, and thus she became his wife. In his love for her, Isaac found solace after the death of his mother Sarah.

Responsorial Psalm 106:1b-2, 3-4a, 4b-5
R. (1b) Give thanks to the Lord, for he is good.

Give thanks to the LORD, for he is good, for his mercy endures forever.

Who can tell the mighty deeds of the LORD, or proclaim all his praises?

R. Give thanks to the Lord, for he is good.

Blessed are they who observe what is right, who do always what is just.

Remember us, O LORD, as you favor your people.

R. Give thanks to the Lord, for he is good.

Visit me with your saving help,

That I may see the prosperity of your chosen ones, rejoice in the joy of your people, and glory with your inheritance.

R. Give thanks to the Lord, for he is good.

Alleluia Mt 11:28

R. Alleluia, alleluia.

Come to me, all you who labor and are burdened, and I will give you rest, says the Lord.

R. Alleluia, alleluia.

Gospel Mt 9:9-13
As Jesus passed by, he saw a man named Matthew sitting at the customs post. He said to him, "Follow me." And he got up and followed him.

While he was at table in his house; many tax collectors and sinners came and sat with Jesus and his disciples. The Pharisees saw this and said to his disciples, "Why does your teacher eat with tax collectors and sinners?" He heard this and said, "Those who are well do not need a physician, but the sick do. Go and learn the meaning of the words, I desire mercy, not sacrifice. I did not come to call the righteous but sinners."

JULY 3RD, 2021
Feast of Saint Thomas, Apostle

1ST Reading Eph 2:19-22
Brothers and sisters:

You are no longer strangers and sojourners, but you are fellow citizens with the holy ones and members of the household of God, built upon the foundation of the Apostles and prophets, with Christ Jesus himself as the capstone. Through him the whole structure is held together and grows into a temple sacred in the Lord; in him you also are being built together into a dwelling place of God in the Spirit.

Responsorial Psalm 117:1bc, 2
R. (Mark 16:15) Go out to all the world and tell the Good News.

Praise the LORD, all you nations; glorify him, all you peoples!

R. Go out to all the world and tell the Good News.

For steadfast is his kindness for us, and the fidelity of the LORD endures forever.

R. Go out to all the world and tell the Good News.

Alleluia Jn 20:29

R. Alleluia, alleluia.

You believe in me, Thomas, because you have seen me, says the Lord; blessed are those who have not seen, but still believe!

R. Alleluia, alleluia.

Gospel Jn 20:24-29
Thomas, called Didymus, one of the Twelve, was not with them when Jesus came. So the other disciples said to him, "We have seen the Lord." But Thomas said to them, "Unless I see the mark of the nails in his hands and put my finger into the nail marks and put my hand into his side, I will not

413

believe." Now a week later his disciples were again inside and Thomas was with them. Jesus came, although the doors were locked, and stood in their midst and said, "Peace be with you." Then he said to Thomas, "Put your finger here and see my hands, and bring your hand and put it into my side, and do not be unbelieving, but believe." Thomas answered and said to him, "My Lord and my God!" Jesus said to him, "Have you come to believe because you have seen me? Blessed are those who have not seen and have believed."

JULY 4TH, 2021
Fourteenth Sunday in Ordinary Time

1ST Reading Ez 2:2-5

As the LORD spoke to me, the spirit entered into me and set me on my feet, and I heard the one who was speaking say to me: Son of man, I am sending you to the Israelites, rebels who have rebelled against me; they and their ancestors have revolted against me to this very day. Hard of face and obstinate of heart are they to whom I am sending you. But you shall say to them:

Thus says the LORD GOD! And whether they heed or resist—for they are arebellious house— they shall know that a prophet has been among them.

Responsorial Psalm Ps 123:1-2, 2, 3-4

R. (2cd) Our eyes are fixed on the Lord, pleading for his mercy.

To you I lift up my eyes who are enthroned in heaven —

As the eyes of servants are on the hands of their masters.

R. Our eyes are fixed on the Lord, pleading for his mercy.

As the eyes of a maid are on the hands of her mistress,

So are our eyes on the LORD, our God, till he have pity on us.

R. Our eyes are fixed on the Lord, pleading for his mercy.

Have pity on us, O LORD, have pity on us, for we are more than sated with contempt; our souls are more than sated with the mockery of the arrogant, with the contempt of the proud.

R. Our eyes are fixed on the Lord, pleading for his mercy.

2ND Reading   Cor 12:7-10
Brothers and sisters:

That I, Paul, might not become too elated, because of the abundance of the revelations, a thorn in the flesh was given to me, an angel of Satan, to beat me, to keep me from being too elated. Three times I begged the Lord about this, that it might leave me, but he said to me, "My grace is sufficient for you, for power is made perfect in weakness." I will rather boast most gladly of my weaknesses, in order that the power of Christ may dwell with me. Therefore, I am content with weaknesses, insults, hardships, persecutions, and constraints, for the sake of Christ; for when I am weak, then I am strong.

Alleluia Cf. Lk 4:18

R. Alleluia, alleluia.

The Spirit of the Lord is upon me, for he sent me to bring glad tidings to the poor.

R. Alleluia, alleluia.

Gospel Mk 6:1-6
Jesus departed from there and came to his native place, accompanied by his disciples. When the sabbath came he began to teach in the synagogue, and many who heard him were astonished. They said, "Where did this man get all this? What kind of wisdom has been given him? What mighty deeds are wrought by his hands! Is he not the carpenter, the son of Mary, and the brother of James and Joses and Judas and Simon? And are not his sisters here with us?" And they took offense at him. Jesus said to them, "A prophet is not without honor except in his native place and among his own kin and in his own house." So he was not able to perform any mighty deed there, apart from curing a few sick people by laying his hands on them. He was amazed at their lack of faith.

JULY 5TH, 2021
Monday of the Fourteenth Week in Ordinary Time

Jacob departed from Beer-sheba and proceeded toward Haran. When he came upon a certain shrine, as the sun had already set, he stopped there for the night. Taking one of the stones at the shrine, he put it under his head and lay down to sleep at that spot.

Then he had a dream: a stairway rested on the ground, with its top reaching to the heavens; and God's messengers were going up and down on it. And there was the LORD standing beside him and saying: "I, the LORD, am the God of your forefather Abraham and the God of Isaac; the land on which you are lying I will give to you and your descendants.

These shall be as plentiful as the dust of the earth, and through them you shall spread out east and west, north and south. In you and your descendants all the nations of the earth shall find blessing. Know that I am with you; I will protect you wherever you go, and bring you back to this land. I will never leave you until I have done what I promised you. "When Jacob awoke from his sleep, he exclaimed, "Truly, the LORD is in this spot, although I did not know it! "In solemn wonder he cried out: "How awesome is this shrine! This is nothing else but an abode of God, and that is the gateway to heaven! "Early the next morning Jacob took the stone that he had put under his head, set it up as a memorial stone, and poured oil on top of it.

He called the site Bethel, whereas the former name of the town had been Luz. Jacob then made this vow: "If God remains with me, to protect me on this journey I am making and to give me enough bread to eat and clothing to wear, and I come back safe to my father's house, the LORD shall be my God. This stone that I have set up as a memorial stone shall be God's abode."

R. (see 2b) In you, my God, I place my trust.

You who dwell in the shelter of the Most High, who abide in the shadow of the Almighty,

Say to the LORD, "My refuge and my fortress, my God, in whom I trust."

R. In you, my God, I place my trust.

For he will rescue you from the snare of the fowler, from the destroying pestilence.

With his pinions he will cover you, and under his wings you shall take refuge.

R. In you, my God, I place my trust.

Because he clings to me, I will deliver him; I will set him on high because he acknowledges my name.

He shall call upon me, and I will answer him; I will be with him in distress.

R. In you, my God, I place my trust.

Alleluia 2 Tm 1:10

R. Alleluia, alleluia.

Our Savior Jesus Christ has destroyed death and brought life to light through the Gospel.

R. Alleluia, alleluia.

Gospel Mt 9:18-26

While Jesus was speaking, an official came forward, knelt down before him, and said,"My daughter has just died. But come, lay your hand on her, and she will live."Jesus rose and followed him, and so did his disciples. A woman suffering hemorrhages for twelve years came up behind him and touched the tassel on his cloak. She said to herself, "If only I can touch his cloak, I shall be cured. "Jesus turned around and saw her, and said, "Courage, daughter! Your faith has saved you. "And from that hour the woman was cured.

When Jesus arrived at the official's house and saw the flute players and the crowd who were making a commotion, he said, "Go away! The girl is not dead but sleeping. "And they ridiculed him. When the crowd was put out, he came and took her by the hand, and the little girl arose. And news of this spread throughout all that land.

JULY 6TH, 2021
Tuesday of the Fourteenth Week in Ordinary Time

1ST Reading Gn 32:23-33

In the course of the night, Jacob arose, took his two wives, with the two maidservants and his eleven children, and crossed the ford of the Jabbok.

After he had taken them across the stream and had brought over all his possessions, Jacob was left there alone.

Then some man wrestled with him until the break of dawn. When the man saw that he could not prevail over him, he struck Jacob's hip at its socket, so that the hip socket was wrenched as they wrestled.

The man then said, "Let me go, for it is daybreak. "But Jacob said, "I will not let you go until you bless me." The man asked, "What is your name?" He answered, "Jacob." Then the man said, "You shall no longer be spoken of as Jacob, but as Israel, because you have contended with divine and human beings and have prevailed." Jacob then asked him, "Do tell me your name, please." He answered, "Why should you want to know my name?" With that, he bade him farewell. Jacob named the place Peniel, "Because I have seen God face to face," he said, "yet my life has been spared." At sunrise, as he left Penuel, Jacob limped along because of his hip. That is why, to this day, the children of Israel do not eat the sciatic muscle that is on the hip socket, inasmuch as Jacob's hip socket was struck at the sciatic muscle.

Responsorial Psalm17:1b, 2-3, 6-7ab, 8b and 15
R. (15a) In justice, I shall behold your face, O Lord.

Hear, O LORD, a just suit; attend to my outcry; hearken to my prayer from lips without deceit.

R. In justice, I shall behold your face, O Lord.

From you let my judgment come; your eyes behold what is right.

Though you test my heart, searching it in the night, though you try me with fire, you shall find no malice in me.

R. In justice, I shall behold your face, O Lord.

I call upon you, for you will answer me, O God incline your ear to me; hear my word.

Show your wondrous mercies, O savior of those who flee from their foes.

R. In justice, I shall behold your face, O Lord.

Hide me in the shadow of your wings.

I in justice shall behold your face; on waking, I shall be content in your presence.

R. In justice, I shall behold your face, O Lord.

Alleluia Jn 10:14

R. Alleluia, alleluia.

I am the good shepherd, says the Lord; I know my sheep, and mine know me.

R. Alleluia, alleluia.

Gospel Mt 9:32-38

A demoniac who could not speak was brought to Jesus, and when the demon was driven out the mute man spoke. The crowds were amazed and said, "Nothing like this has ever been seen in Israel."

But the Pharisees said, "He drives out demons by the prince of demons." Jesus went around to all the towns and villages, teaching in their synagogues, proclaiming the Gospel of the Kingdom, and curing every disease and illness. At the sight of the crowds, his heart was moved with pity for them because they were troubled and abandoned, like sheep without a shepherd. Then he said to his disciples, "The harvest is abundant but the laborers are few; so ask the master of the harvest to send out laborers for his harvest."

JULY 7TH, 2021
Wednesday of the Fourteenth Week in Ordinary Time

1ST Reading Gn 41:55-57; 42:5-7a, 17-24a

When hunger came to be felt throughout the land of Egypt and the people cried to Pharaoh for bread, Pharaoh directed all the Egyptians to go to Joseph and do whatever he told them. When the famine had spread throughout the land, Joseph opened all the cities that had grain and rationed it to the Egyptians, since the famine had gripped the land of Egypt. In fact, all the world came to Joseph to obtain rations of grain, for famine had gripped the whole world.

The sons of Israel were among those who came to procure rations. It was Joseph, as governor of the country, who dispensed the rations to all the people. When Joseph's brothers came and knelt down before him with their faces to the ground, he recognized them as soon as he saw them.

But Joseph concealed his own identity from them and spoke sternly to them. With that, he locked them up in the guardhouse for three days.

On the third day Joseph said to his brothers: "Do this, and you shall live; for I am a God-fearing man. If you have been honest, only one of your brothers need be confined in this prison, while the rest of you may go and take home provisions for your starving families. But you must come back to me with your youngest brother.

Your words will thus be verified, and you will not die." To this they agreed. To one another, however, they said: "Alas, we are being punished because of our brother.

We saw the anguish of his heart when he pleaded with us, yet we paid no heed; that is why this anguish has now come upon us." Reuben broke in, "Did I not tell you not to do wrong to the boy? But you would not listen! Now comes the reckoning for his blood."

The brothers did not know, of course, that Joseph understood what they said, since he spoke with them through an interpreter. But turning away from them, he wept.

Responsorial Psalm 33:2-3, 10-11, 18-19
R. (22) Lord, let your mercy be on us, as we place our trust in you.

Give thanks to the LORD on the harp; with the ten-stringed lyre chant his praises.

Sing to him a new song; pluck the strings skillfully, with shouts of gladness.

R. Lord, let your mercy be on us, as we place our trust in you.

The LORD brings to nought the plans of nations; he foils the designs of peoples.

But the plan of the LORD stands forever; the design of his heart, through all generations.

R. Lord, let your mercy be on us, as we place our trust in you.

But see, the eyes of the LORD are upon those who fear him, upon those who hope for his kindness,

To deliver them from death and preserve them in spite of famine.

R. Lord, let your mercy be on us, as we place our trust in you.

Alleluia Mk 1:15

R. Alleluia, alleluia.

The Kingdom of God is at hand: repent and believe in the Gospel.

R. Alleluia, alleluia.

Gospel Mt 10:1-7
Jesus summoned his Twelve disciples and gave them authority over unclean spirits to drive them out and to cure every disease and every illness. The names of the Twelve Apostles are these: first, Simon called Peter, and his brother Andrew; James, the son of Zebedee, and his brother John; Philip and Bartholomew, Thomas and Matthew the tax collector; James, the son of Alphaeus, and Thaddeus; Simon the Cananean, and Judas Iscariot who betrayed Jesus.

Jesus sent out these Twelve after instructing them thus, "Do not go into pagan territory or enter a Samaritan town. Go rather to the lost sheep of the house of Israel. As you go, make this proclamation: 'The Kingdom of heaven is at hand.'"

JULY 8TH, 2021
Thursday of the Fourteenth Week in Ordinary Time

1ST Reading Gn 44:18-21, 23b-29; 45:1-5
Judah approached Joseph and said: "I beg you, my lord, let your servant speak earnestly to my lord, and do not become angry with your servant, for you are the equal of Pharaoh. My lord asked your servants, 'Have you a father, or another brother?' So we said to my lord, 'We have an aged father, and a young brother, the child of his old age.

This one's full brother is dead, and since he is the only one by that mother who is left, his father dotes on him.' Then you told your servants 'Bring him

421

down to me that my eyes may look on him. Unless your youngest brother comes back with you, you shall not come into my presence again.'

When we returned to your servant our father, we reported to him the words of my lord. "Later, our father told us to come back and buy some food for the family. So we reminded him, '

We cannot go down there; only if our youngest brother is with us can we go, for we may not see the man if our youngest brother is not with us.' Then your servant our father said to us, 'As you know, my wife bore me two sons.

One of them, however, disappeared, and I had to conclude that he must have been torn to pieces by wild beasts; I have not seen him since. If you now take this one away from me, too, and some disaster befalls him, you will send my white head down to the nether world in grief.'"

Joseph could no longer control himself in the presence of all his attendants, so he cried out, "Have everyone withdraw from me!" Thus no one else was about when he made himself known to his brothers. But his sobs were so loud that the Egyptians heard him, and so the news reached Pharaoh's palace. "I am Joseph," he said to his brothers. "Is my father still in good health?" But his brothers could give him no answer, so dumbfounded were they at him. "Come closer to me," he told his brothers.

When they had done so, he said: "I am your brother Joseph, whom you once sold into Egypt. But now do not be distressed, and do not reproach yourselves for having sold me here. It was really for the sake of saving lives that God sent me here ahead of you."

Responsorial Psalm 105:16-17, 18-19, 20-21
R. (5a) Remember the marvels the Lord has done.

or:

R. Alleluia.

When the LORD called down a famine on the land and ruined the crop that sustained them,

He sent a man before them, Joseph, sold as a slave.

R. Remember the marvels the Lord has done.

or:

R. Alleluia.

They had weighed him down with fetters, and he was bound with chains,

Till his prediction came to pass and the word of the LORD proved him true.

R. Remember the marvels the Lord has done.

or:

R. Alleluia.

The king sent and released him, the ruler of the peoples set him free.

He made him lord of his house and ruler of all his possessions.

R. Remember the marvels the Lord has done.

or:

R. Alleluia.

Alleluia Mk 1:15

R. Alleluia, alleluia.

The Kingdom of God is at hand: repent and believe in the Gospel.

R. Alleluia, alleluia.

Gospel Mt 10:7-15

Jesus said to his Apostles:

"As you go, make this proclamation: 'The Kingdom of heaven is at hand.'
Cure the sick, raise the dead, cleanse the lepers, drive out demons. Without
cost you have received; without cost you are to give. Do not take gold or
silver or copper for your belts; no sack for the journey, or a second tunic, or
sandals, or walking stick. The laborer deserves his keep.

Whatever town or village you enter, look for a worthy person in it, and stay
there until you leave. As you enter a house, wish it peace. If the house is
worthy, let your peace come upon it; if not, let your peace return to you.

Whoever will not receive you or listen to your words— go outside that house or town and shake the dust from your feet. Amen, I say to you, it will be more tolerable for the land of Sodom and Gomorrah on the Day of Judgment than for that town."

JULY 9TH, 2021
Friday of the Fourteenth Week in Ordinary Time

1ST Reading Gn 46:1-7, 28-30

Israel set out with all that was his. When he arrived at Beer-sheba, he offered sacrifices to the God of his father Isaac. There God, speaking to Israel in a vision by night, called, "Jacob! Jacob!" He answered, "Here I am." Then he said: "I am God, the God of your father.

Do not be afraid to go down to Egypt, for there I will make you a great nation. Not only will I go down to Egypt with you; I will also bring you back here, after Joseph has closed your eyes." So Jacob departed from Beer-sheba, and the sons of Israel put their father and their wives and children on the wagons that Pharaoh had sent for his transport. They took with them their livestock and the possessions they had acquired in the land of Canaan.

Thus Jacob and all his descendants migrated to Egypt.

His sons and his grandsons, his daughters and his granddaughters all his descendants—he took with him to Egypt. Israel had sent Judah ahead to Joseph, so that he might meet him in Goshen. On his arrival in the region of Goshen, Joseph hitched the horses to his chariot and rode to meet his father Israel in Goshen. As soon as Joseph saw him, he flung himself on his neck and wept a long time in his arms. And Israel said to Joseph, "At last I can die, now that I have seen for myself that Joseph is still alive."

Responsorial Psalm 37:3-4, 18-19, 27-28, 39-40

R. (39a) The salvation of the just comes from the Lord.

Trust in the LORD and do good, that you may dwell in the land and be fed in security.

Take delight in the LORD, and he will grant you your heart's requests.

R. The salvation of the just comes from the Lord.

The LORD watches over the lives of the wholehearted; their inheritance lasts forever.

They are not put to shame in an evil time; in days of famine they have plenty.

R. The salvation of the just comes from the Lord.

Turn from evil and do good, that you may abide forever;

For the LORD loves what is right, and forsakes not his faithful ones.

R. The salvation of the just comes from the Lord.

The salvation of the just is from the LORD; he is their refuge in time of distress.

And the LORD helps them and delivers them; he delivers them from the wicked and saves them, because they take refuge in him.

R. The salvation of the just comes from the Lord.

AlleluiaJn 16:13a, 14:26d

R. Alleluia, alleluia.

When the Spirit of truth comes, he will guide you to all truth and remind you of all I told you.

R. Alleluia, alleluia.

Gospel Mt 10:16-23

Jesus said to his Apostles:

"Behold, I am sending you like sheep in the midst of wolves; so be shrewd as serpents and simple as doves. But beware of men, for they will hand you over to courts and scourge you in their synagogues, and you will be led before governors and kings for my sake as a witness before them and the pagans.

When they hand you over, do not worry about how you are to speak or what you are to say. You will be given at that moment what you are to say. For it will not be you who speak but the Spirit of your Father speaking through you. Brother will hand over brother to death, and the father his child; children will rise up against parents and have them put to death. You will be hated by all because of my name, but whoever endures to the end will be saved. When they persecute you in one town, flee to another. Amen, I say to you, you will not finish the towns of Israel before the Son of Man comes."

JULY 10TH, 2021
Saturday of the Fourteenth Week in Ordinary Time

1ST Reading Gn 49:29-32; 50:15-26a

Jacob gave his sons this charge: "Since I am about to be taken to my people, bury me with my fathers in the cave that lies in the field of Ephron the Hittite, the cave in the field of Machpelah, facing on Mamre, in the land of Canaan, the field that Abraham bought from Ephron the Hittite for a burial ground.

There Abraham and his wife Sarah are buried, and so are Isaac and his wife Rebekah, and there, too, I buried Leah–the field and the cave in it that had been purchased from the Hittites." Now that their father was dead, Joseph's brothers became fearful and thought, "Suppose Joseph has been nursing a grudge against us and now plans to pay us back in full for all the wrong we did him!" So they approached Joseph and said: "Before your father died, he gave us these instructions: 'You shall say to Joseph, Jacob begs you to forgive the criminal wrongdoing of your brothers, who treated you so cruelly.' Please, therefore, forgive the crime that we, the servants of your father's God, committed." When they spoke these words to him, Joseph broke into tears.

Then his brothers proceeded to fling themselves down before him and said, "Let us be your slaves!" But Joseph replied to them: "Have no fear. Can I take the place of God? Even though you meant harm to me, God meant it for good, to achieve his present end, the survival of many people. Therefore have no fear. I will provide for you and for your children." By thus speaking kindly to them, he reassured them. Joseph remained in Egypt, together with his father's family. He lived a hundred and ten years. He saw Ephraim's children to the third generation, and the children of Manasseh's son Machir were also born on Joseph's knees. Joseph said to his brothers: "I am about to die.

God will surely take care of you and lead you out of this land to the land that he promised on oath to Abraham, Isaac and Jacob." Then, putting the sons of Israel under oath, he continued, "When God thus takes care of you, you

426

must bring my bones up with you from this place." Joseph died at the age of a hundred and ten.

Responsorial Psalm 105:1-2, 3-4, 6-7
R. (see Psalm 69:33) Be glad you lowly ones; may your hearts be glad!

Give thanks to the LORD, invoke his name; make known among the nations his deeds.

Sing to him, sing his praise, proclaim all his wondrous deeds.

R. Be glad you lowly ones; may your hearts be glad!

Glory in his holy name; rejoice, O hearts that seek the LORD!

Look to the LORD in his strength; seek to serve him constantly.

R. Be glad you lowly ones; may your hearts be glad!

You descendants of Abraham, his servants, sons of Jacob, his chosen ones!

He, the LORD, is our God; throughout the earth his judgments prevail.

R. Be glad you lowly ones; may your hearts be glad!

Alleluia 1 Pt 4:14

R. Alleluia, alleluia.

If you are insulted for the name of Christ, blessed are you, for the Spirit of God rests upon you.

R. Alleluia, alleluia.

Gospel Mt 10:24-33
Jesus said to his Apostles:

"No disciple is above his teacher, no slave above his master. It is enough for the disciple that he becomes like his teacher, for the slave that he become like his master. If they have called the master of the house Beelzebul, how much more those of his household! "Therefore do not be afraid of them. Nothing is concealed that will not be revealed, nor secret that will not be known. What I say to you in the darkness, speak in the light; what you hear whispered, proclaim on the housetops. And do not be afraid of those who kill the body but cannot kill the soul; rather, be afraid of the one who can destroy both soul and body in Gehenna. Are not two sparrows sold for a small coin? Yet not one of them falls to the ground without your Father's knowledge. Even all the hairs of your head are counted. So do not be afraid; you are worth more than many sparrows.

Everyone who acknowledges me before others I will acknowledge before my heavenly Father. But whoever denies me before others, I will deny before my heavenly Father."

JULY 11TH, 2021
Fifteenth Sunday in Ordinary Time

1ST Reading Am 7:12-15

Amaziah, priest of Bethel, said to Amos, "Off with you, visionary, flee to the land of Judah! There earn your bread by prophesying, but never again prophesy in Bethel; for it is the king's sanctuary and a royal temple." Amos answered Amaziah, "I was no prophet, nor have I belonged to a company of prophets; I was a shepherd and a dresser of sycamores. The LORD took me from following the flock, and said to me, Go, prophesy to my people Israel."

Responsorial Psalm Ps 85:9-10, 11-12, 13-14

R. (8)   Lord, let us see your kindness, and grant us your salvation.

I will hear what God proclaims; the LORD —for he proclaims peace.

Near indeed is his salvation to those who fear him, glory dwelling in our land.

R. Lord, let us see your kindness, and grant us your salvation.

Kindness and truth shall meet; justice and peace shall kiss.

Truth shall spring out of the earth, and justice shall look down from heaven.

R. Lord, let us see your kindness, and grant us your salvation.

The LORD himself will give his benefits; our land shall yield its increase.

Justice shall walk before him, and prepare the way of his steps.

R. Lord, let us see your kindness, and grant us your salvation.

Blessed be the God and Father of our Lord Jesus Christ, who has blessed us in Christ with every spiritual blessing in the heavens, as he chose us in him, before the foundation of the world, to be holy and without blemish before him. In love he destined us for adoption to himself through Jesus Christ, in accord with the favor of his will, for the praise of the glory of his grace that he granted us in the beloved. In him we have redemption by his blood, the forgiveness of transgressions, in accord with the riches of his grace that he lavished upon us.

In all wisdom and insight, he has made known to us the mystery of his will in accord with his favor that he set forth in him as a plan for the fullness of times, to sum up all things in Christ, in heaven and on earth. In him we were also chosen, destined in accord with the purpose of the One who accomplishes all things according to the intention of his will, so that we might exist for the praise of his glory, we who first hoped in Christ.

In him you also, who have heard the word of truth, the gospel of your salvation, and have believed in him, were sealed with the promised holy Spirit, which is the first installment of our inheritance toward redemption as God's possession, to the praise of his glory.

OR:

Blessed be the God and Father of our Lord Jesus Christ, who has blessed us in Christ with every spiritual blessing in the heavens, as he chose us in him, before the foundation of the world, to be holy and without blemish before him.

In love he destined us for adoption to himself through Jesus Christ, in accord with the favor of his will, for the praise of the glory of God's grace that he granted us in the beloved. In him we have redemption by his blood, the forgiveness of transgressions, in accord with the riches of his grace that he lavished upon us. In all wisdom and insight, he has made known to us the mystery of his will in accord with his favor that he set forth in him as a plan for the fullness of times, to sum up all things in Christ, in heaven and on earth.

R. Alleluia, alleluia.

May the Father of our Lord Jesus Christ enlighten the eyes of our hearts, that we may know what is the hope that belongs to our call.

R. Alleluia, alleluia.

Gospel Mk 6:7-13
Jesus summoned the Twelve and began to send them out two by two and gave them authority over unclean spirits. He instructed them to take nothing for the journey but a walking stick—no food, no sack, no money in their belts. They were, however, to wear sandals but not a second tunic. He said to them, "Wherever you enter a house, stay there until you leave. Whatever place does not welcome you or listen to you, leave there and shake the dust off your feet in testimony against them." So they went off and preached repentance. The Twelve drove out many demons, and they anointed with oil many who were sick and cured them.

JULY 12TH, 2021
Monday of the Fifteenth Week in Ordinary Time

1ST Reading Ex 1:8-14, 22
A new king, who knew nothing of Joseph, came to power in Egypt. He said to his subjects, "Look how numerous and powerful the people of the children of Israel are growing, more so than we ourselves! Come, let us deal shrewdly with them to stop their increase; otherwise, in time of war they too may join our enemies to fight against us, and so leave our country."

Accordingly, taskmasters were set over the children of Israel to oppress them with forced labor. Thus they had to build for Pharaoh the supply cities of Pithom and Raamses. Yet the more they were oppressed, the more they multiplied and spread. The Egyptians, then, dreaded the children of Israel and reduced them to cruel slavery, making life bitter for them with hard work in mortar and brick and all kinds of field work—the whole cruel fate of slaves.

Pharaoh then commanded all his subjects, "Throw into the river every boy that is born to the Hebrews, but you may let all the girls live."

Responsorial Psalm 124:1b-3, 4-6, 7-8
R. (8a) Our help is in the name of the Lord.

Had not the LORD been with us– let Israel say, had not the LORD been with us–

When men rose up against us, then would they have swallowed us alive, when their fury was inflamed against us.

R. Our help is in the name of the Lord.

Then would the waters have overwhelmed us;

The torrent would have swept over us; over us then would have swept the raging waters.

Blessed be the LORD, who did not leave us a prey to their teeth.

R. Our help is in the name of the Lord.

We were rescued like a bird from the fowlers' snare;

Broken was the snare, and we were freed.

Our help is in the name of the LORD, who made heaven and earth.

R. Our help is in the name of the Lord.

Alleluia Mt 5:10

R. Alleluia, alleluia.

Blessed are they who are persecuted for the sake of righteousness, for theirs is the Kingdom of heaven.

R. Alleluia, alleluia.

Gospel Mt 10:34—11:1
Jesus said to his Apostles:

"Do not think that I have come to bring peace upon the earth. I have come to bring not peace but the sword. For I have come to set a man against his father, a daughter against her mother, and a daughter-in-law against her mother-in-law; and one's enemies will be those of his household. "Whoever loves father or mother more than me is not worthy of me, and whoever loves son or daughter more than me is not worthy of me; and whoever does not take up his cross and follow after me is not worthy of me.

Whoever finds his life will lose it, and whoever loses his life for my sake will find it. "Whoever receives you receives me, and whoever receives me receives the one who sent me. Whoever receives a prophet because he is a prophet will receive a prophet's reward, and whoever receives a righteous man because he is righteous will receive a righteous man's reward.

And whoever gives only a cup of cold water to one of these little ones to drink because he is a disciple—amen, I say to you, he will surely not lose his reward." When Jesus finished giving these commands to his Twelve disciples, he went away from that place to teach and to preach in their towns.

JULY 13TH, 2021
Tuesday of the Fifteenth Week in Ordinary Time

1ST Reading Ex 2:1-15a

A certain man of the house of Levi married a Levite woman, who conceived and bore a son. Seeing that he was a goodly child, she hid him for three months. When she could hide him no longer, she took a papyrus basket, daubed it with bitumen and pitch, and putting the child in it, placed it among the reeds on the river bank. His sister stationed herself at a distance to find out what would happen to him. Pharaoh's daughter came down to the river to bathe, while her maids walked along the river bank. Noticing the basket among the reeds, she sent her handmaid to fetch it.

On opening it, she looked, and lo, there was a baby boy, crying! She was moved with pity for him and said, "It is one of the Hebrews' children." Then his sister asked Pharaoh's daughter, "Shall I go and call one of the Hebrew women to nurse the child for you?" "Yes, do so," she answered. So the maiden went and called the child's own mother. Pharaoh's daughter said to her, "Take this child and nurse it for me, and I will repay you. "The woman therefore took the child and nursed it.

When the child grew, she brought him to Pharaoh's daughter, who adopted him as her son and called him Moses; for she said, "I drew him out of the water."

On one occasion, after Moses had grown up, when he visited his kinsmen and witnessed their forced labor, he saw an Egyptian striking a Hebrew, one of his own kinsmen. Looking about and seeing no one, he slew the Egyptian and hid him in the sand. The next day he went out again, and now two Hebrews were fighting! So he asked the culprit, "Why are you striking your fellow Hebrew?" But the culprit replied, "Who has appointed you ruler and judge over us? Are you thinking of killing me as you killed the Egyptian?" Then Moses became afraid and thought, "The affair must certainly be known." Pharaoh, too, heard of the affair and sought to put Moses to death. But Moses fled from him and stayed in the land of Midian.

Responsorial Psalm 69:3, 14, 30-31, 33-34
R. (see 33) Turn to the Lord in your need, and you will live.

I am sunk in the abysmal swamp where there is no foothold;

I have reached the watery depths; the flood overwhelms me.

R. Turn to the Lord in your need, and you will live.

But I pray to you, O LORD, for the time of your favor, O God!

In your great kindness answer me with your constant help.

R. Turn to the Lord in your need, and you will live.

But I am afflicted and in pain; let your saving help, O God, protect me;

I will praise the name of God in song, and I will glorify him with thanksgiving.

R. Turn to the Lord in your need, and you will live.

"See, you lowly ones, and be glad; you who seek God, may your hearts revive!

For the LORD hears the poor, and his own who are in bonds he spurns not."

R. Turn to the Lord in your need, and you will live.

Alleluia Ps 95:8

R. Alleluia, alleluia.

If today you hear his voice, harden not your hearts.

R. Alleluia, alleluia.

Jesus began to reproach the towns where most of his mighty deeds had been done, since they had not repented. "Woe to you, Chorazin! Woe to you, Bethsaida! For if the mighty deeds done in your midst had been done in Tyre and Sidon, they would long ago have repented in sackcloth and ashes.

But I tell you, it will be more tolerable for Tyre and Sidon on the day of judgment than for you. And as for you, Capernaum: Will you be exalted to heaven? You will go down to the netherworld for if the mighty deeds done in your midst had been done in Sodom, it would have remained until this day. But I tell you, it will be more tolerable for the land of Sodom on the day of judgment than for you."

JULY 14TH, 2021
Memorial of Saint Kateri Tekakwitha, Virgin

1ST Reading Ex 3:1-6, 9-12

Moses was tending the flock of his father-in-law Jethro, the priest of Midian. Leading the flock across the desert, he came to Horeb, the mountain of God. There an angel of the LORD appeared to him in fire flaming out of a bush. As he looked on, he was surprised to see that the bush, though on fire, was not consumed. So Moses decided, "I must go over to look at this remarkable sight, and see why the bush is not burned."

When the LORD saw him coming over to look at it more closely, God called out to him from the bush, "Moses! Moses!" He answered, "Here I am." God said, "Come no nearer! Remove the sandals from your feet, for the place where you stand is holy ground. I am the God of your father," he continued, "the God of Abraham, the God of Isaac, the God of Jacob.

The cry of the children of Israel has reached me, and I have truly noted that the Egyptians are oppressing them. Come, now! I will send you to Pharaoh to lead my people, the children of Israel, out of Egypt." But Moses said to God, "Who am I that I should go to Pharaoh and lead the children of Israel out of Egypt?" He answered, "I will be with you; and this shall be your proof that it is I who have sent you: when you bring my people out of Egypt, you will worship God on this very mountain."

Responsorial Psalm 103:1b-2, 3-4, 6-7

R. (8a) The Lord is kind and merciful.

Bless the LORD, O my soul; and all my being, bless his holy name.

Bless the LORD, O my soul, and forget not all his benefits.

R. The Lord is kind and merciful.

He pardons all your iniquities; he heals all your ills.

He redeems your life from destruction; he crowns you with kindness and compassion.

R. The Lord is kind and merciful.

The LORD secures justice and the rights of all the oppressed.

He has made known his ways to Moses, and his deeds to the children of Israel.

R. The Lord is kind and merciful.

Alleluia Mt 11:25

R. Alleluia, alleluia.

Blessed are you, Father, Lord of heaven and earth; you have revealed to little ones the mysteries of the Kingdom.

R. Alleluia, alleluia.

Gospel Mt 11:25-27
At that time Jesus exclaimed:

"I give praise to you, Father, Lord of heaven and earth, for although you have hidden these things from the wise and the learned you have revealed them to the childlike. Yes, Father, such has been your gracious will. All things have been handed over to me by my Father.

No one knows the Son except the Father, and no one knows the Father except the Son and anyone to whom the Son wishes to reveal him."

JULY 15TH, 2021
Memorial of Saint Bonaventure, Bishop and Doctor of the Church

Moses, hearing the voice of the LORD from the burning bush, said to him, "When I go to the children of Israel and say to them, 'The God of your fathers has sent me to you,' if they ask me, 'What is his name?' what am I to tell them?" God replied, "I am who am." Then he added, "This is what you shall tell the children of Israel: I AM sent me to you." God spoke further to Moses, "Thus shall you say to the children of Israel:

The LORD, the God of your fathers, the God of Abraham, the God of Isaac, the God of Jacob, has sent me to you. "This is my name forever; this my title for all generations. "Go and assemble the elders of Israel, and tell them: The LORD, the God of your fathers, the God of Abraham, Isaac, and Jacob, has appeared to me and said: I am concerned about you and about the way you are being treated in Egypt; so I have decided to lead you up out of the misery of Egypt into the land of the Canaanites, Hittites, Amorites, Perizzites, Hivites, and Jebusites, a land flowing with milk and honey. "Thus they will heed your message.

Then you and the elders of Israel shall go to the king of Egypt and say to him: "The LORD, the God of the Hebrews, has sent us word. Permit us, then, to go a three- days' journey in the desert, that we may offer sacrifice to the LORD, our God. "Yet I know that the king of Egypt will not allow you to go unless he is forced. I will stretch out my hand, therefore, and smite Egypt by doing all kinds of wondrous deeds there. After that he will send you away."

Responsorial Psalm 105:1 and 5, 8-9, 24-25, 26-27
R. (8a) The Lord remembers his covenant for ever.

or:

R. Alleluia.

Give thanks to the LORD, invoke his name; make known among the nations his deeds.

Recall the wondrous deeds that he has wrought, his portents, and the judgments he has uttered.

R. The Lord remembers his covenant for ever.

or:

R. Alleluia.

He remembers forever his covenant which he made binding for a thousand generations

Which he entered into with Abraham and by his oath to Isaac.

R. The Lord remembers his covenant for ever.

or:

R. Alleluia.

He greatly increased his people and made them stronger than their foes,

Whose hearts he changed, so that they hated his people, and dealt deceitfully with his servants.

R. The Lord remembers his covenant for ever.

or:

R. Alleluia.

He sent Moses his servant; Aaron, whom he had chosen. They wrought his signs among them, and wonders in the land of Ham.

R. The Lord remembers his covenant for ever.

or:

R. Alleluia.

Alleluia Mt 11:28

R. Alleluia, alleluia.

Come to me, all you who labor and are burdened, and I will give you rest, says the Lord.

R. Alleluia, alleluia.

Gospel Mt 11:28-30

Jesus said: "Come to me, all you who labor and are burdened, and I will give you rest. Take my yoke upon you and learn from me, for I am meek and humble of heart; and you will find rest for yourselves. For my yoke is easy, and my burden light."

JULY 16TH, 2021
Friday of the Fifteenth Week in Ordinary Time

1ST Reading Ex 11:10—12:14
Although Moses and Aaron performed various wonders in Pharaoh's presence, the LORD made Pharaoh obstinate, and he would not let the children of Israel leave his land. The LORD said to Moses and Aaron in the land of Egypt, "This month shall stand at the head of your calendar; you shall reckon it the first month of the year.

Tell the whole community of Israel: On the tenth of this month every one of your families must procure for itself a lamb, one apiece for each household. If a family is too small for a whole lamb, it shall join the nearest household in procuring one and shall share in the lamb in proportion to the number of persons who partake of it.

The lamb must be a year-old male and without blemish. You may take it from either the sheep or the goats. You shall keep it until the fourteenth day of this month, and then, with the whole assembly of Israel present, it shall be slaughtered during the evening twilight. They shall take some of its blood and apply it to the two doorposts and the lintel of every house in which they partake of the lamb. That same night they shall eat its roasted flesh with unleavened bread and bitter herbs. It shall not be eaten raw or boiled, but roasted whole, with its head and shanks and inner organs. None of it must be kept beyond the next morning; whatever is left over in the morning shall be burned up.

"This is how you are to eat it: with your loins girt, sandals on your feet and your staff in hand, you shall eat like those who are in flight. It is the Passover of the LORD. For on this same night I will go through Egypt, striking down every first born of the land, both man and beast, and executing judgment on all the gods of Egypt—I, the LORD! But the blood will mark the houses where you are. Seeing the blood, I will pass over you; thus, when I strike the land of Egypt, no destructive blow will come upon you. "This day shall be a memorial feast for you, which all your generations shall celebrate with pilgrimage to the LORD, as a perpetual institution."

Responsorial Psalm 116:12-13, 15 and 16bc, 17-18
R. (13) I will take the cup of salvation, and call on the name of the Lord.

How shall I make a return to the LORD for all the good he has done for me?

The cup of salvation I will take up, and I will call upon the name of the LORD.

R. I will take the cup of salvation, and call on the name of the Lord.

Precious in the eyes of the LORD is the death of his faithful ones.

I am your servant, the son of your handmaid; you have loosed my bonds.

R. I will take the cup of salvation, and call on the name of the Lord.

To you will I offer sacrifice of thanksgiving, and I will call upon the name of the LORD.

My vows to the LORD I will pay in the presence of all his people.

R. I will take the cup of salvation, and call on the name of the Lord.

Alleluia Jn 10:27

R. Alleluia, alleluia.

My sheep hear my voice, says the Lord, I know them, and they follow me.

R. Alleluia, alleluia.

Gospel Mt 12:1-8

Jesus was going through a field of grain on the sabbath. His disciples were hungry and began to pick the heads of grain and eat them. When the Pharisees saw this, they said to him, "See, your disciples are doing what is unlawful to do on the sabbath." He said to them, "Have you not read what David did when he and his companions were hungry, how he went into the house of God and ate the bread of offering, which neither he nor his companions but only the priests could lawfully eat?

Or have you not read in the law that on the Sabbath the priests serving in the temple violate the Sabbath and are innocent? I say to you, something greater than the temple is here. If you knew what this meant, I desire mercy, not sacrifice, you would not have condemned these innocent men. For the Son of Man is Lord of the sabbath."

JULY 17TH, 2021
Saturday of the Fifteenth Week in Ordinary Time

First Reading Ex 12:37-42

The children of Israel set out from Rameses for Succoth, about six hundred thousand men on foot, not counting the little ones. A crowd of mixed ancestry also went up with them, besides their livestock, very numerous flocks and herds. Since the dough they had brought out of Egypt was not leavened, they baked it into unleavened loaves. They had rushed out of Egypt and had no opportunity even to prepare food for the journey.

The time the children of Israel had stayed in Egypt was four hundred and thirty years. At the end of four hundred and thirty years, all the hosts of the LORD left the land of Egypt on this very date.

This was a night of vigil for the LORD, as he led them out of the land of Egypt; so on this same nightfall the children of Israel must keep a vigil for the LORD throughout their generations.

Responsorial Psalm 136:1 and 23-24, 10-12, 13-15
R. His mercy endures forever.

or:

R. Alleluia.

Give thanks to the LORD, for he is good, for his mercy endures forever;

Who remembered us in our abjection, for his mercy endures forever;

And freed us from our foes, for his mercy endures forever.

R. His mercy endures forever.

or:

R. Alleluia.

Who smote the Egyptians in their first-born, for his mercy endures forever;

And brought out Israel from their midst, for his mercy endures forever;

With a mighty hand and an outstretched arm, for his mercy endures forever.

R. His mercy endures forever.

or:

R. Alleluia.

Who split the Red Sea in twain, for his mercy endures forever;

And led Israel through its midst, for his mercy endures forever;

But swept Pharaoh and his army into the Red Sea, for his mercy endures forever.

R. His mercy endures forever.

or:

R. Alleluia.

Alleluia 2 Cor 5:19

R. Alleluia, alleluia.

God was reconciling the world to himself in Christ, and entrusting to us the message of reconciliation.

R. Alleluia, alleluia.

Gospel Mt 12:14-21

The Pharisees went out and took counsel against Jesus to put him to death. When Jesus realized this, he withdrew from that place. Many people followed him, and he cured them all, but he warned them not to make him known.

This was to fulfill what had been spoken through Isaiah the prophet: Behold, my servant whom I have chosen, my beloved in whom I delight; I shall place my Spirit upon him, and he will proclaim justice to the Gentiles.

He will not contend or cry out ,nor will anyone hear his voice in the streets. A bruised reed he will not break, a smoldering wick he will not quench, until he brings justice to victory. And in his name the Gentiles will hope.

JULY 18TH, 2021
Sixteenth Sunday in Ordinary Time

Woe to the shepherds who mislead and scatter the flock of my pasture, says the LORD. Therefore, thus says the LORD, the God of Israel, against the shepherds who shepherd my people: You have scattered my sheep and driven them away. You have not cared for them, but I will take care to punish your evil deeds. I myself will gather the remnant of my flock from all the lands to which I have driven them and bring them back to their meadow; there they shall increase and multiply.

I will appoint shepherds for them who will shepherd them so that they need no longer fear and tremble; and none shall be missing, says the LORD. Behold, the days are coming, says the LORD, when I will raise up a righteous shoot to David; as king he shall reign and govern wisely, he shall do what is just and right in the land. In his days Judah shall be saved, Israel shall dwell in security.

This is the name they give him: "The LORD our justice."

R. (1) The Lord is my shepherd; there is nothing I shall want.

The LORD is my shepherd; I shall not want. In verdant pastures he gives me repose; beside restful waters he leads me; he refreshes my soul.

R. The Lord is my shepherd; there is nothing I shall want.

He guides me in right paths for his name's sake.

Even though I walk in the dark valley I fear no evil; for you are at my side with your rod and your staff that give me courage.

R. The Lord is my shepherd; there is nothing I shall want.

You spread the table before me in the sight of my foes; you anoint my head with oil; my cup overflows.

R. The Lord is my shepherd; there is nothing I shall want.

Only goodness and kindness follow me all the days of my life; and I shall dwell in the house of the LORD for years to come.

R. The Lord is my shepherd; there is nothing I shall want.

2ND Reading Eph 2:13-18

Brothers and sisters:

In Christ Jesus you who once were far off have become near by the blood of Christ. For he is our peace, he who made both one and broke down the dividing wall of enmity, through his flesh, abolishing the law with its commandments and legal claims, that he might create in himself one new person in place of the two, thus establishing peace, and might reconcile both with God, in one body, through the cross, putting that enmity to death by it.

He came and preached peace to you who were far off and peace to those who were near, for through him we both have access in one Spirit to the Father.

Alleluia Jn 10:27

R. Alleluia, alleluia.

My sheep hear my voice, says the Lord; I know them, and they follow me.

R. Alleluia, alleluia.

Gospel Mk 6:30-34

The apostles gathered together with Jesus and reported all they had done and taught. He said to them, "Come away by yourselves to a deserted place and rest a while." People were coming and going in great numbers, and they had no opportunity even to eat. So they went off in the boat by themselves to a deserted place. People saw them leaving and many came to know about it.

They hastened there on foot from all the towns and arrived at the place before them. When he disembarked and saw the vast crowd, his heart was moved with pity for them, for they were like sheep without a shepherd; and he began to teach them many things.

JULY 19TH, 2021
Monday of the Sixteenth Week in Ordinary Time

1ST Reading Ex 14:5-18

When it was reported to the king of Egypt that the people had fled, Pharaoh and his servants changed their minds about them. They exclaimed, "What have we done! Why, we have released Israel from our service!" So Pharaoh made his chariots ready and mustered his soldiers' six hundred first-class chariots and all the other chariots of Egypt, with warriors on them all.

So obstinate had the LORD made Pharaoh that he pursued the children of Israel even while they were marching away in triumph. The Egyptians, then, pursued them; Pharaoh's whole army, his horses, chariots and charioteers, caught up with them as they lay encamped by the sea, at Pi-hahiroth, in front of Baal-zephon. Pharaoh was already near when the children of Israel looked up and saw that the Egyptians were on the march in pursuit of them. In great fright they cried out to the LORD. And they complained to Moses, "Were there no burial places in Egypt that you had to bring us out here to die in the desert? Why did you do this to us? Why did you bring us out of Egypt? Did we not tell you this in Egypt, when we said, 'Leave us alone.

Let us serve the Egyptians'? Far better for us to be the slaves of the Egyptians than to die in the desert." But Moses answered the people, "Fear not! Stand your ground, and you will see the victory the LORD will win for you today.

These Egyptians whom you see today you will never see again. The LORD himself will fight for you; you have only to keep still." Then the LORD said to Moses, "Why are you crying out to me? Tell the children of Israel to go forward. And you, lift up your staff and, with hand outstretched over the sea, split the sea in two, that the children of Israel may pass through it on dry land. But I will make the Egyptians so obstinate that they will go in after them.

Then I will receive glory through Pharaoh and all his army, his chariots and charioteers. The Egyptians shall know that I am the LORD, when I receive glory through Pharaoh and his chariots and charioteers."

Responsorial Psalm Exodus 15:1bc-2, 3-4, 5-6
R. (1b) Let us sing to the Lord; he has covered himself in glory.

I will sing to the LORD, for he is gloriously triumphant; horse and chariot he has cast into the sea.

My strength and my courage is the LORD, and he has been my savior.

He is my God, I praise him; the God of my father, I extol him.

R. Let us sing to the Lord; he has covered himself in glory.

The LORD is a warrior, LORD is his name!

Pharaoh's chariots and army he hurled into the sea; the elite of his officers were submerged in the Red Sea.

R. Let us sing to the Lord; he has covered himself in glory.

The flood waters covered them, they sank into the depths like a stone.

Your right hand, O LORD, magnificent in power, your right hand, O LORD, has shattered the enemy.

R. Let us sing to the Lord; he has covered himself in glory.

Alleluia Ps 95:8

R. Alleluia, alleluia.

If today you hear his voice, harden not your hearts.

R. Alleluia, alleluia.

Gospel Mt 12:38-42

Some of the scribes and Pharisees said to Jesus, "Teacher, we wish to see a sign from you." He said to them in reply, "An evil and unfaithful generation seeks a sign, but no sign will be given it except the sign of Jonah the prophet. Just as Jonah was in the belly of the whale three days and three nights, so will the Son of Man be in the heart of the earth three days and three nights. At the judgment, the men of Nineveh will arise with this generation and condemn it, because they repented at the preaching of Jonah; and there is something greater than Jonah here. At the judgment the queen of the south will arise with this generation and condemn it, because she came from the ends of the earth to hear the wisdom of Solomon; and there is something greater than Solomon here."

JULY 20TH, 2021
Tuesday of the Sixteenth Week in Ordinary Time

1ST Reading Ex 14:21—15:1

Moses stretched out his hand over the sea, and the LORD swept the sea with a strong east wind throughout the night and so turned it into dry land. When the water was thus divided, the children of Israel marched into the midst of the sea on dry land, with the water like a wall to their right and to their left.

The Egyptians followed in pursuit; all Pharaoh's horses and chariots and charioteers went after them right into the midst of the sea. In the night watch just before dawn the LORD cast through the column of the fiery cloud upon the Egyptian force a glance that threw it into a panic; and he so clogged their chariot wheels that they could hardly drive. With that the Egyptians sounded the retreat before Israel, because the LORD was fighting for them against the Egyptians.

Then the LORD told Moses, "Stretch out your hand over the sea,that the water may flow back upon the Egyptians, upon their chariots and their charioteers." So Moses stretched out his hand over the sea, and at dawn the sea flowed back to its normal depth. The Egyptians were fleeing head on toward the sea, when the LORD hurled them into its midst. As the water flowed back, it covered the chariots and the charioteers of Pharaoh's whole army

that had followed the children of Israel into the sea. Not a single one of them escaped. But the children of Israel had marched on dry land through the midst of the sea, with the water like a wall to their right and to their left. Thus the LORD saved Israel on that day from the power of the Egyptians.

When Israel saw the Egyptians lying dead on the seashore and beheld the great power that the LORD had shown against the Egyptians, they feared the LORD and believed in him and in his servant Moses. Then Moses and the children of Israel sang this song to the LORD: I will sing to the LORD, for he is gloriously triumphant; horse and chariot he has cast into the sea.

Responsorial Psalm Exodus 15:8-9, 10 and 12, 17
R. (1b) Let us sing to the Lord; he has covered himself in glory.

At the breath of your anger the waters piled up, the flowing waters stood like a mound, the flood waters congealed in the midst of the sea.

The enemy boasted, "I will pursue and overtake them; I will divide the spoils and have my fill of them;

I will draw my sword; my hand shall despoil them!"

R. Let us sing to the Lord; he has covered himself in glory.

When your wind blew, the sea covered them; like lead they sank in the mighty waters.

When you stretched out your right hand, the earth swallowed them!

R. Let us sing to the Lord; he has covered himself in glory.

And you brought them in and planted them on the mountain of your inheritance— the place where you made your seat, O LORD, the sanctuary, O LORD, which your hands established.

R. Let us sing to the Lord; he has covered himself in glory.

Alleluia Jn 14:23

R. Alleluia, alleluia.

Whoever loves me will keep my word, and my Father will love him and we will come to him.

R. Alleluia, alleluia.

Gospel Mt 12:46-50

While Jesus was speaking to the crowds, his mother and his brothers appeared outside, wishing to speak with him. Someone told him, "Your mother and your brothers are standing outside, asking to speak with you." But he said in reply to the one who told him, "Who is my mother? Who are my brothers?" And stretching out his hand toward his disciples, he said, "Here are my mother and my brothers. For whoever does the will of my heavenly Father is my brother, and sister, and mother."

JULY 21ST, 2021
Wednesday of the Sixteenth Week in Ordinary Time

1ST Reading Ex 16:1-5, 9-15

The children of Israel set out from Elim, and came into the desert of Sin, which is between Elim and Sinai,on the fifteenth day of the second month after their departure from the land of Egypt. Here in the desert the whole assembly of the children of Israel grumbled against Moses and Aaron.

The children of Israel said to them, "Would that we had died at the LORD's hand in the land of Egypt, as we sat by our fleshpots and ate our fill of bread!

But you had to lead us into this desert to make the whole community die of famine! "Then the LORD said to Moses, "I will now rain down bread from heaven for you. Each day the people are to go out and gather their daily portion; thus will I test them, to see whether they follow my instructions or not. On the sixth day, however, when they prepare what they bring in, let it be twice as much as they gather on the other days. "Then Moses said to Aaron, "Tell the whole congregation of the children of Israel: Present yourselves before the LORD, for he has heard your grumbling. "When Aaron announced this to the whole assembly of the children of Israel, they turned toward the desert, and lo, the glory of the LORD appeared in the cloud! The LORD spoke to Moses and said, "I have heard the grumbling of the children of Israel. Tell them: In the evening twilight you shall eat flesh, and in the morning you shall have your fill of bread, so that you may know that I, the LORD, am your God. "In the evening quail came up and covered the camp. In the morning a dew lay all about the camp, and when the dew evaporated, there on the surface of the desert were fine flakes like hoarfrost on the ground. On seeing it, the children of Israel asked one another, "What is this?"for they did not know what it was.But Moses told them, "This is the bread which the LORD has given you to eat."

Responsorial Psalm78:18-19, 23-24, 25-26, 27-28
R. (24b) The Lord gave them bread from heaven.

They tempted God in their hearts by demanding the food they craved.

Yes, they spoke against God, saying, "Can God spread a table in the desert?"

R. The Lord gave them bread from heaven.

Yet he commanded the skies above and the doors of heaven he opened;

He rained manna upon them for food and gave them heavenly bread.

R. The Lord gave them bread from heaven.

Man ate the bread of angels, food he sent them in abundance.

He stirred up the east wind in the heavens, and by his power brought on the south wind.

R. The Lord gave them bread from heaven.

And he rained meat upon them like dust, and, like the sand of the sea, winged fowl,

Which fell in the midst of their camp round about their tents.

R. The Lord gave them bread from heaven.

Alleluia

R. Alleluia, alleluia.

The seed is the word of God, Christ is the sower; all who come to him will live for ever.

R. Alleluia, alleluia.

Gospel Mt 13:1-9

On that day, Jesus went out of the house and sat down by the sea. Such large crowds gathered around him that he got into a boat and sat down, and the whole crowd stood along the shore.

And he spoke to them at length in parables, saying: "A sower went out to sow. and as he sowed, some seed fell on the path, and birds came and ate it up.

Some fell on rocky ground, where it had little soil. It sprang up at once because the soil was not deep, and when the sun rose it was scorched, and it withered for lack of roots. Some seed fell among thorns, and the thorns grew up and choked it. But some seed fell on rich soil, and produced fruit, a hundred or sixty or thirtyfold. Whoever has ears ought to hear."

JULY 22ND, 2021
Feast of Saint Mary Magdalene

1ST Reading Sgs 3:1-4b

The Bride says: On my bed at night I sought him whom my heart loves– I sought him but I did not find him. I will rise then and go about the city; in the streets and crossings I will seek Him whom my heart loves. I sought him but I did not find him. The watchmen came upon me, as they made their rounds of the city: Have you seen him whom my heart loves? I had hardly left them when I found him whom my heart loves.

OR:

2 Cor 5:14-17

Brothers and sisters:

The love of Christ impels us, once we have come to the conviction that one died for all; therefore, all have died. He indeed died for all, so that those who live might no longer live for themselves but for him who for their sake died and was raised. Consequently, from now on we regard no one according to the flesh; even if we once knew Christ according to the flesh, yet now we know him so no longer. So whoever is in Christ is a new creation: the old things have passed away; behold, new things have come.

Responsorial Psalm Ps 63:2, 3-4, 5-6, 8-9
R. (2) My soul is thirsting for you, O Lord my God.

O God, you are my God whom I seek; for you my flesh pines and my soul thirsts like the earth, parched, lifeless and without water.

R. My soul is thirsting for you, O Lord my God.

Thus have I gazed toward you in the sanctuary to see your power and your glory,

For your kindness is a greater good than life; my lips shall glorify you.

R. My soul is thirsting for you, O Lord my God.

Thus will I bless you while I live; lifting up my hands, I will call upon your name.

As with the riches of a banquet shall my soul be satisfied, and with exultant lips my mouth shall praise you.

R. My soul is thirsting for you, O Lord my God.

You are my help, and in the shadow of your wings I shout for joy.

My soul clings fast to you; your right hand upholds me.

R. My soul is thirsting for you, O Lord my God.

Alleluia

R. Alleluia, alleluia.

Tell us Mary, what did you see on the way? I saw the glory of the risen Christ, I saw his empty tomb.

R. Alleluia, alleluia.

On the first day of the week, Mary Magdalene came to the tomb early in the morning, while it was still dark, and saw the stone removed from the tomb. So she ran and went to Simon Peter and to the other disciple whom Jesus loved, and told them, "They have taken the Lord from the tomb, and we don't know where they put him." Mary stayed outside the tomb weeping. And as she wept, she bent over into the tomb and saw two angels in white sitting there, one at the head and one at the feet where the Body of Jesus had been. And they said to her, "Woman, why are you weeping?" She said to them, "They have taken my Lord, and I don't know where they laid him."

When she had said this, she turned around and saw Jesus there, but did not know it was Jesus. Jesus said to her, "Woman, why are you weeping? Whom are you looking for?" She thought it was the gardener and said to him, "Sir, if you carried him away, tell me where you laid him, and I will take him." Jesus said to her, "Mary!" She turned and said to him in Hebrew, "Rabbouni," which means Teacher. Jesus said to her, "Stop holding on to me, for I have not yet ascended to the Father. But go to my brothers and tell them, 'I am going to my Father and your Father, to my God and your God.'" Mary Magdalene went and announced to the disciples, "I have seen the Lord," and then reported what he told her.

JULY 23RD, 2021
Friday of the Sixteenth Week in Ordinary Time

In those days:

God delivered all these commandments: "I, the LORD, am your God, who brought you out of the land of Egypt, that place of slavery. You shall not have other gods besides me.

You shall not carve idols for yourselves in the shape of anything in the sky above or on the earth below or in the waters beneath the earth; you shall not bow down before them or worship them. For I, the LORD, your God, am a jealous God, inflicting punishment for their fathers' wickedness on the children of those who hate me, down to the third and fourth generation; but bestowing mercy down to the thousandth generation on the children of those who love me and keep my commandments "You shall not take the name of the LORD, your God, in vain. For the LORD will not leave unpunished him who takes his name in vain.

"Remember to keep holy the sabbath day. Six days you may labor and do all your work, but the seventh day is the sabbath of the LORD, your God. No work may be done then either by you, or your son or daughter, or your male or female slave, or your beast, or by the alien who lives with you. In six days the LORD made the heavens and the earth, the sea and all that is in them; but on the seventh day he rested.

That is why the LORD has blessed the sabbath day and made it holy. "Honor your father and your mother, that you may have a long life in the land which the LORD, your God, is giving you. "You shall not kill. "You shall not commit adultery. "You shall not steal. "You shall not bear false witness against your neighbor. "You shall not covet your neighbor's house. You shall not covet your neighbor's wife, nor his male or female slave, nor his ox or ass, nor anything else that belongs to him."

Responsorial Psalm 19:8, 9, 10, 11
R. (John 6:68c) Lord, you have the words of everlasting life.

The law of the LORD is perfect, refreshing the soul;

The decree of the LORD is trustworthy, giving wisdom to the simple.

R. Lord, you have the words of everlasting life.

The precepts of the LORD are right, rejoicing the heart;

The command of the LORD is clear, enlightening the eye.

R. Lord, you have the words of everlasting life.

The fear of the LORD is pure, enduring forever;

The ordinances of the LORD are true, all of them just.

R. Lord, you have the words of everlasting life.

They are more precious than gold, than a heap of purest gold;

Sweeter also than syrup or honey from the comb.

R. Lord, you have the words of everlasting life.

Alleluia Lk 8:15

R. Alleluia, alleluia.

Blessed are they who have kept the word with a generous heart and yield a harvest through perseverance.

R. Alleluia, alleluia.

Gospel Mt 13:18-23
Jesus said to his disciples:

"Hear the parable of the sower. The seed sown on the path is the one who hears the word of the Kingdom without understanding it, and the Evil One comes and steals away what was sown in his heart. The seed sown on rocky ground is the one who hears the word and receives it at once with joy. But he has no root and lasts only for a time. When some tribulation or persecution comes because of the word, he immediately falls away. The seed sown among thorns is the one who hears the word, but then worldly anxiety and the lure of riches choke the word and it bears no fruit. But the seed sown on rich soil is the one who hears the word and understands it, who indeed bears fruit and yields a hundred or sixty or thirtyfold."

JULY 24TH, 2021
Saturday of the Sixteenth Week in Ordinary Time

1ST Reading Ex 24:3-8
When Moses came to the people and related all the words and ordinances of the LORD, they all answered with one voice, "We will do everything that the LORD has told us." Moses then wrote down all the words of the LORD and, rising early the next day, he erected at the foot of the mountain an altar and twelve pillars for the twelve tribes of Israel.

Then, having sent certain young men of the children of Israel to offer burnt offerings and sacrifice young bulls as peace offerings to the LORD, Moses took half of the blood and put it in large bowls; the other half he splashed on the altar. Taking the book of the covenant, he read it aloud to the people, who answered, "All that the LORD has said, we will heed and do." Then he took the blood and sprinkled it on the people, saying, "This is the blood of the covenant that the LORD has made with you in accordance with all these words of his."

Responsorial Psalm 50:1b-2, 5-6, 14-15
R. (14a) Offer to God a sacrifice of praise.

God the LORD has spoken and summoned the earth, from the rising of the sun to its setting.

From Zion, perfect in beauty, God shines forth.

R. Offer to God a sacrifice of praise.

"Gather my faithful ones before me, those who have made a covenant with me by sacrifice."

And the heavens proclaim his justice; for God himself is the judge.

R. Offer to God a sacrifice of praise. "Offer to God praise as your sacrifice and fulfill your vows to the Most High;

Then call upon me in time of distress; I will rescue you, and you shall glorify me."

R. Offer to God a sacrifice of praise.

Alleluia Jas 1:21bc

R. Alleluia, alleluia.

Humbly welcome the word that has been planted in you and is able to save your souls.

R. Alleluia, alleluia.

Gospel Mt 13:24-30
Jesus proposed a parable to the crowds. "The Kingdom of heaven may be likened to a man who sowed good seed in his field. While everyone was asleep his enemy came and sowed weeds all through the wheat, and then went off. When the crop grew and bore fruit, the weeds appeared as well.

The slaves of the householder came to him and said, 'Master, did you not sow good seed in your field? Where have the weeds come from?' He answered, 'An enemy has done this.' His slaves said to him, 'Do you want us to go and pull them up?' He replied, 'No, if you pull up the weeds you might uproot the wheat along with them. Let them grow together until harvest; then at harvest time I will say to the harvesters, "First collect the weeds and tie them in bundles for burning; but gather the wheat into my barn."'"

JULY 25TH, 2021
Seventeenth Sunday in Ordinary Time

1ST Reading 2 Kgs 4:42-44
A man came from Baal-shalishah bringing to Elisha, the man of God, twenty barley loaves made from the first fruits, and fresh grain in the ear. Elisha said, "Give it to the people to eat." But his servant objected, "How can I set this before a hundred people?" Elisha insisted, "Give it to the people to eat." "For thus says the LORD, 'They shall eat and there shall be some left over.'" And when they had eaten, there was some left over, as the LORD had said.

Responsorial Psalm Ps 145:10-11, 15-16, 17-18
R. (cf. 16) The hand of the Lord feeds us; he answers all our needs.

Let all your works give you thanks, O LORD, and let your faithful ones bless you.

Let them discourse of the glory of your kingdom and speak of your might.

R. The hand of the Lord feeds us; he answers all our needs.

The eyes of all look hopefully to you, and you give them their food in due season; you open your hand and satisfy the desire of every living thing.

R. The hand of the Lord feeds us; he answers all our needs.

The LORD is just in all his ways and holy in all his works.

The LORD is near to all who call upon him, to all who call upon him in truth.

R. The hand of the Lord feeds us; he answers all our needs.

2ND Reading Eph 4:1-6
Brothers and sisters:

I, a prisoner for the Lord, urge you to live in a manner worthy of the call you have received, with all humility and gentleness, with patience, bearing with one another through love, striving to preserve the unity of the spirit through the bond of peace: one body and one Spirit, as you were also called to the one hope of your call; one Lord, one faith, one baptism; one God and Father of all, who is over all and through all and in all.

Alleluia Lk 7:16

R. Alleluia, alleluia.

A great prophet has risen in our midst. God has visited his people.

R. Alleluia, alleluia.

Gospel Jn 6:1-15
Jesus went across the Sea of Galilee. A large crowd followed him, because they saw the signs he was performing on the sick. Jesus went up on the mountain, and there he sat down with his disciples. The Jewish feast of Passover was near. When Jesus raised his eyes and saw that a large crowd was coming to him, he said to Philip, "Where can we buy enough food for them to eat?"

He said this to test him, because he himself knew what he was going to do. Philip answered him, "Two hundred days' wages worth of food would not be enough for each of them to have a little." One of his disciples, Andrew, the brother of Simon Peter, said to him, "There is a boy here who has five barley loaves and two fish; but what good are these for so many?" Jesus said, "Have the people recline." Now there was a great deal of grass in that place. So the men reclined, about five thousand in number.

Then Jesus took the loaves, gave thanks, and distributed them to those who were reclining, and also as much of the fish as they wanted. When they had had their fill, he said to his disciples, "Gather the fragments left over, so that nothing will be wasted." So they collected them, and filled twelve wicker baskets with fragments from the five barley loaves that had been more than they could eat.

When the people saw the sign he had done, they said, "This is truly the Prophet, the one who is to come into the world." Since Jesus knew that they were going to come and carry him off to make him king, he withdrew again to the mountain alone.

JULY 26TH, 2021
Memorial of Saints Joachim and Anne, Parents of the Blessed Virgin Mary

1ST Reading Ex 32:15-24, 30-34

Moses turned and came down the mountain with the two tablets of the commandments in his hands, tablets that were written on both sides, front and back; tablets that were made by God, having inscriptions on them that were engraved by God himself. Now, when Joshua heard the noise of the people shouting, he said to Moses, "That sounds like a battle in the camp." But Moses answered, "It does not sound like cries of victory, nor does it sound like cries of defeat; the sounds that I hear are cries of revelry." As he drew near the camp, he saw the calf and the dancing. With that, Moses' wrath flared up, so that he threw the tablets down and broke them on the base of the mountain. Taking the calf they had made, he fused it in the fire and then ground it down to powder, which he scattered on the water and made the children of Israel drink.

Moses asked Aaron, "What did this people ever do to you that you should lead them into so grave a sin?" Aaron replied, "Let not my lord be angry. You know well enough how prone the people are to evil. They said to me, 'Make us a god to be our leader; as for the man Moses who brought us out of the land of Egypt, we do not know what has happened to him.' So I told them, 'Let anyone who has gold jewelry take it off.'

They gave it to me, and I threw it into the fire, and this calf came out." On the next day Moses said to the people, "You have committed a grave sin. I will go up to the LORD, then; perhaps I may be able to make atonement for your sin." So Moses went back to the LORD and said, "Ah, this people have indeed committed a grave sin in making a god of gold for themselves! If you would only forgive their sin! If you will not, then strike me out of the book that you have written." The LORD answered, "Him only who has sinned against me will I strike out of my book. Now, go and lead the people to the place I have told you. My angel will go before you. When it is time for me to punish, I will punish them for their sin."

Responsorial Psalm 106:19-20, 21-22, 23
R. (1a) Give thanks to the Lord, for he is good.

Our fathers made a calf in Horeb and adored a molten image;

They exchanged their glory for the image of a grass-eating bullock.

R. Give thanks to the Lord, for he is good.

They forgot the God who had saved them, who had done great deeds in Egypt,

Wondrous deeds in the land of Ham, terrible things at the Red Sea.

R. Give thanks to the Lord, for he is good.

Then he spoke of exterminating them, but Moses, his chosen one,

Withstood him in the breach to turn back his destructive wrath.

R. Give thanks to the Lord, for he is good.

Alleluia Jas 1:18

R. Alleluia, alleluia.

The Father willed to give us birth by the word of truth that we may be a kind of first fruits of his creatures.

R. Alleluia, alleluia.

Gospel Mt 13:31-35

Jesus proposed a parable to the crowds. "The Kingdom of heaven is like a mustard seed that a person took and sowed in a field. It is the smallest of all the seeds, yet when full-grown it is the largest of plants. It becomes a large bush, and the birds of the sky come and dwell in its branches. He spoke to them another parable. "The Kingdom of heaven is like yeast that a woman took and mixed with three measures of wheat flour until the whole batch was leavened." All these things Jesus spoke to the crowds in parables. He spoke to them only in parables, to fulfill what had been said through the prophet:

JULY 27TH, 2021
Tuesday of the Seventeenth Week in Ordinary Time

The tent, which was called the meeting tent, Moses used to pitch at some distance away, outside the camp. Anyone who wished to consult the LORD would go to this meeting tent outside the camp. Whenever Moses went out to the tent, the people would all rise and stand at the entrance of their own tents, watching Moses until he entered the tent. As Moses entered the tent, the column of cloud would come down and stand at its entrance while the LORD spoke with Moses. On seeing the column of cloud stand at the entrance of the tent, all the people would rise and worship at the entrance of their own tents.

The LORD used to speak to Moses face to face, as one man speaks to another. Moses would then return to the camp, but his young assistant, Joshua, son of Nun, would not move out of the tent. Moses stood there with the LORD and proclaimed his name, "LORD." Thus the LORD passed before him and cried out, "The LORD, the LORD, a merciful and gracious God, slow to anger and rich in kindness and fidelity, continuing his kindness for a thousand generations, and forgiving wickedness and crime and sin; yet not declaring the guilty guiltless, but punishing children and grandchildren to the third and fourth generation for their fathers' wickedness!"

Moses at once bowed down to the ground in worship. Then he said, "If I find favor with you, O LORD, do come along in our company. T

his is indeed a stiff-necked people; yet pardon our wickedness and sins, and receive us as your own." So Moses stayed there with the LORD for forty days and forty nights, without eating any food or drinking any water, and he wrote on the tablets the words of the covenant, the Ten Commandments.

Responsorial Psalm 103:6-7, 8-9, 10-11, 12-13
R. (8a) The Lord is kind and merciful.

The LORD secures justice and the rights of all the oppressed.

He has made known his ways to Moses, and his deeds to the children of Israel.

R. The Lord is kind and merciful.

Merciful and gracious is the LORD, slow to anger and abounding in kindness.

He will not always chide, nor does he keep his wrath forever.

R. The Lord is kind and merciful.

Not according to our sins does he deal with us, nor does he requite us according to our crimes.

For as the heavens are high above the earth, so surpassing is his kindness toward those who fear him.

R. The Lord is kind and merciful.

As far as the east is from the west, so far has he put our transgressions from us.

As a father has compassion on his children, so the LORD has compassion on those who fear him.

R. The Lord is kind and merciful.

Alleluia

R. Alleluia, alleluia.

The seed is the word of God, Christ is the sower; all who come to him will live for ever.

R. Alleluia, alleluia

Gospel Mt 13:36-43

Jesus dismissed the crowds and went into the house. His disciples approached him and said, "Explain to us the parable of the weeds in the field." He said in reply, "He who sows good seed is the Son of Man, the field is the world, the good seed the children of the Kingdom. The weeds are the children of the Evil One, and the enemy who sows them is the Devil.

The harvest is the end of the age, and the harvesters are angels. Just as weeds are collected and burned up with fire, so will it be at the end of the age. The Son of Man will send his angels, and they will collect out of his Kingdom all who cause others to sin and all evildoers.

They will throw them into the fiery furnace, where there will be wailing and grinding of teeth. Then the righteous will shine like the sun in the Kingdom of their Father. Whoever has ears ought to hear."

Wednesday of the Seventeenth Week in Ordinary Time

1ST Reading Ex 34:29-35

As Moses came down from Mount Sinai with the two tablets of the commandments in his hands, he did not know that the skin of his face had become radiant while he conversed with the LORD. When Aaron, then, and the other children of Israel saw Moses and noticed how radiant the skin of his face had become, they were afraid to come near him. Only after Moses called to them did Aaron and all the rulers of the community come back to him. Moses then spoke to them. Later on, all the children of Israel came up to him, and he enjoined on them all that the LORD had told him on Mount Sinai. When he finished speaking with them, he put a veil over his face.

Whenever Moses entered the presence of the LORD to converse with him, he removed the veil until he came out again. On coming out, he would tell the children of Israel all that had been commanded. Then the children of Israel would see that the skin of Moses' face was radiant; so he would again put the veil over his face until he went in to converse with the LORD.

Responsorial Psalm 99:5, 6, 7, 9

R. (see 9c) Holy is the Lord our God.

Extol the LORD, our God, and worship at his footstool; holy is he!

R. Holy is the Lord our God.

Moses and Aaron were among his priests, and Samuel, among those who called upon his name; they called upon the LORD, and he answered them.

R. Holy is the Lord our God.

From the pillar of cloud he spoke to them; they heard his decrees and the law he gave them.

R. Holy is the Lord our God.

Extol the LORD, our God, and worship at his holy mountain; for holy is the LORD, our God.

R. Holy is the Lord our God.

Alleluia Jn 15:15b

R. Alleluia, alleluia.

I call you my friends, says the Lord, for I have made known to you all that the Father has told me.

R. Alleluia, alleluia.

Gospel Mt 13:44-46
Jesus said to his disciples: "The Kingdom of heaven is like a treasure buried in a field, which a person finds and hides again, and out of joy goes and sells all that he has and buys that field. Again, the Kingdom of heaven is like a merchant searching for fine pearls. When he finds a pearl of great price, he goes and sells all that he has and buys it."

JULY 29TH, 2021
Memorial of Saint Martha

1ST Reading Ex 40:16-21, 34-38

Moses did exactly as the LORD had commanded him. On the first day of the first month of the second year the Dwelling was erected. It was Moses who erected the Dwelling. He placed its pedestals, set up its boards, put in its bars, and set up its columns. He spread the tent over the Dwelling and put the covering on top of the tent, as the LORD had commanded him. He took the commandments and put them in the ark; he placed poles alongside the ark and set the propitiatory upon it.

He brought the ark into the Dwelling and hung the curtain veil, thus screening off the ark of the commandments, as the LORD had commanded him. Then the cloud covered the meeting tent, and the glory of the LORD filled the Dwelling. Moses could not enter the meeting tent, because the cloud settled down upon it and the glory of the LORD filled the Dwelling. Whenever the cloud rose from the Dwelling, the children of Israel would set out on their journey. But if the cloud did not lift, they would not go forward; only when it lifted did they go forward.

In the daytime the cloud of the LORD was seen over the Dwelling; whereas at night, fire was seen in the cloud by the whole house of Israel in all the stages of their journey.

Responsorial Psalm 84:3, 4, 5-6a and 8a, 11
R. (2)   How lovely is your dwelling place, O Lord, mighty God!

My soul yearns and pines for the courts of the LORD.

My heart and my flesh cry out for the living God.

R. How lovely is your dwelling place, O Lord, mighty God!

Even the sparrow finds a home, and the swallow a nest in which she puts her young–

Your altars, O LORD of hosts, my king and my God!

R. How lovely is your dwelling place, O Lord, mighty God!

Blessed they who dwell in your house! Continually they praise you.

Blessed the men whose strength you are! They go from strength to strength.

R. How lovely is your dwelling place, O Lord, mighty God!

I had rather one day in your courts than a thousand elsewhere;

I had rather lie at the threshold of the house of my God than dwell in the tents of the wicked.

R. How lovely is your dwelling place, O Lord, mighty God!

Alleluia Jn 8:12

R. Alleluia, alleluia.

I am the light of the world, says the Lord; whoever follows me will have the light of life.

R. Alleluia, alleluia.

Gospel Jn 11:19-27

Many of the Jews had come to Martha and Mary to comfort them about their brother [Lazarus, who had died]. When Martha heard that Jesus was coming, she went to meet him; but Mary sat at home. Martha said to Jesus, "Lord, if you had been here, my brother would not have died. But even now I know that whatever you ask of God, God will give you. "Jesus said to her,

"Your brother will rise." Martha said to him, "I know he will rise, in the resurrection on the last day." Jesus told her, "I am the resurrection and the life; whoever believes in me, even if he dies, will live, and anyone who lives and believes in me will never die. Do you believe this?" She said to him, "Yes, Lord. I have come to believe that you are the Christ, the Son of God, the one who is coming into the world."

OR:

Lk 10:38-42

Jesus entered a village where a woman whose name was Martha welcomed him. She had a sister named Mary who sat beside the Lord at his feet listening to him speak. Martha, burdened with much serving, came to him and said, "Lord, do you not care that my sister has left me by myself to do the serving? Tell her to help me."

The Lord said to her in reply, "Martha, Martha, you are anxious and worried about many things. There is need of only one thing. Mary has chosen the better part and it will not be taken from her."

JULY 30TH, 2021
Friday of the Seventeenth Week in Ordinary Time

1ST Reading Lv 23:1, 4-11, 15-16, 27, 34b-37

The LORD said to Moses, "These are the festivals of the LORD which you shall celebrate at their proper time with a sacred assembly. The Passover of the LORD falls on the fourteenth day of the first month, at the evening twilight.

The fifteenth day of this month is the LORD's feast of Unleavened Bread. For seven days you shall eat unleavened bread. On the first of these days you shall hold a sacred assembly and do no sort of work. On each of the seven days you shall offer an oblation to the LORD. Then on the seventh day you shall again hold a sacred assembly and do no sort of work." The LORD said to Moses, "Speak to the children of Israel and tell them:

When you come into the land which I am giving you, and reap your harvest, you shall bring a sheaf of the first fruits of your harvest to the priest, who shall wave the sheaf before the LORD that it may be acceptable for you. On the day after the sabbath the priest shall do this. "Beginning with the day after the sabbath, the day on which you bring the wave-offering sheaf, you shall count seven full weeks, and then on the day after the seventh week, the

fiftieth day, you shall present the new cereal offering to the LORD. "The tenth of this seventh month is the Day of Atonement, when you shall hold a sacred assembly and mortify yourselves and offer an oblation to the LORD.
"

The fifteenth day of this seventh month is the LORD's feast of Booths, which shall continue for seven days. On the first day there shall be a sacred assembly, and you shall do no sort of work. For seven days you shall offer an oblation to the LORD, and on the eighth day you shall again hold a sacred assembly and offer an oblation to the LORD. On that solemn closing you shall do no sort of work. "These, therefore, are the festivals of the LORD on which you shall proclaim a sacred assembly, and offer as an oblation to the LORD burnt offerings and cereal offerings, sacrifices and libations, as prescribed for each day."

Responsorial Psalm 81:3-4, 5-6, 10-11ab
R. (2a) Sing with joy to God our help.

Take up a melody, and sound the timbrel, the pleasant harp and the lyre.

Blow the trumpet at the new moon, at the full moon, on our solemn feast.

R. Sing with joy to God our help.

For it is a statute in Israel, an ordinance of the God of Jacob,

Who made it a decree for Joseph when he came forth from the land of Egypt.

R. Sing with joy to God our help.

There shall be no strange god among you nor shall you worship any alien god.

I, the LORD, am your God who led you forth from the land of Egypt.

R. Sing with joy to God our help.

Alleluia 1 Pt 1:25

R. Alleluia, alleluia.

The word of the Lord remains forever; this is the word that has been proclaimed to you.

465

R. Alleluia, alleluia.

Gospel Mt 13:54-58
Jesus came to his native place and taught the people in their synagogue. They were astonished and said, "Where did this man get such wisdom and mighty deeds? Is he not the carpenter's son? Is not his mother named Mary and his brothers James, Joseph, Simon, and Judas? Are not his sisters all with us? Where did this man get all this?" And they took offense at him. But Jesus said to them, "A prophet is not without honor except in his native place and in his own house." And he did not work many mighty deeds there because of their lack of faith.

JULY 31ST, 2021
Memorial of Saint Ignatius of Loyola, Priest

1ST Reading Lv 25:1, 8-17
The LORD said to Moses on Mount Sinai, "Seven weeks of years shall you count—seven times seven years— so that the seven cycles amount to forty-nine years. Then, on the tenth day of the seventh month, let the trumpet resound; on this, the Day of Atonement, the trumpet blast shall re-echo throughout your land. This fiftieth year you shall make sacred by proclaiming liberty in the land for all its inhabitants.

It shall be a jubilee for you, when every one of you shall return to his own property, everyone to his own family estate. In this fiftieth year, your year of jubilee, you shall not sow, nor shall you reap the after growth or pick the grapes from the untrimmed vines. Since this is the jubilee, which shall be sacred for you, you may not eat of its produce, except as taken directly from the field. "In this year of jubilee, then, every one of you shall return to his own property. Therefore, when you sell any land to your neighbor or buy any from him, do not deal unfairly.

On the basis of the number of years since the last jubilee shall you purchase the land from your neighbor; and so also, on the basis of the number of years for crops, shall he sell it to you. When the years are many, the price shall be so much the more; when the years are few, the price shall be so much the less. For it is really the number of crops that he sells you. Do not deal unfairly, then; but stand in fear of your God. I, the LORD, am your God."

R. (4) O God, let all the nations praise you!

May God have pity on us and bless us; may he let his face shine upon us.

So may your way be known upon earth; among all nations, your salvation.

R. O God, let all the nations praise you!

May the nations be glad and exult because you rule the peoples in equity; the nations on the earth you guide.

R. O God, let all the nations praise you!

The earth has yielded its fruits; God, our God, has blessed us.

May God bless us, and may all the ends of the earth fear him!

R. O God, let all the nations praise you!

Alleluia Mt 5:10

R. Alleluia, alleluia.

Blessed are they who are persecuted for the sake of righteousness for theirs is the Kingdom of heaven.

R. Alleluia, alleluia.

Gospel Mt 14:1-12

Herod the tetrarch heard of the reputation of Jesus and said to his servants, "This man is John the Baptist. He has been raised from the dead; that is why mighty powers are at work in him." Now Herod had arrested John, bound him, and put him in prison on account of Herodias, the wife of his brother Philip, for John had said to him, "It is not lawful for you to have her." Although he wanted to kill him, he feared the people, for they regarded him as a prophet. But at a birthday celebration for Herod, the daughter of Herodias performed a dance before the guests and delighted Herod so much that he swore to give her whatever she might ask for. Prompted by her mother, she said, "Give me here on a platter the head of John the Baptist."

The king was distressed, but because of his oaths and the guests who were present, he ordered that it be given, and he had John beheaded in the prison. His head was brought in on a platter and given to the girl, who took it to her

467

mother. His disciples came and took away the corpse and buried him; and they went and told Jesus.

AUGUST 1ST, 2021
Eighteenth Sunday in Ordinary Time

1ST Reading Ex 16:2-4, 12-15
The whole Israelite community grumbled against Moses and Aaron. The Israelites said to them, "Would that we had died at the LORD's hand in the land of Egypt, as we sat by our fleshpots and ate our fill of bread! But you had to lead us into this desert to make the whole community die of famine!" Then the LORD said to Moses, "I will now rain down bread from heaven for you. Each day the people are to go out and gather their daily portion; thus will I test them, to see whether they follow my instructions or not. "I have heard the grumbling of the Israelites. Tell them: In the evening twilight you shall eat flesh, and in the morning you shall have your fill of bread, so that you may know that I, the LORD, am your God. "In the evening quail came up and covered the camp.

In the morning a dew lay all about the camp, and when the dew evaporated, there on the surface of the desert were fine flakes like hoarfrost on the ground. On seeing it, the Israelites asked one another, "What is this? "for they did not know what it was. But Moses told them, "This is the bread that the LORD has given you to eat."

Responsorial Psalm Ps 78:3-4, 23-24, 25, 54
R. (24b) The Lord gave them bread from heaven.

What we have heard and know, and what our fathers have declared to us,

We will declare to the generation to come the glorious deeds of the LORD and his strength and the wonders that he wrought.

R. The Lord gave them bread from heaven.

He commanded the skies above and opened the doors of heaven; he rained manna upon them for food and gave them heavenly bread.

R. The Lord gave them bread from heaven.

Man ate the bread of angels, food he sent them in abundance.

And he brought them to his holy land, to the mountains his right hand had won.

R. The Lord gave them bread from heaven.

2ND Reading Eph 4:17, 20-24
Brothers and sisters:

I declare and testify in the Lord that you must no longer live as the Gentiles do, in the futility of their minds; that is not how you learned Christ, assuming that you have heard of him and were taught in him, as truth is in Jesus, that you should put away the old self of your former way of life, corrupted through deceitful desires, and be renewed in the spirit of your minds, and put on the new self, created in God's way in righteousness and holiness of truth.

AlleluiaMt 4:4b

R. Alleluia, alleluia.

One does not live on bread alone, but by every word that comes forth from the mouth of God.

R. Alleluia, alleluia.

Gospel Jn 6:24-35
When the crowd saw that neither Jesus nor his disciples were there, they themselves got into boats and came to Capernaum looking for Jesus.

And when they found him across the sea they said to him, "Rabbi, when did you get here?" Jesus answered them and said, "Amen, amen, I say to you, you are looking for me not because you saw signs but because you ate the loaves and were filled. Do not work for food that perishes but for the food that endures for eternal life, which the Son of Man will give you. For on him the Father, God, has set his seal." So they said to him, "What can we do to accomplish the works of God?" Jesus answered and said to them, "This is the work of God that you believe in the one he sent." So they said to him, "What sign can you do, that we may see and believe in you? What can you do? Our ancestors ate manna in the desert, as it is written: He gave them bread from heaven to eat." So Jesus said to them, "Amen, amen, I say to you, it was not Moses who gave the bread from heaven; my Father gives you the true bread from heaven. For the bread of God is that which comes down from heaven and gives life to the world." So they said to him, "Sir, give us this bread always." Jesus said to them, "I am the bread of life; whoever comes to me will never hunger, and whoever believes in me will never thirst."

AUGUST 2ND, 2021
Monday of the Eighteenth Week in Ordinary Time

1ST Reading Nm 11:4b-15

The children of Israel lamented, "Would that we had meat for food! We remember the fish we used to eat without cost in Egypt, and the cucumbers, the melons, the leeks, the onions, and the garlic. But now we are famished; we see nothing before us but this manna." Manna was like coriander seed and had the color of resin. When they had gone about and gathered it up, the people would grind it between millstones or pound it in a mortar, then cook it in a pot and make it into loaves, which tasted like cakes made with oil. At night, when the dew fell upon the camp, the manna also fell. When Moses heard the people, family after family, crying at the entrance of their tents, so that the LORD became very angry, he was grieved. "Why do you treat your servant so badly?" Moses asked the Lord. "Why are you so displeased with me that you burden me with all this people? Was it I who conceived all this people? Or was it I who gave them birth, hat you tell me to carry them at my bosom, like a foster father carrying an infant, to the land you have promised under oath to their fathers? Where can I get meat to give to all this people? For they are crying to me, 'Give us meat for our food.' I cannot carry all this people by myself, for they are too heavy for me. If this is the way you will deal with me, then please do me the favor of killing me at once, so that I need no longer face this distress."

Responsorial Psalm81:12-13, 14-15, 16-17
R. (2a) Sing with joy to God our help.

"My people heard not my voice, and Israel obeyed me not;

So I gave them up to the hardness of their hearts; they walked according to their own counsels."

R. Sing with joy to God our help.

"If only my people would hear me, and Israel walk in my ways,

Quickly would I humble their enemies; against their foes I would turn my hand."

R. Sing with joy to God our help.

"Those who hated the LORD would seek to flatter me, but their fate would endure forever,

While Israel I would feed with the best of wheat, and with honey from the rock I would fill them."

R. Sing with joy to God our help.

Alleluia Mt 4:4

R. Alleluia, alleluia.

One does not live on bread alone, but on every word that comes forth from the mouth of God.

R. Alleluia, alleluia.

Gospel Mt 14:13-21

When Jesus heard of the death of John the Baptist, he withdrew in a boat to a deserted place by himself. The crowds heard of this and followed him on foot from their towns. When he disembarked and saw the vast crowd, his heart was moved with pity for them, and he cured their sick. When it was evening, the disciples approached him and said, "This is a deserted place and it is already late; dismiss the crowds so that they can go to the villages and buy food for themselves." He said to them, "There is no need for them to go away; give them some food yourselves." But they said to him, "Five loaves and two fish are all we have here." Then he said, "Bring them here to me, "and he ordered the crowds to sit down on the grass. Taking the five loaves and the two fish, and looking up to heaven, he said the blessing, broke the loaves, and gave them to the disciples, who in turn gave them to the crowds.

They all ate and were satisfied, and they picked up the fragments left over— twelve wicker baskets full. Those who ate were about five thousand men, not counting women and children.

AUGUST 3RD, 2021
Tuesday of the Eighteenth Week in Ordinary Time

Miriam and Aaron spoke against Moses on the pretext of the marriage he had contracted with a Cushite woman. They complained, "Is it through Moses alone that the LORD speaks? Does he not speak through us also? "And the LORD heard this. Now, Moses himself was by far the meekest man on the face of the earth. So at once the LORD said to Moses and Aaron and Miriam, "Come out, you three, to the meeting tent. "And the three of them went. Then the LORD came down in the column of cloud, and standing at the entrance of the tent, called Aaron and Miriam. When both came forward, he said, "Now listen to the words of the LORD: Should there be a prophet among you, in visions will I reveal myself to him, in dreams will I speak to him; not so with my servant Moses! Throughout my house he bears my trust: face to face I speak to him; plainly and not in riddles. The presence of the LORD he beholds. Why, then, did you not fear to speak against my servant Moses?" So angry was the LORD against them that when he departed, and the cloud withdrew from the tent, there was Miriam, a snow-white leper! When Aaron turned and saw her a leper, he said to Moses, "Ah, my lord! Please do not charge us with the sin that we have foolishly committed! Let her not thus be like the stillborn babe that comes forth from its mother's womb with its flesh half consumed. "Then Moses cried to the LORD, "Please, not this! Pray, heal her!"

Responsorial Psalm51:3-4, 5-6ab, 6cd-7, 12-13
R. (see 3a) Be merciful, O Lord, for we have sinned.

Have mercy on me, O God, in your goodness; in the greatness of your compassion wipe out my offense.

Thoroughly wash me from my guilt and of my sin cleanse me.

R. Be merciful, O Lord, for we have sinned.

For I acknowledge my offense; and my sin is before me always:

"Against you only have I sinned; and done what is evil in your sight."

R. Be merciful, O Lord, for we have sinned.

That you may be justified in your sentence, vindicated when you condemn.

Indeed, in guilt was I born, and in sin my mother conceived me.

R. Be merciful, O Lord, for we have sinned.

A clean heart create for me, O God, and a steadfast spirit renew within me.

Cast me not off from your presence, and your Holy Spirit take not from me.

R. Be merciful, O Lord, for we have sinned.

AlleluiaJn 1:49b

R. Alleluia, alleluia.

Rabbi, you are the Son of God; you are the King of Israel.

R. Alleluia, alleluia.

Gospel Mt 14:22-36

Jesus made the disciples get into a boat and precede him to the other side of the sea, while he dismissed the crowds. After doing so, he went up on the mountain by himself to pray. When it was evening he was there alone. Meanwhile the boat, already a few miles offshore, was being tossed about by the waves, for the wind was against it. During the fourth watch of the night, he came toward them, walking on the sea.

When the disciples saw him walking on the sea they were terrified. "It is a ghost," they said, and they cried out in fear. At once Jesus spoke to them, "Take courage, it is I; do not be afraid" Peter said to him in reply, "Lord, if it is you, command me to come to you on the water."He said, "Come."

Peter got out of the boat and began to walk on the water toward Jesus. But when he saw how strong the wind was he became frightened; and, beginning to sink, he cried out, "Lord, save me! "Immediately Jesus stretched out his hand and caught him, and said to him, "O you of little faith, why did you doubt? "After they got into the boat, the wind died down. Those who were in the boat did him homage, saying, "Truly, you are the Son of God. "After making the crossing, they came to land at Gennesaret.

When the men of that place recognized him, they sent word to all the surrounding country. People brought to him all those who were sick and begged him that they might touch only the tassel on his cloak, and as many as touched it were healed.

Or

Mt 15:1-2, 10-14

473

Some Pharisees and scribes came to Jesus from Jerusalem and said, "Why do your disciples break the tradition of the elders? They do not wash their hands when they eat a meal. "Hesummoned the crowd and said to them, "Hear and understand. It is not what enters one's mouth that defiles the man; but what comes out of the mouth is what defiles one. "Then his disciples approached and said to him, "Do you know that the Pharisees took offense when they heard what you said? "He said in reply, "Every plant that my heavenly Father has not planted will be uprooted. Let them alone; they are blind guides of the blind. If a blind man leads a blind man, both will fall into a pit."

AUGUST 4TH, 2021
Memorial of Saint John Vianney, Priest

1ST Reading Nm 13:1-2, 25–14:1, 26a-29a, 34-35

The LORD said to Moses [in the desert of Paran,] "Send men to reconnoiter the land of Canaan, which I am giving the children of Israel. You shall send one man from each ancestral tribe, all of them princes. "After reconnoitering the land for forty days they returned, met Moses and Aaron and the whole congregation of the children of Israel in the desert of Paran at Kadesh, made a report to them all, and showed the fruit of the country to the whole congregation.

They told Moses: "We went into the land to which you sent us. It does indeed flow with milk and honey, and here is its fruit. However, the people who are living in the land are fierce, and the towns are fortified and very strong. Besides, we saw descendants of the Anakim there. Amalekites live in the region of the Negeb; Hittites, Jebusites, and Amorites dwell in the highlands and Canaanites along the seacoast and the banks of the Jordan." Caleb, however, to quiet the people toward Moses, said, "We ought to go up and seize the land, for we can certainly do so." But the men who had gone up with him said, "We cannot attack these people; they are too strong for us. "So they spread discouraging reports among the children of Israel about the land they had scouted, saying, "The land that we explored is a country that consumes its inhabitants. And all the people we saw there are huge, veritable giants (the Anakim were a race of giants);we felt like mere grasshoppers, and so we must have seemed to them. "At this, the whole community broke out with loud cries, and even in the night the people wailed. The LORD said to Moses and Aaron: "How long will this wicked assembly grumble against me? I have heard the grumblings of the children of Israel against me. Tell them: By my life, says the LORD, I will do to you just what I have heard you say.

Here in the desert shall your dead bodies fall. Forty days you spent in scouting the land; forty years shall you suffer for your crimes: one year for each day.

Thus you will realize what it means to oppose me. I, the LORD, have sworn to do this to all this wicked assembly that conspired against me: here in the desert they shall die to the last man."

Responsorial Psalm106:6-7ab, 13-14, 21-22, 23
R. (4a) Remember us, O Lord, as you favor your people.

We have sinned, we and our fathers; we have committed crimes; we have done wrong.

Our fathers in Egypt considered not your wonders.

R. Remember us, O Lord, as you favor your people.

But soon they forgot his works; they waited not for his counsel.

They gave way to craving in the desert and tempted God in the wilderness.

R. Remember us, O Lord, as you favor your people.

They forgot the God who had saved them, who had done great deeds in Egypt,

Wondrous deeds in the land of Ham, terrible things at the Red Sea.

R. Remember us, O Lord, as you favor your people.

Then he spoke of exterminating them, but Moses, his chosen one,

Withstood him in the breach to turn back his destructive wrath.

R. Remember us, O Lord, as you favor your people.

Alleluia Lk 7:16

R. Alleluia, alleluia.

A great prophet has arisen in our midst and God has visited his people.

R. Alleluia, alleluia.

At that time Jesus withdrew to the region of Tyre and Sidon. And behold, a Canaanite woman of that district came and called out, "Have pity on me, Lord, Son of David! My daughter is tormented by a demon." But he did not say a word in answer to her. His disciples came and asked him, "Send her away, for she keeps calling out after us. "He said in reply, "I was sent only to the lost sheep of the house of Israel. "But the woman came and did him homage, saying, "Lord, help me."

He said in reply, "It is not right to take the food of the children and throw it to the dogs. "She said, "Please, Lord, for even the dogs eat the scraps that fall from the table of their masters. "Then Jesus said to her in reply, "O woman, great is your faith! Let it be done for you as you wish. "And her daughter was healed from that hour.

AUGUST 5TH, 2021
Thursday of the Eighteenth Week in Ordinary Time

1ST Reading Nm 20:1-13

The whole congregation of the children of Israel arrived in the desert of Zin in the first month, and the people settled at Kadesh. It was here that Miriam died, and here that she was buried. As the community had no water, they held a council against Moses and Aaron.

The people contended with Moses, exclaiming, "Would that we too had perished with our kinsmen in the Lord's presence! Why have you brought the LORD's assembly into this desert where we and our livestock are dying? Why did you lead us out of Egypt, only to bring us to this wretched place which has neither grain nor figs nor vines nor pomegranates? Here there is not even water to drink! "But Moses and Aaron went away from the assembly to the entrance of the meeting tent, where they fell prostrate.

Then the glory of the LORD appeared to them, and the LORD said to Moses, "Take your staff and assemble the community, you and your brother Aaron, and in their presence order the rock to yield its waters. From the rock you shall bring forth water for the congregation and their livestock to drink." So Moses took his staff from its place before the LORD, as he was ordered. He and Aaron assembled the community in front of the rock, where he said to them, "Listen to me, you rebels! Are we to bring water for you out of this rock?"

Then, raising his hand, Moses struck the rock twice with his staff, and water gushed out in abundance for the people and their livestock to drink. But the LORD said to Moses and Aaron, "Because you were not faithful to m e n showing forth my sanctity before the children of Israel, you shall not lead this community into the land I will give them."

These are the waters of Meribah, where the children of Israel contended against the Lord, and where the LORD revealed his sanctity among them.

Responsorial Psalm95:1-2, 6-7, 8-9
R. (8) If today you hear his voice, harden not your hearts.

Come, let us sing joyfully to the LORD; let us acclaim the Rock of our salvation.

Let us come into his presence with thanksgiving; let us joyfully sing psalms to him.

R. If today you hear his voice, harden not your hearts.

Come, let us bow down in worship; let us kneel before the LORD who made us.

For he is our God, and we are the people he shepherds, the flock he guides.

R. If today you hear his voice, harden not your hearts.

Oh, that today you would hear his voice: "Harden not your hearts as at Meribah, as in the day of Massah in the desert,

Where your fathers tested me; they tested me though they had seen my works."

R. If today you hear his voice, harden not your hearts.

Alleluia Mt 16:18

R. Alleluia, alleluia.

You are Peter, and upon this rock I will build my Church, and the gates of the netherworld shall not prevail against it.

R. Alleluia, alleluia.

Gospel Mt 16:13-23

Jesus went into the region of Caesarea Philippi and he asked his disciples, "Who do people say that the Son of Man is?" They replied, "Some say John the Baptist, others Elijah, still others Jeremiah or one of the prophets." He said to them, "But who do you say that I am?" Simon Peter said in reply, "You are the Christ, the Son of the living God."

Jesus said to him in reply, "Blessed are you, Simon son of Jonah. For flesh and blood has not revealed this to you, but my heavenly Father. And so I say to you, you are Peter, and upon this rock I will build my Church, and the gates of the netherworld shall not prevail against it. I will give you the keys to the Kingdom of heaven. Whatever you bind on earth shall be bound in heaven; and whatever you loose on earth shall be loosed in heaven." Then he strictly ordered his disciples to tell no one that he was the Christ. From that time on, Jesus began to show his disciples that he must go to Jerusalem and suffer greatly from the elders, the chief priests, and the scribes, and be killed and on the third day be raised. Then Peter took Jesus aside and began to rebuke him, "God forbid, Lord! No such thing shall ever happen to you." He turned and said to Peter, "Get behind me, Satan! You are an obstacle to me. You are thinking not as God does, but as human beings do."

AUGUST 6TH, 2021
Feast of the Transfiguration of the Lord

1ST Reading Dn 7:9-10, 13-14

As I watched: Thrones were set up and the Ancient One took his throne. His clothing was bright as snow, and the hair on his head as white as wool; his throne was flames of fire, with wheels of burning fire.

A surging stream of fire flowed out from where he sat; Thousands upon thousands were ministering to him, and myriads upon myriads attended him. The court was convened and the books were opened. As the visions during the night continued, I saw: One like a Son of man coming, on the clouds of heaven; when he reached the Ancient One and was presented before him, the one like a Son of man received dominion, glory, and kingship; all peoples, nations, and languages serve him. His dominion is an everlasting dominion that shall not be taken away, his kingship shall not be destroyed.

Responsorial Psalm97:1-2, 5-6, 9

R. (1a and 9a) The Lord is king, the Most High over all the earth.

The LORD is king; let the earth rejoice; let the many islands be glad.

Clouds and darkness are round about him, justice and judgment are the foundation of his throne.

R. The Lord is king, the Most High over all the earth.

The mountains melt like wax before the LORD, before the LORD of all the earth.

The heavens proclaim his justice, and all peoples see his glory.

R. The Lord is king, the Most High over all the earth.

Because you, O LORD, are the Most High over all the earth, exalted far above all gods.

R. The Lord is king, the Most High over all the earth.

2ND Reading 2 Pt 1:16-19
Beloved:

We did not follow cleverly devised myths when we made known to you the power and coming of our Lord Jesus Christ, but we had been eyewitnesses of his majesty. For he received honor and glory from God the Father when that unique declaration came to him from the majestic glory, "This is my Son, my beloved, with whom I am well pleased." We ourselves heard this voice come from heaven while we were with him on the holy mountain. Moreover, we possess the prophetic message that is altogether reliable. You will do well to be attentive to it, as to a lamp shining in a dark place, until day dawns and the morning star rises in your hearts.

Alleluia Mt 17:5c

R. Alleluia, alleluia.

This is my beloved Son, with whom I am well pleased; listen to him.

R. Alleluia, alleluia.

Gospel Mk 9:2-10
Jesus took Peter, James, and his brother John, and led them up a high mountain apart by themselves. And he was transfigured before them, and his clothes became dazzling white, such as no fuller on earth could bleach them.

Then Elijah appeared to them along with Moses, and they were conversing with Jesus. Then Peter said to Jesus in reply, "Rabbi, it is good that we are here! Let us make three tents: one for you, one for Moses, and one for Elijah. "He hardly knew what to say, they were so terrified.

Then a cloud came, casting a shadow over them; from the cloud came a voice, "This is my beloved Son. Listen to him. "Suddenly, looking around, they no longer saw anyone but Jesus alone with them. As they were coming down from the mountain, he charged them not to relate what they had seen to anyone, except when the Son of Man had risen from the dead. So they kept the matter to themselves, questioning what rising from the dead meant.

AUGUST 7TH, 2021
Saturday of the Eighteenth Week in Ordinary Time

1ST Reading Dt 6:4-13

Moses said to the people:

"Hear, O Israel! The LORD is our God, the LORD alone! Therefore, you shall love the LORD, your God, with all your heart, and with all your soul, and with all your strength. Take to heart these words which I enjoin on you today. Drill them into your children. Speak of them at home and abroad, whether you are busy or at rest. Bind them at your wrist as a sign and let them be as a pendant on your forehead. Write them on the doorposts of your houses and on your gates. "When the LORD, your God, brings you into the land which he swore to your fathers: Abraham, Isaac and Jacob, that he would give you, a land with fine, large cities that you did not build, with houses full of goods of all sorts that you did not garner, with cisterns that you did not dig, with vineyards and olive groves that you did not plant; and when, therefore, you eat your fill, take care not to forget the LORD, who brought you out of the land of Egypt, that place of slavery. The LORD, your God, shall you fear; him shall you serve, and by his name shall you swear."

Responsorial Psalm18:2-3a, 3bc-4, 47 and 51

R. (2) I love you, Lord, my strength.

I love you, O LORD, my strength LORD, my rock, my fortress, my deliverer.

R. I love you, Lord, my strength.

My God, my rock of refuge, my shield, the horn of my salvation, my stronghold!

Praised be the LORD, I exclaim! And I am safe from my enemies.

R. I love you, Lord, my strength.

The LORD live! And blessed be my Rock! Extolled be God my savior!

You who gave great victories to your king, and showed kindness to your anointed, to David and his posterity forever.

R. I love you, Lord, my strength.

Alleluia 2 Tm 1:10

R. Alleluia, alleluia.

Our Savior Jesus Christ has destroyed death and brought life to light through the Gospel.

R. Alleluia, alleluia.

Gospel Mt 17:14-20

A man came up to Jesus, knelt down before him, and said, "Lord, have pity on my son, who is a lunatic and suffers severely; often he falls into fire, and often into water. I brought him to your disciples, but they could not cure him. "Jesus said in reply, "O faithless and perverse generation, how long will I be with you? How long will I endure you? Bring the boy here to me."

Jesus rebuked him and the demon came out of him, and from that hour the boy was cured. Then the disciples approached Jesus in private and said, "Why could we not drive it out? "He said to them, "Because of your little faith. Amen, I say to you, if you have faith the size of a mustard seed, you will say to this mountain, 'Move from here to there,' and it will move. Nothing will be impossible for you."

AUGUST 8TH, 2021
Nineteenth Sunday in Ordinary Time

Elijah went a day's journey into the desert, until he came to a broom tree and sat beneath it. He prayed for death saying: "This is enough, O LORD! Take my life, for I am no better than my fathers." He lay down and fell asleep under the broom tree, but then an angel touched him and ordered him to get up and eat. Elijah looked and there at his head was a hearth cake and a jug of water. After he ate and drank, he lay down again, but the angel of the LORD came back a second time, touched him, and ordered, "Get up and eat, else the journey will be too long for you!" He got up, ate, and drank; then strengthened by that food, he walked forty days and forty nights to the mountain of God, Horeb.

Responsorial Psalm Ps 34:2-3, 4-5, 6-7, 8-9
R. (9a) Taste and see the goodness of the Lord.

I will bless the LORD at all times; his praise shall be ever in my mouth.

Let my soul glory in the LORD; the lowly will hear me and be glad.

R. Taste and see the goodness of the Lord.

Glorify the LORD with me; Let us together extol his name.

I sought the LORD, and he answered me and delivered me from all my fears.

R. Taste and see the goodness of the Lord.

Look to him that you may be radiant with joy. And your faces may not blush with shame.

When the afflicted man called out, the LORD heard, and from all his distress he saved him.

R. Taste and see the goodness of the Lord.

The angel of the LORD encamps around those who fear him and delivers them.

Taste and see how good the LORD is; blessed the man who takes refuge in him.

R. Taste and see the goodness of the Lord.

2ND Reading Eph 4:30—5:2
Brothers and sisters:

Do not grieve the Holy Spirit of God, with which you were sealed for the day of redemption. All bitterness, fury, anger, shouting, and reviling must be removed from you, along with all malice. And be kind to one another, compassionate, forgiving one another as God has forgiven you in Christ. So be imitators of God, as beloved children, and live in love, as Christ loved us and handed himself over for us as a sacrificial offering to God for a fragrant aroma.

Alleluia Jn 6:51

R. Alleluia, alleluia.

I am the living bread that came down from heaven, says the Lord; whoever eats this bread will live forever.

R. Alleluia, alleluia.

Gospel Jn 6:41-51

The Jews murmured about Jesus because he said, "I am the bread that came down from heaven," and they said, "Is this not Jesus, the son of Joseph? Do we not know his father and mother? Then how can he say, 'I have come down from heaven'?" Jesus answered and said to them, "Stop murmuring among yourselves. No one can come to me unless the Father who sent me draw him, and I will raise him on the last day. It is written in the prophets: They shall all be taught by God. Everyone who listens to my Father and learns from him comes to me. Not that anyone has seen the Father except the one who is from God; he has seen the Father. Amen, amen, I say to you, whoever believes has eternal life. I am the bread of life. Your ancestors ate the manna in the desert, but they died; this is the bread that comes down from heaven so that one may eat it and not die. I am the living bread that came down from heaven; whoever eats this bread will live forever; and the bread that I will give is my flesh for the life of the world."

AUGUST 9TH, 2021
Monday of the Nineteenth Week in Ordinary Time

Moses said to the people: "And now, Israel, what does the LORD, your God, ask of you but to fear the LORD, your God, and follow his ways exactly, to love and serve the LORD, your God, with all your heart and all your soul, to keep the commandments and statutes of the LORD which I enjoin on you today for your own good? Think! The heavens, even the highest heavens, belong to the LORD, your God, as well as the earth and everything on it. Yet in his love for your fathers the LORD was so attached to them as to choose you, their descendants, in preference to all other peoples, as indeed he has now done. Circumcise your hearts, therefore, and be no longer stiff-necked. For the LORD, your God, is the God of gods, the LORD of lords, the great God, mighty and awesome, who has no favorites, accepts no bribes; who executes justice for the orphan and the widow, and befriends the alien, feeding and clothing him. So you too must befriend the alien, for you were once aliens yourselves in the land of Egypt. The LORD, your God, shall you fear, and him shall you serve; hold fast to him and swear by his name. He is your glory, he, your God, who has done for you those great and terrible things which your own eyes have seen. Your ancestors went down to Egypt seventy strong, and now the LORD, your God, has made you as numerous as the stars of the sky."

Responsorial Psalm 147:12-13, 14-15, 19-20

R. (12a) Praise the Lord, Jerusalem.

Glorify the LORD, O Jerusalem; praise your God, O Zion.

For he has strengthened the bars of your gates; he has blessed your children within you.

R. Praise the Lord, Jerusalem.

He has granted peace in your borders; with the best of wheat he fills you.

He sends forth his command to the earth; swiftly runs his word!

R. Praise the Lord, Jerusalem.

He has proclaimed his word to Jacob, his statutes and his ordinances to Israel.

He has not done thus for any other nation; his ordinances he has not made known to them. Alleluia.

R. Praise the Lord, Jerusalem.

Alleluia 2 Thes 2:14

R. Alleluia, alleluia.

God has called you through the Gospel to possess the glory of our Lord
Jesus Christ.

R. Alleluia, alleluia.

Gospel Mt 17:22-27
As Jesus and his disciples were gathering in Galilee, Jesus said to them, "The
Son of Man is to be handed over to men, and they will kill him, and he will
be raised on the third day." And they were overwhelmed with grief. When
they came to Capernaum, the collectors of the temple tax approached Peter
and said, "Does not your teacher pay the temple tax?" "Yes," he said.

When he came into the house, before he had time to speak, Jesus asked him,
"What is your opinion, Simon? From whom do the kings of the earth take
tolls or census tax? From their subjects or from foreigners?" When he said,
"From foreigners," Jesus said to him, "Then the subjects are exempt. But
that we may not offend them, go to the sea, drop in a hook, and take the first
fish that comes up.

Open its mouth and you will find a coin worth twice the temple tax. Give
that to them for me and for you."

AUGUST 10TH, 2021
Feast of Saint Lawrence, Deacon and Martyr
1ST Reading 2 Cor 9:6-10

Brothers and sisters:

Whoever sows sparingly will also reap sparingly, and whoever sows
bountifully will also reap bountifully. Each must do as already determined,
without sadness or compulsion, for God loves a cheerful giver. Moreover,
God is able to make every grace abundant for you, so that in all things,
always having all you need, you may have an abundance for every good work.
As it is written: He scatters abroad, he gives to the poor; his righteousness
endures forever.

The one who supplies seed to the sower and bread for food will supply and multiply your seed and increase the harvest of your righteousness.

Responsorial Psalm 112:1-2, 5-6, 7-8, 9
R. (5) Blessed the man who is gracious and lends to those in need.

Blessed the man who fears the LORD, who greatly delights in his commands.

His posterity shall be mighty upon the earth; the upright generation shall be blessed.

R. Blessed the man who is gracious and lends to those in need.

Well for the man who is gracious and lends, who conducts his affairs with justice;

He shall never be moved; the just one shall be in everlasting remembrance.

R. Blessed the man who is gracious and lends to those in need.

An evil report he shall not fear; his heart is firm, trusting in the LORD.

His heart is steadfast; he shall not fear till he looks down upon his foes.

R. Blessed the man who is gracious and lends to those in need.

Lavishly he gives to the poor, his generosity shall endure forever; his horn shall be exalted in glory.

R. Blessed the man who is gracious and lends to those in need.

Alleluia Jn 8:12bc

R. Alleluia, alleluia.

Whoever follows me will not walk in darkness but will have the light of life, says the Lord.

R. Alleluia, alleluia.

Jesus said to his disciples: "Amen, amen, I say to you, unless a grain of wheat falls to the ground and dies, it remains just a grain of wheat; but if it dies, it produces much fruit.

Whoever loves his life loses it, and whoever hates his life in this world will preserve it for eternal life. Whoever serves me must follow me, and where I am, there also will my servant be. The Father will honor whoever serves me."

AUGUST 11TH, 2021
Memorial of Saint Clare, Virgin

1ST Reading Dt 34:1-12

Moses went up from the plains of Moab to Mount Nebo, the headland of Pisgah which faces Jericho, and the LORD showed him all the land—Gilead, and as far as Dan, all Naphtali, the land of Ephraim and Manasseh, all the land of Judah as far as the Western Sea, the Negeb, the circuit of the Jordan with the lowlands at Jericho, city of palms, and as far as Zoar.

The LORD then said to him, "This is the land which I swore to Abraham, Isaac, and Jacob that I would give to their descendants. I have let you feast your eyes upon it, but you shall not cross over. "So there, in the land of Moab, Moses, the servant of the LORD, died as the LORD had said; and he was buried in the ravine opposite Beth-peor in the land of Moab, but to this day no one knows the place of his burial.

Moses was one hundred and twenty years old when he died, yet his eyes were undimmed and his vigor unabated. For thirty days the children of Israel wept for Moses in the plains of Moab, till they had completed the period of grief and mourning for Moses. Now Joshua, son of Nun, was filled with the spirit of wisdom, since Moses had laid his hands upon him; and so the children of Israel gave him their obedience, thus carrying out the LORD's command to Moses. Since then no prophet has arisen in Israel like Moses, whom the LORD knew face to face. He had no equal in all the signs and wonders the LORD sent him to perform in the land of Egypt against Pharaoh and all his servants and against all his land, and for the might and the terrifying power that Moses exhibited in the sight of all Israel.

Responsorial Psalm66:1-3a, 5 and 8, 16-17
R. (see 20a and 10b) Blessed be God who filled my soul with fire!

Shout joyfully to God, all the earth; sing praise to the glory of his name; proclaim his glorious praise.

Say to God: "How tremendous are your deeds!"

R. Blessed be God who filled my soul with fire!

Come and see the works of God, his tremendous deeds among the children of Adam.

Bless our God, you peoples; loudly sound his praise.

R. Blessed be God who filled my soul with fire!

Hear now, all you who fear God, while I declare what he has done for me.

When I appealed to him in words, praise was on the tip of my tongue.

R. Blessed be God who filled my soul with fire!

Alleluia 2 Cor 5:19

R. Alleluia, alleluia.

God was reconciling the world to himself in Christ, and entrusting to us the message of reconciliation.

R. Alleluia, alleluia.

Gospel Mt 18:15-20

Jesus said to his disciples: "If your brother sins against you, go and tell him his fault between you and him alone. If he listens to you, you have won over your brother. If he does not listen, take one or two others along with you, so that every fact may be established on the testimony of two or three witnesses.

 If he refuses to listen to them, tell the Church. If he refuses to listen even to the Church, then treat him as you would a Gentile or a tax collector. Amen, I say to you, whatever you bind on earth shall be bound in heaven, and whatever you loose on earth shall be loosed in heaven. Again, amen, I say to you, if two of you agree on earth about anything for which they are to pray, it shall be granted to them by my heavenly Father. For where two or three are gathered together in my name, there am I in the midst of them."

Thursday of the Nineteenth Week in Ordinary Time

1ST Reading Jos 3:7-10a, 11, 13-17

The LORD said to Joshua, "Today I will begin to exalt you in the sight of all Israel, that they may know I am with you, as I was with Moses. Now command the priests carrying the Ark of the Covenant to come to a halt in the Jordan when you reach the edge of the waters." So Joshua said to the children of Israel, "Come here and listen to the words of the LORD, your God. This is how you will know that there is a living God in your midst, who at your approach will dispossess the Canaanites. The ark of the covenant of the LORD of the whole earth will precede you into the Jordan. When the soles of the feet of the priests carrying the ark of the LORD, the Lord of the whole earth, touch the water of the Jordan, it will cease to flow; for the water flowing down from upstream will halt in a solid bank."

The people struck their tents to cross the Jordan, with the priests carrying the Ark of the Covenant ahead of them. No sooner had these priestly bearers of the ark waded into the waters at the edge of the Jordan, which overflows all its banks during the entire season of the harvest, than the waters flowing from upstream halted, backing up in a solid mass for a very great distance indeed, from Adam, a city in the direction of Zarethan; while those flowing downstream toward the Salt Sea of the Arabah disappeared entirely. Thus the people crossed over opposite Jericho. While all Israel crossed over on dry ground, the priests carrying the ark of the covenant of the LORD remained motionless on dry ground in the bed of the Jordan until the whole nation had completed the passage.

Responsorial Psalm 114:1-2, 3-4, 5-6

R. Alleluia!

When Israel came forth from Egypt, the house of Jacob from a people of alien tongue,

Judah became his sanctuary, Israel his domain.

R. Alleluia!

The sea beheld and fled; Jordan turned back.

The mountains skipped like rams, the hills like the lambs of the flock.

R. Alleluia!

Why is it, O sea that you flee? O Jordan that you turn back?

You mountains, that you skip like rams? You hills, like the lambs of the flock?

R. Alleluia!

Alleluia Ps 119:135

R. Alleluia, alleluia.

Let your countenance shine upon your servant and teach me your statutes.

R. Alleluia, alleluia.

Gospel Mt 18:21–19:1

Peter approached Jesus and asked him, "Lord, if my brother sins against me, how often must I forgive him? As many as seven times?" Jesus answered, "I say to you, not seven times but seventy-seven times. That is why the Kingdom of heaven may be likened to a king who decided to settle accounts with his servants. When he began the accounting, a debtor was brought before him who owed him a huge amount. Since he had no way of paying it back, his master ordered him to be sold, along with his wife, his children, and all his property, in payment of the debt. At that, the servant fell down, did him homage, and said, 'Be patient with me, and I will pay you back in full.' Moved with compassion the master of that servant let him go and forgave him the loan. When that servant had left, he found one of his fellow servants who owed him a much smaller amount. He seized him and started to choke him, demanding, 'Pay back what you owe.' Falling to his knees, his fellow servant begged him, 'Be patient with me, and I will pay you back.' But he refused. Instead, he had the fellow servant put in prison until he paid back the debt.

Now when his fellow servants saw what had happened, they were deeply disturbed, and went to their master and reported the whole affair.

His master summoned him and said to him, 'You wicked servant! I forgave you your entire debt because you begged me to. Should you not have had pity on your fellow servant, as I had pity on you?' Then in anger his master handed him over to the torturers until he should pay back the whole debt. So will my heavenly Father do to you, unless each of you forgives his brother from his heart. "When Jesus finished these words, he left Galilee and went to the district of Judea across the Jordan.

AUGUST 13TH, 2021
Friday of the Nineteenth Week in Ordinary Time

1ST Reading Jos 24:1-13

Joshua gathered together all the tribes of Israel at Shechem, summoning their elders, their leaders, their judges and their officers. When they stood in ranks before God, Joshua addressed all the people: "Thus says the LORD, the God of Israel: In times past your fathers, down to Terah, father of Abraham and Nahor, dwelt beyond the River and served other gods. But I brought your father Abraham from the region beyond the River and led him through the entire land of Canaan. I made his descendants numerous, and gave him Isaac. To Isaac I gave Jacob and Esau. To Esau I assigned the mountain region of Seir in which to settle, while Jacob and his children went down to Egypt. "Then I sent Moses and Aaron, and smote Egypt with the prodigies which I wrought in her midst.

Afterward I led you out of Egypt, and when you reached the sea, the Egyptians pursued your fathers to the Red Sea with chariots and horsemen. Because they cried out to the LORD, he put darkness between your people and the Egyptians, upon whom he brought the sea so that it engulfed them. After you witnessed what I did to Egypt, and dwelt a long time in the desert, I brought you into the land of the Amorites who lived east of the Jordan.

They fought against you, but I delivered them into your power. You took possession of their land, and I destroyed them, the two kings of the Amorites, before you. Then Balak, son of Zippor, king of Moab, prepared to war against Israel. He summoned Balaam, son of Beor, to curse you; but I would not listen to Balaam. On the contrary, he had to bless you, and I saved you from him. Once you crossed the Jordan and came to Jericho, the men of Jericho fought against you, but I delivered them also into your power. And I sent the hornets ahead of you that drove them (the Amorites, Perizzites, Canaanites, Hittites, Girgashites, Hivites and Jebusites) out of your way; it was not your sword or your bow. "I gave you a land that you had not tilled and cities that you had not built, to dwell in; you have eaten of vineyards and olive groves which you did not plant."

Responsorial Psalm136:1-3, 16-18, 21-22 and 24
R. His mercy endures forever.

Give thanks to the LORD, for he is good, for his mercy endures forever;

Give thanks to the God of gods, for his mercy endures forever;

Give thanks to the LORD of lords, for his mercy endures forever.

R. His mercy endures forever.

Who led his people through the wilderness, for his mercy endures forever;

Who smote great kings, for his mercy endures forever;

And slew powerful kings, for his mercy endures forever.

R. His mercy endures forever.

And made their land a heritage, for his mercy endures forever;

The heritage of Israel his servant, for his mercy endures forever;

And freed us from our foes, for his mercy endures forever.

R. His mercy endures forever.

Alleluia 1 Thes 2:13

R. Alleluia, alleluia.

Receive the word of god, not as the word of men, but, as it truly is, the word of God.

R. Alleluia, alleluia.

Gospel Mt 19:3-12

Some Pharisees approached Jesus, and tested him, saying, "Is it lawful for a man to divorce his wife for any cause whatever?" He said in reply, "Have you not read that from the beginning the Creator made them male and female and said, for this reason a man shall leave his father and mother and be joined to his wife, and the two shall become one flesh? So they are no longer two, but one flesh. Therefore, what God has joined together, man must not separate."

They said to him, "Then why did Moses command that the man give the woman a bill of divorce and dismiss her?" He said to them, "Because of the hardness of your hearts Moses allowed you to divorce your wives, but from the beginning it was not so. I say to you, whoever divorces his wife (unless the marriage is unlawful) and marries another commits adultery."

492

His disciples said to him, "If that is the case of a man with his wife, it is better not to marry." He answered, "Not all can accept this word, but only those to whom that is granted. Some are incapable of marriage because they were born so; some, because they were made so by others; some, because they have renounced marriage for the sake of the Kingdom of heaven. Whoever can accept this ought to accept it."

AUGUST 14TH, 2021
Memorial of Saint Maximilian Kolbe, Priest and Martyr

1ST Reading Jos 24:14-29

Joshua gathered together all the tribes of Israel at Shechem, and addressed them, saying: "Fear the LORD and serve him completely and sincerely. Cast out the gods your fathers served beyond the River and in Egypt, and serve the LORD. If it does not please you to serve the LORD, decide today whom you will serve, the gods your fathers served beyond the River or the gods of the Amorites in whose country you are dwelling. As for me and my household, we will serve the LORD." But the people answered, "Far be it from us to forsake the LORD for the service of other gods. For it was the LORD, our God, who brought us and our fathers up out of the land of Egypt, out of a state of slavery.

He performed those great miracles before our very eyes and protected us along our entire journey and among all the peoples through whom we passed. At our approach the LORD drove out all the peoples, including the Amorites who dwelt in the land.

Therefore we also will serve the LORD, for he is our God." Joshua in turn said to the people, "You may not be able to serve the LORD, for he is a holy God; he is a jealous God who will not forgive your transgressions or your sins. If, after the good he has done for you, you forsake the LORD and serve strange gods; he will do evil to you and destroy you." But the people answered Joshua, "We will still serve the LORD." Joshua therefore said to the people, "You are your own witnesses that you have chosen to serve the LORD." They replied, "We are, indeed!" Joshua continued: "Now, therefore, put away the strange gods that are among you and turn your hearts to the LORD, the God of Israel."

Then the people promised Joshua, "We will serve the LORD, our God, and obey his voice." So Joshua made a covenant with the people that day and made statutes and ordinances for them at Shechem, which he recorded in the book of the law of God. Then he took a large stone and set it up there under the oak that was in the sanctuary of the LORD. And Joshua said to all the people, "This stone shall be our witness, for it has heard all the words which the LORD spoke to us. It shall be a witness against you, should you wish to deny your God." Then Joshua dismissed the people, each to his own heritage. After these events, Joshua, son of Nun, servant of the LORD, died at the age of a hundred and ten.

Responsorial Psalm 16:1-2a and 5, 7-8, 11

R. (see 5a) You are my inheritance, O Lord.

Keep me, O God, for in you I take refuge; I say to the LORD, "My Lord are you."

O LORD, my allotted portion and my cup, you it is who hold fast my lot.

R. You are my inheritance, O Lord.

I bless the LORD who counsels me; even in the night my heart exhorts me.

I set the LORD ever before me; with him at my right hand I shall not be disturbed.

R. You are my inheritance, O Lord.

You will show me the path to life, fullness of joys in your presence, the delights at your right hand forever.

R. You are my inheritance, O Lord.

Alleluia Mt 11:25

R. Alleluia, alleluia.

Blessed are you, Father, Lord of heaven and earth; you have revealed to little ones the mysteries of the Kingdom.

R. Alleluia, alleluia.

Gospel Mt 19:13-15

Children were brought to Jesus that he might lay his hands on them and pray. The disciples rebuked them, but Jesus said, "Let the children come to me, and do not prevent them; for the Kingdom of heaven belongs to such as these." After he placed his hands on them, he went away.

AUGUST 15TH, 2021
Solemnity of the Assumption of the Blessed Virgin Mary
Vigil

1ST Reading 1 Chr 15:3-4, 15-16; 16:1-2

David assembled all Israel in Jerusalem to bring the ark of the Lord to the place which he had prepared for it. David also called together the sons of Aaron and the Levites. The Levites bore the ark of God on their shoulders with poles, as Moses had ordained according to the word of the Lord. David commanded the chiefs of the Levites to appoint their kinsmen as chanters, to play on musical instruments, harps, lyres, and cymbals, to make a loud sound of rejoicing.

They brought in the ark of God and set it within the tent which David had pitched for it. Then they offered up burnt offerings and peace offerings to God. When David had finished offering up the burnt offerings and peace offerings, he blessed the people in the name of the Lord.

Responsorial Psalm 132:6-7, 9-10, 13-14

R. (8) Lord, go up to the place of your rest, you and the ark of your holiness.

Behold, we heard of it in Ephrathah; we found it in the fields of Jaar.

Let us enter his dwelling, let us worship at his footstool.

R. Lord, go up to the place of your rest, you and the ark of your holiness.

May your priests be clothed with justice; let your faithful ones shout merrily for joy.

For the sake of David your servant, reject not the plea of your anointed.

R. Lord, go up to the place of your rest, you and the ark of your holiness.

For the LORD has chosen Zion; he prefers her for his dwelling.

"Zion is my resting place forever; in her will I dwell, for I prefer her."

R. Lord, go up to the place of your rest, you and the ark of your holiness.

2ND Reading 1 Cor 15:54b-57

Brothers and sisters:

When that which is mortal clothes itself with immortality, then the word that is written shall come about: Death is swallowed up in victory. Where, O death, is your victory? Where, O death, is your sting? The sting of death is sin, and the power of sin is the law. But thanks be to God who gives us the victory through our Lord Jesus Christ.

Alleluia Lk 11:28

R. Alleluia, alleluia.

Blessed are they who hear the word of God and observe it.

R. Alleluia, alleluia.

Gospel Lk 11:27-28
While Jesus was speaking, a woman from the crowd called out and said to him, "Blessed is the womb that carried you and the breasts at which you nursed." He replied, "Rather, blessed are those who hear the word of God and observe it."

AUGUST 16TH, 2021
Monday of the Twentieth Week in Ordinary Time

1ST Reading Jgs 2:11-19
The children of Israel offended the LORD by serving the Baals. Abandoning the LORD, the God of their fathers, who led them out of the land of Egypt, they followed the other gods of the various nations around them, and by their worship of these gods provoked the LORD. Because they had thus abandoned him and served Baal and the Ashtaroth, the anger of the LORD flared up against Israel,and he delivered them over to plunderers who despoiled them. He allowed them to fall into the power of their enemies round about whom they were no longer able to withstand. Whatever they undertook, the LORD turned into disaster for them, as in his warning he had sworn he would do, till they were in great distress. Even when the LORD raised up judges to deliver them from the power of their despoilers, they did not listen to their judges, but abandoned themselves to the worship of other gods. They were quick to stray from the way their fathers had taken, and did not follow their example of obedience to the commandments of the LORD.

Whenever the LORD raised up judges for them, he would be with the judge and save them from the power of their enemies as long as the judge lived; it was thus the LORD took pity on their distressful cries of affliction under their oppressors. But when the judge died, they would relapse and do worse than their ancestors, following other gods in service and worship, relinquishing none of their evil practices or stubborn conduct.

Responsorial Psalm 106:34-35, 36-37, 39-40, 43ab and 44
R. (4a) Remember us, O Lord, as you favor your people.

They did not exterminate the peoples, as the LORD had commanded them,

But mingled with the nations and learned their works.

R. Remember us, O Lord, as you favor your people.

They served their idols, which became a snare for them.

They sacrificed their sons and their daughters to demons.

R. Remember us, O Lord, as you favor your people.

They became defiled by their works, and wanton in their crimes.

And the LORD grew angry with his people, and abhorred his inheritance.

R. Remember us, O Lord, as you favor your people.

Many times did he rescue them, but they embittered him with their counsels.

Yet he had regard for their affliction when he heard their cry.

R. Remember us, O Lord, as you favor your people.

Alleluia Mt 5:3

R. Alleluia, alleluia.

Blessed are the poor in spirit; for theirs is the Kingdom of heaven.

R. Alleluia, alleluia.

Gospel Mt 19:16-22
A young man approached Jesus and said, "Teacher, what good must I do to gain eternal life?" He answered him, "Why do you ask me about the good? There is only one who is good. If you wish to enter into life, keep the commandments." He asked him, "Which ones?" And Jesus replied, "You

shall not kill; you shall not commit adultery; you shall not steal; you shall not bear false witness; honor your father and your mother; and you shall love your neighbor as yourself."

The young man said to him, "All of these I have observed. What do I still lack?" Jesus said to him, "If you wish to be perfect, go, sell what you have and give to the poor, and you will have treasure in heaven. Then come, follow me." When the young man heard this statement, he went away sad, for he had many possessions.

AUGUST 17TH, 2021
Tuesday of the Twentieth Week in Ordinary Time

1ST Reading Jgs 6:11-24a

The angel of the LORD came and sat under the terebinth in Ophrah that belonged to Joash the Abiezrite. While his son Gideon was beating out wheat in the wine press to save it from the Midianites, the angel of the LORD appeared to him and said, "

The LORD is with you, O champion!" Gideon said to him, "My Lord, if the LORD is with us, why has all this happened to us? Where are his wondrous deeds of which our fathers told us when they said, 'Did not the LORD bring us up from Egypt?' For now the LORD has abandoned us and has delivered us into the power of Midian."

The LORD turned to him and said, "Go with the strength you have and save Israel from the power of Midian. It is I who send you." But Gideon answered him, "Please, my lord, how can I save Israel? My family is the lowliest in Manasseh, and I am the most insignificant in my father's house." "I shall be with you," the LORD said to him, "and you will cut down Midian to the last man." Gideon answered him, "If I find favor with you, give me a sign that you are speaking with me. Do not depart from here, I pray you, until I come back to you and bring out my offering and set it before you." He answered, "I will await your return." So Gideon went off and prepared a kid and a measure of flour in the form of unleavened cakes.

Putting the meat in a basket and the broth in a pot, he brought them out to him under the terebinth and presented them. The angel of God said to him, "Take the meat and unleavened cakes and lay them on this rock; then pour out the broth." When he had done so, the angel of the LORD stretched out the tip of the staff he held, and touched the meat and unleavened cakes.

Thereupon a fire came up from the rock that consumed the meat and unleavened cakes, and the angel of the LORD disappeared from sight. Gideon, now aware that it had been the angel of the LORD, said, "Alas, Lord GOD, that I have seen the angel of the LORD face to face!" The LORD answered him, "Be calm, do not fear. You shall not die." So Gideon built there an altar to the LORD and called it Yahweh-shalom.

Responsorial Psalm 85:9, 11-12, 13-14
R. (see 9b) The Lord speaks of peace to his people.

I will hear what God proclaims; the LORD–for he proclaims peace

To his people, and to his faithful ones, and to those who put in him their hope.

R. The Lord speaks of peace to his people.

Kindness and truth shall meet; justice and peace shall kiss.

Truth shall spring out of the earth, and justice shall look down from heaven.

R. The Lord speaks of peace to his people.

The LORD himself will give his benefits; our land shall yield its increase.

Justice shall walk before him, and salvation, along the way of his steps.

R. The Lord speaks of peace to his people.

Alleluia 2 Cor 8:9

R. Alleluia, alleluia.

Jesus Christ became poor although he was rich so that by his poverty you might become rich.

R. Alleluia, alleluia.

Gospel Mt 19:23-30
Jesus said to his disciples:

"Amen, I say to you, it will be hard for one who is rich to enter the Kingdom of heaven. Again I say to you, it is easier for a camel to pass through the eye of a needle than for one who is rich to enter the Kingdom of God." When the disciples heard this, they were greatly astonished and said, "Who then can be saved?" Jesus looked at them and said, "For men this is impossible, but for God all things are possible." Then Peter said to him in reply, "We have given up everything and followed you. What will there be for us?" Jesus said to them, "Amen, I say to you that you who have followed me, in the new age, when the Son of Man is seated on his throne of glory, will yourselves sit on twelve thrones, judging the twelve tribes of Israel.

And everyone who has given up houses or brothers or sisters or father or mother or children or lands for the sake of my name will receive a hundred times more, and will inherit eternal life. But many who are first will be last, and the last will be first."

AUGUST 18TH, 2021
Wednesday of the Twentieth Week in Ordinary Time

1ST Reading Jgs 9:6-15

All the citizens of Shechem and all Beth-millo came together and proceeded to make Abimelech king by the terebinth at the memorial pillar in Shechem. When this was reported to him, Jotham went to the top of Mount Gerizim and, standing there, cried out to them in a loud voice: "Hear me, citizens of Shechem, that God may then hear you! Once the trees went to anoint a king over themselves. So they said to the olive tree, 'Reign over us.' But the olive tree answered them, 'Must I give up my rich oil, whereby men and gods are honored, and go to wave over the trees?' Then the trees said to the fig tree, 'Come; you reign over us!' But the fig tree answered them, 'Must I give up my sweetness and my good fruit, and go to wave over the trees?'

Then the trees said to the vine, 'Come you, and reign over us.' But the vine answered them, 'Must I give up my wine that cheers gods and men, and go to wave over the trees?' Then all the trees said to the buckthorn, 'Come; you reign over us!' But the buckthorn replied to the trees, 'If you wish to anoint me king over you in good faith, come and take refuge in my shadow. Otherwise, let fire come from the buckthorn and devour the cedars of Lebanon.'"

Responsorial Psalm 21:2-3, 4-5, 6-7
R. (2a) Lord, in your strength the king is glad.

O LORD, in your strength the king is glad; in your victory how greatly he rejoices!

You have granted him his heart's desire; you refused not the wish of his lips.

R. Lord, in your strength the king is glad.

For you welcomed him with goodly blessings, you placed on his head a crown of pure gold.

He asked life of you: you gave him length of days forever and ever.

R. Lord, in your strength the king is glad.

Great is his glory in your victory; majesty and splendor you conferred upon him.

You made him a blessing forever, you gladdened him with the joy of your face.

R. Lord, in your strength the king is glad.

Alleluia Heb 4:12

R. Alleluia, alleluia.

The word of God is living and effective, able to discern the reflections and thoughts of the heart.

R. Alleluia, alleluia.

Gospel Mt 20:1-16
Jesus told his disciples this parable:

"The Kingdom of heaven is like a landowner who went out at dawn to hire laborers for his vineyard. After agreeing with them for the usual daily wage, he sent them into his vineyard. Going out about nine o'clock, he saw others standing idle in the marketplace, and he said to them, 'You too go into my vineyard, and I will give you what is just.' So they went off. And he went out again around noon, and around three o'clock, and did likewise. Going out about five o'clock, he found others standing around, and said to them, 'Why do you stand here idle all day?' They answered, 'Because no one has hired us.' He said to them, 'You too go into my vineyard.' When it was evening the owner of the vineyard said to his foreman, 'Summon the laborers and give them their pay, beginning with the last and ending with the first.'

When those who had started about five o'clock came, each received the usual daily wage. So when the first came, they thought that they would receive more, but each of them also got the usual wage. And on receiving it they grumbled against the landowner, saying, 'These last ones worked only one hour, and you have made them equal to us, who bore the day's burden and the heat.' He said to one of them in reply, 'My friend, I am not cheating you. Did you not agree with me for the usual daily wage?

Take what is yours and go. What if I wish to give this last one the same as you? Or am I not free to do as I wish with my own money? Are you envious because I am generous?' Thus, the last will be first, and the first will be last."

AUGUST 19TH, 2021
Thursday of the Twentieth Week in Ordinary Time

1ST Reading Jgs 11:29-39a

The Spirit of the LORD came upon Jephthah. He passed through Gilead and Manasseh, and through Mizpah-Gilead as well, and from there he went on to the Ammonites. Jephthah made a vow to the LORD. "If you deliver the Ammonites into my power," he said, "whoever comes out of the doors of my house to meet me when I return in triumph from the Ammonites shall belong to the LORD.

I shall offer him up as a burnt offering." Jephthah then went on to the Ammonites to fight against them, and the LORD delivered them into his power, so that he inflicted a severe defeat on them, from Aroer to the approach of Minnith (twenty cities in all) and as far as Abel-keramim. Thus were the Ammonites brought into subjection by the children of Israel. When Jephthah returned to his house in Mizpah, it was his daughter who came forth, playing the tambourines and dancing. She was an only child: he had neither son nor daughter besides her. When he saw her, he rent his garments and said, "Alas, daughter, you have struck me down and brought calamity upon me. For I have made a vow to the LORD and I cannot retract." She replied, "Father, you have made a vow to the LORD. Do with me as you have vowed, because the LORD has wrought vengeance for you on your enemies the Ammonites." Then she said to her father, "Let me have this favor. Spare me for two months, that I may go off down the mountains to mourn my virginity with my companions." "Go," he replied, and sent her away for two months.

So she departed with her companions and mourned her virginity on the mountains. At the end of the two months she returned to her father, who did to her as he had vowed.

Responsorial Psalm 40:5, 7-8a, 8b-9, 10
R. (8a and 9a) Here I am, Lord; I come to do your will.

Blessed the man who makes the LORD his trust; who turns not to idolatry or to those who stray after falsehood.

R. Here I am, Lord; I come to do your will.

Sacrifice or oblation you wished not, but ears open to obedience you gave me.

Burnt offerings or sin-offerings you sought not; then said I, "Behold I come."

R. Here I am, Lord; I come to do your will.

"In the written scroll it is prescribed for me.

To do your will, O my God, is my delight, and your law is within my heart!"

R. Here I am, Lord; I come to do your will.

I announced your justice in the vast assembly; I did not restrain my lips, as you, O LORD, know.

R. Here I am, Lord; I come to do your will.

Alleluia Ps 95:8

R. Alleluia, alleluia.

If today you hear his voice, harden not your hearts.

R. Alleluia, alleluia.

Gospel Mt 22:1-14
Jesus again in reply spoke to the chief priests and the elders of the people in parables saying, "The Kingdom of heaven may be likened to a king who gave a wedding feast for his son. He dispatched his servants to summon the invited guests to the feast, but they refused to come. A second time he sent

other servants, saying, 'Tell those invited: "Behold, I have prepared my banquet, my calves and fattened cattle are killed, and everything is ready; come to the feast."' Some ignored the invitation and went away, one to his farm, another to his business.

The rest laid hold of his servants, mistreated them, and killed them. The king was enraged and sent his troops, destroyed those murderers, and burned their city. Then the king said to his servants, 'The feast is ready, but those who were invited were not worthy to come. Go out, therefore, into the main roads and invite to the feast whomever you find. 'The servants went out into the streets and gathered all they found, bad and good alike, and the hall was filled with guests. But when the king came in to meet the guest she saw a man there not dressed in a wedding garment. He said to him, 'My friend, how is it that you came in here without a wedding garment? 'But he was reduced to silence. Then the king said to his attendants, 'Bind his hands and feet, and cast him into the darkness outside, where there will be wailing and grinding of teeth. 'Many are invited, but few are chosen."

AUGUST 20TH, 2021
Memorial of Saint Bernard, Abbot and Doctor of the Church

1ST Reading Ru 1:1, 3-6, 14b-16, 22

Once in the time of the judges there was a famine in the land; so a man from Bethlehem of Judah departed with his wife and two sons to reside on the plateau of Moab. Elimelech, the husband of Naomi, died, and she was left with her two sons, who married Moabite women, one named Orpah, the other Ruth. When they had lived there about ten years, both Mahlon and Chilion died also, and the woman was left with neither her two sons nor her husband. She then made ready to go back from the plateau of Moab because word reached her there that the LORD had visited his people and given them food. Orpah kissed her mother-in-law good-bye, but Ruth stayed with her. Naomi said, "See now! Your sister-in-law has gone back to her people and her god. Go back after your sister-in-law!" But Ruth said, "Do not ask me to abandon or forsake you! For wherever you go,

I will go, wherever you lodge I will lodge, your people shall be my people and your God my God." Thus it was that Naomi returned with the Moabite daughter-in-law, Ruth, who accompanied her back from the plateau of Moab. They arrived in Bethlehem at the beginning of the barley harvest.

504

R. (1b) Praise the Lord, my soul!

Blessed is he whose help is the God of Jacob, whose hope is in the LORD, his God,

Who made heaven and earth, the sea and all that is in them.

R. Praise the Lord, my soul!

The LORD keeps faith forever, secures justice for the oppressed, gives food to the hungry.

The LORD sets captives free.

R. Praise the Lord, my soul!

The LORD gives sight to the blind. The LORD raises up those who were bowed down;

The LORD loves the just. The LORD protects strangers.

R. Praise the Lord, my soul!

The fatherless and the widow he sustains, but the way of the wicked he thwarts.

The LORD shall reign forever; your God, O Zion, through all generations. Alleluia.

R Praise the Lord, my soul!

R. Alleluia, alleluia.

Teach me your paths, my God, guide me in your truth.

R. Alleluia, alleluia.

When the Pharisees heard that Jesus had silenced the Sadducees, they gathered together, and one of them, a scholar of the law, tested him by asking, "Teacher, which commandment in the law is the greatest?" He said to

505

him, "You shall love the Lord, your God, with all your heart, with all your soul, and with all your mind. This is the greatest and the first commandment. The second is like it: You shall love your neighbor as yourself. The whole law and the prophets depend on these two commandments."

AUGUST 21ST, 2021
Memorial of Saint Pius X, Pope

1ST Reading Ru 2:1-3, 8-11; 4:13-17

Naomi had a prominent kinsman named Boaz, of the clan of her husband Elimelech. Ruth the Moabite said to Naomi, "Let me go and glean ears of grain in the field of anyone who will allow me that favor." Naomi said to her, "Go, my daughter," and she went. The field she entered to glean after the harvesters happened to be the section belonging to Boaz of the clan of Elimelech. Boaz said to Ruth, "Listen, my daughter! Do not go to glean in anyone else's field; you are not to leave here. Stay here with my women servants. Watch to see which field is to be harvested, and follow them; I have commanded the young men to do you no harm.

When you are thirsty, you may go and drink from the vessels the young men have filled." Casting herself prostrate upon the ground, Ruth said to him, "Why should I, a foreigner, be favored with your notice?" Boaz answered her: "I have had a complete account of what you have done for your mother-in-law after your husband's death; you have left your father and your mother and the land of your birth, and have come to a people whom you did not know previously." Boaz took Ruth. When they came together as man and wife, the LORD enabled her to conceive and she bore a son. Then the women said to Naomi, "Blessed is the LORD who has not failed to provide you today with an heir! May he become famous in Israel!

He will be your comfort and the support of your old age, for his mother is the daughter-in-law who loves you. She is worth more to you than seven sons!" Naomi took the child, placed him on her lap, and became his nurse. And the neighbor women gave him his name, at the news that a grandson had been born to Naomi. They called him Obed. He was the father of Jesse, the father of David.

Responsorial Psalm 128:1b-2, 3, 4, 5

R. (4) See how the Lord blesses those who fear him.

Blessed are you who fear the LORD, who walk in his ways!

506

For you shall eat the fruit of your handiwork; blessed shall you be, and favored.

R. See how the Lord blesses those who fear him.

You wife shall be like a fruitful vine in the recesses of your home;

Your children like olive plants around your table.

R. See how the Lord blesses those who fear him.

Behold, thus is the man blessed who fears the LORD.

R. See how the Lord blesses those who fear him.

The LORD bless you from Zion: may you see the prosperity of Jerusalem all the days of your life.

R. See how the Lord blesses those who fear him.

Alleluia Mt 23:9b, 10b

R. Alleluia, alleluia.

You have but one Father in heaven; you have but one master, the Christ.

R. Alleluia, alleluia.

Gospel Mt 23:1-12

Jesus spoke to the crowds and to his disciples, saying, "The scribes and the Pharisees have taken their seat on the chair of Moses. Therefore, do and observe all things whatsoever they tell you, but do not follow their example.

For they preach but they do not practice. They tie up heavy burdens hard to carry and lay them on people's shoulders, but they will not lift a finger to move them. All their works are performed to be seen. They widen their phylacteries and lengthen their tassels. They love places of honor at banquets, seats of honor in synagogues, greetings in marketplaces, and the salutation 'Rabbi.' As for you, do not be called 'Rabbi.' You have but one teacher, and you are all brothers. Call no one on earth your father; you have but one Father in heaven. Do not be called 'Master'; you have but one master, the Christ. The greatest among you must be your servant. Whoever exalts himself will be humbled; but whoever humbles himself will be exalted."

1ST Reading Jos 24:1-2a, 15-17, 18b

Joshua gathered together all the tribes of Israel at Shechem, summoning their elders, their leaders, their judges, and their officers. When they stood in ranks before God, Joshua addressed all the people: "If it does not please you to serve the LORD, decide today whom you will serve, the gods your fathers served beyond the River or the gods of the Amorites in whose country you are now dwelling. As for me and my household, we will serve the LORD." But the people answered, "Far be it from us to forsake the LORD for the service of other gods. For it was the LORD, our God, who brought us and our fathers up out of the land of Egypt, out of a state of slavery.

He performed those great miracles before our very eyes and protected us along our entire journey and among the peoples through whom we passed. Therefore we also will serve the LORD, for he is our God."

Responsorial Psalm Ps 34:2-3, 16-17, 18-19, 20-21

R. (9a) Taste and see the goodness of the Lord.

I will bless the LORD at all times; his praise shall be ever in my mouth.

Let my soul glory in the LORD; the lowly will hear me and be glad.

R. Taste and see the goodness of the Lord.

The LORD has eyes for the just, and ears for their cry.

The LORD confronts the evildoers, to destroy remembrance of them from the earth.

R. Taste and see the goodness of the Lord.

When the just cry out, the LORD hears them, and from all their distress he rescues them.

He is close to the brokenhearted; and those who are crushed in spirit he saves.

R. Taste and see the goodness of the Lord.

Many are the troubles of the just one, but out of them all the LORD delivers him;

He watches over all his bones; not one of them shall be broken.

R. Taste and see the goodness of the Lord.

Brothers and sisters:

Be subordinate to one another out of reverence for Christ. Wives should be subordinate to their husbands as to the Lord. For the husband is head of his wife just as Christ is head of the church, he himself the savior of the body. As the church is subordinate to Christ, so wives should be subordinate to their husbands in everything. Husbands, love your wives, even as Christ loved the church and handed himself over for her to sanctify her, cleansing her by the bath of water with the word, that he might present to himself the church in splendor, without spot or wrinkle or any such thing, that she might be holy and without blemish. So also husbands should love their wives as their own bodies.

He who loves his wife loves himself. For no one hates his own flesh but rather nourishes and cherishes it, even as Christ does the church, because we are members of his body. For this reason a man shall leave his father and his mother and be joined to his wife, and the two shall become one flesh. This is a great mystery, but I speak in reference to Christ and the church.

OR:

Brothers and sisters:

Live in love, as Christ loved us. Husbands, love your wives, even as Christ loved the church and handed himself over for her to sanctify her, cleansing her by the bath of water with the word, that he might present to himself the church in splendor, without spot or wrinkle or any such thing, that she might be holy and without blemish. So also husbands should love their wives as their own bodies.

He who loves his wife loves himself. For no one hates his own flesh but rather nourishes and cherishes it, even as Christ does the church, because we are members of his body. For this reason a man shall leave his father and his mother and be joined to his wife, and the two shall become one flesh. This is a great mystery, but I speak in reference to Christ and the church.

R. Alleluia, alleluia.

Your words, Lord, are Spirit and life; you have the words of everlasting life.

R. Alleluia, alleluia.

Gospel Jn 6:60-69

Many of Jesus' disciples who were listening said, "This saying is hard; who can accept it?" Since Jesus knew that his disciples were murmuring about this, he said to them, "Does this shock you? What if you were to see the Son of Man ascending to where he was before? It is the spirit that gives life, while the flesh is of no avail. The words I have spoken to you are Spirit and life. But there are some of you who do not believe." Jesus knew from the beginning the ones who would not believe and the one who would betray him. And he said, "For this reason I have told you that no one can come to me unless it is granted him by my Father." As a result of this, many of his disciples returned to their former way of life and no longer accompanied him.

Jesus then said to the Twelve, "Do you also want to leave?" Simon Peter answered him, "Master, to whom shall we go? You have the words of eternal life. We have come to believe and are convinced that you are the Holy One of God."

AUGUST 23RD, 2021
Monday of the Twenty-first Week in Ordinary Time

1ST Reading 1 Thes 1:1-5, 8b-10

Paul, Silvanus, and Timothy to the Church of the Thessalonians in God the Father and the Lord Jesus Christ: grace to you and peace. We give thanks to God always for all of you, remembering you in our prayers, unceasingly calling to mind your work of faith and labor of love and endurance in hope of our Lord Jesus Christ, before our God and Father, knowing, brothers and sisters loved by God, how you were chosen. For our Gospel did not come to you in word alone, but also in power and in the Holy Spirit and with much conviction. You know what sort of people we were among you for your sake. In every place your faith in God has gone forth, so that we have no need to say anything. For they themselves openly declare about us what sort of reception we had among you, and how you turned to God from idols to serve the living and true God and to await his Son from heaven, whom he raised from the dead, Jesus, who delivers us from the coming wrath.

Responsorial Psalm 149:1b-2, 3-4, 5-6a and 9b
R. (see 4a) The Lord takes delight in his people.

or:

R. Alleluia.

Sing to the LORD a new song of praise in the assembly of the faithful.

Let Israel be glad in their maker, let the children of Zion rejoice in their king.

R. The Lord takes delight in his people.

or:

R. Alleluia.

Let them praise his name in the festive dance, let them sing praise to him with timbrel and harp.

For the LORD loves his people, and he adorns the lowly with victory.

R. The Lord takes delight in his people.

or:

R. Alleluia.

Let the faithful exult in glory; let them sing for joy upon their couches;

Let the high praises of God be in their throats. This is the glory of all his faithful. Alleluia.

R. The Lord takes delight in his people.

or:

R. Alleluia.

Alleluia Jn 10:27

R. Alleluia, alleluia.

My sheep hear my voice, says the Lord; I know them, and they follow me.

R. Alleluia, alleluia.

Jesus said to the crowds and to his disciples:

"Woe to you, scribes and Pharisees, you hypocrites. You lock the Kingdom of heaven before men. You do not enter yourselves, nor do you allow entrance to those trying to enter. "Woe to you, scribes and Pharisees, you hypocrites. Y

ou traverse sea and land to make one convert, and when that happens you make him a child of Gehenna twice as much as yourselves. "Woe to you, blind guides, who say, 'If one swears by the temple, it means nothing, but if one swears by the gold of the temple, one is obligated.' Blind fools, which is greater, the gold, or the temple that made the gold sacred? And you say, 'If one swears by the altar, it means nothing, but if one swears by the gift on the altar, one is obligated.' You blind ones, which is greater, the gift, or the altar that makes the gift sacred?

One who swears by the altar swears by it and all that is upon it; one who swears by the temple swears by it and by him who dwells in it; one who swears by heaven swears by the throne of God and by him who is seated on it."

AUGUST 24TH, 2021
Feast of Saint Bartholomew, Apostle

1ST Reading Rv 21:9b-14
The angel spoke to me, saying, "Come here. I will show you the bride, the wife of the Lamb." He took me in spirit to a great, high mountain and showed me the holy city Jerusalem coming down out of heaven from God. It gleamed with the splendor of God. Its radiance was like that of a precious stone, like jasper, clear as crystal. It had a massive, high wall, with twelve gates where twelve angels were stationed and on which names were inscribed, the names of the twelve tribes of the children of Israel. There were three gates facing east, three north, three south, and three west. The wall of the city had twelve courses of stones as its foundation, on which were inscribed the twelve names of the twelve Apostles of the Lamb.

R. (12) Your friends make known, O Lord, the glorious splendor of your Kingdom.

Let all your works give you thanks, O LORD, and let your faithful ones bless you.

Let them discourse of the glory of your Kingdom and speak of your might.

R. Your friends make known, O Lord, the glorious splendor of your Kingdom.

Making known to men your might and the glorious splendor of your Kingdom.

Your Kingdom is a Kingdom for all ages, and your dominion endures through all generations.

R. Your friends make known, O Lord, the glorious splendor of your Kingdom.

The LORD is just in all his ways and holy in all his works.

The LORD is near to all who call upon him, to all who call upon him in truth.

R. Your friends make known, O Lord, the glorious splendor of your Kingdom.

Alleluia Jn 1:49b

R. Alleluia, alleluia.

Rabbi, you are the Son of God; you are the King of Israel.

R. Alleluia, alleluia.

Gospel Jn 1:45-51

Philip found Nathanael and told him, "We have found the one about whom Moses wrote in the law, and also the prophets, Jesus son of Joseph, from Nazareth." But Nathanael said to him, "Can anything good come from Nazareth?" Philip said to him, "Come and see." Jesus saw Nathanael coming toward him and said of him, "Here is a true child of Israel.

There is no duplicity in him." Nathanael said to him, "How do you know me?" Jesus answered and said to him, "Before Philip called you, I saw you under the fig tree." Nathanael answered him, "Rabbi, you are the Son of God; you are the King of Israel." Jesus answered and said to him, "Do you believe because I told you that I saw you under the fig tree? You will see greater things than this." And he said to him, "Amen, amen, I say to you, you will see heaven opened and the angels of God ascending and descending on the Son of Man."

AUGUST 25TH, 2021
Wednesday of the Twenty-first Week in Ordinary Time

1ST Reading 1 Thes 2:9-13

You recall, brothers and sisters, our toil and drudgery. Working night and day in order not to burden any of you, we proclaimed to you the Gospel of God. You are witnesses, and so is God, how devoutly and justly and blamelessly we behaved toward you believers. As you know, we treated each one of you as a father treats his children, exhorting and encouraging you and insisting that you walk in a manner worthy of the God who calls you into his Kingdom and glory. And for this reason we too give thanks to God unceasingly, that, in receiving the word of God from hearing us, you received it not as the word of men, but as it truly is, the word of God, which is now at work in you who believe.

Responsorial Psalm 139:7-8, 9-10, 11-12ab

R. (1) You have searched me and you know me, Lord.

Where can I go from your spirit? From your presence where can I flee?

If I go up to the heavens, you are there; if I sink to the nether world, you are present there.

R. You have searched me and you know me, Lord.

If I take the wings of the dawn, if I settle at the farthest limits of the sea,

Even there your hand shall guide me, and your right hand hold me fast.

R. You have searched me and you know me, Lord.

If I say, "Surely the darkness shall hide me, and night shall be my light"–

For you darkness itself is not dark, and night shines as the day.

R. You have searched me and you know me, Lord.

Alleluia 1 Jn 2:5

R. Alleluia, alleluia.

Whoever keeps the word of Christ, the love of God is truly perfected in him.

R. Alleluia, alleluia.

Gospel Mt 23:27-32
Jesus said, "Woe to you, scribes and Pharisees, you hypocrites. You are like whitewashed tombs, which appear beautiful on the outside, but inside are full of dead men's bones and every kind of filth. Even so, on the outside you appear righteous, but inside you are filled with hypocrisy and evildoing. "Woe to you, scribes and Pharisees, you hypocrites.

You build the tombs of the prophets and adorn the memorials of the righteous, and you say, 'If we had lived in the days of our ancestors, we would not have joined them in shedding the prophets' blood.' Thus you bear witness against yourselves that you are the children of those who murdered the prophets; now fill up what your ancestors measured out!"

AUGUST 26TH, 2021
Thursday of the Twenty-first Week in Ordinary Time

1ST Reading Thes 3:7-13
We have been reassured about you, brothers and sisters, in our every distress and affliction, through your faith. For we now live, if you stand firm in the Lord.

What thanksgiving, then, can we render to God for you, for all the joy we feel on your account before our God? Night and day we pray beyond measure to see you in person and to remedy the deficiencies of your faith.

Now may God himself, our Father, and our Lord Jesus direct our way to you, and may the Lord make you increase and abound in love for one another and for all, just as we have for you, so as to strengthen your hearts, to be blameless in holiness before our God and Father at the coming of our Lord Jesus with all his holy ones. Amen.

R. (14) Fill us with your love, O Lord, and we will sing for joy!

You turn man back to dust, saying, "Return, O children of men."

For a thousand years in your sight are as yesterday, now that it is past, or as a watch of the night.

R. Fill us with your love, O Lord, and we will sing for joy!

Teach us to number our days aright, that we may gain wisdom of heart.

Return, O LORD! How long? Have pity on your servants!

R. Fill us with your love, O Lord, and we will sing for joy!

Fill us at daybreak with your kindness, that we may shout for joy and gladness all our days.

And may the gracious care of the LORD our God be ours; prosper the work of our hands for us!

Prosper the work of our hands!

R. Fill us with your love, O Lord, and we will sing for joy!

Alleluia Mt 24:42a, 44

R. Alleluia, alleluia.

Stay awake! For you do not know when the Son of Man will come.

R. Alleluia, alleluia.

Gospel Mt 24:42-51
Jesus said to his disciples:

"Stay awake! For you do not know on which day your Lord will come. Be sure of this: if the master of the house had known the hour of night when the thief was coming, he would have stayed awake and not let his house be broken into. So too, you also must be prepared, for at an hour you do not expect, the Son of Man will come. "Who, then, is the faithful and prudent servant, whom the master has put in charge of his household to distribute to them their food at the proper time?

Blessed is that servant whom his master on his arrival finds doing so. Amen, I say to you, he will put him in charge of all his property. But if that wicked servant says to himself, 'My master is long delayed,' and begins to beat his fellow servants, and eat and drink with drunkards, the servant's master will come on an unexpected day and at an unknown hour and will punish him severely and assign him a place with the hypocrites, where there will be wailing and grinding of teeth."

AUGUST 27TH, 2021
Memorial of Saint Monica

1ST Reading 1 Thes 4:1-8
Brothers and sisters, we earnestly ask and exhort you in the Lord Jesus that, as you received from us how you should conduct yourselves to please God– and as you are conducting yourselves– you do so even more. For you know what instructions we gave you through the Lord Jesus.

This is the will of God, your holiness: that you refrain from immorality, that each of you know how to acquire a wife for himself in holiness and honor, not in lustful passion as do the Gentiles who do not know God; not to take advantage of or exploit a brother or sister in this matter, for the Lord is an avenger in all these things, as we told you before and solemnly affirmed. For God did not call us to impurity but to holiness. Therefore, whoever disregards this, disregards not a human being but God, who also gives his Holy Spirit to you.

Responsorial Psalm 97:1 and 2b, 5-6, 10, 11-12
R. (12a) Rejoice in the Lord, you just!

The LORD is king; let the earth rejoice; let the many isles be glad. Justice and judgment are the foundation of his throne.

R. Rejoice in the Lord, you just!

The mountains melt like wax before the LORD, before the LORD of all the earth.

The heavens proclaim his justice, and all peoples see his glory.

R. Rejoice in the Lord, you just!

The LORD loves those who hate evil; he guards the lives of his faithful ones; from the hand of the wicked he delivers them.

R. Rejoice in the Lord, you just!

Light dawns for the just; and gladness, for the upright of heart.

Be glad in the LORD, you just, and give thanks to his holy name.

R. Rejoice in the Lord, you just!

Alleluia Lk 21:36

R. Alleluia, alleluia.

Be vigilant at all times and pray, that you may have the strength to stand before the Son of Man.

R. Alleluia, alleluia.

Gospel Mt 25:1-13

Jesus told his disciples this parable:

"The Kingdom of heaven will be like ten virgins who took their lamps and went out to meet the bridegroom. Five of them were foolish and five were wise. The foolish ones, when taking their lamps, brought no oil with them, but the wise brought flasks of oil with their lamps. Since the bridegroom was long delayed, they all became drowsy and fell asleep. At midnight, there was a cry, 'Behold, the bridegroom! Come out to meet him!'

Then all those virgins got up and trimmed their lamps. The foolish ones said to the wise, 'Give us some of your oil, for our lamps are going out.' But the wise ones replied, 'No, for there may not be enough for us and you. Go instead to the merchants and buy some for yourselves.'

While they went off to buy it, the bridegroom came and those who were ready went into the wedding feast with him. Then the door was locked. Afterwards the other virgins came and said, 'Lord, Lord, open the door for us!' But he said in reply, 'Amen, I say to you, I do not know you.' Therefore, stay awake, for you know neither the day nor the hour."

AUGUST 28TH, 2021
Memorial of Saint Augustine, Bishop and Doctor of the Church

1ST Reading 1 Thes 4:9-11
Brothers and sisters:

On the subject of fraternal charity you have no need for anyone to write you, for you yourselves have been taught by God to love one another. Indeed, you do this for all the brothers throughout Macedonia. Nevertheless we urge you, brothers and sisters, to progress even more, and to aspire to live a tranquil life, to mind your own affairs, and to work with your own hands, as we instructed you.

Responsorial Psalm 98:1, 7-8, 9
R. (9) The Lord comes to rule the earth with justice.

Sing to the LORD a new song, for he has done wondrous deeds;

His right hand has won victory for him, his holy arm.

R. The Lord comes to rule the earth with justice.

Let the sea and what fills it resound, the world and those who dwell in it;

Let the rivers clap their hands, the mountains shout with them for joy.

R. The Lord comes to rule the earth with justice.

Before the LORD, for he comes, for he comes to rule the earth;

He will rule the world with justice and the peoples with equity.

R. The Lord comes to rule the earth with justice.

Alleluia Jn 13:34

R. Alleluia, alleluia.

I give you a new commandment: love one another as I have loved you.

R. Alleluia, alleluia.

519

Jesus told his disciples this parable: "A man going on a journey called in his servants and entrusted his possessions to them. To one he gave five talents; to another, two; to a third, one– to each according to his ability. Then he went away. Immediately the one who received five talents went and traded with them, and made another five. Likewise, the one who received two made another two. But the man who received one went off and dug a hole in the ground and buried his master's money. After a long time the master of those servants came back and settled accounts with them. The one who had received five talents came forward bringing the additional five.

He said, 'Master, you gave me five talents. See, I have made five more.' His master said to him, 'Well done, my good and faithful servant. Since you were faithful in small matters, I will give you great responsibilities. Come, share your master's joy. 'Then the one who had received two talents also came forward and said, 'Master, you gave me two talents. See, I have made two more.' His master said to him, 'Well done, my good and faithful servant. Since you were faithful in small matters,

I will give you great responsibilities. Come, share your master's joy.' Then the one who had received the one talent came forward and said, 'Master, I knew you were a demanding person, harvesting where you did not plant and gathering where you did not scatter; so out of fear I went off and buried your talent in the ground. Here it is back.' His master said to him in reply, 'You wicked, lazy servant! So you knew that I harvest where I did not plant and gather where I did not scatter? Should you not then have put my money in the bank so that I could have got it back with interest on my return? Now then!

Take the talent from him and give it to the one with ten. For to everyone who has, more will be given and he will grow rich; but from the one who has not, even what he has will be taken away. And throw this useless servant into the darkness outside, where there will be wailing and grinding of teeth.'"

AUGUST 29TH, 2021
Twenty-second Sunday in Ordinary Time

1ST Reading Dt 4:1-2, 6-8
Moses said to the people:

"Now, Israel, hear the statutes and decrees which I am teaching you to observe, that you may live, and may enter in and take possession of the land which the LORD, the God of your fathers, is giving you. In your observance of the commandments of the LORD, your God, which I enjoin upon you, you shall not add to what I command you nor subtract from it. Observe them carefully, for thus will you give evidence of your wisdom and intelligence to the nations, who will hear of all these statutes and say, 'This great nation is truly a wise and intelligent people.' For what great nation is there that has gods so close to it as the LORD, our God, is to us whenever we call upon him? Or what great nation has statutes and decrees that are as just as this whole law which I am setting before you today?"

Responsorial Psalm Ps 15:2-3, 3-4, 4-5
R. (1a) One who does justice will live in the presence of the Lord.

Whoever walks blamelessly and does justice; who thinks the truth in his heart and slanders not with his tongue.

R. One who does justice will live in the presence of the Lord.

Who harms not his fellow man, nor takes up a reproach against his neighbor; by whom the reprobate is despised, while he honors those who fear the LORD.

R. One who does justice will live in the presence of the Lord.

Who lends not his money at usury and accepts no bribe against the innocent.

Whoever does these things shall never be disturbed.

R. One who does justice will live in the presence of the Lord.

2ND Reading Jas 1:17-18, 21b-22, 27
Dearest brothers and sisters:

All good giving and every perfect gift is from above, coming down from the Father of lights, with whom there is no alteration or shadow caused by change. He willed to give us birth by the word of truth that we may be a kind of first fruits of his creatures. Humbly welcome the word that has been planted in you and is able to save your souls. Be doers of the word and not hearers only, deluding yourselves. Religion that is pure and undefiled before God and the Father is this: to care for orphans and widows in their affliction and to keep oneself unstained by the world.

Alleluia Jas 1:18

R. Alleluia, alleluia.

The Father willed to give us birth by the word of truth that we may be a kind of first fruits of his creatures.

R. Alleluia, alleluia.

Gospel Mk 7:1-8, 14-15, 21-23

When the Pharisees with some scribes who had come from Jerusalem gathered around Jesus, they observed that some of his disciples ate their meals with unclean, that is, unwashed, hands. —For the Pharisees and, in fact, all Jews, do not eat without carefully washing their hands,

keeping the tradition of the elders. And on coming from the marketplace they do not eat without purifying themselves. And there are many other things that they have traditionally observed, the purification of cups and jugs and kettles and beds. —So the Pharisees and scribes questioned him, "Why do your disciples not follow the tradition of the elders but instead eat a meal with unclean hands?" He responded, "Well did Isaiah prophesy about you hypocrites, as it is written:

This people honors me with their lips, but their hearts are far from me; in vain do they worship me, teaching as doctrines human precepts. You disregard God's commandment but cling to human tradition." He summoned the crowd again and said to them, "Hear me, all of you, and understand. Nothing that enters one from outside can defile that person; but the things that come out from within are what defile. "From within people, from their hearts, come evil thoughts, unchastity, theft, murder, adultery, greed, malice, deceit, licentiousness, envy, blasphemy, arrogance, folly. All these evils come from within and they defile."

AUGUST 30TH, 2021
Monday of the Twenty-second Week in Ordinary Time

1ST Reading 1 Thes 4:13-18

We do not want you to be unaware, brothers and sisters, about those who have fallen asleep, so that you may not grieve like the rest, who have no hope. For if we believe that Jesus died and rose, so too will God, through Jesus, bring with him those who have fallen asleep. Indeed, we tell you this, on the word of the Lord, that we who are alive, who are left until the coming of the Lord, will surely not precede those who have fallen asleep. For the Lord himself, with a word of command, with the voice of an archangel and with the trumpet of God, will come down from heaven, and the dead in Christ will rise first. Then we who are alive, who are left, will be caught up together with them in the clouds to meet the Lord in the air. Thus we shall always be with the Lord. Therefore, console one another with these words.

Responsorial Psalm 96:1 and 3, 4-5, 11-12, 13
R. (13b) The Lord comes to judge the earth.

Sing to the LORD a new song; sing to the LORD, all you lands.

Tell his glory among the nations; among all peoples, his wondrous deeds.

R. The Lord comes to judge the earth.

For great is the LORD and highly to be praised; awesome is he, beyond all gods.

For all the gods of the nations are things of nought, but the LORD made the heavens.

R. The Lord comes to judge the earth.

Let the heavens be glad and the earth rejoice; let the sea and what fills it resound; let the plains be joyful and all that is in them!

Then shall all the trees of the forest exult.

R. The Lord comes to judge the earth.

Before the LORD, for he comes; for he comes to rule the earth.

He shall rule the world with justice and the peoples with his constancy.

R. The Lord comes to judge the earth.

Alleluia Lk 4:18

R. Alleluia, alleluia.

The Spirit of the Lord is upon me; he has sent me to bring glad tidings to the poor.

R. Alleluia, alleluia.

Gospel Lk 4:16-30

Jesus came to Nazareth, where he had grown up, and went according to his custom into the synagogue on the sabbath day. He stood up to read and was handed a scroll of the prophet Isaiah. He unrolled the scroll and found the passage where it was written:

The Spirit of the Lord is upon me, because he has anointed me to bring glad tidings to the poor. He has sent me to proclaim liberty to captives and recovery of sight to the blind, to let the oppressed go free, and to proclaim a year acceptable to the Lord. Rolling up the scroll, he handed it back to the attendant and sat down, and the eyes of all in the synagogue looked intently at him.

He said to them, "Today this Scripture passage is fulfilled in your hearing." And all spoke highly of him and were amazed at the gracious words that came from his mouth. They also asked, "Is this not the son of Joseph?"

He said to them, "Surely you will quote me this proverb, 'Physician, cure yourself,' and say, 'Do here in your native place the things that we heard were done in Capernaum.'" And he said, "Amen, I say to you, no prophet is accepted in his own native place. Indeed, I tell you, there were many widows in Israel in the days of Elijah when the sky was closed for three and a half years and a severe famine spread over the entire land. It was to none of these that Elijah was sent, but only to a widow in Zarephath in the land of Sidon. Again, there were many lepers in Israel during the time of Elisha the prophet; yet not one of them was cleansed, but only Naaman the Syrian." When the people in the synagogue heard this, they were all filled with fury. They rose up, drove him out of the town, and led him to the brow of the hill on which their town had been built, to hurl him down headlong. But he passed through the midst of them and went away.

AUGUST 31ST, 2021
Tuesday of the Twenty-second Week in Ordinary Time

1ST Reading 1 Thes 5:1-6, 9-11

Concerning times and seasons, brothers and sisters, you have no need for anything to be written to you. For you yourselves know very well that the day of the Lord will come like a thief at night. When people are saying, "Peace and security," then sudden disaster comes upon them, like labor pains upon a pregnant woman, and they will not escape. But you, brothers and sisters, are not in darkness, for that day to overtake you like a thief. For all of you are children of the light and children of the day.

We are not of the night or of darkness. Therefore, let us not sleep as the rest do, but let us stay alert and sober. For God did not destine us for wrath, but to gain salvation through our Lord Jesus Christ, who died for us, so that whether we are awake or asleep we may live together with him. Therefore, encourage one another and build one another up, as indeed you do.

Responsorial Psalm 27:1, 4, 13-14

R. (13) I believe that I shall see the good things of the Lord in the land of the living.

The LORD is my light and my salvation; whom should I fear?

The LORD is my life's refuge; of whom should I be afraid?

R. I believe that I shall see the good things of the Lord in the land of the living.

One thing I ask of the LORD; this I seek:

To dwell in the house of the LORD all the days of my life,

That I may gaze on the loveliness of the LORD and contemplate his temple.

R. I believe that I shall see the good things of the Lord in the land of the living.

I believe that I shall see the bounty of the LORD in the land of the living.

Wait for the LORD with courage; be stouthearted, and wait for the LORD.

R. I believe that I shall see the good things of the Lord in the land of the living.

Alleluia Lk 7:16

R. Alleluia, alleluia.

A great prophet has arisen in our midst and God has visited his people.

R. Alleluia, alleluia.

Gospel Lk 4:31-37

Jesus went down to Capernaum, a town of Galilee. He taught them on the sabbath, and they were astonished at his teaching because he spoke with authority. In the synagogue there was a man with the spirit of an unclean demon, and he cried out in a loud voice, "What have you to do with us, Jesus of Nazareth? Have you come to destroy us? I know who you are–the Holy One of God!" Jesus rebuked him and said, "Be quiet! Come out of him!"

Then the demon threw the man down in front of them and came out of him without doing him any harm. They were all amazed and said to one another, "What is there about his word? For with authority and power he commands the unclean spirits, and they come out." And news of him spread everywhere in the surrounding region.

SEPTEMBER 1ST, 2021
Wednesday of the Twenty-second Week in Ordinary Time

1ST Reading Col 1:1-8

Paul, an Apostle of Christ Jesus by the will of God, and Timothy our brother, to the holy ones and faithful brothers and sisters in Christ in Colossae: grace to you and peace from God our Father. We always give thanks to God, the Father of our Lord Jesus Christ, when we pray for you, for we have heard of your faith in Christ Jesus and the love that you have for all the holy ones because of the hope reserved for you in heaven. Of this you have already heard through the word of truth, the Gospel, that has come to you. Just as in the whole world it is bearing fruit and growing, so also among you, from the day you heard it and came to know the grace of God in truth, as you learned it from Epaphras our beloved fellow slave, who is a trustworthy minister of Christ on your behalf and who also told us of your love in the Spirit.

Responsorial Psalm52:10, 11

R. (10) I trust in the mercy of God for ever.

I, like a green olive tree in the house of God, Trust in the mercy of God forever and ever.

R. I trust in the mercy of God for ever.

I will thank you always for what you have done, and proclaim the goodness of your name before your faithful ones.

R. I trust in the mercy of God for ever.

R. Alleluia, alleluia.

The Lord sent me to bring glad tidings to the poorand to proclaim liberty to captives.

R. Alleluia, alleluia.

Gospel Lk 4:38-44

After Jesus left the synagogue, he entered the house of Simon. Simon's mother-in-law was afflicted with a severe fever, and they interceded with him about her. He stood over her, rebuked the fever, and it left her. She got up immediately and waited on them. At sunset, all who had people sick with various diseases brought them to him.

He laid his hands on each of them and cured them. And demons also came out from many, shouting, "You are the Son of God." But he rebuked them and did not allow them to speak because they knew that he was the Christ. At daybreak, Jesus left and went to a deserted place.

The crowds went looking for him, and when they came to him, they tried to prevent him from leaving them. But he said to them, "To the other towns also I must proclaim the good news of the Kingdom of God, because for this purpose I have been sent." And he was preaching in the synagogues of Judea.

SEPTEMBER 2ND, 2021
Thursday of the Twenty-second Week in Ordinary Time

1ST Reading Col 1:9-14
Brothers and sisters:

From the day we heard about you, we do not cease praying for you and asking that you may be filled with the knowledge of God's will through all spiritual wisdom and understanding to walk in a manner worthy of the Lord, so as to be fully pleasing, in every good work bearing fruit and growing in the knowledge of God, strengthened with every power, in accord with his glorious might, for all endurance and patience, with joy giving thanks to the

Father, who has made you fit to share in the inheritance of the holy ones in light.

He delivered us from the power of darkness and transferred us to the Kingdom of his beloved Son, in whom we have redemption, the forgiveness of sins.

Responsorial Psalm 98:2-3ab, 3cd-4, 5-6
R. (2) The Lord has made known his salvation.

The LORD has made his salvation known: in the sight of the nations he has revealed his justice.

He has remembered his kindness and his faithfulness toward the house of Israel.

R. The Lord has made known his salvation.

All the ends of the earth have seen the salvation by our God.

Sing joyfully to the LORD, all you lands; break into song; sing praise.

R. The Lord has made known his salvation.

Sing praise to the LORD with the harp, with the harp and melodious song.

With trumpets and the sound of the horn sing joyfully before the King, the LORD.

R. The Lord has made known his salvation.

Alleluia Mt 4:19

R. Alleluia, alleluia.

Come after me, says the Lord, and I will make you fishers of men.

R. Alleluia, alleluia.

Gospel Lk 5:1-11
While the crowd was pressing in on Jesus and listening to the word of God, he was standing by the Lake of Gennesaret. He saw two boats there alongside the lake; the fishermen had disembarked and were washing their nets. Getting into one of the boats, the one belonging to Simon, he asked

him to put out a short distance from the shore. Then he sat down and taught the crowds from the boat. After he had finished speaking, he said to Simon, "Put out into deep water and lower your nets for a catch." Simon said in reply, "Master, we have worked hard all night and have caught nothing, but at your command I will lower the nets." When they had done this, they caught a great number of fish and their nets were tearing. They signaled to their partners in the other boat to come to help them. They came and filled both boats so that the boats were in danger of sinking. When Simon Peter saw this, he fell at the knees of Jesus and said, "Depart from me, Lord, for I am a sinful man." For astonishment at the catch of fish they had made seized him and all those with him, and likewise James and John, the sons of Zebedee, who were partners of Simon. Jesus said to Simon, "Do not be afraid; from now on you will be catching men." When they brought their boats to the shore, they left everything and followed him.

SEPTEMBER 3RD, 2021
Memorial of Saint Gregory the Great, Pope and Doctor of the Church

1ST Reading Col 1:15-20
Brothers and sisters:

Christ Jesus is the image of the invisible God, the firstborn of all creation. For in him were created all things in heaven and on earth, the visible and the invisible, whether thrones or dominions or principalities or powers; all things were created through him and for him. He is before all things, and in him all things hold together. He is the head of the Body, the Church. He is the beginning, the firstborn from the dead, that in all things he himself might be preeminent. For in him all the fullness was pleased to dwell, and through him to reconcile all things for him, making peace by the Blood of his cross through him, whether those on earth or those in heaven.

Responsorial Psalm 100:1b-2, 3, 4, 5
R. (2b) Come with joy into the presence of the Lord.

Sing joyfully to the LORD, all you lands; serve the LORD with gladness; come before him with joyful song.

R. Come with joy into the presence of the Lord.

Know that the LORD is God; he made us, his we are; his people, the flock he tends.

R. Come with joy into the presence of the Lord.

Enter his gates with thanksgiving, his courts with praise;

Give thanks to him; bless his name.

R. Come with joy into the presence of the Lord.

For he is good, the LORD, whose kindness endures forever, and his faithfulness, to all generations.

R. Come with joy into the presence of the Lord.

Alleluia Jn 8:12

R. Alleluia, alleluia.

I am the light of the world, says the Lord; whoever follows me will have the light of life.

R. Alleluia, alleluia.

Gospel Lk 5:33-39

The scribes and Pharisees said to Jesus, "The disciples of John the Baptist fast often and offer prayers, and the disciples of the Pharisees do the same; but yours eat and drink." Jesus answered them, "Can you make the wedding guests fast while the bridegroom is with them? But the days will come, and when the bridegroom is taken away from them, then they will fast in those days." And he also told them a parable. "No one tears a piece from a new cloak to patch an old one. Otherwise, he will tear the new and the piece from it will not match the old cloak. Likewise, no one pours new wine into old wineskins.

Otherwise, the new wine will burst the skins, and it will be spilled, and the skins will be ruined. Rather, new wine must be poured into fresh wineskins. And no one who has been drinking old wine desires new, for he says, 'The old is good.'"

SEPTEMBER 4TH, 2021
Saturday of the Twenty-second Week in Ordinary Time

Brothers and sisters:

You once were alienated and hostile in mind because of evil deeds; God has now reconciled you in the fleshly Body of Christ through his death, to present you holy, without blemish, and irreproachable before him, provided that you persevere in the faith, firmly grounded, stable, and not shifting from the hope of the Gospel that you heard, which has been preached to every creature under heaven, of which I, Paul, am a minister.

Responsorial Psalm 54:3-4, 6 and 8

R. (6) God himself is my help.

O God, by your name save me, and by your might defend my cause.

O God, hear my prayer; hearken to the words of my mouth.

R. God himself is my help.

Behold, God is my helper; the Lord sustains my life.

Freely will I offer you sacrifice; I will praise your name, O LORD, for its goodness.

R. God himself is my help.

Alleluia Jn 14:6

R. Alleluia, alleluia.

I am the way and the truth and the life, says the Lord; no one comes to the Father except through me.

R. Alleluia, alleluia.

Gospel Lk 6:1-5

While Jesus was going through a field of grain on a sabbath, his disciples were picking the heads of grain, rubbing them in their hands, and eating them. Some Pharisees said, "Why are you doing what is unlawful on the sabbath?"

Jesus said to them in reply, "Have you not read what David did when he and those who were with him were hungry? How he went into the house of God, took the bread of offering, which only the priests could lawfully eat, ate of it, and shared it with his companions?" Then he said to them, "The Son of Man is lord of the sabbath."

SEPTEMBER 5TH, 2021
Twenty-third Sunday in Ordinary Time

1ST Reading Is 35:4-7a
Thus says the LORD:

Say to those whose hearts are frightened: Be strong, fear not! Here is your God, he comes with vindication; with divine recompense he comes to save you.

Then will the eyes of the blind be opened, the ears of the deaf be cleared; then will the lame leap like a stag, then the tongue of the mute will sing. Streams will burst forth in the desert, and rivers in the steppe. The burning sands will become pools, and the thirsty ground, springs of water.

Responsorial Psalm Ps 146:6-7, 8-9, 9-10
R. (1b) Praise the Lord, my soul!

or:

R. Alleluia.

The God of Jacob keeps faith forever, secures justice for the oppressed, gives food to the hungry.

The LORD sets captives free.

R. Praise the Lord, my soul!

or:

R. Alleluia.

The LORD gives sight to the blind; the LORD raises up those who were bowed down.

The LORD loves the just; the LORD protects strangers.

R. Praise the Lord, my soul!

or:

R. Alleluia.

The fatherless and the widow the LORD sustains, but the way of the wicked he thwarts.

The LORD shall reign forever; your God, O Zion, through all generations. Alleluia.

R. Praise the Lord, my soul!

or:

R. Alleluia.

2ND Reading Jas 2:1-5

My brothers and sisters, show no partiality as you adhere to the faith in our glorious Lord Jesus Christ. For if a man with gold rings and fine clothes comes into your assembly, and a poor person in shabby clothes also comes in, and you pay attention to the one wearing the fine clothes and say, "Sit here, please, " while you say to the poor one, "Stand there, " or "Sit at my feet, " have you not made distinctions among yourselves and become judges with evil designs? Listen, my beloved brothers and sisters. Did not God choose those who are poor in the world to be rich in faith and heirs of the kingdom that he promised to those who love him?

Alleluia Cf. Mt 4:23

R. Alleluia, alleluia.

Jesus proclaimed the Gospel of the kingdom and cured every disease among the people.

R. Alleluia, alleluia.

Gospel Mk 7:31-37

Again Jesus left the district of Tyre and went by way of Sidon to the Sea of Galilee, into the district of the Decapolis. And people brought to him a deaf man who had a speech impediment and begged him to lay his hand on him. He took him off by himself away from the crowd.

He put his finger into the man's ears and, spitting, touched his tongue; then he looked up to heaven and groaned, and said to him, "Ephphatha!"— that is, "Be opened!" — And immediately the man's ears were opened, his speech impediment was removed, and he spoke plainly. He ordered them not to tell anyone. But the more he ordered them not to, the more they proclaimed it.

They were exceedingly astonished and they said, "He has done all things well. He makes the deaf hear and the mute speak."

SEPTEMBER 6TH, 2021
Monday of the Twenty-third Week in Ordinary Time

1ST Reading Col 1:24–2:3

Brothers and sisters:

I rejoice in my sufferings for your sake, and in my flesh I am filling up what is lacking in the afflictions of Christ on behalf of his Body, which is the Church, of which I am a minister in accordance with God's stewardship given to me to bring to completion for you the word of God, the mystery hidden from ages and from generations past. But now it has been manifested to his holy ones, to whom God chose to make known the riches of the glory of this mystery among the Gentiles; it is Christ in you, the hope for glory. It is he whom we proclaim, admonishing everyone and teaching everyone with all wisdom, that we may present everyone perfect in Christ. For this I labor and struggle, in accord with the exercise of his power working within me. For I want you to know how great a struggle I am having for you and for those in Laodicea and all who have not seen me face to face, that their hearts may be encouraged as they are brought together in love, to have all the richness of assured understanding, for the knowledge of the mystery of God, Christ, in whom are hidden all the treasures of wisdom and knowledge.

Responsorial Psalm 62:6-7, 9

R. (8) In God is my safety and my glory.

Only in God be at rest, my soul, for from him comes my hope.

He only is my rock and my salvation, my stronghold; I shall not be disturbed.

R. In God is my safety and my glory.

Trust in him at all times, O my people! Pour out your hearts before him; God is our refuge!

R. In God is my safety and my glory.

R. Alleluia, alleluia.

My sheep hear my voice, says the Lord; I know them, and they follow me.

R. Alleluia, alleluia.

Gospel Lk 6:6-11
On a certain sabbath Jesus went into the synagogue and taught, and there was a man there whose right hand was withered. The scribes and the Pharisees watched him closely to see if he would cure on the Sabbath so that they might discover a reason to accuse him. But he realized their intentions and said to the man with the withered hand, "Come up and stand before us."

And he rose and stood there. Then Jesus said to them, "I ask you, is it lawful to do good on the Sabbath rather than to do evil, to save life rather than to destroy it?" Looking around at them all, he then said to him, "Stretch out your hand." He did so and his hand was restored. But they became enraged and discussed together what they might do to Jesus.

SEPTEMBER 7TH, 2021
Tuesday of the Twenty-third Week in Ordinary Time

1ST Reading Col 2:6-15
Brothers and sisters:

As you received Christ Jesus the Lord, walk in him, rooted in him and built upon him and established in the faith as you were taught, abounding in thanksgiving. See to it that no one captivate you with an empty, seductive philosophy according to the tradition of men, according to the elemental powers of the world and not according to Christ. For in him dwells the whole fullness of the deity bodily, and you share in this fullness in him, who is the head of every principality and power. In him you were also circumcised with a circumcision not administered by hand, by stripping off the carnal body, with the circumcision of Christ. You were buried with him in baptism, in which you were also raised with him through faith in the power of God,

535

who raised him from the dead. And even when you were dead in transgressions and the uncircumcision of your flesh, he brought you to life along with him, having forgiven us all our transgressions; obliterating the bond against us, with its legal claims, which was opposed to us, he also removed it from our midst, nailing it to the cross; despoiling the principalities and the powers, he made a public spectacle of them, leading them away in triumph by it.

Responsorial Psalm 145:1b-2, 8-9, 10-11
R. (9) The Lord is compassionate toward all his works.

I will extol you, O my God and King, and I will bless your name forever and ever.

Every day will I bless you, and I will praise your name forever and ever.

R. The Lord is compassionate toward all his works.

The LORD is gracious and merciful, slow to anger and of great kindness.

The LORD is good to all and compassionate toward all his works.

R. The Lord is compassionate toward all his works.

Let all your works give you thanks, O LORD, and let your faithful ones bless you.

Let them discourse of the glory of your Kingdom and speak of your might.

R. The Lord is compassionate toward all his works.

Alleluia Jn 15:16

R. Alleluia, alleluia.

I chose you from the world, that you may go and bear fruit that will last, says the Lord.

R. Alleluia, alleluia.

Gospel Lk 6:12-19
Jesus departed to the mountain to pray, and he spent the night in prayer to God. When day came, he called his disciples to himself, and from them he chose twelve, whom he also named Apostles: Simon, whom he named Peter,

and his brother Andrew, James, John, Philip, Bartholomew, Matthew, Thomas, James the son of Alphaeus, Simon who was called a Zealot, and Judas the son of James, and Judas Iscariot, who became a traitor. And he came down with them and stood on a stretch of level ground. A great crowd of his disciples and a large number of the people from all Judea and Jerusalem and the coastal region of Tyre and Sidon came to hear him and to be healed of their diseases; and even those who were tormented by unclean spirits were cured. Everyone in the crowd sought to touch him because power came forth from him and healed them all.

SEPTEMBER 8TH, 2021
Feast of the Nativity of the Blessed Virgin Mary

1ST Reading Mi 5:1-4a
The LORD says

You, Bethlehem-Ephrathah, too small to be among the clans of Judah, From you shall come forth for me one who is to be ruler in Israel; Whose origin is from of old, from ancient times. (Therefore the Lord will give them up, until the time when she who is to give birth has borne, and the rest of his brethren shall return to the children of Israel.) He shall stand firm and shepherd his flock by the strength of the LORD, in the majestic name of the LORD, his God; And they shall remain, for now his greatness shall reach to the ends of the earth; he shall be peace.

OR:

Rom 8:28-30

Brothers and sisters:

We know that all things work for good for those who love God, who are called according to his purpose. For those he foreknew he also predestined to be conformed to the image of his Son, so that he might be the firstborn among many brothers. And those he predestined he also called; and those he called he also justified; and those he justified he also glorified.

Responsorial Psalm 13:6ab, 6c
R. (Isaiah 61:10) With delight I rejoice in the Lord.

Though I trusted in your mercy, let my heart rejoice in your salvation.

537

R. With delight I rejoice in the Lord.

Let me sing of the LORD, "He has been good to me."

R. With delight I rejoice in the Lord.

Alleluia

R. Alleluia, alleluia.

Blessed are you, holy Virgin Mary, deserving of all praise; from you rose the sun of Justice, Christ our God.

R. Alleluia, alleluia.

Gospel Mt 1:1-16, 18-23 or 1:18-23

The Book of the genealogy of Jesus Christ, the son of David, the son of Abraham. Abraham became the father of Isaac, Isaac the father of Jacob, Jacob the father of Judah and his brothers. Judah became the father of Perez and Zerah, whose mother was Tamar. Perez became the father of Hezron, Hezron the father of Ram, Ram the father of Amminadab. Amminadab became the father of Nahshon, Nahshon the father of Salmon, Salmon the father of Boaz, whose mother was Rahab.

Boaz became the father of Obed, whose mother was Ruth. Obed became the father of Jesse, Jesse the father of David the king. David became the father of Solomon, whose mother had been the wife of Uriah. Solomon became the father of Rehoboam, Rehoboam the father of Abijah, Abijah the father of Asaph. Asaph became the father of Jehoshaphat, Jehoshaphat the father of Joram, Joram the father of Uzziah. Uzziah became the father of Jotham, Jotham the father of Ahaz, Ahaz the father of Hezekiah. Hezekiah became the father of Manasseh, Manasseh the father of Amos, Amos the father of Josiah.

Josiah became the father of Jechoniah and his brothers at the time of the Babylonian exile. After the Babylonian exile, Jechoniah became the father of Shealtiel, Shealtiel the father of Zerubbabel, Zerubbabel the father of Abiud. Abiud became the father of Eliakim, Eliakim the father of Azor, Azor the father of Zadok. Zadok became the father of Achim, Achim the father of Eliud, Eliud the father of Eleazar. Eleazar became the father of Matthan, Matthan the father of Jacob, Jacob the father of Joseph, the husband of Mary. Of her was born Jesus who is called the Christ. Now this is how the birth of Jesus Christ came about. When his mother Mary was betrothed to

Joseph, but before they lived together, she was found with child through the Holy Spirit. Joseph her husband, since he was a righteous man, yet unwilling to expose her to shame, decided to divorce her quietly. Such was his intention when, behold, the angel of the Lord appeared to him in a dream and said, "Joseph, son of David, do not be afraid to take Mary your wife into your home. For it is through the Holy Spirit that this child has been conceived in her.

She will bear a son and you are to name him Jesus, because he will save his people from their sins." All this took place to fulfill what the Lord had said through the prophet: Behold, the virgin shall be with child and bear a son, and they shall name him Emmanuel, which means "God is with us."

OR:

This is how the birth of Jesus Christ came about. When his mother Mary was betrothed to Joseph, but before they lived together, she was found with child through the Holy Spirit. Joseph her husband, since he was a righteous man, yet unwilling to expose her to shame, decided to divorce her quietly. Such was his intention when, behold, the angel of the Lord appeared to him in a dream and said, "Joseph, son of David, do not be afraid to take Mary your wife into your home. For it is through the Holy Spirit that this child has been conceived in her. She will bear a son and you are to name him Jesus, because he will save his people from their sins." All this took place to fulfill what the Lord had said through the prophet: Behold, the virgin shall be with child and bear a son, and they shall name him Emmanuel, which means "God is with us."

SEPTEMBER 9TH, 2021
Memorial of Saint Peter Claver, Priest

1ST Reading Col 3:12-17
Brothers and sisters:

Put on, as God's chosen ones, holy and beloved, heartfelt compassion, kindness, humility, gentleness, and patience, bearing with one another and forgiving one another, if one has a grievance against another; as the Lord has forgiven you, so must you also do. And over all these put on love, that is, the bond of perfection. And let the peace of Christ control your hearts, the peace into which you were also called in one Body. And be thankful.

539

Let the word of Christ dwell in you richly, as in all wisdom you teach and admonish one another, singing psalms, hymns, and spiritual songs with gratitude in your hearts to God. And whatever you do, in word or in deed, do everything in the name of the Lord Jesus, giving thanks to God the Father through him.

Responsorial Psalm 150:1b-2, 3-4, 5-6
R. (6) Let everything that breathes praise the Lord!

Praise the LORD in his sanctuary, praise him in the firmament of his strength.

Praise him for his mighty deeds, praise him for his sovereign majesty.

R. Let everything that breathes praise the Lord!

Praise him with the blast of the trumpet, praise him with lyre and harp,

Praise him with timbrel and dance, praise him with strings and pipe.

R. Let everything that breathes praise the Lord!

Praise him with sounding cymbals, praise him with clanging cymbals.

Let everything that has breath praise the LORD! Alleluia.

R. Let everything that breathes praise the Lord!

Alleluia 1 Jn 4:12

R. Alleluia, alleluia.

If we love one another, God remains in us, and his love is brought to perfection in us.

R. Alleluia, alleluia.

Gospel Lk 6:27-38
Jesus said to his disciples:

"To you who hear I say, love your enemies, do good to those who hate you, bless those who curse you, pray for those who mistreat you. To the person who strikes you on one cheek, offer the other one as well, and from the person who takes your cloak, do not withhold even your tunic. Give to

540

everyone who asks of you, and from the one who takes what is yours do not demand it back.

Do to others as you would have them do to you. For if you love those who love you, what credit is that to you? Even sinners love those who love them. And if you do good to those who do good to you, what credit is that to you? Even sinners do the same. If you lend money to those from whom you expect repayment, what credit is that to you? Even sinners lend to sinners, and get back the same amount. But rather, love your enemies and do good to them, and lend expecting nothing back; then your reward will be great and you will be children of the Most High, for he himself is kind to the ungrateful and the wicked. Be merciful, just as also your Father is merciful. "Stop judging and you will not be judged. Stop condemning and you will not be condemned. Forgive and you will be forgiven.

Give and gifts will be given to you; a good measure, packed together, shaken down, and overflowing, will be poured into your lap. For the measure with which you measure will in return be measured out to you."

SEPTEMBER 10TH, 2021
Friday of the Twenty-third Week in Ordinary Time

1ST Reading 1 Tm 1:1-2, 12-14
Paul, an Apostle of Christ Jesus by command of God our savior and of Christ Jesus our hope, to Timothy, my true child in faith: grace, mercy, and peace from God the Father and Christ Jesus our Lord. I am grateful to him who has strengthened me, Christ Jesus our Lord, because he considered me trustworthy in appointing me to the ministry. I was once a blasphemer and a persecutor and an arrogant man, but I have been mercifully treated because I acted out of ignorance in my unbelief. Indeed, the grace of our Lord has been abundant, along with the faith and love that are in Christ Jesus.

Responsorial Psalm 16:1b-2a and 5, 7-8, 11
R. (see 5) You are my inheritance, O Lord.

Keep me, O God, for in you I take refuge; I say to the LORD, "My Lord are you."

O LORD, my allotted portion and my cup, you it is who hold fast my lot.

R. You are my inheritance, O Lord.

I bless the LORD who counsels me; even in the night my heart exhorts me.

I set the LORD ever before me; with him at my right hand I shall not be disturbed.

R. You are my inheritance, O Lord.

You will show me the path to life, fullness of joys in your presence, the delights at your right hand forever.

R. You are my inheritance, O Lord.

Alleluia Jn 17:17b, 17a

R. Alleluia, alleluia.

Your word, O Lord, is truth; consecrate us in the truth.

R. Alleluia, alleluia.

Gospel Lk 6:39-42

Jesus told his disciples a parable: "Can a blind person guide a blind person? Will not both fall into a pit? No disciple is superior to the teacher; but when fully trained, every disciple will be like his teacher. Why do you notice the splinter in your brother's eye, but do not perceive the wooden beam in your own? How can you say to your brother, 'Brother, let me remove that splinter in your eye,' when you do not even notice the wooden beam in your own eye? You hypocrite! Remove the wooden beam from your eye first; then you will see clearly to remove the splinter in your brother's eye."

SEPTEMBER 11TH, 2021
Saturday of the Twenty-third Week in Ordinary Time

1ST Reading 1 Tm 1:15-17

Beloved:

This saying is trustworthy and deserves full acceptance: Christ Jesus came into the world to save sinners. Of these I am the foremost. But for that reason I was mercifully treated, so that in me, as the foremost, Christ Jesus might display all his patience as an example for those who would come to believe in him for everlasting life. To the king of ages, incorruptible, invisible, the only God, honor and glory forever and ever. Amen.

R. (2) Blessed be the name of the Lord for ever.

Praise, you servants of the LORD, praise the name of the LORD.

Blessed be the name of the LORD both now and forever.

R. Blessed be the name of the Lord for ever.

From the rising to the setting of the sun is the name of the LORD to be praised.

High above all nations is the LORD; above the heavens is his glory.

R. Blessed be the name of the Lord for ever.

Who is like the LORD, our God, and looks upon the heavens and the earth below?

He raises up the lowly from the dust; from the dunghill he lifts up the poor.

R. Blessed be the name of the Lord for ever.

Alleluia Jn 14:23

R. Alleluia, alleluia.

Whoever loves me will keep my word, and my Father will love him, and we will come to him.

R. Alleluia, alleluia.

Gospel Lk 6:43-49

Jesus said to his disciples: "A good tree does not bear rotten fruit, nor does a rotten tree bear good fruit. For every tree is known by its own fruit. For people do not pick figs from thorn bushes, nor do they gather grapes from brambles. A good person out of the store of goodness in his heart produces good, but an evil person out of a store of evil produces evil; for from the fullness of the heart the mouth speaks. "Why do you call me, 'Lord, Lord,' but not do what I command? I will show you what someone is like who comes to me, listens to my words, and acts on them. That one is like a man building a house, who dug deeply and laid the foundation on rock; when the flood came, the river burst against that house but could not shake it because it had been well built. But the one who listens and does not act is like a person who built a house on the ground without a foundation. When the river burst against it, it collapsed at once and was completely destroyed."

SEPTEMBER 12TH, 2021
Twenty-fourth Sunday in Ordinary Time

1ST Reading Is 50:5-9a
The Lord GOD opens my ear that I may hear; and I have not rebelled, have not turned back. I gave my back to those who beat me, my cheeks to those who plucked my beard; my face I did not shield from buffets and spitting.

The Lord GOD is my help therefore I am not disgraced; I have set my face like flint, knowing that I shall not be put to shame. He is near who upholds my right; if anyone wishes to oppose me, let us appear together. Who disputes my right? Let that man confront me. See, the Lord GOD is my help; who will prove me wrong?

Responsorial Psalm Ps 114:1-2, 3-4, 5-6, 8-9
R. (9)   I will walk before the Lord, in the land of the living.

or:

R. Alleluia.

I love the LORD because he has heard my voice in supplication,

Because he has inclined his ear to me the day I called.

R. I will walk before the Lord, in the land of the living.

or:

R. Alleluia.

The cords of death encompassed me; the snares of the netherworld seized upon me; I fell into distress and sorrow,

And I called upon the name of the LORD, "O LORD, save my life!"

R. I will walk before the Lord, in the land of the living.

or:

R. Alleluia.

Gracious is the LORD and just; yes, our God is merciful.

The LORD keeps the little ones; I was brought low, and he saved me.

R. I will walk before the Lord, in the land of the living.

or:

R. Alleluia.

For he has freed my soul from death, my eyes from tears, my feet from stumbling.

I shall walk before the Lord in the land of the living.

R. I will walk before the Lord, in the land of the living.

or:

R. Alleluia.

2ND Reading Jas 2:14-18

What good is it, my brothers and sisters, if someone says he has faith but does not have works? Can that faith save him? If a brother or sister has nothing to wear and has no food for the day, and one of you says to them, "Go in peace, keep warm, and eat well," but you do not give them the necessities of the body, what good is it? So also faith of itself, if it does not have works, is dead. Indeed someone might say, "You have faith and I have works." Demonstrate your faith to me without works, and I will demonstrate my faith to you from my works.

Alleluia Gal 6:14

R. Alleluia, alleluia.

May I never boast except in the cross of our Lord through which the world has been crucified to me and I to the world.

R. Alleluia, alleluia.

Gospel Mk 8:27-35

Jesus and his disciples set out for the villages of Caesarea Philippi. Along the way he asked his disciples, "Who do people say that I am?" They said in reply, "John the Baptist, others Elijah, still others one of the prophets." And he asked them, "But who do you say that I am?" Peter said to him in reply, "You are the Christ." Then he warned them not to tell anyone about him. He began to teach them that the Son of Man must suffer greatly and be rejected by the elders, the chief priests, and the scribes, and be killed, and rise after three days.

He spoke this openly. Then Peter took him aside and began to rebuke him. At this he turned around and, looking at his disciples, rebuked Peter and said, "Get behind me, Satan.

You are thinking not as God does, but as human beings do." He summoned the crowd with his disciples and said to them, "Whoever wishes to come after me must deny himself, take up his cross, and follow me. For whoever wishes to save his life will lose it, but whoever loses his life for my sake and that of the gospel will save it."

SEPTEMBER 13TH, 2021
Memorial of Saint John Chrysostom, Bishop and Doctor of the Church

1ST Reading 1 Tm 2:1-8
Beloved:

First of all, I ask that supplications, prayers, petitions, and thanksgivings be offered for everyone, for kings and for all in authority, that we may lead a quiet and tranquil life in all devotion and dignity. This is good and pleasing to God our savior, who wills everyone to be saved and to come to knowledge of the truth. For there is one God. There is also one mediator between God and men, the man Christ Jesus, who gave himself as ransom for all. This was the testimony at the proper time. For this I was appointed preacher and Apostle (I am speaking the truth, I am not lying), teacher of the Gentiles in faith and truth. It is my wish, then, that in every place the men should pray, lifting up holy hands, without anger or argument.

Responsorial Psalm 28:2, 7, 8-9
R. (6) Blessed be the Lord, for he has heard my prayer.

Hear the sound of my pleading, when I cry to you, lifting up my hands toward your holy shrine.

R. Blessed be the Lord, for he has heard my prayer.

The LORD is my strength and my shield.

In him my heart trusts, and I find help; then my heart exults, and with my song I give him thanks.

R. Blessed be the Lord, for he has heard my prayer.

The LORD is the strength of his people, the saving refuge of his anointed.

Save your people, and bless your inheritance; feed them, and carry them forever!

R. Blessed be the Lord, for he has heard my prayer.

Alleluia Jn 3:16

R. Alleluia, alleluia.

God so loved the world that he gave his only-begotten Son, so that everyone who believes in him might have eternal life.

R. Alleluia, alleluia.

Gospel Lk 7:1-10

When Jesus had finished all his words to the people, he entered Capernaum. A centurion there had a slave who was ill and about to die, and he was valuable to him. When he heard about Jesus, he sent elders of the Jews to him, asking him to come and save the life of his slave. They approached Jesus and strongly urged him to come, saying, "He deserves to have you do this for him, for he loves our nation and he built the synagogue for us." And Jesus went with them, but when he was only a short distance from the house, the centurion sent friends to tell him, "Lord, do not trouble yourself, for I am not worthy to have you enter under my roof. Therefore, I did not consider myself worthy to come to you; but say the word and let my servant be healed. For I too am a person subject to authority, with soldiers subject to me.

And I say to one, Go, and he goes; and to another, Come here, and he comes; and to my slave, Do this, and he does it." When Jesus heard this he was amazed at him and, turning, said to the crowd following him, "I tell you, not even in Israel have I found such faith." When the messengers returned to the house, they found the slave in good health.

SEPTEMBER 14TH, 2021
Feast of the Exaltation of the Holy Cross

1ST Reading Nm 21:4b-9

With their patience worn out by the journey, the people complained against God and Moses, "Why have you brought us up from Egypt to die in this desert, where there is no food or water? We are disgusted with this wretched food!" In punishment the LORD sent among the people saraph serpents, which bit the people so that many of them died.

Then the people came to Moses and said, "We have sinned in complaining against the LORD and you. Pray the LORD to take the serpents from us." So Moses prayed for the people, and the LORD said to Moses, "Make a saraph and mount it on a pole, and if any who have been bitten look at it, they will live." Moses accordingly made a bronze serpent and mounted it on a pole, and whenever anyone who had been bitten by a serpent looked at the bronze serpent, he lived.

Responsorial Psalm 78:1bc-2, 34-35, 36-37, 38

R. (see 7b) Do not forget the works of the Lord!

Hearken, my people, to my teaching; incline your ears to the words of my mouth.

I will open my mouth in a parable, I will utter mysteries from of old.

R. Do not forget the works of the Lord!

While he slew them they sought him and inquired after God again,

Remembering that God was their rock and the Most High God, their redeemer.

R. Do not forget the works of the Lord!

But they flattered him with their mouths and lied to him with their tongues,

Though their hearts were not steadfast toward him, nor were they faithful to his covenant.

R. Do not forget the works of the Lord!

But he, being merciful, forgave their sin and destroyed them not;

Often he turned back his anger and let none of his wrath be roused.

R. Do not forget the works of the Lord!

2ND Reading Phil 2:6-11
Brothers and sisters:

Christ Jesus, though he was in the form of God, did not regard equality with God something to be grasped. Rather, he emptied himself, taking the form of a slave, coming in human likeness; and found human in appearance, he humbled himself, becoming obedient to death, even death on a cross. Because of this, God greatly exalted him and bestowed on him the name that is above every name, that at the name of Jesus every knee should bend, of those in heaven and on earth and under the earth, and every tongue confess that Jesus Christ is Lord, to the glory of God the Father.

Alleluia

R. Alleluia, alleluia.

We adore you, O Christ, and we bless you, because by your Cross you have redeemed the world.

R. Alleluia, alleluia.

Gospel Jn 3:13-17
Jesus said to Nicodemus:

"No one has gone up to heaven except the one who has come down from heaven, the Son of Man. And just as Moses lifted up the serpent in the desert, so must the Son of Man be lifted up, so that everyone who believes in him may have eternal life." For God so loved the world that he gave his only Son, so that everyone who believes in him might not perish but might have eternal life. For God did not send his Son into the world to condemn the world, but that the world might be saved through him.

SEPTEMBER 15TH, 2021

Memorial of Our Lady of Sorrows

1ST Reading 1 Tm 3:14-16

Beloved:

I am writing you, although I hope to visit you soon. But if I should be delayed, you should know how to behave in the household of God, which is the Church of the living God, the pillar and foundation of truth. Undeniably great is the mystery of devotion, who was manifested in the flesh, vindicated in the spirit, seen by angels, proclaimed to the Gentiles, believed in throughout the world, taken up in glory.

Responsorial Psalm 111:1-2, 3-4, 5-6

R. (2) How great are the works of the Lord!

I will give thanks to the LORD with all my heart in the company and assembly of the just.

Great are the works of the LORD, exquisite in all their delights.

R. How great are the works of the Lord!

Majesty and glory are his work, and his justice endures forever.

He has won renown for his wondrous deeds; gracious and merciful is the LORD.

R. How great are the works of the Lord!

He has given food to those who fear him; he will forever be mindful of his covenant.

He has made known to his people the power of his works, giving them the inheritance of the nations.

R. How great are the works of the Lord!

Sequence (Optional)

At the cross her station keeping, Stood the mournful Mother weeping,

Close to Jesus to the last. Through her heart, his sorrow sharing,

All his bitter anguish bearing, now at length the sword had passed.

Oh, how sad and sore distressed was that Mother highly blessed

Of the sole begotten One! Christ above in torment hangs,

She beneath beholds the pangs of her dying, glorious Son.

Is there one who would not weep, 'Whelmed in miseries so deep,

Christ's dear Mother to behold?

Can the human heart refrain?

From partaking in her pain, in that mother's pain untold?

Bruised, derided, cursed, defiled, she beheld her tender Child,

All with bloody scourges rent. For the sins of his own nation

Saw him hang in desolation Till his spirit forth he sent.

O sweet Mother! Font of love, Touch my spirit from above,

Make my heart with yours accord. Make me feel as you have felt;

Make my soul to glow and melt with the love of Christ, my Lord.

Holy Mother, pierce me through, in my heart each wound renew

Of my Savior crucified. Let me share with you his pain,

Who for all our sins was slain, who for me in torments died.

Let me mingle tears with you, mourning him who mourned for me,

All the days that I may live. By the cross with you to stay,

There with you to weep and pray, is all I ask of you to give.

Virgin of all virgins blest! Listen to my fond request:

Let me share your grief divine. Let me to my latest breath,

In my body bear the death of that dying Son of yours.

R. Alleluia, alleluia.

Blessed are you, O Virgin Mary; without dying you won the Martyr's crown beneath the Cross of the Lord.

R. Alleluia, alleluia.

Gospel Jn 19:25-27

Standing by the cross of Jesus were his mother and his mother's sister, Mary the wife of Clopas, and Mary Magdalene. When Jesus saw his mother and the disciple there whom he loved he said to his mother, "Woman, behold, your son." Then he said to the disciple, "Behold, your mother." And from that hour the disciple took her into his home.

OR:

Lk 2:33-35

Jesus' father and mother were amazed at what was said about him; and Simeon blessed them and said to Mary his mother, "Behold, this child is destined for the fall and rise of many in Israel, and to be a sign that will be contradicted and you yourself a sword will pierce so that the thoughts of many hearts may be revealed."

SEPTEMBER 16TH, 2021
Memorial of Saints Cornelius, Pope, and Saint Cyprian, Bishop, Martyrs

1ST Reading 1 Tm 4:12-16
Beloved:

Let no one have contempt for your youth, but set an example for those who believe, in speech, conduct, love, faith, and purity. Until I arrive, attend to the reading, exhortation, and teaching. Do not neglect the gift you have, which was conferred on you through the prophetic word with the imposition of hands by the presbyterate. Be diligent in these matters, be absorbed in them, so that your progress may be evident to everyone. Attend to yourself and to your teaching; persevere in both tasks, for by doing so you will save both yourself and those who listen to you.

R. (2) How great are the works of the Lord!

The works of his hands are faithful and just; sure are all his precepts,

Reliable forever and ever, wrought in truth and equity.

R. How great are the works of the Lord!

He has sent deliverance to his people; he has ratified his covenant forever; holy and awesome is his name.

R. How great are the works of the Lord!

The fear of the LORD is the beginning of wisdom; prudent are all who live by it.

His praise endures forever.

R. How great are the works of the Lord!

Alleluia Mt 11:28

R. Alleluia, alleluia.

Come to me, all you who labor and are burdened, and I will give you rest, says the Lord.

R. Alleluia, alleluia.

Gospel Lk 7:36-50

A certain Pharisee invited Jesus to dine with him, and he entered the Pharisee's house and reclined at table. Now there was a sinful woman in the city who learned that he was at table in the house of the Pharisee. Bringing an alabaster flask of ointment, she stood behind him at his feet weeping and began to bathe his feet with her tears. Then she wiped them with her hair, kissed them, and anointed them with the ointment. When the Pharisee who had invited him saw this he said to himself, "If this man were a prophet, he would know who and what sort of woman this is who Jesus said to him in reply, "Simon, I have something to say to you." "Tell me, teacher," he said. "Two people were in debt to a certain creditor; one owed five hundred days' wages and the other owed fifty.

Since they were unable to repay the debt, he forgave it for both. Which of them will love him more?" Simon said in reply, "The one, I suppose, whose larger debt was forgiven." He said to him, "You have judged rightly."

Then he turned to the woman and said to Simon, "Do you see this woman? When I entered your house, you did not give me water for my feet, but she has bathed them with her tears and wiped them with her hair. You did not give me a kiss, but she has not ceased kissing my feet since the time I entered. You did not anoint my head with oil, but she anointed my feet with ointment. So I tell you, her many sins have been forgiven; hence, she has shown great love. But the one to whom little is forgiven, loves little." He said to her, "Your sins are forgiven." The others at table said to themselves, "Who is this who even forgives sins?" But he said to the woman, "Your faith has saved you; go in peace."

SEPTEMBER 17TH, 2021
Friday of the Twenty-fourth Week in Ordinary Time

1ST Reading 1 Tm 6:2c-12
Beloved:

Teach and urge these things. Whoever teaches something different and does not agree with the sound words of our Lord Jesus Christ and the religious teaching is conceited, understanding nothing, and has a morbid disposition for arguments and verbal disputes. From these come envy, rivalry, insults, evil suspicions, and mutual friction among people with corrupted minds, who are deprived of the truth, supposing religion to be a means of gain. Indeed, religion with contentment is a great gain.

For we brought nothing into the world, just as we shall not be able to take anything out of it. If we have food and clothing, we shall be content with that. Those who want to be rich are falling into temptation and into a trap and into many foolish and harmful desires, which plunge them into ruin and destruction. For the love of money is the root of all evils, and some people in their desire for it have strayed from the faith and have pierced themselves with many pains.

But you, man of God, avoid all this. Instead, pursue righteousness, devotion, faith, love, patience, and gentleness. Compete well for the faith. Lay hold of eternal life, to which you were called when you made the noble confession in the presence of many witnesses.

Responsorial Psalm 49:6-7, 8-10, 17-18, 19-20
R. Blessed the poor in spirit; the Kingdom of heaven is theirs!

Why should I fear in evil days when my wicked ensnarers ring me round?

They trust in their wealth; the abundance of their riches is their boast.

R. Blessed the poor in spirit; the Kingdom of heaven is theirs!

Yet in no way can a man redeem himself, or pay his own ransom to God;

Too high is the price to redeem one's life; he would never have enough to remain alive always and not see destruction.

R. Blessed the poor in spirit; the Kingdom of heaven is theirs!

Fear not when a man grows rich, when the wealth of his house becomes great,

For when he dies, he shall take none of it; his wealth shall not follow him down.

R. Blessed the poor in spirit; the Kingdom of heaven is theirs!

Though in his lifetime he counted himself blessed, "They will praise you for doing well for yourself,"

He shall join the circle of his forebears who shall never more see light.

R. Blessed the poor in spirit; the Kingdom of heaven is theirs!

Alleluia Mt 11:25

R. Alleluia, alleluia.

Blessed are you, Father, Lord of heaven and earth; you have revealed to little ones the mysteries of the Kingdom.

R. Alleluia, alleluia.

Gospel Lk 8:1-3
Jesus journeyed from one town and village to another, preaching and proclaiming the good news of the Kingdom of God. Accompanying him were the Twelve and some women who had been cured of evil spirits and

infirmities, Mary, called Magdalene, from whom seven demons had gone out, Joanna, the wife of Herod's steward Chuza, Susanna, and many others who provided for them out of their resources.

SEPTEMBER 18TH, 2021
Saturday of the Twenty-fourth Week in Ordinary Time

1ST Reading 1 Tm 6:13-16
Beloved:

I charge you before God, who gives life to all things, and before Christ Jesus,

who gave testimony under Pontius Pilate for the noble confession, to keep the commandment without stain or reproach until the appearance of our Lord Jesus Christ that the blessed and only ruler will make manifest at the proper time, the King of kings and Lord of lords, who alone has immortality, who dwells in unapproachable light, and whom no human being has seen or can see. To him be honor and eternal power. Amen.

Responsorial Psalm 100:1b-2, 3, 4, 5
R. (2) Come with joy into the presence of the Lord.

Sing joyfully to the LORD all you lands; serve the LORD with gladness; come before him with joyful song.

R. Come with joy into the presence of the Lord.

Know that the LORD is God; he made us, his we are; his people, the flock he tends.

R. Come with joy into the presence of the Lord.

Enter his gates with thanksgiving, his courts with praise; Give thanks to him; bless his name.

R. Come with joy into the presence of the Lord.

For he is good: the LORD, whose kindness endures forever, and his faithfulness, to all generations.

R. Come with joy into the presence of the Lord.

Alleluia Lk 8:15

R. Alleluia, alleluia.

Blessed are they who have kept the word with a generous heart and yield a harvest through perseverance.

R. Alleluia, alleluia.

Gospel Lk 8:4-15
When a large crowd gathered, with people from one town after another journeying to Jesus, he spoke in a parable. "A sower went out to sow his seed. And as he sowed, some seed fell on the path and was trampled, and the birds of the sky ate it up. Some seed fell on rocky ground, and when it grew, it withered for lack of moisture. Some seed fell among thorns, and the thorns grew with it and choked it. And some seed fell on good soil, and when it grew, it produced fruit a hundredfold." After saying this, he called out, "Whoever has ears to hear ought to hear." Then his disciples asked him what the meaning of this parable might be. He answered, "Knowledge of the mysteries of the Kingdom of God has been granted to you; but to the rest, they are made known through parables so that they may look but not see, and hear but not understand. "This is the meaning of the parable. The seed is the word of God. Those on the path are the ones who have heard, but the Devil comes and takes away the word from their hearts that they may not believe and be saved.

Those on rocky ground are the ones who, when they hear, receive time and fall away in time of temptation. As for the seed that fell among thorns, they are the ones who have heard, but as they go along, they are choked by the anxieties and riches and pleasures of life, and they fail to produce mature fruit. But as for the seed that fell on rich soil, they are the ones who, when they have heard the word, embrace it with a generous and good heart, and bear fruit through perseverance."

SEPTEMBER 19TH, 2021
Twenty-fifth Sunday in Ordinary Time

First Reading Wis 2:12, 17-20
The wicked say:

Let us beset the just one, because he is obnoxious to us; he sets himself against our doings, reproaches us for transgressions of the law and charges us with violations of our training. Let us see whether his words be true; let us find out what will happen to him. For if the just one be the son of God, God will defend him and deliver him from the hand of his foes. With revilement and torture let us put the just one to the test that we may have proof of his gentleness and try his patience. Let us condemn him to a shameful death; for according to his own words, God will take care of him.

Responsorial Psalm Ps 54:3-4, 5, 6 and 8
R. (6b)   The Lord upholds my life.

O God, by your name save me, and by your might defend my cause.

O God, hear my prayer; hearken to the words of my mouth.

R. The Lord upholds my life.

For the haughty men have risen up against me, the ruthless seek my life; they set not God before their eyes.

R. The Lord upholds my life.

Behold, God is my helper; the Lord sustains my life.

Freely will I offer you sacrifice; I will praise your name, O LORD, for its goodness.

R. The Lord upholds my life.

2ND Reading Jas 3:16—4:3
Beloved:

Where jealousy and selfish ambition exist, there is disorder and every foul practice. But the wisdom from above is first of all pure, then peaceable, gentle, compliant, full of mercy and good fruits, without inconstancy or insincerity. And the fruit of righteousness is sown in peace for those who cultivate peace. Where do the wars and where do the conflicts among you come from? Is it not from your passions that make war within your members? You covet but do not possess. You kill and envy but you cannot obtain; you fight and wage war. You do not possess because you do not ask. You ask but do not receive, because you ask wrongly, to spend it on your passions.

Alleluia Cf. 2 Thes 2:14

R. Alleluia, alleluia.

God has called us through the Gospel to possess the glory of our Lord Jesus Christ.

R. Alleluia, alleluia.

Jesus and his disciples left from there and began a journey through Galilee, but he did not wish anyone to know about it. He was teaching his disciples and telling them, "The Son of Man is to be handed over to men and they will kill him, and three days after his death the Son of Man will rise." But they did not understand the saying, and they were afraid to question him. They came to Capernaum and, once inside the house, he began to ask them, "What were you arguing about on the way?" But they remained silent. They had been discussing among themselves on the way who was the greatest. Then he sat down, called the Twelve, and said to them, "If anyone wishes to be first, he shall be the last of all and the servant of all." Taking a child, he placed it in the their midst, and putting his arms around it, he said to them, "Whoever receives one child such as this in my name, receives me; and whoever receives me, receives not me but the One who sent me."

SEPTEMBER 20TH, 2021
Memorial of Saints Andrew Kim Tae-gŏn, Priest, and Paul Chŏng Ha-sang, and Companions, Martyrs

1ST Reading Ezr 1:1-6
In the first year of Cyrus, king of Persia, in order to fulfill the word of the Lord spoken by Jeremiah, the Lord inspired King Cyrus of Persia to issue this proclamation throughout his kingdom, both by word of mouth and in writing: "Thus says Cyrus, king of Persia: 'All the kingdoms of the earth the Lord, the God of heaven, has given to me, and he has also charged me to build him a house in Jerusalem, which is in Judah. Therefore, whoever among you belongs to any part of his people, let him go up, and may his God be with him! Let everyone who has survived, in whatever place he may have dwelt, be assisted by the people of that place with silver, gold, goods, and cattle, together with free-will offerings for the house of God in Jerusalem.'" Then the family heads of Judah and Benjamin and the priests and Levites—everyone, that is, whom God had inspired to do so— prepared to go up to build the house of the Lord in Jerusalem. All their neighbors gave

them help in every way, with silver, gold, goods, and cattle, and with many precious gifts besides all their free-will offerings.

R. (3) The Lord has done marvels for us.

When the LORD brought back the captives of Zion, we were like men dreaming.

Then our mouth was filled with laughter, and our tongue with rejoicing.

R. The Lord has done marvels for us.

Then they said among the nations, "The LORD has done great things for them."

The LORD has done great things for us; we are glad indeed.

R. The Lord has done marvels for us.

Restore our fortunes, O LORD, like the torrents in the southern desert.

Those that sow in tears shall reap rejoicing.

R. The Lord has done marvels for us.

Although they go forth weeping, carrying the seed to be sown,

They shall come back rejoicing, carrying their sheaves.

R. The Lord has done marvels for us.

R. Alleluia, alleluia.

Let your light shine before others, that they may see your good deeds and glorify your heavenly Father.

R. Alleluia, alleluia.

Jesus said to the crowd: "No one who lights a lamp conceals it with a vessel or sets it under a bed; rather, he places it on a lamp stand so that those who enter may see the light. For there is nothing hidden that will not become visible, and nothing secret that will not be known and come to light. Take care, then, how you hear. To anyone who has, more will be given, and from the one who has not, even what he seems to have will be taken away."

SEPTEMBER 21ST, 2021
Feast of Saint Matthew, Apostle and evangelist

1ST Reading Eph 4:1-7, 11-13
Brothers and sisters:

I, a prisoner for the Lord, urge you to live in a manner worthy of the call you have received, with all humility and gentleness, with patience, bearing with one another through love, striving to preserve the unity of the Spirit through the bond of peace: one Body and one Spirit, as you were also called to the one hope of your call; one Lord, one faith, one baptism; one God and Father of all, who is over all and through all and in all. But grace was given to each of us according to the measure of Christ's gift. And he gave some as Apostles, others as prophets, others as evangelists, others as pastors and teachers, to equip the holy ones for the work of ministry, for building up the Body of Christ, until we all attain to the unity of faith and knowledge of the Son of God, to mature manhood, to the extent of the full stature of Christ.

Responsorial Psalm 19:2-3, 4-5
R. (5) Their message goes out through all the earth.

The heavens declare the glory of God; and the firmament proclaims his handiwork.

Day pours out the word to day, and night to night imparts knowledge.

R. Their message goes out through all the earth.

Not a word nor a discourse whose voice is not heard;

Through all the earth their voice resounds, and to the ends of the world, their message.

R. Their message goes out through all the earth.

Alleluia Te Deum

R. Alleluia, alleluia.

We praise you, O God, we acclaim you as Lord; the glorious company of Apostles praise you.

R. Alleluia, alleluia.

Gospel Mt 9:9-13

As Jesus passed by, he saw a man named Matthew sitting at the customs post. He said to him, "Follow me." And he got up and followed him. While he was at table in his house, many tax collectors and sinners came and sat with Jesus and his disciples. The Pharisees saw this and said to his disciples, "Why does your teacher eat with tax collectors and sinners?" He heard this and said, "Those who are well do not need a physician, but the sick do. Go and learn the meaning of the words, I desire mercy, not sacrifice. I did not come to call the righteous but sinners."

SEPTEMBER 22ND, 2021
Wednesday of the Twenty-fifth Week in Ordinary Time

1ST Reading Ezr 9:5-9

At the time of the evening sacrifice, I, Ezra, rose in my wretchedness, and with cloak and mantle torn I fell on my knees, stretching out my hands to the LORD, my God. I said: "My God, I am too ashamed and confounded to raise my face to you, O my God, for our wicked deeds are heaped up above our heads and our guilt reaches up to heaven. From the time of our fathers even to this day great has been our guilt, and for our wicked deeds we have been delivered up, we and our kings and our priests, to the will of the kings of foreign lands, to the sword, to captivity, to pillage, and to disgrace, as is the case today. "And now, but a short time ago, mercy came to us from the LORD, our God, who left us a remnant and gave us a stake in his holy place; thus our God has brightened our eyes and given us relief in our servitude. For slaves we are, but in our servitude our God has not abandoned us; rather, he has turned the good will of the kings of Persia toward us. Thus he has given us new life to raise again the house of our God and restore its ruins, and has granted us a fence in Judah and Jerusalem."

Responsorial Psalm Tobit 13:2, 3-4a, 4befghn, 7-8
R. (1b) Blessed be God, who lives for ever.

He scourges and then has mercy; he casts down to the depths of the nether world, and he brings up from the great abyss.

No one can escape his hand.

R. Blessed be God, who lives for ever.

Praise him, you children of Israel, before the Gentiles, for though he has scattered you among them, he has shown you his greatness even there.

R. Blessed be God, who lives for ever.

So now consider what he has done for you, and praise him with full voice.

Bless the Lord of righteousness, and exalt the King of ages.

R. Blessed be God, who lives for ever.

In the land of my exile I praise him and show his power and majesty to a sinful nation.

R. Blessed be God, who lives for ever.

Bless the Lord, all you his chosen ones, and may all of you praise his majesty.

Celebrate days of gladness, and give him praise.

R. Blessed be God, who lives for ever.

Alleluia Mk 1:15

R. Alleluia, alleluia.

The Kingdom of God is at hand; repent and believe in the Gospel.

R. Alleluia, alleluia.

Gospel Lk 9:1-6

Jesus summoned the Twelve and gave them power and authority over all demons and to cure diseases, and he sent them to proclaim the Kingdom of God and to heal the sick. He said to them, "Take nothing for the journey, neither walking stick, nor sack, nor food, nor money, and let no one take a second tunic. Whatever house you enter, stay there and leave from there. And as for those who do not welcome you, when you leave that town, shake the dust from your feet in testimony against them." Then they set out and went from village to village proclaiming the good news and curing diseases everywhere.

Memorial of Saint Pius of Pietrelcina, Priest

1ST Reading Hg 1:1-8

On the first day of the sixth month in the second year of King Darius, The word of the LORD came through the prophet Haggai to the governor of Judah, Zerubbabel, son of Shealtiel, and to the high priest Joshua, son of Jehozadak: Thus says the LORD of hosts: This people says: "The time has not yet come to rebuild the house of the LORD." (Then this word of the LORD came through Haggai, the prophet:) Is it time for you to dwell in your own paneled houses, while this house lies in ruins? Now thus says the LORD of hosts: Consider your ways!

You have sown much, but have brought in little; you have eaten, but have not been satisfied; You have drunk, but have not been exhilarated; have clothed yourselves, but not been warmed; And whoever earned wages earned them for a bag with holes in it. Thus says the LORD of hosts: Consider your ways! Go up into the hill country; bring timber, and build the house That I may take pleasure in it and receive my glory, says the LORD.

Responsorial Psalm 149:1b-2, 3-4, 5-6a and 9b

R. (see 4a) The Lord takes delight in his people.

Sing to the LORD a new song of praise in the assembly of the faithful.

Let Israel be glad in their maker, let the children of Zion rejoice in their king.

R. The Lord takes delight in his people.

Let them praise his name in the festive dance, let them sing praise to him with timbrel and harp.

For the LORD loves his people, and he adorns the lowly with victory.

R. The Lord takes delight in his people.

Let the faithful exult in glory; let them sing for joy upon their couches;

Let the high praises of God be in their throats. This is the glory of all his faithful. Alleluia.

R. The Lord takes delight in his people.

R. Alleluia, alleluia.

I am the way and the truth and the life, says the Lord; no one comes to the Father except through me.

R. Alleluia, alleluia.

Gospel Lk 9:7-9

Herod the tetrarch heard about all that was happening, and he was greatly perplexed because some were saying, "John has been raised from the dead"; others were saying, "Elijah has appeared"; still others, "One of the ancient prophets has arisen." But Herod said, "John I beheaded. Who then is this about whom I hear such things?" And he kept trying to see him.

SEPTEMBER 24TH, 2021
Friday of the Twenty-fifth Week in Ordinary Time

1ST Reading Hg 2:1-9

In the second year of King Darius, on the twenty-first day of the seventh month, the word of the LORD came through the prophet Haggai: Tell this to the governor of Judah, Zerubbabel, son of Shealtiel, and to the high priest Joshua, son of Jehozadak, and to the remnant of the people: Who is left among you that saw this house in its former glory? And how do you see it now? Does it not seem like nothing in your eyes? But now take courage, Zerubbabel, says the LORD, and take courage, Joshua, high priest, son of Jehozadak, and take courage, all you people of the land, says the LORD, and work! For I am with you, says the LORD of hosts. This is the pact that I made with you when you came out of Egypt, and my spirit continues in your midst; do not fear! For thus says the LORD of hosts: One moment yet, a little while, and I will shake the heavens and the earth, the sea and the dry land. I will shake all the nations, and the treasures of all the nations will come in, And I will fill this house with glory, says the LORD of hosts. Mine is the silver and mine the gold, says the LORD of hosts. Greater will be the future glory of this house than the former, says the LORD of hosts; And in this place I will give you peace, says the LORD of hosts!

Responsorial Psalm 43:1, 2, 3, 4
R. (5) Hope in God; I will praise him, my savior and my God.

Do me justice, O God, and fight my fight against a faithless people; from the deceitful and impious man rescue me.

R. Hope in God; I will praise him, my savior and my God.

For you, O God, are my strength. Why do you keep me so far away?

Why must I go about in mourning, with the enemy oppressing me?

R. Hope in God; I will praise him, my savior and my God.

Send forth your light and your fidelity; they shall lead me on

And bring me to your holy mountain, to your dwelling place.

R. Hope in God; I will praise him, my savior and my God.

Then will I go in to the altar of God, the God of my gladness and joy;

Then will I give you thanks upon the harp, O God, my God!

R. Hope in God; I will praise him, my savior and my God.

Alleluia Mk 10:45

R. Alleluia, alleluia.

The Son of Man came to serve and to give his life as a ransom for many.

R. Alleluia, alleluia.

Gospel Lk 9:18-22

Once when Jesus was praying in solitude, and the disciples were with him, he asked them, "Who do the crowds say that I am?" They said in reply, "John the Baptist; others, Elijah; still others, 'One of the ancient prophets has arisen.'" Then he said to them, "But who do you say that I am?" Peter said in reply, "The Christ of God." He rebuked them and directed them not to tell this to anyone. He said, "The Son of Man must suffer greatly and be rejected by the elders, the chief priests, and the scribes, and be killed and on the third day be raised."

SEPTEMBER 25TH, 2021
Saturday of the Twenty-fifth Week in Ordinary Time

I, Zechariah, raised my eyes and looked: there was a man with a measuring line in his hand. I asked, "Where are you going?" He answered, "To measure Jerusalem, to see how great is its width and how great its length." Then the angel who spoke with me advanced, and another angel came out to meet him and said to him, "Run, tell this to that young man:

People will live in Jerusalem as though in open country, because of the multitude of men and beasts in her midst. But I will be for her an encircling wall of fire, says the LORD, and I will be the glory in her midst." Sing and rejoice, O daughter Zion! See, I am coming to dwell among you, says the LORD. Many nations shall join themselves to the LORD on that day, and they shall be his people and he will dwell among you.

Responsorial Psalm Jeremiah 31:10, 11-12ab, 13

R. (see 10d) The Lord will guard us as a shepherd guards his flock.

Hear the word of the LORD, O nations, proclaim it on distant isles, and say:

He who scattered Israel, now gathers them together, he guards them as a shepherd guards his flock.

R. The Lord will guard us as a shepherd guards his flock.

The LORD shall ransom Jacob, he shall redeem him from the hand of his conqueror.

Shouting, they shall mount the heights of Zion, they shall come streaming to the LORD's blessings.

R. The Lord will guard us as a shepherd guards his flock.

Then the virgins shall make merry and dance, and young men and old as well.

I will turn their mourning into joy, I will console and gladden them after their sorrows.

R. The Lord will guard us as a shepherd guards his flock.

Alleluia 2 Tm 1:10

R. Alleluia, alleluia.

567

Our Savior Jesus Christ destroyed death and brought life to light through the Gospel.

R. Alleluia, alleluia.

Gospel Lk 9:43b-45
While they were all amazed at his every deed, Jesus said to his disciples, "Pay attention to what I am telling you. The Son of Man is to be handed over to men." But they did not understand this saying; its meaning was hidden from them so that they should not understand it, and they were afraid to ask him about this saying.

SEPTEMBER 26TH, 2021
Twenty-sixth Sunday in Ordinary Time

1ST Reading Nm 11:25-29
The LORD came down in the cloud and spoke to Moses. Taking some of the spirit that was on Moses, the LORD bestowed it on the seventy elders; and as the spirit came to rest on them, they prophesied. Now two men, one named Eldad and the other Medad, were not in the gathering but had been left in the camp. They too had been on the list, but had not gone out to the tent; yet the spirit came to rest on them also, and they prophesied in the camp. So, when a young man quickly told Moses, "Eldad and Medad are prophesying in the camp," Joshua, son of Nun, who from his youth had been Moses' aide, said, "Moses, my lord, stop them." But Moses answered him, "Are you jealous for my sake? Would that all the people of the LORD were prophets! Would that the LORD might bestow his spirit on them all!"

Responsorial Psalm Ps 19:8, 10, 12-13, 14
R. (9a) The precepts of the Lord give joy to the heart.

The law of the LORD is perfect, refreshing the soul; the decree of the LORD is trustworthy, giving wisdom to the simple.

R. The precepts of the Lord give joy to the heart.

The fear of the LORD is pure, enduring forever; the ordinances of the LORD are true, all of them just.

R. The precepts of the Lord give joy to the heart.

Though your servant is careful of them, very diligent in keeping them,

Yet who can detect failings? Cleanse me from my unknown faults!

R. The precepts of the Lord give joy to the heart.

From wanton sin especially, restrain your servant; let it not rule over me.

Then shall I be blameless and innocent of serious sin.

R. The precepts of the Lord give joy to the heart.

2ND Reading Jas 5:1-6

Come now, you rich, weep and wail over your impending miseries. Your wealth has rotted away, your clothes have become moth-eaten, your gold and silver have corroded, and that corrosion will be a testimony against you; it will devour your flesh like a fire. You have stored up treasure for the last days. Behold, the wages you withheld from the workers who harvested your fields are crying aloud; and the cries of the harvesters have reached the ears of the Lord of hosts. You have lived on earth in luxury and pleasure; you have fattened your hearts for the day of slaughter. You have condemned; you have murdered the righteous one; he offers you no resistance.

Alleluia Cf. Jn 17:17b, 17a

R. Alleluia, alleluia.

Your word, O Lord, is truth; consecrate us in the truth.

R. Alleluia, alleluia.

Gospel Mk 9:38-43, 45, 47-48

At that time, John said to Jesus,

"Teacher, we saw someone driving out demons in your name, and we tried to prevent him because he does not follow us."

Jesus replied, "Do not prevent him. There is no one who performs a mighty deed in my name who can at the same time speak ill of me. For whoever is not against us is for us. Anyone who gives you a cup of water to drink because you belong to Christ, amen, I say to you, will surely not lose his reward. "Whoever causes one of these little ones who believe in me to sin, it would be better for him if a great millstone were put around his neck and he were thrown into the sea. If your hand causes you to sin, cut it off. It is better for you to enter into life maimed than with two hands to go into

Gehenna, into the unquenchable fire. And if your foot causes you to sin, cut if off. It is better for you to enter into life crippled than with two feet to be thrown into Gehenna. And if your eye causes you to sin, pluck it out.

Better for you to enter into the kingdom of God with one eye than with two eyes to be thrown into Gehenna, where 'their worm does not die, and the fire is not quenched.'"

SEPTEMBER 27TH, 2021
Memorial of Saint Vincent de Paul, Priest

1ST Reading Zec 8:1-8

This word of the LORD of hosts came: Thus says the LORD of hosts: I am intensely jealous for Zion, stirred to jealous wrath for her. Thus says the LORD: I will return to Zion, and I will dwell within Jerusalem; Jerusalem shall be called the faithful city, and the mountain of the LORD of hosts, the holy mountain. Thus says the LORD of hosts: Old men and old women, each with staff in hand because of old age, shall again sit in the streets of Jerusalem. The city shall be filled with boys and girls playing in its streets. Thus says the LORD of hosts: Even if this should seem impossible in the eyes of the remnant of this people, shall it in those days be impossible in my eyes also, says the LORD of hosts? Thus says the LORD of hosts: Lo, I will rescue my people from the land of the rising sun, and from the land of the setting sun. I will bring them back to dwell within Jerusalem. They shall be my people, and I will be their God, with faithfulness and justice.

Responsorial Psalm 102:16-18, 19-21, 29 and 22-23

R. (17) The Lord will build up Zion again, and appear in all his glory.

The nations shall revere your name, O LORD, and all the kings of the earth your glory,

When the LORD has rebuilt Zion and appeared in his glory;

When he has regarded the prayer of the destitute, and not despised their prayer.

R. The Lord will build up Zion again, and appear in all his glory.

Let this be written for the generation to come, and let his future creatures praise the Lord:

"The LORD looked down from his holy height, from heaven he beheld the earth,

To hear the groaning of the prisoners, to release those doomed to die."

R. The Lord will build up Zion again, and appear in all his glory.

The children of your servants shall abide, and their posterity shall continue in your presence.

That the name of the LORD may be declared in Zion; and his praise, in Jerusalem,

When the peoples gather together, and the kingdoms, to serve the LORD.

R. The Lord will build up Zion again, and appear in all his glory.

Alleluia Mk 10:45

R. Alleluia, alleluia.

The Son of Man came to serve and to give his life as a ransom for many.

R. Alleluia, alleluia.

Gospel Lk 9:46-50

An argument arose among the disciples about which of them was the greatest. Jesus realized the intention of their hearts and took a child and placed it by his side and said to them, "Whoever receives this child in my name receives me, and whoever receives me receives the one who sent me. For the one who is least among all of you is the one who is the greatest.

Then John said in reply, "Master, we saw someone casting out demons in your name and we tried to prevent him because he does not follow in our company." Jesus said to him, "Do not prevent him, for whoever is not against you is for you."

SEPTEMBER 28TH, 2021
Tuesday of the Twenty-sixth Week in Ordinary Time

1ST Reading Zec 8:20-23
Thus says the LORD of hosts:

There shall yet come peoples, the inhabitants of many cities; and the inhabitants of one city shall approach those of another, and say, "Come! Let us go to implore the favor of the LORD"; and, "I too will go to seek the LORD." Many peoples and strong nations shall come to seek the Lord of hosts in Jerusalem and to implore the favor of the LORD. Thus says the LORD of hosts: In those days ten men of every nationality, speaking different tongues, shall take hold, yes, take hold of every Jew by the edge of his garment and say, "Let us go with you, for we have heard that God is with you."

Responsorial Psalm 87:1b-3, 4-5, 6-7
R. (Zec 8:23) God is with us.

His foundation upon the holy mountains the LORD loves:

The gates of Zion, more than any dwelling of Jacob.

Glorious things are said of you, O city of God!

R. God is with us.

I tell of Egypt and Babylon among those that know the LORD;

Of Philistia, Tyre, Ethiopia: "This man was born there."

And of Zion they shall say: "One and all were born in her;

And he who has established her is the Most High LORD."

R. God is with us.

They shall note, when the peoples are enrolled: "This man was born there."

And all shall sing, in their festive dance: "My home is within you."

R. God is with us.

Alleluia Mk 10:45

R. Alleluia, alleluia.

The Son of Man came to serve and to give his life as a ransom for many.

R. Alleluia, alleluia.

When the days for Jesus to be taken up were fulfilled, he resolutely determined to journey to Jerusalem, and he sent messengers ahead of him. On the way they entered a Samaritan village to prepare for his reception there, but they would not welcome him because the destination of his journey was Jerusalem.

When the disciples James and John saw this they asked, "Lord, do you want us to call down fire from heaven to consume them?" Jesus turned and rebuked them, and they journeyed to another village.

SEPTEMBER 29TH, 2021
Feast of Saints Michael, Gabriel, and Raphael, archangels

1ST Reading Dn 7:9-10, 13-14

As I watched: Thrones were set up and the Ancient One took his throne. His clothing was bright as snow, and the hair on his head as white as wool; His throne was flames of fire, with wheels of burning fire. A surging stream of fire flowed out from where he sat; Thousands upon thousands were ministering to him, and myriads upon myriads attended him. The court was convened, and the books were opened. As the visions during the night continued, I saw One like a son of man coming, on the clouds of heaven; When he reached the Ancient One and was presented before him, He received dominion, glory, and kingship; nations and peoples of every language serve him. His dominion is an everlasting dominion that shall not be taken away, his kingship shall not be destroyed.

OR:

Rv 12:7-12ab

War broke out in heaven; Michael and his angels battled against the dragon. The dragon and its angels fought back, but they did not prevail and there was no longer any place for them in heaven. The huge dragon, the ancient serpent, who is called the Devil and Satan, who deceived the whole world, was thrown down to earth, and its angels were thrown down with it. Then I heard a loud voice in heaven say: "Now have salvation and power come, and the Kingdom of our God and the authority of his Anointed.

For the accuser of our brothers is cast out, who accuses them before our God day and night. They conquered him by the Blood of the Lamb and by the word of their testimony; love for life did not deter them from death. Therefore, rejoice, you heavens, and you who dwell in them."

Responsorial Psalm 138:1-2ab, 2cde-3, 4-5
R. (1) In the sight of the angels I will sing your praises, Lord.

I will give thanks to you, O LORD, with all my heart, for you have heard the words of my mouth; in the presence of the angels I will sing your praise;

I will worship at your holy temple and give thanks to your name.

R. In the sight of the angels I will sing your praises, Lord.

Because of your kindness and your truth; for you have made great above all things your name and your promise.

When I called, you answered me; you built up strength within me.

R. In the sight of the angels I will sing your praises, Lord.

All the kings of the earth shall give thanks to you, O LORD when they hear the words of your mouth;

And they shall sing of the ways of the LORD "Great is the glory of the LORD

R. In the sight of the angels I will sing your praises, Lord.

Alleluia Ps 103:21

R. Alleluia, alleluia.

Bless the LORD, all you angels, you ministers, who do his will.

R. Alleluia, alleluia.

Gospel Jn 1:47-51
Jesus saw Nathanael coming toward him and said of him, "Here is a true child of Israel. There is no duplicity in him." Nathanael said to him, "How do you know me?" Jesus answered and said to him, "Before Philip called you, I saw you under the fig tree." Nathanael answered him, "Rabbi, you are the Son of God; you are the King of Israel." Jesus answered and said to him, "Do you believe because I told you that I saw you under the fig tree? You will see greater things than this." And he said to him, "Amen, amen, I say to

you, you will see heaven opened and the angels of God ascending and descending on the Son of Man."

SEPTEMBER 30TH, 2021
Memorial of Saint Jerome, Priest and Doctor of the Church

1ST Reading Neh 8:1-4a, 5-6, 7b-12

The whole people gathered as one in the open space before the Water Gate, and they called upon Ezra the scribe to bring forth the book of the Law of Moses which the LORD prescribed for Israel. On the first day of the seventh month, therefore, Ezra the priest brought the law before the assembly, which consisted of men, women, and those children old enough to understand. Standing at one end of the open place that was before the Water Gate, he read out of the book from daybreak until midday, in the presence of the men, the women, and those children old enough to understand; and all the people listened attentively to the book of the law. Ezra the scribe stood on a wooden platform that had been made for the occasion.

He opened the scroll so that all the people might see it (for he was standing higher up than any of the people); and, as he opened it, all the people rose. Ezra blessed the LORD, the great God, and all the people, their hands raised high, answered, "Amen, amen!" Then they bowed down and prostrated themselves before the LORD, their faces to the ground. As the people remained in their places, Ezra read plainly from the book of the law of God, interpreting it so that all could understand what was read. Then Nehemiah, that is, His Excellency, and Ezra the priest-scribe and the Levites who were instructing the people said to all the people: "Today is holy to the LORD your God. Do not be sad, and do not weep"– for all the people were weeping as they heard the words of the law. He said further: "Go, eat rich foods and drink sweet drinks, and allot portions to those who had nothing prepared; for today is holy to our LORD. Do not be saddened this day, for rejoicing in the LORD must be your strength!" And the Levites quieted all the people, saying, "Hush, for today is holy, and you must not be saddened." Then all the people went to eat and drink, to distribute portions, and to celebrate with great joy, for they understood the words that had been expounded to them.

Responsorial Psalm 19:8, 9, 10, 11

R. (9ab) The precepts of the Lord give joy to the heart.

The law of the LORD is perfect, refreshing the soul;

The decree of the LORD is trustworthy, giving wisdom to the simple.

R. The precepts of the Lord give joy to the heart.

The precepts of the LORD are right, rejoicing the heart;

The command of the LORD is clear, enlightening the eye;

R. The precepts of the Lord give joy to the heart.

The fear of the LORD is pure, enduring forever;

The ordinances of the LORD are true, all of them just.

R. The precepts of the Lord give joy to the heart.

They are more precious than gold, than a heap of purest gold;

Sweeter also than syrup or honey from the comb.

R. The precepts of the Lord give joy to the heart.

Alleluia Mk 1:15

R. Alleluia, alleluia.

The Kingdom of God is at hand; repent and believe in the Gospel.

R. Alleluia, alleluia.

Gospel Lk 10:1-12

Jesus appointed seventy-two other disciples whom he sent ahead of him in pairs to every town and place he intended to visit. He said to them, "The harvest is abundant but the laborers are few; so ask the master of the harvest to send out laborers for his harvest. Go on your way; behold, I am sending you like lambs among wolves. Carry no money bag, no sack, no sandals; and greet no one along the way. Into whatever house you enter, first say, 'Peace to this household.' If a peaceful person lives there, your peace will rest on him; but if not, it will return to you. Stay in the same house and eat and drink what is offered to you, for the laborer deserves his payment.

Do not move about from one house to another. Whatever town you enter and they welcome you, eat what is set before you, cure the sick in it and say to them, 'The Kingdom of God is at hand for you.' Whatever town you enter and they do not receive you, go out into the streets and say, 'The dust of your town that clings to our feet, even that we shake off against you.' Yet know this: the Kingdom of God is at hand. I tell you, it will be more tolerable for Sodom on that day than for that town."

OCTOBER 1ST, 2021
Memorial of Saint Thérèse of the Child Jesus, Virgin and Doctor of the Church

1ST Reading Bar 1:15-22

During the Babylonian captivity, the exiles prayed:"Justice is with the Lord, our God; and we today are flushed with shame, we men of Judah and citizens of Jerusalem, that we, with our kings and rulers and priests and prophets, and with our ancestors, have sinned in the Lord's sight and disobeyed him. We have neither heeded the voice of the Lord, our God, nor followed the precepts which the Lord set before us. From the time the Lord led our ancestors out of the land of Egypt until the present day, we have been disobedient to the Lord, our God, and only too ready to disregard his voice. And the evils and the curse that the Lord enjoined upon Moses, his servant, at the time he led our ancestors forth from the land of Egypt to give us the land flowing with milk and honey, cling to us even today. For we did not heed the voice of the Lord, our God, in all the words of the prophets whom he sent us, but each one of us went off after the devices of his own wicked heart, served other gods, and did evil in the sight of the Lord, our God."

Responsorial Psalm79:1b-2, 3-5, 8, 9

R. (9) For the glory of your name, O Lord, deliver us.

O God, the nations have come into your inheritance; they have defiled your holy temple, they have laid Jerusalem in ruins.

They have given the corpses of your servants as food to the birds of heaven, the flesh of your faithful ones to the beasts of the earth.

R. For the glory of your name, O Lord, deliver us.

They have poured out their blood like water round about Jerusalem, and there is no one to bury them.

We have become the reproach of our neighbors, the scorn and derision of those around us.

O LORD, how long? Will you be angry forever? Will your jealousy burn like fire?

R. For the glory of your name, O Lord, deliver us.

Remember not against us the iniquities of the past; may your compassion quickly come to us, for we are brought very low.

R. For the glory of your name, O Lord, deliver us.

Help us, O God our savior, because of the glory of your name;

Deliver us and pardon our sins for your name's sake.

R. For the glory of your name, O Lord, deliver us.

AlleluiaPs 95:8

R. Alleluia, alleluia.

If today you hear his voice, harden not your hearts.

R. Alleluia, alleluia.

Gospel Lk 10:13-16
Jesus said to them,

"Woe to you, Chorazin! Woe to you, Bethsaida! For if the mighty deeds done in your midst had been done in Tyre and Sidon, they would long ago have repented, sitting in sackcloth and ashes. But it will be more tolerable for Tyre and Sidonat the judgment than for you. And as for you, Capernaum, 'Will you be exalted to heaven? You will go down to the netherworld. 'Whoever listens to you listens to me. Whoever rejects you rejects me. And whoever rejects me rejects the one who sent me."

OCTOBER 2ND, 2021
Memorial of the Holy Guardian Angels

Fear not, my people! Remember, Israel, You were sold to the nations not for your destruction; It was because you angered God that you were handed over to your foes. For you provoked your Maker with sacrifices to demons, to no-gods; you forsook the Eternal God who nourished you, and you grieved Jerusalem who fostered you. She indeed saw coming upon you the anger of God; and she said: "Hear, you neighbors of Zion! God has brought great mourning upon me, for I have seen the captivity that the Eternal God has brought upon my sons and daughters. With joy I fostered them; but with mourning and lament I let them go. Let no one gloat over me, a widow, bereft of many: For the sins of my children I am left desolate, because they turned from the law of God. Fear not, my children; call out to God! He who brought this upon you will remember you. As your hearts have been disposed to stray from God, turn now ten times the more to seek him; For he who has brought disaster upon you will, in saving you, bring you back enduring joy."

R. (34) The Lord listens to the poor.

"See, you lowly ones, and be glad; you who seek God, may your hearts revive!

For the LORD hears the poor, and his own who are in bonds he spurns not.

Let the heavens and the earth praise him, the seas and whatever moves in them!"

R. The Lord listens to the poor.

For God will save Zion and rebuild the cities of Judah.

They shall dwell in the land and own it, and the descendants of his servants shall inherit it, and those who love his name shall inhabit it.

R. The Lord listens to the poor.

R. Alleluia, alleluia.

Bless the LORD, all you angels, you ministers, who do his will.

R. Alleluia, alleluia.

The disciples approached Jesus and said, "Who is the greatest in the Kingdom of heaven?"

He called a child over, placed it in their midst, and said, "Amen, I say to you, unless you turn and become like children, you will not enter the Kingdom of heaven. Whoever humbles himself like this child is the greatest in the Kingdom of heaven. And whoever receives one child such as this in my name receives me. "See that you do not despise one of these little ones, for I say to you that their angels in heaven always look upon the face of my heavenly Father."

OCTOBER 3RD, 2021
Twenty-seventh Sunday in Ordinary Time

The LORD God said: "It is not good for the man to be alone. I will make a suitable partner for him. "So the LORD God formed out of the ground various wild animals and various birds of the air, and he brought them to the man to see what he would call them; whatever the man called each of them would be its name.

The man gave names to all the cattle, all the birds of the air, and all wild animals; but none proved to be the suitable partner for the man. So the LORD God cast a deep sleep on the man, and while he was asleep, he took out one of his ribs and closed up its place with flesh. The LORD God then built up into a woman the rib that he had taken from the man. When he brought her to the man, the man said: "This one, at last, is bone of my bones and flesh of my flesh; this one shall be called 'woman, 'for out of 'her man' this one has been taken." That is why a man leaves his father and mother and clings to his wife, and the two of them become one flesh.

R. (cf. 5) May the Lord bless us all the days of our lives.

Blessed are you who fear the LORD, who walk in his ways!

For you shall eat the fruit of your handiwork; blessed shall you be, and favored.

R. May the Lord bless us all the days of our lives.

Your wife shall be like a fruitful vine in the recesses of your home; your children like olive plants around your table.

R. May the Lord bless us all the days of our lives.

Behold, thus is the man blessed who fears the LORD.

The LORD bless you from Zion: may you see the prosperity of Jerusalem all the days of your life.

R. May the Lord bless us all the days of our lives.

May you see your children's children.

Peace be upon Israel!

R. May the Lord bless us all the days of our lives.

2ND Reading Heb 2:9-11
Brothers and sisters:

He "for a little while" was made "lower than the angels," that by the grace of God he might taste death for everyone. For it was fitting that he, for whom and through whom all things exist, in bringing many children to glory, should make the leader to their salvation perfect through suffering. He who consecrates and those who are being consecrated all have one origin. Therefore, he is not ashamed to call them "brothers."

Alleluia 1 Jn 4:12

R. Alleluia, alleluia.

If we love one another, God remains in us and his love is brought to perfection in us.

R. Alleluia, alleluia.

Gospel Mk 10:2-16 or 10:2-12

The Pharisees approached Jesus and asked, "Is it lawful for a husband to divorce his wife?" They were testing him. He said to them in reply, "What did Moses command you?" They replied, "Moses permitted a husband to write a bill of divorce and dismiss her." But Jesus told them, "Because of the hardness of your hearts he wrote you this commandment. But from the beginning of creation, God made them male and female. For this reason a man shall leave his father and mother and be joined to his wife, and the two shall become one flesh. So they are no longer two but one flesh. Therefore what God has joined together, no human being must separate." In the house the disciples again questioned Jesus about this.

He said to them, "Whoever divorces his wife and marries another commits adultery against her; and if she divorces her husband and marries another, she commits adultery." And people were bringing children to him that he might touch them, but the disciples rebuked them. When Jesus saw this he became indignant and said to them, "Let the children come to me; do not prevent them, for the kingdom of God belongs to such as these. Amen, I say to you, whoever does not accept the kingdom of God like a child will not enter it." Then he embraced them and blessed them, placing his hands on them.

OR:

The Pharisees approached Jesus and asked, "Is it lawful for a husband to divorce his wife?" They were testing him. He said to them in reply, "What did Moses command you?" They replied, "Moses permitted a husband to write a bill of divorce and dismiss her." But Jesus told them, "Because of the hardness of your hearts he wrote you this commandment. But from the beginning of creation, God made them male and female. For this reason a man shall leave his father and mother and be joined to his wife, and the two shall become one flesh. So they are no longer two but one flesh. Therefore what God has joined together, no human being must separate." In the house the disciples again questioned Jesus about this. He said to them, "Whoever divorces his wife and marries another commits adultery against her; and if she divorces her husband and marries another, she commits adultery."

OCTOBER 4TH, 2021
Memorial of Saint Francis of Assisi

This is the word of the LORD that came to Jonah, son of Amittai: "Set out for the great city of Nineveh, and preach against it; their wickedness has come up before me." But Jonah made ready to flee to Tarshish away from the LORD. He went down to Joppa, found a ship going to Tarshish, paid the fare, and went aboard to journey with them to Tarshish, away from the LORD. The LORD, however, hurled a violent wind upon the sea, and in the furious tempest that arose the ship was on the point of breaking up. Then the mariners became frightened and each one cried to his god. To lighten the ship for themselves, they threw its cargo into the sea. Meanwhile, Jonah had gone down into the hold of the ship, and lay there fast asleep.

The captain came to him and said, "What are you doing asleep? Rise up, call upon your God! Perhaps God will be mindful of us so that we may not perish." Then they said to one another, "Come, let us cast lots to find out on whose account we have met with this misfortune." So they cast lots, and thus singled out Jonah. "Tell us," they said, "what is your business? Where do you come from? What is your country, and to what people do you belong?" Jonah answered them, "I am a Hebrew, I worship the LORD, the God of heaven, who made the sea and the dry land."

Now the men were seized with great fear and said to him, "How could you do such a thing! – They knew that he was fleeing from the LORD, because he had told them.–They asked, "What shall we do with you, that the sea may quiet down for us?" For the sea was growing more and more turbulent. Jonah said to them, "Pick me up and throw me into the sea, that it may quiet down for you; since I know it is because of me that this violent storm has come upon you." Still the men rowed hard to regain the land, but they could not, for the sea grew ever more turbulent. Then they cried to the LORD: "We beseech you, O LORD, let us not perish for taking this man's life; do not charge us with shedding innocent blood, for you, LORD, have done as you saw fit." Then they took Jonah and threw him into the sea, and the sea's raging abated. Struck with great fear of the LORD, the men offered sacrifice and made vows to him. But the LORD sent a large fish, that swallowed Jonah; and Jonah remained in the belly of the fish three days and three nights. From the belly of the fish Jonah prayed to the LORD, his God. Then the LORD commanded the fish to spew Jonah upon the shore.

Responsorial Psalm Jonah 2:3, 4, 5, 8
R. You will rescue my life from the pit, O Lord.

Out of my distress I called to the LORD, and he answered me;

From the midst of the nether world I cried for help, and you heard my voice.

R. You will rescue my life from the pit, O Lord.

For you cast me into the deep, into the heart of the sea, and the flood enveloped me;

All your breakers and your billows passed over me.

R. You will rescue my life from the pit, O Lord.

Then I said, "I am banished from your sight! yet would I again look upon your holy temple."

R. You will rescue my life from the pit, O Lord.

When my soul fainted within me, I remembered the LORD;

My prayer reached you in your holy temple.

R. You will rescue my life from the pit, O Lord.

Alleluia Jn 13:34

R. Alleluia, alleluia.

I give you a new commandment: love one another as I have loved you.

R. Alleluia, alleluia.

Gospel Lk 10:25-37

There was a scholar of the law who stood up to test Jesus and said, "Teacher, what must I do to inherit eternal life?" Jesus said to him, "What is written in the law? How do you read it?" He said in reply, "You shall love the Lord, your God, with all your heart, with all your being, with all your strength, and with all your mind, and your neighbor as yourself." He replied to him, "You have answered correctly; do this and you will live." But because he wished to justify himself, he said to Jesus, "And who is my neighbor?" Jesus replied, "A man fell victim to robbers as he went down from Jerusalem to Jericho.

They stripped and beat him and went off leaving him half-dead. A priest happened to be going down that road, but when he saw him, he passed by on the opposite side. Likewise a Levite came to the place, and when he saw him, he passed by on the opposite side. But a Samaritan traveler who came upon him was moved with compassion at the sight.

He approached the victim, poured oil and wine over his wounds and bandaged them. Then he lifted him up on his own animal, took him to an inn, and cared for him. The next day he took out two silver coins and gave them to the innkeeper with the instruction, 'Take care of him. If you spend more than what I have given you, I shall repay you on my way back.' Which of these three, in your opinion, was neighbor to the robbers' victim?" He answered, "The one who treated him with mercy." Jesus said to him, "Go and do likewise."

OCTOBER 5TH, 2021
Tuesday of the Twenty-seventh Week in Ordinary Time

1ST Reading Jon 3:1-10

The word of the LORD came to Jonah a second time: "Set out for the great city of Nineveh, and announce to it the message that I will tell you." So Jonah made ready and went to Nineveh, according to the LORD's bidding. Now Nineveh was an enormously large city; it took three days to go through it. Jonah began his journey through the city, and had gone but a single day's walk announcing, "Forty days more and Nineveh shall be destroyed," when the people of Nineveh believed God; they proclaimed a fast and all of them, great and small, put on sackcloth. When the news reached the king of Nineveh, he rose from his throne, laid aside his robe, covered himself with sackcloth, and sat in the ashes.

Then he had this proclaimed throughout Nineveh, by decree of the king and his nobles: "Neither man nor beast, neither cattle nor sheep, shall taste anything; they shall not eat, nor shall they drink water. Man and beast shall be covered with sackcloth and call loudly to God; every man shall turn from his evil way and from the violence he has in hand. Who knows, God may relent and forgive, and withhold his blazing wrath, so that we shall not perish." When God saw by their actions how they turned from their evil way, he repented of the evil that he had threatened to do to them; he did not carry it out.

Responsorial Psalm 130:1b-2, 3-4ab, 7-8

R. (3) If you, O Lord, mark iniquities, who can stand?

Out of the depths I cry to you, O LORD

LORD, hear my voice! Let your ears be attentive to my voice in supplication.

R. If you, O Lord, mark iniquities, who can stand?

If you, O LORD, mark iniquities, LORD, who can stand?

But with you is forgiveness, that you may be revered.

R. If you, O Lord, mark iniquities, who can stand?

Let Israel wait for the LORD,

For with the LORD is kindness and with him is plenteous redemption;

And he will redeem Israel from all their iniquities.

R. If you, O Lord, mark iniquities, who can stand?

Alleluia Lk 11:28

R. Alleluia, alleluia.

Blessed are those who hear the word of God and observe it.

R. Alleluia, alleluia.

Gospel Lk 10:38-42

Jesus entered a village where a woman whose name was Martha welcomed him. She had a sister named Mary who sat beside the Lord at his feet listening to him speak. Martha, burdened with much serving, came to him and said, "Lord, do you not care that my sister has left me by myself to do the serving? Tell her to help me." The Lord said to her in reply, "Martha, Martha, you are anxious and worried about many things. There is need of only one thing. Mary has chosen the better part and it will not be taken from her."

OCTOBER 6TH, 2021
Wednesday of the Twenty-seventh Week in Ordinary Time

Jonah was greatly displeased and became angry that God did not carry out the evil he threatened against Nineveh. He prayed, "I beseech you, LORD, is not this what I said while I was still in my own country? This is why I fled at first to Tarshish. I knew that you are a gracious and merciful God, slow to anger, rich in clemency, loath to punish. And now, LORD, please take my life from me; for it is better for me to die than to live." But the LORD asked, "Have you reason to be angry?"

Jonah then left the city for a place to the east of it, where he built himself a hut and waited under it in the shade, to see what would happen to the city. And when the LORD God provided a gourd plant that grew up over Jonah's head, giving shade that relieved him of any discomfort, Jonah was very happy over the plant. But the next morning at dawn God sent a worm that attacked the plant, so that it withered. And when the sun arose, God sent a burning east wind; and the sun beat upon Jonah's head till he became faint. Then Jonah asked for death, saying, "I would be better off dead than alive."

But God said to Jonah, "Have you reason to be angry over the plant?" "I have reason to be angry," Jonah answered, "angry enough to die." Then the LORD said, "You are concerned over the plant which cost you no labor and which you did not raise; it came up in one night and in one night it perished. And should I not be concerned over Nineveh, the great city, in which there are more than a hundred and twenty thousand persons who cannot distinguish their right hand from their left, not to mention the many cattle?"

Responsorial Psalm 86:3-4, 5-6, 9-10

R. (15) Lord, you are merciful and gracious.

Have mercy on me, O Lord, for to you I call all the day.

Gladden the soul of your servant, for to you, O Lord, I lift up my soul.

R. Lord, you are merciful and gracious.

For you, O Lord, are good and forgiving, abounding in kindness to all who call upon you.

Hearken, O LORD, to my prayer and attend to the sound of my pleading.

R. Lord, you are merciful and gracious.

All the nations you have made shall come and worship you, O Lord, and glorify your name.

For you are great, and you do wondrous deeds; you alone are God.

R. Lord, you are merciful and gracious.

Alleluia Rom 8:15bc

R. Alleluia, alleluia.

You have received a spirit of adoption as sons through which we cry: Abba! Father!

R. Alleluia, alleluia.

Gospel Lk 11:1-4
Jesus was praying in a certain place, and when he had finished, one of his disciples said to him, "Lord, teach us to pray just as John taught his disciples." He said to them, "When you pray, say: Father, hallowed be your name, your Kingdom come. Give us each day our daily bread and forgive us our sins for we ourselves forgive everyone in debt to us, and do not subject us to the final test."

OCTOBER 7TH, 2021
Memorial of Our Lady of the Rosary

1ST Reading Mal 3:13-20b
You have defied me in word, says the LORD, yet you ask, "What have we spoken against you?" You have said, "It is vain to serve God, and what do we profit by keeping his command, and going about in penitential dress in awe of the LORD of hosts? Rather must we call the proud blessed; for indeed evildoers prosper, and even tempt God with impunity." Then they who fear the LORD spoke with one another, and the LORD listened attentively; and a record book was written before him of those who fear the LORD and trust in his name. And they shall be mine, says the LORD of hosts, my own special possession, on the day I take action. And I will have compassion on them, as a man has compassion on his son who serves him.

Then you will again see the distinction between the just and the wicked; between the one who serves God, and the one who does not serve him. For lo, the day is coming, blazing like an oven, when all the proud and all evildoers will be stubble, And the day that is coming will set them on fire, leaving them neither root nor branch, says the LORD of hosts. But for you who fear my name, there will arise the sun of justice with its healing rays.

Responsorial Psalm 1:1-2, 3, 4 and 6
R. (Ps 40:5a) Blessed are they who hope in the Lord.

Blessed the man who follows not the counsel of the wicked

Nor walks in the way of sinners, nor sits in the company of the insolent,

But delights in the law of the LORD and meditates on his law day and night.

R. Blessed are they who hope in the Lord.

He is like a tree planted near running water,

That yields its fruit in due season, and whose leaves never fade.

Whatever he does, prospers.

R. Blessed are they who hope in the Lord.

Not so the wicked, not so; they are like chaff which the wind drives away.

For the LORD watches over the way of the just, but the way of the wicked vanishes.

R. Blessed are they who hope in the Lord.

Alleluia Acts 16:14b

R. Alleluia, alleluia.

Open your hearts, O Lord, to listen to the words of your Son.

R. Alleluia, alleluia.

Gospel Lk 11:5-13
Jesus said to his disciples: "Suppose one of you has a friend to whom he goes at midnight and says, 'Friend, lend me three loaves of bread, for a friend of mine has arrived at my house from a journey and I have nothing to offer him,' and he says in reply from within, 'Do not bother me; the door has already been locked and my children and I are already in bed.

589

I cannot get up to give you anything.' I tell you, if he does not get up to give him the loaves because of their friendship, he will get up to give him whatever he needs because of his persistence. "And I tell you, ask and you will receive; seek and you will find; knock and the door will be opened to you. For everyone who asks, receives; and the one who seeks, finds; and to the one who knocks, the door will be opened. What father among you would hand his son a snake when he asks for a fish?

Or hand him a scorpion when he asks for an egg? If you then, who are wicked, know how to give good gifts to your children, how much more will the Father in heaven give the Holy Spirit to those who ask him?

OCTOBER 8TH, 2021
Friday of the Twenty-seventh Week in Ordinary Time

1ST Reading Jl 1:13-15; 2:1-2

Gird yourselves and weep, O priests! Wail, O ministers of the altar! Come, spend the night in sackcloth, O ministers of my God! The house of your God is deprived of offering and libation. Proclaim a fast, call an assembly; Gather the elders, all who dwell in the land, into the house of the LORD, your God, and cry to the LORD! Alas, the day! For near is the day of the LORD, and it comes as ruin from the Almighty. Blow the trumpet in Zion, sound the alarm on my holy mountain! Let all who dwell in the land tremble, for the day of the LORD is coming; Yes, it is near, a day of darkness and of gloom, a day of clouds and somberness! Like dawn spreading over the mountains, a people numerous and mighty! Their like has not been from of old, nor will it be after them, even to the years of distant generations.

Responsorial Psalm 9:2-3, 6 and 16, 8-9

R. (9) The Lord will judge the world with justice.

I will give thanks to you, O LORD, with all my heart; I will declare all your wondrous deeds.

I will be glad and exult in you; I will sing praise to your name, Most High.

R. The Lord will judge the world with justice.

You rebuked the nations and destroyed the wicked; their name you blotted out forever and ever.

The nations are sunk in the pit they have made; in the snare they set, their foot is caught.

R. The Lord will judge the world with justice.

But the LORD sits enthroned forever; he has set up his throne for judgment.

He judges the world with justice; he governs the peoples with equity.

R. The Lord will judge the world with justice.

Alleluia Jn 12:31b-32

R. Alleluia, alleluia.

The prince of this world will now be cast out, and when I am lifted up from the earth I will draw all to myself, says the Lord.

R. Alleluia, alleluia.

Gospel Lk 11:15-26

When Jesus had driven out a demon, some of the crowd said: "By the power of Beelzebul, the prince of demons, he drives out demons." Others, to test him, asked him for a sign from heaven. But he knew their thoughts and said to them, "Every kingdom divided against itself will be laid waste and house will fall against house. And if Satan is divided against himself, how will his kingdom stand? For you say that it is by Beelzebul that I drive out demons.

If I, then, drive out demons by Beelzebul, by whom do your own people drive them out? Therefore they will be your judges. But if it is by the finger of God that I drive out demons, then the Kingdom of God has come upon you. When a strong man fully armed guards his palace, his possessions are safe. But when one stronger than he attacks and overcomes him, he takes away the armor on which he relied and distributes the spoils. Whoever is not with me is against me, and whoever does not gather with me scatters. "When an unclean spirit goes out of someone, it roams through arid regions searching for rest but, finding none, it says, 'I shall return to my home from which I came.' But upon returning, it finds it swept clean and put in order. Then it goes and brings back seven other spirits more wicked than itself who move in and dwell there, and the last condition of that man is worse than the first."

OCTOBER 9TH, 2021

Saturday of the Twenty-seventh Week in Ordinary Time

1ST Reading Jl 4:12-21

Thus says the LORD:

Let the nations bestir themselves and come up to the Valley of Jehoshaphat; for there will I sit in judgment upon all the neighboring nations. Apply the sickle, for the harvest is ripe; Come and tread, for the wine press is full; the vats overflow, for great is their malice. Crowd upon crowd in the valley of decision; for near is the day of the LORD in the valley of decision. Sun and moon are darkened, and the stars withhold their brightness.

The LORD roars from Zion, and from Jerusalem raises his voice; the heavens and the earth quake, but the LORD is a refuge to his people, a stronghold to the children of Israel. Then shall you know that I, the LORD, am your God, dwelling on Zion, my holy mountain; Jerusalem shall be holy, and strangers shall pass through her no more. And then, on that day, the mountains shall drip new wine, and the hills shall flow with milk; and the channels of Judah shall flow with water: A fountain shall issue from the house of the LORD, to water the Valley of Shittim. Egypt shall be a waste, and Edom a desert waste, Because of violence done to the people of Judah, because they shed innocent blood in their land. But Judah shall abide forever, and Jerusalem for all generations. I will avenge their blood, and not leave it unpunished. The LORD dwells in Zion.

Responsorial Psalm 97:1-2, 5-6, 11-12

R. (12a) Rejoice in the Lord, you just!

The LORD is king; let the earth rejoice; let the many isles be glad.

Clouds and darkness are round about him, justice and judgment are the foundation of his throne.

R. Rejoice in the Lord, you just!

The mountains melt like wax before the LORD, before the LORD of all the earth.

The heavens proclaim his justice, and all peoples see his glory.

R. Rejoice in the Lord, you just!

Light dawns for the just; and gladness, for the upright of heart.

Be glad in the LORD, you just, and give thanks to his holy name.

R. Rejoice in the Lord, you just!

Alleluia Lk 11:28

R. Alleluia, alleluia.

Blessed are those who hear the word of God and observe it.

R. Alleluia, alleluia.

Gospel Lk 11:27-28

While Jesus was speaking, a woman from the crowd called out and said to him, "Blessed is the womb that carried you and the breasts at which you nursed." He replied, "Rather, blessed are those who hear the word of God and observe it."

OCTOBER 10TH, 2021
Twenty-eighth Sunday in Ordinary Time

1ST Reading Wis 7:7-11

Prudence was given me; I pleaded, and the spirit of wisdom came to me. I preferred her to scepter and throne, and deemed riches nothing in comparison with her, nor did I liken any priceless gem to her; because all gold, in view of her, is a little sand, and before her, silver is to be accounted mire. Beyond health and comeliness I loved her, and I chose to have her rather than the light, because the splendor of her never yields to sleep. Yet all good things together came to me in her company, and countless riches at her hands.

Responsorial Psalm Ps 90:12-13, 14-15, 16-17
R. (14) Fill us with your love, O Lord, and we will sing for joy!

Teach us to number our days aright, that we may gain wisdom of heart.

Return, O LORD! How long? Have pity on your servants!

R. Fill us with your love, O Lord, and we will sing for joy!

Fill us at daybreak with your kindness, that we may shout for joy and gladness all our days.

Make us glad, for the days when you afflicted us, for the years when we saw evil.

R. Fill us with your love, O Lord, and we will sing for joy!

Let your work be seen by your servants and your glory by their children; and may the gracious care of the LORD our God be ours; prosper the work of our hands for us!

Prosper the work of our hands!

R. Fill us with your love, O Lord, and we will sing for joy!

2ND Reading Heb 4:12-13

Brothers and sisters:

Indeed the word of God is living and effective, sharper than any two-edged sword, penetrating even between soul and spirit, joints and marrow, and able to discern reflections and thoughts of the heart. No creature is concealed from him, but everything is naked and exposed to the eyes of him to whom we must render an account.

Alleluia Mt 5:3

R. Alleluia, alleluia.

Blessed are the poor in spirit, for theirs is the kingdom of heaven.

R. Alleluia, alleluia.

Gospel Mk 10:17-30 or 10:17-27

As Jesus was setting out on a journey, a man ran up, knelt down before him, and asked him, "Good teacher, what must I do to inherit eternal life?" Jesus answered him, "Why do you call me good? No one is good but God alone. You know the commandments: You shall not kill; you shall not commit adultery; you shall not steal; you shall not bear false witness; you shall not defraud; honor your father and your mother." He replied and said to him, "Teacher, all of these I have observed from my youth." Jesus, looking at him, loved him and said to him, "You are lacking in one thing. Go, sell what you have, and give to the poor and you will have treasure in heaven; then come, follow me." At that statement his face fell, and he went away sad, for he had many possessions. Jesus looked around and said to his disciples, "How hard it is for those who have wealth to enter the kingdom of God!" The disciples were amazed at his words. So Jesus again said to them in reply,

"Children, how hard it is to enter the kingdom of God! It is easier for a camel to pass through the eye of a needle than for one who is rich to enter the kingdom of God." They were exceedingly astonished and said among themselves, "Then who can be saved?" Jesus looked at them and said, "For human beings it is impossible, but not for God. All things are possible for God." Peter began to say to him, "We have given up everything and followed you." Jesus said, "Amen, I say to you, there is no one who has given up house or brothers or sisters or mother or father or children or lands for my sake and for the sake of the gospel who will not receive a hundred times more now in this present age: houses and brothers and sisters and mothers and children and lands, with persecutions, and eternal life in the age to come."

OR:

As Jesus was setting out on a journey, a man ran up, knelt down before him, and asked him, "Good teacher, what must I do to inherit eternal life?" Jesus answered him, "Why do you call me good? No one is good but God alone. You know the commandments:

You shall not kill; you shall not commit adultery; you shall not steal; you shall not bear false witness; you shall not defraud; honor your father and your mother." He replied and said to him, "Teacher, all of these I have observed from my youth." Jesus, looking at him, loved him and said to him, "You are lacking in one thing. Go, sell what you have, and give to the poor and you will have treasure in heaven; then come, follow me." At that statement his face fell, and he went away sad, for he had many possessions.

Jesus looked around and said to his disciples, "How hard it is for those who have wealth to enter the kingdom of God!" The disciples were amazed at his words. So Jesus again said to them in reply, "Children, how hard it is to enter the kingdom of God! It is easier for a camel to pass through the eye of a needle than for one who is rich to enter the kingdom of God." They were exceedingly astonished and said among themselves, "Then who can be saved?" Jesus looked at them and said, "For human beings it is impossible, but not for God. All things are possible for God."

OCTOBER 11TH, 2021
Monday of the Twenty-eighth Week in Ordinary Time

1ST Reading Rom 1:1-7

Paul, a slave of Christ Jesus, called to be an Apostle and set apart for the Gospel of God, which he promised previously through his prophets in the holy Scriptures, the Gospel about his Son, descended from David according to the flesh, but established as Son of God in power according to the Spirit of holiness through resurrection from the dead, Jesus Christ our Lord. Through him we have received the grace of apostleship, to bring about the obedience of faith, for the sake of his name, among all the Gentiles, among whom are you also, who are called to belong to Jesus Christ; to all the beloved of God in Rome, called to be holy. Grace to you and peace from God our Father and the Lord Jesus Christ.

Responsorial Psalm 98:1bcde, 2-3ab, 3cd-4
R. (2a) The Lord has made known his salvation.

Sing to the LORD a new song, for he has done wondrous deeds;

His right hand has won victory for him, his holy arm.

R. The Lord has made known his salvation.

The LORD has made his salvation known: in the sight of the nations he has revealed his justice.

He has remembered his kindness and his faithfulness toward the house of Israel.

R. The Lord has made known his salvation.

All the ends of the earth have seen the salvation by our God.

Sing joyfully to the LORD, all you lands; break into song; sing praise.

R. The Lord has made known his salvation.

Alleluia Ps 95:8

R. Alleluia, alleluia.

If today you hear his voice, harden not your hearts.

R. Alleluia, alleluia.

Gospel Lk 11:29-32
While still more people gathered in the crowd, Jesus said to them, "This generation is an evil generation; it seeks a sign, but no sign will be given it, except the sign of Jonah. Just as Jonah became a sign to the Ninevites, so will the Son of Man be to this generation. At the judgment the queen of the south will rise with the men of this generation and she will condemn them, because she came from the ends of the earth to hear the wisdom of Solomon, and there is something greater than Solomon here. At the judgment the men of Nineveh will arise with this generation and condemn it, because at the preaching of Jonah they repented, and there is something greater than Jonah here."

OCTOBER 12TH, 2021
Tuesday of the Twenty-eighth Week in Ordinary Time

1ST Reading Rom 1:16-25
Brothers and sisters:

I am not ashamed of the Gospel. It is the power of God for the salvation of everyone who believes: for Jew first, and then Greek. For in it is revealed the righteousness of God from faith to faith; as it is written, "The one who is righteous by faith will live." The wrath of God is indeed being revealed from heaven against every impiety and wickedness of those who suppress the truth by their wickedness. For what can be known about God is evident to them, because God made it evident to them. Ever since the creation of the world, his invisible attributes of eternal power and divinity have been able to be understood and perceived in what he has made. As a result, they have no excuse; for although they knew God they did not accord him glory as God or give him thanks. Instead, they became vain in their reasoning, and their senseless minds were darkened. While claiming to be wise, they became fools and exchanged the glory of the immortal God for the likeness of an image of mortal man or of birds or of four-legged animals or of snakes.

Therefore, God handed them over to impurity through the lusts of their hearts for the mutual degradation of their bodies. They exchanged the truth of God for a lie and revered and worshiped the creature rather than the creator, who is blessed forever. Amen.

Responsorial Psalm 19:2-3, 4-5
R. (2a) The heavens proclaim the glory of God.

The heavens declare the glory of God, and the firmament proclaims his handiwork.

Day pours out the word to day, and night to night imparts knowledge.

R. The heavens proclaim the glory of God.

Not a word nor a discourse whose voice is not heard;

Through all the earth their voice resounds, and to the ends of the world, their message.

R. The heavens proclaim the glory of God.

Alleluia Heb 4:12

R. Alleluia, alleluia.

The word of God is living and effective, able to discern reflections and thoughts of the heart.

R. Alleluia, alleluia.

Gospel Lk 11:37-41
After Jesus had spoken, a Pharisee invited him to dine at his home. He entered and reclined at table to eat. The Pharisee was amazed to see that he did not observe the prescribed washing before the meal. The Lord said to him, "Oh you Pharisees! Although you cleanse the outside of the cup and the dish, inside you are filled with plunder and evil. You fools! Did not the maker of the outside also make the inside? But as to what is within, give alms, and behold, everything will be clean for you."

OCTOBER 13TH, 2021
Wednesday of the Twenty-eighth Week in Ordinary Time

1ST Reading Rom 2:1-11
You, O man, are without excuse, every one of you who passes judgment. For by the standard by which you judge another you condemn yourself, since you, the judge, do the very same things.

We know that the judgment of God on those who do such things is true. Do you suppose, then, you who judge those who engage in such things and yet do them yourself, that you will escape the judgment of God? Or do you hold his priceless kindness, forbearance, and patience in low esteem, unaware that the kindness of God would lead you to repentance? By your stubbornness and impenitent heart, you are storing up wrath for yourself for the day of wrath and revelation of the just judgment of God, who will repay everyone according to his works, eternal life to those who seek glory, honor, and immortality through perseverance in good works, but wrath and fury to those who selfishly disobey the truth and obey wickedness. Yes, affliction and distress will come upon everyone who does evil, Jew first and then Greek. But there will be glory, honor, and peace for everyone who does good, Jew first and then Greek. There is no partiality with God.

Responsorial Psalm 62:2-3, 6-7, 9

R. (13b) Lord, you give back to everyone according to his works.

Only in God is my soul at rest; from him comes my salvation.

He only is my rock and my salvation, my stronghold; I shall not be disturbed at all.

R. Lord, you give back to everyone according to his works.

Only in God be at rest, my soul, for from him comes my hope.

He only is my rock and my salvation, my stronghold; I shall not be disturbed.

R. Lord, you give back to everyone according to his works.

Trust in him at all times, O my people! Pour out your hearts before him;

God is our refuge!

R. Lord, you give back to everyone according to his works.

Alleluia Jn 10:27

R. Alleluia, alleluia.

My sheep hear my voice, says the Lord; I know them, and they follow me.

R. Alleluia, alleluia.

The Lord said:

"Woe to you Pharisees! You pay tithes of mint and of rue and of every garden herb, but you pay no attention to judgment and to love for God. These you should have done, without overlooking the others. Woe to you Pharisees! You love the seat of honor in synagogues and greetings in marketplaces. Woe to you! You are like unseen graves over which people unknowingly walk." Then one of the scholars of the law said to him in reply, "Teacher, by saying this you are insulting us too." And he said, "Woe also to you scholars of the law! You impose on people burdens hard to carry, but you yourselves do not lift one finger to touch them."

OCTOBER 14TH, 2021
Thursday of the Twenty-eighth Week in Ordinary Time

1ST Reading Rom 3:21-30a
Brothers and sisters:

Now the righteousness of God has been manifested apart from the law, though testified to by the law and the prophets, the righteousness of God through faith in Jesus Christ for all who believe. For there is no distinction; all have sinned and are deprived of the glory of God.

They are justified freely by his grace through the redemption in Christ Jesus, whom God set forth as an expiation, through faith, by his Blood, to prove his righteousness because of the forgiveness of sins previously committed, through the forbearance of God– to prove his righteousness in the present time, that he might be righteous and justify the one who has faith in Jesus.

What occasion is there then for boasting? It is ruled out. On what principle, that of works? No, rather on the principle of faith. For we consider that a person is justified by faith apart from works of the law. Does God belong to Jews alone? Does he not belong to Gentiles, too? Yes, also to Gentiles, for God is one and will justify the circumcised on the basis of faith and the uncircumcised through faith.

Responsorial Psalm 130:1b-2, 3-4, 5-6ab
R. (7) With the Lord there is mercy, and fullness of redemption.

Out of the depths I cry to you, O LORD;

LORD, hear my voice!

Let your ears be attentive to my voice in supplication.

R. With the Lord there is mercy, and fullness of redemption.

If you, O LORD, mark iniquities, Lord, who can stand?

But with you is forgiveness, that you may be revered.

R. With the Lord there is mercy, and fullness of redemption.

I trust in the LORD; my soul trusts in his word.

My soul waits for the LORD more than sentinels wait for the dawn.

R. With the Lord there is mercy, and fullness of redemption.

Alleluia Jn 14:6

R. Alleluia, alleluia.

I am the way and the truth and the life, says the Lord; no one comes to the Father except through me.

R. Alleluia, alleluia.

Gospel Lk 11:47-54
The Lord said:

"Woe to you who build the memorials of the prophets whom your fathers killed. Consequently, you bear witness and give consent to the deeds of your ancestors, for they killed them and you do the building. Therefore, the wisdom of God said, 'I will send to them prophets and Apostles; some of them they will kill and persecute' in order that this generation might be charged with the blood of all the prophets shed since the foundation of the world, from the blood of Abel to the blood of Zechariah who died between the altar and the temple building. Yes, I tell you, this generation will be charged with their blood! Woe to you, scholars of the law!

You have taken away the key of knowledge. You yourselves did not enter and you stopped those trying to enter." When Jesus left, the scribes and Pharisees began to act with hostility toward him and to interrogate him about many things, for they were plotting to catch him at something he might say.

OCTOBER 15TH, 2021
Memorial of Saint Teresa of Jesus, Virgin and Doctor of the Church

1ST Reading Rom 4:1-8

Brothers and sisters: Feast of Saint Luke, evangelist what can we say that Abraham found, our ancestor according to the flesh? Indeed, if Abraham was justified on the basis of his works, he has reason to boast; but this was not so in the sight of God. For what does the Scripture say? Abraham believed God, and it was credited to him as righteousness.

A worker's wage is credited not as a gift, but as something due. But when one does not work, yet believes in the one who justifies the ungodly, his faith is credited as righteousness. So also David declares the blessedness of the person to whom God credits righteousness apart from works: Blessed are they whose iniquities are forgiven and whose sins are covered. Blessed is the man whose sin the Lord does not record.

Responsorial Psalm 32:1b-2, 5, 11

R. (see 7) I turn to you, Lord, in time of trouble, and you fill me with the joy of salvation.

Blessed is he whose fault is taken away, whose sin is covered.

Blessed the man to whom the LORD imputes not guilt, in whose spirit there is no guile.

R. I turn to you, Lord, in time of trouble, and you fill me with the joy of salvation.

Then I acknowledged my sin to you, my guilt I covered not.

I said, "I confess my faults to the LORD," and you took away the guilt of my sin.

R. I turn to you, Lord, in time of trouble, and you fill me with the joy of salvation.

Be glad in the LORD and rejoice, you just; exult, all you upright of heart.

R. I turn to you, Lord, in time of trouble, and you fill me with the joy of salvation.

Alleluia Ps 33:22

R. Alleluia, alleluia.

May your kindness, O LORD, be upon us; who have put our hope in you.

R. Alleluia, alleluia.

Gospel Lk 12:1-7
At that time: So many people were crowding together that they were trampling one another underfoot. Jesus began to speak, first to his disciples, "Beware of the leaven—that is, the hypocrisy—of the Pharisees. "There is nothing concealed that will not be revealed, nor secret that will not be known. Therefore whatever you have said in the darkness will be heard in the light, and what you have whispered behind closed doors will be proclaimed on the housetops.

I tell you, my friends, do not be afraid of those who kill the body but after that can do no more. I shall show you whom to fear. Be afraid of the one who after killing has the power to cast into Gehenna; yes, I tell you, be afraid of that one. Are not five sparrows sold for two small coins? Yet not one of them has escaped the notice of God. Even the hairs of your head have all been counted. Do not be afraid. You are worth more than many sparrows."

OCTOBER 16TH, 2021
Saturday of the Twenty-eighth Week in Ordinary Time

1ST Reading Rom 4:13, 16-18
Brothers and sisters:

It was not through the law that the promise was made to Abraham and his descendants that he would inherit the world, but through the righteousness that comes from faith. For this reason, it depends on faith, so that it may be a gift, and the promise may be guaranteed to all his descendants, not to those who only adhere to the law but to those who follow the faith of Abraham, who is the father of all of us, as it is written, I have made you father of many nations. He is our father in the sight of God, in whom he believed, who gives life to the dead and calls into being what does not exist. He believed, hoping against hope, that he would become the father of many nations, according to what was said, Thus shall your descendants be.

Responsorial Psalm 105:6-7, 8-9, 42-43
R. (8a) The Lord remembers his covenant for ever.

You descendants of Abraham, his servants, sons of Jacob, his chosen ones!

He, the LORD, is our God; throughout the earth his judgments prevail.

R. The Lord remembers his covenant for ever.

He remembers forever his covenant which he made binding for a thousand generations –

Which he entered into with Abraham and by his oath to Isaac.

R. The Lord remembers his covenant for ever.

For he remembered his holy word to his servant Abraham.

And he led forth his people with joy; with shouts of joy, his chosen ones.

R. The Lord remembers his covenant for ever.

Alleluia Jn 15:26b, 27a

R. Alleluia, alleluia.

The Spirit of truth will testify to me, says the Lord, and you also will testify.

R. Alleluia, alleluia.

Gospel Lk 12:8-12
Jesus said to his disciples:

"I tell you, everyone who acknowledges me before others the Son of Man will acknowledge before the angels of God. But whoever denies me before others will be denied before the angels of God. "Everyone who speaks a word against the Son of Man will be forgiven, but the one who blasphemes against the Holy Spirit will not be forgiven. When they take you before synagogues and before rulers and authorities, do not worry about how or what your defense will be or about what you are to say. For the Holy Spirit will teach you at that moment what you should say."

OCTOBER 17TH, 2021
Twenty-ninth Sunday in Ordinary Time

The LORD was pleased to crush him in infirmity. If he gives his life as an offering for sin, he shall see his descendants in a long life, and the will of the LORD shall be accomplished through him. Because of his affliction he shall see the light in fullness of days; through his suffering, my servant shall justify many, and their guilt he shall bear.

Responsorial Psalm Ps 33:4-5, 18-19, 20, 22

R. (22) Lord, let your mercy be on us, as we place our trust in you.

Upright is the word of the LORD, and all his works are trustworthy.

He loves justice and right; of the kindness of the LORD the earth is full.

R. Lord, let your mercy be on us, as we place our trust in you.

See, the eyes of the LORD are upon those who fear him, upon those who hope for his kindness,

To deliver them from death and preserve them in spite of famine.

R. Lord, let your mercy be on us, as we place our trust in you.

Our soul waits for the LORD, who is our help and our shield.

May your kindness, O LORD, be upon us who have put our hope in you.

R. Lord, let your mercy be on us, as we place our trust in you.

2ND Reading Heb 4:14-16

Brothers and sisters:

Since we have a great high priest who has passed through the heavens, Jesus, the Son of God, let us hold fast to our confession. For we do not have a high priest who is unable to sympathize with our weaknesses, but one who has similarly been tested in every way, yet without sin. So let us confidently approach the throne of grace to receive mercy and to find grace for timely help.

Alleluia Mk 10:45

R. Alleluia, alleluia.

The Son of Man came to serve and to give his life as a ransom for many.

R. Alleluia, alleluia.

Gospel Mk 10:35-45 or 10:42-45
James and John, the sons of Zebedee, came to Jesus and said to him,
"Teacher, we want you to do for us whatever we ask of you." He replied,
"What do you wish me to do for you?" They answered him, "Grant that in
your glory we may sit one at your right and the other at your left." Jesus said
to them, "You do not know what you are asking. Can you drink the cup that
I drink or be baptized with the baptism with which I am baptized?"

They said to him, "We can." Jesus said to them, "The cup that I drink, you
will drink, and with the baptism with which I am baptized, you will be
baptized; but to sit at my right or at my left is not mine to give but is for
those for whom it has been prepared." When the ten heard this, they
became indignant at James and John. Jesus summoned them and said to
them, "You know that those who are recognized as rulers over the Gentiles
lord it over them, and their great ones make their authority over them felt.
But it shall not be so among you. Rather, whoever wishes to be great among
you will be your servant; whoever wishes to be first among you will be the
slave of all. For the Son of Man did not come to be served but to serve and
to give his life as a ransom for many."

OR:

Jesus summoned the twelve and said to them, "You know that those who are
recognized as rulers over the Gentiles lord it over them, and their great ones
make their authority over them felt. But it shall not be so among you.
Rather, whoever wishes to be great among you will be your servant; whoever
wishes to be first among you will be the slave of all. For the Son of Man did
not come to be served but to serve and to give his life as a ransom for
many."

OCTOBER 18TH, 2021
Feast of Saint Luke, evangelist

1ST Reading 2 Tm 4:10-17b
Beloved:

Demas, enamored of the present world, deserted me and went to
Thessalonica, Crescens to Galatia, and Titus to Dalmatia. Luke is the only
one with me. Get Mark and bring him with you, for he is helpful to me in the

ministry. I have sent Tychicus to Ephesus. When you come, bring the cloak I left with Carpus in Troas, the papyrus rolls, and especially the parchments. Alexander the coppersmith did me a great deal of harm; the Lord will repay him according to his deeds. You too be on guard against him, for he has strongly resisted our preaching. At my first defense no one appeared on my behalf, but everyone deserted me. May it not be held against them! But the Lord stood by me and gave me strength, so that through me the proclamation might be completed and all the Gentiles might hear it.

Responsorial Psalm 145:10-11, 12-13, 17-18
R. (12) Your friends make known, O Lord, the glorious splendor of your Kingdom.

Let all your works give you thanks, O LORD, and let your faithful ones bless you.

Let them discourse of the glory of your Kingdom and speak of your might.

R. Your friends make known, O Lord, the glorious splendor of your Kingdom.

Making known to men your might and the glorious splendor of your Kingdom.

Your Kingdom is a Kingdom for all ages, and your dominion endures through all generations.

R. Your friends make known, O Lord, the glorious splendor of your Kingdom.

The LORD is just in all his ways and holy in all his works.

The LORD is near to all who call upon him, to all who call upon him in truth.

R. Your friends make known, O Lord, the glorious splendor of your Kingdom.

Alleluia Jn 15:16

R. Alleluia, alleluia.

I chose you from the world, to go and bear fruit that will last, says the Lord.

R. Alleluia, alleluia.

Gospel Lk 10:1-9

The Lord Jesus appointed seventy-two disciples whom he sent ahead of him in pairs to every town and place he intended to visit. He said to them, "The harvest is abundant but the laborers are few; so ask the master of the harvest to send out laborers for his harvest. Go on your way; behold, I am sending you like lambs among wolves. Carry no money bag, no sack, no sandals; and greet no one along the way. Into whatever house you enter, first say, 'Peace to this household.' If a peaceful person lives there, your peace will rest on him; but if not, it will return to you. Stay in the same house and eat and drink what is offered to you, for the laborer deserves payment. Do not move about from one house to another. Whatever town you enter and they welcome you, eat what is set before you, cure the sick in it and say to them, 'The Kingdom of God is at hand for you.'"

OCTOBER 19TH, 2021
Memorial of Saints John de Brébeuf and Isaac Jogues, Priests, and Companions, Martyrs

1ST Reading Rom 5:12, 15b, 17-19, 20b-21
Brothers and sisters:

Through one man sin entered the world, and through sin, death, and thus death came to all men, inasmuch as all sinned. If by that one person's transgression the many died, how much more did the grace of God and the gracious gift of the one man Jesus Christ overflow for the many. For if, by the transgression of the one, death came to reign through that one, how much more will those who receive the abundance of grace and the gift of justification come to reign in life through the one Jesus Christ. In conclusion, just as through one transgression condemnation came upon all, so, through one righteous act acquittal and life came to all. For just as through the disobedience of one man the many were made sinners, so, through the obedience of the one the many will be made righteous. Where sin increased, grace overflowed all the more, so that, as sin reigned in death, grace also might reign through justification for eternal life through Jesus Christ our Lord.

Responsorial Psalm 40:7-8a, 8b-9, 10, 17
R (8a and 9a) Here I am, Lord; I come to do your will.

Sacrifice or oblation you wished not, but ears open to obedience you gave me.

Burnt offerings or sin offerings you sought not; then said I, "Behold I come."

R. Here I am, Lord; I come to do your will.

"In the written scroll it is prescribed for me,

To do your will, O my God, is my delight, and your law is within my heart!"

R. Here I am, Lord; I come to do your will.

I announced your justice in the vast assembly; I did not restrain my lips, as you, O LORD, know.

R. Here I am, Lord; I come to do your will.

May all who seek you exult and be glad in you,

And may those who love your salvation say ever, "The LORD be glorified."

R. Here I am, Lord; I come to do your will.

Alleluia Lk 21:36

R. Alleluia, alleluia.

Be vigilant at all times and pray that you may have the strength to stand before the Son of Man.

R. Alleluia, alleluia.

Gospel Lk 12:35-38
Jesus said to his disciples:

"Gird your loins and light your lamps and be like servants who await their master's return from a wedding, ready to open immediately when he comes and knocks. Blessed are those servants whom the master finds vigilant on his arrival. Amen, I say to you, he will gird himself, have them recline at table, and proceed to wait on them. And should he come in the second or third watch and find them prepared in this way, blessed are those servants."

OCTOBER 20TH, 2021
Wednesday of the Twenty-ninth Week in Ordinary Time

1ST Reading Rom 6:12-18
Brothers and sisters:

Sin must not reign over your mortal bodies so that you obey their desires.
And do not present the parts of your bodies to sin as weapons for
wickedness, but present yourselves to God as raised from the dead to life
and the parts of your bodies to God as weapons for righteousness. For sin is
not to have any power over you, since you are not under the law but under
grace. What then? Shall we sin because we are not under the law but under
grace? Of course not! Do you not know that if you present yourselves to
someone as obedient slaves, you are slaves of the one you obey, either of sin,
which leads to death, or of obedience, which leads to righteousness? But
thanks be to God that, although you were once slaves of sin, you have
become obedient from the heart to the pattern of teaching to which you
were entrusted. Freed from sin, you have become slaves of righteousness.

Responsorial Psalm 124:1b-3, 4-6, 7-8
R. (8a) Our help is in the name of the Lord.

Had not the LORD been with us, let Israel say, had not the LORD been
with us–

When men rose up against us, then would they have swallowed us alive;

When their fury was inflamed against us.

R. Our help is in the name of the Lord.

Then would the waters have overwhelmed us;

The torrent would have swept over us; over us then would have swept the
raging waters.

Blessed be the LORD, who did not leave us a prey to their teeth.

R. Our help is in the name of the Lord.

We were rescued like a bird from the fowlers' snare;

Broken was the snare, and we were freed.

Our help is in the name of the LORD, who made heaven and earth.

R. Our help is in the name of the Lord.

Alleluia Mt 24:42a, 44

R. Alleluia, alleluia.

Stay awake! For you do not know when the Son of Man will come.

R. Alleluia, alleluia.

Gospel Lk 12:39-48
Jesus said to his disciples:

"Be sure of this: if the master of the house had known the hour when the thief was coming, he would not have let his house be broken into. You also must be prepared, for at an hour you do not expect, the Son of Man will come." Then Peter said, "Lord, is this parable meant for us or for everyone?" And the Lord replied, "Who, then, is the faithful and prudent steward whom the master will put in charge of his servants to distribute the food allowance at the proper time? Blessed is that servant whom his master on arrival finds doing so. Truly, I say to you, he will put him in charge of all his property. But if that servant says to himself, 'My master is delayed in coming,' and begins to beat the menservants and the maidservants, to eat and drink and get drunk, then that servant's master will come on an unexpected day and at an unknown hour and will punish the servant severely and assign him a place with the unfaithful. That servant who knew his master's will but did not make preparations nor act in accord with his will shall be beaten severely; and the servant who was ignorant of his master's will but acted in a way deserving of a severe beating shall be beaten only lightly. Much will be required of the person entrusted with much, and still more will be demanded of the person entrusted with more."

OCTOBER 21ST, 2021
Thursday of the Twenty-ninth Week in Ordinary Time

1ST Reading Rom 6:19-23
Brothers and sisters:

I am speaking in human terms because of the weakness of your nature. For just as you presented the parts of your bodies as slaves to impurity and to lawlessness for lawlessness, so now present them as slaves to righteousness for sanctification. For when you were slaves of sin, you were free from righteousness. But what profit did you get then from the things of which you are now ashamed? For the end of those things is death. But now that you have been freed from sin and have become slaves of God, the benefit that you have leads to sanctification, and its end is eternal life. For the wages of sin is death, but the gift of God is eternal life in Christ Jesus our Lord.

Responsorial Psalm 1:1-2, 3, 4 and 6
R. (Ps 40:5) Blessed are they who hope in the Lord.

Blessed the man who follows not the counsel of the wicked

Nor walks in the way of sinners, nor sits in the company of the insolent,

But delights in the law of the LORD and meditates on his law day and night.

R. Blessed are they who hope in the Lord.

He is like a tree planted near running water,

That yields its fruit in due season, and whose leaves never fade.

Whatever he does, prospers.

R. Blessed are they who hope in the Lord.

Not so the wicked, not so; they are like chaff which the wind drives away.

For the LORD watches over the way of the just, but the way of the wicked vanishes.

R. Blessed are they who hope in the Lord.

Alleluia Phil 3:8-9

R. Alleluia, alleluia.

I consider all things so much rubbish that I may gain Christ and be found in him.

R. Alleluia, alleluia.

Jesus said to his disciples:

"I have come to set the earth on fire, and how I wish it were already blazing! There is a baptism with which I must be baptized, and how great is my anguish until it is accomplished! Do you think that I have come to establish peace on the earth? No, I tell you, but rather division. From now on a household of five will be divided, three against two and two against three; a father will be divided against his son and a son against his father, a mother against her daughter and a daughter against her mother, a mother-in-law against her daughter-in-law and a daughter-in-law against her mother-in-law."

OCTOBER 22ND, 2021
Friday of the Twenty-ninth Week in Ordinary Time

1ST Reading Rom 7:18-25a
Brothers and sisters:

I know that good does not dwell in me, that is, in my flesh. The willing is ready at hand, but doing the good is not. For I do not do the good I want, but I do the evil I do not want. Now if I do what I do not want, it is no longer I who do it, but sin that dwells in me. So, then, I discover the principle that when I want to do right, evil is at hand. For I take delight in the law of God, in my inner self, but I see in my members another principle at war with the law of my mind, taking me captive to the law of sin that dwells in my members. Miserable one that I am! Who will deliver me from this mortal body? Thanks be to God through Jesus Christ our Lord.

Responsorial Psalm 119:66, 68, 76, 77, 93, 94
R. (68b) Lord, teach me your statutes.

Teach me wisdom and knowledge, for in your commands I trust.

R. Lord, teach me your statutes.

You are good and bountiful; teach me your statutes.

R. Lord, teach me your statutes.

Let your kindness comfort me according to your promise to your servants.

R. Lord, teach me your statutes.

Let your compassion come to me that I may live, for your law is my delight.

R. Lord, teach me your statutes.

Never will I forget your precepts, for through them you give me life.

R. Lord, teach me your statutes.

I am yours; save me, for I have sought your precepts.

R. Lord, teach me your statutes.

Alleluia Mt 11:25

R. Alleluia, alleluia.

Blessed are you, Father, Lord of heaven and earth; you have revealed to little ones the mysteries of the Kingdom.

R. Alleluia, alleluia.

Gospel Lk 12:54-59

Jesus said to the crowds, "When you see a cloud rising in the west you say immediately that it is going to rain—and so it does; and when you notice that the wind is blowing from the south you say that it is going to be hot—and so it is. You hypocrites! You know how to interpret the appearance of the earth and the sky; why do you not know how to interpret the present time?

Why do you not judge for yourselves what is right? If you are to go with your opponent before a magistrate, make an effort to settle the matter on the way; otherwise your opponent will turn you over to the judge, and the judge hand you over to the constable, and the constable throw you into prison. I say to you, you will not be released until you have paid the last penny."

OCTOBER 23RD, 2021
Saturday of the Twenty-ninth Week in Ordinary Time

1ST Reading Rom 8:1-11October 24, 2021

Brothers and sisters:

Now there is no condemnation for those who are in Christ Jesus. For the law of the spirit of life in Christ Jesus has freed you from the law of sin and death. For what the law, weakened by the flesh, was powerless to do, this God has done: by sending his own Son in the likeness of sinful flesh and for the sake of sin, he condemned sin in the flesh, so that the righteous decree of the law might be fulfilled in us, who live not according to the flesh but according to the spirit. For those who live according to the flesh are concerned with the things of the flesh, but those who live according to the spirit with the things of the spirit.

The concern of the flesh is death, but the concern of the spirit is life and peace. For the concern of the flesh is hostility toward God; it does not submit to the law of God, nor can it; and those who are in the flesh cannot please God. But you are not in the flesh; on the contrary, you are in the spirit, if only the Spirit of God dwells in you. Whoever does not have the Spirit of Christ does not belong to him. But if Christ is in you, although the body is dead because of sin, the spirit is alive because of righteousness. If the Spirit of the one who raised Jesus from the dead dwells in you, the one who raised Christ from the dead will give life to your mortal bodies also, through his Spirit that dwells in you.

Responsorial Psalm 24:1b-2, 3-4ab, 5-6
R. (see 6) Lord, this is the people that longs to see your face.

The LORD's are the earth and its fullness; the world and those who dwell in it.

For he founded it upon the seas and established it upon the rivers.

R. Lord, this is the people that longs to see your face.

Who can ascend the mountain of the LORD? or who may stand in his holy place?

He whose hands are sinless, whose heart is clean, who desires not what is vain.

R. Lord, this is the people that longs to see your face.

He shall receive a blessing from the LORD, a reward from God his savior.

Such is the race that seeks for him, that seeks the face of the God of Jacob.

R. Lord, this is the people that longs to see your face.

Alleluia Ez 33:11

R. Alleluia, alleluia.

I take no pleasure in the death of the wicked man, says the Lord, but rather in his conversion that he may live.

R. Alleluia, alleluia.

Gospel Lk 13:1-9

Some people told Jesus about the Galileans whose blood Pilate had mingled with the blood of their sacrifices. He said to them in reply, "Do you think that because these Galileans suffered in this way they were greater sinners than all other Galileans? By no means! But I tell you, if you do not repent, you will all perish as they did! Or those eighteen people who were killed when the tower at Siloam fell on them—do you think they were more guilty than everyone else who lived in Jerusalem? By no means! But I tell you, if you do not repent, you will all perish as they did!" And he told them this parable: "There once was a person who had a fig tree planted in his orchard, and when he came in search of fruit on it but found none, he said to the gardener, 'For three years now I have come in search of fruit on this fig tree but have found none. So cut it down. Why should it exhaust the soil?' He said to him in reply, 'Sir, leave it for this year also, and I shall cultivate the ground around it and fertilize it; it may bear fruit in the future. If not you can cut it down.'"

OCTOBER 24TH, 2021
Thirtieth Sunday in Ordinary Time

1ST Reading Jer 31:7-9

Thus says the LORD:

Shout with joy for Jacob, exult at the head of the nations; proclaim your praise and say: The LORD has delivered his people, the remnant of Israel. Behold, I will bring them back from the land of the north; I will gather them from the ends of the world, with the blind and the lame in their midst, the mothers and those with child; they shall return as an immense throng.

They departed in tears, but I will console them and guide them; I will lead them to brooks of water, on a level road, so that none shall stumble. For I am a father to Israel,

Ephraim is my first-born.

Responsorial Psalm Ps 126:1-2, 2-3, 4-5, 6
R. (3)   The Lord has done great things for us; we are filled with joy.

When the LORD brought back the captives of Zion, we were like men dreaming.

Then our mouth was filled with laughter, and our tongue with rejoicing.

R. The Lord has done great things for us; we are filled with joy.

Then they said among the nations, "The LORD has done great things for them."

The LORD has done great things for us; we are glad indeed.

R. The Lord has done great things for us; we are filled with joy.

Restore our fortunes, O LORD, like the torrents in the southern desert.

Those that sow in tears shall reap rejoicing.

R. The Lord has done great things for us; we are filled with joy.

Although they go forth weeping, carrying the seed to be sown,

They shall come back rejoicing, carrying their sheaves.

R. The Lord has done great things for us; we are filled with joy.

2ND Reading Heb 5:1-6
Brothers and sisters: Every high priest is taken from among men and made their representative before God, to offer gifts and sacrifices for sins. He is able to deal patiently with the ignorant and erring, for he himself is beset by weakness and so, for this reason, must make sin offerings for himself as well as for the people. No one takes this honor upon himself but only when called by God, just as Aaron was. In the same way, it was not Christ who glorified himself in becoming high priest, but rather the one who said to him:

You are my son: this day I have begotten you; just as he says in another place: You are a priest forever according to the order of Melchizedek.

Alleluia Cf. 2 Tm 1:10

R. Alleluia, alleluia.

Our Savior Jesus Christ destroyed death and brought life to light through the Gospel.

R. Alleluia, alleluia.

Gospel Mk 10:46-52
As Jesus was leaving Jericho with his disciples and a sizable crowd, Bartimaeus, a blind man, the son of Timaeus, sat by the roadside begging. On hearing that it was Jesus of Nazareth, he began to cry out and say, "Jesus, son of David, have pity on me." And many rebuked him, telling him to be silent. But he kept calling out all the more, "Son of David, have pity on me." Jesus stopped and said, "Call him. "So they called the blind man, saying to him, "Take courage; get up, Jesus is calling you. "He threw aside his cloak, sprang up, and came to Jesus. Jesus said to him in reply, "What do you want me to do for you?" The blind man replied to him, "Master, I want to see." Jesus told him, "Go your way; your faith has saved you." Immediately he received his sight and followed him on the way.

OCTOBER 25TH, 2021
Monday of the Thirtieth Week in Ordinary Time

1ST Reading Rom 8:12-17
Brothers and sisters, we are not debtors to the flesh, to live according to the flesh. For if you live according to the flesh, you will die, but if by the spirit you put to death the deeds of the body,

you will live. For those who are led by the Spirit of God are sons of God. For you did not receive a spirit of slavery to fall back into fear, but you received a spirit of adoption, through which we cry, "Abba, Father!" The Spirit himself bears witness with our spirit that we are children of God, and if children, then heirs, heirs of God and joint heirs with Christ, if only we suffer with him so that we may also be glorified with him.

R (21a) Our God is the God of salvation.

God arises; his enemies are scattered, and those who hate him flee before him.

But the just rejoice and exult before God; they are glad and rejoice.

R. Our God is the God of salvation.

The father of orphans and the defender of widow is God in his holy dwelling.

God gives a home to the forsaken; he leads forth prisoners to prosperity.

R. Our God is the God of salvation.

Blessed day by day be the Lord, who bears our burdens; God, who is our salvation.

God is a saving God for us; the LORD, my Lord, controls the passageways of death.

R. Our God is the God of salvation.

Alleluia Jn 17:17b, 17a

R. Alleluia, alleluia.

Your word, O Lord, is truth; consecrate us in the truth.

R. Alleluia, alleluia.

Gospel Lk 13:10-17

Jesus was teaching in a synagogue on the Sabbath. And a woman was there who for eighteen years had been crippled by a spirit; she was bent over, completely incapable of standing erect. When Jesus saw her, he called to her and said, "Woman, you are set free of your infirmity." He laid his hands on her, and she at once stood up straight and glorified God. But the leader of the synagogue, indignant that Jesus had cured on the Sabbath, said to the crowd in reply, "There are six days when work should be done. Come on those days to be cured, not on the Sabbath day." The Lord said to him in reply, "Hypocrites! Does not each one of you on the Sabbath untie his ox or his ass from the manger and lead it out for watering? This daughter of

Abraham, whom Satan has bound for eighteen years now, ought she not to have been set free on the sabbath day from this bondage?" When he said this, all his adversaries were humiliated; and the whole crowd rejoiced at all the splendid deeds done by him.

OCTOBER 26TH, 2021
Tuesday of the Thirtieth Week in Ordinary Time

1ST Reading Rom 8:18-25

Brothers and sisters:

I consider that the sufferings of this present time are as nothing compared with the glory to be revealed for us. For creation awaits with eager expectation the revelation of the children of God; for creation was made subject to futility, not of its own accord but because of the one who subjected it, in hope that creation itself would be set free from slavery to corruption and share in the glorious freedom of the children of God.

We know that all creation is groaning in labor pains even until now; and not only that, but we ourselves, who have the first fruits of the Spirit, we also groan within ourselves as we wait for adoption, the redemption of our bodies. For in hope we were saved. Now hope that sees for itself is not hope. For who hopes for what one sees? But if we hope for what we do not see, we wait with endurance.

Responsorial Psalm126:1b-2ab, 2cd-3, 4-5, 6

R. 3a) The Lord has done marvels for us.

When the LORD brought back the captives of Zion, we were like men dreaming.

Then our mouth was filled with laughter, and our tongue with rejoicing.

R. The Lord has done marvels for us.

Then they said among the nations, "The LORD has done great things for them."

The LORD has done great things for us; we are glad indeed.

R. The Lord has done marvels for us.

Restore our fortunes, O LORD, like the torrents in the southern desert.

Those that sow in tears shall reap rejoicing.

R. The Lord has done marvels for us.

Although they go forth weeping, carrying the seed to be sown,

They shall come back rejoicing, carrying their sheaves.

R. The Lord has done marvels for us.

Alleluia Mt 11:25

R. Alleluia, alleluia.

Blessed are you, Father, Lord of heaven and earth; you have revealed to little ones the mysteries of the Kingdom.

R. Alleluia, alleluia.

Gospel Lk 13:18-21
Jesus said, "What is the Kingdom of God like? To what can I compare it? It is like a mustard seed that a man took and planted in the garden. When it was fully grown, it became a large bush and the birds of the sky dwelt in its branches." Again he said, "To what shall I compare the Kingdom of God? It is like yeast that a woman took and mixed in with three measures of wheat flour until the whole batch of dough was leavened."

OCTOBER 27TH, 2021
Wednesday of the Thirtieth Week in Ordinary Time

1ST Reading Rom 8:26-30
Brothers and sisters:

The Spirit comes to the aid of our weakness; for we do not know how to pray as we ought, but the Spirit himself intercedes with inexpressible groanings. And the one who searches hearts knows what is the intention of the Spirit, because he intercedes for the holy ones according to God's will. We know that all things work for good for those who love God, who are called according to his purpose. For those he foreknew he also predestined to be conformed to the image of his Son, so that he might be the firstborn among many brothers. And those he predestined he also called; and those he called he also justified; and those he justified he also glorified.

Responsorial Psalm13:4-5, 6
R. (6a) My hope, O Lord, is in your mercy.

Look, answer me, O LORD, my God!

Give light to my eyes that I may not sleep in death lest my enemy say,

"I have overcome him"; lest my foes rejoice at my downfall.

R. My hope, O Lord, is in your mercy.

Though I trusted in your mercy,

Let my heart rejoice in your salvation; let me sing of the LORD, "He has been good to me."

R. My hope, O Lord, is in your mercy.

Alleluia 2 Thes 2:14

R. Alleluia, alleluia.

God has called us through the Gospel to possess the glory of our Lord Jesus Christ.

R. Alleluia, alleluia.

Gospel Lk 13:22-30
Jesus passed through towns and villages, teaching as he went and making his way to Jerusalem. Someone asked him, "Lord, will only a few people be saved?" He answered them, "Strive to enter through the narrow gate, for many, I tell you, will attempt to enter but will not be strong enough. After the master of the house has arisen and locked the door, then will you stand outside knocking and saying, 'Lord, open the door for us.' He will say to you in reply, 'I do not know where you are from.' And you will say, 'We ate and drank in your company and you taught in our streets.' Then he will say to you, 'I do not know where you are from. Depart from me, all you evildoers!' And there will be wailing and grinding of teeth when you see Abraham, Isaac, and Jacob and all the prophets in the Kingdom of God and you yourselves cast out. And people will come from the east and the we stand

from the north and the south and will recline at table in the Kingdom of God. For behold, some are last who will be first, and some are first who will be last."

October 28TH, 2021
Feast of Saints Simon and Jude, Apostles

First Reading Eph 2:19-22
Brothers and sisters:

You are no longer strangers and sojourners, but you are fellow citizens with the holy one sand members of the household of God, built upon the foundation of the Apostles and prophets, with Christ Jesus himself as the capstone. Through him the whole structure is held together and grows into a temple sacred in the Lord; in him you also are being built together into a dwelling place of God in the Spirit.

Responsorial Psalm19:2-3, 4-5
R. (5a) Their message goes out through all the earth.

The heavens declare the glory of God, and the firmament proclaims his handiwork.

Day pours out the word to day, and night to night imparts knowledge.

R. Their message goes out through all the earth.

Not a word nor a discourse whose voice is not heard;

Through all the earth their voice resounds, and to the ends of the world, their message.

R. Their message goes out through all the earth.

Alleluia

R. Alleluia, alleluia.

We praise you, O God, we acclaim you as Lord; the glorious company of Apostles praise you.

R. Alleluia, alleluia.

Gospel Lk 6:12-16

Jesus went up to the mountain to pray, and he spent the night in prayer to God. When day came, he called his disciples to himself, and from them he chose Twelve, whom he also named Apostles: Simon, whom he named Peter, and his brother Andrew, James, John, Philip, Bartholomew, Matthew, Thomas, James the son of Alphaeus, Simon who was called a Zealot, and Judas the son of James, and Judas Iscariot, who became a traitor.

OCTOBER 29TH, 2021
Friday of the Thirtieth Week in Ordinary Time

1ST Reading Rom 9:1-5
Brothers and sisters:

I speak the truth in Christ, I do not lie; my conscience joins with the Holy Spirit in bearing me witness that I have great sorrow and constant anguish in my heart. For I could wish that I myself were accursed and cut off from Christ for the sake of my own people, my kindred according to the flesh. They are children of Israel; theirs the adoption, the glory, the covenants, the giving of the law, the worship, and the promises; theirs the patriarchs, and from them, according to the flesh, is the Christ, who is over all, God blessed forever. Amen.

Responsorial Psalm147:12-13, 14-15, 19-20
R. Praise the Lord, Jerusalem.

Glorify the LORD, O Jerusalem; praise your God, O Zion.

For he has strengthened the bars of your gates; he has blessed your children within you.

R. Praise the Lord, Jerusalem.

He has granted peace in your borders; with the best of wheat he fills you.

He sends forth his command to the earth; swiftly runs his word!

R. Praise the Lord, Jerusalem.

He has proclaimed his word to Jacob, his statutes and his ordinances to Israel.

He has not done thus for any other nation; his ordinances he has not made known to them. Alleluia.

R. Praise the Lord, Jerusalem.

Alleluia Jn 10:27

R. Alleluia, alleluia.

My sheep hear my voice, says the Lord; I know them, and they follow me.

R. Alleluia, alleluia.

Gospel Lk 14:1-6

On a sabbath Jesus went to dine at the home of one of the leading Pharisees, and the people there were observing him carefully. In front of him there was a man suffering from dropsy. Jesus spoke to the scholars of the law and Pharisees in reply, asking, "Is it lawful to cure on the sabbath or not?" But they kept silent; so he took the man and, after he had healed him, dismissed him.

Then he said to them "Who among you, if your son or ox falls into a cistern, would not immediately pull him out on the sabbath day?" But they were unable to answer his question.

OCTOBER 30TH, 2021
Saturday of the Thirtieth Week in Ordinary Time

1ST Reading Rom 11:1-2a, 11-12, 25-29

Brothers and sisters:

I ask, then, has God rejected his people? Of course not! For I too am a child of Israel, a descendant of Abraham, of the tribe of Benjamin. God has not rejected his people whom he foreknew. Do you not know what the Scripture says about Elijah,how he pleads with God against Israel? Hence I ask, did they stumble so as to fall? Of course not! But through their transgression salvation has come to the Gentiles, so as to make them jealous. Now if their transgression is enrichment for the world, and if their diminished number is enrichment for the Gentiles, how much more their full number. I do not want you to be unaware of this mystery, brothers and sisters, so that you will not become wise in your own estimation: a hardening has come upon Israel in part, until the full number of the Gentiles comes in, and thus all Israel will be saved, as it is written: The deliverer will come out of Zion, he will turn away godlessness from Jacob; and this is my covenant with them when I take away their sins. In respect to the Gospel, they are enemies on your account; but in respect to election, they are beloved because of the patriarch. For the gifts and the call of God are irrevocable.

Responsorial Psalm94:12-13a, 14-15, 17-18
R. (14a) The Lord will not abandon his people.

Blessed the man whom you instruct, O LORD, whom by your law you teach,

Giving him rest from evil days.

R. The Lord will not abandon his people.

For the LORD will not cast off his people, nor abandon his inheritance;

But judgment shall again be with justice, and all the upright of heart shall follow it.

R. The Lord will not abandon his people.

Were not the LORD my help, my soul would soon dwell in the silent grave.

When I say, "My foot is slipping," your mercy, O LORD, sustains me.

R. The Lord will not abandon his people.

Alleluia Mt 11:29ab

R. Alleluia, alleluia.

Take my yoke upon you and learn from me, For I am meek and humble of heart.

R. Alleluia, alleluia.

Gospel Lk 14:1, 7-11
On a sabbath Jesus went to dine at the home of one of the leading Pharisees, and the people there were observing him carefully. He told a parable to those who had been invited, noticing how they were choosing the places of honor at the table. "When you are invited by someone to a wedding banquet, do not recline at table in the place of honor. A more distinguished guest than you may have been invited by him, and the host who invited both of you

may approach you and say, 'Give your place to this man, 'and then you would proceed with embarrassment to take the lowest place. Rather, when you are invited, go and take the lowest place so that when the host comes to you he may say, 'My friend, move up to a higher position. 'Then you will enjoy the esteem of your companions at the table. For everyone who exalts himself will be humbled, but the one who humbles himself will be exalted."

OCTOBER 31ST, 2021
Thirty-first Sunday in Ordinary Time

1ST Reading Dt 6:2-6

Moses spoke to the people, saying: "Fear the LORD, your God,

and keep, throughout the days of your lives, all his statutes and commandments which I enjoin on you, and thus have long life. Hear then, Israel, and be careful to observe them, that you may grow and prosper the more, in keeping with the promise of the LORD, the God of your fathers, to give you a land flowing with milk and honey. "Hear, O Israel! The LORD is our God, the LORD alone! Therefore, you shall love the LORD, your God, with all your heart, and with all your soul, and with all your strength. Take to heart these words which I enjoin on you today."

Responsorial Psalm Ps 18:2-3, 3-4, 47, 51

R. (2)   I love you, Lord, my strength.

I love you, O LORD, my strength, O LORD, my rock, my fortress, my deliverer.

R. I love you, Lord, my strength.

My God, my rock of refuge, my shield, the horn of my salvation, my stronghold!

Praised be the LORD, I exclaim, and I am safe from my enemies.

R. I love you, Lord, my strength.

The LORD lives! And blessed be my rock! Extolled be God my savior.

You who gave great victories to your king and showed kindness to your anointed.

R. I love you, Lord, my strength.

2ND Reading Heb 7:23-28
Brothers and sisters:

The levitical priests were many because they were prevented by death from remaining in office, but Jesus, because he remains forever, has a priesthood that does not pass away. Therefore, he is always able to save those who approach God through him, since he lives forever to make intercession for them. It was fitting that we should have such a high priest: holy, innocent, undefiled, separated from sinners, higher than the heavens. He has no need, as did the high priests, to offer sacrifice day after day, first for his own sins and then for those of the people; he did that once for all when he offered himself. For the law appoints men subject to weakness to be high priests, but the word of the oath, which was taken after the law, appoints a son, who has been made perfect forever.

Alleluia Jn 14:23

R. Alleluia, alleluia.

Whoever loves me will keep my word, says the Lord; and my father will love him and we will come to him.

R. Alleluia, alleluia.

Gospel Mk 12:28b-34
One of the scribes came to Jesus and asked him, "Which is the first of all the commandments?" Jesus replied, "The first is this: Hear, O Israel! The Lord our God is Lord alone! You shall love the Lord your God with all your heart, with all your soul, with all your mind, and with all your strength. The second is this: You shall love your neighbor as yourself. There is no other commandment greater than these." The scribe said to him, "Well said, teacher. You are right in saying, 'He is One and there is no other than he. 'And 'to love him with all your heart, with all your understanding, with all your strength, and to love your neighbor as yourself 'is worth more than all burnt offerings and sacrifices." And when Jesus saw that he answered with understanding, he said to him, "You are not far from the kingdom of God." And no one dared to ask him any more questions.

1ST Reading Rv 7:2-4, 9-14

I, John, saw another angel come up from the East, holding the seal of the living God. He cried out in a loud voice to the four angels who were given power to damage the land and the sea, "Do not damage the land or the sea or the trees until we put the seal on the foreheads of the servants of our God." I heard the number of those who had been marked with the seal, one hundred and forty-four thousand marked from every tribe of the children of Israel. After this I had a vision of a great multitude, which no one could count, from every nation, race, people, and tongue. They stood before the throne and before the Lamb, wearing white robes and holding palm branches in their hands.

They cried out in a loud voice: "Salvation comes from our God, who is seated on the throne, and from the Lamb." All the angels stood around the throne and around the elders and the four living creatures.

They prostrated themselves before the throne, worshiped God, and exclaimed: "Amen. Blessing and glory, wisdom and thanksgiving, honor, power, and might be to our God forever and ever. Amen." Then one of the elders spoke up and said to me, "Who are these wearing white robes, and where did they come from?" I said to him, "My lord, you are the one who knows." He said to me, "These are the ones who have survived the time of great distress; they have washed their robes and made them white in the Blood of the Lamb."

Responsorial Psalm 24:1bc-2, 3-4ab, 5-6

R. (see 6) Lord, this is the people that longs to see your face.

The LORD's are the earth and its fullness; the world and those who dwell in it.

For he founded it upon the seas and established it upon the rivers.

R. Lord, this is the people that longs to see your face.

Who can ascend the mountain of the LORD? Or who may stand in his holy place?

One whose hands are sinless, whose heart is clean, who desires not what is vain.

629

R. Lord, this is the people that longs to see your face.

He shall receive a blessing from the LORD, a reward from God his savior.

Such is the race that seeks him, that seeks the face of the God of Jacob.

R. Lord, this is the people that longs to see your face.

2nd Reading 1 Jn 3:1-3
Beloved:

See what love the Father has bestowed on us that we may be called the children of God. Yet so we are. The reason the world does not know us is that it did not know him. Beloved, we are God's children now; what we shall be has not yet been revealed. We do know that when it is revealed we shall be like him, for we shall see him as he is. Everyone who has this hope based on him makes himself pure, as he is pure.

Alleluia Mt 11:28

R. Alleluia, alleluia.

Come to me, all you who labor and are burdened, and I will give you rest, says the Lord.

R. Alleluia, alleluia.

Gospel Mt 5:1-12a
When Jesus saw the crowds, he went up the mountain, and after he had sat down, his disciples came to him. He began to teach them, saying: "Blessed are the poor in spirit, for theirs is the Kingdom of heaven. Blessed are they who mourn, for they will be comforted. Blessed are the meek, for they will inherit the land. Blessed are they who hunger and thirst for righteousness, for they will be satisfied. Blessed are the merciful, for they will be shown mercy. Blessed are the clean of heart, for they will see God. Blessed are the peacemakers, for they will be called children of God. Blessed are they who are persecuted for the sake of righteousness, for theirs is the Kingdom of heaven. Blessed are you when they insult you and persecute you and utter every kind of evil against you falsely because of me. Rejoice and be glad, for your reward will be great in heaven."

NOVEMBER 2ND, 2021
The Commemoration of All the Faithful Departed
(All Souls)

1st Reading Wis 3:1-9

The souls of the just are in the hand of God, and no torment shall touch them. They seemed, in the view of the foolish, to be dead; and their passing away was thought an affliction and their going forth from us, utter destruction. But they are in peace. For if before men, indeed, they be punished, yet is their hope full of immortality; chastised a little, they shall be greatly blessed, because God tried them and found them worthy of himself. As gold in the furnace, he proved them, and as sacrificial offerings he took them to himself. In the time of their visitation they shall shine, and shall dart about as sparks through stubble; they shall judge nations and rule over peoples, and the Lord shall be their King forever. Those who trust in him shall understand truth, and the faithful shall abide with him in love: because grace and mercy are with his holy ones, and his care is with his elect.

Responsorial Psalm 23:1-3a, 3b-4, 5, 6

R. (1) The Lord is my shepherd; there is nothing I shall want.

or:

R. Though I walk in the valley of darkness, I fear no evil, for you are with me.

The LORD is my shepherd; I shall not want. In verdant pastures he gives me repose; beside restful waters he leads me; he refreshes my soul.

R. The Lord is my shepherd; there is nothing I shall want.

or:

R. Though I walk in the valley of darkness, I fear no evil, for you are with me.

He guides me in right paths for his name's sake.

Even though I walk in the dark valley I fear no evil; for you are at my side with your rod and your staff that give me courage.

R. The Lord is my shepherd; there is nothing I shall want.

631

or:

R. Though I walk in the valley of darkness, I fear no evil, for you are with me.

You spread the table before me in the sight of my foes; You anoint my head with oil; my cup overflows.

R. The Lord is my shepherd; there is nothing I shall want.

or:

R. Though I walk in the valley of darkness, I fear no evil, for you are with me.

Only goodness and kindness follow me all the days of my life; and I shall dwell in the house of the LORD for years to come.

R. The Lord is my shepherd; there is nothing I shall want.

or:

R. Though I walk in the valley of darkness, I fear no evil, for you are with me.

2ND Reading Rom 5:5-11
Brothers and sisters:

Hope does not disappoint, because the love of God has been poured out into our hearts through the Holy Spirit that has been given to us. For Christ, while we were still helpless, died at the appointed time for the ungodly.

Indeed, only with difficulty does one die for a just person, though perhaps for a good person one might even find courage to die. But God proves his love for us in that while we were still sinners Christ died for us. How much more then, since we are now justified by his Blood, will we be saved through him from the wrath. Indeed, if, while we were enemies, we were reconciled to God through the death of his Son, how much more, once reconciled, will we be saved by his life. Not only that, but we also boast of God through our Lord Jesus Christ, through whom we have now received reconciliation.

Alleluia Mt 25:34

R. Alleluia, alleluia.

Come, you who are blessed by my Father; inherit the Kingdom prepared for you from the foundation of the world.

R. Alleluia, alleluia.

Gospel Jn 6:37-40
Jesus said to the crowds:

"Everything that the Father gives me will come to me, and I will not reject anyone who comes to me, because I came down from heaven not to do my own will but the will of the one who sent me. And this is the will of the one who sent me, that I should not lose anything of what he gave me, but that I should raise it on the last day. For this is the will of my Father, that everyone who sees the Son and believes in him may have eternal life, and I shall raise him on the last day."

NOVEMBER 3RD, 2021
Wednesday of the Thirty-first Week in Ordinary Time

1ST Reading Rom 13:8-10
Brothers and sisters:

Owe nothing to anyone, except to love one another; for the one who loves another has fulfilled the law. The commandments, You shall not commit adultery; you shall not kill; you shall not steal; you shall not covet, and whatever other commandment there may be, are summed up in this saying, namely, You shall love your neighbor as yourself. Love does no evil to the neighbor; hence, love is the fulfillment of the law.

Responsorial Psalm 112:1b-2, 4-5, 9
R. (5a) Blessed the man who is gracious and lends to those in need.

or:

R. Alleluia.

Blessed the man who fears the LORD, who greatly delights in his commands.

His posterity shall be mighty upon the earth; the upright generation shall be blessed.

R. Blessed the man who is gracious and lends to those in need.

or:

R. Alleluia.

He dawns through the darkness, a light for the upright; he is gracious and merciful and just.

Well for the man who is gracious and lends, who conducts his affairs with justice.

R. Blessed the man who is gracious and lends to those in need.

or:

R. Alleluia.

Lavishly he gives to the poor; his generosity shall endure forever; his horn shall be exalted in glory.

R. Blessed the man who is gracious and lends to those in need.

or:

R. Alleluia.

Alleluia 1 Pt 4:14

R. Alleluia, alleluia.

If you are insulted for the name of Christ, blessed are you, for the Spirit of God rests upon you.

R. Alleluia, alleluia.

Gospel Lk 14:25-33

Great crowds were traveling with Jesus, and he turned and addressed them, "If anyone comes to me without hating his father and mother, wife and children, brothers and sisters, and even his own life, he cannot be my disciple. Whoever does not carry his own cross and come after me cannot be my disciple. Which of you wishing to construct a tower does not first sit down and calculate the cost to see if there is enough for its completion? Otherwise, after laying the foundation and finding himself unable to finish the work the onlookers should laugh at him and say, 'This one began to build but did not have the resources to finish.' Or what king marching into battle would not first sit down and decide whether with ten thousand troops he can successfully oppose another king advancing upon him with twenty thousand troops? But if not, while he is still far away, he will send a delegation to ask for peace terms. In the same way, everyone of you who does not renounce all his possessions cannot be my disciple."

NOVEMBER 4TH, 2021
Memorial of Saint Charles Borromeo, Bishop

1ST Reading Rom 14:7-12
Brothers and sisters:

None of us lives for oneself, and no one dies for oneself. For if we live, we live for the Lord, and if we die, we die for the Lord; so then, whether we live or die, we are the Lord's. For this is why Christ died and came to life, that he might be Lord of both the dead and the living. Why then do you judge your brother or sister? Or you, why do you look down on your brother or sister? For we shall all stand before the judgment seat of God; for it is written: As I live, says the Lord, every knee shall bend before me, and every tongue shall give praise to God. So then each of us shall give an account of himself to God.

Responsorial Psalm 27:1bcde, 4, 13-14
R. (13) I believe that I shall see the good things of the Lord in the land of the living.

The LORD is my light and my salvation; whom should I fear?

The LORD is my life's refuge; of whom should I be afraid?

R. I believe that I shall see the good things of the Lord in the land of the living.

One thing I ask of the LORD; this I seek:

To dwell in the house of the LORD all the days of my life,

That I may gaze on the loveliness of the LORD and contemplate his temple.

R. I believe that I shall see the good things of the Lord in the land of the living.

I believe that I shall see the bounty of the LORD in the land of the living.

Wait for the LORD with courage; be stouthearted, and wait for the LORD.

R. I believe that I shall see the good things of the Lord in the land of the living.

Alleluia Mt 11:28

R. Alleluia, alleluia.

Come to me, all you who labor and are burdened, and I will give you rest, says the Lord.

R. Alleluia, alleluia.

Gospel Lk 15:1-10

The tax collectors and sinners were all drawing near to listen to Jesus, but the Pharisees and scribes began to complain, saying, "This man welcomes sinners and eats with them." So Jesus addressed this parable to them. "What man among you having a hundred sheep and losing one of them would not leave the ninety-nine in the desert and go after the lost one until he finds it? And when he does find it, he sets it on his shoulders with great joy and, upon his arrival home, he calls together his friends and neighbors and says to them, 'Rejoice with me because I have found my lost sheep.' I tell you, in just the same way there will be more joy in heaven over one sinner who repents than over ninety-nine righteous people who have no need of repentance. "Or what woman having ten coins and losing one would not light a lamp and sweep the house, searching carefully until she finds it?

And when she does find it, she calls together her friends and neighbors and says to them, 'Rejoice with me because I have found the coin that I lost.' In just the same way, I tell you, there will be rejoicing among the angels of God over one sinner who repents."

NOVEMBER 5TH, 2021
Friday of the Thirty-first Week in Ordinary Time

I myself am convinced about you, my brothers and sisters, that you yourselves are full of goodness, filled with all knowledge, and able to admonish one another. But I have written to you rather boldly in some respects to remind you, because of the grace given me by God to be a minister of Christ Jesus to the Gentiles in performing the priestly service of the Gospel of God, so that the offering up of the Gentiles may be acceptable, sanctified by the Holy Spirit.

In Christ Jesus, then, I have reason to boast in what pertains to God. For I will not dare to speak of anything except what Christ has accomplished through me to lead the Gentiles to obedience by word and deed, by the power of signs and wonders, by the power of the Spirit of God, so that from Jerusalem all the way around to Illyricum I have finished preaching the Gospel of Christ. Thus I aspire to proclaim the Gospel not where Christ has already been named, so that I do not build on another's foundation, but as it is written: Those who have never been told of him shall see, and those who have never heard of him shall understand.

Responsorial Psalm 98:1, 2-3ab, 3cd-4

R. (see 2b) The Lord has revealed to the nations his saving power.

Sing to the LORD a new song, for he has done wondrous deeds;

His right hand has won victory for him, his holy arm.

R. The Lord has revealed to the nations his saving power.

The LORD has made his salvation known: in the sight of the nations he has revealed his justice.

He has remembered his kindness and his faithfulness toward the house of Israel.

R. The Lord has revealed to the nations his saving power.

All the ends of the earth have seen the salvation by our God.

Sing joyfully to the LORD, all you lands; break into song; sing praise.

R. The Lord has revealed to the nations his saving power.

Alleluia 1 Jn 2:5

R. Alleluia, alleluia.

Whoever keeps the word of Christ, the love of God is truly perfected in him.

R. Alleluia, alleluia.

Gospel Lk 16:1-8
Jesus said to his disciples, "A rich man had a steward who was reported to him for squandering his property. He summoned him and said, 'What is this I hear about you? Prepare a full account of your stewardship, because you can no longer be my steward.' The steward said to himself, 'What shall I do, now that my master is taking the position of steward away from me? I am not strong enough to dig and I am ashamed to beg. I know what I shall do so that, when I am removed from the stewardship, they may welcome me into their homes.' He called in his master's debtors one by one. To the first he said, 'How much do you owe my master?' He replied, 'One hundred measures of olive oil.' He said to him, 'Here is your promissory note. Sit down and quickly write one for fifty.' Then to another he said, 'And you, how much do you owe?'

He replied, 'One hundred measures of wheat.' He said to him, 'Here is your promissory note; write one for eighty.' And the master commended that dishonest steward for acting prudently. For the children of this world are more prudent in dealing with their own generation than the children of light."

NOVEMBER 6TH, 2021
Saturday of the Thirty-first Week in Ordinary Time

1ST Reading Rom 16:3-9, 16, 22-27
Brothers and sisters:

Greet Prisca and Aquila, my co-workers in Christ Jesus, who risked their necks for my life, to whom not only I am grateful but also all the churches of the Gentiles; greet also the Church at their house. Greet my beloved Epaenetus, who was the first fruits in Asia for Christ. Greet Mary, who has worked hard for you. Greet Andronicus and Junia, my relatives and my fellow prisoners; they are prominent among the Apostles and they were in Christ before me. Greet Ampliatus, my beloved in the Lord. Greet Urbanus, our co-worker in Christ, and my beloved Stachys. Greet one another with a holy kiss. All the churches of Christ greet you.

I, Tertius, the writer of this letter, greet you in the Lord. Gaius, who is host to me and to the whole Church, greets you. Erastus, the city treasurer, and our brother Quartus greet you. Now to him who can strengthen you, according to my Gospel and the proclamation of Jesus Christ, according to the revelation of the mystery kept secret for long ages but now manifested through the prophetic writings and, according to the command of the eternal God, made known to all nations to bring about the obedience of faith, to the only wise God, through Jesus Christ be glory forever and ever. Amen.

Responsorial Psalm 145:2-3, 4-5, 10-11
R. (1b) I will praise your name for ever, Lord.

Every day will I bless you, and I will praise your name forever and ever.

Great is the LORD and highly to be praised; his greatness is unsearchable.

R. I will praise your name for ever, Lord.

Generation after generation praises your works and proclaims your might.

They speak of the splendor of your glorious majesty and tell of your wondrous works.

R. I will praise your name for ever, Lord.

Let all your works give you thanks, O LORD, and let your faithful ones bless you.

Let them discourse of the glory of your Kingdom and speak of your might.

R. I will praise your name for ever, Lord.

Alleluia 2 Cor 8:9

R. Alleluia, alleluia.

Jesus Christ became poor although he was rich, so that by his poverty you might become rich.

R. Alleluia, alleluia.

Gospel Lk 16:9-15
Jesus said to his disciples:

639

"I tell you, make friends for yourselves with dishonest wealth, so that when it fails, you will be welcomed into eternal dwellings. The person who is trustworthy in very small matters is also trustworthy in great ones; and the person who is dishonest in very small matters is also dishonest in great ones. If, therefore, you are not trustworthy with dishonest wealth, who will trust you with true wealth? If you are not trustworthy with what belongs to another, who will give you what is yours? No servant can serve two masters. He will either hate one and love the other, or be devoted to one and despise the other. You cannot serve God and mammon." The Pharisees, who loved money, heard all these things and sneered at him. And he said to them, "You justify yourselves in the sight of others, but God knows your hearts; for what is of human esteem is an abomination in the sight of God."

NOVEMBER 7TH, 2021
Thirty-second Sunday in Ordinary Time

1ST Reading 1 Kgs 17:10-16

In those days, Elijah the prophet went to Zarephath. As he arrived at the entrance of the city, a widow was gathering sticks there; he called out to her, "Please bring me a small cupful of water to drink." She left to get it, and he called out after her, "Please bring along a bit of bread." She answered, "As the LORD, your God, lives, I have nothing baked; there is only a handful of flour in my jar and a little oil in my jug. Just now I was collecting a couple of sticks, to go in and prepare something for myself and my son; when we have eaten it, we shall die." Elijah said to her, "Do not be afraid. Go and do as you propose. But first make me a little cake and bring it to me. Then you can prepare something for yourself and your son. For the LORD, the God of Israel, says, The jar of flour shall not go empty, nor the jug of oil run dry, until the day when the LORD sends rain upon the earth.'" She left and did as Elijah had said. She was able to eat for a year, and he and her son as well; the jar of flour did not go empty, nor the jug of oil run dry, as the LORD had foretold through Elijah.

Responsorial Psalm Ps 146:7, 8-9, 9-10
R. (1b) Praise the Lord, my soul!

or:

R. Alleluia.

The LORD keeps faith forever, secures justice for the oppressed, gives food to the hungry.

The LORD sets captives free.

R. Praise the Lord, my soul!

or:

R. Alleluia.

The LORD gives sight to the blind. The LORD raises up those who were bowed down; the LORD loves the just.

The LORD protects strangers.

R. Praise the Lord, my soul!

or:

R. Alleluia.

The fatherless and the widow he sustains, but the way of the wicked he thwarts.

The LORD shall reign forever; your God, O Zion, through all generations. Alleluia.

R. Praise the Lord, my soul!

or:

R. Alleluia.

2ND Reading Heb 9:24-28

Christ did not enter into a sanctuary made by hands, a copy of the true one, but heaven itself, that he might now appear before God on our behalf. Not that he might offer himself repeatedly, as the high priest enters each year into the sanctuary with blood that is not his own; if that were so, he would have had to suffer repeatedly from the foundation of the world. But now once for all he has appeared at the end of the ages to take away sin by his sacrifice. Just as it is appointed that human beings die once, and after this the judgment, so also Christ, offered once to take away the sins of many, will appear a second time, not to take away sin but to bring salvation to those who eagerly await him.

Alleluia Mt 5:3

R. Alleluia, alleluia.

Blessed are the poor in spirit, for theirs is the kingdom of heaven.

R. Alleluia, alleluia.

Gospel Mk 12:38-44 or 12:41-44
In the course of his teaching Jesus said to the crowds, "Beware of the scribes, who like to go around in long robes and accept greetings in the marketplaces, seats of honor in synagogues, and places of honor at banquets. They devour the houses of widows and, as a pretext recite lengthy prayers. They will receive a very severe condemnation." He sat down opposite the treasury and observed how the crowd put money into the treasury. Many rich people put in large sums.

A poor widow also came and put in two small coins worth a few cents. Calling his disciples to himself, he said to them, "Amen, I say to you, this poor widow put in more than all the other contributors to the treasury. For they have all contributed from their surplus wealth, but she, from her poverty, has contributed all she had, her whole livelihood."

OR:

Jesus sat down opposite the treasury and observed how the crowd put money into the treasury. Many rich people put in large sums. A poor widow also came and put in two small coins worth a few cents. Calling his disciples to himself, he said to them, "Amen, I say to you, this poor widow put in more than all the other contributors to the treasury. For they have all contributed from their surplus wealth, but she, from her poverty, has contributed all she had, her whole livelihood."

NOVEMBER 8TH, 2021
Monday of the Thirty-second Week in Ordinary Time

1ST Reading Wis 1:1-7
Love justice, you who judge the earth; think of the Lord in goodness, and seek him in integrity of heart; because he is found by those who test him not,

and he manifests himself to those who do not disbelieve him. For perverse counsels separate a man from God, and his power, put to the proof, rebukes the foolhardy; because into a soul that plots evil, wisdom enters not, nor dwells she in a body under debt of sin. For the Holy Spirit of discipline flees deceit and withdraws from senseless counsels; and when injustice occurs it is rebuked. For wisdom is a kindly spirit, yet she acquits not the blasphemer of his guilty lips; Because God is the witness of his inmost self and the sure observer of his heart and the listener to his tongue. For the Spirit of the Lord fills the world, is all-embracing, and knows what man says.

Responsorial Psalm 139:1b-3, 4-6, 7-8, 9-10
R. (24b) Guide me, Lord, along the everlasting way.

O LORD, you have probed me and you know me; you know when I sit and when I stand; you understand my thoughts from afar.

My journeys and my rest you scrutinize, with all my ways you are familiar.

R. Guide me, Lord, along the everlasting way.

Even before a word is on my tongue, behold, O LORD, you know the whole of it.

Behind me and before, you hem me in and rest your hand upon me.

Such knowledge is too wonderful for me; too lofty for me to attain.

R. Guide me, Lord, along the everlasting way.

Where can I go from your spirit? From your presence where can I flee?

If I go up to the heavens, you are there; if I sink to the nether world, you are present there.

R. Guide me, Lord, along the everlasting way.

If I take the wings of the dawn, if I settle at the farthest limits of the sea,

Even there your hand shall guide me, and your right hand hold me fast.

R. Guide me, Lord, along the everlasting way.

Alleluia Phil 2:15d, 16a

R. Alleluia, alleluia.

Shine like lights in the world, as you hold on to the word of life.

R. Alleluia, alleluia.

Gospel Lk 17:1-6
Jesus said to his disciples, "Things that cause sin will inevitably occur, but woe to the one through whom they occur. It would be better for him if a millstone were put around his neck and he be thrown into the sea than for him to cause one of these little ones to sin. Be on your guard! If your brother sins, rebuke him; and if he repents, forgive him. And if he wrongs you seven times in one day and returns to you seven times saying, 'I am sorry,' you should forgive him." And the Apostles said to the Lord, "Increase our faith." The Lord replied, "If you have faith the size of a mustard seed, you would say to this mulberry tree, 'Be uprooted and planted in the sea,' and it would obey you."

NOVEMBER 9TH, 2021
Feast of the Dedication of the Lateran Basilica in Rome

1ST Reading Ez 47:1-2, 8-9, 12

The angel brought me back to the entrance of the temple, and I saw water flowing out from beneath the threshold of the temple toward the east, for the façade of the temple was toward the east; the water flowed down from the southern side of the temple, south of the altar. He led me outside by the north gate, and around to the outer gate facing the east, where I saw water trickling from the southern side.

He said to me, "This water flows into the eastern district down upon the Arabah, and empties into the sea, the salt waters, which it makes fresh. Wherever the river flows, every sort of living creature that can multiply shall live, and there shall be abundant fish, for wherever this water comes the sea shall be made fresh. Along both banks of the river, fruit trees of every kind shall grow; their leaves shall not fade, nor their fruit fail. Every month they shall bear fresh fruit, for they shall be watered by the flow from the sanctuary. Their fruit shall serve for food, and their leaves for medicine."

Responsorial Psalm 46:2-3, 5-6, 8-9

R. (5) The waters of the river gladden the city of God, the holy dwelling of the Most High!

God is our refuge and our strength, an ever-present help in distress.

Therefore, we fear not, though the earth be shaken and mountains plunge into the depths of the sea.

R. The waters of the river gladden the city of God, the holy dwelling of the Most High!

There is a stream whose runlets gladden the city of God, the holy dwelling of the Most High.

God is in its midst; it shall not be disturbed; God will help it at the break of dawn.

R. The waters of the river gladden the city of God, the holy dwelling of the Most High!

The LORD of hosts is with us; our stronghold is the God of Jacob.

Come! behold the deeds of the LORD, the astounding things he has wrought on earth.

R. The waters of the river gladden the city of God, the holy dwelling of the Most High!

2ND Reading 1 Cor 3:9c-11, 16-17
Brothers and sisters:

You are God's building. According to the grace of God given to me, like a wise master builder I laid a foundation, and another is building upon it. But each one must be careful how he builds upon it, for no one can lay a foundation other than the one that is there, namely, Jesus Christ. Do you not know that you are the temple of God, and that the Spirit of God dwells in you? If anyone destroys God's temple, God will destroy that person; for the temple of God, which you are, is holy.

Alleluia 2 Chr 7:16

R. Alleluia, alleluia.

I have chosen and consecrated this house, says the Lord, that my name may be there forever.

R. Alleluia, alleluia.

645

Since the Passover of the Jews was near, Jesus went up to Jerusalem. He found in the temple area those who sold oxen, sheep, and doves, as well as the money-changers seated there. He made a whip out of cords and drove them all out of the temple area, with the sheep and oxen, and spilled the coins of the money-changers and overturned their tables, and to those who sold doves he said, "Take these out of here, and stop making my Father's house a marketplace."

His disciples recalled the words of Scripture, Zeal for your house will consume me. At this the Jews answered and said to him, "What sign can you show us for doing this?" Jesus answered and said to them, "Destroy this temple and in three days I will raise it up." The Jews said, "This temple has been under construction for forty-six years, and you will raise it up in three days?" But he was speaking about the temple of his Body. Therefore, when he was raised from the dead, his disciples remembered that he had said this, and they came to believe the Scripture and the word Jesus had spoken.

NOVEMBER 10TH, 2021
Memorial of Saint Leo the Great, Pope and Doctor of the Church

1ST Reading Wis 6:1-11

Hear, O kings, and understand; learn, you magistrates of the earth's expanse! Hearken, you who are in power over the multitude and lord it over throngs of peoples! Because authority was given you by the Lord and sovereignty by the Most High, who shall probe your works and scrutinize your counsels. Because, though you were ministers of his kingdom, you judged not rightly, and did not keep the law, nor walk according to the will of God, Terribly and swiftly shall he come against you, because judgment is stern for the exalted– For the lowly may be pardoned out of mercy but the mighty shall be mightily put to the test. For the Lord of all shows no partiality, nor does he fear greatness, Because he himself made the great as well as the small, and he provides for all alike; but for those in power a rigorous scrutiny impends. To you, therefore, O princes, are my words addressed that you may learn wisdom and that you may not sin. For those who keep the holy precepts hallowed shall be found holy, and those learned in them will have ready a response. Desire therefore my words; long for them and you shall be instructed.

R. (8a) Rise up, O God, bring judgment to the earth.

Defend the lowly and the fatherless; render justice to the afflicted and the destitute.

Rescue the lowly and the poor; from the hand of the wicked deliver them.

R. Rise up, O God, bring judgment to the earth.

I said: "You are gods, all of you sons of the Most High; yet like men you shall die, and fall like any prince."

R. Rise up, O God, bring judgment to the earth.

Alleluia 1 Thes 5:18

R. Alleluia, alleluia.

In all circumstances, give thanks, for this is the will of God for you in Christ Jesus.

R. Alleluia, alleluia.

Gospel Lk 17:11-19

As Jesus continued his journey to Jerusalem, he traveled through Samaria and Galilee. As he was entering a village, ten lepers met him. They stood at a distance from him and raised their voice, saying, "Jesus, Master! Have pity on us!" And when he saw them, he said, "Go show yourselves to the priests." As they were going they were cleansed. And one of them, realizing he had been healed, returned, glorifying God in a loud voice; and he fell at the feet of Jesus and thanked him. He was a Samaritan. Jesus said in reply, "Ten were cleansed, were they not? Where are the other nine? Has none but this foreigner returned to give thanks to God?" Then he said to him, "Stand up and go; your faith has saved you."

NOVEMBER 11TH, 2021
Memorial of Saint Martin of Tours, Bishop

1ST Reading Wis 7:22b–8:1

In Wisdom is a spirit intelligent, holy, unique, Manifold, subtle, agile, clear, unstained, certain, Not baneful, loving the good, keen, unhampered, beneficent, kindly, Firm, secure, tranquil, all-powerful, all-seeing, And pervading all spirits, though they be intelligent, pure and very subtle. For Wisdom is mobile beyond all motion, and she penetrates and pervades all things by reason of her purity. For she is an aura of the might of God and a pure effusion of the glory of the Almighty; therefore nought that is sullied enters into her. For she is the refulgence of eternal light, the spotless mirror of the power of God, the image of his goodness. And she, who is one, can do all things, and renews everything while herself perduring; And passing into holy souls from age to age, she produces friends of God and prophets. For there is nought God loves, be it not one who dwells with Wisdom. For she is fairer than the sun and surpasses every constellation of the stars. Compared to light, she takes precedence; for that, indeed, night supplants, but wickedness prevails not over Wisdom. Indeed, she reaches from end to end mightily and governs all things well.

Responsorial Psalm119:89, 90, 91, 130, 135, 175
R. (89a) Your word is for ever, O Lord.

Your word, O LORD, endures forever; it is firm as the heavens.

R. Your word is for ever, O Lord.

Through all generations your truth endures; you have established the earth, and it stands firm.

R. Your word is for ever, O Lord.

According to your ordinances they still stand firm: all things serve you.

R. Your word is for ever, O Lord.

The revelation of your words sheds light, giving understanding to the simple.

R. Your word is for ever, O Lord.

Let your countenance shine upon your servant, and teach me your statutes.

R. Your word is for ever, O Lord.

Let my soul live to praise you, and may your ordinances help me.

R. Your word is for ever, O Lord.

AlleluiaJn 15:5

R. Alleluia, alleluia.

I am the vine, you are the branches, says the Lord: whoever remains in me and I in him will bear much fruit.

R. Alleluia, alleluia.

Asked by the Pharisees when the Kingdom of God would come, Jesus said in reply, "The coming of the Kingdom of God cannot be observed, and no one will announce, 'Look, here it is,' or, 'There it is.' For behold, the Kingdom of God is among you." Then he said to his disciples, "The days will come when you will long to see one of the days of the Son of Man, but you will not see it.

There will be those who will say to you, 'Look, there he is,' or 'Look, here he is.' Do not go off, do not run in pursuit. For just as lightning flashes and lights up the sky from one side to the other so will the Son of Man be in his day. But first he must suffer greatly and be rejected by this generation."

NOVEMBER 12TH, 2021
Memorial of Saint Josaphat, Bishop and Martyr

1ST Reading Wis 13:1-9
All men were by nature foolish who were in ignorance of God, and who from the good things seen did not succeed in knowing him who is, and from studying the works did not discern the artisan; But either fire, or wind, or the swift air, or the circuit of the stars, or the mighty water, or the luminaries of heaven, the governors of the world, they considered gods. Now if out of joy in their beauty they thought them gods, let them know how far more excellent is the Lord than these; for the original source of beauty fashioned them. Or if they were struck by their might and energy, let them from these things realize how much more powerful is he who made them. For from the greatness and the beauty of created things their original author, by analogy, is seen. But yet, for these the blame is less; for they indeed have gone astray perhaps, though they seek God and wish to find him. For they search busily among his works, but are distracted by what they see, because the things seen are fair. But again, not even these are pardonable. For if they so far succeeded in knowledge that they could speculate about the world, how did they not more quickly find its Lord?

Responsorial Psalm19:2-3, 4-5ab
R. (2a) The heavens proclaim the glory of God.

The heavens declare the glory of God, and the firmament proclaims his handiwork.

Day pours out the word to day, and night to night imparts knowledge.

R. The heavens proclaim the glory of God.

Not a word nor a discourse whose voice is not heard;

Through all the earth their voice resounds, and to the ends of the world, their message.

R. The heavens proclaim the glory of God.

Alleluia Lk 21:28

R. Alleluia, alleluia.

Stand erect and raise your heads because your redemption is at hand.

R. Alleluia, alleluia.

Gospel Lk 17:26-37
Jesus said to his disciples:

"As it was in the days of Noah, so it will be in the days of the Son of Man; they were eating and drinking, marrying and giving in marriage up to the day that Noah entered the ark, and the flood came and destroyed them all. Similarly, as it was in the days of Lot: they were eating, drinking, buying, selling, planting, building; on the day when Lot left Sodom, fire and brimstone rained from the sky to destroy them all. So it will be on the day the Son of Man is revealed. On that day, someone who is on the housetop and whose belongings are in the house must not go down to get them, and likewise one in the field must not return to what was left behind. Remember the wife of Lot. Whoever seeks to preserve his life will lose it, but whoever loses it will save it. I tell you, on that night there will be two people in one bed; one will be taken, the other left. And there will be two women grinding meal together; one will be taken, the other left." They said to him in reply, "Where, Lord?" He said to them, "Where the body is, there also the vultures will gather."

Memorial of Saint Frances Xavier Cabrini, Virgin

When peaceful stillness compassed everything and the night in its swift course was half spent, your all-powerful word, from heaven's royal throne bounded, a fierce warrior, into the doomed land, bearing the sharp sword of your inexorable decree. And as he alighted, he filled every place with death; he still reached to heaven, while he stood upon the earth. For all creation, in its several kinds, was being made over anew, serving its natural laws, that your children might be preserved unharmed.

The cloud overshadowed their camp; and out of what had before been water, dry land was seen emerging: Out of the Red Sea an unimpeded road, and a grassy plain out of the mighty flood. Over this crossed the whole nation sheltered by your hand, after they beheld stupendous wonders. For they ranged about like horses, and bounded about like lambs, praising you, O Lord! Their deliverer.

R. (5a) Remember the marvels the Lord has done!

or:

R. Alleluia.

Sing to him, sing his praise, proclaim all his wondrous deeds.

Glory in his holy name; rejoice, O hearts that seek the LORD!

R. Remember the marvels the Lord has done!

or:

R. Alleluia.

Then he struck every firstborn throughout their land, the first fruits of all their manhood.

And he led them forth laden with silver and gold, with not a weakling among their tribes.

R. Remember the marvels the Lord has done!

or:

R. Alleluia.

For he remembered his holy word to his servant Abraham.

And he led forth his people with joy; with shouts of joy, his chosen ones.

R. Remember the marvels the Lord has done!

or:

R. Alleluia.

Alleluia 2 Thes 2:14

R. Alleluia, alleluia.

God has called us through the Gospel, to possess the glory of our Lord Jesus Christ.

R. Alleluia, alleluia.

Gospel Lk 18:1-8

Jesus told his disciples a parable about the necessity for them to pray always without becoming weary. He said, "There was a judge in a certain town who neither feared God nor respected any human being. And a widow in that town used to come to him and say,

'Render a just decision for me against my adversary.' For a long time the judge was unwilling, but eventually he thought, 'While it is true that I neither fear God nor respect any human being, because this widow keeps bothering me I shall deliver a just decision for her lest she finally come and strike me.'" The Lord said, "Pay attention to what the dishonest judge says. Will not God then secure the rights of his chosen ones who call out to him day and night? Will he be slow to answer them? I tell you, he will see to it that justice is done for them speedily. But when the Son of Man comes, will he find faith on earth?"

NOVEMBER 14TH, 2021
Thirty-third Sunday in Ordinary Time

In those days, I Daniel, heard this word of the Lord: "At that time there shall arise Michael, the great prince, guardian of your people; it shall be a time unsurpassed in distress since nations began until that time. At that time your people shall escape, everyone who is found written in the book. "Many of those who sleep in the dust of the earth shall awake; some shall live forever, others shall be an everlasting horror and disgrace. "But the wise shall shine brightly like the splendor of the firmament, and those who lead the many to justice shall be like the stars forever."

R. (1) You are my inheritance, O Lord!

O LORD, my allotted portion and my cup, you it is who hold fast my lot.

I set the LORD ever before me; with him at my right hand I shall not be disturbed.

R. You are my inheritance, O Lord!

Therefore my heart is glad and my soul rejoices, my body, too, abides in confidence; because you will not abandon my soul to the netherworld, nor will you suffer your faithful one to undergo corruption.

R. You are my inheritance, O Lord!

You will show me the path to life, fullness of joys in your presence, the delights at your right hand forever.

R. You are my inheritance, O Lord!

Brothers and sisters:

Every priest stands daily at his ministry, offering frequently those same sacrifices that can never take away sins. But this one offered one sacrifice for sins, and took his seat forever at the right hand of God; now he waits until his enemies are made his footstool. For by one offering he has made perfect forever those who are being consecrated. Where there is forgiveness of these, there is no longer offering for sin.

R. Alleluia, alleluia.

Be vigilant at all times and pray that you have the strength to stand before the Son of Man.

R. Alleluia, alleluia.

Gospel Mk 13:24-32
Jesus said to his disciples:

"In those days after that tribulation the sun will be darkened, and the moon will not give its light, and the stars will be falling from the sky, and the powers in the heavens will be shaken." And then they will see 'the Son of Man coming in the clouds' with great power and glory, and then he will send out the angels and gather his elect from the four winds, from the end of the earth to the end of the sky. "Learn a lesson from the fig tree.

When its branch becomes tender and sprouts leaves, you know that summer is near. In the same way, when you see these things happening, know that he is near, at the gates. Amen, I say to you, this generation will not pass away until all these things have taken place. Heaven and earth will pass away, but my words will not pass away. "But of that day or hour, no one knows, neither the angels in heaven, nor the Son, but only the Father."

NOVEMBER 15TH, 2021
Monday of the Thirty-third Week in Ordinary Time

1ST Reading 1 Mc 1:10-15, 41-43, 54-57, 62-63
[From the descendants of Alexander's officers] there sprang a sinful offshoot, Antiochus Epiphanes, son of King Antiochus, once a hostage at Rome. He became king in the year one hundred and thirty-seven of the kingdom of the Greeks. In those days there appeared in Israel men who were breakers of the law, and they seduced many people, saying: "Let us go and make an alliance with the Gentiles all around us; since we separated from them, many evils have come upon us." The proposal was agreeable; some from among the people promptly went to the king, and he authorized them to introduce the way of living of the Gentiles. Thereupon they built a gymnasium in Jerusalem according to the Gentile custom. They covered over the mark of their circumcision and abandoned the holy covenant; they allied themselves with the Gentiles and sold themselves to wrongdoing.

Then the king wrote to his whole kingdom that all should be one people, each abandoning his particular customs. All the Gentiles conformed to the command of the king, and many children of Israel were in favor of his religion; they sacrificed to idols and profaned the sabbath. On the fifteenth day of the month Chislev, in the year one hundred and forty-five, the king erected the horrible abomination upon the altar of burnt offerings and in the surrounding cities of Judah they built pagan altars. They also burned incense at the doors of the houses and in the streets. Any scrolls of the law which they found they tore up and burnt. Whoever was found with a scroll of the covenant, and whoever observed the law, was condemned to death by royal decree. But many in Israel were determined and resolved in their hearts not to eat anything unclean; they preferred to die rather than to be defiled with unclean food or to profane the holy covenant; and they did die. Terrible affliction was upon Israel.

Responsorial Psalm 119:53, 61, 134, 150, 155, 158
R. (see 88) Give me life, O Lord, and I will do your commands.

Indignation seizes me because of the wicked who forsake your law.

R. Give me life, O Lord, and I will do your commands.

Though the snares of the wicked are twined about me, your law I have not forgotten.

R. Give me life, O Lord, and I will do your commands.

Redeem me from the oppression of men, that I may keep your precepts.

R. Give me life, O Lord, and I will do your commands.

I am attacked by malicious persecutors who are far from your law.

R. Give me life, O Lord, and I will do your commands.

Far from sinners is salvation, because they seek not your statutes.

R. Give me life, O Lord, and I will do your commands.

I beheld the apostates with loathing, because they kept not to your promise.

R. Give me life, O Lord, and I will do your commands.

Alleluia Jn 8:12

R. Alleluia, alleluia.

I am the light of the world, says the Lord; whoever follows me will have the light of life.

R. Alleluia, alleluia.

Gospel Lk 18:35-43
As Jesus approached Jericho a blind man was sitting by the roadside begging, and hearing a crowd going by, he inquired what was happening. They told him, "Jesus of Nazareth is passing by." He shouted, "Jesus, Son of David, have pity on me!" The people walking in front rebuked him, telling him to be silent, but he kept calling out all the more, "Son of David, have pity on me!" Then Jesus stopped and ordered that he be brought to him; and when he came near, Jesus asked him, "What do you want me to do for you?" He replied, "Lord, please let me see." Jesus told him, "Have sight; your faith has saved you." He immediately received his sight and followed him, giving glory to God. When they saw this, all the people gave praise to God.

NOVEMBER 16TH, 2021
Tuesday of the Thirty-third Week in Ordinary Time

1ST Reading 2 Mc 6:18-31
Eleazar, one of the foremost scribes, a man of advanced age and noble appearance, was being forced to open his mouth to eat pork. But preferring a glorious death to a life of defilement, he spat out the meat, and went forward of his own accord to the instrument of torture, as people ought to do who have the courage to reject the food which it is unlawful to taste even for love of life. Those in charge of that unlawful ritual meal took the man aside privately, because of their long acquaintance with him, and urged him to bring meat of his own providing, such as he could legitimately eat, and to pretend to be eating some of the meat of the sacrifice prescribed by the king; in this way he would escape the death penalty, and be treated kindly because of their old friendship with him.

But Eleazar made up his mind in a noble manner, worthy of his years, the dignity of his advanced age, the merited distinction of his gray hair, and of the admirable life he had lived from childhood; and so he declared that above all he would be loyal to the holy laws given by God. He told them to send him at once to the abode of the dead, explaining: "At our age it would be unbecoming to make such a pretense; many young people would think the ninety-year-old Eleazar had gone over to an alien religion.

Should I thus pretend for the sake of a brief moment of life, they would be led astray by me, while I would bring shame and dishonor on my old age. Even if, for the time being, I avoid the punishment of men, I shall never, whether alive or dead, escape the hands of the Almighty. Therefore, by manfully giving up my life now, I will prove myself worthy of my old age, and I will leave to the young a noble example of how to die willingly and generously for the revered and holy laws." Eleazar spoke thus, and went immediately to the instrument of torture.

Those who shortly before had been kindly disposed, now became hostile toward him because what he had said seemed to them utter madness. When he was about to die under the blows, he groaned and said: "The Lord in his holy knowledge knows full well that, although I could have escaped death, I am not only enduring terrible pain in my body from this scourging, but also suffering it with joy in my soul because of my devotion to him." This is how he died, leaving in his death a model of courage and an unforgettable example of virtue not only for the young but for the whole nation.

Responsorial Psalm 3:2-3, 4-5, 6-7
R. (6b) The Lord upholds me.

O LORD, how many are my adversaries! Many rise up against me!

Many are saying of me, "There is no salvation for him in God."

R. The Lord upholds me.

But you, O LORD, are my shield; my glory, you lift up my head!

When I call out to the LORD, he answers me from his holy mountain.

R. The Lord upholds me.

When I lie down in sleep, I wake again, for the LORD sustains me.

I fear not the myriads of people arrayed against me on every side.

R. The Lord upholds me.

Alleluia 1 Jn 4:10b

R. Alleluia, alleluia.

God loved us, and sent his Son as expiation for our sins.

R. Alleluia, alleluia.

Gospel Lk 19:1-10
At that time Jesus came to Jericho and intended to pass through the town.
Now a man there named Zacchaeus, who was a chief tax collector and also a
wealthy man, was seeking to see who Jesus was; but he could not see him
because of the crowd, for he was short in stature. So he ran ahead and
climbed a sycamore tree in order to see Jesus, who was about to pass that
way. When he reached the place, Jesus looked up and said, "Zacchaeus,
come down quickly, for today I must stay at your house." And he came
down quickly and received him with joy. When they saw this, they began to
grumble, saying, "He has gone to stay at the house of a sinner." But
Zacchaeus stood there and said to the Lord, "Behold, half of my
possessions, Lord, I shall give to the poor, and if I have extorted anything
from anyone I shall repay it four times over." And Jesus said to him, "Today
salvation has come to this house because this man too is a descendant of
Abraham. For the Son of Man has come to seek and to save what was lost."

NOVEMBER 17TH, 2021
Memorial of Saint Elizabeth of Hungary, Religious

1ST Reading 2 Mc 7:1, 20-31
It happened that seven brothers with their mother were arrested and tortured
with whips and scourges by the king, to force them to eat pork in violation
of God's law. Most admirable and worthy of everlasting remembrance was
the mother, who saw her seven sons perish in a single day, yet bore it
courageously because of her hope in the Lord. Filled with a noble spirit that
stirred her womanly heart with manly courage, she exhorted each of them in
the language of their ancestors with these words: "I do not know how you
came into existence in my womb; it was not I who gave you the breath of
life, nor was it I who set in order the elements of which each of you is
composed. Therefore, since it is the Creator of the universe who shapes each
man's beginning, as he brings about the origin of everything, he, in his
mercy, will give you back both breath and life, because you now disregard
yourselves for the sake of his law."

Antiochus, suspecting insult in her words, thought he was being ridiculed. As the youngest brother was still alive, the king appealed to him, not with mere words, but with promises on oath, to make him rich and happy if he would abandon his ancestral customs: he would make him his Friend and entrust him with high office. When the youth paid no attention to him at all, the king appealed to the mother, urging her to advise her boy to save his life. After he had urged her for a long time, she went through the motions of persuading her son. In derision of the cruel tyrant, she leaned over close to her son and said in their native language: "Son, have pity on me, who carried you in my womb for nine months, nursed you for three years, brought you up, educated and supported you to your present age.

I beg you, child, to look at the heavens and the earth and see all that is in them; then you will know that God did not make them out of existing things; and in the same way the human race came into existence. Do not be afraid of this executioner, but be worthy of your brothers and accept death, so that in the time of mercy I may receive you again with them." She had scarcely finished speaking when the youth said: "What are you waiting for? I will not obey the king's command. I obey the command of the law given to our fathers through Moses. But you, who have contrived every kind of affliction for the Hebrews, will not escape the hands of God."

Responsorial Psalm 17:1bcd, 5-6, 8b and 15

R. (15b) Lord, when your glory appears, my joy will be full.

Hear, O LORD, a just suit; attend to my outcry; hearken to my prayer from lips without deceit.

R. Lord, when your glory appears, my joy will be full.

My steps have been steadfast in your paths, my feet have not faltered.

I call upon you, for you will answer me, O God; incline your ear to me; hear my word.

R. Lord, when your glory appears, my joy will be full.

Keep me as the apple of your eye; hide me in the shadow of your wings.

But I in justice shall behold your face; on waking, I shall be content in your presence.

R. Lord, when your glory appears, my joy will be full.

659

R. Alleluia, alleluia.

I chose you from the world, to go and bear fruit that will last, says the Lord.

R. Alleluia, alleluia.

Gospel Lk 19:11-28

While people were listening to Jesus speak, he proceeded to tell a parable because he was near Jerusalem and they thought that the Kingdom of God would appear there immediately. So he said, "A nobleman went off to a distant country to obtain the kingship for himself and then to return. He called ten of his servants and gave them ten gold coins and told them, 'Engage in trade with these until I return.' His fellow citizens, however, despised him and sent a delegation after him to announce, 'We do not want this man to be our king.' But when he returned after obtaining the kingship, he had the servants called, to whom he had given the money, to learn what they had gained by trading.

The first came forward and said, 'Sir, your gold coin has earned ten additional ones.' He replied, 'Well done, good servant! You have been faithful in this very small matter; take charge of ten cities.' Then the second came and reported, 'Your gold coin, sir, has earned five more.'

And to this servant too he said, 'You, take charge of five cities.' Then the other servant came and said, 'Sir, here is your gold coin; I kept it stored away in a handkerchief, for I was afraid of you, because you are a demanding man; you take up what you did not lay down and you harvest what you did not plant.' He said to him, 'With your own words I shall condemn you, you wicked servant. You knew I was a demanding man, taking up what I did not lay down and harvesting what I did not plant; why did you not put my money in a bank? Then on my return I would have collected it with interest.' And to those standing by he said, 'Take the gold coin from him and give it to the servant who has ten.' But they said to him, 'Sir, he has ten gold coins.'

He replied, 'I tell you, to everyone who has, more will be given, but from the one who has not, even what he has will be taken away. Now as for those enemies of mine who did not want me as their king, bring them here and slay them before me.'" After he had said this, he proceeded on his journey up to Jerusalem.

1ST Reading 1 Mc 2:15-29

The officers of the king in charge of enforcing the apostasy came to the city of Modein to organize the sacrifices. Many of Israel joined them, but Mattathias and his sons gathered in a group apart. Then the officers of the king addressed Mattathias: "You are a leader, an honorable and great man in this city, supported by sons and kin. Come now, be the first to obey the king's command, as all the Gentiles and the men of Judah and those who are left in Jerusalem have done. Then you and your sons shall be numbered among the King's Friends, and shall be enriched with silver and gold and many gifts." But Mattathias answered in a loud voice: "Although all the Gentiles in the king's realm obey him, so that each forsakes the religion of his fathers and consents to the king's orders, yet I and my sons and my kin will keep to the covenant of our fathers. God forbid that we should forsake the law and the commandments.

We will not obey the words of the king nor depart from our religion in the slightest degree." As he finished saying these words, a certain Jew came forward in the sight of all to offer sacrifice on the altar in Modein according to the king's order. When Mattathias saw him, he was filled with zeal; his heart was moved and his just fury was aroused; he sprang forward and killed him upon the altar. At the same time, he also killed the messenger of the king who was forcing them to sacrifice, and he tore down the altar.

Thus he showed his zeal for the law, just as Phinehas did with Zimri, son of Salu. Then Mattathias went through the city shouting, "Let everyone who is zealous for the law and who stands by the covenant follow after me!" Thereupon he fled to the mountains with his sons, leaving behind in the city all their possessions. Many who sought to live according to righteousness and religious custom went out into the desert to settle there.

Responsorial Psalm 50:1b-2, 5-6, 14-15

R. (23b) To the upright I will show the saving power of God.

God the LORD has spoken and summoned the earth, from the rising of the sun to its setting.

From Zion, perfect in beauty, God shines forth.

R. To the upright I will show the saving power of God.

"Gather my faithful ones before me, those who have made a covenant with me by sacrifice."

And the heavens proclaim his justice; for God himself is the judge.

R. To the upright I will show the saving power of God.

"Offer to God praise as your sacrifice and fulfill your vows to the Most High;

Then call upon me in time of distress; I will rescue you, and you shall glorify me."

R. To the upright I will show the saving power of God.

Alleluia Ps 95:8

R. Alleluia, alleluia.

If today you hear his voice, harden not your hearts.

R. Alleluia, alleluia.

Gospel Lk 19:41-44

As Jesus drew near Jerusalem, he saw the city and wept over it, saying," If this day you only knew what makes for peace– but now it is hidden from your eyes. For the days are coming upon you when your enemies will raise a palisade against you; they will encircle you and hem you in on all sides. They will smash you to the ground and your children within you, and they will not leave one stone upon another within you because you did not recognize the time of your visitation."

NOVEMBER 19TH, 2021
Friday of the Thirty-third Week in Ordinary Time

1ST Reading 1 Mc 4:36-37, 52-59

Judas and his brothers said, "Now that our enemies have been crushed, let us go up to purify the sanctuary and rededicate it." So the whole army assembled, and went up to Mount Zion. Early in the morning on the twenty-fifth day of the ninth month, that is, the month of Chislev, in the year one hundred and forty-eight, they arose and offered sacrifice according to the law on the new altar of burnt offerings that they had made. On the anniversary of the day on which the Gentiles had defiled it, on that very day it was reconsecrated with songs, harps, flutes, and cymbals. All the people prostrated themselves and adored and praised Heaven, who had given them success. For eight days they celebrated the dedication of the altar and joyfully offered burnt offerings and sacrifices of deliverance and praise.

They ornamented the facade of the temple with gold crowns and shields; they repaired the gates and the priests' chambers and furnished them with doors. There was great joy among the people now that the disgrace of the Gentiles was removed. Then Judas and his brothers and the entire congregation of Israel decreed that the days of the dedication of the altar should be observed with joy and gladness on the anniversary every year for eight days, from the twenty-fifth day of the month Chislev.

Responsorial Psalm 1 Chronicles 29:10bcd, 11abc, 11d-12a, 12bcd

R. (13b) We praise your glorious name, O mighty God.

"Blessed may you be, O LORD, God of Israel our father, from eternity to eternity."

R. We praise your glorious name, O mighty God.

"Yours, O LORD, are grandeur and power, majesty, splendor, and glory.

For all in heaven and on earth is yours."

R. We praise your glorious name, O mighty God.

"Yours, O LORD, is the sovereignty; you are exalted as head over all.

Riches and honor are from you."

R. We praise your glorious name, O mighty God.

"You have dominion over all,

In your hand are power and might; it is yours to give grandeur and strength to all."

R. We praise your glorious name, O mighty God.

Alleluia Jn 10:27

R. Alleluia, alleluia.

My sheep hear my voice, says the Lord; I know them, and they follow me.

R. Alleluia, alleluia.

Gospel Lk 19:45-48
Jesus entered the temple area and proceeded to drive out those who were selling things, saying to them, "It is written, My house shall be a house of prayer, but you have made it a den of thieves." And every day he was teaching in the temple area. The chief priests, the scribes, and the leaders of the people, meanwhile, were seeking to put him to death, but they could find no way to accomplish their purpose because all the people were hanging on his words.

NOVEMBER 20TH, 2021
Saturday of the Thirty-third Week in Ordinary Time

1ST Reading 1 Mc 6:1-13
As King Antiochus was traversing the inland provinces, he heard that in Persia there was a city called Elymais, famous for its wealth in silver and gold, and that its temple was very rich, containing gold helmets, breastplates, and weapons left there by Alexander, son of Philip, king of Macedon, the first king of the Greeks.

He went therefore and tried to capture and pillage the city. But he could not do so, because his plan became known to the people of the city who rose up in battle against him. So he retreated and in great dismay withdrew from there to return to Babylon. While he was in Persia, a messenger brought him news that the armies sent into the land of Judah had been put to flight; that Lysias had gone at first with a strong army and been driven back by the children of Israel; that they had grown strong by reason of the arms, men, and abundant possessions taken from the armies they had destroyed; that they had pulled down the Abomination which he had built upon the altar in Jerusalem; and that they had surrounded with high walls both the sanctuary, as it had been before, and his city of Beth-zur. When the king heard this news, he was struck with fear and very much shaken. Sick with grief because his designs had failed, he took to his bed. There he remained many days, overwhelmed with sorrow, for he knew he was going to die.

So he called in all his Friends and said to them: "Sleep has departed from my eyes, for my heart is sinking with anxiety. I said to myself: 'Into what tribulation have I come, and in what floods of sorrow am I now! Yet I was kindly and beloved in my rule.' But I now recall the evils I did in Jerusalem, when I carried away all the vessels of gold and silver that were in it, and for no cause gave orders that the inhabitants of Judah be destroyed. I know that this is why these evils have overtaken me; and now I am dying, in bitter grief, in a foreign land."

Responsorial Psalm 9:2-3, 4 and 6, 16 and 19
R. (see 16a) I will rejoice in your salvation, O Lord.

I will give thanks to you, O LORD, with all my heart; I will declare all your wondrous deeds.

I will be glad and exult in you; I will sing praise to your name, Most High.

R. I will rejoice in your salvation, O Lord.

Because my enemies are turned back, overthrown and destroyed before you.

You rebuked the nations and destroyed the wicked; their name you blotted out forever and ever.

R. I will rejoice in your salvation, O Lord.

The nations are sunk in the pit they have made; in the snare they set, their foot is caught.

For the needy shall not always be forgotten, nor shall the hope of the afflicted forever perish.

R. I will rejoice in your salvation, O Lord.

Alleluia 2 Tm 1:10

R. Alleluia, alleluia.

Our Savior Jesus Christ has destroyed death and brought life to light through the Gospel.

R. Alleluia, alleluia.

Gospel Lk 20:27-40
Some Sadducees, those who deny that there is a resurrection, came forward and put this question to Jesus, saying, "Teacher, Moses wrote for us, If someone's brother dies leaving a wife but no child, his brother must take the

wife and raise up descendants for his brother. Now there were seven brothers; the first married a woman but died childless. Then the second and the third married her, and likewise all the seven died childless. Finally the woman also died. Now at the resurrection whose wife will that woman be? For all seven had been married to her."

Jesus said to them, "The children of this age marry and remarry; but those who are deemed worthy to attain to the coming age and to the resurrection of the dead neither marry nor are given in marriage. They can no longer die, for they are like angels; and they are the children of God because they are the ones who will rise. That the dead will rise even Moses made known in the passage about the bush, when he called 'Lord' the God of Abraham, the God of Isaac, and the God of Jacob; and he is not God of the dead, but of the living, for to him all are alive." Some of the scribes said in reply, "Teacher, you have answered well." And they no longer dared to ask him anything.

NOVEMBER 21ST, 2021
The Solemnity of Our Lord Jesus Christ, King of the Universe

1ST Reading Dn 7:13-14

As the visions during the night continued, I saw one like a Son of man coming, on the clouds of heaven; when he reached the Ancient One and was presented before him, the one like a Son of man received dominion, glory, and kingship; all peoples, nations, and languages serve him. His dominion is an everlasting dominion that shall not be taken away, his kingship shall not be destroyed.

Responsorial Psalm Ps 93:1, 1-2, 5

R. (1a) The LORD is king; he is robed in majesty.

The LORD is king, in splendor robed; robed is the LORD and girt about with strength.

R. The LORD is king; he is robed in majesty.

And he has made the world firm, not to be moved.

Your throne stands firm from of old; from everlasting you are, O LORD.

R. The LORD is king; he is robed in majesty.

Your decrees are worthy of trust indeed; holiness befits your house,

O LORD, for length of days.

R. The LORD is king; he is robed in majesty.

2ND Reading Rv 1:5-8
Jesus Christ is the faithful witness, the firstborn of the dead and ruler of the kings of the earth. To him who loves us and has freed us from our sins by his blood, who has made us into a kingdom, priests for his God and Father, to him be glory and power forever and ever. Amen. Behold, he is coming amid the clouds, and every eye will see him, even those who pierced him. All the peoples of the earth will lament him. Yes. Amen. "I am the Alpha and the Omega," says the Lord God, "the one who is and who was and who is to come, the almighty."

Alleluia Mk 11:9, 10

R. Alleluia, alleluia.

Blessed is he who comes in the name of the Lord! Blessed is the kingdom of our father David that is to come!

R. Alleluia, alleluia.

Gospel Jn 18:33b-37
Pilate said to Jesus, "Are you the King of the Jews?" Jesus answered, "Do you say this on your own or have others told you about me?" Pilate answered, "I am not a Jew, am I? Your own nation and the chief priests handed you over to me. What have you done?" Jesus answered, "My kingdom does not belong to this world. If my kingdom did belong to this world, my attendants would be fighting to keep me from being handed over to the Jews. But as it is, my kingdom is not here." So Pilate said to him, "Then you are a king?" Jesus answered, "You say I am a king. For this I was born and for this I came into the world, to testify to the truth. Everyone who belongs to the truth listens to my voice."

NOVEMBER 22ND, 2021
Memorial of Saint Cecilia, Virgin and Martyr

1ST Reading Dn 1:1-6, 8-20
In the third year of the reign of Jehoiakim, king of Judah, King Nebuchadnezzar of Babylon came and laid siege to Jerusalem. The Lord

handed over to him Jehoiakim, king of Judah, and some of the vessels of the temple of God; he carried them off to the land of Shinar, and placed the vessels in the temple treasury of his god.

The king told Ashpenaz, his chief chamberlain, to bring in some of the children of Israel of royal blood and of the nobility, young men without any defect, handsome, intelligent and wise, quick to learn, and prudent in judgment, such as could take their place in the king's palace; they were to be taught the language and literature of the Chaldeans; after three years' training they were to enter the king's service.

The king allotted them a daily portion of food and wine from the royal table. Among these were men of Judah: Daniel, Hananiah, Mishael, and Azariah. But Daniel was resolved not to defile himself with the king's food or wine; so he begged the chief chamberlain to spare him this defilement. Though God had given Daniel the favor and sympathy of the chief chamberlain, he nevertheless said to Daniel, "I am afraid of my lord the king; it is he who allotted your food and drink. If he sees that you look wretched by comparison with the other young men of your age, you will endanger my life with the king." Then Daniel said to the steward whom the chief chamberlain had put in charge of Daniel, Hananiah, Mishael, and Azariah, "Please test your servants for ten days. Give us vegetables to eat and water to drink.

Then see how we look in comparison with the other young men who eat from the royal table, and treat your servants according to what you see." He acceded to this request, and tested them for ten days; after ten days they looked healthier and better fed than any of the young men who ate from the royal table. So the steward continued to take away the food and wine they were to receive, and gave them vegetables. To these four young men God gave knowledge and proficiency in all literature and science, and to Daniel the understanding of all visions and dreams. At the end of the time the king had specified for their preparation, the chief chamberlain brought them before Nebuchadnezzar.

When the king had spoken with all of them, none was found equal to Daniel, Hananiah, Mishael, and Azariah; and so they entered the king's service. In any question of wisdom or prudence which the king put to them, he found them ten times better than all the magicians and enchanters in his kingdom.

Responsorial Psalm Daniel 3:52, 53, 54, 55, 56

R. (52b) Glory and praise for ever!

"Blessed are you, O Lord, the God of our fathers, praiseworthy and exalted above all forever;

And blessed is your holy and glorious name, praiseworthy and exalted above all for all ages."

R. Glory and praise for ever!

"Blessed are you in the temple of your holy glory, praiseworthy and glorious above all forever."

R. Glory and praise for ever!

"Blessed are you on the throne of your Kingdom, praiseworthy and exalted above all forever."

R. Glory and praise for ever!

"Blessed are you who look into the depths from your throne upon the cherubim, praiseworthy and exalted above all forever."

R. Glory and praise for ever!

"Blessed are you in the firmament of heaven, praiseworthy and glorious forever."

R. Glory and praise for ever!

Alleluia Mt 24:42a, 44

R. Alleluia, alleluia.

Stay awake! For you do not know when the Son of Man will come.

R. Alleluia, alleluia.

Gospel Lk 21:1-4

When Jesus looked up he saw some wealthy people putting their offerings into the treasury and he noticed a poor widow putting in two small coins. He said, "I tell you truly, this poor widow put in more than all the rest; for those others have all made offerings from their surplus wealth, but she, from her poverty, has offered her whole livelihood."

Tuesday of the Thirty-fourth Week in Ordinary Time

1ST Reading Dn 2:31-45

Daniel said to Nebuchadnezzar: "In your vision, O king, you saw a statue, very large and exceedingly bright, terrifying in appearance as it stood before you. The head of the statue was pure gold, its chest and arms were silver, its belly and thighs bronze, the legs iron, its feet partly iron and partly tile. While you looked at the statue, a stone which was hewn from a mountain without a hand being put to it, struck its iron and tile feet, breaking them in pieces.

The iron, tile, bronze, silver, and gold all crumbled at once, fine as the chaff on the threshing floor in summer, and the wind blew them away without leaving a trace. But the stone that struck the statue became a great mountain and filled the whole earth. "This was the dream; the interpretation we shall also give in the king's presence. You, O king, are the king of kings; to you the God of heaven has given dominion and strength, power and glory; men, wild beasts, and birds of the air, wherever they may dwell, he has handed over to you, making you ruler over them all; you are the head of gold. Another kingdom shall take your place, inferior to yours, then a third kingdom, of bronze, which shall rule over the whole earth.

There shall be a fourth kingdom, strong as iron; it shall break in pieces and subdue all these others, just as iron breaks in pieces and crushes everything else. The feet and toes you saw, partly of potter's tile and partly of iron, mean that it shall be a divided kingdom, but yet have some of the hardness of iron.

As you saw the iron mixed with clay tile, and the toes partly iron and partly tile, the kingdom shall be partly strong and partly fragile. The iron mixed with clay tile means that they shall seal their alliances by intermarriage, but they shall not stay united, any more than iron mixes with clay. In the lifetime of those kings the God of heaven will set up a kingdom that shall never be destroyed or delivered up to another people; rather, it shall break in pieces all these kingdoms and put an end to them, and it shall stand forever. That is the meaning of the stone you saw hewn from the mountain without a hand being put to it, which broke in pieces the tile, iron, bronze, silver, and gold. The great God has revealed to the king what shall be in the future; this is exactly what you dreamed, and its meaning is sure."

Responsorial Psalm Daniel 3:57, 58, 59, 60, 61
R. (59b) Give glory and eternal praise to him.

"Bless the Lord, all you works of the Lord, praise and exalt him above all forever."

R. Give glory and eternal praise to him.

"Angels of the Lord, bless the Lord, praise and exalt him above all forever."

R. Give glory and eternal praise to him. "You heavens, bless the Lord, praise and exalt him above all forever."

R. Give glory and eternal praise to him.

"All you waters above the heavens, bless the Lord, praise and exalt him above all forever."

R. Give glory and eternal praise to him.

"All you hosts of the Lord, bless the Lord; praise and exalt him above all forever."

R. Give glory and eternal praise to him.

Alleluia Rv 2:10c

R. Alleluia, alleluia.

Remain faithful until death, and I will give you the crown of life.

R. Alleluia, alleluia.

Gospel Lk 21:5-11

While some people were speaking about how the temple was adorned with costly stones and votive offerings, Jesus said, "All that you see here– the days will come when there will not be left a stone upon another stone that will not be thrown down." Then they asked him, "Teacher, when will this happen?

And what sign will there be when all these things are about to happen?"

He answered, "See that you not be deceived, for many will come in my name, saying, 'I am he,' and 'The time has come.' Do not follow them! When you hear of wars and insurrections, do not be terrified; for such things must happen first, but it will not immediately be the end." Then he said to them, "Nation will rise against nation, and kingdom against kingdom. There will be powerful earthquakes, famines, and plagues from place to place; and awesome sights and mighty signs will come from the sky."

NOVEMBER 24TH, 2021
Memorial of Saint Andrew Dŭng-Lạc, Priest, and Companions, Martyrs

1ST Reading Dn 5:1-6, 13-14, 16-17, 23-28

King Belshazzar gave a great banquet for a thousand of his lords, with whom he drank. Under the influence of the wine, he ordered the gold and silver vessels which Nebuchadnezzar, his father, had taken from the temple in Jerusalem, to be brought in so that the king, his lords, his wives and his entertainers might drink from them. When the gold and silver vessels taken from the house of God in Jerusalem had been brought in, and while the king, his lords, his wives and his entertainers were drinking wine from them, they praised their gods of gold and silver, bronze and iron, wood and stone. Suddenly, opposite the lamp stand, the fingers of a human hand appeared, writing on the plaster of the wall in the king's palace.

When the king saw the wrist and hand that wrote, his face blanched; his thoughts terrified him, his hip joints shook, and his knees knocked. Then Daniel was brought into the presence of the king. The king asked him, "Are you the Daniel, the Jewish exile, whom my father, the king, brought from Judah? I have heard that the Spirit of God is in you, that you possess brilliant knowledge and extraordinary wisdom. I have heard that you can interpret dreams and solve difficulties; if you are able to read the writing and tell me what it means, you shall be clothed in purple, wear a gold collar about your neck, and be third in the government of the kingdom."

Daniel answered the king: "You may keep your gifts, or give your presents to someone else; but the writing I will read for you, O king, and tell you what it means. You have rebelled against the Lord of heaven. You had the vessels of his temple brought before you, so that you and your nobles, your wives and your entertainers, might drink wine from them; and you praised the gods of silver and gold, bronze and iron, wood and stone, that neither see nor hear nor have intelligence. But the God in whose hand is your life breath and the whole course of your life, you did not glorify. By him were the wrist and hand sent, and the writing set down. "This is the writing that was inscribed: MENE, TEKEL, and PERES.

These words mean:

MENE, God has numbered your kingdom and put an end to it; TEKEL, you have been weighed on the scales and found wanting; PERES, your kingdom has been divided and given to the Medes and Persians."

Responsorial Psalm Daniel 3:62, 63, 64, 65, 66, 67
R. (59b) Give glory and eternal praise to him.

"Sun and moon, bless the Lord; praise and exalt him above all forever."

R. Give glory and eternal praise to him.

"Stars of heaven, bless the Lord; praise and exalt him above all forever."

R. Give glory and eternal praise to him.

"Every shower and dew, bless the Lord; praise and exalt him above all forever."

R. Give glory and eternal praise to him.

"All you winds, bless the Lord; praise and exalt him above all forever."

R. Give glory and eternal praise to him.

"Fire and heat, bless the Lord; praise and exalt him above all forever."

R. Give glory and eternal praise to him.

"Cold and chill, bless the Lord; praise and exalt him above all forever."

R. Give glory and eternal praise to him.

Alleluia Rv 2:10c

R. Alleluia, alleluia.

Remain faithful until death, and I will give you the crown of life.

R. Alleluia, alleluia.

Gospel Lk 21:12-19
Jesus said to the crowd:

"They will seize and persecute you, they will hand you over to the synagogues and to prisons, and they will have you led before kings and governors because of my name. It will lead to your giving testimony. Remember, you are not to prepare your defense beforehand, for I myself shall give you a wisdom in speaking that all your adversaries will be powerless to resist or refute. You will even be handed over by parents, brothers, relatives, and friends, and they will put some of you to death. You will be hated by all because of my name, but not a hair on your head will be destroyed. By your perseverance you will secure your lives."

NOVEMBER 25TH, 2021
Thanksgiving Day

1ST Reading Sir 50:22-24
And now, bless the God of all, who has done wondrous things on earth; who fosters people's growth from their mother's womb, and fashions them according to his will! May he grant you joy of heart and may peace abide among you; May his goodness toward us endure in Israel to deliver us in our days.

Responsorial Psalm 145:2-3, 4-5, 6-7, 8-9, 10-11
R. (see 1) I will praise your name for ever, Lord.

Every day will I bless you, and I will praise your name forever and ever.

Great is the Lord and highly to be praised; his greatness is unsearchable.

R. I will praise your name for ever, Lord.

Generation after generation praises your works and proclaims your might.

They speak of the splendor of your glorious majesty and tell of your wondrous works.

R. I will praise your name for ever, Lord.

They discourse of the power of your terrible deeds and declare your greatness.

They publish the fame of your abundant goodness and joyfully sing of your justice.

R. I will praise your name for ever, Lord.

The Lord is gracious and merciful, slow to anger and of great kindness.

The Lord is good to all and compassionate toward all his works.

R. I will praise your name for ever, Lord.

Let all your works give you thanks, O Lord, and let your faithful ones bless you.

Let them discourse of the glory of your Kingdom and speak of your might.

R. I will praise your name for ever, Lord

2ND Reading 1 Cor 1:3-9
Brothers and sisters:

Grace to you and peace from God our Father and the Lord Jesus Christ. I give thanks to my God always on your account for the grace of God bestowed on you in Christ Jesus, that in him you were enriched in every way, with all discourse and all knowledge, as the testimony to Christ was confirmed among you, so that you are not lacking in any spiritual gift as you wait for the revelation of our Lord Jesus Christ. He will keep you firm to the end, irreproachable on the day of our Lord Jesus Christ. God is faithful, and by him you were called to fellowship with his Son, Jesus Christ our Lord.

Alleluia 1 Thes 5:18

R. Alleluia, alleluia.

In all circumstances, give thanks, for this is the will of God for you in Christ Jesus.

R. Alleluia, alleluia.

Gospel Lk 17:11-19
As Jesus continued his journey to Jerusalem, he traveled through Samaria and Galilee. As he was entering a village, ten persons with leprosy met him. They stood at a distance from him and raised their voices, saying, "Jesus, Master! Have pity on us!" And when he saw them, he said, "Go show yourselves to the priests." As they were going they were cleansed. And one of them, realizing he had been healed, returned, glorifying God in a loud voice; and he fell at the feet of Jesus and thanked him. He was a Samaritan. Jesus said in reply, "Ten were cleansed, were they not? Where are the other nine? Has

none but this foreigner returned to give thanks to God?" Then he said to him, "Stand up and go; your faith has saved you."

November 26TH, 2021
Friday of the Thirty-fourth Week in Ordinary Time

1ST Reading Dn 7:2-14

In a vision I, Daniel, saw during the night, the four winds of heaven stirred up the great sea, from which emerged four immense beasts, each different from the others. The first was like a lion, but with eagle's wings. While I watched, the wings were plucked; it was raised from the ground to stand on two feet like a man, and given a human mind.

The second was like a bear; it was raised up on one side, and among the teeth in its mouth were three tusks. It was given the order, "Up, devour much flesh." After this I looked and saw another beast, like a leopard; on its back were four wings like those of a bird, and it had four heads. To this beast dominion was given. After this, in the visions of the night I saw the fourth beast, different from all the others, terrifying, horrible, and of extraordinary strength; it had great iron teeth with which it devoured and crushed, and what was left it trampled with its feet. I was considering the ten horns it had, when suddenly another, a little horn, sprang out of their midst, and three of the previous horns were torn away to make room for it. This horn had eyes like a man, and a mouth that spoke arrogantly. As I watched, Thrones were set up and the Ancient One took his throne. His clothing was snow bright, and the hair on his head as white as wool; His throne was flames of fire, with wheels of burning fire.

A surging stream of fire flowed out from where he sat; Thousands upon thousands were ministering to him, and myriads upon myriads attended him. The court was convened, and the books were opened. I watched, then, from the first of the arrogant words which the horn spoke, until the beast was slain and its body thrown into the fire to be burnt up. The other beasts, which also lost their dominion, were granted a prolongation of life for a time and a season. As the visions during the night continued, I saw One like a son of man coming, on the clouds of heaven; When he reached the Ancient One and was presented before him, He received dominion, glory, and kingship; nations and peoples of every language serve him. His dominion is an everlasting dominion that shall not be taken away, his kingship shall not be destroyed.

Responsorial Psalm Daniel 3:75, 76, 77, 78, 79, 80, 81
R. Give glory and eternal praise to him!

"Mountains and hills, bless the Lord; praise and exalt him above all forever."

R. Give glory and eternal praise to him!

"Everything growing from the earth, bless the Lord; praise and exalt him above all forever.

R. Give glory and eternal praise to him!"

"You springs, bless the Lord; praise and exalt him above all forever."

R. Give glory and eternal praise to him!

"Seas and rivers, bless the Lord; praise and exalt him above all forever."

R. Give glory and eternal praise to him!

"You dolphins and all water creatures, bless the Lord; praise and exalt him above all forever."

R. Give glory and eternal praise to him!

"All you birds of the air, bless the Lord; praise and exalt him above all forever."

R. Give glory and eternal praise to him!

"All you beasts, wild and tame, bless the Lord; praise and exalt him above all forever."

R. Give glory and eternal praise to him!

Alleluia Lk 21:28

R. Alleluia, alleluia.

Stand erect and raise your heads because your redemption is at hand.

R. Alleluia, alleluia.

Jesus told his disciples a parable. "Consider the fig tree and all the other trees. When their buds burst open, you see for yourselves and know that summer is now near; in the same way, when you see these things happening, know that the Kingdom of God is near. Amen, I say to you, this generation will not pass away until all these things have taken place. Heaven and earth will pass away, but my words will not pass away."

NOVEMBER 27TH, 2021
Saturday of the Thirty-fourth Week in Ordinary Time

1ST Reading Dn 7:15-27

I, Daniel, found my spirit anguished within its covering of flesh, and I was terrified by the visions of my mind. I approached one of those present and asked him what all this meant in truth; in answer, he made known to me the meaning of the things: "These four great beasts stand for four kingdoms which shall arise on the earth. But the holy ones of the Most High shall receive the kingship, to possess it forever and ever." But I wished to make certain about the fourth beast, so very terrible and different from the others, devouring and crushing with its iron teeth and bronze claws, and trampling with its feet what was left; about the ten horns on its head, and the other one that sprang up, before which three horns fell; about the horn with the eyes and the mouth that spoke arrogantly, which appeared greater than its fellows. For, as I watched, that horn made war against the holy ones and was victorious until the Ancient One arrived; judgment was pronounced in favor of the holy ones of the Most High, and the time came when the holy ones possessed the kingdom. He answered me thus: "The fourth beast shall be a fourth kingdom on earth different from all the others; It shall devour the whole earth, beat it down, and crush it. The ten horns shall be ten kings rising out of that kingdom; another shall rise up after them, Different from those before him, who shall lay low three kings.

He shall speak against the Most High and oppress the holy ones of the Most High, thinking to change the feast days and the law. They shall be handed over to him for a year, two years, and a half-year. But when the court is convened, and his power is taken away by final and absolute destruction, then the kingship and dominion and majesty of all the kingdoms under the heavens shall be given to the holy people of the Most High, Whose Kingdom shall be everlasting: all dominions shall serve and obey him."

R. Give glory and eternal praise to him.

"You sons of men, bless the Lord; praise and exalt him above all forever."

R. Give glory and eternal praise to him.

"O Israel, bless the Lord; praise and exalt him above all forever."

R. Give glory and eternal praise to him.

"Priests of the Lord, bless the Lord; praise and exalt him above all forever."

R. Give glory and eternal praise to him.

"Servants of the Lord, bless the Lord; praise and exalt him above all forever."

R. Give glory and eternal praise to him.

"Spirits and souls of the just, bless the Lord; praise and exalt him above all forever."

R. Give glory and eternal praise to him.

"Holy men of humble heart, bless the Lord; praise and exalt him above all forever."

R. Give glory and eternal praise to him.

Alleluia Lk 21:36

R. Alleluia, alleluia.

Be vigilant at all times and pray that you may have the strength to stand before the Son of Man.

R. Alleluia, alleluia.

Gospel Lk 21:34-36
Jesus said to his disciples:

"Beware that your hearts do not become drowsy from carousing and drunkenness and the anxieties of daily life, and that day catch you by surprise like a trap. For that day will assault everyone who lives on the face of the earth. Be vigilant at all times and pray that you have the strength to escape the tribulations that are imminent and to stand before the Son of Man."

NOVEMBER 28TH, 2021
First Sunday of Advent

1ST Reading Jer 33:14-16

The days are coming, says the LORD, when I will fulfill the promise I made to the house of Israel and Judah. In those days, in that time, I will raise up for David a just shoot; he shall do what is right and just in the land. In those days Judah shall be safe and Jerusalem shall dwell secure; this is what they shall call her: "The LORD our justice."

Responsorial Psalm Ps 25:4-5, 8-9, 10, 14

R. (1b) To you, O Lord, I lift my soul.

Your ways, O LORD, make known to me; teach me your paths,

Guide me in your truth and teach me, for you are God my savior, and for you I wait all the day.

R. To you, O Lord, I lift my soul.

Good and upright is the LORD; thus he shows sinners the way.

He guides the humble to justice, and teaches the humble his way.

R. To you, O Lord, I lift my soul.

All the paths of the LORD are kindness and constancy toward those who keep his covenant and his decrees.

The friendship of the LORD is with those who fear him, and his covenant, for their instruction.

R. To you, O Lord, I lift my soul.

2ND Reading 1 Thes 3:12—4:2

Brothers and sisters:

May the Lord make you increase and abound in love for one another and for all, just as we have for you, so as to strengthen your hearts, to be blameless in holiness before our God and Father at the coming of our Lord Jesus with all his holy ones. Amen. Finally, brothers and sisters, we earnestly ask and exhort you in the Lord Jesus that, as you received from us how you should conduct yourselves to please God and as you are conducting yourselves you do so even more. For you know what instructions we gave you through the Lord Jesus.

Alleluia Ps 85:8

R. Alleluia, alleluia.

Show us, Lord, your love; and grant us your salvation.

R. Alleluia, alleluia.

Gospel Lk 21:25-28, 34-36
Jesus said to his disciples:

"There will be signs in the sun, the moon, and the stars, and on earth nations will be in dismay, perplexed by the roaring of the sea and the waves. People will die of fright in anticipation of what is coming upon the world, for the powers of the heavens will be shaken. And then they will see the Son of Man coming in a cloud with power and great glory. But when these signs begin to happen, stand erect and raise your heads because your redemption is at hand.

"Beware that your hearts do not become drowsy from carousing and drunkenness and the anxieties of daily life, and that day catch you by surprise like a trap. For that day will assault everyone who lives on the face of the earth. Be vigilant at all times and pray that you have the strength to escape the tribulations that are imminent and to stand before the Son of Man."

NOVEMBER 29TH, 2021
Monday of the First Week of Advent

1ST Reading Is 2:1-5
This is what Isaiah, son of Amoz, saw concerning Judah and Jerusalem. In days to come, The Mountain of the LORD's house shall be established as the highest mountain and raised above the hills. All nations shall stream toward it; many peoples shall come and say: "Come, let us climb the LORD's mountain, to the house of the God of Jacob, that he may instruct us in his ways, and we may walk in his paths." For from Zion shall go forth instruction, and the word of the LORD from Jerusalem. He shall judge

between the nations, and impose terms on many peoples. They shall beat their swords into plowshares and their spears into pruning hooks; one nation shall not raise the sword against another, nor shall they train for war again. O house of Jacob, come, let us walk in the light of the LORD!

Responsorial Psalm 122:1-2, 3-4b, 4cd-5, 6-7, 8-9
R. Let us go rejoicing to the house of the Lord.

I rejoiced because they said to me, "We will go up to the house of the LORD."

And now we have set foot within your gates, O Jerusalem.

R. Let us go rejoicing to the house of the Lord.

Jerusalem, built as a city with compact unity.

To it the tribes go up, the tribes of the LORD.

R. Let us go rejoicing to the house of the Lord.

According to the decree for Israel, to give thanks to the name of the LORD.

In it are set up judgment seats, seats for the house of David.

R. Let us go rejoicing to the house of the Lord.

Pray for the peace of Jerusalem! May those who love you prosper!

May peace be within your walls, prosperity in your buildings.

R. Let us go rejoicing to the house of the Lord.

Because of my relatives and friends I will say, "Peace be within you!"

Because of the house of the LORD, our God, I will pray for your good.

R. Let us go rejoicing to the house of the Lord.

Alleluia Ps 80:4

R. Alleluia, alleluia.

Come and save us, LORD our God; let your face shine upon us, that we may be saved.

R. Alleluia, alleluia.

Gospel Mt 8:5-11

When Jesus entered Capernaum, a centurion approached him and appealed
to him, saying, "Lord, my servant is lying at home paralyzed, suffering
dreadfully." He said to him, "I will come and cure him." The centurion said
in reply, "Lord, I am not worthy to have you enter under my roof; only say
the word and my servant will be healed. For I too am a man subject to
authority, with soldiers subject to me. And I say to one, 'Go,' and he goes;
and to another, 'Come here,' and he comes; and to my slave, 'Do this,' and
he does it."

When Jesus heard this, he was amazed and said to those following him,
"Amen, I say to you, in no one in Israel have I found such faith. I say to you,
many will come from the east and the west, and will recline with Abraham,
Isaac, and Jacob at the banquet in the Kingdom of heaven."

NOVEMBER 30TH, 2021
Feast of Saint Andrew, Apostle

1ST Reading Rom 10:9-18
Brothers and sisters:

If you confess with your mouth that Jesus is Lord and believe in your heart
that God raised him from the dead, you will be saved. For one believes with
the heart and so is justified, and one confesses with the mouth and so is
saved. The Scripture says, No one who believes in him will be put to shame.
There is no distinction between Jew and Greek; the same Lord is Lord of all,
enriching all who call upon him. For everyone who calls on the name of the
Lord will be saved. But how can they call on him in whom they have not
believed? And how can they believe in him of whom they have not heard?
And how can they hear without someone to preach? And how can people
preach unless they are sent? As it is written, how beautiful are the feet of
those who bring the good news! But not everyone has heeded the good
news; for Isaiah says, Lord, who has believed what was heard from us? Thus
faith comes from what is heard, and what is heard comes through the word
of Christ. But I ask, did they not hear? Certainly they did; for their voice has
gone forth to all the earth, and their words to the ends of the world.

Responsorial Psalm 19:8, 9, 10, 11
R. (10) The judgments of the Lord are true, and all of them are just.

or:

R. (John 6:63) Your words, Lord, are Spirit and life.

The law of the LORD is perfect, refreshing the soul;

The decree of the LORD is trustworthy, giving wisdom to the simple.

R. The judgments of the Lord are true, and all of them are just.

or:

R. Your words, Lord, are Spirit and life.

The precepts of the LORD are right, rejoicing the heart;

The command of the LORD is clear, enlightening the eye.

R. The judgments of the Lord are true, and all of them are just.

or:

R. Your words, Lord, are Spirit and life.

The fear of the LORD is pure, enduring forever;

The ordinances of the LORD are true, all of them just.

R. The judgments of the Lord are true, and all of them are just.

or:

R. Your words, Lord, are Spirit and life.

They are more precious than gold, than a heap of purest gold;

Sweeter also than syrup or honey from the comb.

R. The judgments of the Lord are true, and all of them are just.

or:

R. Your words, Lord, are Spirit and life.

Alleluia Mt 4:19

R. Alleluia, alleluia.

Come after me, says the Lord, and I will make you fishers of men.

R. Alleluia, alleluia.

Gospel Mt 4:18-22
As Jesus was walking by the Sea of Galilee, he saw two brothers, Simon who is called Peter, and his brother Andrew, casting a net into the sea; they were fishermen.

He said to them, "Come after me, and I will make you fishers of men." At once they left their nets and followed him. He walked along from there and saw two other brothers, James, the son of Zebedee, and his brother John. They were in a boat, with their father Zebedee, mending their nets. He called them, and immediately they left their boat and their father and followed him.

DECEMBER 1ST, 2021
Wednesday of the First Week of Advent

1ST Reading Is 25:6-10a
On this mountain the LORD of host will provide for all peoples

A feast of rich food and choice wines, juicy, rich food and pure, choice wines.

On this mountain he will destroy the veil that veils all peoples,

The web that is woven over all nations; he will destroy death forever.

The Lord GOD will wipe away the tears from all faces;

The reproach of his people he will remove from the whole earth; for the Lord has spoken.

On that day it will be said: "Behold our God, to whom we looked to save us! This is the LORD for whom we looked; let us rejoice and be glad that he has saved us!"

For the hand of the LORD will rest on this mountain!

Responsorial Psalm PS 23:1-3a, 3b-4, 5, 6
R. (6cd) I shall live in the house of the Lord all the days of my life.

685

The LORD is my shepherd; I shall not want. In verdant pastures he gives me repose;

Beside restful waters he leads me; he refreshes my soul.

R. I shall live in the house of the Lord all the days of my life.

He guides me in right paths for his name's sake. Even though I walk in the dark valley I fear no evil; for you are at my side

With your rod and your staff that give me courage.

R. I shall live in the house of the Lord all the days of my life.

You spread the table before me in the sight of my foes;

You anoint my head with oil; my cup overflows.

R. I shall live in the house of the Lord all the days of my life.

Only goodness and kindness follow me all the days of my life;

And I shall dwell in the house of the LORD for years to come.

R. I shall live in the house of the Lord all the days of my life.

Alleluia

R. Alleluia, alleluia.

Behold, the Lord comes to save his people; blessed are those prepared to meet him.

R. Alleluia, alleluia.

Gospel MT 15:29-37
At that time:

Jesus walked by the Sea of Galilee, went up on the mountain, and sat down there.

Great crowds came to him, having with them the lame, the blind, the deformed, the mute, and many others. They placed them at his feet, and he cured them. The crowds were amazed when they saw the mute speaking, the deformed made whole, the lame walking, and the blind able to see, and they glorified the God of Israel.

Jesus summoned his disciples and said, "My heart is moved with pity for the crowd, for they have been with me now for three days and have nothing to eat.

I do not want to send them away hungry, for fear they may collapse on the way." The disciples said to him, "Where could we ever get enough bread in this deserted place to satisfy such a crowd?"

Jesus said to them, "How many loaves do you have?" "Seven," they replied, "and a few fish."

He ordered the crowd to sit down on the ground.

Then he took the seven loaves and the fish, gave thanks, broke the loaves, and gave them to the disciples, who in turn gave them to the crowds. They all ate and were satisfied.

They picked up the fragments left over–seven baskets full

DECEMBER 2ND, 2021
Thursday of the First Week of Advent

1ST Reading
On that day they will sing this song in the land of Judah: "A strong city have we; he sets up walls and ramparts to protect us.

Open up the gates to let in a nation that is just, one that keeps faith. A nation of firm purpose you keep in peace; in peace, for its trust in you." Trust in the LORD forever! For the LORD is an eternal Rock. He humbles those in high places, and the lofty city he brings down; He tumbles it to the ground, levels it with the dust. It is trampled underfoot by the needy, by the footsteps of the poor.

Responsorial Psalm PS 118:1 AND 8-9, 19-21, 25-27A
R... (26a) Blessed is he who comes in the name of the Lord.

or:

R. Alleluia.

Give thanks to the LORD, for he is good, for his mercy endures forever. It is better to take refuge in the LORD than to trust in man. It is better to take refuge in the LORD than to trust in princes.

R. Blessed is he who comes in the name of the Lord.

or:

R. Alleluia.

Open to me the gates of justice; I will enter them and give thanks to the LORD. This gate is the LORD's; the just shall enter it. I will give thanks to you, for you have answered me and have been my savior.

R. Blessed is he who comes in the name of the Lord.

or:

R. Alleluia.

O LORD, grant salvation! O LORD, grant prosperity! Blessed is he who comes in the name of the LORD; we bless you from the house of the LORD. The LORD is God, and he has given us light.

R. Blessed is he who comes in the name of the Lord.

or:

R. Alleluia.

Alleluia IS 55:6

R. Alleluia, alleluia.

Seek the LORD while he may be found; call him while he is near.

R. Alleluia, alleluia.

Gospel MT 7:21, 24-27
Jesus said to his disciples:

"Not everyone who says to me, 'Lord, Lord,' will enter the Kingdom of heaven, but only the one who does the will of my Father in heaven.

"Everyone who listens to these words of mine and acts on them will be like a wise man who built his house on rock. The rain fell, the floods came, and the winds blew and buffeted the house. But it did not collapse; it had been set solidly on rock. And everyone who listens to these words of mine but does not act on them will be like a fool who built his house on sand.

The rain fell, the floods came, and the winds blew and buffeted the house. And it collapsed and was completely ruined."

DECEMBER 3RD, 2021
Memorial of Saint Francis Xavier, Priest

1ST Reading IS 29:17-24
Thus says the Lord GOD:

But a very little while, and Lebanon shall be changed into an orchard, and the orchard be regarded as a forest! On that day the deaf shall hear the words of a book; And out of gloom and darkness, the eyes of the blind shall see. The lowly will ever find joy in the LORD, and the poor rejoice in the Holy One of Israel. For the tyrant will be no more and the arrogant will have gone; All who are alert to do evil will be cut off, those whose mere word condemns a man, Who ensnare his defender at the gate, and leave the just man with an empty claim. Therefore thus says the LORD, the God of the house of Jacob, who redeemed Abraham:

Now Jacob shall have nothing to be ashamed of, nor shall his face grow pale. When his children see the work of my hands in his midst,

They shall keep my name holy; they shall reverence the Holy One of Jacob, and be in awe of the God of Israel. Those who err in spirit shall acquire understanding, and those who find fault shall receive instruction.

Responsorial Psalm PS 27:1, 4, 13-14
R... (1a) The Lord is my light and my salvation.

The LORD is my light and my salvation; whom should I fear? The LORD is my life's refuge; of whom should I be afraid?

R... The Lord is my light and my salvation.

One thing I ask of the LORD; this I seek: To dwell in the house of the LORD all the days of my life, That I may gaze on the loveliness of the LORD and contemplate his temple.

R... The Lord is my light and my salvation.

I believe that I shall see the bounty of the LORD in the land of the living. Wait for the LORD with courage; be stouthearted, and wait for the LORD.

R... The Lord is my light and my salvation.

Alleluia

R. Alleluia, alleluia.

Behold, our Lord shall come with power; he will enlighten the eyes of his servants.

R. Alleluia, alleluia.

Gospel MT 9:27-31
As Jesus passed by, two blind men followed him, crying out, "Son of David, have pity on us!" When he entered the house, the blind men approached him and Jesus said to them, "Do you believe that I can do this?" "Yes, Lord," they said to him. Then he touched their eyes and said,"Let it be done for you according to your faith."

And their eyes were opened. Jesus warned them sternly, "See that no one knows about this." But they went out and spread word of him through all that land.

DECEMBER 4TH, 2021
Saturday of the First Week of Advent

1ST Reading IS 30:19-21, 23-26
Thus says the Lord GOD, the Holy One of Israel: O people of Zion, who dwell in Jerusalem, no more will you weep; He will be gracious to you when you cry out, as soon as he hears he will answer you. The Lord will give you the bread you need and the water for which you thirst. No longer will your Teacher hide himself, but with your own eyes you shall see your Teacher, While from behind, a voice shall sound in your ears: "This is the way; walk in it," when you would turn to the right or to the left.

He will give rain for the seed that you sow in the ground, And the wheat that the soil produces will be rich and abundant. On that day your flock will be given pasture and the lamb will graze in spacious meadows; The oxen and the asses that till the ground will eat silage tossed to them with shovel and pitchfork. Upon every high mountain and lofty hill there will be streams of running water. On the day of the great slaughter, when the towers fall, The light of the moon will be like that of the sun and the light of the sun will be seven times greater like the light of seven days. On the day the LORD binds up the wounds of his people, he will heal the bruises left by his blows.

Responsorial Psalm PS 147:1-2, 3-4, 5-6
R... (see Isaiah 30:18d) Blessed are all who wait for the Lord.

Praise the LORD, for he is good; sing praise to our God, for he is gracious; it is fitting to praise him. The LORD rebuilds Jerusalem; the dispersed of Israel he gathers.

R. Blessed are all who wait for the Lord.

He heals the brokenhearted and binds up their wounds. He tells the number of the stars; he calls each by name.

R. Blessed are all who wait for the Lord.

Great is our LORD and mighty in power: to his wisdom there is no limit. The LORD sustains the lowly; the wicked he casts to the ground.

R. Blessed are all who wait for the Lord.

Alleluia IS 33:22

R. Alleluia, alleluia.

The LORD is our Judge, our Lawgiver, our King; he it is who will save us.

R. Alleluia, alleluia.

Gospel MT 9:35–10:1, 5A, 6-8
Jesus went around to all the towns and villages, teaching in their synagogues, proclaiming the Gospel of the Kingdom, and curing every disease and illness. At the sight of the crowds, his heart was moved with pity for them because they were troubled and abandoned, like sheep without a shepherd. Then he

said to his disciples, "The harvest is abundant but the laborers are few; so ask the master of the harvest to send out laborers for his harvest."

Then he summoned his Twelve disciples and gave them authority over unclean spirits to drive them out and to cure every disease and every illness. Jesus sent out these twelve after instructing them thus, "Go to the lost sheep of the house of Israel. As you go, make this proclamation: 'The Kingdom of heaven is at hand.' Cure the sick, raise the dead, cleanse lepers, drive out demons. Without cost you have received; without cost you are to give."

DECEMBER 5TH, 2021
Second Sunday of Advent

1ST Reading Bar 5:1-9

Jerusalem, take off your robe of mourning and misery; put on the splendor of glory from God forever: wrapped in the cloak of justice from God, bear on your head the mitre that displays the glory of the eternal name.

For God will show all the earth your splendor: you will be named by God forever the peace of justice, the glory of God's worship.

Up, Jerusalem! stand upon the heights; look to the east and see your children gathered from the east and the west at the word of the Holy One, rejoicing that they are remembered by God.

Led away on foot by their enemies they left you: but God will bring them back to you borne aloft in glory as on royal thrones.

For God has commanded that every lofty mountain be made low, and that the age-old depths and gorges be filled to level ground, that Israel may advance secure in the glory of God.

The forests and every fragrant kind of tree have overshadowed Israel at God's command; for God is leading Israel in joy by the light of his glory, with his mercy and justice for company..

Responsorial Psalm PS 126:1-2, 2-3, 4-5, 6.

R. (3) The Lord has done great things for us; we are filled with joy.

When the LORD brought back the captives of Zion, we were like men dreaming. Then our mouth was filled with laughter, and our tongue with rejoicing.

R. The Lord has done great things for us; we are filled with joy.

Then they said among the nations, "The LORD has done great things for them."

The LORD has done great things for us; we are glad indeed.

R. The Lord has done great things for us; we are filled with joy.

Restore our fortunes, O LORD, like the torrents in the southern desert. Those who sow in tears shall reap rejoicing.

R. The Lord has done great things for us; we are filled with joy.

Although they go forth weeping, carrying the seed to be sown. They shall come back rejoicing, carrying their sheaves.

R. The Lord has done great things for us; we are filled with joy.

2ND Reading Phil 1:4-6, 8-11
Brothers and sisters:

I pray always with joy in my every prayer for all of you, because of your partnership for the gospel from the first day until now.

I am confident of this, that the one who began a good work in you will continue to complete it until the day of Christ Jesus.

God is my witness, how I long for all of you with the affection of Christ Jesus. And this is my prayer: that your love may increase ever more and more in knowledge and every kind of perception, to discern what is of value, so that you may be pure and blameless for the day of Christ, filled with the fruit of righteousness that comes through Jesus Christ for the glory and praise of God.

Alleluia Lk 3:4, 6

R. Alleluia, alleluia.

Prepare the way of the Lord, make straight his paths: all flesh shall see the salvation of God.

R. Alleluia, alleluia..

In the fifteenth year of the reign of Tiberius Caesar, when Pontius Pilate was governor of Judea, and Herod was tetrarch of Galilee, and his brother Philip tetrarch of the region of Ituraea and Trachonitis, and Lysanias was tetrarch of Abilene, during the high priesthood of Annas and Caiaphas, the word of God came to John the son of Zechariah in the desert.

John went throughout the whole region of the Jordan, proclaiming a baptism of repentance for the forgiveness of sins, as it is written in the book of the words of the prophet Isaiah:

A voice of one crying out in the desert:

"Prepare the way of the Lord, make straight his paths.

Every valley shall be filled and every mountain and hill shall be made low.

The winding roads shall be made straight, and the rough ways made smooth, and all flesh shall see the salvation of God."

DECEMBER 6TH, 2021
Monday of the Second Week of Advent

1ST Reading Is 35:1-10
The desert and the parched land will exult; the steppe will rejoice and bloom. They will bloom with abundant flowers, and rejoice with joyful song. The glory of Lebanon will be given to them, the splendor of Carmel and Sharon; They will see the glory of the LORD, the splendor of our God. Strengthen the hands that are feeble, make firm the knees that are weak, Say to those whose hearts are frightened:

Be strong, fear not! Here is your God; he comes with vindication; with divine recompense he comes to save you.

Then will the eyes of the blind be opened, the ears of the deaf be cleared;

Then will the lame leap like a stag, then the tongue of the mute will sing. Streams will burst forth in the desert, and rivers in the steppe.

The burning sands will become pools, and the thirsty ground, springs of water; The abode where jackals lurk will be a marsh for the reed and papyrus. A highway will be there, called the holy way;

No one unclean may pass over it, nor fools go astray on it. No lion will be there, nor beast of prey go up to be met upon it. It is for those with a journey to make, and on it the redeemed will walk.

Those whom the LORD has ransomed will return and enter Zion singing, crowned with everlasting joy; They will meet with joy and gladness, sorrow and mourning will flee.

Responsorial Psalm PS 98:1, 2-3AB, 3CD-4
R. (Isaiah 35:4f) Our God will come to save us!

I will hear what God proclaims; the LORD –for he proclaims peace to his people.

Near indeed is his salvation to those who fear him, glory dwelling in our land.

R. Our God will come to save us!

Kindness and truth shall meet; justice and peace shall kiss.

Truth shall spring out of the earth, and justice shall look down from heaven.

R. Our God will come to save us!

The LORD himself will give his benefits; our land shall yield its increase.

Justice shall walk before him, and salvation, along the way of his steps.

R. Our God will come to save us!

Alleluia

R. Alleluia, alleluia.

Behold the king will come, the Lord of the earth, and he himself will lift the yoke of our capacity.

R. Alleluia, alleluia..

Gospel Lk 5:17-26
One day as Jesus was teaching,

Pharisees and teachers of the law, who had come from every village of Galilee and Judea and Jerusalem, were sitting there, and the power of the Lord was with him for healing.

And some men brought on a stretcher a man who was paralyzed; they were trying to bring him in and set him in his presence.

But not finding a way to bring him in because of the crowd, they went up on the roof and lowered him on the stretcher through the tiles into the middle in front of Jesus. When Jesus saw their faith, he said, "As for you, your sins are forgiven."

Then the scribes and Pharisees began to ask themselves, "Who is this who speaks blasphemies? Who but God alone can forgive sins?" Jesus knew their thoughts and said to them in reply, "What are you thinking in your hearts? Which is easier, to say, 'Your sins are forgiven,' or to say, 'Rise and walk'?

But that you may know that the Son of Man has authority on earth to forgive sins"–he said to the one who was paralyzed,

"I say to you, rise, pick up your stretcher, and go home." He stood up immediately before them, picked up what he had been lying on, and went home, glorifying God. Then astonishment seized them all and they glorified God, and, struck with awe, they said,"We have seen incredible things today.".

DECEMBER 7TH, 2021
Memorial of Saint Ambrose, Bishop and Doctor of the Church

1ST Reading IS 40:1-11
Comfort, give comfort to my people, says your God. Speak tenderly to Jerusalem, and proclaim to her that her service is at an end, her guilt is expiated; Indeed, she has received from the hand of the LORD double for all her sins.

A voice cries out:

In the desert prepare the way of the LORD! Make straight in the wasteland a highway for our God! Every valley shall be filled in, every mountain and hill shall be made low; The rugged land shall be made a plain, the rough country, a broad valley.

Then the glory of the LORD shall be revealed, and all people shall see it together; for the mouth of the LORD has spoken.

A voice says, "Cry out!" I answer, "What shall I cry out?"

"All flesh is grass, and all their glory like the flower of the field.

The grass withers, the flower wilts, when the breath of the LORD blows upon it. So then, the people is the grass. Though the grass withers and the flower wilts, the word of our God stands forever."

Go up onto a high mountain, Zion, herald of glad tidings; Cry out at the top of your voice, Jerusalem, herald of good news! Fear not to cry out and say to the cities of Judah: Here is your God! Here comes with power the Lord GOD, who rules by his strong arm; Here is his reward with him, his recompense before him. Like a shepherd he feeds his flock; in his arms he gathers the lambs, Carrying them in his bosom, and leading the ewes with care.

Responsorial Psalm PS 96:1-2, 3 AND 10AC, 11-12, 13
R... (see Isaiah 40:10ab) The Lord our God comes with power.

Sing to the LORD a new song; sing to the LORD, all you lands. Sing to the LORD; bless his name; announce his salvation, day after day.

R... The Lord our God comes with power.

Tell his glory among the nations; among all peoples, his wondrous deeds. Say among the nations: The LORD is king; he governs the peoples with equity.

R... The Lord our God comes with power.

Let the heavens be glad and the earth rejoice; let the sea and what fills it resound; let the plains be joyful and all that is in them! Then let all the trees of the forest rejoice.

R... The Lord our God comes with power.

They shall exult before the LORD, for he comes; for he comes to rule the earth. He shall rule the world with justice and the peoples with his constancy.

R… The Lord our God comes with power.

Alleluia

R. Alleluia, alleluia.

The day of the Lord is near; Behold, he comes to save us.

R. Alleluia, alleluia.

Gospel MT 18:12-14

Jesus said to his disciples: "What is your opinion? If a man has a hundred sheep and one of them goes astray, will he not leave the ninety-nine in the hills and go in search of the stray? And if he finds it, amen, I say to you, he rejoices more over it than over the ninety-nine that did not stray.

In just the same way, it is not the will of your heavenly Father that one of these little ones be lost."

DECEMBER 8TH, 2021
Solemnity of the Immaculate Conception of the Blessed Virgin Mary

1ST Reading GN 3:9-15, 20

After the man, Adam, had eaten of the tree, the LORD God called to the man and asked him, "Where are you?" He answered, "I heard you in the garden; but I was afraid, because I was naked, so I hid myself." Then he asked, "Who told you that you were naked? You have eaten, then, from the tree of which I had forbidden you to eat!" The man replied, "The woman whom you put here with me— she gave me fruit from the tree, and so I ate it." The LORD God then asked the woman, "Why did you do such a thing?"

The woman answered, "The serpent tricked me into it, so I ate it." Then the LORD God said to the serpent: "Because you have done this, you shall be banned from all the animals and from all the wild creatures; on your belly shall you crawl, and dirt shall you eat all the days of your life. I will put enmity between you and the woman, and between your offspring and hers; he will strike at your head, while you strike at his heel."

The man called his wife Eve, because she became the mother of all the living.

Responsorial Psalm PS 98:1, 2-3AB, 3CD-4

R... (1) Sing to the Lord a new song, for he has done marvelous deeds.

Sing to the LORD a new song, for he has done wondrous deeds; His right hand has won victory for him, his holy arm.

698

R. Sing to the Lord a new song, for he has done marvelous deeds.

The LORD has made his salvation known: in the sight of the nations he has revealed his justice. He has remembered his kindness and his faithfulness toward the house of Israel.

R. Sing to the Lord a new song, for he has done marvelous deeds.

All the ends of the earth have seen the salvation by our God. Sing joyfully to the LORD, all you lands; break into song; sing praise.

R. Sing to the Lord a new song, for he has done marvelous deeds.

2ND Reading EPH 1:3-6, 11-12
Brothers and sisters:

Blessed be the God and Father of our Lord Jesus Christ, who has blessed us in Christ with every spiritual blessing in the heavens, as he chose us in him, before the foundation of the world, to be holy and without blemish before him.

In love he destined us for adoption to himself through Jesus Christ, in accord with the favor of his will, for the praise of the glory of his grace that he granted us in the beloved.

In him we were also chosen, destined in accord with the purpose of the One who accomplishes all things according to the intention of his will, so that we might exist for the praise of his glory, we who first hoped in Christ.

Alleluia SEE LK 1:28

R. Alleluia, alleluia.

Hail, Mary, full of grace, the Lord is with you; blessed are you among women.

R. Alleluia, alleluia.

Gospel LK 1:26-38
The angel Gabriel was sent from God to a town of Galilee called Nazareth, to a virgin betrothed to a man named Joseph, of the house of David, and the virgin's name was Mary. And coming to her, he said, "Hail, full of grace! The Lord is with you." But she was greatly troubled at what was said and

pondered what sort of greeting this might be. Then the angel said to her, "Do not be afraid, Mary, for you have found favor with God. Behold, you will conceive in your womb and bear a son, and you shall name him Jesus.

He will be great and will be called Son of the Most High, and the Lord God will give him the throne of David his father, and he will rule over the house of Jacob forever, and of his Kingdom there will be no end." But Mary said to the angel, "How can this be, since I have no relations with a man?" And the angel said to her in reply,

"The Holy Spirit will come upon you, and the power of the Most High will overshadow you. Therefore the child to be born will be called holy, the Son of God. And behold, Elizabeth, your relative, has also conceived a son in her old age, and this is the sixth month for her who was called barren; for nothing will be impossible for God."

Mary said, "Behold, I am the handmaid of the Lord. May it be done to me according to your word." Then the angel departed from her.

DECEMBER 9TH, 2021
Thursday of the Second Week of Advent

1ST Reading Is 41:13-20

I am the LORD, your God, who grasp your right hand; It is I who say to you, "Fear not, I will help you."

Fear not, O worm Jacob, O maggot Israel;

I will help you, says the LORD; your redeemer is the Holy One of Israel. I will make of you a threshing sledge, sharp, new, and double-edged,

To thresh the mountains and crush them, to make the hills like chaff.

When you winnow them, the wind shall carry them off and the storm shall scatter them. But you shall rejoice in the LORD, and glory in the Holy One of Israel.

The afflicted and the needy seek water in vain, their tongues are parched with thirst. I, the LORD, will answer them; I, the God of Israel, will not forsake them.

I will open up rivers on the bare heights and fountains in the broad valleys;

I will turn the desert into a marshland, and the dry ground into springs of water. I will plant in the desert the cedar, acacia, myrtle, and olive;

I will set in the wasteland the cypress, together with the plane tree and the pine, That all may see and know, observe and understand,

That the hand of the LORD has done this, the Holy One of Israel has created it.

Responsorial Psalm PS 145:1 and 9, 10-11, 12-13ab
R (8) The Lord is gracious and merciful; slow to anger, and of great kindness.

I will extol you, O my God and King and I will bless your name forever and ever.

The LORD is good to all and compassionate toward all his works.

R. The Lord is gracious and merciful; slow to anger, and of great kindness.

Let all your works give you thanks, O LORD, and let your faithful ones bless you.

Let them discourse of the glory of your Kingdom and speak of your might.

R. The Lord is gracious and merciful; slow to anger, and of great kindness.

Let them make known to men your might and the glorious splendor of your Kingdom.

Your Kingdom is a Kingdom for all ages, and your dominion endures through all generations.

R. The Lord is gracious and merciful; slow to anger, and of great kindness.

Alleluia: See Is 45:8

R. Alleluia, alleluia.

Let the clouds rain down the Just One, and the earth bring forth a Savior.

R. Alleluia, alleluia..

DECEMBER 10TH, 2021

Memorial of Saint Lucy, Virgin and Martyr

1ST Reading IS 48:17-19

Thus says the LORD, your redeemer, the Holy One of Israel: I, the LORD, your God, teach you what is for your good, and lead you on the way you should go. If you would hearken to my commandments, your prosperity would be like a river, and your vindication like the waves of the sea; Your descendants would be like the sand, and those born of your stock like its grains, Their name never cut off or blotted out from my presence.

Responsorial Psalm PS 1:1-2, 3, 4 AND 6

R... (see John 8:12) Those who follow you, Lord, will have the light of life.

Blessed the man who follows not the counsel of the wicked Nor walks in the way of sinners, nor sits in the company of the insolent, But delights in the law of the LORD and meditates on his law day and night.

R. Those who follow you, Lord, will have the light of life.

He is like a tree planted near running water, That yields its fruit in due season, and whose leaves never fade. Whatever he does, prospers.

R... Those who follow you, Lord, will have the light of life.

Not so the wicked, not so; they are like chaff which the wind drives away. For the LORD watches over the way of the just, but the way of the wicked vanishes.

R... Those who follow you, Lord, will have the light of life.

Alleluia

R. Alleluia, alleluia.

The Lord will come; go out to meet him! He is the prince of peace.

R. Alleluia, alleluia.

Gospel MT 11:16-19

Jesus said to the crowds:

"To what shall I compare this generation? It is like children who sit in marketplaces and call to one another, 'We played the flute for you, but you

702

did not dance, we sang a dirge but you did not mourn.' For John came neither eating nor drinking, and they said, 'He is possessed by a demon.' The Son of Man came eating and drinking and they said, 'Look, he is a glutton and a drunkard, a friend of tax collectors and sinners.' But wisdom is vindicated by her works."

Gospel Mt 11:11-15
Jesus said to the crowds:

"Amen, I say to you, among those born of women there has been none greater than John the Baptist; yet the least in the Kingdom of heaven is greater than he.

From the days of John the Baptist until now, the Kingdom of heaven suffers violence, and the violent are taking it by force.

All the prophets and the law prophesied up to the time of John. And if you are willing to accept it, he is Elijah, the one who is to come.

Whoever has ears ought to hear."."

DECEMBER 11TH, 2021
Memorial of Saint John of the Cross, Priest and Doctor of the Church

1ST Reading SIR 48:1-4, 9-11
In those days, like a fire there appeared the prophet Elijah whose words were as a flaming furnace. Their staff of bread he shattered, in his zeal he reduced them to straits; By the Lord's word he shut up the heavens and three times brought down fire. How awesome are you, Elijah, in your wondrous deeds! Whose glory is equal to yours? You were taken aloft in a whirlwind of fire, in a chariot with fiery horses. You were destined, it is written, in time to come to put an end to wrath before the day of the LORD, To turn back the hearts of fathers toward their sons, and to re-establish the tribes of Jacob. Blessed is he who shall have seen you and who falls asleep in your friendship.

Responsorial Psalm PS 80:2AC AND 3B, 15-16, 18-19
R. (4) Lord, make us turn to you; let us see your face and we shall be saved.

O shepherd of Israel, hearken, From your throne upon the cherubim, shine forth. Rouse your power.

R. Lord, make us turn to you; let us see your face and we shall be saved.

Once again, O LORD of hosts, look down from heaven, and see; Take care of this vine, and protect what your right hand has planted the son of man whom you yourself made strong.

R. Lord, make us turn to you; let us see your face and we shall be saved.

May your help be with the man of your right hand, with the son of man whom you yourself made strong. Then we will no more withdraw from you; give us new life, and we will call upon your name.

R. Lord, make us turn to you; let us see your face and we shall be saved.

Alleluia LK 3:4, 6

R. Alleluia, alleluia.

Prepare the way of the Lord, make straight his paths: All flesh shall see the salvation of God.

R. Alleluia, alleluia.

Gospel MT 17:9A, 10-13
As they were coming down from the mountain, the disciples asked Jesus, "Why do the scribes say that Elijah must come first?" He said in reply, "Elijah will indeed come and restore all things; but I tell you that Elijah has already come, and they did not recognize him but did to him whatever they pleased.

So also will the Son of Man suffer at their hands." Then the disciples understood that he was speaking to them of John the Baptist.

DECEMBER 12TH, 2021
Third Sunday of Advent

1ST Reading Zep 3:14-18a
Shout for joy, O daughter Zion! Sing joyfully, O Israel! Be glad and exult with all your heart, O daughter Jerusalem!

The LORD has removed the judgment against you he has turned away your enemies; the King of Israel, the LORD, is in your midst, you have no further misfortune to fear. On that day, it shall be said to Jerusalem: Fear not, O Zion, be not discouraged!

The LORD, your God, is in your midst, a mighty savior; he will rejoice over you with gladness, and renew you in his love, he will sing joyfully because of you, as one sings at festivals.

Responsorial Psalm Is 12:2-3, 4, 5-6..
R. (6) Cry out with joy and gladness: for among you is the great and Holy One of Israel.

God indeed is my savior; I am confident and unafraid.

My strength and my courage is the LORD, and he has been my savior. With joy you will draw water at the fountain of salvation.

R. Cry out with joy and gladness: for among you is the great and Holy One of Israel.

Give thanks to the LORD, acclaim his name; among the nations make known his deeds, proclaim how exalted is his name.

R. Cry out with joy and gladness: for among you is the great and Holy One of Israel.

Sing praise to the LORD for his glorious achievement; let this be known throughout all the earth.

Shout with exultation, O city of Zion, for great in your midst is the Holy One of Israel!

R. Cry out with joy and gladness: for among you is the great and Holy One of Israel.

2ND Reading Phil 4:4-7
Brothers and sisters:

Rejoice in the Lord always. I shall say it again: rejoice! Your kindness should be known to all. The Lord is near. Have no anxiety at all, but in everything, by prayer and petition, with thanksgiving, make your requests known to God.

Then the peace of God that surpasses all understanding will guard your hearts and minds in Christ Jesus.

Alleluia: Is 61:1 (cited in Lk 4:18)

R. Alleluia, alleluia.

The Spirit of the Lord is upon me, because he has anointed me to bring glad tidings to the poor.

R. Alleluia, alleluia.

Gospel Lk 3:10-18
The crowds asked John the Baptist, "What should we do?"

He said to them in reply, "Whoever has two cloaks should share with the person who has none. And whoever has food should do likewise."

Even tax collectors came to be baptized and they said to him, "Teacher, what should we do?" He answered them, "Stop collecting more than what is prescribed." Soldiers also asked him,

"And what is it that we should do?" He told them,

"Do not practice extortion, do not falsely accuse anyone, and be satisfied with your wages."

Now the people were filled with expectation, and all were asking in their hearts whether John might be the Christ.

John answered them all, saying, "I am baptizing you with water, but one mightier than I is coming. I am not worthy to loosen the thongs of his sandals. He will baptize you with the Holy Spirit and fire.

His winnowing fan is in his hand to clear his threshing floor and to gather the wheat into his barn, but the chaff he will burn with unquenchable fire." Exhorting them in many other ways, he preached good news to the people

DECEMBER 13TH, 2021
Memorial of Saint Lucy, Virgin and Martyr

1ST Reading NM 24:2-7, 15-17A
When Balaam raised his eyes and saw Israel encamped, tribe by tribe, the spirit of God came upon him, and he gave voice to his oracle: The utterance of Balaam, son of Beor, the utterance of a man whose eye is true, The utterance of one who hears what God says, and knows what the Most High knows, Of one who sees what the Almighty sees, enraptured, and with eyes unveiled:

How goodly are your tents, O Jacob; your encampments, O Israel! They are like gardens beside a stream, like the cedars planted by the LORD.

His wells shall yield free-flowing waters, he shall have the sea within reach; His king shall rise higher, and his royalty shall be exalted. Then Balaam gave voice to his oracle: The utterance of Balaam, son of Beor, the utterance of the man whose eye is true, The utterance of one who hears what God says, and knows what the Most High knows, Of one who sees what the Almighty sees, enraptured, and with eyes unveiled. I see him, though not now; I behold him, though not near: A star shall advance from Jacob, and a staff shall rise from Israel.

Responsorial Psalm PS 25:4-5AB, 6 AND 7BC, 8-9
R. (4) Teach me your ways, O Lord.

Your ways, O LORD, make known to me; teach me your paths, Guide me in your truth and teach me, for you are God my savior.

R. Teach me your ways, O Lord.

Remember that your compassion, O LORD, and your kindness are from of old. In your kindness remember me, because of your goodness, O LORD.

R. Teach me your ways, O Lord.

Good and upright is the LORD; thus he shows sinners the way. He guides the humble to justice, he teaches the humble his way.

R. Teach me your ways, O Lord.

Alleluia PS 85:8

R. Alleluia, alleluia.

Show us, LORD, your love, and grant us your salvation.

R. Alleluia, alleluia.

Gospel MT 21:23-27
When Jesus had come into the temple area, the chief priests and the elders of the people approached him as he was teaching and said, "By what authority are you doing these things? And who gave you this authority?"

Jesus said to them in reply, "I shall ask you one question, and if you answer it for me, then I shall tell you by what authority I do these things. Where was John's baptism from? Was it of heavenly or of human origin?" They discussed this among themselves and said, "If we say 'Of heavenly origin,' he will say to us, 'Then why did you not believe him?' But if we say, 'Of human origin,' we fear the crowd, for they all regard John as a prophet."

So they said to Jesus in reply, "We do not know." He himself said to them, "Neither shall I tell you by what authority I do these things."

DECEMBER 14TH, 2021
Memorial of Saint John of the Cross, Priest and Doctor of the Church

1ST Reading Zep 3:1-2, 9-13
Thus says the Lord:

Woe to the city, rebellious and polluted, to the tyrannical city!

She hears no voice, accepts no correction; In the Lord she has not trusted, to her God she has not drawn near.

For then I will change and purify the lips of the peoples,

That they all may call upon the name of the Lord, to serve him with one accord;

From beyond the rivers of Ethiopia and as far as the recesses of the North, they shall bring me offerings. On that day You need not be ashamed of all your deeds, your rebellious actions against me;

For then will I remove from your midst the proud braggarts, And you shall no longer exalt yourself on my holy mountain.

But I will leave as a remnant in your midst a people humble and lowly, Who shall take refuge in the name of the Lord: the remnant of Israel. They shall do no wrong and speak no lies;

Nor shall there be found in their mouths a deceitful tongue;

They shall pasture and couch their flocks with none to disturb them. The word of the Lord."

R..(7a) The Lord hears the cry of the poor.

I will bless the Lord at all times; his praise shall be ever in my mouth. Let my soul glory in the Lord; the lowly will hear me and be glad.

R. The Lord hears the cry of the poor.

Look to him that you may be radiant with joy, and your faces may not blush with shame. When the poor one called out, the Lord heard, and from all his distress he saved him.

R. The Lord hears the cry of the poor.

The Lord confronts the evildoers, to destroy remembrance of them from the earth. When the just cry out, the Lord hears them, and from all their distress he rescues them.

R. The Lord hears the cry of the poor.

The Lord is close to the brokenhearted; and those who are crushed in spirit he saves.

The Lord redeems the lives of his servants; no one incurs guilt who takes refuge in him.

R. The Lord hears the cry of the poor.

Alleluia

R. Alleluia, alleluia.

Come, O Lord, do not delay; forgive the sins of your people.

R. Alleluia, alleluia.

Gospel Mt 21:28-32
Jesus said to the chief priests and the elders of the people:

"What is your opinion? A man had two sons. He came to the first and said, 'Son, go out and work in the vineyard today.'

The son said in reply, 'I will not,' but afterwards he changed his mind and went. The man came to the other son and gave the same order. He said in reply, 'Yes, sir,' but did not go.

Which of the two did his father's will?" They answered, "The first." Jesus said to them, "Amen, I say to you, tax collectors and prostitutes are entering the Kingdom of God before you.

When John came to you in the way of righteousness, you did not believe him; but tax collectors and prostitutes did. Yet even when you saw that, you did not later change your minds and believe him."

DECEMBER 15TH, 2021
Wednesday of the Third Week of Advent

1ST Reading Is 45:6c-8, 18, 21c-25
I am the LORD, there is no other; I form the light, and create the darkness, I make well-being and create woe; I, the LORD, do all these things.

Let justice descend, O heavens, like dew from above, like gentle rain let the skies drop it down.

Let the earth open and salvation bud forth; let justice also spring up! I, the LORD, have created this. For thus says the LORD,

The creator of the heavens, who is God, The designer and maker of the earth who established it, Not creating it to be a waste, but designing it be lived in:

I am the LORD, and there is no other.

Who announced this from the beginning and foretold it from of old? Was it not I, the LORD, besides whom there is no other God? There is no just and saving God but me.

Turn to me and be safe, all you ends of the earth, for I am God; there is no other!

By myself I swear, uttering my just decree and my unalterable word: To me every knee shall bend; by me every tongue shall swear,

Saying, "Only in the LORD are just deeds and power. Before him in shame shall come all who vent their anger against him. In the LORD shall be the vindication and the glory of all the descendants of Israel.".

Responsorial Psalm 85:9ab and 10, 11-12, 13-14
R. (Isaiah 45:8) Let the clouds rain down the Just One, and the earth bring forth a Savior.

I will hear what God proclaims; the Lord–for he proclaims peace to his people.

Near indeed is his salvation to those who fear him, glory dwelling in our land.

R. Let the clouds rain down the Just One, and the earth bring forth a Savior.

Kindness and truth shall meet; justice and peace shall kiss.

Truth shall spring out of the earth, and justice shall look down from heaven.

R. Let the clouds rain down the Just One, and the earth bring forth a Savior.

The Lord himself will give his benefits; our land shall yield its increase. Justice shall walk before him, and salvation, along the way of his steps.

R. Let the clouds rain down the Just One, and the earth bring forth a Savior.

Alleluia: See Isaiah 40:9-10

R. Alleluia, alleluia.

Raise your voice and tell the Good News: Behold, the Lord God comes with power.

R. Alleluia, alleluia.

Gospel Lk 7:18b-23
At that time,

John summoned two of his disciples and sent them to the Lord to ask,

"Are you the one who is to come, or should we look for another?" When the men came to the Lord, they said," John the Baptist has sent us to you to ask, 'Are you the one who is to come, or should we look for another?'" At that time Jesus cured many of their diseases, sufferings, and evil spirits; he also granted sight to many who were blind.

And Jesus said to them in reply, "Go and tell John what you have seen and heard: the blind regain their sight, the lame walk, lepers are cleansed, the deaf hear, the dead are raised, the poor have the good news proclaimed to them.

And blessed is the one who takes no offense at me.

DECEMBER 16TH, 2021
Thursday of the Third Week of Advent

1ST Reading Is 54:1-10

Raise a glad cry, you barren one who did not bear, Break forth in jubilant song, you who were not in labor, For more numerous are the children of the deserted wife than the children of her who has a husband, says the Lord.

Enlarge the space for your tent, spread out your tent cloths unsparingly; lengthen your ropes and make firm your stakes. For you shall spread abroad to the right and to the left; your descendants shall dispossess the nations and shall people the desolate cities.

Fear not, you shall not be put to shame; you need not blush, for you shall not be disgraced. The shame of your youth you shall forget, the reproach of your widowhood no longer remember.

For he who has become your husband is your Maker; his name is the Lord of hosts;

Your redeemer is the Holy One of Israel, called God of all the earth.

The Lord calls you back, like a wife forsaken and grieved in spirit, A wife married in youth and then cast off, says your God. For a brief moment I abandoned you, but with great tenderness I will take you back. In an outburst of wrath, for a moment. I hid my face from you, But with enduring love I take pity on you, says the Lord, your redeemer.

This is for me like the days of Noah, when I swore that the waters of Noah should never again deluge the earth; So I have sworn not to be angry with you, or to rebuke you. Though the mountains leave their place and the hills be shaken, My love shall never leave you nor my covenant of peace be shaken, says the Lord, who has mercy on you

712

R. (2a) I will praise you, Lord, for you have rescued me.

I will extol you, O Lord, for you drew me clear and did not let my enemies rejoice over me.

O Lord, you brought me up from the nether world; you preserved me from among those going down into the pit.

R. I will praise you, Lord, for you have rescued me.

Sing praise to the Lord, you his faithful ones, and give thanks to his holy name. For his anger lasts but a moment; a lifetime, his good will.

At nightfall, weeping enters in but with the dawn, rejoicing.

R. I will praise you, Lord, for you have rescued me.

"Hear, O Lord, and have pity on me; O Lord, be my helper."

You changed my mourning into dancing; O Lord, my God, forever will I give you thanks.

R. I will praise you, Lord, for you have rescued me.

Alleluia: Luke 3:4, 6

R. Alleluia, alleluia.

Prepare the way of the Lord, make straight his paths: All flesh shall see the salvation of God.

R. Alleluia, alleluia.

Gospel Lk 7:24-30
When the messengers of John the Baptist had left,

Jesus began to speak to the crowds about John.

"What did you go out to the desert to see a reed swayed by the wind? Then what did you go out to see? Someone dressed in fine garments?

Those who dress luxuriously and live sumptuously are found in royal palaces. Then what did you go out to see? A prophet? Yes, I tell you, and more than a prophet.

This is the one about whom Scripture says: Behold, I am sending my messenger ahead of you, he will prepare your way before you.

I tell you, among those born of women, no one is greater than John; yet the least in the Kingdom of God is greater than he."

(All the people who listened, including the tax collectors, who were baptized with the baptism of John, acknowledged the righteousness of God; but the Pharisees and scholars of the law, who were not baptized by him, rejected the plan of God for themselves.)

DECEMBER 17TH, 2021
Friday of the Third Week of Advent

1ST Reading Gn 49:2, 8-10

Jacob called his sons and said to them: "Assemble and listen, sons of Jacob, listen to Israel, your father. "You, Judah, shall your brothers praise–your hand on the neck of your enemies; the sons of your father shall bow down to you. Judah, like a lion's whelp, you have grown up on prey, my son. He crouches like a lion recumbent, the king of beasts–who would dare rouse him?

The scepter shall never depart from Judah, or the mace from between his legs, While tribute is brought to him, and he receives the people's homage.".

Responsorial Psalm 72:1-2, 3-4ab, 7-8, 17

R..(see 7) Justice shall flourish in his time, and fullness of peace for ever.

O God, with your judgment endow the king, and with your justice, the king's son;

He shall govern your people with justice and your afflicted ones with judgment.

R. Justice shall flourish in his time, and fullness of peace for ever.

The mountains shall yield peace for the people, and the hills justice. He shall defend the afflicted among the people, save the children of the poor.

R. Justice shall flourish in his time, and fullness of peace for ever.

Justice shall flower in his days, and profound peace, till the moon be no more. May he rule from sea to sea, and from the River to the ends of the earth.

R. Justice shall flourish in his time, and fullness of peace for ever.

May his name be blessed forever; as long as the sun his name shall remain. In him shall all the tribes of the earth be blessed; all the nations shall proclaim his happiness.

R. Justice shall flourish in his time, and fullness of peace for ever.

Alleluia

R. Alleluia, alleluia.

O Wisdom of our God Most High, guiding creation with power and love: come to teach us the path of knowledge!

R. Alleluia, alleluia..

Gospel Mt 1:1-17
The book of the genealogy of Jesus Christ, the son of David, the son of Abraham.

Abraham became the father of Isaac, Isaac the father of Jacob, Jacob the father of Judah and his brothers. Judah became the father of Perez and Zerah, whose mother was Tamar. Perez became the father of Hezron, Hezron the father of Ram, Ram the father of Amminadab. Amminadab became the father of Nahshon, Nahshon the father of Salmon, Salmon the father of Boaz, whose mother was Rahab. Boaz became the father of Obed, whose mother was Ruth. Obed became the father of Jesse, Jesse the father of David the king.

David became the father of Solomon, whose mother had been the wife of Uriah. Solomon became the father of Rehoboam, Rehoboam the father of Abijah, Abijah the father of Asaph. Asaph became the father of Jehoshaphat, Jehoshaphat the father of Joram, Joram the father of Uzziah. Uzziah became the father of Jotham, Jotham the father of Ahaz, Ahaz the father of Hezekiah.

Hezekiah became the father of Manasseh, Manasseh the father of Amos, Amos the father of Josiah. Josiah became the father of Jechoniah and his brothers at the time of the Babylonian exile.

After the Babylonian exile, Jechoniah became the father of Shealtiel, Shealtiel the father of Zerubbabel, Zerubbabel the father of Abiud. Abiud became the father of Eliakim, Eliakim the father of Azor, Azor the father of Zadok. Zadok became the father of Achim, Achim the father of Eliud, Eliud the father of Eleazar. Eleazar became the father of Matthan,

Matthan the father of Jacob, Jacob the father of Joseph, the husband of Mary. Of her was born Jesus who is called the Christ.

Thus the total number of generations from Abraham to David is fourteen generations; from David to the Babylonian exile, fourteen generations; from the Babylonian exile to the Christ, fourteen generations..

DECEMBER 18TH, 2021
Saturday of the Third Week of Advent

1ST Reading Jer 23:5-8
Behold, the days are coming, says the LORD, when I will raise up a righteous shoot to David;

As king he shall reign and govern wisely, he shall do what is just and right in the land. In his days Judah shall be saved, Israel shall dwell in security. This is the name they give him: "The LORD our justice."

Therefore, the days will come, says the LORD, when they shall no longer say, "As the LORD lives, who brought the children of Israel out of the land of Egypt"; but rather, "As the LORD lives, who brought the descendants of the house of Israel up from the land of the north"– and from all the lands to which I banished them; they shall again live on their own land.

Responsorial Psalm 72:1-2, 12-13, 18-19
R. (see 7) Justice shall flourish in his time, and fullness of peace for ever.

O God, with your judgment endow the king, and with your justice, the king's son; He shall govern your people with justice and your afflicted ones with judgment.

R. Justice shall flourish in his time, and fullness of peace for ever.

For he shall rescue the poor when he cries out, and the afflicted when he has no one to help him.

He shall have pity for the lowly and the poor; the lives of the poor he shall save.

R. Justice shall flourish in his time, and fullness of peace for ever.

Blessed be the LORD, the God of Israel, who alone does wondrous deeds.

And blessed forever be his glorious name; may the whole earth be filled with his glory.

R. Justice shall flourish in his time, and fullness of peace for ever.

Alleluia

R. Alleluia, alleluia.

O Leader of the House of Israel, giver of the Law to Moses on Sinai: come to rescue us with your mighty power!

R. Alleluia, alleluia..

Gospel Mt 1:18-25

This is how the birth of Jesus Christ came about.

When his mother Mary was betrothed to Joseph, but before they lived together, she was found with child through the Holy Spirit.

Joseph her husband, since he was a righteous man, yet unwilling to expose her to shame, decided to divorce her quietly. Such was his intention when, behold, the angel of the Lord appeared to him in a dream and said,

"Joseph, son of David, do not be afraid to take Mary your wife into your home. For it is through the Holy Spirit that this child has been conceived in her. She will bear a son and you are to name him Jesus, because he will save his people from their sins."

All this took place to fulfill what the Lord had said through the prophet: Behold, the virgin shall be with child and bear a son, and they shall name him Emmanuel, which means "God is with us."

When Joseph awoke, he did as the angel of the Lord had commanded him and took his wife into his home.

He had no relations with her until she bore a son, and he named him Jesus."

DECEMBER 19TH, 2021
Fourth Sunday of Advent

1ST Reading Mi 5:1-4a

Thus says the LORD: You, Bethlehem-Ephrathah too small to be among the clans of Judah, from you shall come forth for me one who is to be ruler in Israel; whose origin is from of old, from ancient times. Therefore the Lord will give them up, until the time when she who is to give birth has borne, and the rest of his kindred shall return to the children of Israel.

He shall stand firm and shepherd his flock by the strength of the LORD, in the majestic name of the LORD, his God; and they shall remain, for now his greatness shall reach to the ends of the earth; he shall be peace.

Responsorial Psalm Ps 80:2-3, 15-16, 18-19.

R (4) Lord, make us turn to you; let us see your face and we shall be saved.

O shepherd of Israel, hearken, from your throne upon the cherubim, shine forth.

Rouse your power, and come to save us.

R. Lord, make us turn to you; let us see your face and we shall be saved.

Once again, O LORD of hosts, look down from heaven, and see; take care of this vine, and protect what your right hand has planted the son of man whom you yourself made strong.

R. Lord, make us turn to you; let us see your face and we shall be saved.

May your help be with the man of your right hand, with the son of man whom you yourself made strong.

Then we will no more withdraw from you; give us new life, and we will call upon your name.

R. Lord, make us turn to you; let us see your face and we shall be saved.

Brothers and sisters:

When Christ came into the world, he said: "Sacrifice and offering you did not desire, but a body you prepared for me; in holocausts and sin offerings you took no delight.

Then I said, 'As is written of me in the scroll, behold, I come to do your will, O God.'"

First he says, "Sacrifices and offerings, holocausts and sin offerings, you neither desired nor delighted in." These are offered according to the law. Then he says, Behold, I come to do your will." He takes away the first to establish the second. By this "will," we have been consecrated through the offering of the body of Jesus Christ once for all.

Alleluia: Lk 1:38

R. Alleluia, alleluia.

Behold, I am the handmaid of the Lord. May it be done to me according to your word.

R. Alleluia, alleluia..

Gospel Lk 1:39-45
Mary set out and traveled to the hill country in haste to a town of Judah, where she entered the house of Zechariah and greeted Elizabeth.

When Elizabeth heard Mary's greeting, the infant leaped in her womb, and Elizabeth, filled with the Holy Spirit, cried out in a loud voice and said,

"Blessed are you among women, and blessed is the fruit of your womb.

And how does this happen to me, that the mother of my Lord should come to me? For at the moment the sound of your greeting reached my ears, the infant in my womb leaped for joy.

Blessed are you who believed that what was spoken to you by the Lord would be fulfilled."

1ST Reading IS 7:10-14

The LORD spoke to Ahaz:

Ask for a sign from the LORD, your God; let it be deep as the nether world, or high as the sky! But Ahaz answered,

"I will not ask! I will not tempt the LORD!"

Then Isaiah said: Listen, O house of David! Is it not enough for you to weary men, must you also weary my God? Therefore the Lord himself will give you this sign: the virgin shall conceive and bear a son, and shall name him Emmanuel.

Responsorial Psalm PS 24:1-2, 3-4AB, 5-6

R... (see 7c and 10b) Let the Lord enter; he is the king of glory.

The LORD's are the earth and its fullness; the world and those who dwell in it. For he founded it upon the seas and established it upon the rivers.

R. Let the Lord enter; he is the king of glory.

Who can ascend the mountain of the LORD? or who may stand in his holy place? He whose hands are sinless, whose heart is clean, who desires not what is vain.

R. Let the Lord enter; he is the king of glory.

He shall receive a blessing from the LORD, a reward from God his savior. Such is the race that seeks for him, that seeks the face of the God of Jacob.

R. Let the Lord enter; he is the king of glory.

Alleluia

R. Alleluia, alleluia.

O Key of David, opening the gates of God's eternal Kingdom: come and free the prisoners of darkness!

R. Alleluia, alleluia.

Gospel LK 1:26-38

In the sixth month, the angel Gabriel was sent from God to a town of Galilee called Nazareth, to a virgin betrothed to a man named Joseph, of the house of David, and the virgin's name was Mary. And coming to her, he said, "Hail, full of grace! The Lord is with you." But she was greatly troubled at what was said and pondered what sort of greeting this might be. Then the angel said to her, "Do not be afraid, Mary, for you have found favor with God.

Behold, you will conceive in your womb and bear a son, and you shall name him Jesus. He will be great and will be called Son of the Most High, and the Lord God will give him the throne of David his father, and he will rule over the house of Jacob forever, and of his Kingdom there will be no end."

But Mary said to the angel, "How can this be, since I have no relations with a man?" And the angel said to her in reply, "The Holy Spirit will come upon you, and the power of the Most High will overshadow you. Therefore the child to be born will be called holy, the Son of God.

And behold, Elizabeth, your relative, has also conceived a son in her old age, and this is the sixth month for her who was called barren; for nothing will be impossible for God."

Mary said, "Behold, I am the handmaid of the Lord.

May it be done to me according to your word." Then the angel departed from her.

DECEMBER 21ST, 2021
Tuesday of the Fourth Week of Advent

1ST Reading SG 2:8-14

Hark! my lover–here he comes springing across the mountains, leaping across the hills. My lover is like a gazelle or a young stag. Here he stands behind our wall, gazing through the windows, peering through the lattices. My lover speaks; he says to me, "Arise, my beloved, my dove, my beautiful one, and come!

"For see, the winter is past, the rains are over and gone. The flowers appear on the earth, the time of pruning the vines has come, and the song of the dove is heard in our land.

The fig tree puts forth its figs, and the vines, in bloom, give forth fragrance. Arise, my beloved, my beautiful one, and come!

"O my dove in the clefts of the rock, in the secret recesses of the cliff, Let me see you, let me hear your voice, For your voice is sweet, and you are lovely."

Or ZEP 3:14-18A

Shout for joy, O daughter Zion! Sing joyfully, O Israel! Be glad and exult with all your heart, O daughter Jerusalem! The LORD has removed the judgment against you, he has turned away your enemies;

The King of Israel, the LORD, is in your midst, you have no further misfortune to fear. On that day, it shall be said to Jerusalem: Fear not, O Zion, be not discouraged! The LORD, your God, is in your midst, a mighty savior; He will rejoice over you with gladness, and renew you in his love, He will sing joyfully because of you, as one sings at festivals.

Responsorial Psalm PS 33:2-3, 11-12, 20-21
R... (1a; 3a) Exult, you just, in the Lord! Sing to him a new song.

Give thanks to the LORD on the harp; with the ten-stringed lyre chant his praises. Sing to him a new song; pluck the strings skillfully, with shouts of gladness.

R. Exult, you just, in the Lord! Sing to him a new song.

But the plan of the LORD stands forever; the design of his heart, through all generations. Blessed the nation whose God is the LORD, the people he has chosen for his own inheritance.

R. Exult, you just, in the Lord! Sing to him a new song.

Our soul waits for the LORD, who is our help and our shield, For in him our hearts rejoice; in his holy name we trust.

R. Exult, you just, in the Lord! Sing to him a new song.

Alleluia

R. Alleluia, alleluia.

O Emmanuel, our King and Giver of Law: come to save us, Lord our God!

R. Alleluia, alleluia.

Gospel LK 1:39-45
Mary set out in those days and traveled to the hill country in haste to a town of Judah, where she entered the house of Zechariah and greeted Elizabeth. When Elizabeth heard Mary's greeting, the infant leaped in her womb, and Elizabeth, filled with the Holy Spirit, cried out in a loud voice and said, "Most blessed are you among women, and blessed is the fruit of your womb.

And how does this happen to me, that the mother of my Lord should come to me? For at the moment the sound of your greeting reached my ears, the infant in my womb leaped for joy. Blessed are you who believed that what was spoken to you by the Lord would be fulfilled."

DECEMBER 22ND, 2021
Wednesday of the Fourth Week of Advent

1ST Reading 1 Sm 1:24-28
In those days,

Hannah brought Samuel with her, along with a three-year-old bull, an ephah of flour, and a skin of wine, and presented him at the temple of the LORD in Shiloh. After the boy's father had sacrificed the young bull,

Hannah, his mother, approached Eli and said: "Pardon, my lord!

As you live, my lord, I am the woman who stood near you here, praying to the LORD. I prayed for this child, and the LORD granted my request.

Now I, in turn, give him to the LORD; as long as he lives, he shall be dedicated to the LORD." She left Samuel there.

Responsorial Psalm   1 Samuel 2:1, 4-5, 6-7, 8abcd
R. (see 1a) My heart exults in the Lord, my Savior.

"My heart exults in the LORD, my horn is exalted in my God.

I have swallowed up my enemies; I rejoice in my victory."

R. My heart exults in the Lord, my Savior.

"The bows of the mighty are broken, while the tottering gird on strength. The well-fed hire themselves out for bread, while the hungry batten on spoil.

The barren wife bears seven sons, while the mother of many languishes."

R. My heart exults in the Lord, my Savior.

"The LORD puts to death and gives life; he casts down to the nether world; he raises up again.

The LORD makes poor and makes rich, he humbles, he also exalts."

R. My heart exults in the Lord, my Savior.

"He raises the needy from the dust; from the dung heap he lifts up the poor, To seat them with nobles and make a glorious throne their heritage."

R. My heart exults in the Lord, my Savior.

Alleluia

R. Alleluia, alleluia.

O King of all nations and keystone of the Church: come and save man, whom you formed from the dust!

R. Alleluia, alleluia..

Gospel Lk 1:46-56
Mary said:

"My soul proclaims the greatness of the Lord; my spirit rejoices in God my savior. for he has looked upon his lowly servant. From this day all generations will call me blessed: the Almighty has done great things for me, and holy is his Name.

He has mercy on those who fear him in every generation.

He has shown the strength of his arm, and has scattered the proud in their conceit. He has cast down the mighty from their thrones and has lifted up the lowly.

He has filled the hungry with good things, and the rich he has sent away empty. He has come to the help of his servant Israel for he remembered his

724

promise of mercy, the promise he made to our fathers, to Abraham and his children for ever."

Mary remained with Elizabeth about three months and then returned to her home.

The Nativity of the Lord (Christmas) - Mass During the Day

DECEMBER 23RD, 2021
Thursday of the Fourth Week of Advent

1ST Reading Mal 3:1-4, 23-24
Thus says the Lord GOD:

Lo, I am sending my messenger to prepare the way before me;

And suddenly there will come to the temple the LORD whom you seek, And the messenger of the covenant whom you desire. Yes, he is coming, says the LORD of hosts.

But who will endure the day of his coming? And who can stand when he appears? For he is like the refiner's fire, or like the fuller's lye.

He will sit refining and purifying silver, and he will purify the sons of Levi,

Refining them like gold or like silver that they may offer due sacrifice to the LORD. Then the sacrifice of Judah and Jerusalem will please the LORD, as in the days of old, as in years gone by.

Lo, I will send you Elijah, the prophet, Before the day of the LORD comes, the great and terrible day,

To turn the hearts of the fathers to their children, and the hearts of the children to their fathers,

Lest I come and strike the land with doom."

Responsorial Psalm PS 25:4-5ab, 8-9, 10 and 14
R...(see Luke 21:28) Lift up your heads and see; your redemption is near at hand.

Your ways, O LORD, make known to me; teach me your paths,

Guide me in your truth and teach me, for you are God my savior.

R. Lift up your heads and see; your redemption is near at hand.

Good and upright is the LORD; thus he shows sinners the way. He guides the humble to justice, he teaches the humble his way.

R. Lift up your heads and see; your redemption is near at hand.

All the paths of the LORD are kindness and constancy toward those who keep his covenant and his decrees.

The friendship of the LORD is with those who fear him, and his covenant, for their instruction.

R. Lift up your heads and see; your redemption is near at hand.

Alleluia

R. Alleluia, alleluia.

O King of all nations and keystone of the Church; come and save man, whom you formed from the dust!

R. Alleluia, alleluia.

Gospel Lk 1:57-66

When the time arrived for Elizabeth to have her child she gave birth to a son. Her neighbors and relatives heard that the Lord had shown his great mercy toward her, and they rejoiced with her.

When they came on the eighth day to circumcise the child, they were going to call him Zechariah after his father, but his mother said in reply,

"No. He will be called John." But they answered her, "There is no one among your relatives who has this name." So they made signs, asking his father what he wished him to be called.

He asked for a tablet and wrote, "John is his name," and all were amazed. Immediately his mouth was opened, his tongue freed, and he spoke blessing God.

Then fear came upon all their neighbors, and all these matters were discussed throughout the hill country of Judea.

All who heard these things took them to heart, saying,

"What, then, will this child be? For surely the hand of the Lord was with him."

DECEMBER 24TH, 2021
Friday of the Fourth Week of Advent

Mass in the Morning

1ST Reading   2 SM 7:1-5, 8B-12, 14A, 16

When King David was settled in his palace, and the LORD had given him rest from his enemies on every side, he said to Nathan the prophet, "Here I am living in a house of cedar, while the ark of God dwells in a tent!" Nathan answered the king, "Go, do whatever you have in mind, for the LORD is with you." But that night the LORD spoke to Nathan and said:

"Go, tell my servant David, 'Thus says the LORD: Should you build me a house to dwell in? '"It was I who took you from the pasture and from the care of the flock to be commander of my people Israel. I have been with you wherever you went, and I have destroyed all your enemies before you. And I will make you famous like the great ones of the earth.

I will fix a place for my people Israel; I will plant them so that they may dwell in their place without further disturbance. Neither shall the wicked continue to afflict them as they did of old, since the time I first appointed judges over my people Israel. I will give you rest from all your enemies. The LORD also reveals to you that he will establish a house for you. And when your time comes and you rest with your ancestors, I will raise up your heir after you, sprung from your loins, and I will make his Kingdom firm. I will be a father to him, and he shall be a son to me. Your house and your Kingdom shall endure forever before me; your throne shall stand firm forever.'"

Responsorial Psalm PS 89:2-3, 4-5, 27 AND 29

R... (2) For ever I will sing the goodness of the Lord.

The favors of the LORD I will sing forever; through all generations my mouth shall proclaim your faithfulness. For you have said, "My kindness is established forever"; in heaven you have confirmed your faithfulness.

R. For ever I will sing the goodness of the Lord.

"I have made a covenant with my chosen one, I have sworn to David my servant: Forever will I confirm your posterity and establish your throne for all generations."

R. For ever I will sing the goodness of the Lord.

"He shall say of me, 'You are my father, my God, the rock, my savior.' Forever I will maintain my kindness toward him, and my covenant with him stands firm."

R. For ever I will sing the goodness of the Lord.

Alleluia

R. Alleluia, alleluia.

O Radiant Dawn, splendor of eternal light, sun of justice: come and shine on those who dwell in darkness and in the shadow of death.

R. Alleluia, alleluia.

Gospel LK 1:67-79
Zechariah his father, filled with the Holy Spirit, prophesied, saying:

"Blessed be the Lord, the God of Israel; for he has come to his people and set them free. He has raised up for us a mighty Savior, born of the house of his servant David. Through his prophets he promised of old that he would save us from our enemies, from the hands of all who hate us. He promised to show mercy to our fathers and to remember his holy covenant.

This was the oath he swore to our father Abraham: to set us free from the hand of our enemies, free to worship him without fear, holy and righteous in his sight all the days of our life. You, my child, shall be called the prophet of the Most High, for you will go before the Lord to prepare his way, to give his people knowledge of salvation by the forgiveness of their sins.

In the tender compassion of our God the dawn from on high shall break upon us, to shine on those who dwell in darkness and the shadow of death, and to guide our feet into the way of peace.

DECEMBER 25TH, 2021
The Nativity of the Lord (Christmas) - Mass at Dawn

The people who walked in darkness have seen a great light; upon those who dwelt in the land of gloom a light has shone. You have brought them abundant joy and great rejoicing, as they rejoice before you as at the harvest, as people make merry when dividing spoils.

For the yoke that burdened them, the pole on their shoulder, and the rod of their taskmaster you have smashed, as on the day of Midian. For every boot that tramped in battle, every cloak rolled in blood, will be burned as fuel for flames.

For a child is born to us, a son is given us; upon his shoulder dominion rests. They name him Wonder-Counselor, God-Hero, Father-Forever, Prince of Peace. His dominion is vast and forever peaceful, from David's throne, and over his kingdom, which he confirms and sustains by judgment and justice, both now and forever. The zeal of the LORD of hosts will do this!

Responsorial Psalm Ps 96: 1-2, 2-3, 11-12, 13.
R. (Lk 2:11) Today is born our Savior, Christ the Lord.

Sing to the LORD a new song; sing to the LORD, all you lands.

Sing to the LORD; bless his name.

R. Today is born our Savior, Christ the Lord.

Announce his salvation, day after day. Tell his glory among the nations; among all peoples, his wondrous deeds.

R. Today is born our Savior, Christ the Lord.

Let the heavens be glad and the earth rejoice; let the sea and what fills it resound; let the plains be joyful and all that is in them!

Then shall all the trees of the forest exult.

R. Today is born our Savior, Christ the Lord.

They shall exult before the LORD, for he comes; for he comes to rule the earth.

He shall rule the world with justice and the peoples with his constancy.

R. Today is born our Savior, Christ the Lord..

2ND Reading Ti 2:11-14

Beloved:

The grace of God has appeared, saving all and training us to reject godless ways and worldly desires and to live temperately, justly, and devoutly in this age, as we await the blessed hope, the appearance of the glory of our great God and savior Jesus Christ, who gave himself for us to deliver us from all lawlessness and to cleanse for himself a people as his own, eager to do what is good.

Alleluia: Lk 2:10-11

R. Alleluia, alleluia.

I proclaim to you good news of great joy: today a Savior is born for us, Christ the Lord.

R. Alleluia, alleluia..

Gospel Lk 2:1-14

In those days a decree went out from Caesar Augustus that the whole world should be enrolled.

This was the first enrollment, when Quirinius was governor of Syria.So all went to be enrolled, each to his own town.

And Joseph too went up from Galilee from the town of Nazareth to Judea, to the city of David that is called Bethlehem, because he was of the house and family of David, to be enrolled with Mary, his betrothed, who was with child.

While they were there, the time came for her to have her child, and she gave birth to her firstborn son.

She wrapped him in swaddling clothes and laid him in a manger, because there was no room for them in the inn.

Now there were shepherds in that region living in the fields and keeping the night watch over their flock.

The angel of the Lord appeared to them and the glory of the Lord shone around them, and they were struck with great fear.

The angel said to them, "Do not be afraid; for behold, I proclaim to you good news of great joy that will be for all the people.

For today in the city of David a savior has been born for you who is Christ and Lord. And this will be a sign for you: you will find an infant wrapped in swaddling clothes and lying in a manger."

And suddenly there was a multitude of the heavenly host with the angel, praising God and saying: "Glory to God in the highest and on earth peace to those on whom his favor rests."

DECEMBER 26TH, 2021
Feast of the Holy Family of Jesus, Mary and Joseph

1ST Sir 3:2-6, 12-14

God sets a father in honor over his children; a mother's authority he confirms over her sons. Whoever honors his father atones for sins, and preserves himself from them.

When he prays, he is heard; he stores up riches who reveres his mother. Whoever honors his father is gladdened by children, and, when he prays, is heard.

Whoever reveres his father will live a long life; he who obeys his father brings comfort to his mother.

My son, take care of your father when he is old; grieve him not as long as he lives. Even if his mind fail, be considerate of him; revile him not all the days of his life; kindness to a father will not be forgotten, firmly planted against the debt of your sins—a house raised in justice to you.

OR:

1 Sm 1:20-22, 24-28

In those days Hannah conceived, and at the end of her term bore a son whom she called Samuel, since she had asked the LORD for him. The next time her husband Elkanah was going up with the rest of his household to offer the customary sacrifice to the LORD and to fulfill his vows,

Hannah did not go, explaining to her husband,

"Once the child is weaned, I will take him to appear before the LORD and to remain there forever;

I will offer him as a perpetual nazirite."

Once Samuel was weaned, Hannah brought him up with her, along with a three-year-old bull, an ephah of flour, and a skin of wine, and presented him at the temple of the LORD in Shiloh.

After the boy's father had sacrificed the young bull,

Hannah, his mother, approached Eli and said: "Pardon, my lord! As you live, my lord, I am the woman who stood near you here, praying to the LORD.

I prayed for this child, and the LORD granted my request.

Now I, in turn, give him to the LORD;as long as he lives, he shall be dedicated to the LORD."

Hannah left Samuel there.

Responsorial Psalm Ps 128:1-2, 3, 4-5.
R. (cf. 1) Blessed are those who fear the Lord and walk in his ways.

Blessed is everyone who fears the LORD, who walks in his ways!

For you shall eat the fruit of your handiwork; blessed shall you be, and favored.

R. Blessed are those who fear the Lord and walk in his ways.

Your wife shall be like a fruitful vine in the recesses of your home; your children like olive plants around your table.

R. Blessed are those who fear the Lord and walk in his ways.

Behold, thus is the man blessed who fears the LORD.

The LORD bless you from Zion: may you see the prosperity of Jerusalem all the days of your life.

R. Blessed are those who fear the Lord and walk in his ways.

OR:

Ps 84:2-3, 5-6, 9-10.

R. (cf. 5a) Blessed are they who dwell in your house, O Lord.

How lovely is your dwelling place, O LORD of hosts! My soul yearns and pines for the courts of the LORD.

My heart and my flesh cry out for the living God.

R. Blessed are they who dwell in your house, O Lord.

Happy they who dwell in your house! Continually they praise you.

Happy the men whose strength you are! Their hearts are set upon the pilgrimage.

R. Blessed are they who dwell in your house, O Lord.

O LORD of hosts, hear our prayer; hearken, O God of Jacob!

O God, behold our shield, and look upon the face of your anointed.

R. Blessed are they who dwell in your house, O Lord.

2ND Reading Col 3:12-21 or 3:12-17

Brothers and sisters:

Put on, as God's chosen ones, holy and beloved, heartfelt compassion, kindness, humility, gentleness, and patience, bearing with one another and forgiving one another, if one has a grievance against another; as the Lord has forgiven you, so must you also do.

And over all these put on love, that is, the bond of perfection. And let the peace of Christ control your hearts, the peace into which you were also called in one body. And be thankful.

Let the word of Christ dwell in you richly, as in all wisdom you teach and admonish one another, singing psalms, hymns, and spiritual songs with gratitude in your hearts to God.

733

And whatever you do, in word or in deed, do everything in the name of the Lord Jesus, giving thanks to God the Father through him. Wives, be subordinate to your husbands, as is proper in the Lord.

Husbands, love your wives, and avoid any bitterness toward them.

Children, obey your parents in everything, for this is pleasing to the Lord. Fathers, do not provoke your children, so they may not become discouraged.

OR:

Brothers and sisters:

Put on, as God's chosen ones, holy and beloved, heartfelt compassion, kindness, humility, gentleness, and patience, bearing with one another and forgiving one another, if one has a grievance against another; as the Lord has forgiven you, so must you also do.

And over all these put on love, that is, the bond of perfection. And let the peace of Christ control your hearts, the peace into which you were also called in one body.

And be thankful. Let the word of Christ dwell in you richly, as in all wisdom you teach and admonish one another, singing psalms, hymns, and spiritual songs with gratitude in your hearts to God.

And whatever you do, in word or in deed, do everything in the name of the Lord Jesus, giving thanks to God the Father through him.

OR:

1 Jn 3:1-2, 21-24

Beloved:

See what love the Father has bestowed on us that we may be called the children of God.

And so we are. The reason the world does not know us is that it did not know him. Beloved, we are God's children now; what we shall be has not yet been revealed.

We do know that when it is revealed we shall be like him, for we shall see him as he is.

Beloved, if our hearts do not condemn us, we have confidence in God and receive from him whatever we ask, because we keep his commandments and do what pleases him.

And his commandment is this: we should believe in the name of his Son, Jesus Christ, and love one another just as he commanded us.

Those who keep his commandments remain in him, and he in them, and the way we know that he remains in us is from the Spirit he gave us.

Alleluia

Col 3:15a, 16a

R. Alleluia, alleluia.

Let the peace of Christ control your hearts; Let the word of Christ dwell in you richly.

R. Alleluia, alleluia.

OR:

Cf. Acts 16:14b

R. Alleluia, alleluia.

Open our hearts, O Lord, to listen to the words of your Son.

R. Alleluia, alleluia.

Gospel Lk 2:41-52
Each year Jesus' parents went to Jerusalem for the feast of Passover, and when he was twelve years old, they went up according to festival custom.

After they had completed its days, as they were returning, the boy Jesus remained behind in Jerusalem, but his parents did not know it.

Thinking that he was in the caravan, they journeyed for a day and looked for him among their relatives and acquaintances, but not finding him, they returned to Jerusalem to look for him.

After three days they found him in the temple, sitting in the midst of the teachers, listening to them and asking them questions, and all who heard him were astounded at his understanding and his answers.

When his parents saw him, they were astonished, and his mother said to him, "Son, why have you done this to us?

Your father and I have been looking for you with great anxiety." And he said to them, "Why were you looking for me? Did you not know that I must be in my Father's house?" But they did not understand what he said to them. He went down with them and came to Nazareth, and was obedient to them; and his mother kept all these things in her heart.

And Jesus advanced in wisdom and age and favor before God and man.

DECEMBER 27TH, 2021
Feast of Saint John, Apostle and evangelist

1ST Reading 1 JN 1:1-4
Beloved:

What was from the beginning, what we have heard, what we have seen with our eyes, what we looked upon and touched with our hands concerns the Word of life — for the life was made visible; we have seen it and testify to it and proclaim to you the eternal life that was with the Father and was made visible to us— what we have seen and heard we proclaim now to you, so that you too may have fellowship with us; for our fellowship is with the Father and with his Son, Jesus Christ.

We are writing this so that our joy may be complete.

Responsorial Psalm PS 97:1-2, 5-6, 11-12
R. (12) Rejoice in the Lord, you just!

The LORD is king; let the earth rejoice; let the many isles be glad. Clouds and darkness are around him, justice and judgment are the foundation of his throne.

R. Rejoice in the Lord, you just!

The mountains melt like wax before the LORD, before the LORD of all the earth. The heavens proclaim his justice, and all peoples see his glory.

R. Rejoice in the Lord, you just!

Light dawns for the just; and gladness, for the upright of heart. Be glad in the LORD, you just, and give thanks to his holy name.

R. Rejoice in the Lord, you just!

Alleluia See Te Deum

R. Alleluia, alleluia.

We praise you, O God, we acclaim you as Lord; the glorious company of Apostles praise you.

R. Alleluia, alleluia.

Gospel JN 20:1A AND 2-8
On the first day of the week, Mary Magdalene ran and went to Simon Peter and to the other disciple whom Jesus loved, and told them, "They have taken the Lord from the tomb, and we do not know where they put him." So Peter and the other disciple went out and came to the tomb. They both ran, but the other disciple ran faster than Peter and arrived at the tomb first; he bent down and saw the burial cloths there, but did not go in.

When Simon Peter arrived after him, he went into the tomb and saw the burial cloths there, and the cloth that had covered his head, not with the burial cloths but rolled up in a separate place. Then the other disciple also went in, the one who had arrived at the tomb first, and he saw and believed

DECEMBER 28TH, 2021
Feast of the Holy Innocents, martyrs

1ST Reading 1 JN 1:5—2:2
Beloved:

This is the message that we have heard from Jesus Christ and proclaim to you: God is light, and in him there is no darkness at all. If we say, "We have fellowship with him," while we continue to walk in darkness, we lie and do not act in truth. But if we walk in the light as he is in the light, then we have fellowship with one another, and the Blood of his Son Jesus cleanses us from all sin. If we say, "We are without sin," we deceive ourselves, and the truth is not in us. If we acknowledge our sins, he is faithful and just and will forgive our sins and cleanse us from every wrongdoing. If we say, "We have not sinned," we make him a liar, and his word is not in us. My children, I am writing this to you so that you may not commit sin. But if anyone does sin, we have an Advocate with the Father, Jesus Christ the righteous one. He is expiation for our sins, and not for our sins only but for those of the whole world.

Responsorial Psalm PS 124:2-3, 4-5, 7CD-8
R... (7) Our soul has been rescued like a bird from the fowler's snare.

Had not the LORD been with us— When men rose up against us, then would they have swallowed us alive, When their fury was inflamed against us.

R. Our soul has been rescued like a bird from the fowler's snare.

Then would the waters have overwhelmed us; The torrent would have swept over us; over us then would have swept the raging waters.

R. Our soul has been rescued like a bird from the fowler's snare.

Broken was the snare, and we were freed. Our help is in the name of the LORD, who made heaven and earth.

R. Our soul has been rescued like a bird from the fowler's snare.

Alleluia See Te Deum

R. Alleluia, alleluia.

We praise you, O God, we acclaim you as Lord; the white-robed army of martyrs praise you.

R. Alleluia, alleluia.

Gospel MT 2:13-18
When the magi had departed, behold, the angel of the Lord appeared to Joseph in a dream and said, "Rise, take the child and his mother, flee to Egypt, and stay there until I tell you. Herod is going to search for the child to destroy him." Joseph rose and took the child and his mother by night and departed for Egypt. He stayed there until the death of Herod, that what the Lord had said through the prophet might be fulfilled, Out of Egypt I called my son.

When Herod realized that he had been deceived by the magi, he became furious. He ordered the massacre of all the boys in Bethlehem and its vicinity two years old and under, in accordance with the time he had ascertained from the magi. Then was fulfilled what had been said through Jeremiah the prophet: A voice was heard in Ramah, sobbing and loud lamentation;

Rachel weeping for her children, and she would not be consoled, since they were no more.

DECEMBER 29TH, 2021
The Fifth Day in the Octave of Christmas

1ST Reading 1 Jn 2:3-11
Beloved:

The way we may be sure that we know Jesus is to keep his commandments.

Whoever says, "I know him," but does not keep his commandments is a liar, and the truth is not in him.

But whoever keeps his word, the love of God is truly perfected in him.

This is the way we may know that we are in union with him: whoever claims to abide in him ought to walk just as he walked.

Beloved, I am writing no new commandment to you but an old commandment that you had from the beginning. The old commandment is the word that you have heard.

And yet I do write a new commandment to you, which holds true in him and among you, for the darkness is passing away, and the true light is already shining.

Whoever says he is in the light, yet hates his brother, is still in the darkness. Whoever loves his brother remains in the light, and there is nothing in him to cause a fall.

Whoever hates his brother is in darkness; he walks in darkness and does not know where he is going because the darkness has blinded his eyes..

Responsorial Psalm 96:1-2a, 2b-3, 5b-6.
R. (11a) Let the heavens be glad and the earth rejoice!

Sing to the LORD a new song; sing to the LORD, all you lands.

Sing to the LORD; bless his name.

R. Let the heavens be glad and the earth rejoice!

Announce his salvation, day after day.

Tell his glory among the nations; among all peoples, his wondrous deeds.

R. Let the heavens be glad and the earth rejoice!

The LORD made the heavens. Splendor and majesty go before him; praise and grandeur are in his sanctuary.

R. Let the heavens be glad and the earth rejoice!

Alleluia: Lk 2:32

R. Alleluia, alleluia.

A light of revelation to the Gentiles and glory for your people Israel.

R. Alleluia, alleluia..

Gospel Lk 2:22-35

When the days were completed for their purification according to the law of Moses, the parents of Jesus took him up to Jerusalem to present him to the Lord, just as it is written in the law of the Lord,

Every male that opens the womb shall be consecrated to the Lord, and to offer the sacrifice of a pair of turtledoves or two young pigeons, in accordance with the dictate in the law of the Lord.

Now there was a man in Jerusalem whose name was Simeon. This man was righteous and devout, awaiting the consolation of Israel, and the Holy Spirit was upon him.

It had been revealed to him by the Holy Spirit that he should not see death before he had seen the Christ of the Lord.

He came in the Spirit into the temple; and when the parents brought in the child Jesus to perform the custom of the law in regard to him, he took him into his arms and blessed God, saying:

"Lord, now let your servant go in peace; your word has been fulfilled: my own eyes have seen the salvation which you prepared in the sight of every people, a light to reveal you to the nations and the glory of your people Israel."

The child's father and mother were amazed at what was said about him; and Simeon blessed them and said to Mary his mother,

"Behold, this child is destined for the fall and rise of many in Israel, and to be a sign that will be contradicted (and you yourself a sword will pierce) so that the thoughts of many hearts may be revealed."

DECEMBER 30TH, 2021
The Sixth Day in the Octave of Christmas

1ST Reading 1 JN 2:12-17
I am writing to you, children, because your sins have been forgiven for his name's sake. I am writing to you, fathers, because you know him who is from the beginning. I am writing to you, young men, because you have conquered the Evil One. I write to you, children, because you know the Father.

I write to you, fathers, because you know him who is from the beginning. I write to you, young men, because you are strong and the word of God remains in you, and you have conquered the Evil One.

Do not love the world or the things of the world. If anyone loves the world, the love of the Father is not in him. For all that is in the world, sensual lust, enticement for the eyes, and a pretentious life, is not from the Father but is from the world. Yet the world and its enticement are passing away. But whoever does the will of God remains forever.

Responsorial Psalm PS 96:7-8A, 8B-9, 10
R... (11a) Let the heavens be glad and the earth rejoice!

Give to the LORD, you families of nations, give to the LORD glory and praise; give to the LORD the glory due his name!

R. Let the heavens be glad and the earth rejoice!

Bring gifts, and enter his courts; worship the LORD in holy attire. Tremble before him, all the earth.

R. Let the heavens be glad and the earth rejoice!

Say among the nations: The LORD is king. He has made the world firm, not to be moved; he governs the peoples with equity.

R. Let the heavens be glad and the earth rejoice!

Alleluia

R. Alleluia, alleluia.

A holy day has dawned upon us. Come, you nations, and adore the Lord. Today a great light has come upon the earth.

R. Alleluia, alleluia.

Gospel LK 2:36-40

There was a prophetess, Anna, the daughter of Phanuel, of the tribe of Asher. She was advanced in years, having lived seven years with her husband after her marriage, and then as a widow until she was eighty-four. She never left the temple, but worshiped night and day with fasting and prayer. And coming forward at that very time, she gave thanks to God and spoke about the child to all who were awaiting the redemption of Jerusalem.

When they had fulfilled all the prescriptions of the law of the Lord, they returned to Galilee, to their own town of Nazareth. The child grew and became strong, filled with wisdom; and the favor of God was upon him.

DECEMBER 31ST, 2021

The Seventh Day in the Octave of Christmas

1ST Reading 1 JN 2:18-21

Children, it is the last hour; and just as you heard that the antichrist was coming, so now many antichrists have appeared. Thus we know this is the last hour. They went out from us, but they were not really of our number; if they had been, they would have remained with us. Their desertion shows that none of them was of our number. But you have the anointing that comes from the Holy One, and you all have knowledge. I write to you not because you do not know the truth but because you do, and because every lie is alien to the truth.

Responsorial Psalm PS 96:1-2, 11-12, 13
R. (11a) Let the heavens be glad and the earth rejoice!

Sing to the LORD a new song; sing to the LORD, all you lands. Sing to the LORD; bless his name; announce his salvation, day after day.

R. Let the heavens be glad and the earth rejoice!

Let the heavens be glad and the earth rejoice; let the sea and what fills it resound; let the plains be joyful and all that is in them! Then shall all the trees of the forest exult before the LORD.

R. Let the heavens be glad and the earth rejoice!

The LORD comes, he comes to rule the earth. He shall rule the world with justice and the peoples with his constancy.

R. Let the heavens be glad and the earth rejoice!

Alleluia JN 1:14A, 12A

R. Alleluia, alleluia.

The Word of God became flesh and dwelt among us. To those who accepted him he gave power to become the children of God.

R. Alleluia, alleluia.

Gospel JN 1:1-18
In the beginning was the Word, and the Word was with God, and the Word was God. He was in the beginning with God. All things came to be through him, and without him nothing came to be. What came to be through him was life, and this life was the light of the human race; the light shines in the darkness, and the darkness has not overcome it. A man named John was sent from God. He came for testimony, to testify to the light, so that all might believe through him. He was not the light, but came to testify to the light. The true light, which enlightens everyone, was coming into the world. He was in the world, and the world came to be through him, but the world did not know him. He came to what was his own, but his own people did not accept him.

But to those who did accept him he gave power to become children of God, to those who believe in his name, who were born not by natural generation nor by human choice nor by a man's decision but of God. And the Word became flesh and made his dwelling among us, and we saw his glory, the glory as of the Father's only-begotten Son, full of grace and truth.

John testified to him and cried out, saying, "This was he of whom I said, 'The one who is coming after me ranks ahead of me because he existed before me.'" From his fullness we have all received, grace in place of grace, because while the law was given through Moses, grace and truth came through Jesus Christ.

No one has ever seen God. The only-begotten Son, God, who is at the Father's side, has revealed him.

Made in the USA
Las Vegas, NV
28 October 2021